Java EE to Jakarta EE 10 Recipes

A Problem-Solution Approach for Enterprise Java

Third Edition

Josh Juneau
Tarun Telang

Apress®

Java EE to Jakarta EE 10 Recipes: A Problem-Solution Approach for Enterprise Java

Josh Juneau
Hinckley, IL, USA

Tarun Telang
Hyderabad, Telangana, India

ISBN-13 (pbk): 978-1-4842-8078-2
https://doi.org/10.1007/978-1-4842-8079-9

ISBN-13 (electronic): 978-1-4842-8079-9

Managing Director, Apress Media LLC: Welmoed Spahr
Acquisitions Editor: Steve Anglin
Development Editor: Laura Berendson
Coordinating Editor: Mark Powers

Cover designed by eStudioCalamar

Cover image by Said Alamri on Unsplash (www.unsplash.com)

Distributed to the book trade worldwide by Apress Media, LLC, 1 New York Plaza, New York, NY 10004, U.S.A. Phone 1-800-SPRINGER, fax (201) 348-4505, e-mail orders-ny@springer-sbm.com, or visit www.springeronline.com. Apress Media, LLC is a California LLC and the sole member (owner) is Springer Science + Business Media Finance Inc (SSBM Finance Inc). SSBM Finance Inc is a Delaware corporation.

For information on translations, please e-mail booktranslations@springernature.com; for reprint, paperback, or audio rights, please e-mail bookpermissions@springernature.com.

Apress titles may be purchased in bulk for academic, corporate, or promotional use. eBook versions and licenses are also available for most titles. For more information, reference our Print and eBook Bulk Sales web page at http://www.apress.com/bulk-sales.

Any source code or other supplementary material referenced by the author in this book is available to readers on GitHub (https://github.com/Apress). For more detailed information, please visit http://www.apress.com/source-code.

Printed on acid-free paper

This book is dedicated to my wife Angela and my five children: Kaitlyn, Jacob, Matthew, Zachary, and Lucas. You are my joy and inspiration. It is also dedicated to the many Java developers worldwide. I hope that these recipes can lead you to developing the sophisticated solutions of tomorrow.

—Josh Juneau

This book is dedicated to my grandparents, parents, wife Nikita, and son Vihan. They have always been a source of inspiration and encouragement to me. It's also for all of the software and technology creators who work hard to make our planet a better place to live.

—Tarun Telang

Table of Contents

About the Authors

Josh Juneau has been developing software and database systems for several years. Database application development and sophisticated web apps have been the focus of his career since the beginning. Early in his career, he became an Oracle database administrator and adopted the PL/SQL language for performing administrative tasks and developing applications for Oracle database. In an effort to build more complex solutions, he began to incorporate Java into his PL/SQL applications and later developed stand-alone and web applications with Java. Josh wrote his early Java web applications utilizing JDBC to work with backend databases. Later, he incorporated frameworks into his enterprise solutions, including Java EE, Spring, and JBoss Seam. Today, he primarily develops enterprise web solutions utilizing Java EE.

He extended his knowledge of the JVM by developing applications with other JVM languages such as Jython and Groovy. In 2006, Josh became the editor and publisher for the *Jython Monthly* newsletter. In late 2008, he began a podcast dedicated to the Jython programming language. Josh was the lead author for *The Definitive Guide to Jython, Oracle PL/SQL Recipes*, and *Java 7 Recipes*, which were published by Apress. Since then, he has continued to author Java-related books for Apress, including his most recent work entitled *Java 9 Recipes*. He is an avid contributor to Oracle's *Java Magazine*, and he speaks at Java User Groups and conferences when he has the opportunity.

He works as an application developer and systems analyst, and he is a contributor to the Chicago Java Users Group. Josh is an Apache NetBeans committer and a Java Champion. He participates in the JCP and has been a part of the Jakarta Faces expert group for the development of Java EE 8. Josh has a wonderful wife and five children with whom he loves to spend time. To hear more from Josh, follow his blog, which can be found at http://jj-blogger.blogspot.com. You can also follow him on Twitter via @javajuneau.

Tarun Telang is a hands-on technologist with extensive experience in the design and implementation of multitiered, highly scalable software applications. He has been part of several well-known companies such as Microsoft, Oracle, Polycom, and SAP. He has over 17 years of experience in architecting and developing business applications.

He began his career as an enterprise Java developer at SAP, where he has developed distributed application software for big firms. He got his start with enterprise session beans and message-driven beans, as well as instrumenting enterprise applications' configuration and management using the Java Management Extensions (JMX) technology.

He quickly mastered various enterprise technologies like Enterprise Beans, Java Management Extensions, Servlets, and Server Pages technologies, and in his first year as a developer, he became Sun Certified Programmer for the Java Platform, Standard Edition 6, and SAP Certified Development Consultant for the SAP NetWeaver Java Web Application Server (which was a Java EE 5–compliant application server).

He also gained expertise in XML technologies like XSLT and XSD, using which he developed several solutions using session beans and message-driven beans to handle message-oriented communications across numerous systems. In 2007, Tarun was named SAP Mentor and Community Influencer for his articles and blog posts on emerging technologies and promoting innovative solutions in the SAP Developer Community. He frequently writes articles on Java and related technologies. Tarun has also authored multiple online courses including a best-selling course on YAML data serialization language.

He has presented technical lectures at several developer conferences, including SAP TechEd and the Great Indian Developer Summit. It has been more than 15 years since he has been presenting at conferences about software technology, actively publishing technical papers and blogs to assist everyone to better grasp the fundamentals of software technology. Tarun has also developed cloud-based video conferencing applications using a microservices architecture with the Spring framework and has experience working with Persistence APIs and Hazelcast framework for building REST-based services.

Later, he led the development of many end-to-end cloud-based solutions using various architectural patterns including microservices and service-oriented architecture. Tarun has gained expertise in web, mobile, and cloud technologies. He is also thorough in applied agile methodologies including user-centric and mobile-first design for managing projects with cross-functional teams located in multiple geographies.

Having previously worked in Canada and Germany, Tarun currently resides in Hyderabad, India, with his wife and child. You can follow him over LinkedIn or Twitter (@taruntelang).

About the Technical Reviewer

Manuel Jordan Elera is an autodidactic developer and researcher who enjoys learning new technologies for his own experiments and creating new integrations. Manuel won the Springy Award–Community Champion and Spring Champion 2013. In his little free time, he reads the Bible and composes music on his guitar. Manuel is known as dr_pompeii. He has tech-reviewed numerous books for Apress, including *Pro Spring MVC with WebFlux* (2020), *Pro Spring Boot 2* (2019), *Rapid Java Persistence and Microservices* (2019), *Java Language Features* (2018), *Spring Boot 2 Recipes* (2018), and *Java APIs, Extensions and Libraries* (2018). Read his 13 detailed tutorials about many Spring technologies, contact him through his blog at www.manueljordanelera.blogspot.com, and follow him on his Twitter account, @dr_pompeii.

Acknowledgments

To my wife Angela: I am still amazed by you and always will be. Thanks again for helping to inspire me and keep me moving forward in my endeavors. You continue to be my rock, and I am so grateful for all you do.

To my children, Kaitlyn, Jacob, Matthew, Zachary, and Lucas – I love you all so much, and I cherish every moment we have together. I hope that you'll find your passion in life and enjoy each day as much as I enjoy each day spending time with you. I wish I could slow time down…you are growing up too fast!

I want to thank my family for their continued support in my career. I also want to thank my coworkers for allowing me to guide the organization's application development efforts and build successful solutions to keep us moving forward.

To the folks at Apress – I thank you for providing me with the chance to share my knowledge with others, once again. I especially thank Jonathan Gennick for the continued support of my work and for providing the continued guidance to produce useful content for our readers. I also thank Jill Balzano for doing a great job coordinating this project and many of my others before it. Lastly, I'd like to thank everyone else at Apress who had a hand in this book.

To the Java community – thanks again for helping to make the Java platform such an innovative and effective realm for application development. I especially want to thank those in the Java EE community who have a hand in helping to move things forward via EE4J, the Eclipse Working Group, Java EE Guardians, and other speakers, writers, and evangelists of Java EE and Jakarta EE. To the members of the Chicago Java Users Group, I want to thank you for helping Chicago be one of the best locations for Java expertise. I also want to thank my fellow members of the Java OffHeap podcast – Freddy Guime, Bob Paulin, Michael Minella, and Jeff Palmer – you help me remain engaged in all of Java technologies, and it is a privilege to have the opportunity to meet and discuss Java each month.

—Josh Juneau

I would like to thank my wife, Nikita, and son, Vihan, for their patience and love throughout the process of writing this book. I am indebted to all my mentors and friends who always encouraged me to keep on growing in every phase of my professional career.

I'd like to thank my parents for pushing me in the right direction with technology and always supporting me every step of the way, even when I decided to do something completely different than they expected. It's also important to note that without them, I probably wouldn't have become a developer and had such a great career. Lastly, thanks again go out to my wife (and soulmate), Nikita. It's an incredible feeling to be with someone who keeps you motivated and challenges you not only professionally but personally as well. Thank you for always being there for me!

I'd like to send a special thanks to Josh Juneau (coauthor) and Manuel Jordan Elera (technical reviewer) for their impeccable work on this book. I also greatly appreciate Steve Anglin, Mark Powers, and everyone at Apress Media (apress.com) for their support in getting this book published.

Last, but not least, I would like to thank you, the reader, for taking the time to read this book. I hope that it will help you in your journey of becoming a better Jakarta EE developer.

—Tarun Telang

Introduction

The Java platform is one of the most popular platforms for application development in the world. This platform is so popular that several different editions of Java exist and can be used to develop applications that run in several environments. From developing desktop, mobile, or web applications and operating systems, developers can utilize Java to create just about any solution. Java has become extremely popular for building web and enterprise applications, offering web services with its strengths, including security, reliability, and much more.

Enterprise Java (currently known as Jakarta Enterprise Edition) is the most widely adopted platform for building and deploying enterprise applications. It has come a long way since its inception in 1997. It first started as an extension of the Java 2 Platform, Standard Edition (J2SE), and gradually evolved into a modular programming model with many different specifications supporting middleware technologies. Sun Microsystems originally released it in 1999 as Java 2 Platform, Enterprise Edition (J2EE). The first version of J2EE came intending to build a component-based n-tier distributed client-server application using JSP as view technology for rendering HTML pages on web browsers and Servlets for processing Java code on the server-side.

Although several enterprise frameworks were available to develop reliable and secure applications on the Java platform, it made sense to standardize specific solutions to minimize customization and aid in the adoption of industry standards around Java Enterprise development. The platform initially included a terse number of specifications for standardization, including Java Servlet, Java Server Pages, RMI, Java Database Connectivity (JDBC), Java Message Service API (JMS), Java Transaction API (JTA), and Enterprise JavaBean. The early development of J2EE applications had a significant learning curve, and it was cumbersome because it required lots of XML configuration. Even with these setbacks, it became popular among larger organizations and companies due to the prevalence of Java and its well-known security benefits.

In 2001, J2EE 1.3 was released, adding more specifications to the platform, including the Java Server Pages Standard Tag Library (JSTL) and Java Authentication and Authorization Service (JAAS). Other specifications, such as Java Servlets, also gained enhancements under the J2EE 1.3 release, making evolutionary enhancements to the platform.

The release of J2EE 1.4 in 2003 marked a significant milestone for Java Enterprise, as many new specifications were added to the platform, providing standards for even more Java technologies. J2EE 1.4 marked the first iteration of Web Services for J2EE 1.1, Java Server Faces, and Java APIs for XML solutions such as JAXP, JAXR, and more. Although the release of J2EE 1.4 included many specifications, it was still deemed as "difficult to learn," "cumbersome," and "not productive." Over the next few years, J2EE was reworked in an attempt to make it easier to learn and utilize for the construction of modern web applications. Although XML is an excellent means for configuration, it can be cumbersome and challenging to manage, so the configuration was a big item addressed for the next release. Technologies such as Enterprise JavaBean (EJB) included some redundant characteristics, making EJB coding time-consuming and complex to manage, so an overhaul of EJB was also in order.

In May of 2006, Sun Microsystems released Java EE 5, leaving the J2EE acronym behind and changing to simply Java EE instead. The Java EE 5 platform was significantly easier to use and maintain because it introduced features such as annotations, considerably cutting down the amount of XML configuration. It could now inject configurations via annotations. It made EJBs easier to develop, and the Java Persistence API

(JPA) became a marketable technology for object-relational mapping. As a result, Java Enterprise Edition has become a widely adopted and mature platform for enterprise development.

After acquiring Sun Microsystems, Oracle Corporation released Java EE 6 in 2009, making configuration and APIs even easier and adding more specifications to the platform. Specifications such as Contexts and Dependency Injection (CDI) and Bean Validation were introduced, vastly changing the landscape of the platform and streamlining development.

Java EE 7 (released in 2013) continued to strengthen and modernize the platform, adding the WebSockets and JSON-P specifications. In the Java EE 7 release, specifications such as Java Server Faces and EJB were also enhanced, adding more features to increase productivity and functionality and working better for more modern web solutions.

What occurred next in the timeline was a definitive game changer for the Java EE platform. The Java EE 8 initiative had begun in 2015, and many of the specifications that make up the platform had begun to work. The focus of Java EE 8 was to continue to work toward Java SE 8 compatibility throughout the APIs and to continue making the APIs easier to use. There was also a focus on creating new specifications around making microservices easier to develop with Java EE.

In late 2015, many of the specifications stopped moving forward, and there was a halt in progress across the board. A few specifications, such as Java Server Faces, CDI, and JSON-B, continued to progress, while many of the others stalled. The community became concerned about the future of Java EE, and there was a perception that Oracle was going to discontinue it. Oracle was silent on the progress of Java EE 8, and uncertainty was in the air. During this same timeframe, the Java EE Guardians group was formed, focusing on trying to make Oracle produce a statement about the future direction of the platform and make the platform open source rather than dropping it. Around that same time, the Microprofile project also got started as a collaborative effort by a number of the Java EE container vendors, focusing on providing a genuine microservices profile for the Java EE platform.

In late 2016, Oracle changed the direction of Java EE 8 by removing some of the previously planned specification updates and adding others. There took place a renewed effort to keep Java EE 8 moving forward to produce a final release in 2017, working toward a better platform for building microservices-based applications. The Java EE 8 release was finalized in the fall of 2017, and it included updates to many of the specifications. However, Oracle dropped some of the specifications planned to enhance microservices development to produce a timely release, including MVC and the Health Checking API.

Just before Java EE 8, Oracle announced that they would open source Java EE. After a short while, Oracle also announced that it would contribute all of the Java EE sources (for each of the underlying specifications) along with all documentation and TCKs (Technology Compatibility Kits) to the Eclipse Foundation. In late 2017, the EE4J (Eclipse Enterprise for Java) project was formed, and the transfer of each specification began.

In early 2018, the new name for the platform under the open source EE4J project became Jakarta EE. Platform vendors use TCKs to test the compatibility of their Jakarta EE implementations with the Jakarta EE specification. TCKs provide a comprehensive set of tests that ensure that all specification feature implementations are correct and consistent. Once Oracle transferred all specification sources, documentation, and TCKs, Jakarta EE 8 was the first release in parity with Java EE 8.

In November 2020, Eclipse Foundation released Jakarta EE 9. It does not include any significant changes to the platform. The most crucial milestone was moving all the APIs from the *.javax* namespace to the *.jakarta* namespace, as modification in the *.javax* namespace was not allowed due to trademark restrictions.

In February 2021, Eclipse Foundation released Jakarta EE 9.1. Jakarta EE 9.1 added support for Java SE 11 on top of Jakarta EE 9. The Jakarta EE platform now aims to provide enterprise-grade cloud-native development features. It is set to improve and simplify its enterprise-ready APIs with every new release.

Jakarta EE 10 is the first major Jakarta EE release after the *.jakarta* namespace migration. It is also the third release of Jakarta EE since the transition from the Java Community Process (JCP) to the Eclipse Foundation. The key themes for this release are around features like CDI alignment, Java SE alignment, and closing the standardization gap. With Jakarta EE 10, some of these component specifications significantly change their APIs, necessitating a major version upgrade from the previous release. At the same time, many other component specifications introduced updates that are binary compatible and only need a minor version update.

The Jakarta EE Platform contained all the component specifications. It is targeted at enterprise applications that need the full power of Jakarta EE. In contrast, the following profile specifications include the individual specifications focused on developing web platforms and microservices architectures.

The Jakarta EE Web Profile is a subset of the Jakarta EE platform that provides a set of most essential components required for developing web platforms.

The Jakarta EE Core Profile is a subset of the Jakarta EE platform that provides a smaller, more lightweight runtime for developing cloud-native applications. It includes only the most essential APIs and components, making it ideal for microservices that require a fast startup time and a small footprint.

As you move from Jakarta EE 8 to 10, the community has added many new capabilities. I've listed some of the more interesting ones in the following.

HTTP/2 is now enabled by default for all Servlets and Filters. It uses multiplexed connections to handle multiple requests simultaneously instead of serially, significantly reducing latency over HTTP 1.1. You can now inject environment properties directly into your application, and you can configure resources using application contexts. It lets you configure resources such as classes and templates for components like RESTful web services or Model-View-Controllers (MVC) in a single location rather than scattered throughout multiple deployment descriptors.

If the preceding new features aren't enough, there are also significant performance improvements with this release of Jakarta EE over Jakarta EE 8. Jakarta EE 10 works with Java SE 11, leveraging the latest optimizations in both the JVM and platform libraries.

This book focuses on the Jakarta EE 10 release. Throughout this book, I will refer to the platform as Jakarta EE. The platform is covered as a whole, touching upon most of the widely used specifications that make up Jakarta EE. You will learn how to use each of the major specifications, using real-world examples and solutions. This book will cover APIs that have been enhanced, providing complete coverage for those who are newer to the platform. It also features recipes that cover the platform's latest features so that seasoned Enterprise Java developers can skip those introductory concepts and delve into newer material.

I work with Jakarta EE daily, and I have a deep passion for the technologies involved in the platform. I hope that this book increases your passion and productivity using the platform in its entirety.

Who This Book Is For

Java developers who want to develop effective and proven solutions without reading a lengthy manual and scrubbing for techniques will benefit from this book. A beginning Java programmer will find the book handy for learning a variety of different solutions for the platform, while advanced developers will enjoy the ease of the problem-solution approach to quickly broaden their knowledge of the platform's latest technologies.

This book is intended for Java developers who are interested in learning Jakarta Enterprise Edition (Jakarta EE) development and/or already know Java EE/Jakarta EE but would like some information regarding the new features included in Jakarta EE 10. Those who are new to Jakarta EE development can read this book, and it will allow them to start from scratch to get up and running quickly. Intermediate and advanced Java developers who are looking to update their arsenal with the latest features that Jakarta EE 10 has to offer can also read the book to quickly update and refresh their skillset. It can also be used as a guide by developers of organizations migrating their applications from Java EE to Jakarta EE.

How This Book Is Structured

This book is structured so that it does not have to be read from cover to cover. In fact, it is structured so that developers can choose which topic(s) they'd like to read about and jump right to them. Each recipe contains a problem to solve, one or more solutions to solve that problem, and a detailed explanation of how the solution works. Although some recipes may build on concepts that have been discussed in other recipes, they will contain the appropriate references so that the developer can find other related recipes that are beneficial to the solution. The book is designed to allow developers to get up and running quickly with a solution so that they can be home in time for dinner.

Conventions

Throughout the book, I've kept a consistent style for presenting Java code, SQL, command-line text, and results. Where pieces of code, SQL, reserved words, or code fragments are presented in the text, they are presented in fixed-width Courier font, such as this (working) example:

```java
public class MyExample {
    public static void main(String[] args){
        System.out.println("Jakarta EE is excellent!");
    }
}
```

Downloading the Code

The code for the examples shown in this book is available at github.com/apress/javaEE-to-jakartaEE10-recipes.

■ **Note**   The sources for this book may change over time, to provide new implementations that incorporate the most up-to-date features in Jakarta EE. That said, if any issues are found within the sources, please submit them via the book's GitHub repo, and code will be adjusted accordingly.

Testing Jakarta EE Application Projects

Testing is extremely important and essential for a project's success. That said, I want to get you pointed in the correct direction with my approach to testing Jakarta EE application projects.

Certainly, testing is one of those objectives that meet the "more is the better" mantra, so I believe it is important to take a multiheaded approach to the test. The most obvious testing is that you must test your application user interface and ensure that the application UI and business logic function as expected during user testing. This is perhaps the easiest testing, as it only requires user-documented testing of each form within a web application. Before user testing can begin, automated unit testing and UI testing should take place. By automated unit testing, I mean using a framework such as JUnit (https://junit.org/junit5/) to test the business logic of the application. Such tests can be configured to run each time a project is built and compiled.

Automated UI testing can be achieved via the use of a testing API such as Arquillian (https://arquillian.org/), along with an add-on like Graphene (http://arquillian.org/arquillian-graphene/). My approach is to utilize Arquillian for configuration and coordination of all unit tests via JUnit and also for orchestration of the automated UI testing via Graphene.

While this topic is too big to cover in this section, I want to point you to some online resources that you can use to get started with Arquillian testing of your Jakarta EE application projects. It is important to gain a decent understanding of the Arquillian framework by reading through the documentation (`https://arquillian.org/docs/`).

One of the most difficult pieces of the puzzle is setting up the Maven POM file with the correct dependencies. You will find a sample POM file dependency list for setting up Arquillian with Graphene extension here: `https://arquillian.org/guides/getting_started/#add_the_arquillian_apis`. Once the dependencies are set up, it is very easy to create tests that will be executed each time the project is built.

An Arquillian test file is simply a Java class that contains JUnit (or another testing framework) tests and runs under the Arquillian harness. The harness allows one to set up a custom deployment package for each test class, packaging only the required dependencies for running the individual tests. The deployment package can then be deployed to a running application server container, or it can be deployed to an embedded container. In my experience, I've had the best luck deploying to an existing server...typically the same server that I develop against on my local machine.

The Graphene extension can be used to code the web interaction on a specific page of an application. You can code the completion of a web form, which is the clicking of a button, and test for a specified result.

Use the guides available at the following links to get started with Arquillian and Graphene:

- *Getting Started (`http://arquillian.org/guides/getting_started/`)*: How to add the Arquillian test suite to your project and create your first Arquillian test.

- *Getting Started: Rinse and Repeat (`http://arquillian.org/guides/getting_started_rinse_and_repeat/`)*: Learn how to use remote containers for testing more complex Jakarta EE projects.

- *Creating Deployable Archives with ShrinkWrap (`http://arquillian.org/guides/shrinkwrap_introduction/`)*: Create archives using ShrinkWrap to more easily test Jakarta EE deployments.

- *Functional Testing using Graphene (`http://arquillian.org/guides/functional_testing_using_graphene/`)*: Learn how to perform functional testing using the Arquillian Graphene extension.

CHAPTER 1

■ ■ ■

Jakarta Servlets

Jakarta Servlets (formerly Java Servlets) is the technology for building dynamic web applications. In 1997, Sun Microsystems released the first version of servlets. Since then, it has undergone significant evolution, becoming more powerful and easier to use with each release. Jakarta EE 10 includes the 6.0 version of Jakarta Servlets.

Jakarta Servlets are at the base of all Jakarta EE applications. However, developers can utilize servlet frameworks such as Jakarta Server Pages (formerly known as Java Server Pages or JSP) and Jakarta Server Faces (formerly known as Java Server Faces or JSF). Both these frameworks compile pages into Jakarta Servlets in the background using the servlet container. That said, a basic understanding of Jakarta servlet technology is very beneficial for anyone working on Java-based web application development.

Jakarta Servlets are Java classes that respond to requests and conform to the Jakarta Servlet API. They can respond to various types of requests, but they are mostly written to respond to web-based requests. A servlet must be deployed to a servlet container, be it a full application server or a micro-container, to become usable. The Servlet API provides several objects that are used to enable the functionality of a servlet within a web container. These objects include the request and response objects, pageContext, and many others. When these objects are used properly, they enable a servlet to perform just about any task a web-based application needs to do.

Dynamic web applications are those that change based on user input. This contrasts with static web applications, where the content is generally viewed as unchanging and determined by the web server administrator. Since a servlet is written in Java, any valid Java code can be used inside the servlet class. This allows Jakarta servlets to interact with other Java classes, the web container, the underlying file server, and much more.

With Jakarta EE 8 came the Servlet 4.0 specification; it was a significant revision around an upgrade from HTTP 1.1 to HTTP/2. The updated version of the HTTP protocol brings forth many enhancements, including request/response multiplexing, server push, binary framing, and stream prioritization. Some of the functionality enhancements occur underneath the covers, meaning that no API enhancements were required to support them. Other features, such as server push, exposed new APIs for the developer.

Servlet 5.0 was released as part of Jakarta EE 9 using the Eclipse EE Specification Process. It includes migration from the *javax.** to the *jakarta.** namespace. However, it was functionally identical to Servlet 4.0.

Jakarta EE 10 is adopting a microservices-first strategy, using containers as its primary deployment vehicle. This means that applications are expected to split into multiple service components. Servlets are ideal for this approach because they are scalable and can handle many concurrent requests with minimal overhead.

This chapter will get you started developing and deploying servlets. You will be taught the basics of developing servlets, how to use them with client web sessions, and how to link a servlet to another application. All the while, you will learn to use standards from the latest release of the Java Servlet API under the Jakarta EE platform, which modernizes servlet development and makes it much easier and more productive than in years past.

© Josh Juneau and Tarun Telang 2022
J. Juneau and T. Telang, *Java EE to Jakarta EE 10 Recipes*, https://doi.org/10.1007/978-1-4842-8079-9_1

To begin with, you need to install the Eclipse GlassFish application server (https://glassfish.org/) or Payara server (https://www.payara.fish/), both robust servlet containers, to deploy your sophisticated Jakarta EE applications.

Throughout this book, I would be sharing the solution using Eclipse GlassFish only. Because the Payara Server is mostly based on GlassFish, in case required, you will be able to switch to it with ease.

You will learn the basics of developing servlets, how to use them with client web sessions, and how to link a servlet to another application. All the while, you will learn to use standards from the latest release of the Jakarta Servlet API, which modernizes servlet development and makes it considerably simpler and more productive.

1-1. Setting Up a Jakarta EE Application Server

Problem

You want to set up an environment that you can use to deploy and run Jakarta servlets and other Jakarta EE technologies.

Solution

Download and install the Eclipse GlassFish application server from the GlassFish website (https://glassfish.org/). The version used for this book is the open source edition, release *7.0.0*, and it can be downloaded from the Downloads page (http://projects.eclipse.org/projects/ee4j.glassfish/downloads). Navigate into the promoted directory and grab a copy of the *glassfish-7.x.x.zip*, where x.x determines the MINOR.PATCH version. Decompress the downloaded files within a directory on your workstation. I will refer to that directory as /JAVA_DEV/glassfish7. The GlassFish distribution comes prepackaged with a domain known as *domain1* so that developers can get up and running quickly. Once the *.zip* file has been unpacked, you can start the domain by opening a command prompt or terminal and starting GlassFish using the following statement:

```
/JAVA_DEV/glassfish7/bin/asadmin start-domain domain1
```

The domain will start, and it will be ready for use. You will see output from the server that looks like the one shown in Figure 1-1.

```
$ ./asadmin start-domain domain1
Waiting for domain1 to start .............
Successfully started the domain : domain1
domain  Location: /Users/home/glassfish7/glassfish/domains/domain1
Log File: /Users/home/glassfish7/glassfish/domains/domain1/logs/server.log
Admin Port: 4848
Command start-domain executed successfully.
$
```

Figure 1-1. *Command to start the GlassFish server*

Once started, the domain can be stopped via the administrative console or from the command line:

```
/JAVA_DEV/glassfish7/bin/asadmin stop-domain domain1
```

Now, you will see output from the server that looks like the one shown in Figure 1-2.

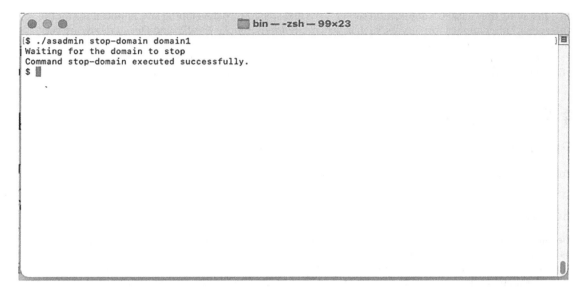

Figure 1-2. *Command to stop the GlassFish server*

How It Works

The development of Jakarta EE applications begins with a Jakarta EE-compliant application server. A Jakarta EE-compliant server contains all the essential components to provide a robust environment for deploying and hosting enterprise Java applications. The GlassFish 7 application server is a compatible implementation for Jakarta EE 10 (Full Platform and Web Profile).

Installing the GlassFish application server is very easy. The installation consists of downloading an archive and uncompressing it on your machine. Once you've completed this, the application server will use your locally installed Java Development Kit (JDK) when it is started. Once the server starts, you can validate this by opening a browser and navigating to http://localhost:8080 to view the Eclipse GlassFish start page.

Figure 1-3 shows the screenshot of the GlassFish start page.

Figure 1-3. *GlassFish start page*

Installing the GlassFish application server is the first step toward developing Java applications for the enterprise. Other application servers, such as *Payara*, *WildFly*, *Apache TomEE*, and *Open Liberty*, are very well adapted for development and production use.

GlassFish offers an excellent environment for starting development with Jakarta EE. Many servers also offer open source options, and they are the compatible implementation of Jakarta EE.

1-2. Developing a Servlet

Problem

You wish to develop a web page that enables the use of dynamic content.

Solution

Develop a Jakarta Servlet class, compile it, and deploy it within a compliant Jakarta Servlet container, such as Eclipse GlassFish. In this example, a simple servlet is created, which will be used to display dynamic content onto a web page. The following example demonstrates how to code a servlet which will display HTML content. In this example, the content is hard-coded, but it could be easily modified to pull in dynamic content from a database or external properties file:

```
package org.jakartaeerecipe.chapter01.recipe01_02;

import jakarta.servlet.annotation.*;
import jakarta.servlet.http.*;

import java.io.*;

public class SimpleServlet extends HttpServlet {

    private String message;

    @Override
    public void init() {
        message = "Welcome to Java EE to Jakarta EE 10 Recipes!";
    }

    /**
     * Processes requests for both HTTP
     * <code>GET</code> and
     * <code>POST</code> methods.
     *
     * @param request servlet request
     * @param response servlet response
     * @throws ServletException if a servlet-specific error occurs
     * @throws IOException if an I/O error occurs
     */
    protected void processRequest(HttpServletRequest request, HttpServletResponse response)
            throws ServletException, IOException {
        response.setContentType("text/html;charset=UTF-8");
        try (PrintWriter out = response.getWriter()) {
```

```
        // Place page output here
        out.printf("""
          <html>
                  <head>
                      <title>Simple Servlet</title>
                  </head>
                  <body>
                    <h2>Simple Servlet at %s</h2>
                    <br/>%s
                </body>
            </html>
                """, request.getContextPath(), message);
    }
}

/**
 * Handles the HTTP GET
 *
 * @param request servlet request
 * @param response servlet response
 * @throws ServletException if a servlet-specific error occurs
 * @throws IOException if an I/O error occurs
 */
@Override
protected void doGet(HttpServletRequest request, HttpServletResponse response)
        throws ServletException, IOException {
    processRequest(request, response);
}

/**
 * Handles the HTTP POST
 *
 * @param request servlet request
 * @param response servlet response
 * @throws ServletException if a servlet-specific error occurs
 * @throws IOException if an I/O error occurs
 */
@Override
protected void doPost(HttpServletRequest request, HttpServletResponse response)
        throws ServletException, IOException {
    processRequest(request, response);
}
}
```

The following code is the web deployment descriptor (*web.xml*). The deployment descriptor must be placed within the *WEB-INF* folder, which is located at the web sources root. In Recipe 1-4, you will learn how to omit the servlet configuration and to map from the web.xml file to make servlet development, deployment, and maintenance easier.

```
<?xml version="1.0" encoding="UTF-8"?>
<web-app xmlns="https://jakarta.ee/xml/ns/jakartaee"
        xmlns:xsi="http://www.w3.org/2001/XMLSchema-instance"
```

5

```
        xsi:schemaLocation="https://jakarta.ee/xml/ns/jakartaee https://jakarta.ee/xml/ns/
        jakartaee/web-app_5_0.xsd"
        version="5.0">
    <servlet>
        <servlet-name>SimpleServlet</servlet-name>
        <servlet-class>org.jakartaeerecipe.chapter01.recipe01_02.SimpleServlet
        </servlet-class>
    </servlet>
    <servlet-mapping>
        <servlet-name>SimpleServlet</servlet-name>
        <url-pattern>/SimpleServlet</url-pattern>
    </servlet-mapping>
    <welcome-file-list>
        <welcome-file>/SimpleServlet </welcome-file>
    </welcome-file-list>
</web-app>
```

To compile the servlet, use the `javac` command-line utility or a Java integrated development environment (IDE) such as Apache NetBeans. The following line was excerpted from the command line, and it compiles the `SimpleServlet.java` file into a class file. First, traverse into the directory containing the `SimpleServlet.java` file. Next, execute the following command:

```
javac -cp /JAVA_DEV/glassfish7/glassfish/modules/jakarta.servlet-api.jar SimpleServlet.java
```

Note that the path in the preceding example utilizes the `jakarta.servlet-api.jar` file which is part of GlassFish 7.0.x. Once the servlet code has been compiled into a Java class file, then it is ready to package for deployment to a servlet container.

■ **Note**   You may want to consider installing an integrated development environment (IDE) to increase your development productivity. There are several very good IDEs available to developers, so be sure to choose one that contains the features you find most important and useful for development. I recommend installing the latest version of any of these IDEs: IntelliJ IDEA (Ultimate Edition), Apache NetBeans, or an Eclipse IDE for Enterprise Java and Web Developers for development.

Apache NetBeans is an open source IDE that is maintained by Apache, and it includes support for all the cutting-edge features that the Java industry has to offer, including development with Jakarta EE, OpenJFX support, and more.

IntelliJ IDEA Ultimate Edition is a Java integrated development environment (IDE) for developing computer software developed by JetBrains with features such as code analysis, refactoring, version control systems integration, unit testing, and code inspections.

The Eclipse IDE is a cross-platform integrated development environment (IDE) for programming in many languages. It is written primarily in Java, and its primary use is for developing Java applications, but it can be used to develop applications in other programming languages including C++, PHP, Python, and Ruby.

All these IDEs support development of Jakarta EE applications. Which one to use is up to personal preference. In this book, I would be using IntelliJ IDEA Ultimate Edition, but the same concepts apply to NetBeans or the Eclipse IDE.

How It Works

Jakarta Servlets provide developers with the flexibility to design applications using a request-response programming model. It plays a key role in the development of microservices and web applications on the Java platform. There are different types of servlets that can be created, and each of them is geared toward providing a different functionality. The first type is known as a GenericServlet, which provides protocol-independent services and functionalities. The second type, HttpServlet, is a subclass of GenericServlet and provides functionality and a response utilizing HTTP. The solution to this recipe demonstrates the latter type of servlet because it displays a result for the user to see within a web browser.

Servlets conform to a life cycle for processing requests and posting results. First, the Jakarta Servlet container calls the servlet's constructor. The constructor of every servlet must accept no arguments. Next, the container calls the servlet init() method, which is responsible for initializing the servlet. Once the servlet has been initialized, it is ready for use. At that point, the servlet can begin processing. Each servlet contains a service() method, which handles the requests being made and dispatches them to the appropriate methods for request handling. Implementing the service() method is optional. Finally, the container calls upon the servlet destroy() method, which takes care of finalizing the servlet and taking it out of service.

Every servlet class must implement the jakarta.servlet.Servlet interface or extend another class that does. In the solution to this recipe, the servlet named SimpleServlet extends the HttpServlet class, which provides methods for handling HTTP processes. In this scenario, a browser client request is sent from the container to the servlet; then the servlet service() method dispatches the HttpServletRequest object to the appropriate method provided by HttpServlet. Namely, the HttpServlet class provides the doGet(), doPut(), doPost(), and doDelete() methods for working with an HTTP request. The most often used methods are the doGet() and doPost(). The HttpServlet class is abstract, so it must be subclassed, and then an implementation can be provided for its methods. Table 1-1 describes each of the methods available to an HttpServlet.

Table 1-1. *HttpServlet Methods*

Method Name	Description
doGet	Used to process HTTP GET requests. Input sent to the servlet must be included in the URL address. For example: ?publisher=Apress&topic=JakartaEE10
doPost	Used to process HTTP POST requests. Input can be sent to the servlet within HTML form fields
doPut	Used to process HTTP PUT requests
doDelete	Used to process HTTP DELETE requests
doHead	Used to process HTTP HEAD requests
doOptions	Called by the container to allow OPTIONS request handling
doTrace	Called by the container to handle TRACE requests
getLastModified	Returns the time that the HttpServletRequest object was last modified
init	Initializes the servlet
service	Called by the servlet container after the init() method. It allows the servlet to respond to a request
destroy	Finalizes the servlet
getServletInfo	Provides information regarding the servlet

A servlet generally performs some processing within the implementation of its methods and then returns a response to the client. The HttpServletRequest object can be used to process arguments that are sent via the request. For instance, if an HTML form contains some input fields that are sent to the server, those fields would be contained within the HttpServletRequest object. The HttpServletResponse object is used to send responses to the client browser. Both the doGet() and doPost() methods within a servlet accept the same arguments, namely, the HttpServletRequest and HttpServletResponse objects.

▪ **Note** The doGet() method is used to intercept HTTP GET requests, and doPost() is used to intercept HTTP POST requests. Generally, the doGet() method is used to prepare a request before displaying for a client, and the doPost() method is used to process a request and gather information from an HTML form.

In the solution to this recipe, both the doGet() and doPost() methods pass the HttpServletRequest and HttpServletResponse objects to the processRequest() method for further processing. The HttpServletResponse object is used to set the content type of the response and to obtain a handle on the PrintWriter object in the processRequest() method. The following lines of code show how this is done, if the identifier referencing the HttpServletResponse object is response:

```
response.setContentType("text/html;charset=UTF-8");
PrintWriter out = response.getWriter();
```

A GenericServlet can be used for providing services to web applications. This type of servlet is oftentimes used for logging events because it implements the log() method. A GenericServlet implements both the Servlet and ServletConfig interfaces, and to write a generic servlet, only the service() method must be overridden.

1-3. Packaging, Compiling, and Deploying a Servlet

Problem

You have written a Jakarta servlet and now want to package it and deploy it for use.

Solution

Compile the sources, set up a deployable application, and copy the contents into the GlassFish deployment directory. From the command line, use the javac command to compile the sources:

```
javac -cp /JAVA_DEV/glassfish7/glassfish/modules/jakarta.servlet-api.jar SimpleServlet.java
```

After the class has been compiled, deploy it along with the web.xml deployment descriptor, conforming to the appropriate directory structure.

Quick Start

To quickly get started with packaging, compiling, and deploying the example application for the servlet recipes in this chapter on GlassFish 7.0, follow these steps:

1. Create an application named SimpleServlet by making a directory named SimpleServlet.

2. Create the WEB-INF, WEB-INF/classes, and WEB-INF/lib directories inside SimpleServlet.

3. Copy the Chapter 1 sources (beginning with the org directory) in the WEB-INF/ classes directory you created, as well as the contents of the web folder, into the root of your SimpleServlet directory.

4. Copy the web.xml file that is in the source's recipe01_01 directory into the WEB-INF directory you created.

5. Download the Jakarta Mail API code from the Jakarta Mail website https:// eclipse-ee4j.github.io/mail/, and copy the jakarta.mail.jar file into the WEB-INF/lib directory you created. This API will be used to send mail in future recipes.

6. Set your CLASSPATH to include the jakarta.mail.jar file you downloaded in step 5 by giving the following command:

   CLASSPATH=${CLASSPATH}:/PATH_TO_PROJECT/SimpleServlet/WEB-INF/lib

7. At the command prompt, change directories so that you are in the classes directory you created in step 2. Compile each recipe with the command javac org\jakartaeerecipe\chapter01\recipe1_x*.java, where x is equal to the recipe number.

8. Copy your SimpleServlet application directory to the /JAVA_DEV/glassfish7/ glassfish/domains/domain1/autodeploy directory for GlassFish.

Test the application by launching a browser and going to http://localhost:8080/JakartaEERecipes_ Chapter01-1.0-SNAPSHOT/<servlet_name>, where <servlet_name> corresponds to the servlet name in each recipe.

How It Works

To compile the sources, you can use your favorite Java development environment such as Apache NetBeans (http://netbeans.apache.org/), Eclipse IDE (www.eclipse.org/eclipseide/), or IntelliJ IDEA (www. jetbrains.com/idea/), or you can use the command line. If you're using the command line, you must ensure you are using the javac command that is associated with the same Java release that you will be using to run your servlet container. In this example, the location of the Java SE 17 installation was at the following path:

/Library/Java/JavaVirtualMachines/jdk-17.0.1.jdk/Contents/Home

---

■ **Note** The Java JDK that is used to compile is dependent upon the application server container that is being used for deployment. At the time of this writing, most containers were compatible with JDK 17.

This path may differ in your environment if you are using a different operating system and/or installation location. To ensure you are using the Java runtime that is located at this path, set the JAVA_HOME environment variable equal to this path. On OS X and *nix operating systems, you can set the environment variable by opening the terminal and typing the following:

```
export JAVA_HOME=/Library/Java/JavaVirtualMachines/jdk-17.0.1.jdk/Contents/Home
```

If you are using Windows, use the SET command within the command line to set up the JAVA_HOME environment variable:

```
set JAVA_HOME=C:\your-java-se-path\
```

Next, compile your Java servlet sources, and be sure to include the jakarta.servlet-api.jar file that is packaged with your servlet container (use servlet-api.jar for Tomcat) in your CLASSPATH. You can set the CLASSPATH by using the –cp flag of the javac command. The following command should be executed at the command line from within the same directory that contains the sources. In this case, the source file is named *SimpleServlet.java*:

```
javac -cp /path_to_jar/jakarta.servlet-api.jar SimpleServlet.java
```

Next, package your application by creating a directory and naming it after your application. In this case, create a directory and name it *SimpleServlet*. Within that directory, create another directory named *WEB-INF*. Traverse into the *WEB-INF* directory, and create another directory named classes. Lastly, create directories within the classes directory to replicate your Java servlet package structure. For this recipe, the *SimpleServlet.java* class resides within the Java package *org.jakartaeerecipe.chapter01.recipe01_01* so create a directory for each of those packages within the classes directory. Create a final directory within *WEB-INF* and name it *lib*; any JAR files containing external libraries should be placed within the lib directory. In the end, your directory structure should resemble the following:

```
SimpleServlet
└── WEB-INF
    ├── classes
    │   └── org
    │       └── jakartaeerecipe
    │           └── chapter01
    │               └── recipe01_03
    │                   └── SimpleServlet.class
    ├── lib
    │   └── jakarta.mail.jar
    └── web.xml
```

Place your web.xml deployment descriptor within the WEB-INF directory and place the compiled SimpleServlet.class file within the recipe01_03 directory. The entire contents of the SimpleServlet directory can now be copied within the deployment directory for your application server container to deploy the application. Restart the application server if using Tomcat and launch the URL http://localhost:8080/SimpleServlet/SimpleServlet to see the servlet in action as per the screenshot in Figure 1-4.

Simple Servlet at /JakartaEERecipes_Chapter01-1.0-SNAPSHOT

Welcome to Java EE to Jakarta EE 10 Recipes!

Figure 1-4. *SimpleServlet output*

> ■ **Note** If using an integrated development environment or a build tool such as Maven, all the manual work of generating directories and placing files into the correct locations is done automatically. In general, the use of an IDE is greatly recommended, as it can increase productivity and reduce the chance for errors.

1-4. Registering a Servlet Without web.xml

Problem

Registering servlets in the web.xml file is cumbersome, and you want to deploy servlets without modifying web.xml at all.

Solution

Use the @WebServlet annotation to register the servlet and omit the web.xml registration. This will alleviate the need to modify the web.xml file each time a servlet is added to your application. The following adaptation of the SimpleServlet class that was used in Recipe 1-2 includes the @WebServlet annotation and demonstrates its use:

```
package org.jakartaeerecipe.chapter01.recipe01_04;
import jakarta.servlet.annotation.*;
import jakarta.servlet.http.*;

import java.io.*;

@WebServlet(name = "SimpleServletNoDescriptor", urlPatterns = {"/
SimpleServletNoDescriptor"})
public class SimpleServletNoDescriptor extends HttpServlet {

        private String message;

        @Override
        public void init() {
            message = "Look ma, no WEB-XML!";
        }

        protected void processRequest(HttpServletRequest request,
                HttpServletResponse response) throws ServletException, IOException {

            response.setContentType("text/html;charset=UTF-8");

            try(PrintWriter out = response.getWriter()) {
                    out.printf("""
                        <html>
                            <head>
                                    <title>Servlet SimpleServlet</title>
                            </head>
```

```
                    <body>
                            <h2>Servlet SimpleServlet at %s</h2>
                                    <br/>%s
                    </body>
            </html>
            """, request.getContextPath(), message);
    }
}

@Override
protected void doGet(HttpServletRequest request, HttpServletResponse response)
        throws ServletException, IOException {
    processRequest(request, response);
}

@Override
protected void doPost(HttpServletRequest request, HttpServletResponse response)
        throws ServletException, IOException {
    processRequest(request, response);
}
}
```

In the end, the servlet will be accessible via a URL in the same way that it would if the servlet were registered within web.xml. You should see the page loaded as in Figure 1-5.

Servlet SimpleServlet at /JakartaEERecipes_Chapter01-1.0-SNAPSHOT

Look ma, no WEB-XML!

Figure 1-5. *SimpleServletNoDescriptor output*

■■ **Note** Remove any existing servlet mapping within the web.xml file to make use of the @WebServlet annotation.

How It Works

There are several ways to register servlets with a web container. The first way is to register them using the web.xml deployment descriptor, as demonstrated in Recipe 1-1. The second way to register them is to use the @WebServlet annotation, which provides an easier technique to use for mapping a servlet to a URL. The @WebServlet annotation is placed before the declaration of a class, and it accepts the elements listed in Table 1-2.

Table 1-2. *@WebServlet Annotation Elements*

Element	Description
description	Description of the servlet
displayName	The display name of the servlet
initParams	Accepts a list of `@WebInitParam` annotations
largeIcon	The large icon of the servlet
loadOnStartup	Load on startup order of the servlet
name	Servlet name
smallIcon	The small icon of the servlet
urlPatterns	URL patterns that invoke the servlet
asyncSupported	Whether the servlet supports async operation mode

In the solution to this recipe, the `@WebServlet` annotation maps the servlet class named `SimpleServletNoDescriptor` to the URL pattern of `/SimpleServletNoDescriptor`, and it also names the servlet `SimpleServletNoDescriptor`:

```
@WebServlet(name="SimpleServletNoDescriptor", urlPatterns={"/SimpleServletNoDescriptor"})
```

1-5. Displaying Dynamic Content with a Servlet

Problem

You want to display some content to a web page that may change depending upon server-side activity or user input.

Solution

Define a field within your servlet to contain the dynamic content that is to be displayed. Post the dynamic content on the page by appending the field containing it using the `PrintWriter` `println()` method. The following example servlet declares a `Date` field and updates it with the current date each time the page is loaded:

```
package org.jakartaeerecipe.chapter01.recipe01_05;

import java.io.*;
import java.util.Date;

import jakarta.servlet.annotation.*;
import jakarta.servlet.http.*;

@WebServlet(name = "CurrentDateAndTime", urlPatterns = {"/CurrentDateAndTime"})
public class CurrentDateAndTime extends HttpServlet {
    Date currDateAndTime = new Date();
```

13

```
    protected void processRequest(HttpServletRequest request, HttpServletResponse response)
            throws ServletException, IOException {
        response.setContentType("text/html;charset=UTF-8");

            synchronized(currDateAndTime){
                currDateAndTime = new Date();
        }

        try (PrintWriter out = response.getWriter()) {
            out.printf("""
              <html>
                            <head>
                                <title>Servlet Current Date And Time</title>
                            </head>
                            <body>
                                    <h1>Servlet CurrentDateAndTime at %s</h1><br/>
                                    The current date and time is: %s
                            </body>
                    </html>""", request.getContextPath(), currDateAndTime);
        }
    }

    @Override
    protected void doGet(HttpServletRequest request, HttpServletResponse response)
            throws ServletException, IOException {
        processRequest(request, response);
    }

    @Override
    protected void doPost(HttpServletRequest request, HttpServletResponse response)
            throws ServletException, IOException {
        processRequest(request, response);
    }
}
```

■ **Note** Servlets are multithreaded, and many client requests may be using a servlet concurrently. When a field is declared as a servlet class member (not within a method) as you have done with currDateAndTime, you must assure that only one client request can manipulate the field at any instance. You do this by synchronizing around the use of the field, as shown in the processRequest() method. You synchronize around the smallest block of code you can manage in order to minimize latency. The resulting output from this servlet will be the current date and time.

```
synchronized( currDateAndTime ) {
    currDateAndTime = new Date();
}
```

How It Works

One of the reasons why Java servlets are so useful is because they allow dynamic content to be displayed on a web page. The content can be taken from the server itself, a database, another website, or any other web-accessible resource. If you refresh the web page after some time, you would see the current time updated dynamically to your present time. Servlets are not static web pages; they are dynamic, and that is arguably their biggest strength.

In the solution to this recipe, a servlet is used to display the current time and date on the server. When the servlet is processed, the `doGet()` method is called, which subsequently makes a call to the `processRequest()` method, passing the request and response objects. Therefore, the `processRequest()` method is where the bulk of the work occurs. The `processRequest()` method creates a `PrintWriter` by calling the `response.getWriter()` method, and the `PrintWriter` is used to display content on the resulting web page. Next, the current date and time are obtained from the server by creating a new `Date` and assigning it to the `currDateAndTime` field.

Lastly, the `processRequest()` method sends the web content through the `out.println()` method, and the contents of the `currDateAndTime` field are concatenated to a String and sent to `out.println()` as well. Each time the servlet is processed, it will display the current date and time at the time in which the servlet is invoked because a new `Date` is created with each request.

This example just scratches the surface of what is possible with a Jakarta servlet. Although displaying the current date and time is trivial, you could alter that logic to display the contents of any field contained within the servlet. Whether it be an `int` field that displays a calculation that was performed by the servlet container or a `String` field containing some information, the possibilities are endless. Figure 1-6 shows the output for this page.

Servlet CurrentDateAndTime at /JakartaEERecipes_Chapter01-1.0-SNAPSHOT

The current date and time is: Thu Mar 31 18:49:03 IST 2022

Figure 1-6. *CurrentDateAndTime servlet output*

1-6. Handling Requests and Responses

Problem

You want to create a web form that accepts user input and supplies a response based upon the input that has been received.

Solution

Create a standard HTML-based web form, and when the submit button is clicked, invoke a servlet to process the end-user input and post a response. To examine this technique, you will see two different pieces of code. The following code is HTML that is used to generate the input form. This code exists within the file

15

recipe01_06.html. Please browse to /chapter01/recipe01_06.html to execute the example. Pay particular attention to the <form> and <input> tags. You will see that the form's action parameter lists a servlet name, MathServlet:

```html
<html>
    <head>
    <title>Simple Math Servlet</title>
    </head>
    <body>
        <h1>This is a simple Math Servlet</h1>
        <form method="POST" action="../MathServlet">
            <label for="numa">Enter Number A: </label>
            <input type="text" id="numa" name="numa"/><br><br>
                            <label for="numb">Enter Number B: </label>
                            <input type="text" id="numb" name="numb"/><br/><br/>
            <input type="submit" value="Submit Form"/>
            <input type="reset" value="Reset Form"/>
        </form>
    </body>
</html>
```

Next, look at the following code for a servlet named MathServlet. This is the Java code that receives the input from the HTML code listed earlier, processes it accordingly, and posts a response:

```java
package org.jakartaeerecipe.chapter01.recipe01_06;

import jakarta.servlet.annotation.*;
import jakarta.servlet.http.*;
import jakarta.servlet.ServletException;

import java.io.*;

@WebServlet(name="MathServlet", urlPatterns={"/MathServlet"})
public class MathServlet extends HttpServlet {
    @Override
      public void doPost(HttpServletRequest req, HttpServletResponse res)
            throws IOException, ServletException {

        res.setContentType("text/html");

        // Store the input parameter values into Strings
        String numA = req.getParameter("numa");
        String numB = req.getParameter("numb");
        int solution = 0;
        try (PrintWriter out = res.getWriter()) {
        try {
                solution= Integer.valueOf(numA) + Integer.valueOf(numB);
            } catch (java.lang.NumberFormatException ex) {
            // Display error if an exception is raised
            out.println("Please use numbers only...try again.");
            return;
        }
```

```
        out.printf("""
                <html>
                    <head>
                      <title>Test Math Servlet</title>
                    </head>
                    <body>
                        Solution: %d + %d = %d
                        <br/>
                        <a href='recipe01_05.html'>Add Two More Numbers</a>
                            </body>
                </html>""", numA, numB, solution);
    }
}
```

■ **Note** To run the example, copy the previous HTML code into an HTML file within the web root of your JakartaEERecipes_Chapter01 application named recipe01_06.html, and then enter the following address into your browser: http://localhost:8080/JakartaEERecipes_Chapter01-1.0-SNAPSHOT/ chapter01/recipe01_06.html. This assumes you are using default port numbers for your application server installation.

How It Works

Servlets make it easy to create web applications that adhere to a request and response life cycle. They can provide HTTP responses and process business logic within the same body of code. The ability to process business logic makes servlets much more powerful than standard HTML code. The solution to this recipe demonstrates a standard servlet structure for processing requests and sending responses. An HTML web form contains parameters that are sent to a servlet. The servlet then processes those parameters in some manner and publishes a response that can be seen by the client. In the case of an HttpServlet object, the client is a web browser, and the response is a web page.

This is a simple MathServlet

Enter Number A: | 10 |

Enter Number B: | 5 |

| Submit Form | | Reset Form |

Figure 1-7. *HTML form which calls MathServlet*

Values can be obtained from an HTML form by using HTML <input> tags embedded within an HTML <form>. In the solution to this recipe, two values are accepted as input, and they are referenced by their id attributes as numa and numb. There are two more <input> tags within the form; one of them is used to submit the values to the form action, and the other is used to reset the form fields to blank. The form action is the name of the servlet that the form values will be passed to as parameters. In this case, the action is set to MathServlet. The <form> tag also accepts a form-processing method, either GET or POST. In the example, the POST method is used because form data is being sent to the action; in this case, data is being sent to MathServlet. You could, of course, create an HTML form as detailed as you would like and then have that data sent to any servlet in the same manner. This example is relatively basic; it serves to give you an understanding of how the processing is performed.

The <form> action attribute states that the MathServlet should be used to process the values that are contained within the form. The MathServlet name can be mapped back to the MathServlet class via the web.xml deployment descriptor or the @WebServlet annotation. Looking at the MathServlet code, you can see that a doPost() method is implemented to handle the processing of the POST form values. The doPost() method accepts HttpServletRequest and HttpServletResponse objects as arguments. The values contained within the HTML form are embedded within the HttpServletRequest object. To obtain those values, call upon the request object's getParameter() method, passing the id of the input parameter you want to obtain. In the solution to this recipe, those values are obtained and stored within local String fields:

```
String numA = req.getParameter("numa");
String numB = req.getParameter("numb");
```

Solution: 10 + 5 = 15
Add Two More Numbers

Figure 1-8. *MathServlet output*

Once the values are obtained, they can be processed as needed. In this case, those String values are converted into int values, and then they are added together to generate a sum and stored into an int field. That field is then presented as a response on a resulting web page:

```
int solution = Integer.valueOf(numA) + Integer.valueOf(numB);
```

As mentioned, the HTML form could be much more complex, containing any number of <input> fields. Likewise, the servlet could perform more complex processing of those field values.

This example is merely the tip of the iceberg, and the possibilities are without bounds. Servlet-based web frameworks such as Jakarta Server Pages and Jakarta Server Faces hide many of the complexities of passing form values to a servlet and processing a response. However, the same basic framework is used behind the scenes.

1-7. Listening for Servlet Container Events

Problem

You want to have the ability to listen for application startup and shutdown events.

Solution

Create a servlet context event listener to alert when the application has started up or when it has been shut down. The following solution demonstrates the code for a context listener, which will log application startup and shutdown events and send email alerting of such events:

```
package org.jakartaeerecipe.chapter01.recipe01_07;

import java.util.Properties;
import jakarta.mail.*;
import jakarta.mail.internet.*;
import jakarta.servlet.*;
import jakarta.servlet.annotation.WebListener;

@WebListener
public class StartupShutdownListener implements ServletContextListener {

    private final String TAG = "StartupShutdownListener: ";

    @Override
     public void contextInitialized(ServletContextEvent event) {
        System.out.println(TAG + "Servlet startup...");
        System.out.println(TAG + event.getServletContext().getServerInfo());
        System.out.println(TAG + System.currentTimeMillis());

        sendEmail("Servlet context has initialized");
     }

    @Override
    public void contextDestroyed(ServletContextEvent event) {
        System.out.println(TAG + "Servlet shutdown...");
        System.out.println(TAG + event.getServletContext().getServerInfo());
        System.out.println(TAG + System.currentTimeMillis());

        // See error in server.log if mail is unsuccessful
        sendEmail("Servlet context has been destroyed...");
    }

    /**
     * This implementation uses the GMail smtp server
     * @param message text to be sent in the mail
     */
    private void sendEmail(String message) {
        String smtpHost = "smtp.someserver.com"; // for e.g smtp.smtp2go.com
        String smtpUsername = "username"; // username for the SMTP server
        String smtpPassword = "password";  // password for the SMTP server
        String from = "fromaddress@domain.com"; // sender email address
        String to = "toaddress@domain.com"; // recipient email address
        int smtpPort = 2525; // SMTP server port

         System.out.println(TAG + "sending email...");
         try {
            // Send email here

            //Set the host smtp address
            Properties props = new Properties();
            props.put("mail.smtp.host", smtpHost);
```

```
        props.put("mail.smtp.auth", "true");
        props.put("mail.smtp.starttls.enable", "false");

        // create some properties and get the default Session
        Session session = Session.getInstance(props);

        // create a message
        Message msg = new MimeMessage(session);

        // set the from and to address
        InternetAddress addressFrom = new InternetAddress(from);
        msg.setFrom(addressFrom);
        InternetAddress[] address = new InternetAddress[1];
        address[0] = new InternetAddress(to);
        msg.setRecipients(Message.RecipientType.TO, address);
        msg.setSubject( TAG + "Servlet container shutting down");

        // Append Footer
        msg.setContent(msg, "text/plain");
        Transport transport = session.getTransport("smtp");
        transport.connect(smtpHost, smtpPort, smtpUsername, smtpPassword);
        Transport.send(msg, smtpUsername, smtpPassword);
    } catch (jakarta.mail.MessagingException ex) {
        System.out.println(TAG + e.getMessage());
    }
    System.out.println(TAG + "email successfully sent");
  }
}
```

■ **Note**   To run this example, make sure you have added `jakarta.mail.jar` as described earlier in this chapter in Recipe 1-2.

Once the servlet is successfully initialized, it should generate the log messages for the same in the GlassFish server log file which can be found in the following location:

`JAVA_DEV/glassfish7/glassfish/domain/domain1/logs/server.log`

You can also view this from your IntelliJ IDEA by going to the *Services* ➤ *GlassFish Log*; see Figure 1-9.

Figure 1-9. *Viewing GlassFish Log using the Services tab of IntelliJ IDEA*

How It Works

Sometimes, it is useful to know when certain events occur within the application server container. This concept can be useful under many different circumstances, but most often it would be used for initializing an application upon startup or cleaning up after an application upon shutdown. A servlet listener can be registered with an application to indicate when it has been started up or shut down. Therefore, by listening for such events, the servlet can perform some actions when they occur.

To create a listener that performs actions based on a container event, you must develop a class that implements the ServletContextListener interface. The methods that need to be implemented are contextInitialized() and contextDestroyed(). Both methods accept a ServletContextEvent as an argument, and they are automatically called each time the servlet container is initialized or shut down, respectively. To register the listener with the container, you can use one of the following techniques:

- Utilize the @WebListener annotation, as demonstrated by the solution to this recipe.

- Register the listener within the web.xml application deployment descriptor.

- Use the addListener() method defined in ServletContext.

For example, to register this listener within web.xml, you need to add the following lines of XML:

```
<listener>
    <listener-class> org.jakartaeerecipe.chapter01.recipe01_06.StartupShutdownListener</
    listener-class>
</listener>
```

Neither way is better than the other. The only time that listener registration within the application deployment descriptor (web.xml) would be more helpful is if you had the need to disable the listener in some cases. On the other hand, to disable a listener when it is registered using @WebListener, you must remove the annotation and recompile the code. Altering the web deployment descriptor does not require any code to be recompiled.

There are many different listener types, and the interface that the class implements is what determines the listener type. For instance, in the solution to this recipe, the class implements the ServletContextListener interface. Doing so creates a listener for servlet context events. If, however, the class implements HttpSessionListener, it would be a listener for HTTP session events. The following is a complete listing of listener interfaces:

```
jakarta.servlet.ServletRequestListener
jakarta.servlet.ServletRequestAttributeListener
jakarta.servlet.ServletContextListener
jakarta.servlet.ServletContextAttributeListener
jakarta.servlet.http.HttpSessionListener
jakarta.servlet.http.HttpSessionAttributeListener
jakarta.servlet.http.HttpSessionIdListener
```

It is also possible to create a listener that implements multiple listener interfaces. To learn more about listening for different situations such as attribute changes, see Recipe 1-10.

1-8. Setting Initialization Parameters

Problem

A servlet you are writing requires the ability to accept one or more parameters to be set upon initialization.

Solution #1

Set the servlet initialization parameters using the @WebInitParam annotation. The following code sets an initialization parameter that is equal to a String value:

```
package org.jakartaeerecipe.chapter01.recipe01_08;

import java.io.*;

import jakarta.servlet.*;
import jakarta.servlet.annotation.*;
import jakarta.servlet.http.*;

@WebServlet(name="SimpleServletCtx1", urlPatterns={"/SimpleServletCtx1"},
    initParams={ @WebInitParam(name="name", value="Duke") })
public class SimpleServletCtx1 extends HttpServlet {
        @Override
    public void doGet(HttpServletRequest req, HttpServletResponse res)
        throws IOException, ServletException {
        response.setContentType("text/html");

        try (PrintWriter out = response.getWriter()) {
            out.printf("""
                    <html>
                        <head>
                            <title> Simple Servlet Context Example</title>
                        </head>
                        <body>
                            <p>This is a simple servlet to demonstrate context!
                            Hello %s </p>
                        </body>
                    </html>
                    """, getServletConfig().getInitParameter("name"));
        }
    }
}
```

To execute the example using the sources for this book, load the following URL into your web browser: http://localhost:8080/JakartaEERecipes_Chapter01-1.0-SNAPSHOT/SimpleServletCtx1. The resulting web page will display the text as in Figure 1-10.

Figure 1-10. SimpleServletCtx1 servlet output

Solution #2

Place the init parameters inside the web.xml deployment descriptor file. The following lines are excerpted from the web.xml deployment descriptor for the SimpleServlet application. They include the initialization parameter names and values:

```xml
<web-app>
    <servlet>
        <servlet-name>SimpleServletCtx1</servlet-name>
        <servlet-class> org.jakartaeerecipe.chapter01.recipe01_08.SimpleServletCtx1
        </servlet-class>
        <init-param>
            <param-name>name</param-name>
            <param-value>Duke</param-value>
        </init-param>
    ...
    </servlet>
    ...
</web-app>
```

How It Works

Oftentimes, there is a requirement to set initialization parameters for a servlet in order to initialize certain values. Servlets can accept any number of initialization parameters, and there are a couple of ways in which they can be set. The first solution is to annotate the servlet class with the @WebInitParam annotation, as demonstrated in Solution #1, and the second way to set an initialization parameter is to declare the parameter within the web.xml deployment descriptor, as demonstrated in Solution #2. Either way will work; however, the solution using @WebInitParam is based on the newer Jakarta Servlet 5.0 API. Therefore, Solution #1 is the more contemporary approach, but Solution #2 remains valid for following an older model or using an older servlet release.

To use the @WebInitParam annotation, it must be embedded within the @WebServlet annotation. Therefore, the servlet must be registered with the web application via the @WebServlet annotation rather than within the web.xml file. For more information on registering a servlet via the @WebServlet annotation, see Recipe 1-4.

The @WebInitParam annotation accepts a name-value pair as an initialization parameter. In the solution to this recipe, the parameter name is name, and the value is Duke:

```java
@WebInitParam(name="name", value="Duke")
```

23

Once set, the parameter can be used within code by calling getServletConfig(). getInitializationParameter() and passing the name of the parameter.

The annotations have the benefit of providing ease of development, and they also make it easier to maintain servlets as a single package rather than jumping back and forth between the servlet and the deployment descriptor. However, those benefits come at the cost of compilation because to change the value of an initialization parameter using the @WebInitParam annotation, you must recompile the code. This is not the case when using the web.xml deployment descriptor. It is best to evaluate your application circumstances before committing to a standard for setting initialization parameters.

1-9. Filtering Web Requests

Problem

You want to invoke certain processing if a specified URL is used to access your application. For instance, if a specific URL were used to access your application, you would want to log the user's IP address.

Solution

Create a servlet filter that will be processed when the specified URL format is used to access the application. In this example, the filter will be executed when a URL conforming to the format of /* is used. This format pertains to any URL in the application. Therefore, any page will cause the servlet to be invoked.

```
package org.jakartaeerecipe.chapter01.recipe01_09;

import java.io.IOException;

import jakarta.servlet.*;
import jakarta.servlet.annotation.WebFilter;

@WebFilter("/*")
public class LoggingFilter implements Filter {
    private FilterConfig filterConfig = null;
    @Override
    public void init(FilterConfig filterConf) {
        this.filterConf = filterConf;
    }

    @Override
    public void doFilter(ServletRequest request,
            ServletResponse response,
            FilterChain chain)
            throws IOException, ServletException {
        String userIP = request.getRemoteHost();
        System.out.println("Visitor User IP: " + userAddy);
        chain.doFilter(request, response);
    }
    @Override
    public void destroy() {
        throw new UnsupportedOperationException("Not supported yet.");
    }
}
```

How It Works

Web filters are useful for preprocessing requests and invoking certain functionality when a given URL is visited. Rather than invoking a servlet that exists at a given URL directly, any filter that contains the same URL pattern will be invoked prior to the servlet. This can be helpful in many situations, perhaps the most useful for performing logging, authentication, or other services that occur in the background without user interaction.

Filters must implement the jakarta.servlet.Filter interface. Methods contained within this interface include init, destroy, and doFilter. The init and destroy methods are invoked by the container. The doFilter method is used to implement tasks for the filter class. As you can see from the solution to this recipe, the filter class has access to the ServletRequest and ServletResponse objects. This means the request can be captured, and information can be obtained from it. This also means the request can be modified if need be. For example, including the username in the request after an authentication filter has been used.

If you want to chain filters or if more than one filter exists for a given URL pattern, they will be invoked in the order in which they are configured in the web.xml deployment descriptor. It is best to manually configure the filters if you are using more than one per URL pattern rather than using the @WebFilter annotation. To manually configure the web.xml file to include a filter, use the <filter> and <filter-mapping> XML elements along with their associated child element tags. The following excerpt shows how the filter can be manually configured within the web.xml file configuration file:

```
<filter>
    <filter-name>LoggingFilter</filter-name>
    <filter-class>LoggingFilter</filter-class>
</filter>
<filter-mapping>
    <filter-name>LoggingFilter</filter-name>
    <url-pattern>/*</url-pattern>
</filter-mapping>
```

Of course, the @WebFilter annotation takes care of the configuration for you, so in this case the manual configuration is not required.

■ **Note**   If a filter invokes the next entity in the chain, each of the filter service methods must run in the same thread as all filters that apply to the servlet.

In addition to the Services tab in the IDE, GlassFish Server Log can also be viewed by visiting the URL http://localhost:4848/management/domain/view-log through a browser. The screenshot in Figure 1-11 demonstrates how you can verify the functioning of your filters by looking into the server logs.

Figure 1-11. *GlassFish Server Log*

1-10. Listening for Attribute Changes

Problem

You want to have the ability to perform an action within a servlet when a servlet attribute is added, removed, or updated.

Solution

Generate an attribute listener servlet to listen for such events as attributes being added, removed, or modified, and invoke an action when these events occur. The following class demonstrates this technique by implementing HttpSessionAttributeListener and listening for attributes that are added, removed, or replaced within the HTTP session:

```java
package org.jakartaeerecipe.chapter01.recipe01_10;

import jakarta.servlet.*;
import jakarta.servlet.annotation.WebListener;
import jakarta.servlet.http.*;

@WebListener
public final class AttributeListener implements ServletContextListener,
        HttpSessionAttributeListener {

    private ServletContext context = null;

    @Override
    public void attributeAdded(HttpSessionBindingEvent se) {
        HttpSession session = se.getSession();
        String id = session.getId();
        String name = se.getName();
        String value = (String) se.getValue();
        String message = new StringBuffer("New attribute has been added to session: \n")
.append("Attribute Name: ").append(name).append("\n")
.append("Attribute Value:").append(value).toString();
        log(message);
    }

@Override
public void attributeRemoved(HttpSessionBindingEvent se) {
        HttpSession session = se.getSession();
        String id = session.getId();
        String name = se.getName();
        if (name == null) {
            name = "Unknown";
        }
        String value = (String) se.getValue();
        String message = new StringBuffer("Attribute has been removed from session: \n").
        append(id).append("\n")
                .append("Attribute Name: ").append(name).append("\n").append("Attribute
                Value:")
```

```
                .append(value).toString();
        log(message);
    }

    @Override
    public void attributeReplaced(HttpSessionBindingEvent se) {
        String name = se.getName();
        if (name == null) {
            name = "Unknown";
        }
        String value = (String) se.getValue();
        String message = new StringBuffer("Attribute has been replaced: \n ").append(name).
        toString();
        log(message);
    }

    private void log(String message) {
        if (context != null) {
            context.log("SessionListener: " + message);
        } else {
            System.out.println("SessionListener: " + message);
        }
    }

    @Override
    public void contextInitialized(ServletContextEvent event) {
        this.context = event.getServletContext();
        log("contextInitialized()");
    }

    @Override
    public void contextDestroyed(ServletContextEvent event) {
    }
}
```

In this example, messages will be displayed within the server log file indicating when attributes have been added, removed, or replaced.

How It Works

In some situations, it can be useful to know when an attribute has been set or what an attribute value has been set to. The solution to this recipe demonstrates how to create an attribute listener in order to determine this information. To create a servlet listener, you must implement one or more of the servlet listener interfaces. To listen for HTTP session attribute changes, implement HttpSessionAttributeListener. In doing so, the listener will implement the attributeAdded, attributeRemoved, and attributeReplaced methods. Each of these methods accepts HttpSessionBindingEvent as an argument, and their implementation defines what will occur when an HTTP session attribute is added, removed, or changed, respectively.

In the solution to this recipe, you can see that each of the three methods listed in the previous paragraph contains a similar implementation. Within each method, the HttpSessionBindingEvent is interrogated and broken down into String values, which represent the ID, name, and value of the attribute that caused the listener to react. For instance, in the attributeAdded method, the session is obtained from

27

HttpSessionBindingEvent, and then the session ID is retrieved via the use of getSession. The attribute information can be obtained directly from the HttpSessionBindingEvent using the getId and getName methods, as shown in the following lines of code:

```
HttpSession session = se.getSession();
String id = session.getId();
String name = se.getName();
String value = (String) se.getValue();
```

After these values are obtained, the application can do whatever it needs to do with them. In this recipe, the attribute ID, name, and session ID are simply logged and printed:

```
String message = new StringBuffer("New attribute has been added to session: \n")
.append("Attribute Name: ").append(name).append("\n")
.append("Attribute Value:").append(value).toString();
log(message);
```

The body of the attributeReplaced and attributeRemoved methods contains similar functionality. In the end, the same routine is used within each to obtain the attribute name and value, and then something is done with those values.

A few different options can be used to register the listener with the container. The @WebListener annotation is the easiest way to do so, and the only downfall to using it is that you will need to recompile code to remove the listener annotation if you ever need to do so. The listener can be registered within the web deployment descriptor, or it can be registered using one of the addListener methods contained in ServletContext.

Although the example in the recipe does not perform any life-changing events, it does demonstrate how to create and use an attribute listener. In the real world, such a listener could become handy if an application needed to capture the username of everyone who logs in or needed to send an email whenever a specified attribute is set.

Note that it is possible to develop more sophisticated solutions using interfaces such as the ServletRequestAttributeListener or ServletContextAttributeListener, which can be useful for receiving events regarding ServletRequest or ServletContext attribute changes, respectively.

1-11. Applying a Listener to a Session

Problem

You want to listen for sessions to be created and destroyed so that you can count how many active sessions your application currently contains as well as perform some initialization for each session.

Solution

Create a session listener and implement the sessionCreated and sessionDestroyed methods accordingly. In the following example, a servlet is used to keep track of active sessions. Each time someone works with the application, a counter has one added to it. Likewise, each time a person leaves the application, the counter goes down by one:

```
package org.jakartaeerecipe.chapter01.recipe01_11;

import jakarta.servlet.annotation.WebListener;
import jakarta.servlet.http.*;

@WebListener
public class SessionListener implements HttpSessionListener {

    private int numberOfSessions;

    public SessionListener() {
        numberOfSessions = 0;
    }

    public int getNumberOfSessions() {
        return numberOfSessions;
    }

    @Override
    public void sessionCreated(HttpSessionEvent event) {
        HttpSession session = event.getSession();
        session.setMaxInactiveInterval(60);
        session.setAttribute("testAttr", "testVal");
        synchronized (this) {
            numberOfSessions++;
        }
        System.out.println("Session created, current count: " + numberOfSessions);
    }

    @Override
    public void sessionDestroyed(HttpSessionEvent event) {
        HttpSession session = event.getSession();
        synchronized (this) {
            numberOfSessions--;
        }
        System.out.println("Session destroyed, current count: " + numberOfSessions);
        System.out.println("The attribute value: " + session.getAttribute(("testAttr")));
    }
}
```

Each time a new visitor visits the application, a new session is started, and testAttr is set. When the session times out, it will be destroyed, and any attributes that have been set for the session will be removed.

In this example, messages will be displayed within the server log file as shown in Figure 1-12 indicating when sessions have been created or destroyed.

Record Number	Log Level	Message
3352	INFO	Session destroyed, current count: 0(details)
3351	INFO	The attribute value: testVal(details)
3350	INFO	Session destroyed, current count: 1(details)

Figure 1-12. *GlassFish Server Log Viewer output*

How It Works

A meaningful way to track web application users is to place values in their HttpSession object. Using a Jakarta servlet, session attributes can be set, which will exist for the life of the HttpSession. Once the session is invalidated, the attributes will be removed. To set up a session listener, create a Jakarta servlet, annotate it with the @WebListener annotation, and implement jakarta.servlet.http.HttpSessionListener. Doing so will force the implementation of both the sessionCreated and sessionDestroyed methods, which is where the session magic occurs.

In the example to this recipe, the sessionCreated method first obtains a handle on the current HttpSession object by calling the HttpSessionEvent object's getSession method. The handle is assigned to an HttpSession variable named session. Now that you have that variable initialized with the session object, it can be used to set the time of life and place attributes that will live and die with the session's life. The first session configuration performed in the example is to set the maximum inactive life to 60 (seconds), after which time the servlet container will invalidate the session. Next, an attribute named testAttr is set in the session and given a value of testVal:

```
HttpSession session = arg.getSession();
session.setMaxInactiveInterval(60);
session.setAttribute("testAttr", "testVal");
```

A field within the servlet named numberOfSessions is declared, and it is incremented each time a new session is started. Following the session.setAttribute() call, the counter is incremented within a synchronized statement. Finally, a message is printed to the server log indicating that a new session was created and providing the total active session count.

■ **Note**   Placing the increment within the synchronized statement helps avoid concurrency issues with the field. For more information on Java synchronization and concurrency, see the online documentation at http://docs.oracle.com/javase/tutorial/essential/concurrency/locksync.html.

The sessionDestroyed method is called on a session once the maximum number of inactive seconds has passed. In this example, the method will be called after 60 seconds of inactivity. Within the sessionDestroyed method, another synchronization statement decrements the numberOfSessions field value by one, and then a couple of lines are printed to the server log indicating that a session has been destroyed and providing the new total number of active sessions.

Session listeners can be used to set cookies and perform other useful tactics to help manage a user's experience. They are easy to use and very powerful.

1-12. Managing Session Attributes

Problem

You want to maintain some information regarding an individual session on a per-session basis when a user visits your site.

Solution

Use session attributes to retain session-based information. To do so, use the HttpServletRequest object to obtain access to the session, and then use the getAttribute() and setAttribute() methods accordingly. In the following scenario, an HTML page is used to capture a user's email address, and then the email address is placed into a session attribute. The attribute is then used by Jakarta servlets across different pages of the application in order to maintain state.

The following code demonstrates what the HTML form (recipe01_12.html) may look like in this scenario:

```
<html lang="en">
<head>
    <title></title>
    <meta http-equiv="Content-Type" content="text/html; charset=UTF-8">
</head>
<body>
<h1>Provide an email address to use with this transaction</h1>
</br>
<form method="POST" action="SessionServlet">
    <label for="email">Email</label>
    <input type="email" id="email" name="email" formnovalidate="false" required/>
    <br/></br>
    <input type="submit" value="Submit"/>
</form>
</body>
</html>
```

Next, the Jakarta servlet named SessionServlet using a URL pattern of /SessionServlet is initiated when the form is submitted. Any form input values are passed to SessionServlet and processed accordingly.

```
package org.jakartaeerecipe.chapter01.recipe01_12;

import java.io.*;
import jakarta.servlet.*;
import jakarta.servlet.annotation.WebServlet;
import jakarta.servlet.http.*;

@WebServlet(name="SessionServlet", urlPatterns={"/SessionServlet"})
public class SessionServlet extends HttpServlet {

@Override
public void doPost (HttpServletRequest req, HttpServletResponse res)
        throws ServletException, IOException {
    // Obtain the Session object
    HttpSession session = req.getSession(true);
    // Set up a session attribute
    String email = (String)
    session.getAttribute ("session.email");
    if (email == null) {
        email = req.getParameter("email");
        session.setAttribute ("session.email", email);
    }
```

```
String sessionId = session.getId();
res.setContentType("text/html");
try (PrintWriter out = response.getWriter()) {
    out.printf("""
        <html>
            <head>
                <title>Working with sessions</title>
            </head>
            <body>
                <h1>Session Test</h1>
                Your email address is: %s <br/>
                Your session id: %s
            </body>
        </html>""", email, sessionId);

    }
}
}
```

In the end, the email address that was entered within the original HTML form was captured and used throughout the different pages in the application.

Session Test

Your email address is: someone@domain.com
Your session id: 392dfb6af66931bd25c6f984fc69

Figure 1-13. *SessionServlet output*

How It Works

Since the beginning of web development, session attributes have been used to retain important information regarding a user's session. This concept holds true when developing using Jakarta servlets as well, and servlets make it easy to set and get the attribute values. All HttpServlet classes must implement doGet or doPost methods in order to process web application events. In doing so, these methods have access to the HttpServletRequest object as it is passed to them as an argument. An HttpSession object can be gleaned from the HttpServletRequest, and, therefore, it can be used to retrieve and set attributes as needed.

In the solution to this recipe, an HTTP session attribute is used to store an email address. That address is then used throughout the application within different servlet classes by obtaining the session object and then retrieving the attribute value:

```
// Obtain the Session object
    HttpSession session = req.getSession(true);
// Set up a session attribute
    String email = (String)
    session.getAttribute ("session.email");
```

```
if (email == null) {
    email = req.getParameter("email");
    session.setAttribute ("session.email", email);
}
```

Any attributes will remain in the HttpSession object as long as the session remains valid. The session ID will remain consistent when traversing between pages. You can see that the solution to this recipe obtains and prints the current session ID for reference. Using attributes in the HttpSession is a good way to pass data around to maintain a session's state.

1-13. Downloading a File

Problem

You want to enable your servlet application to have the ability to download a given file.

Solution

Write a servlet that will accept the name and path of a chosen file and then read the file and stream it to the file requestor. The following web page can be used to select a file for the servlet to download. Although the following HTML (recipe01_13.html) contains a statically typed file name, it could very well contain a dynamic list of files from a database or other source:

```
<html>
    <head>
        <meta charset="UTF-8">
    </head>
    <body>
        <h1>Click on the link below to download the file.</h1>
        <br/>
        <a href="DownloadServlet?filename=downloadTest.txt">Download test file</a>
        <br/>
    </body>
</html>
```

▪ **Note**   For the example in this recipe, you can create and edit a file in your root directory next to the WEB-INF folder and name the file downloadTest.txt to see the servlet transfer the data to your browser client.

When a user clicks the link presented on the web page from the previous HTML, the following servlet will be used to download the given file by passing the HttpServletRequest and HttpServletResponse objects to it along with the file that should be downloaded:

```
package org.jakartaeerecipe.chapter01.recipe01_13;

import jakarta.servlet.*;
import jakarta.servlet.http.*;
import jakarta.servlet.annotation.*;
```

```java
import java.io.IOException;
import java.io.InputStream;

@WebServlet(name = "DownloadServlet", value = "/DownloadServlet")
public class DownloadServlet extends HttpServlet {
    /**
     * Handles the HTTP
     * <code>GET</code> method.
     *
     * @param request servlet request
     * @param response servlet response
     * @throws ServletException if a servlet-specific error occurs
     * @throws IOException if an I/O error occurs
     */
    @Override
    protected void doGet(HttpServletRequest request, HttpServletResponse response)
            throws ServletException, IOException {

        // Read parameter from form that contains the file name to download
        String fileToDownload = request.getParameter("filename");

        // Call the download method with the given file
        System.err.println("Downloading file now...");

        doDownload(request, response, fileToDownload);
    }

    /**
     * Send a file to the output stream.
     *
     * @param request The request
     * @param response The response
     * @param originalFile The name the browser should receive.
     */
    private void doDownload( HttpServletRequest request, HttpServletResponse response,
                            String originalFile) throws IOException {
        final int BYTES = 1024;
        int length;

        ServletOutputStream outStream = response.getOutputStream();
        ServletContext context = getServletConfig().getServletContext();

        response.setContentType((context.getMimeType( originalFile ) != null) ?
                context.getMimeType( originalFile ) : "text/plain" );
        response.setHeader("Content-Disposition", "attachment; filename=\"" + originalFile
        + "\"" );

        InputStream in = context.getResourceAsStream("/" + originalFile);
        byte[] bbuf = new byte[BYTES];
        while ((in != null) && ((length = in.read(bbuf)) != -1))
        {
```

```
            outStream.write(bbuf,0,length);
        }
        outStream.flush();
        outStream.close();
    }

    /**
     * Returns a short description of the servlet.
     *
     * @return a String containing servlet description
     */
    @Override
    public String getServletInfo() {
        return "Short description";
    }
}
```

The servlet will not produce a response; it will simply download the given file to the end user when the user clicks the link to download the file.

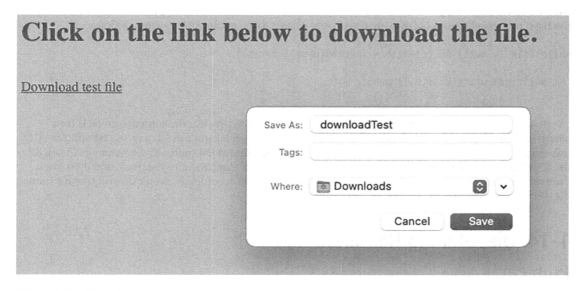

Figure 1-14. *DownloadServlet output*

How It Works

Downloading files is an essential task for almost any web application. Performing the steps that are provided by this recipe will make it easy to achieve this task. The example in this recipe demonstrates an easy case in which users can visit a web page, click a file to download, and have the file retrieved from the server and copied to their machine. The HTML is very simplistic in this example, and it lists a URL link that invokes the servlet and passes the name of the file that is to be downloaded. When the user clicks the link, the name of the file is passed to /DownloadServlet as a parameter with the name filename. When the link is clicked, the servlet doGet method is invoked. The first task that is performed in the doGet method is to read the filename parameter from the invoking web page. That information is then passed to the doDownload method along with the HttpServletRequest and HttpServletResponse objects.

In the doDownload method, the ServletOutputStream is obtained from the HttpServletResponse object, and the ServletContext is obtained for later use. To download a file, the servlet must provide a response of the same type that matches that of the file to be downloaded. It must also indicate in the response header that an attachment is to be included. Therefore, the first tasks to be performed by the doDownload method involve setting up the HttpServletResponse appropriately:

```
response.setContentType( (context.getMimeType( originalFile ) != null) ?
              context.getMimeType( originalFile ) : "text/plain" );
response.setHeader( "Content-Disposition", "attachment; filename=\"" + originalFile + "\"" );
```

The file name, in this case originalFile, is used to obtain the MIME type of the file. If the MIME type of the file is null, then text/plain will be returned. The attachment is set up in the response header as well, by appending the file name as an attachment to the Content-Disposition. Next, the doDownload method obtains a reference to the file that is to be downloaded by calling the ServletContext getResourceAsStream method and passing the name of the file. This will return an InputStream object that can be used to read the contents of the indicated file. A byte buffer is then created, which will be used to obtain chunks of data from the file when it is being read. The final real task is to read the file contents and copy them to the output stream. This is done using a while loop, which will continue to read from the InputStream until everything has been processed. Chunks of data are read in and written to the output stream using the loop:

```
while ((in != null) && ((length = in.read(bbuf)) != -1))
{
    outStream.write(bbuf,0,length);
}
```

Lastly, the ServletOutputStream object's flush method is called to clear the contents, and it is then closed to release resources. The magic of downloading files using a Jakarta servlet may be a bit obfuscated by this example, however, because a static file is being used as the download source in this example. In real life, the HTML page would probably contain a list of files that are contained within a database, and then when the user selects a file to download, the servlet will process that file accordingly, even extracting the file from the database if necessary.

1-14. Dispatching Requests

Problem

You want to write a servlet that hands off requests to other servlets based on the task that needs to be accomplished. Furthermore, you want the requests to be handed off without redirecting the client to another site, and, therefore, the URL in the browser should not change.

Solution

Create a request dispatcher servlet, which will decide which task needs to be completed, and then send the request to an appropriate servlet to achieve that task. The following example demonstrates this concept via an HTML form that accepts two numbers from the user and allows the user to decide what type of mathematical evaluation should be performed by the server. The servlet processes the request by first determining which type of mathematical evaluation should be performed and then dispatching the request to the appropriate servlet to perform the task.

The following HTML form accepts two numbers from the user and allows them to choose which type of math to perform against the numbers:

```
<html>
    <head>
        <title></title>
        <meta http-equiv="Content-Type" content="text/html; charset=UTF-8">
    </head>
    <body>
        <h1>Request Dispatch Example</h1>
        <p>Perform a mathematical evaluation.  Insert two numbers to be evaluated and then
            choose the type of evaluation to perform.</p>
        <form method="POST" action="MathDispatcher">
            <label for="numa">Enter Number A: </label>
            <input type="text" id="numa" name="numa"/><br><br>
            <label for="numb">Enter Number B: </label>
            <input type="text" id="numb" name="numb"/><br/><br/>
            <select id="eval" name="eval">
                <option value="add">Add the numbers</option>
                <option value="subtract">Subtract the numbers</option>
                <option value="multiply">Multiply the numbers</option>
                <option value="divide">Divide the numbers</option>
            </select>
            <input type="submit" value="Submit Form"/>
            <input type="reset" value="Reset Form"/>
        </form>
    </body>
</html>
```

The next piece of code is the servlet, which will dispatch requests accordingly depending on the value of the matheval field:

```
package org.jakartaeerecipe.chapter01.recipe01_14;

import java.io.IOException;

import jakarta.servlet.*;
import jakarta.servlet.annotation.WebServlet;
import jakarta.servlet.http.*;

@WebServlet(name = "MathDispatcher", urlPatterns = {"/MathDispatcher"})
public class MathDispatcher extends HttpServlet {
    /**
     * Handles the HTTP
     * <code>POST</code> method.
     *
     * @param request servlet request
     * @param response servlet response
```

```
 * @throws ServletException if a servlet-specific error occurs
 * @throws IOException if an I/O error occurs
 */
@Override
protected void doPost(HttpServletRequest request, HttpServletResponse response)
        throws ServletException, IOException {
    System.out.println("In the servlet...");

    // Store the input parameter values into Strings
    String eval = request.getParameter("eval");

    ServletContext sc = getServletConfig().getServletContext();
    RequestDispatcher rd = null;

    switch(eval){
        case "add" -> rd =  sc.getRequestDispatcher("/AddServlet");
        case "subtract" -> rd =  sc.getRequestDispatcher("/SubtractServlet");
        case "multiply" -> rd = sc.getRequestDispatcher("/MultiplyServlet");
        case "divide" -> rd = sc.getRequestDispatcher("/DivideServlet");
    }
    rd.forward(request, response);
}
/**
 * Returns a short description of the servlet.
 *
 * @return a String containing servlet description
 */
@Override
public String getServletInfo() {
    return "Short description";
}
}
```

Next is an example of one of the servlets that the request will be dispatched to. The following is the code for the AddServlet, which will add the two numbers and return the sum to the user:

```
package org.jakartaeerecipe.chapter01.recipe01_14;

import java.io.*;

import jakarta.servlet.ServletException;
import jakarta.servlet.annotation.WebServlet;
import jakarta.servlet.http.*;

@WebServlet(name = "AddServlet", urlPatterns = {"/AddServlet"})
public class AddServlet extends HttpServlet {
    /**
     * Processes requests for both HTTP
     * <code>GET</code> and
     * <code>POST</code> methods.
     *
```

```
     * @param request servlet request
     * @param response servlet response
     * @throws ServletException if a servlet-specific error occurs
     * @throws IOException if an I/O error occurs
     */
    protected void processRequest(HttpServletRequest request, HttpServletResponse response)
            throws ServletException, IOException {
        response.setContentType("text/html;charset=UTF-8");
                // Store the input parameter values into Strings
                String numA = request.getParameter("numa");
                String numB = request.getParameter("numb");
                int sum = Integer.valueOf(numA) + Integer.valueOf(numB);
        try (PrintWriter out = response.getWriter())
{

            out.printf("""<html>
                    <head>
                        <title>The Sum of the Numbers</title>");
                    </head>
                    <body>
                        <h1>Sum: %s </h1>
                        <br/>
                        <a href=recipe01_14.html>Try Again</a>
                        </body>
                </html>""", sum);
    }
    /**
     * Handles the HTTP
     * <code>GET</code> method.
     *
     * @param request servlet request
     * @param response servlet response
     * @throws ServletException if a servlet-specific error occurs
     * @throws IOException if an I/O error occurs
     */
    @Override
    protected void doGet(HttpServletRequest request, HttpServletResponse response)
            throws ServletException, IOException {
        processRequest(request, response);
    }
    /**
     * Handles the HTTP
     * <code>POST</code> method.
     *
     * @param request servlet request
     * @param response servlet response
     * @throws ServletException if a servlet-specific error occurs
     * @throws IOException if an I/O error occurs
     */
    @Override
    protected void doPost(HttpServletRequest request, HttpServletResponse response)
            throws ServletException, IOException {
```

```
        processRequest(request, response);
    }
    /**
     * Returns a short description of the servlet.
     *
     * @return a String containing servlet description
     */
    @Override
    public String getServletInfo() {
        return "Short description";
    }
}
```

Each of the other servlets is very similar to AddServlet, except the mathematical evaluation is different. To see a full listing of the code, take a look at the sources for this book.

How It Works

Sometimes, it is a good idea to hide the forwarding of requests from the end user. Other times, it just makes sense to hand off a request from one servlet to another so that another type of processing can occur. These are just two examples of when it is handy to perform a request dispatch within a servlet. Forwarding a request vs. dispatching a request is different because a forwarded request hands off the request on the client-side, whereas a dispatched request hands off the request on the server-side. The difference can be quite large since the end user has no idea of server-side dispatches, whereas the browser is redirected to a different URL when the request is forwarded on the client-side.

Dispatching requests is an easy task. The facilities for doing so are built right into the ServletContext, so once you obtain a reference to ServletContext, you simply call the getRequestDispatcher method to obtain a RequestDispatcher object that can be used to dispatch the request. When calling the getRequestDispatcher method, pass a string containing the name of the servlet that you want to hand off the request to. You can actually obtain a RequestDispatcher object for any valid HTTP resource within the application by passing the appropriate URL for the resource in String format to the getRequestDispatcher method. Therefore, if you'd rather dispatch to a JSP or HTML page, you can do that as well. After a RequestDispatcher object has been obtained, invoke its forward method by passing the HttpServletRequest and HttpServletResponse objects to it. The forward method performs the task of handing off the request:

```
rd = sc.getRequestDispatcher("/AddServlet");
rd.forward(request, response);
```

In the case of the example in this recipe, you can dispatch requests to different servlets to perform a specific task. Once handed off, the servlet that has obtained the request is responsible for providing the response to the client. In this case, the servlet returns the result of the specified mathematical evaluation.

Request Dispatch Example

Perform a mathematical evaluation. Insert two numbers to be evaluated and then choose the type of evaluation to perform.

Enter Number A: `15`

Enter Number B: `4`

`Add the numbers ⌄` `Submit Form` `Reset Form`

Figure 1-15. *HTML form for calling the MathDispatcher servlet*

Sum: 19

<u>Try Again</u>

Figure 1-16. *AddServlet servlet output*

1-15. Redirecting to a Different Site

Problem

You need to redirect the browser to another URL when a specific URL within your application is visited.

Solution

Use the HttpServletResponse object's sendRedirect() method to redirect from the servlet to another URL. In the following example, when a URL that matches the /redirect pattern is used, then the servlet will redirect the browser to another site:

```
import java.io.IOException;
import jakarta.servlet.*;
import jakarta.servlet.annotation.WebServlet;
import jakarta.servlet.http.*;

@WebServlet(name="RedirectServlet", urlPatterns={"/redirect"})
public class RedirectServlet extends HttpServlet {
    @Override
    protected void doGet(HttpServletRequest req, HttpServletResponse res)
        throws IOException, ServletException {
            String site = "http://www.apress.com";
        res.sendRedirect(site);
    }
}
```

In this example, the servlet will redirect to the www.apress.com website.

41

How It Works

There are some cases in which a web application needs to redirect traffic to another site or URL within the same or another application. For such cases, the HttpServletResponse sendRedirect method can be of use. The sendRedirect method accepts a URL in String format and then redirects the web browser to the given URL. The fact that sendRedirect accepts a string-based URL makes it easy to build dynamic URLs as well. For instance, some applications may redirect to a different URL based on certain parameters that are passed from a user. Dynamic generation of a URL in such cases may look something like the following:

```
String redirectUrl = null;
if(parameter.equals("SOME STRING")
    redirectUrl = "/" + urlPathA;
else
    redirectUrl = "/" + urlPathB;
res.sendRedirect(redirectUrl);
```

The sendRedirect() method can also come in handy for creating the control for web menus and other page items that can send web traffic to different locations.

■ **Note**   This simple redirect, as opposed to servlet chaining, does not pass the `HttpRequest` object along to the target address.

1-16. Securely Maintaining State Within the Browser

Problem

You have the requirement to save a user's state within the browser for your application.

Solution

Use "HTTP only" browser cookies to save the state. In the following example, one servlet is used to place some session information into a cookie in the browser. Another servlet is then called, which reads the cookie information and displays it to the user. The following servlet demonstrates how to store a cookie in the browser using a Jakarta servlet:

```
package org.jakartaeerecipe.chapter01.recipe01_16;

import java.io.*;
import jakarta.servlet.ServletException;
import jakarta.servlet.annotation.WebServlet;
import jakarta.servlet.http.*;

@WebServlet(name = "SetCookieServlet", urlPatterns = {"/SetCookieServlet"})
public class SetCookieServlet extends HttpServlet {
    protected void processRequest(HttpServletRequest request, HttpServletResponse response)
            throws ServletException, IOException {
        response.setContentType("text/html;charset=UTF-8");
        PrintWriter out = response.getWriter();
```

```
            Cookie cookie = new Cookie("sessionId","12345");
            cookie.setHttpOnly(true);
            cookie.setMaxAge(-30);
            response.addCookie(cookie);
            try {
                out.println("""<html>
                            <head>
                            <title>Set Cookie</title>
                            </head>
                            <body>
                                    <h1>Servlet SetCookieServlet is setting a cookie into the
                                    browser</h1>
                                    <br/><br/>
                                    <a href='DisplayCookieServlet'>Display the cookie
                                    contents.</a>
                            </body>
                    </html>""");
            } finally {
                out.close();
            }
        }
        @Override
        protected void doGet(HttpServletRequest request, HttpServletResponse response)
                throws ServletException, IOException {
            processRequest(request, response);
        }
        @Override
        protected void doPost(HttpServletRequest request, HttpServletResponse response)
                throws ServletException, IOException {
            processRequest(request, response);
        }
    }
```

Servlet SetCookieServlet is setting a cookie into the browser

Display the cookie contents.

Figure 1-17. *SetCookieServlet servlet output*

The next code listing demonstrates a servlet that reads the cookies in the browser and prints the contents:

```
package org.jakartaeerecipe.chapter01.recipe01_16;

import java.io.*;
import jakarta.servlet.ServletException;
import jakarta.servlet.annotation.WebServlet;
import jakarta.servlet.http.*;
```

```
@WebServlet(name = "DisplayCookieServlet", urlPatterns = {"/DisplayCookieServlet"})
public class DisplayCookieServlet extends HttpServlet {
    protected void processRequest(HttpServletRequest request, HttpServletResponse response)
            throws ServletException, IOException {
        response.setContentType("text/html;charset=UTF-8");
        Cookie[] cookies = request.getCookies();
        try (PrintWriter out = response.getWriter()) {
            out.print("""
                <html>
                    <head>
                        <title>Display Cookies</title>
                    </head>
                    <body>
                """);

            for(Cookie cookie:cookies){
                out.printf("""
                    <p>Cookie Name: %s <br/>
                      Value: %s
                    </p>
                    """, cookie.getName(), cookie.getValue());
            }
            out.println("</body>");
            out.println("</html>");
        }
    }
    @Override
    protected void doGet(HttpServletRequest request, HttpServletResponse response)
            throws ServletException, IOException {
        processRequest(request, response);
    }
    @Override
    protected void doPost(HttpServletRequest request, HttpServletResponse response)
            throws ServletException, IOException {
        processRequest(request, response);
    }
}
```

How It Works

Using cookies to store data in the browser is a technique that has been in practice for years. Since the Servlet 3.0 API, the ability to mark a cookie as HTTP only has become available. This allows the cookie to be safeguarded against client-side scripting attacks, making the cookie more secure. Any standard servlet can create a cookie and place it into the current session. Similarly, any servlet that is contained within the same session can read or update a session's cookie values. In the example for this recipe, two servlets are used to demonstrate how cookies work. The first servlet that is listed is responsible for creating a new cookie and setting it into the browser session. The second servlet is responsible for displaying the contents of the cookie to the user.

To create a cookie, simply instantiate a new jakarta.servlet.http.Cookie object and assign a name and value to it. Passing both the name and value into the Cookie constructor at the time of instantiation can assign a name and value, or it can be done by passing values to the cookie's setName and setValue methods.

Once the cookie has been instantiated, properties can be set that will help to configure the cookie. In the example to this recipe, the cookie's setMaxAge and setHttpOnly methods are called, setting the time of life for the cookie and ensuring that it will be guarded against client-side scripting. For a complete listing of cookie properties, refer to Table 1-3. Finally, the cookie is placed into the response by passing it to the response object's addCookie method:

```
Cookie cookie = new Cookie("sessionId","12345");
cookie.setHttpOnly(true);
cookie.setMaxAge(-30);
response.addCookie(cookie);
```

Table 1-3. *Cookie Property Methods*

Property	Description
setComment	Sets a comment to describe the cookie
setDomain	Specifies the domain in which the cookie belongs
setHttpOnly	Marks the cookie as HTTP only
setMaxAge	Sets the maximum lifetime of the cookie. A negative value indicates that the cookie will expire when the session ends
setPath	Specifies a path for the cookie to which the client should return it
setSecure	Indicates that the cookie should be sent only using a secure protocol
setValue	Assigns a value to the cookie
setVersion	Specifies the version of the cookie protocol that the cookie will comply with

The second servlet in the example, DisplayCookieServlet, is responsible for reading and displaying the session's cookie values. When DisplayCookieServlet is invoked, its processRequest method is called, which obtains the cookies within the response object by calling response.getCookies() and setting the result to an array of Cookie objects:

```
Cookie[] cookies = request.getCookies();
```

The cookie object array can now be iterated over in order to obtain each cookie and print its contents. The servlet does so by using a for loop and printing each cookie's name and value:

```
for(Cookie cookie:cookies){
            out.printf("""
                <p>
                    Cookie Name: %s <br/>
                     Value: %s
                </p>
                """, cookie.getName(), cookie.getValue());
}
```

Figure 1-18 shows the output of the DisplayCookie servlet.

Cookie Name: sessionId
Value: 12345

Figure 1-18. *DisplayCookieServlet servlet output*

1-17. Finalizing Servlet Tasks

Problem

There are some resources you want to have your servlet clean up once the servlet is no longer in use.

Solution

The solution to the problem is twofold. First, provide code for performing any cleanup within the servlet destroy method. Second, in the case that there are potentially long-running methods, code them so that you will become aware of a shutdown and, if necessary, halt and return so that the servlet can shut down cleanly. The following code excerpt is a small example of a destroy method. In this code, it is being used to initialize local variables and is setting the beingDestroyed boolean value to indicate that the servlet is shutting down:

```
...
    /**
     * Used to finalize the servlet
     */
    @Override
    public void destroy() {
        // Tell the servlet it is shutting down
        setBeingDestroyed(true);
        // Perform any cleanup
        thisString = null;
    }
...
```

The code within the destroy method may successfully achieve a full cleanup of the servlet, but in the case where there may be a long-running task, then it must be notified of a shutdown. The following excerpt is a block of code that signifies a long-running task. The task should stop processing once the shutdown is indicated by the beingDestroyed value becoming true:

```
for (int x = 0; (x <= 100000 && !isBeingDestroyed()); x++) {
    doSomething();
}
```

■ **Note** If you want to perform cleanup prior to calling the destroy method, then create a public, protected, or private method that returns void and annotate it with @PreDestroy. The @PreDestroy annotation marks a method to be called prior to the component being removed from the container. This method must not throw a checked exception.

How It Works

The finalization of a servlet can be very important, especially if the servlet is using some resources that may lead to a memory leak, using a reusable resource such as a database connection, or needs to persist some values for another session. In such cases, it is a good idea to perform cleanup within the servlet destroy method. Every servlet contains a destroy method (which may be implemented to overload default behavior) that is initiated once the servlet container determines that a servlet should be taken out of service.

The destroy method is called once all of a servlet's service methods have stopped running. However, if there is a long-running service method, then a server grace period can be set that would cause any running service to be shut down when the grace period is reached. As mentioned earlier, the destroy method is the perfect place to clean up resources. However, the destroy method is also a good place to help clean up after long-running services. Cleanup can be done by setting a servlet-specific local variable to indicate that the servlet is being destroyed and by having the long-running service check the state of that variable periodically. If the variable indicates that the destroy method has been called, then it should stop executing.

1-18. Reading and Writing with Nonblocking I/O

Problem

You want to read and write I/O in an asynchronous, nonblocking manner.

Solution

Use the Non-Blocking I/O API that was part of the Servlet 3.1 release. To use the technology, implement the ReadListener interface when performing nonblocking reads, and implement the WriteListener interface for performing nonblocking writes.

The implementation class can then be registered to a ServletInputStream or ServletOutputStream so that reads or writes can be performed when the listener finds that servlet content can be read or written without blocking.

The following sources are those of a ReadListener implementation that reside in the source file org.jakartaeerecipe.chapter01.recipe01_07.AcmeReadListenerImpl.java, and they demonstrate how to implement the ReadListener:

```
package org.jakartaeerecipe.chapter01.recipe01_07;

import java.io.IOException;
import java.util.logging.*;
import jakarta.servlet.*;

public class AcmeReadListenerImpl implements ReadListener {
```

```java
    private ServletInputStream is = null;
    private AsyncContext async = null;

    public AcmeReadListenerImpl(ServletInputStream in, AsyncContext ac) {
        this.is = in;
        this.async = ac;
        System.out.println("read listener initialized");
    }

    @Override
    public void onDataAvailable() {
        System.out.println("onDataAvailable");
        try {
            StringBuilder sb = new StringBuilder();
            int len = -1;
            byte b[] = new byte[1024];
            while (is.isReady()
                    && (len = is.read(b)) != -1) {
                String data = new String(b, 0, len);
                System.out.println(data);
            }
        } catch (IOException ex) {
            Logger.getLogger(AcmeReadListenerImpl.class.getName()).log(Level.SEVERE,
            null, ex);
        }
    }

    @Override
    public void onAllDataRead() {
        System.out.println("onAllDataRead");
        async.complete();
    }

    @Override
    public void onError(Throwable throwable) {
        System.out.println("Error: " + throwable);
        async.complete();
    }
}
```

Next, use the listener by registering it to a ServletInputStream (in the case of the ReadListener) or a ServletOutputStream (in the case of a WriteListener). For this example, I show a servlet that utilizes the AcmeReadListenerImpl class. The sources for the following class reside in the org.jakartaeerecipe. chapter01.recipe01_07.AcmeReaderExample.java file:

```java
package org.jakartaeerecipe.chapter01.recipe01_07;

import java.io.IOException;
import java.io.PrintWriter;

import jakarta.servlet.*;
```

```java
import jakarta.servlet.annotation.WebServlet;
import jakarta.servlet.http.*;

@WebServlet(urlPatterns = {"/AcmeReaderServlet"}, asyncSupported = true)
public class AcmeReaderServlet extends HttpServlet {
    protected void processRequest(HttpServletRequest request, HttpServletResponse response)
            throws ServletException, IOException {
        response.setContentType("text/html;charset=UTF-8");
        try (PrintWriter output = response.getWriter()) {
            AsyncContext asyncCtx = request.startAsync();
            ServletInputStream input = request.getInputStream();
            input.setReadListener(new AcmeReadListenerImpl(input, asyncCtx));
        } catch (Exception ex) {
            System.out.println("Exception Occurred: " + ex);
        }
    }
  // Http Servlet Methods ...
...
}
```

The last piece of code that we need is the servlet that invokes the AcmeReaderServlet, passing the message that needs to be processed. In this example, a file from the server is passed to the AcmeReaderServlet as input, which then is asynchronously processed via the AcmeReadListenerImpl class. The following code is taken from org.jakartaeerecipe.chapter01.recipe01_07.ReaderExample.java:

```java
package org.jakartaeerecipe.chapter01.recipe01_07;

import java.io.*;
import java.net.*;
import java.util.logging.*;
import jakarta.servlet.*;
import jakarta.servlet.annotation.WebServlet;
import jakarta.servlet.http.*;

@WebServlet(name = "ReaderExample", urlPatterns = {"/ReaderExample"})
public class ReaderExample extends HttpServlet {
    protected void processRequest(HttpServletRequest request, HttpServletResponse response)
    throws ServletException, IOException {
        response.setContentType("text/html;charset=UTF-8");
        String filename = "/WEB-INF/test.txt";
        ServletContext context = getServletContext();
        InputStream in = context.getResourceAsStream(filename);
        try (PrintWriter out = response.getWriter()) {
            String path = "http://"
                    + request.getServerName()
                    + ":"
                    + request.getServerPort()
                    + request.getContextPath()
                    + "/AcmeReaderServlet";
            out.println("""<html>
                    <head>
```

```
                    <title>Intro to Jakarta EE 10 - Servlet Reader Example</title>
                </head>
                <body>
                        <h1>Servlet ReaderExample at %s</h1>
                        Invoking the endpoint: %s
                        <br>
         """, request.getContextPath(), path);
        out.flush();
        URL url = new URL(path);
        HttpURLConnection conn = (HttpURLConnection) url.openConnection();
        conn.setChunkedStreamingMode(2);
        conn.setDoOutput(true);
        conn.connect();
        if (in != null) {
            InputStreamReader inReader = new InputStreamReader(in);
            BufferedReader reader = new BufferedReader(inReader);
            String text = "";
            out.println("Beginning Read");
            try (BufferedWriter output = new BufferedWriter(new OutputStreamWriter(conn.
            getOutputStream())))) {
                out.println("got the output...beginning loop");
                while ((text = reader.readLine()) != null) {
                    out.println("reading text: " + text);
                    out.flush();
                    output.write(text);
                    Thread.sleep(1000);
                    output.write("Ending example now..");
                    out.flush();
                }
                output.flush();
                output.close();
            }
        }
        out.println("Review the Glassfish server log for messages...");
        out.println("</body>");
        out.println("</html>");
    } catch (InterruptedException | IOException ex) {
        Logger.getLogger(ReaderExample.class.getName()).log(Level.SEVERE, null, ex);
    }
}
// Http Servlet Methods ...
...
}
```

When the servlet is visited, the asynchronous, nonblocking read of the test.txt file will occur, and its text will be displayed in the server log.

How It Works

Servlet technology has allowed only traditional (blocking) input/output during request processing since its inception. In the Servlet 3.1 release, the Non-Blocking I/O API was introduced to make it possible for servlets to read or write without any blocking. This means other tasks can be performed while a read or write is occurring, without any wait.

To implement a nonblocking I/O solution, programming interfaces were added to ServletInputStream and ServletOutputStream with the release of Servlet 3.1, as well as two event listeners: ReadListener and WriteListener. ReadListener and WriteListener interfaces make the servlet I/O processing occur in a nonblocking manner via callback methods that are invoked when servlet content can be read or written without blocking. Use the ServletInputStream.setReadListener(ServletInputStream, AsyncContext) method to register a ReadListener with a ServletInputStream, and use the ServletInputStream.setWrit eListener(ServletOutputStream, AsyncContext) method for registering a WriteListener. The following lines of code demonstrate how to register a ReadListener implementation with a ServletInputStream:

```
AsyncContext context = request.startAsync();
ServletInputStream input = request.getInputStream();
input.setReadListener(new ReadListenerImpl(input, context));
```

■ **Note** In Servlet 3.0, AsyncContext was introduced to represent an execution context for an asynchronous operation that is initiated on a servlet request. To use the asynchronous context, a servlet should be annotated as a @WebServlet, and the asyncSupported attribute of the annotation must be set to true. The @WebFilter annotation also contains the asyncSupported() attribute.

After a listener has been registered with a ServletInputStream, the status on a nonblocking read can be checked by calling the methods ServletInputStream.isReady() and ServletInputStream.isFinished(). For instance, a read can begin once the ServletInputStream.isReady() method returns a true, as shown here:

```
while (is.isReady() && (b = input.read()) != -1)) {
    len = is.read(b);
    String data = new String(b, 0, len);
}
```

To create a ReadListener or WriteListener, three methods must be overridden: onDataAvailable(), onAllDataRead(), and onError(). The onDataAvailable() method is invoked when data is available to be read or written, onAllDataRead() is invoked once all the data has been read or written, and onError() is invoked if an error is encountered. The code for AcmeReadListenerImpl in the solution to this recipe demonstrates how to override these methods.

The AsyncContext.complete() method is called in the onAllDataRead() method to indicate that the read has been completed and to commit the response. This method is also called in the onError() implementation so that the read will complete, so it is important to perform any cleanup within the body of the onError() method to ensure that no resources are leaked, and so on.

To implement a WriteListener, use the ServletOutputStream.canWrite method, which determines whether data can be written in a nonblocking fashion. A WriteListener implementation class must override the following methods: onWritePossible() and onError(). The onWritePossible() method is invoked when a nonblocking write can occur. The write implementation should take place within the body of this method. The onError() method is much the same as its ReadListener implementation counterpart, because it is invoked when an error occurs.

The following lines of code demonstrate how to register a WriteListener with a ServletOutputStream:

```
AsyncContext context = request.startAsync();
ServletOutputStream os = response.getOutputStream();
os.setWriteListener(new WriteListenerImpl(os, context));
```

The WriteListener implementation class must include overriding methods for onWritePossible() and onError(). The following is an example for a WriteListener implementation class:

```
import jakarta.servlet.AsyncContext;
import jakarta.servlet.ServletOutputStream;
import jakarta.servlet.WriteListener;
public class WriteListenerImpl implements WriteListener {
    ServletOutputStream os;
    AsyncContext context;
    public WriteListenerImpl(ServletOutputStream out, AsyncContext ctx){
        this.os = out;
        this.context = ctx;
        System.out.println("Write Listener Initialized");
    }
    @Override
    public void onWritePossible() {
        System.out.println("Now possible to write...");
        // Write implementation here...
    }
    @Override
    public void onError(Throwable throwable) {
        System.out.println("Error occurred");
        context.complete();
    }
}
```

■ **Note** In most cases, the ReadListener and WriteListener implementation classes can be embedded within the calling servlet. They have been broken out into separate classes for the examples in this book for demonstration purposes.

The Non-Blocking I/O API helps bring the Servlet API into compliance with current web standards while making it possible to create web-based applications that perform well in an asynchronous fashion.

Servlet ReaderExample at /JakartaEERecipes_Chapter01-1.0-SNAPSHOT

Invoking the endpoint: http://localhost:8080/JakartaEERecipes_Chapter01-1.0-SNAPSHOT/AcmeReaderServlet
Review the Glassfish server log for messages...

Figure 1-19. *DisplayCookieServlet servlet output*

1-19. Pushing Resources from a Server to a Client

Problem

You want to push resources to your clients automatically when they visit a particular page within your web application, rather than sending multiple requests.

Solution

Use the Servlet HTTP/2 Push API to push the resources before the page is loaded. This will cause all of the resources to be included with the single response, rather than multiple responses that used to be needed for HTTP 1.1 implementations. In the following example, a PushBuilder is created, and then a few statically typed resources are pushed to the client prior to loading the page:

```java
@WebServlet(name = "PushServlet", urlPatterns = {"/PushServlet"})
public class PushServlet extends HttpServlet {

        protected void processRequest(HttpServletRequest request,
                HttpServletResponse response)  throws ServletException, IOException {

        response.setContentType("text/html;charset=UTF-8");

        try (PrintWriter out = response.getWriter()) {
            out.printf("""<html>
                    <head>
                            <title>Push Servlet</title>");
                    </head>
                    <body>
                            <h1>Servlet PushServlet at %s!</h1>
                    </body>
                    </html>""",request.getContextPath());
        }
    }

    @Override
    protected void doGet(HttpServletRequest request, HttpServletResponse response)
            throws ServletException, IOException {

        System.out.println("In the servlet");

        if (request.getRequestURI().equals("/JakartaEERecipes/PushServlet")
                && request.getPushBuilder() != null) {
            System.out.println("Pushing resources");
            PushBuilder builder =
            request.newPushBuilder().path("/resources/images/jakartaee10recipes.png");
            builder.path("/resources/images/jakartaee10recipes.png");
            builder.push();
        }
        processRequest(request, response);
    }
. . .
}
```

How It Works

A significant problem with serving content from the Web has always been the request and response life cycle. HTTP 1.1 requires multiple TCP connections issuing parallel requests in order to load page content containing various resources such as JavaScript files and images. This can not only lead to significant performance issues but also starves network resources. HTTP/2 is fundamentally different in that it is fully multiplexed, rather than being ordered and blocking. It also allows a single connection to be used for issuing requests in parallel, making performance much better and using much less network resources. Other differences for HTTP/2 include using header compression to help reduce overhead and allowing servers to have the ability to push resources proactively to active clients. This latter feature of HTTP/2 is covered by the example in this recipe, pushing resources from the server, rather than making the client fetch each required resource.

The PushBuilder interface was introduced with Servlet 4.0, which is part of the Java EE 8 and Jakarta EE platforms. The PushBuilder is used to build a push request based on the HttpServletRequest. Once the PushBuilder is obtained, it can be used to add resources via the path() method, which are subsequently pushed to the client while the target page is being processed. In the example, a PNG image resource is added using the path method. However, an application can be coded such that any resource that is required by a specific page can be pushed preemptively to the client and loaded into the browser cache. Once obtained, the PushBuilder can be used as many times as required. After all resources have been loaded, initiate the PushBuilder.push() method to perform the push action.

After the resources have been pushed, the invoked page will be loaded to process resources, determining which resources have already been cached and which need to be loaded from the server push. If a client browser already has the resource in the cache, it returns an RST_STREAM to indicate that the server does not need to end it.

CHAPTER 2

Jakarta Server Pages

The Jakarta Server Pages web framework provides a tremendous boost in productivity for Java web developers over the Jakarta Servlet API. Jakarta Server Pages is a framework that allows web developers to quickly create dynamic online content. It may contain eXtensible Markup Language (XML) or HyperText Markup Language (HTML), and it can even include embedded Java code within *scriptlets*, which are pieces of scripting code. The Jakarta Server Pages framework is simple to master and allows developers to quickly produce dynamic content while also allowing them to use their preferred HTML editor to create attractive websites. Jakarta Server Pages was developed several years ago and is still one of the most essential Java web technologies. Despite its evolution throughout time, many applications still use its older variants.

The development of dynamic web content has become more stable now, with the techniques used to create web applications becoming simpler to maintain in the future. The separation of markup from business logic is becoming increasingly essential. Earlier versions of Jakarta Server Pages were often written as a mix of Java and XML syntax. Today's Jakarta Server Pages, on the other hand, necessitates a greater distinction between markup and business logic than its predecessors or other competing web frameworks. These changes in the web environment have been met by newer versions of Jakarta Server Pages, which provide developers more freedom to create highly dynamic content without the use of any embedded Java code, but instead utilizing markup and custom tags inside pages.

This chapter shows you the ins and outs of Jakarta Server development. Starting with creating a simple Jakarta Server application, you learn how to develop applications using Jakarta Server technology from the ground up and harness the productivity and power that the technology has to offer. The chapter also brushes on advanced techniques such as the development of custom Jakarta Server tags and the invocation of Java functions utilizing conditional tags. The recipes within this chapter lay a solid foundation on which you can begin to develop applications utilizing Jakarta Server Pages.

Note Utilizing an integrated development environment (IDE) can save a lot of time when developing with Java-based web technologies like Jakarta Server Pages. Please see the appendix of this book to learn how to develop a Jakarta Server Pages application in the NetBeans IDE.

2-1. Creating a Simple Jakarta Server Page

Problem

You want to develop a web page using HTML markup that enables you to include dynamic content.

J. Juneau and T. Telang, *Java EE to Jakarta EE 10 Recipes*, https://doi.org/10.1007/978-1-4842-8079-9_2

Solution

Use Jakarta Server Pages to create a web page that combines standard markup with blocks of Java code that are embedded within the markup. Create a jsp file named recipe02_01.jsp inside the /webapp folder. The project folder structure is shown in Figure 2-1 for your reference.

Figure 2-1. *IntelliJ IDEA project folder structure*

The following Jakarta Server Page markup demonstrates how to include dynamic code in a page:

```
<%@page contentType="text/html" pageEncoding="UTF-8"%>
<!DOCTYPE html>
<html>
<head>
    <meta http-equiv="Content-Type" content="text/html; charset=UTF-8">
    <title>Jakarta Server Page Example</title>
</head>
<body>
<jsp:useBean id="dateBean" scope="application" class="org.jakartaeerecipe.chapter02.
recipe02_01.DateBean"/>
Hello World!<br/>
The current date is: ${dateBean.currentDate}!
</body>
</html>
```

The code uses a JavaBean to pull the current date into the page. The following Java code is the JavaBean that is used by the Jakarta Server Page code:

```
package org.jakartaeerecipe.chapter02.recipe02_01;

import java.util.Date;

public class DateBean {
    private Date currentDate = new Date();
    /**
     * @return the currentDate
     */
    public Date getCurrentDate() {
        return currentDate;
    }
    /**
     * @param currentDate the currentDate to set
     */
    public void setCurrentDate(Date currentDate) {
        this.currentDate = currentDate;
    }
}
```

The output would be as shown in Figure 2-2. Of course, the page will display the current date when you run the code.

← → C ⓘ localhost:8080/JakartaEERecipies-1.0-SNAPSHOT/chapter02/recipe02_01.jsp

Hello World!
The current date is: Fri Dec 24 00:48:21 IST 2021!

Figure 2-2. *Jakarta Server Pages recipe 02-01 output*

How It Works

The Jakarta Server Pages technology makes it easy to develop web pages that can utilize both static and dynamic web content by providing a set of tags and value expressions to expose dynamic Java fields to a web page. Using the Jakarta Server Page technology, a page developer can access the underlying JavaBean classes to pass content between the client and the server. In the example within this recipe, a Jakarta Server Page is used to display the current date and time, which is obtained from a JavaBean class on the server. Therefore, when a user visits the Jakarta Server Page in a browser, the current time and date on the server will be displayed.

A Jakarta Server Page should have an extension of .jsp if it is a standard HTML-based Jakarta Server Page. Other types of Jakarta Server Pages contain different extensions; one of those is the Jakarta Server Page document type with .jspx extension. A Jakarta Server Page document is an XML-based well-formed Jakarta Server Page. You can learn more about Jakarta Server Page documents in Recipe 2-6. Jakarta Server Pages can contain HTML markup, special Jakarta Server Page tags, page directives, JavaScript, embedded Java code, and more. This example contains the <jsp:useBean> tag, as well as a value expression to display the content of a field that is contained within the JavaBean. The <jsp:useBean> tag is used to include a reference to a Java class that will be referenced in the Jakarta Server Page markup. In this case, the class that is referenced is named org.jakartaeerecipe.chapter02.recipe02_01.DateBean, and it will be referenced as dateBean within the page. For a full description of the <jsp:useBean> tag, reference Recipe 2-3.

```
<jsp:useBean id="dateBean" scope="application" class="org.jakartaeerecipe.chapter02.
recipe02_01.DateBean"/>
```

Since the <jsp:useBean> tag contains a reference to the DateBean Java class, the Jakarta Server Page that includes the tag can use any public fields or methods that are contained within the class or private fields through public "getter" methods. This is demonstrated by using the Expression Language value expression, which is enclosed within the ${} characters. To learn more about Jakarta Expression Language expressions, see Recipe 2-4. In the example, the value of the JavaBean field named currentDate is displayed on the page. The value of the private field is retrieved automatically via the public "getter" method, getCurrentDate.

```
The current date is: ${dateBean.currentDate}!
```

LIFE CYCLE OF A JAKARTA SERVER PAGE PAGE

The life cycle of a Jakarta Server Page is very much the same as that of a Java servlet. This is because a Jakarta Server Page is translated to a servlet (the HttpJspBase class) behind the scenes by a special servlet. When a request is sent to a Jakarta Server Page, the special servlet checks to ensure that the Jakarta Server Page's servlet is not older than the page itself. If it is, the Jakarta Server Page is retranslated into a servlet class and compiled. The Jakarta Server Page-to-servlet translation is automatic, which makes Jakarta Server Page very productive.

When a Jakarta Server Page is translated, a servlet with a name such as 0002f<name>_jsp.java is automatically created, where <name> is the name of the Jakarta Server Page. If errors result during the translation, they will be displayed when the Jakarta Server Page response is displayed.

Different portions of the Jakarta Server Page are treated differently during the translation to a Java servlet.

If the Jakarta Server Page's servlet does not already exist, then the container does the following:

- Template data is translated into code.

- Jakarta Server Page scripting elements are inserted into the Jakarta Server Page's servlet class.

- <jsp:XXX .../> elements are converted into method calls.

After translation, the life cycle works similarly to the servlet life cycle:

1. Loads the servlet class

2. Instantiates the servlet class

3. Initializes the servlet instance with a call to the jspInit method

This recipe contains only beginning knowledge of what is possible with the Jakarta Server Page technology. To learn more regarding the technology and best practices when using Jakarta Server Page, continue reading the recipes in this chapter.

2-2. Embedding Java into a Jakarta Server Page

Problem

You want to embed some Java code into a standard Jakarta Server Page web page for dynamic content creation.

Solution

Use Jakarta Server Page scripting elements to embed Java code into the page and then display Java field content. Create a jsp file named recipe02_02.jsp inside the /webapp folder. The following Jakarta Server Page code demonstrates how to import the Java Date class and then use it to obtain the current date without using a server-side JavaBean class:

```
<%@page import="java.util.Date"%>
<%@page contentType="text/html" pageEncoding="UTF-8"%>
<%! Date currDate = null; %>
<% currDate = new Date(); %>
<html>
<head>
    <meta http-equiv="Content-Type" content="text/html; charset=UTF-8">
    <title>Jakarta Server Page Example</title>
</head>
<body>
Hello World!<br/>
The current date is: <%= currDate %>
</body>
</html>
```

This page will display the current system date from the server that hosts the Jakarta Server Page application. The Figure 2-3 shows the output of this recipe.

Hello World!
The current date is: Fri Dec 24 01:03:46 IST 2021

Figure 2-3. Jakarta Server Pages recipe 02-02 output

How It Works

Using scripting elements within a Jakarta Server Page allows you to embed Java code directly in a web page. However, it should be noted that this is not the best approach to web development. Scripting element programming used to be thought of as one of the best ways to code web applications using Jakarta Server Page technology. However, when it came time to perform maintenance activities on a Jakarta Server Page or to introduce new developers to a code base that used scripting elements in Jakarta Server Page, nightmares ensued because in order to debug a problem, the developer had to search through scripts embedded within

HTML, as well as Java classes themselves. Sometimes, it is still nice to have the ability to embed Java code directly into a page, even if for nothing more than testing, so that is why I show how it is done in this recipe. A better approach would be to separate the business logic from the view code, which you saw in Recipe 2-1 and will also see in subsequent recipes.

In this example, the current date is pulled into the Jakarta Server Page via the Java Date class. A new Date instance is assigned to a field that is named currDate. An import page directive is used to import the java.util.Date class into the Jakarta Server Page using the following line:

```
<%@page import="java.util.Date"%>
```

The declaration of currDate is done within a declaration scripting element. Declaration scripting elements begin with the character sequence <%! and end with the character sequence %>. Excerpted from the example, the currDate field is declared in the following line of code:

```
<%! Date currDate = null; %>
```

Anything that is contained inside declarations goes directly to the jspService() method of the generated Jakarta Server Page servlet class, creating a global declaration for the entire servlet to use. Any variable or method can be declared within declarations' character sequences.

■ **Note** Declarations are executed only once for the Jakarta Server Page, when it is initially converted into a servlet. If any code on the Jakarta Server Page changes, it will be translated to a servlet again, and the declaration will be evaluated again at that time. If you want code to be executed each time the Jakarta Server Page is loaded by the browser, do not place it in a declaration.

In the example for this recipe, you can see that there are no Jakarta Server Page tags used to reference a server-side JavaBean class to create a new instance of the Date class, and that is because the instantiation is done right within the Jakarta Server Page code in between character sequences known as *scriptlets*, <% %>. Scriptlets basically have the same syntax as declarations, except that they do not include the exclamation point in the first character sequence. Scriptlets are used to embed any Java code that you want to have run each time the Jakarta Server Page is loaded, at request-processing time. At translation time, anything contained within a scriptlet is placed into a method named _jspService within the translated Jakarta Server Page servlet, and that method is executed with each request on the Jakarta Server Page. Scriptlets are the most common place to use embedded Java in a Jakarta Server Page. Since in this example you want the current date to be displayed each time the page is loaded, the new Date class is instantiated and assigned to the currDate variable within a scriptlet:

```
<% currDate = new Date(); %>
```

Later in the Jakarta Server Page, the currDate field is displayed using an expression, which is enclosed using the <%= and %> character sequences. Expressions are used to display content, and anything that is contained within an expression is automatically converted to a string when a request is processed. After the string conversion, it is displayed as output on the page:

```
The current date and time is: <%= currDate %>
```

■ **Note** If the code within an expression is unable to be converted into a String, an exception will occur.

While embedding Java code in a Jakarta Server Page is possible to do, it is frowned upon within the Java community since the Model-View-Controller (MVC) paradigm makes coding much cleaner. To learn more about coding Jakarta Server Page applications without using scripting elements, see the next example, Recipe 2-3.

2-3. Separating Business Logic from View Code

Problem

You want to separate the business logic from the code that is used to create a view within your web application.

Solution

Separate the business logic into a JavaBean class and use Jakarta Server Page tags to incorporate the logic into the view. In the following example, a JavaBean is referenced from within a Jakarta Server Page, and one of the JavaBean fields is displayed on the page. Each time the page is refreshed, the field value is updated because the page calls the underlying JavaBean field's getter method, where the field is initialized.

Create a jsp file named recipe02_03.jsp inside the /webapp folder. The following Jakarta Server Page markup contains a reference to a JavaBean named RandomBean and displays a field from the bean on the page:

```
<%@page contentType="text/html" pageEncoding="UTF-8"%>
<html>
<head>
    <title>Recipe 2-3: Separating Business Logic from View Code</title>
</head>
<body>
    <jsp:useBean id="randomBean" scope="application"
                 class="org.jakartaeerecipe.chapter02.recipe02_03.RandomBean"/>
    Display a Random Number!<br/>
    Your random number is ${randomBean.randomNumber}. Refresh page to see another!
</body>
</html>
```

The next code is that of the JavaBean class referenced in the Jakarta Server Page code, known as RandomBean:

```
package org.jakartaeerecipe.chapter02.recipe02_03;
import java.util.Random;

public class RandomBean {
    Random randomGenerator = new Random();
    private int randomNumber = 0;
    /**
     * @return the randomNumber
     */
```

```
    public int getRandomNumber() {
        randomNumber = randomGenerator.nextInt();
        return randomNumber;
    }
}
```

To execute the preceding code, open the URL http://localhost:8080/JakartaEERecipies-1.0-SNAPSHOT/chapter02/recipe02_03.jsp in your browser. The resulting output for the page resembles Figure 2-4, although the random number will be different every time the page is loaded.

Display a Random Number!
Your random number is 2063341895. Refresh page to see another!

Figure 2-4. Jakarta Server Pages recipe 02-03 output

How It Works

Sometimes, embedding Java code directly into a Jakarta Server Page can be helpful, and it can satisfy the requirement. However, in most cases, it is a good idea to separate any Java code from markup code that is used to create the web view. Doing so makes maintenance easier, and it allows a page developer to focus on creating nice-looking web pages rather than wading through Java code. In some organizations, a Java developer can then write the server-side business logic code, and a web developer can focus on the view. In many organizations today, the same person is performing both tasks, and using the MVC methodology can help separate the logic and increase productivity.

In the early days of Jakarta Server Page, embedding Java directly into a Jakarta Server Page was considered the best way to go, but as time went on, the MVC paradigm caught on, and Jakarta Server Page has been updated to follow suit. As a best practice, it is good to use Jakarta Server Page tags to separate Java code from page markup. In the example, the <jsp:useBean> element is used to reference a server-side JavaBean class so that the public fields and methods from that class, as well as private fields via public "getter" methods, can be incorporated into the Jakarta Server Page. The jsp:useBean element requires that you provide an ID and a scope, along with a class name or a beanName. In the example, the id attribute is set to randomBean, and this id is used to reference the bean within the Jakarta Server Page. The scope attribute is set to application, which means that the bean can be used from any Jakarta Server Page within the application. Table 2-1 displays all the possible scopes and what they mean. The class attribute is set to the fully qualified name of the Java class that will be referenced via the name that is set with the id attribute, which in this case is randomBean.

Table 2-1. *jsp:useBean Element Scopes*

Scope	Description
page (default)	The bean can be used within the same Jakarta Server Page that contains the jsp:useBean element
request	The bean can be used from any Jakarta Server Page processing the same request
session	The bean can be used from any Jakarta Server Page within the same session as the Jakarta Server Page that contains the jsp:useBean element that created the bean. The page that creates the bean must have a page directive with session="true"
application	The bean can be used from any Jakarta Server Page within the same application as the Jakarta Server Page that created it

After the jsp:useBean element has been added to a page, JavaBean properties can be used in the Jakarta Server Page, and public methods can be called from the page. The example demonstrates how to display the value of a JavaBean property using the ${ } notation. Any variable that contains a "getter" and a "setter" method in the JavaBean can be accessed from a Jakarta Server Page by referencing the class member field in between the ${ and } character sequences, better known as a Jakarta Expression Language expression. To learn more about Jakarta Expression Language expressions, see Recipe 2-4. The following excerpt from the example demonstrates how to display the randomNumber field from the JavaBean:

```
Your random number is ${randomBean.randomNumber}. Refresh page to see another!
```

The key to separating business logic from view logic in the Jakarta Server Page technology is the jsp:useBean element. This will allow you to use JavaBean classes from within the Jakarta Server Page, without embedding the code directly in the page. Separating business logic from view code can help make it easier to maintain code in the future and make the code easier to follow.

2-4. Yielding or Setting Values

Problem

You want to display values from a JavaBean in a Jakarta Server Page. Furthermore, you want to have the ability to set values in a Jakarta Server Page.

Solution

Create a jsp file named recipe02_04.jsp inside the /webapp folder. Expose the values from a Bean in a Jakarta Server Page using Jakarta Expression Language expressions with the ${bean.value} syntax. In the following Jakarta Server Page code, a Java class by the name of EasyBean will be used to hold the value that is entered into a text field by a user. The value will then be read from the bean and displayed on the page using Jakarta Expression Language expressions.

The following code shows a Jakarta Server Page that contains an input form and displays the value that is entered into the text box:

```
<%@page contentType="text/html; charset=UTF-8"%>
<html>
    <head>
        <title>Recipe 2-4: Yielding or Setting Values</title>
    </head>
```

```
    <body>
        <jsp:useBean id="easyBean" scope="page" class="org.jakartaeerecipe.chapter02.
        recipe02_04.EasyBean"/>
        <jsp:setProperty name="easyBean" property="*"/>
        <form method="post">
                Use the input text box below to set the value, and then hit submit.
                <br/><br/>
                <label for="fieldValue">Set the field value: </label>
                <input id="fieldValue" name="fieldValue" type="text" size="30"/>
                <br/>
                The value contained within the field is currently:
                <jsp:getProperty name="easyBean" property="fieldValue"/>
                <input type="submit">
        </form>
    </body>
</html>
```

Next, create the JavaBean class within the /src folder, which is used to hold the value that is used by the page; it looks like the following:

```
package org.jakartaeerecipe.chapter02.recipe02_04;

public class EasyBean implements java.io.Serializable {

    private String fieldValue;

    public EasyBean(){
        fieldValue = null;
    }

    /**
     * @return the fieldValue
     */
    public String getFieldValue() {
        return fieldValue;
    }

    /**
     * @param fieldValue the fieldValue to set
     */
    public void setFieldValue(String fieldValue) {
        this.fieldValue = fieldValue;
    }
}
```

This simple example demonstrates how to enter a value, "set" it into the Bean variable, and then display it on the page. To view this page, open the URL http://localhost:8080/JakartaEERecipies-1.0-SNAPSHOT/chapter02/recipe02_04.jsp in your browser. The output would be as shown in Figure 2-5.

Use the input text box below to set the value, and then hit submit.

Set the field value: Hello World!
The value contained within the field is currently: Hello World! Submit

Figure 2-5. *Jakarta Server Pages recipe 02-04 output*

How It Works

Perhaps one of the most useful web constructs is the input form, which allows a user to enter information into text boxes or other input constructs on the page and submit them to a server for processing. Jakarta Server Page makes it easy to submit values from an HTML form, and it is equally easy to display data back onto a page. To do so, a field is declared in a Java class, and accessor methods (a.k.a. getters and setters) are provided so that other classes can save values to the field and obtain values that are currently stored in it. Sometimes, Java classes that contain fields with accessor methods are referred to as JavaBean *classes*. The classes can also contain other methods that can be used to perform tasks, but it is a best practice to keep Beans as simple as possible. JavaBean classes should also implement java.io.Serializable so that they can be easily stored as a byte stream and resurrected.

In the example for this recipe, a Java class named EasyBean contains a private field named fieldValue. The accessor methods getFieldValue and setFieldValue can be used to obtain and store the value in fieldValue, respectively. Those accessor methods are declared as public, and thus they can be used from another Java class or Jakarta Server Page. The Jakarta Server Page uses the jsp:useBean element to obtain a reference to the EasyBean class. The scope is set to page so that the class can be used only within the Jakarta Server Page that contains the jsp:useBean element. Table 2-1, which can be found in the previous recipe, lists the different scopes available for use with the jsp:useBean element:

```
<jsp:useBean id="easyBean" scope="page" class="org.jakartaeerecipe.chapter02.recipe02_04.
EasyBean"/>
```

Next, an HTML form is defined in the Jakarta Server Page with the POST method, and it contains an input field named fieldValue, which allows a user to enter a string of text that will be submitted as a request parameter when the form is submitted. Note that the form in the example does not have an action specified; this means that the same URL will be used for form submission, and the same Jakarta Server Page will be used for form submission and will be displayed again once the form is submitted. Since the Jakarta Server Page has a jsp:useBean element specified on the page, all request parameters will be sent to that bean when the page is submitted. The key to ensuring that the value entered into the fieldValue input text field is stored into the fieldValue variable within the Java class is using the jsp:setProperty element within the form. The jsp:setProperty element allows one or more properties to be set in a JavaBean class using the corresponding setter methods. In the example, <jsp:useBean> is used to instantiate the EasyBean Java class, and <jsp:setProperty> is used to set the value that is entered within the fieldValue input text box to the fieldValue variable within the EasyBean class. The jsp:setProperty name attribute must equal the value of the jsp:useBean id attribute. The jsp:setProperty property attribute can equal the name of the field within the Java class that you want to set in the bean, or it can be a wildcard * character to submit all input fields to the bean. The value attribute of jsp:setProperty can be used to specify a static value for the property. The following excerpt from the example shows how the jsp:setProperty tag is used:

```
<jsp:setProperty name="easyBean" property="*"/>
```

■ **Note**   The ordering of the Jakarta Server Page elements is very important. `<jsp:useBean>` must come before `<jsp:setProperty>` because the `jsp:useBean` element is responsible for instantiating its corresponding Java class. Since the Jakarta Server Page is executed from the top of the page downward, the bean would be unavailable for use to any elements prior to when `jsp:useBean` is specified.

When the user enters a value into the input field and submits the request, it is submitted as a request parameter to the Java class that corresponds to the `jsp:useBean` element for that page. There are a couple of different ways to display the data that has been populated in the JavaBean field. The example demonstrates how to use the `jsp:getProperty` element to display the value of the `fieldValue` variable. The `<jsp:getProperty>` element must specify a `name` attribute, which corresponds to the `id` of the Java class that was specified within the `jsp:useBean` element. It must also specify a `property` attribute, which corresponds to the name of the JavaBean property that you want to display. The following excerpt from the example demonstrates the use of the `jsp:getProperty` tag:

```
<jsp:getProperty name="easyBean" property="fieldValue"/>
```

It is also possible to display the value of a JavaBean property using Jakarta Expression Language expressions, using the `id specified` in the `jsp:useBean` element, along with the property name. To try this, you can replace the `jsp:getProperty` element with the following Jakarta Expression Language expression:

```
${easyBean.fieldValue}
```

The Jakarta Server framework makes the development of web applications using Java technology much easier than using servlets. Input forms such as the one demonstrated in this example show how much more productive Jakarta Server Page is compared to standard servlet coding. As with anything, both servlets and Jakarta Server Page technology have their place in your toolbox. For creating simple data entry forms, Jakarta Server Page definitely takes the cake.

2-5. Invoking a Function in a Conditional Expression

Problem

You want to use a Java function to perform a conditional evaluation within your Jakarta Server Page. However, you do not want to embed Java code into your Jakarta Server Page.

Solution

Code the function in a JavaBean class and then register the bean with the Jakarta Server Page via the `<jsp:useBean>` tag. You will then need to register the function within a tag library descriptor (TLD) so that it can be made usable on the Jakarta Server Page via a tag. Finally, set up a page directive for the TLD in which the function is registered, and use the function tag within the page. In the example that follows, a Jakarta Server Page will use a function to tell the user whether a given Java type is a primitive type. The user will enter a string value into a text box, and that value will be submitted to a JavaBean field. The contents of the field will then be compared against a list of Java primitive types to determine whether it is a match. If the value entered into the field is a primitive, a message will be displayed to the user. The following is the folder structure for this project:

```
├── src
│   ├── main
│   │   ├── java
│   │   │   └── org
│   │   │       └── jakartaeerecipe
│   │   │           ├── chapter02
│   │   │           │   ├── recipe02_05
│   │   │           │   │   └── ConditionalClass.java
│   │   └── webapp
│   │       ├── WEB-INF
│   │       │   ├── tlds
│   │       │   │   ├── functions.tld
│   │       │   └── web.xml
│   │       ├── chapter02
│   │       │   ├── recipe02_05.jsp
```

The following code is the Java class that contains the implementation of the function, which is going to be used from within the Jakarta Server Page. The bean also contains a field that will be used from the Jakarta Server Page for setting and getting the value that is entered by the user:

```java
package org.jakartaeerecipe.chapter02.recipe02_05;

import java.io.Serializable;
import java.util.*;

public class ConditionalClass implements Serializable {
    private String typename = null;
    public static Set<String> javaTypes = new HashSet<>();

    public ConditionalClass() {
        javaTypes.add("byte");
        javaTypes.add("short");
        javaTypes.add("int");
        javaTypes.add("long");
        javaTypes.add("float");
        javaTypes.add("double");
        javaTypes.add("boolean");
        javaTypes.add("char");
    }

    public static boolean isPrimitive(String value){
        return javaTypes.contains(value.toLowerCase());
    }

    /**
     * @return the typename
     */
    public String getTypename() {
        return typename;
    }
```

```
    /**
     * @param typename the typename to set
     */
    public void setTypename(String typename) {
        this.typename = typename;
    }
}
```

The field typename will be used from the Jakarta Server Page to set the value that is entered by the user and to retrieve it for passing to the function named isPrimitive();, which is used to compare the given value to a list of Java primitives. Next is a listing of the TLD that is used to register the function so that it can be used as a tag within the Jakarta Server Page. For simplicity, the TLD file is named functions.tld and is placed within the /webapp folder:

```
<?xml version="1.0" encoding="UTF-8"?>
<taglib xmlns="http://java.sun.com/xml/ns/javaee"
        xmlns:xsi="http://www.w3.org/2001/XMLSchema-instance"
        xsi:schemaLocation="http://java.sun.com/xml/ns/javaee
        http://java.sun.com/xml/ns/javaee/web-jsptaglibrary_2_1.xsd"
        version="2.1" >
    <tlib-version>1.0</tlib-version>
    <short-name>fct</short-name>
    <uri>functions</uri>
    <function>
        <name>isPrimitive</name>
        <function-class>org.jakartaeerecipe.chapter02.recipe02_05.ConditionalClass
        </function-class>
        <function-signature>boolean isPrimitive(java.lang.String)</function-signature>
    </function>
</taglib>
```

Last is the Jakarta Server Page code that contains the page directive for using the TLD and the conditional call to the function isPrimitive() via a tag:

```
<%@ page contentType="text/html;charset=UTF-8" %>
<%@ taglib uri="http://java.sun.com/jsp/jstl/core"
           prefix="c" %>
<%@ taglib uri="/WEB-INF/tlds/functions.tld" prefix="fct" %>
<html>
<head>
    <title>Recipe 2-5: Invoking a Function in an Expression</title>
</head>
<body>
<form method="get">
    <label for="typename">
        Name one of the primitive Java types:
    </label>
    <input type="text" id="typename" name="typename" size="40"/>
    <br/>
    <input type="submit">
</form>
```

```
<jsp:useBean id="conditionalBean" scope="page" class="org.jakartaeerecipe.chapter02.
recipe02_05.ConditionalClass"/>
<jsp:setProperty name="conditionalBean" property="typename"/>
<c:if test="${fct:isPrimitive(conditionalBean.typename)}">
    ${ conditionalBean.typename } is a primitive type.
</c:if>
<c:if test="${conditionalBean.typename ne null and !fct:isPrimitive(conditionalBean.
typename)}">
    ${ conditionalBean.typename } is not a primitive type.
</c:if>
</body>
</html>
```

Following the strategy used in this solution, you can create a conditional test that is usable via a Jakarta Server Page tag for your pages. The output is shown in the Figure 2-6.

Figure 2-6. *Jakarta Server Pages recipe 02-05 output*

How It Works

A Jakarta Expression Language function must be declared with a public static modifier so that it could be executed by the framework. In this recipe, the function isPrimitive is declared as public static, and it returns a boolean value indicating whether the user types the name of a Java primitive type.

The next step toward making a function accessible via a Jakarta Server Page is to register it with a TLD. In the example, a TLD named functions.tld is created. If there is already a custom TLD in your application, then you could register the function with it rather than creating an additional one if you want. The TLD in this example has a short-name attribute of fct, which will be used from within Jakarta Server Page tags. To actually register the function, you must create a function element within the TLD, provide a function name, indicate the class that the function resides within, and, finally, specify the function signature:

```
<function>
    <name>isPrimitive</name>
    <function-class>org.jakartaeerecipe.chapter02.recipe02_05.ConditionalClass
    </function-class>
    <function-signature>boolean isPrimitive(java.lang.String)</function-signature>
</function>
```

The function is now ready for use within the Jakarta Server Page. To make the function accessible via the Jakarta Server Page, register the TLD that contains the function element by including a `taglib` directive specifying the `uri` and prefix for the TLD. The `uri` is the path to the TLD, and the prefix should match the name given in the `short-name` element of the TLD. The following excerpt from the Jakarta Server Page in this example shows the `taglib` directive:

```
<%@ taglib uri="/WEB-INF/tlds/functions.tld" prefix="fct" %>
```

The function will now be accessible via a Jakarta Expression Language expression within the Jakarta Server Page by specifying the `taglib` prefix along with the name of the function as it is registered in the TLD. The Jakarta Expression Language expression in the example calls the function, passing the `typename` parameter. The `isPrimitive` function is used to determine whether the text contained within the `typename` bean field is equal to one of the Java primitive types:

```
<c:if test="${fct:isPrimitive(conditionalBean.typename)}" >
```

The solution in this recipe also uses the Jakarta Standard Tag Library core. Depending on the server environment being used, this may be a separate download. The Jakarta Standard Tag Library provides an extension to the standard set of tags provided with the Jakarta Server Page API. For more information regarding Jakarta Standard Tag Library, refer to the online documentation, which can be found at `https://jakarta.ee/specifications/tags/2.0/jakarta-tags-spec-2.0.pdf`.

The Jakarta Standard Tag Library `<c:if>` tag can be used to test conditions, executing the markup between its opening and closing tags if the condition test returns a `true` value. Not surprisingly, the `<c:if>` tag includes a `test` attribute that specifies a Jakarta Expression Language expression that indicates the test that needs to be performed. In the example, the `isPrimitive` function is called within the Jakarta Expression Language expression, passing the bean value. If the test returns a `true`, then a message is printed indicating that the given value is equal to a Java primitive type. Another `<c:if>` test follows the first in the example, and this time it tests to ensure that the property value is not equal to `null` and that it is not a Java primitive type. Expression Language is used to determine whether the property value is equal to `null` via the `new expression`. The and expression ties the first and second conditional expressions together within the Jakarta Expression Language expression, meaning that both of the expressions must evaluate to a `true` value in order for the condition to be met. If both conditions are met, then the value specified by the user is not a Java primitive type, and a corresponding message is printed:

```
<c:if test="${conditionalBean.typename ne null and !fct:isPrimitive(conditionalBean.
typename)}" >
           ${ conditionalBean.typename } is not a primitive type.
</c:if>
```

Below is the snippet from pom.xml file which adds the Jakarta Standard Tag Library support to your project:
```
<dependency>
    <groupId>jakarta.servlet.jsp.jstl</groupId>
    <artifactId>jakarta.servlet.jsp.jstl-api</artifactId>
    <version>2.0.0</version>
    <scope>compile</scope>
</dependency>
```

It takes only a few easy steps to create a conditional function for use within Jakarta Server Pages. First, in the JavaBean class, you must create a public static function, which returns a boolean value. Second, create a TLD, which will make the function available via a Jakarta Server Page tag. Lastly, use the custom tag from within the Jakarta Server Page along with Jakarta Standard Tag Library conditional test tags to display the content conditionally.

2-6. Creating a Jakarta Server Page Document

Problem

Rather than using standard HTML format, you want to ensure that your Jakarta Server Page code follows the XML standard and contains only valid HTML and Jakarta Server Page tags.

Solution

Create a Jakarta Server Page document rather than a standard Jakarta Server Page. A Jakarta Server Page document is an XML-based representation of a standard Jakarta Server Page document that conforms to the XML standard. The following Jakarta Server Page document contains the same code that is used in the Jakarta Server Page code for Recipe 2-4, but it uses the Jakarta Server Page document format instead. As you can see, not much is different because well-formed tags were already used to create the standard Jakarta Server Page document. The page is also saved with an extension of jspx rather than jsp:

```
<html xmlns:jsp="http://java.sun.com/JSP/Page"
      version="2.0">
    <head>
        <title>Recipe 2-4: Yielding or Setting Values</title>
    </head>
    <body>
        <jsp:directive.page contentType="text/html" pageEncoding="UTF-8"/>
        <jsp:useBean id="easyBean" class="org.jakartaeerecipe.chapter02.recipe02_04.
        EasyBean"/>
        <jsp:setProperty name="easyBean" property="*"/>
        <form method="post">
            Use the input text box below to set the value, and then hit submit.
            <br/><br/>
            <label for="fieldValue">Set the field value: </label>
            <input id="fieldValue" name="fieldValue" type="text" size="30"/>
            <br/>
            The value contained within the field is currently:
            <jsp:getProperty name="easyBean" property="fieldValue"/>
            <input type="submit"/>
        </form>
    </body>
</html>
```

This Jakarta Server Page document will yield the same output as the one in recipe02_04.jsp. However, a well-formed document will be enforced, and this will exclude the use of scripting elements within the page.

How It Works

As foreshadowed in Recipe 2-3, separating business logic from markup code can be important for many reasons. Standard Jakarta Server Pages can adhere to the MVC paradigm, but they are not forced into doing so. Sometimes, it makes sense to enforce the separation of business logic, by strictly adhering to a well-formed XML document using only Jakarta Server Page tags to work with server-side Java classes. Well-formed means that there should be only one root element, and each starting tag must have a corresponding ending tag. Creating a Jakarta Server Page document is one answer because such documents enforce well-formed XML and do not allow scripting elements to be used within the Jakarta Server Page. It is still possible to display the value of scripting expressions in the body of a Jakarta Server Page document using the `<jsp:expression/>` tag or value expressions, as demonstrated in Recipe 2-8.

Several Jakarta Server Page tags can be used to communicate with Java classes, perform Jakarta Server Page–specific functionality, and make markup easy to follow. As such, modern Jakarta Server Page–based applications should use well-formed Jakarta Server Page documents utilizing such Jakarta Server Page tags, rather than embedding scripting elements throughout markup. Table 2-2 describes what the different Jakarta Server Page tags do.

Table 2-2. *Jakarta Server Page Tags*

Tag	Description
`<jsp:attribute>`	Defines attributes for a Jakarta Server Page
`<jsp:body>`	Defines an element body
`<jsp:declaration>`	Defines page declarations
`<jsp:directive>`	Defines page includes and page directives
`<jsp:doBody>`	Executes the body of the Jakarta Server Page tag that is used by the calling Jakarta Server Page to invoke the tag
`<jsp:element>`	Generates an XML element dynamically
`<jsp:expression>`	Inserts the value of a scripting language expression, converted into a string
`<jsp:forward>`	Forwards a request to another page. The new page can be HTML, Jakarta Server Page, or servlet
`<jsp:getProperty>`	Obtains the value of a bean property and places it in the page
`<jsp:include>`	Includes another Jakarta Server Page or web resource in the page
`<jsp:invoke>`	Invokes a specified Jakarta Server Page fragment
`<jsp:output>`	Specifies the document type declaration
`<jsp:plugin>`	Executes an applet or bean with the specified plug-in
`<jsp:root>`	Defines standard elements and tag library namespaces
`<jsp:scriptlet>`	Embeds code fragments into a page if necessary
`<jsp:setProperty>`	Sets specified value(s) into a bean property
`<jsp:text>`	Encloses template data
`<jsp:useBean>`	References and instantiates (if needed) a JavaBean class using a name and providing a scope

Creating a well-formed Jakarta Server Page can lead to easier development, ease of maintenance, and better overall design. Since it is so important, the remaining recipes in this chapter use the Jakarta Server Page document format.

2-7. Embedding Expressions in Jakarta Expression Language

Problem

You want to use some conditional expressions and/or arithmetic within your Jakarta Server Page without embedding Java code using scripting elements.

Solution

Use Jakarta Expression Language expressions within Jakarta Server Page tags to perform conditional and/or arithmetic expressions. This solution will look at two examples of Jakarta Expression Language expressions. The first example demonstrates how to perform conditional logic using Jakarta Expression Language expressions. Note that the Jakarta Standard Tag Library tag library is also used in this case, to conditionally display a message on the page if the expression results to true:

```
<html xmlns:jsp="http://java.sun.com/JSP/Page"
    xmlns:c="http://java.sun.com/jsp/jstl/core"
    version="2.0">
    <jsp:directive.page contentType="text/html" pageEncoding="UTF-8"/>
    <head>
        <title>Recipe 2-7: Embedding Expressions in Jakarta Expression Language </title>
    </head>
    <body>
        <h1>Conditional Expressions</h1>
        <p>
            The following portion of the page will only display conditional
            expressions which result in a true value.
        </p>
        <c:if test="${1 + 1 == 2}">
            The conditional expression (1 + 1 == 2) results in TRUE.
            <br/>
        </c:if>
        <c:if test="${'x' == 'y'}">
            The conditional expression (x == y) results in TRUE.
            <br/>
        </c:if>
        <c:if test="${(100/10) gt 5}">
            The conditional expression ((100/10) > 5) results in TRUE.
            <br/>
        </c:if>
        <c:if test="${20 mod 3 eq 2}">
            The conditional expression (20 mod 3 eq 2) results in TRUE.
            <br/>
        </c:if>
```

```
    </body>
</html>
```

This Jakarta Server Page will result in the following output being displayed:

```
...
The conditional expression (1 + 1 == 2) results in TRUE.
The conditional expression ((100/10) > 5) results in TRUE.
The conditional expression (20 mod 3 eq 2) results in TRUE.
...
```

The output is shown in the Figure 2-7.

Conditional Expressions

The following portion of the page will only display conditional expressions which result in a true value.

The conditional expression (1 + 1 == 2) results in TRUE.
The conditional expression ((100/10) > 5) results in TRUE.
The conditional expression (20 mod 3 eq 2) results in TRUE.

Figure 2-7. *Jakarta Server Pages recipe 02-07 output*

Arithmetic expressions can also be evaluated using Jakarta Expression Language. The following Jakarta Server Page code demonstrates some examples of using arithmetic within Jakarta Expression Language:

```
<html xmlns="http://www.w3.org/1999/xhtml" version="2.0">
    <head>
        <title>Recipe 2-7: Embedding Expressions in Jakarta Expression Language </title>
    </head>
    <body>
        <h1>Arithmetic Expressions</h1>
        <p>The following expressions demonstrate how to perform arithmetic using Jakarta
        Expression Language.</p>
        10 - 4 = ${10 - 4}<br/>
        85 / 15 = ${85 / 15}<br/>
        847 divided by 6 = ${847 div 6}<br/>
    </body>
</html>
```

The preceding Jakarta Server Page will result in the following output being displayed:

```
...
10 - 4 = 6
85 / 15 = 5.666666666666667
847 divided by 6 = 141.16666666666666
...
```

The output is shown in the Figure 2-8.

Arithmetic Expressions

The following expressions demonstrate how to perform arithmetic using Jakarta Expression Language.

10 - 4 = 6
85 / 15 = 5.666666666666667
847 divided by 6 = 141.16666666666666

Figure 2-8. Jakarta Server Pages recipe 02-07a output

How It Works

The Jakarta Server Page technology makes it easy to work with expressions. Conditional page rendering can be performed using a combination of Jakarta Expression Language value expressions, which are enclosed within the ${ } character sequences and Jakarta Standard Tag Library tags. Arithmetic expressions can also be performed using Jakarta Expression Language expressions. To make things easier, the Expression Language contains keywords or characters that can be used to help form expressions. The example for this recipe contains various expressions and conditional page rendering using the Jakarta Standard Tag Library <c:if> tag.

In the first Jakarta Server Page displayed in the example, there are some examples of conditional page rendering. To use the <c:if> tag to perform the conditional tests, you must be sure to import the Jakarta Standard Tag Library with the Jakarta Server Page. To do so, add an import for the Jakarta Standard Tag Library and assign it to a character or string of characters. In the following excerpt from the recipe, the Jakarta Standard Tag Library library is assigned to the character c:

```
<html xmlns:jsp="http://java.sun.com/JSP/Page"
      xmlns:c="http://java.sun.com/jsp/jstl/core"
      version="2.0">
```

A Jakarta Expression Language value expression is contained within the ${ and } character sequences. Anything within these characters will be treated as Jakarta Expression Language, and, as such, the syntax must be correct, or the Jakarta Server Page will not be able to compile into a servlet, and it will throw an error. All expressions using the ${ } syntax are evaluated immediately, and they are read-only expressions. That is, no expressions using this syntax can be used to set values into a JavaBean property. The Jakarta Server Page engine first evaluates the expression, and then it converts into a String and lastly returns the value to the tag handler. Four types of objects can be referenced within a value expression. Those are JavaBean components, collections, enumerated types, and implicit objects. If using a JavaBean component, the JavaBean must be registered with the Jakarta Server Page using the jsp:useBean element (see Recipe 2-3 for details). Collections or enumerated types can also be referenced from a JavaBean that has been registered with the page. Implicit objects are those that allow access to page context, scoped variables, and other such objects. Table 2-3 lists different implicit objects that can be referenced from within Jakarta Expression Language expressions.

Table 2-3. *Implicit Jakarta Server Page Objects*

Object	Type	Description
pageContext	Context	Provides access to the context of the page and various subobjects
servletContext	Page context	Context for Jakarta Server Page servlet and web components
session	Page context	Session object for the client
request	Page context	Request that invoked the execution of the page
response	Page context	Response that is returned by the Jakarta Server Page
param	N/A	Responsible for mapping parameter names to values
paramValues	N/A	Maps a request parameter to an array of values
header	N/A	Responsible for mapping a header name to a value
headerValues	N/A	Maps a header name to an array of values
cookie	N/A	Maps a cookie name to a single cookie
initParam	N/A	Maps a context initialization parameter to a value
pageScope	Scope	Maps page scope variables
requestScope	Scope	Maps request scope variables
sessionScope	Scope	Maps session scope variables
applicationScope	Scope	Maps application scope variables

The following are some examples of expressions that use JavaBean components, collections, enumerated types, and implicit objects:

```
// Displays the value of a variable named myVar within a JavaBean referenced as elTester
${ elTester.myVar }
// Does the same thing as the line above
${ elTester["myVar"] }

// Evaluates an Enumerated Type in which myEnum is an instance of MyEnum
${ myEnum == "myValue" }
// Reference a getter method of the Enum named getTestVal()
${ myEnum.testVal}

// References a collection named myCollection within the JavaBean referenced as elTester
${ elTester.myCollection }

// Obtain the parameter named "testParam"
${ param.testParam }  // Same as: request.getParameter("testParam")
// Obtain session attribute named "testAttr"
${ sessionScope.testAttr } // Same as: session.getAttribute("testAttr")
```

In the recipe example, the `<c:if>` tag is used to test a series of value expressions and conditionally display page content. The test attribute of `<c:if>` is used to register a test condition, and if the test condition returns a `true` result, then the content contained between the `<c:if>` starting and ending tags is displayed. The following excerpt from the example demonstrates how a test is performed:

```
<c:if test="${'x' == 'y'}">
        The conditional expression (x == y) results in TRUE.
        <br/>
</c:if>
```

Jakarta Expression Language expressions can contain a series of reserved words that can be used to help evaluate the expression. For instance, the following expression utilizes the gt reserved word to return a value indicating whether the value returned from the calculation of 100/10 is greater than 5:

```
<c:if test="${(100/10) gt 5}">
        The conditional expression ((100/10) > 5) results in TRUE.
        <br/>
</c:if>
```

Table 2-4 lists all the Jakarta Server Page Jakarta Expression Language expression reserved words and their meanings.

Table 2-4. *Jakarta Expression Language Expression Reserved Words*

Reserved Word	Description
and	Combines expressions and returns `true` if all of them evaluate to `true`
or	Combines expressions and returns `true` if one of them evaluates to `true`
not	Negates an expression
eq	Equal
ne	Not equal
lt	Less than
gt	Greater than
le	Less than or equal
ge	Greater than or equal
true	True value
false	False value
null	Null value
instanceof	Used to test whether an object is an instance of another object
empty	Determines whether a list or collection is empty
div	Divided by
mod	Modulus

Arithmetic expressions are demonstrated by the second example in this recipe. The following arithmetic operators can be utilized within expressions:

- + (addition), - (binary and unary), * (multiplication), / and div (division), %, and mod (modulus)

- and, &&, or, | |, not, !

- ==, ! =, <, >, <=, >=

- X ? Y : Z (ternary conditional)

Entire chapters of books have been written on the use of Jakarta Expression Language expressions within Jakarta Server Pages. This recipe only touches on the possibilities of using value expressions. The best way to get used to expressions is to create a test Jakarta Server Page and experiment with the different options that are available.

2-8. Accessing Parameters in Multiple Pages

Problem

You want to access a parameter from within multiple pages of your web application.

Solution

Create an input form to submit parameters to the request object, and then utilize the request object to retrieve the values in another page. In the example that follows, a Jakarta Server Page that contains an input form is used to pass values to another Jakarta Server Page by setting the HTML form action attribute to the value of the Jakarta Server Page that will utilize the parameters. In the case of this example, the receiving Jakarta Server Page merely displays the parameter values, but other work could be performed as well.

The following Jakarta Server Page code demonstrates the use of an input form to save parameters into the request object and pass them to a page named recipe02_08b.jspx:

```
<html xmlns:jsp="http://java.sun.com/JSP/Page">
<jsp:directive.page contentType="text/html" pageEncoding="UTF-8"/>
<head>
    <style>div {
        padding: 10px;
    }</style>
    <title>Recipe 2-8: Accessing Parameters in Multiple Pages </title>
</head>
<body>
<h1>Passing Parameters</h1>
<p>
    The following parameters will be passed to the next Jakarta Server.
</p>
<form method="get" action="recipe02_08b.jspx">
    <div>
        <label for="param1">Param 1: </label>
        <input id="param1" name="param1" type="text" value="1"/>
    </div>
    <div>
```

```
        <label for="param2">Param 2: </label>
        <input id="param2" name="param2" type="text" value="2 + 0"/>
    </div>
    <div>
        <label for="param3">Param 3: </label>
        <input id="param3" name="param3" type="text" value="three"/>
    </div>
    <div>
        <input type="submit" value="Go to next page"/>
    </div>
</form>
</body>
</html>
```

The next Jakarta Server Page code receives the parameters and displays their values:

```
<html xmlns:jsp="http://java.sun.com/JSP/Page" version="2.0">
    <jsp:directive.page contentType="text/html" pageEncoding="UTF-8"/>
    <head>
        <title>Recipe 2-8: Accessing Parameters in Multiple Pages </title>
    </head>
    <body>
        <h1>Passing Parameters</h1>
        <p>
            The following parameters were passed from the original Jakarta Server Pages.
        </p>
        <form method="post" action="recipe02_08a.jspx">
        Param 1: <jsp:expression>request.getParameter("param1") </jsp:expression>
        <br/>
        Param 2: <jsp:expression> request.getParameter("param2") </jsp:expression>
        <br/>
        Param 3: <jsp:expression> request.getParameter("param3") </jsp:expression>
        <br/>
        OR using value expressions
        <br/>
        Param 1: ${ param.param1 }
        <br/>
        Param 2: ${ param.param2 }
        <br/>
        Param 3: ${ param.param3 }
        <br/>
        <input type="submit" value="Back to Page 1"/>
        </form>
    </body>
</html>
```

As you can see, a couple of variations can be used to display the parameter values. Both of the variations will display the same result.

How It Works

Request parameters are one of the most useful features of web applications. When a user enters some data into a web form and submits the form, the request contains the parameters that were entered into the form. Parameters can also be statically embedded in a web page or concatenated onto a URL and sent to a receiving servlet or Jakarta Server Page. The data contained in request parameters can then be inserted into a database, redisplayed on another Jakarta Server Page, used to perform a calculation, or a myriad of other possibilities. The Jakarta Server technology provides an easy mechanism for using request parameters in other Jakarta Server Pages, and the example in this recipe demonstrates how to do just that.

> ■ **Note** Request parameters are always translated into `String` values.

Note that in the example, the first Jakarta Server Page uses a simple HTML form to obtain values from a user and submit them to the request. The form will look as shown in the Figure 2-9. Another Jakarta Server Page named `recipe02_08b.jspx` is set as the form action attribute, so when the form is submitted, it will send the request to `recipe02_08b.jspx`. The input fields on the first Jakarta Server Page specify both an `id` attribute and a `name` attribute, although only the `name` attribute is required. The name that is given to the input fields is the name that will be used to reference the value entered into it as a request parameter.

> ■ **Note** It is a good programming practice to always include an `id` attribute. The ID is useful for performing work with the DOM and for referencing elements via a scripting language such as JavaScript.

The receiving action, `recipe02_08b.jspx` in this example, can make a call to `response. getParameter()`, passing the name of a parameter (input field name) to obtain the value that was entered into its corresponding text field. To adhere to Jakarta Server document standards, the scriptlet containing the call to `response.getParameter()` must be enclosed in `<jsp:expression>` tags. The following excerpt demonstrates how this is done:

```
Param 1: <jsp:expression>request.getParameter("param1") </jsp:expression>
```

Optionally, a Jakarta Expression Language expression can contain a reference to the implicit `param` object and obtain the request parameter in the same way. When the expression `${param.param1}` is called, it is evaluated by the Jakarta Server engine, and it is translated into `response.getParameter("param1")`. The following excerpt demonstrates this use of Jakarta Expression Language expressions:

```
Param 1: ${ param.param1 }
```

Either technique will perform the same task; the named request parameter will be obtained and displayed on the page. The output is shown in Figure 2-10.

Figure 2-9. *Jakarta Server Pages recipe 02-08a output*

Figure 2-10. *Jakarta Server Pages recipe 02-08b output*

2-9. Creating a Custom Jakarta Server Tag

Problem

You want to create a Jakarta Server tag that provides custom functionality for your application.

Solution

Create a custom Jakarta Server tag using Jakarta Server 2.0 *simple tag support*. Suppose you want to create a custom tag that will insert a signature into the Jakarta Server where the tag is placed. The custom tag will print a default signature, but it will also accept an `authorName` attribute, which will include a given author's name to the signature if provided. To get started, you'll need to define a Java class that extends the `SimpleTagSupport` class. This class will provide the implementation for your tag. The following code is the implementation for a class named `Signature`, which provides the implementation for the custom tag:

```java
package org.jakartaeerecipe.chapter02.recipe02_09;

import jakarta.servlet.jsp.JspException;
import jakarta.servlet.jsp.JspWriter;
import jakarta.servlet.jsp.PageContext;
import jakarta.servlet.jsp.tagext.SimpleTagSupport;

public class Signature extends SimpleTagSupport {
    private String authorName = null;
    /**
     * @param authorName the authorName to set
     */
    public void setAuthorName(String authorName) {
        this.authorName = authorName;
    }
    @Override
    public void doTag() throws JspException {
        PageContext pageContext = (PageContext) getJspContext();
        JspWriter out = pageContext.getOut();
        try {
            if(authorName != null){
                out.println("Written by " + authorName);
                out.println("<br/>");
            }
            out.println("Published by Apress");
        } catch (Exception e) {
            System.out.println(e);
        }
    }
}
```

The following is the folder structure for this project:

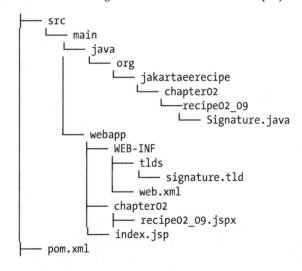

```
├── src
│   └── main
│       └── java
│           └── org
│               └── jakartaeerecipe
│                   └── chapter02
│                       └──recipe02_09
│                           └── Signature.java
│       └── webapp
│           ├── WEB-INF
│           │   ├── tlds
│           │   │   └── signature.tld
│           │   └── web.xml
│           ├── chapter02
│           │   ├── recipe02_09.jspx
│           └── index.jsp
├── pom.xml
```

■ **Note**   To compile the following code, you need to add `jakarta.servlet.jsp-api.jar` to `classpath`:

```
cd recipe02_09

javac -cp ...\glassfish\modules\jakarta.servlet.jsp-api.jar *.java
```

Next, a TLD needs to be created to map the Signature class tag implementation to a tag. The file signature.tld is the TLD source file that includes the custom tag mapping; its code is listed as follows:

```xml
<?xml version="1.0" encoding="UTF-8"?>
<taglib version="2.1" xmlns="http://java.sun.com/xml/ns/javaee" xmlns:xsi="http://www.
w3.org/2001/XMLSchema-instance" xsi:schemaLocation="http://java.sun.com/xml/ns/javaee
http://java.sun.com/xml/ns/javaee/web-jsptaglibrary_2_1.xsd">
  <tlib-version>1.0</tlib-version>
  <short-name>cust</short-name>
  <uri>custom</uri>
  <tag>
   <name>signature</name>
   <tag-class>org.jakartaeerecipe.chapter02.recipe02_09.Signature</tag-class>
   <body-content>empty</body-content>
   <attribute>
       <name>authorName</name>
       <rtexprvalue>true</rtexprvalue>
       <required>false</required>
   </attribute>
 </tag>
</taglib>
```

Once the class implementation and the TLD are in place, the tag can be used from within a Jakarta Server Pages page. The following Jakarta Server code is taken from recipe_02_09.jspx; it uses the custom tag:

```xml
<html xmlns:jsp="http://java.sun.com/JSP/Page"
      xmlns:cust="custom">
<jsp:directive.page contentType="text/html" pageEncoding="UTF-8"/>
<head>
      <title>Recipe 2-9: Creating a Custom Jakarta Server Tag</title>
</head>
<body>
<h1>Custom Jakarta Server Tag</h1>
<p>The custom Jakarta Server tag is used as the footer for this page.</p>
<br/>
<cust:signature authorName="Josh Juneau and Tarun Telang"/>
</body>
</html>
```

The custom tag output will now be displayed in place of the `cust:signature` element on the Jakarta Server Page. The output will be as shown in Figure 2-11.

Custom Jakarta Server Tag

The custom Jakarta Server tag is used as the footer for this page.

Written by Josh Juneau and Tarun Telang
Published by Apress

Figure 2-11. *Jakarta Server Pages recipe 02-09 output*

How It Works

One of the most useful new features of JSP 2.0 was the inclusion of the `SimpleTagSupport` class, which provides an easy way for developers to create custom tags. Prior to the 2.0 release, custom tag creation took a good deal of more work, because the developer had to provide much more code to implement the tag within the tag's implementation class. The `SimpleTagSupport` class takes care of much implementation for the developer so that the only thing left to do is implement the `doTag` method in order to provide an implementation for the custom tag.

In the example for this recipe, a custom tag is created that will print a signature on the Jakarta Server Page in the position where the tag is located. To create a custom tag implementation, create a Java class that will extend the `SimpleTagSupport` class, and provide an implementation for the `doTag` method. The example class also contains a field named `authorName`, which will be mapped within the TLD as an attribute for the custom tag. In the `doTag` method, a handle on the Jakarta Server Page context is obtained by calling the `getJspContext` method. `getJspContext` is a custom method that is implemented for you in `SimpleTagSupport` and makes it easy to get a hold of the Jakarta Server Page context. Next, to provide the ability to write to the Jakarta Server output, a handle is obtained on the `JspWriter` by calling `PageContext`'s `getOut` method:

```
PageContext pageContext = (PageContext) getJspContext();
JspWriter out = pageContext.getOut();
```

The next lines within `doTag` provide the implementation for writing to the Jakarta Server output via a series of calls to `out.println`. Any content that is passed to `out.println` will be displayed on the page. Note that in the example, the `authorName` field is checked to see whether it contains a `null` value. If it does not contain a `null` value, then it is displayed on the page; otherwise, it is omitted. Therefore, if the tag within the Jakarta Server Page contains a value for the `authorName` attribute, then it will be printed on the page. The `out.println` code is contained within a `try-catch` block in case any exceptions occur.

■ **Note** To allow your tag to accept scriptlets, you will need to use the *classic tag handlers*. The classic tag handlers existed before the Jakarta Server 2.0 era and can still be used today alongside the simple tag handlers. The simple tag handlers revolve around the `doTag()` method, whereas the classic tag handlers deal with a `doStartTag()` method and a `doEndTag()` method, as well as others. Since the simple tag handlers can be used alongside the classic tag handlers, it is possible to use some of the more complex classic tag methods while utilizing simple tag methods in the same application. This eases the transition from the classic tag handlers to the simple tag handlers. For more information regarding the differences between the two APIs, see some online documentation by searching for the keywords *Simple vs. Classic Tag Handlers*.

That's it; the implementation for the tag is complete. To map the implementation class to the Document Object Model (DOM) via a tag name, a TLD must contain a mapping to the class. In the example, a TLD is created named `custom.tld`, and it contains the mapping for the class. The `short-name` element specifies the name that must be used within the Jakarta Server Page to reference the tag. The `uri` element specifies the name of the TLD, and it is used from within the Jakarta Server Page to reference the TLD file itself. The meat of the TLD is contained within the `tag` element. The `name` element is used to specify the name for the tag, and it will be used within a Jakarta Server Page in combination with the `short-name` element to provide the complete tag name. The `tag-class` element provides the name of the class that implements the tag, and `body-content` specifies a value to indicate whether the body content for the Jakarta Server Page will be made available for the tag implementation class. It is set to `empty` for this example. To specify an attribute for the tag, the `attribute` element must be added to the TLD, including the `name`, `rtexprvalue`, and `required` elements. The `name` element of attribute specifies the name of the attribute, `rtexprvalue` indicates whether the attribute can contain a Jakarta Expression Language expression, and `required` indicates whether the attribute is required.

To use the tag in a Jakarta Server Page, the `custom.tld` TLD must be mapped to the page within the `<html>` element in a Jakarta Server document or a `taglib` directive within a standard Jakarta Server. The following lines show the difference between these two:

```
<!—Jakarta Server Document syntax -->
<html
xmlns:cust="custom"
. . .(more taglib directives) . . .>
<!—Jakarta Server syntax -->
<%@taglib prefix="cust" uri="custom" %>
```

To use the tag within the page, simply specify the TLD `short-name` along with the mapping name for the tag implementation and any attributes you want to provide:

```
<cust:signature authorName="Josh Juneau and Tarun Telang"/>
```

Creating custom tags within Jakarta Server is easier than it was in the past. Custom tags provide developers with the ability to define custom actions and/or content that can be made accessible from within a Jakarta Server Page via a tag rather than scriptlets. Custom tags help developers follow the MVC architecture, separating code from business logic.

2-10. Including Other Jakarta Server Pages into a Page

Problem

Rather than coding the same header or footer into each Jakarta Server, you want to place the content for those page sections into a separate Jakarta Server Page and then pull them into Jakarta Server Pages by reference.

Solution

Use the `<jsp:include>` tag to embed other static or dynamic pages in your Jakarta Server Page. The following example demonstrates the inclusion of two Jakarta Server Pages within another. One of the Jakarta Server Pages is used to formulate the header of the page, and another is used for the footer. The following page demonstrates the main Jakarta Server Page, which includes two others using the `<jsp:include>` tag.

The JSPX files named `recipe02_10-header.jspx` and `recipe02_10-footer.jspx` are included in the body of the main Jakarta Server Page in order to provide the header and footer sections of the page:

```
<html xmlns:jsp="http://java.sun.com/JSP/Page">
<jsp:directive.page contentType="text/html" pageEncoding="UTF-8"/>
<head>
  <title>Recipe 2-10: Including Other Jakarta Server Pages into a Page</title>
</head>
<body>
<jsp:include page="recipe02_10-header.jspx" />
<h1>This is the body of the main Jakarta Server Page.</h1>
<p>
  Both the header and footer for this page were created as separate Jakarta Server Pages.
</p>
<jsp:include page="recipe02_10-footer.jspx"/>
</body>
</html>
```

Next is the Jakarta Server code that comprises the page header. It's nothing fancy but is a separate Jakarta Server Page nonetheless:

```
<html xmlns:jsp="http://java.sun.com/JSP/Page">
    <jsp:directive.page contentType="text/html" pageEncoding="UTF-8"/>
    <p>This is the page header</p>
</html>
```

The following Jakarta Server code makes up the page footer:

```
<html xmlns:jsp="http://java.sun.com/JSP/Page">
    <jsp:directive.page contentType="text/html" pageEncoding="UTF-8"/>
    <p>This is the page footer</p>
</html>
```

In the end, these three pages create a single page that contains a header, a body, and a footer. The output of this page would be as shown in Figure 2-12.

How It Works

Including other Jakarta Server Pages helps increase developer productivity and reduces maintenance time. Using this technique, a developer can extract any Jakarta Server features that appear in multiple pages and place them into a separate Jakarta Server Page. Doing so will allow a single point of maintenance when one of these features needs to be updated.

To include another page within a Jakarta Server Page, use the `<jsp:include>` tag. The `<jsp:include>` tag allows embedding a static file or another web component. The tag includes a page attribute, which is used to specify the relative URL or an expression that results in another file or web component to include in the page.

This is the page header

This is the body of the main Jakarta Server Page.

Both the header and footer for this page were created as separate akarta Server Pages.

This is the page footer

Figure 2-12. *Jakarta Server Pages recipe 02-10 output*

■ **Note**   The tag also has an optional `flush` attribute, which can be set to `true` or `false` to indicate whether the output buffer should be flushed prior to the page inclusion. The default value for the `flush` attribute is `false`.

Optionally, `<jsp:param>` clauses can be placed between the opening and closing `<jsp:include>` tags to pass one or more name-value pairs to the included resource if the resource is dynamic. An example of performing this technique would resemble something like the following lines of code. In the following lines, a parameter with a name of bookAuthor and a value of Juneau is passed to the header Jakarta Server Page:

```
<jsp:include page="header.jspx">
    <jsp:param name="bookAuthor" value="Juneau and Telang"/>
</jsp:include>
```

The ability to include other content within a Jakarta Server Page provides a means to encapsulate resources and static content. This allows developers to create content once and include it in many pages.

2-11. Creating an Input Form for a Database Record

Problem

You want to create a Jakarta Server Page that will be used to input information that will be inserted as a database record.

Solution

Create an input form and use a Jakarta servlet action method to insert the values into the database. This solution requires a Jakarta Server Pages document and a Jakarta servlet in order to complete the database input form. In the following example, an input form is created within a Jakarta Server document to populate records within a database table named `RECIPES`. When the user enters the information into the text fields on the form and clicks the Submit button, a servlet is called that performs the database insert transaction.

The following code is the Jakarta Server document that is used to create the input form for the database application:

```
<html xmlns:jsp="http://java.sun.com/JSP/Page"
     version="2.0">
    <jsp:directive.page contentType="text/html" pageEncoding="UTF-8"/>
    <head>
        <title>Recipe 2-11: Creating an Input Form for a Database Record </title>
    </head>

<body>
        <h1>Recipe Input Form</h1>
        <p>
            Please insert recipe details using the text fields below.
        </p>

        <form method="POST" action="../RecipeServlet">
            <label for="recipeNumber">Recipe Number:</label><br/>
            <input id="recipeNumber" type="number" name="recipeNumber"/><br/>
            <label for="name">Recipe Name: </label><br/>
            <input type="text" name="name" size="30"/><br/>
            <label for="description">Recipe Description: </label><br/>
            <textarea name="description" rows="5" cols="50"> Enter description here...
            </textarea><br/>

            <label for="text">Recipe Text: </label><br/>
            <textarea id="text" name="text" rows="10" cols="50"> Enter text here...
            </textarea><br/><br/>
            <input type="submit"/><input type="reset"/>
        </form>
    </body>
</html>
```

Next is the code for a servlet named RecipeServlet. It is responsible for reading the request parameters from the Jakarta Server document input form and inserting the fields into the database:

```
package org.jakartaeerecipe.chapter02.recipe02_11;

import java.io.*;
import java.sql.*;
import javax.servlet.ServletException;
import javax.servlet.annotation.WebServlet;
import javax.servlet.http.*;

@WebServlet(name = "RecipeServlet", urlPatterns = {"/RecipeServlet"})
public class RecipeServlet extends HttpServlet {
    /**
     * Processes requests for both HTTP
     * <code>GET</code> and
     * <code>POST</code> methods.
     *
```

```java
 * @param request servlet request
 * @param response servlet response
 * @throws ServletException if a servlet-specific error occurs
 * @throws IOException if an I/O error occurs
 */
protected void processRequest(HttpServletRequest request, HttpServletResponse response)
        throws ServletException, IOException {
    response.setContentType("text/html;charset=UTF-8");
    PrintWriter out = response.getWriter();
    int result = -1;
    try {
        /*
         * TODO Perform validation on the request parameters here
         */
        result = insertRow (request.getParameter("recipeNumber"),
                    request.getParameter("name"),
                    request.getParameter("description"),
                    request.getParameter("text"));
        out.println("""
            <html>
            <head>
            <title>Servlet RecipeServlet</title>
            </head>
            <body>
        """);
        out.printf("<h1>Servlet RecipeServlet at " + request.getContextPath() + "</h1>");
        out.println("<br/><br/>");
        if(result > 0){
            out.println("""
                <font color='green'>Record successfully inserted!</font>
                <br/><br/>
          <a href='/JakartaEERecipes_Chapter02-1.0-SNAPSHOT/chapter02/recipe02_11.jspx'>
          Insert another record
        </a>
                """);
        } else {
            out.println("""
                <font color='red'>Record NOT inserted!</font>"
                <br/><br/>
              <a href='/JakartaEERecipes_Chapter02-1.0-SNAPSHOT/chapter02/recipe02_11.jspx'>
            Try Again
                    </a>
            """);
        }
        out.println("</body>");
        out.println("</html>");
    } finally {
        out.close();
    }
}
```

```java
    public int insertRow(String recipeNumber,
                        String name,
                        String description,
                        String text) {
        String sql = "INSERT INTO RECIPES VALUES(" +
                    "RECIPES_SEQ.NEXTVAL,?,?,?,?)";
        PreparedStatement stmt = null;
        int result = -1;
        try {
            CreateConnection createConn = new CreateConnection();
            Connection conn = createConn.getConnection();
            stmt = (PreparedStatement) conn.prepareStatement(sql);
            stmt.setString(1, recipeNumber);
            stmt.setString(2, name);
            stmt.setString(3, description);
            stmt.setString(4, text);
            // Returns row-count or 0 if not successful
            result = stmt.executeUpdate();
            if (result > 0){
                System.out.println("-- Record created --");
            } else {
                System.out.println("!! Record NOT Created !!");
            }
        } catch (SQLException e) {
            e.printStackTrace();
        } finally {
            if (stmt != null) {
                try {
                    stmt.close();
                } catch (SQLException ex) {
                    ex.printStackTrace();
                }
            }
        }
        return result;
    }
    @Override
    protected void doGet(HttpServletRequest request, HttpServletResponse response)
            throws ServletException, IOException {
        processRequest(request, response);
    }
    @Override
    protected void doPost(HttpServletRequest request, HttpServletResponse response)
            throws ServletException, IOException {
        processRequest(request, response);
    }
}
```

If the request is successful, the record will be inserted into the database, and the user will be able to click a link to add another record. Of course, in a real-life application, you would want to code some validation using JavaScript either within the input form or within the server-side Java code to help ensure database integrity.

How It Works

A fundamental task to almost every enterprise application is the use of a database input form. Database input forms make it easy for end users to populate database tables with data. When using Jakarta Server technology along with servlets, this operation can become fairly simple.

The Apache Derby database comes preinstalled with the GlassFish server within the directory:

`JAVA_DEV/glassfish7/javadb`

To run the code of this recipe, you need to first create a new database. The Apache Derby database comes with an interactive SQL scripting tool, ij. You can start it from the command prompt by going to the directory:

`JAVA_DEV/glassfish7/javadb/bin`

and then running the ij command. You should see the output as follows:

`ij version 10.5`

`ij>`

To create a new database with name acmedb, you can use the connect command by providing create=true:

`ij> connect 'jdbc:derby:/path/to/database/acmedb;create=true;`

You can replace /path/to/database with your database folder within your project folder. Next, create a database table with the help of the following command:

```
ij> create table RECIPE >
( ID INTEGER not null
> constraint RECIPE_PK primary key,
> NAME VARCHAR(30) not null,
> DESCRIPTION VARCHAR(250),
> TEXT VARCHAR(1000)
> );
```

After the table is created, you can disconnect from the database by giving the following command:

`ij > disconnect;`

Figure 2-13 shows the structure of the table created as a result of the preceding commands.

Figure 2-13. *Table structure for the RECIPE table*

As you have seen in the example to this recipe, writing a Jakarta Server input form is straightforward and can be coded using basic HTML. The key is to set up a Java servlet to receive a submitted request and process the records using the servlet. This provides an easy mechanism for separating web content from the application logic.

In the example, a Jakarta Server document named recipe02_11.jspx contains a standard HTML form with a method of POST and an action of /JakartaEERecipes/RecipeServlet. The input form contains four fields, which map to database columns into which the data will eventually be inserted. The input tags contain the name of four corresponding fields (recipeNumber, name, description, and text), which will be passed to the form action when submitted. As you can see, the only reference to the Java code is the name of the servlet that is contained within the form action attribute.

The Java servlet named RecipeServlet is responsible for obtaining the request parameters that were submitted via the Jakarta Server document, validating them accordingly (not shown in the example), and inserting them into the database. When the page is submitted, RecipeServlet is invoked, and the request is sent to the doPost method since the HTML action method is POST. Both the doGet and doPost methods are really just wrapper methods for a processing method named processRequest, which is responsible for most of the work. The processRequest method is responsible for obtaining the request parameters, inserting them into the database, and sending a response to the client.

A PrintWriter object is declared and created by making a call to response.getWriter() first because this object will be used later to help form the response that is sent to the client. Next, an int value named result is set up and initialized to -1. This variable will be used for determining whether the SQL insert worked or failed. After those declarations, a try-catch block is opened, and the first line of the try block is a call to the insertRow method, passing the request parameters as values. The result variable is going to accept the int value that is returned from the execution of the insertRows method, indicating whether the insert was successful:

```
result = insertRow (request.getParameter("recipeNumber"),
                    request.getParameter("name"),
                    request.getParameter("description"),
                    request.getParameter("text"));
```

As such, an SQL insert statement is assigned to a string named sql, and it is set up using the PreparedStatement format. Each question mark in the SQL string corresponds to a parameter that will be substituted in the string when the SQL is executed:

```
String sql = "INSERT INTO RECIPES VALUES(" + "RECIPES_SEQ.NEXTVAL,?,?,?,?)";
```

Next, the `PreparedStatement` and `int` values are initialized, and then a `try-catch-finally` block is opened, which will contain the SQL insert code. Within the block, a `Connection` object is created by calling a helper class named `CreateConnection`. If you want to read more about this helper class, you can read Chapter 7 on JDBC. For now, all you need to know is that `CreateConnection` will return a database connection that can then be used to work with the database. If for some reason the connection fails, the `catch` block will be executed, followed by the `finally` block. A `PreparedStatement` object is created from the successful connection, and the SQL string that contains the database insert is assigned to it. Each of the request parameter values, in turn, is then set as a parameter to the `PreparedStatement`. Lastly, the `PreparedStatement`'s `executeUpdate` method is called, which performs an insert to the database. The return value of `executeUpdate` is assigned to the result variable and then returned to the `processRequest` method. Once the control is returned to `processRequest`, the servlet response is created using a series of `PrintWriter` statements. If the insert was successful, then a message indicating success is displayed. Likewise, if unsuccessful, then a message indicating failure is displayed.

Figure 2-14. *Jakarta Server Pages recipe 02-11 output*

Figure 2-14 shows the output of this recipe. Developing database input forms with Jakarta Server is fairly easy to do. To preserve the MVC structure, using a Java servlet for handling the request and database logic is the best choice.

2-12. Looping Through Database Records Within a Page

Problem

You want to display the records from a database table on your Jakarta Server Page.

Solution

Encapsulate the database logic in a Java class and access it from the Jakarta Server Page. Use the Jakarta Standards Tag Library c:forEach element to iterate through the database rows and display them on the page. Two Java classes would be used for working with the data in this situation. One of the classes would represent the table, which you are querying from the database, and it would contain fields for each column in that table. Another JavaBean class would be used to contain the database business logic for querying the database. The following is the project structure:

```
.
├── src
│   └── main
│       ├── java
│       │   └── org
│       │       └── jakartaeerecipe
│       │           └── chapter02
│       │               └── recipe02_12
│       │                   ├── Author.java
│       │                   └── AuthorBean.java
│       └── webapp
│           ├── WEB-INF
│           │   └── web.xml
│           └── chapter02
│               └── recipe02_12.jspx
└──pom.xml
```

The example for this recipe will display the first and last names of each author contained within the BOOK_AUTHORS database table. The table should be created as per the structure in Figure 2-15.

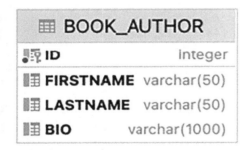

Figure 2-15. *Table structure for the BOOK_AUTHOR table*

Here is the SQL command to create this table:

```
create table BOOK_AUTHOR
(
    ID INTEGER not null
        constraint BOOK_AUTHOR_PK
        primary key,
```

```
    FIRSTNAME VARCHAR(50),
    LASTNAME  VARCHAR(50),
    BIO VARCHAR(1000)
);
```

You can also create a sequence to autogenerate IDs by using the following command:

```
create sequence book_author_s
start with 1
increment by 1;
```

Next, you can run the following INSERT statements to populate data into the BOOK_AUTHOR table:

```
insert into BOOK_AUTHOR (ID, FIRSTNAME, LASTNAME, BIO) values (
next value for book_author_s,
'Josh',
'Juneau'
'Author of Apress Books',
);

insert into BOOK_AUTHOR (ID, FIRSTNAME, LASTNAME, BIO) values (
next value for book_author_s,
'Tarun',
'Telang'
'Author of Apress Books',
);
```

The following code is used to create the Jakarta Server document that will display the data from the table using a standard HTML-based table along with the Jakarta Standard Tag Library <c:forEach> tag to loop through the rows:

```
<html xmlns:jsp="http://java.sun.com/JSP/Page"
    xmlns:c="http://java.sun.com/jsp/jstl/core"
    version="2.0">
    <jsp:directive.page contentType="text/html" pageEncoding="UTF-8"/>
    <jsp:useBean id="authorBean" scope="session" class="org.jakartaeerecipe.chapter02.
    recipe02_12.AuthorBean"/>
    <head>
        <title>Recipe 2-12: Looping Through Database Records Within a Page </title>
    </head>
    <body>
        <h1>Authors</h1>
        <p>
            The authors from the books which Josh Juneau has worked on are printed below.
        </p>
        <table border="1">
        <c:forEach items="${authorBean.authorList }" var="author">
            <tr>
                <td> ${ author.first } ${ author.last }</td>
            </tr>
```

```
        </c:forEach>
        </table>
    </body>
</html>
```

As you can see, `<c:forEach>` is used to loop through the items contained within `${authorBean.authorList}`. Each item within the list is an object of type `Author`. The following Java code is that of the `Author` class, which is used for holding the data contained within each table row:

```java
package org.jakartaeerecipe.chapter02.recipe02_12;

public class Author implements java.io.Serializable {
    private int id;
    private String first;
    private String last;
    public Author(){
        id = -1;
        first = null;
        last = null;
    }
    /**
     * @return the id
     */
    public int getId() {
        return id;
    }
    /**
     * @param id the id to set
     */
    public void setId(int id) {
        this.id = id;
    }
    /**
     * @return the first
     */
    public String getFirst() {
        return first;
    }
    /**
     * @param first the first to set
     */
    public void setFirst(String first) {
        this.first = first;
    }
    /**
     * @return the last
     */
    public String getLast() {
        return last;
    }
    /**
```

```
     * @param last the last to set
     */
    public void setLast(String last) {
        this.last = last;
    }
}
```

Lastly, the Jakarta Server document makes reference to a JavaBean named AuthorBean, which contains the business logic to query the data and return it as a list to the Jakarta Server Page. The following code is contained in the AuthorBean class:

```
package org.jakartaeerecipe.chapter02.recipe02_12;

import java.sql.Connection;
import java.sql.PreparedStatement;
import java.sql.ResultSet;
import java.sql.SQLException;
import java.util.ArrayList;
import java.util.List;
import org.jakartaeerecipe.common.CreateConnection;

public class AuthorBean implements java.io.Serializable {
    public static Connection conn = null;
    private List authorList = null;
    public List queryAuthors(){
        String sql = "SELECT ID, FIRST, LAST FROM BOOK_AUTHOR";
        List<Author> authorList = new ArrayList<>();
        PreparedStatement stmt = null;
        ResultSet rs = null;
        int result = -1;
        try {
            CreateConnection createConn = new CreateConnection();
            conn = createConn.getConnection();
            stmt = (PreparedStatement) conn.prepareStatement(sql);
            // Returns row-count or 0 if not successful
            rs = stmt.executeQuery();
            while (rs.next()){
                Author author = new Author();
                author.setId(rs.getInt("ID"));
                author.setFirst(rs.getString("FIRST"));
                author.setLast(rs.getString("LAST"));
                authorList.add(author);
            }
        } catch (SQLException e) {
            e.printStackTrace();
        } finally {
            if (stmt != null) {
                try {
                    stmt.close();
                } catch (SQLException ex) {
                    ex.printStackTrace();
                }
```

```
            }
        }
        return authorList;
    }
    public List getAuthorList(){
        authorList = queryAuthors();
        return authorList;
    }
}
```

The names of the authors contained in the records in the table will be displayed on the page. Figure 2-16 shows the screenshot of the output generated from this recipe:

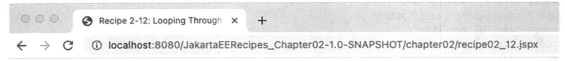

Authors

The authors from the books are printed below.

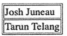

Figure 2-16. *The output of recipe 2-12*

How It Works

Almost any enterprise application performs some sort of database querying. Oftentimes, results from a database query are displayed in a table format. The example in this recipe demonstrates how to query a database and return the results to a Jakarta Server Page for display in a standard HTML table. The Jakarta Server Page in this example uses the Jakarta Standard Tag Library c:forEach element to iterate through the results of the database query. Note that there is more than one way to develop this type of database query using Jakarta Server; however, the format demonstrated in this recipe is most recommended for use in a production enterprise environment.

As mentioned previously, the Jakarta Server Page in this recipe uses a combination of the jsp:useBean element and the c:forEach element to iterate over the results of a database query. The logic for querying the database resides within a server-side JavaBean class that is referenced within the jsp:useBean element on the page. In the example, the JavaBean is named AuthorBean, and it is responsible for querying a database table named AUTHORS and populating a list of Author objects with the results of the query. When the c:forEach element is evaluated with the items attribute set to ${authorBean.authorList }, it calls on the JavaBean method named getAuthorList because Jakarta Server expressions always append "get" to a method call behind the scenes and capitalizes the first letter of the method name within the call. When the getAuthorList method is called, the authorList field is populated via a call to queryAuthors. The queryAuthors method utilizes a Java Database Connectivity (JDBC) database call to obtain the authors from the AUTHORS table. A new Author object is created for each row returned by the database query, and each new Author object is, in turn, added to the authorList. In the end, the populated authorList contains a number of Author objects, and it is returned to the Jakarta Server Page and iterated over utilizing the c:forEach element.

The `c:forEach` element contains an attribute named `var`, and this should be set equal to a string that will represent each element in the list that is being iterated over. The `var` is then used between the opening and closing `c:forEach` element tags to reference each element in the list, printing each author's first and last names.

This recipe provides some insight on how to combine the power of Jakarta Standard Tag Library tags with other technologies such as JDBC to produce very useful results. To learn more about the different Jakarta Standard Tag Library tags that are part of Jakarta Server, visit the online documentation at `www.oracle.com/technetwork/java/jstl-137486.html`. To learn more about JDBC, read Chapter 7 of this book.

2-13. Handling Errors in Jakarta Server Pages

Problem

You want to display a nicely formatted error page when a Jakarta Server Page encounters an error.

Solution

Create a standard error page and forward control to the error page if an exception occurs within the Jakarta Server Page. The following Jakarta Server Page, with .jsp format (not .jspx), demonstrates a standard error page to display when an error occurs within a Jakarta Server Pages application. If an exception occurs within any Jakarta Server Page in the application, the following error page will be displayed.

■ **Note** The example in the solution for this recipe uses the Jakarta Standard Tag Library fmt library, which provides convenient access to formatting capabilities that allow for localization of text as well as date and number formatting. Text localization capabilities allow locales to be set so that text can be formatted into different languages, depending on the user locale. Tags used for date manipulation make it easy for developers to format dates and times within a Jakarta Server Page and provide a way to parse dates and times for data input. Lastly, number-formatting tags provide a way to format and parse numeric data within pages. To learn more about the fmt Jakarta Standard Tag Library, refer to the online documentation at `https://jakarta.ee/specifications/tags/2.0/tagdocs/`.

```
<%@page contentType="text/html" pageEncoding="UTF-8"%>
<%@ page isErrorPage="true" %>
<%@ taglib uri="http://java.sun.com/jsp/jstl/core"
    prefix="c" %>
<%@ taglib uri="http://java.sun.com/jsp/jstl/fmt"
    prefix="fmt" %>
<!DOCTYPE html>
<html>
    <head>
        <title>Jakarta Server Pages - Error Page</title>
    </head>
    <body>
        <h1>Error Encountered</h1>
        <br/>
        <br/>
```

```
    <p>
        The application has encountered the following error:
        <br/>
        <fmt:message key="ServerError"/>: ${pageContext.errorData.statusCode}
    </p>
    </body>
</html>
```

For example, the following Jakarta Server would create an error (NullPointerException) if the parameter designated as param is null. If this occurs, the indicated error page would be displayed:

```
<html xmlns:jsp="http://java.sun.com/JSP/Page"
    xmlns:c="http://java.sun.com/jsp/jstl/core"
    version="2.0">
    <jsp:directive.page contentType="text/html" pageEncoding="UTF-8"/>
    <jsp:directive.page errorPage="recipe02_13_errorPage.jsp"/>
    <head>
        <title>Recipe 2-13: Handling Jakarta Server Errors </title>
    </head>
    <body>
        <h1>There is an error on this page</h1>
        <p>
            This will produce an error:
            <jsp:scriptlet>
             if (request.getParameter("param").equals("value")) {
                System.out.println("test");
             }
            </jsp:scriptlet>
        </p>
    </body>
</html>
```

How It Works

One of the most annoying issues for users while working with applications is when an error is thrown. A nasty, long stack trace is often produced, and the user is left with no idea how to resolve the error. It is better to display a user-friendly error page when such an error occurs. The Jakarta Server technology allows an error page to be designated by adding a page directive to each Jakarta Server Page that may produce an error. The directive should designate an error page that will be displayed if the page containing the directive produces an error.

The second Jakarta Server document in the solution to this recipe demonstrates a Jakarta Server Page that will throw an error if the parameter being requested within the page is null. If this were to occur and there were no error page specified, then a NullPointerException error message would be displayed. However, this Jakarta Server indicates an error page by designating it within a page directive using the following syntax:

```
<jsp:directive.page errorPage="recipe02_13_errorPage.jsp"/>
```

When an error occurs on the example page, recipe02_13.errorPage.jsp is displayed. The output would be as shown in Figure 2-17. The first Jakarta Server document listed in the solution to this recipe contains the sources for the recipe02_13.errorPage.jsp page. It is flagged as an error page because it includes a page directive indicating as such:

```
<%@ page isErrorPage="true" %>
```

An error page is able to determine the error code, status, exception, and an array of other information by using the pageContext implicit object. In the example, the ${pageContext.errorData.statusCode} expression is used to display the status code of the exception. Table 2-5 displays the other possible pieces of information that can be gleaned from the pageContext object.

Table 2-5. *pageContext Implicit Object Exception Information*

Expression	Value
pageContext.errorData	Provides access to the error information
pageContext.exception	Returns the current value of the exception object
pageContext.errorData.requestURI	Returns the request URI
pageContext.errorData.servletName	Returns the name of the servlet invoked
pageContext.errorData.statusCode	Returns the error status code
pageContext.errorData.throwable	Returns the throwable that caused the error

Providing user-friendly error pages in any application can help create a more usable and overall more functional experience for the end user. Jakarta Server and Java technology provide robust exception handling and mechanisms that can be used to help users and administrators alike when exceptions occur.

Error Encountered

The application has encountered the following error:
: 500

Figure 2-17. *Jakarta Server Pages recipe 02-13 output*

2-14. Disabling Scriptlets in Pages

Problem

You want to ensure that Java code cannot be embedded into Jakarta Server Pages within your web application.

Solution

Set the `scripting-invalid` element within the web deployment descriptor to `true`. The following excerpt from a `web.xml` deployment descriptor demonstrates how to do so:

```
<jsp-config>
    <jsp-property-group>
        <scripting-invalid>true</scripting-invalid>
    </jsp-property-group>
</jsp-config>
```

How It Works

When working in an environment that encourages the use of the Model-View-Controller architecture, it can be useful to prohibit the use of scriptlets within Jakarta Server Pages and documents. When Jakarta Server 2.1 was released, it provided solutions to help developers move Java code out of Jakarta Server Pages and into server-side Java classes where it belonged. In the early years of Jakarta Server, pages were cluttered with scriptlets and markup. This made it difficult for developers to separate business logic from content, and it was hard to find good tools to help develop such pages effectively. Jakarta Server 2.1 introduced tags, which make it possible to eliminate the use of scriptlets within Jakarta Server Pages, and this helps maintain the use of the MVC architecture.

To prohibit the use of scriptlets within Jakarta Server Pages in an application, add the `jsp-config` element within the `web.xml` file of the application of which you want to enforce the rule. Add a subelement of `jsp-property-group` along with the `scripting-invalid` element. The value of the `scripting-invalid` element should be set to `true`.

2-15. Ignoring Jakarta Expression Language in Pages

Problem

You want to turn off Jakarta Expression Language expression translation within your Jakarta Server Page so that older applications will be able to pass through expressions verbatim.

Solution #1

Escape the Jakarta Expression Language expressions within the page by using the \ character before any expressions. For instance, the following expressions will be ignored because the \ character appears before them:

```
\${elBean.myProperty}
\${2 + 4}
```

Solution #2

Configure a Jakarta Server Pages property group within the `web.xml` file for the application. Within the `web.xml` file, a `<jsp-property-group>` element can contain child elements that characterize how the Jakarta Server Page evaluates specified items. By including an `<el-ignored>true</el-ignored>` element, all Jakarta Expression Language within the application's Jakarta Server documents will be ignored and treated as literals. The following excerpt from `web.xml` demonstrates this feature:

```
<jsp-property-group>
    <el-ignored>true</el-ignored>
 </jsp-property-group>
```

Solution #3

Include a page directive including the isELIgnored attribute and set it to true. The following page directive can be placed at the top of a given Jakarta Server document to allow each Jakarta Expression Language expression to be treated as a literal:

```
<jsp:directive.page isELIgnored="true"/>
```

or in a standard Jakarta Server Pages:

```
<%@ page isELIgnored="true" %>
```

How It Works

There may be a situation in which the evaluation of Jakarta Expression Language expressions should be turned off. This occurs most often in cases of legacy applications using older versions of Jakarta Server technology; Jakarta Expression Language expressions were not yet available. There are a few different ways to turn off the evaluation of Jakarta Expression Language expressions, and this recipe demonstrates each of them.

In the first solution to this recipe, the escape technique is demonstrated. A Jakarta Expression Language expression can be escaped by placing the \ character directly before the expression, as shown in the example. Doing so will cause the Jakarta Server interpreter to treat the expression as a string literal, and the output on the page will be the expression itself, rather than its evaluation. The second solution to this recipe demonstrates adding a jsp-property-group to the web.xml deployment descriptor in order to ignore Jakarta Expression Language. All Jakarta Expression Language within an application will be ignored by including the isELIgnored element and providing a true value for it. Lastly, the final solution demonstrates how to ignore Jakarta Expression Language on a page-by-page basis by including a page directive with the isELIgnored attribute set to true.

Each of the different solutions for ignoring Jakarta Expression Language allows coverage to different parts of the application. The solution you choose should depend on how broadly you want to ignore Jakarta Expression Language throughout an application.

CHAPTER 3

■ ■ ■

Jakarta Server Faces

Jakarta Server Faces was released in 2004 by Sun Microsystems as Java Server Faces. It was intended to make web application creation easier and uses server-side rendering. It's an improvement on the Jakarta Server Pages framework with a more structured development cycle and greater flexibility in using contemporary web technologies. The Jakarta Server Faces framework is built on the Model-View-Controller (MVC) architecture and uses XML files for constructing views and Java classes for application logic. The Jakarta Server Faces framework also supports annotations to simplify view construction.

The Jakarta Server Faces framework is request driven, which means that it responds to requests from clients and each request is processed by a special servlet named the `FacesServlet`. The `FacesServlet` is responsible for building the component trees, processing events, determining which view to process next, and rendering the response. The `faces-config.xml` file was a specific resource file for Jakarta Server Faces 1.x that defined application information such as navigation rules, listener registration, and so on. While the `faces-config.xml` file is still useful in Jakarta Server Faces 2.x, modern Jakarta Server Faces releases have focused on making things easier to use by limiting XML configuration and using annotations instead. The faces-config.xml is an XML file that specifies the configuration for Jakarta Server Faces. It's typically located in the WEB-INF directory of a web application.

The framework is very powerful, including easy integration with technologies such as Ajax and making it effortless to develop dynamic content. Jakarta Server Faces works well with databases, using RESTful data calls, JDBC, or EJB technology to work with the backend. JavaBean, known as Jakarta Server Faces *controller class* or *Controllers*, are used for application business logic and support the dynamic content in each view. They can adhere to different life cycles, depending on the scope that is specified. Views can invoke methods within the beans to perform actions such as data manipulation and form processing. Properties can also be declared within the beans and exposed within the views, providing a convenient way to make dynamic content available within a view or pass request values. Jakarta Server Faces allows developers to customize their applications with preexisting validation and conversion tags that can be used on components with the view to validate or convert data. It is also easy to build custom validators, as well as custom components that can be applied to components in a view.

This chapter includes recipes that will be useful for those who are getting started with Jakarta Server Faces and also those who are looking to beef up their basic knowledge of the framework with some of the latest Jakarta Server Faces techniques. You learn how to create controller classes, work with standard components, and handle page navigation. There are also recipes that cover useful techniques such as building custom validators and creating bookmarkable URLs. The recipes are refined to include the most current techniques and provide the most useful methodologies for using them. After studying the recipes in this chapter, you will be ready to build standard Jakarta Server Faces applications, sprinkling in some custom features as well.

© Josh Juneau and Tarun Telang 2022
J. Juneau and T. Telang, *Java EE to Jakarta EE 10 Recipes*, https://doi.org/10.1007/978-1-4842-8079-9_3

■ **Note** Many people prefer to work within an integrated development environment (IDE) for increased productivity. To get started learning how to create a new Jakarta Server Faces project and manage it with the NetBeans IDE, see the appendix of this book.

3-1. Writing a Simple Jakarta Server Faces Application

Problem

You want to get up and running quickly by creating a simple Jakarta Server Faces application.

Solution #1

Create a simple Jakarta Server Faces web application that is composed of a single XHTML page and a simple Java class known as a backing bean and a bean that activates Jakarta Server Faces. The application in this recipe simply displays a message that is initialized in the backing bean. Figure 3-1 shows the project structure for this solution.

Figure 3-1. *Project folder structure*

■ **Note** It is recommended that you utilize a Java IDE to make life easier. There are many excellent IDE choices. You can choose the IDE you prefer and follow along with its instructions for working with Jakarta Server Faces.

Project Dependencies

The following is the snippet from pom.xml showing the required dependencies for this project:

```
<dependencies>
    <dependency>
        <groupId>jakarta.faces</groupId>
        <artifactId>jakarta.faces-api</artifactId>
        <version>4.0.0</version>
        <scope>provided</scope>
    </dependency>
    <dependency>
        <groupId>jakarta.platform</groupId>
        <artifactId>jakarta.jakartaee-api</artifactId>
        <version>10.0.0</version>
    </dependency>
</dependencies>
```

Displaying a Jakarta Server Faces Controller Field Value

The following code within the \webapp\chapter03\recipe03_01.xhtml file makes the XHTML view that will be used to display the Jakarta Server Faces backing bean's field value:

```
<?xml version='1.0' encoding='UTF-8' ?>
<!DOCTYPE html>
<html xmlns="http://www.w3.org/1999/xhtml" xmlns:h="http://xmlns.jcp.org/jsf/html">
    <h:head>
        <title>Recipe 3-1:  A Simple Jakarta Server Faces Application</title>
    </h:head>
    <h:body>
        <p>
            This simple application utilizes a request-scoped Jakarta Server Faces
            controller class
            to display the message below.  If you change the message within the
            controller class's constructor and then recompile the application, the
            a new message appears.
            <br/>
            <br/>
            #{helloWorldController.hello}
            <br/>
            or
            <br/>
            <h:outputText id="helloMessage" value="#{helloWorldController.hello}"/>
        </p>
    </h:body>
</html>
```

As you can see, the Jakarta Server Faces page utilizes a Jakarta Server Faces expression; #{helloWorldController.hello} is referenced in the expression along with the field to expose.

Also, ensure you have the web.xml configuration file as follows:

```xml
<?xml version="1.0" encoding="UTF-8"?>
<web-app xmlns="https://jakarta.ee/xml/ns/jakartaee"
    xmlns:xsi="http://www.w3.org/2001/XMLSchema-instance"
    xsi:schemaLocation="https://jakarta.ee/xml/ns/jakartaee https://jakarta.ee/xml/ns/
    jakartaee/web-app_5_0.xsd" version="5.0">
<context-param>
      <param-name>jakarta.faces.CONFIG_FILES</param-name>
      <param-value>/faces-config.xml</param-value>
</context-param>
<servlet>
      <servlet-name>Faces Servlet</servlet-name>
      <servlet-class>jakarta.faces.webapp.FacesServlet</servlet-class>
      <load-on-startup>1</load-on-startup>
</servlet>
      <servlet-mapping>
      <servlet-name>Faces Servlet</servlet-name>
          <url-pattern>*.xhtml</url-pattern>
      </servlet-mapping>
</web-app>
```

Examining the Jakarta Server Faces Controller

The following code is that of HelloWorldController, the Jakarta Server Faces Controller for this recipe example:

```java
package org.jakartaeerecipe.chapter03.recipe03_01;

import jakarta.enterprise.context.RequestScoped;
import jakarta.inject.Named;

@Named
@RequestScoped
public class HelloWorldController {
    private String hello = "Hello World!";
    public String getHello() {
        return hello;
    }
}
```

■ **Note** Prior to JSF 2.0, in order to enable the JSF servlet to translate the XHTML page, you needed to ensure that the web.xml file contained a servlet element indicating the jakarta.faces.webapp.FacesServlet class and its associated servlet-mapping URL. If you're using a Servlet 3.x container, the FacesServlet is automatically mapped for you, so there is no requirement to adjust the web.xml configuration.

To load the application in your browser, visit http://localhost:8080/JakartaEERecipes_ Chapter03-1.0-SNAPSHOT/chapter03/recipe03_01.xhtml, and you will see the text shown in Figure 3-2.

Figure 3-2. *Resulting Jakarta Server Faces view page*

Breaking Down a Jakarta Server Faces Application

Now for the real reason you are reading this recipe...the explanation for building a Jakarta Server Faces application! A Jakarta Server Faces application is comprised of the following parts:

- If it's using or maintaining Jakarta Server Faces applications written using Jakarta Server Faces 1.*x*, it includes the web.xml deployment descriptor that is responsible for mapping the FacesServlet instance to a URL path.

- One or more web pages on which Jakarta Server Faces components are used to provide the page layout (may or may not utilize Facelets view technology). Typically, these web pages are referred to as "views."

- Jakarta Server Faces component tags within the views.

- One or more controller classes, which are simple, lightweight container-managed objects that are responsible for supporting page constructs and basic services.

- Optionally, one or more configuration files such as faces-config.xml that can be used to define navigation rules and configure beans and other custom objects.

- Optionally, supporting objects such as listeners, converters, or custom components.

- Optionally, custom tags for use on a Jakarta Server Faces view.

LIFE CYCLE OF A JAKARTA SERVER FACES APPLICATION

The Jakarta Server Faces view processing life cycle contains six stages. These stages are as follows:

1. Restore View

2. Apply Request Values

3. Process Validations

4. Update Model Values

5. Invoke Application

6. Render Response

Restore View is the first phase in the Jakarta Server Faces life cycle, and it is responsible for constructing the view. The component tree then applies the request parameters to each of the corresponding component values using the component tree's decode method. This occurs during the Apply Request Values phase. During this phase, any value conversion errors will be added to FacesContext for display as error messages during the Render Response phase. Next, all of the validations are processed. During the Process Validations phase, each component that has a registered validator is examined, and local values are compared to the validation rules. If any validation errors arise, the Render Response phase is entered, rendering the page with the corresponding validation errors.

If the Process Validations phase exists without errors, the Update Model Values phase begins. During this phase, controller class properties are set for each of the corresponding input components within the tree that contain local values. Once again, if any errors occur, then the Render Response phase is entered, rendering the page with the corresponding errors displayed. After the successful completion of the Update Model Values phase, the application-level events are handled during the Invoke Application phase. Such events include page submits or redirects to other pages. Finally, the Render Response phase occurs, and the page is rendered to the user. If the application is using Jakarta Server Pages pages, then the Jakarta Server Faces implementation allows the Jakarta Server Pages container to render the page.

The example in this recipe uses the minimum number of these parts. To run the example, you need to ensure that the web.xml file contains the proper Jakarta Server Faces configuration if it's running in a pre-Jakarta Server Faces 2.*x* environment. You need to have a backing bean declaring the field that is exposed on the Jakarta Server Faces view along with the necessary accessor methods to make it work properly. And lastly, you need to have the XHTML Jakarta Server Faces view page containing the Jakarta Server Faces expression that exposes the field declared in the backing bean. A backing bean is the model behind a UI. It contains properties that are used in the application to populate its view with data. The JSF container manages these objects by instantiating them when needed and injecting them instance variables via Jakarta Expression Language expressions using their names prefixed with "#".

The backing bean class is much like Jakarta Server Page's JavaBean in that it provides the application logic for a particular page so that Java code does not need to be embedded into the view code. Components (a.k.a. Jakarta Server Faces tags) that are used within a Jakarta Server Faces view are mapped to server-side fields and methods contained within the Jakarta Server Faces backing bean. In the example, the Jakarta Server Faces controller class is named HelloWorldController, and a field named hello is declared, exposing itself to the public via the getHello() method. The Jakarta Server Faces bean class is instantiated and initialized when a page that contains a reference to the bean is requested, and its scope determines the lifespan of the backing bean. In the case of this example, the backing bean contains a request scope, via the @RequestScoped annotation. Therefore, its lifespan is that of a single request, and it is reinstantiated each time a request is made. In this case, when the page in the example is reloaded. To learn more about the scope and annotations that are available for a controller class, see Recipe 3-2.

Jakarta Server Faces technology utilizes a web view declaration framework known as Facelets. Facelets uses a special set of XML tags, similar in style to the standard Jakarta Server Faces tags, to help build componentized web views. While this example does not use Facelets, it is a vital part of Jakarta Server Faces view technology. Facelets pages typically use XHTML, which is an HTML page that is composed of well-formed XML components. The example Jakarta Server Faces view in this recipe is well structured, and it contains two Jakarta Expression Language expressions that are responsible for instantiating the controller class and displaying the content for the hello field. When the Jakarta Expression Language expression #{helloWorldController.hello} is translated by the FacesServlet, it makes the call to the getHello() method of HelloWorldController.

Lots of information was thrown at you in this introductory recipe. The simple example in this recipe provides a good starting point for working with Jakarta Server Faces technology. Continue with the recipes in this chapter to gain a broader knowledge of each component that is used for developing Jakarta Server Faces web applications.

3-2. Writing a Controller Class

Problem

You want to use a server-side Java class from within your Jakarta Server Faces application web pages.

Solution

Develop a Jakarta Server Faces controller class, a lightweight container-managed component, which will provide the application logic for use within your Jakarta Server Faces application web pages. The example in this recipe is a Jakarta Server Faces view and a Jakarta Server Faces controller class. The application calculates two numbers that are entered by the user and then adds, subtracts, multiplies, or divides them depending on the user's selection. The following code is the controller class that is responsible for declaring fields for each of the numbers that will be entered by the user, as well as a field for the result of the calculation. The controller class is also responsible for creating a list of Strings that will be displayed within an h:selectOneMenu element within the Jakarta Server Faces view and retaining the value that is chosen by the user.

Although it may seem as though this controller class is doing a lot of work, it is very simple to make it happen! The controller class is really a beefed-up Plain Old Java Object (POJO) that includes some methods that can be called from Jakarta Server Faces view components.

Controller Class

The following code is for the controller class that is used for the calculation example. The class is named CalculationController, and it is referenced as calculationController from within the Jakarta Server Faces view. Jakarta Server Faces uses convention over configuration for its naming conventions. By default, Jakarta Server Faces views can contain Jakarta Expression Language that references a controller class by specifying the class name with the first character in lowercase.

```
package org.jakartaeerecipe.chapter03.recipe03_02;

import java.io.Serializable;
import java.util.*;

import jakarta.enterprise.context.SessionScoped;
import jakarta.faces.application.FacesMessage;
import jakarta.faces.context.FacesContext;
import jakarta.faces.model.SelectItem;
import jakarta.inject.Named;
```

```java
@Named
@SessionScoped
public class CalculationController implements Serializable {
    private int num1;
    private int num2;
    private int result;

    private String calculationType;

    private static final String ADDITION = "Addition";
    private static final String SUBTRACTION = "Subtraction";
    private static final String MULTIPLICATION = "Multiplication";
    private static final String DIVISION = "Division";

    List<SelectItem> calculationList;

    /**
     * Creates a new instance of CalculationController
     */
    public CalculationController() {
        // Initialize variables
        num1 = 0;
        num2 = 0;
        result = 0;
        calculationType = null;
        // Initialize the list of values for the SelectOneMenu
        populateCalculationList();
        System.out.println("initialized the bean!");
    }

    // getters and setters
    // ...

    private void populateCalculationList(){
        calculationList = new ArrayList<>();
        calculationList.add(new SelectItem(ADDITION));
        calculationList.add(new SelectItem(SUBTRACTION));
        calculationList.add(new SelectItem(MULTIPLICATION));
        calculationList.add(new SelectItem(DIVISION));
    }
    public void performCalculation() {
        switch (getCalculationType()) {
            case ADDITION -> setResult(num1 + num2);
            case SUBTRACTION -> setResult(num1 - num2);
            case MULTIPLICATION -> setResult(num1 * num2);
            case DIVISION -> {
                try {
                    setResult(num1 / num2);
                } catch (Exception ex) {
                    FacesMessage facesMsg = new FacesMessage(FacesMessage.SEVERITY_ERROR,
                    "Invalid Calculation", "Invalid Calculation");
```

```
                    FacesContext.getCurrentInstance().addMessage(null, facesMsg);
                }
            }
        }
    }
}
```

Next is the view that composes the web page, which is displayed to the user. The view is composed within an XHTML document and is a well-formed XML.

Jakarta Server Faces View

The view contains Jakarta Server Faces components that are displayed as text boxes into which the user can enter information, a pick list of different calculation types for the user to choose from, a component responsible for displaying the result of the calculation, and an h:commandButton component for submitting the form values:

```
<html xmlns="http://www.w3.org/1999/xhtml"
    xmlns:f="http://xmlns.jcp.org/jsf/core"
    xmlns:h="http://xmlns.jcp.org/jsf/html">
    <h:head>
        <meta http-equiv="Content-Type" content="text/html; charset=UTF-8"/>
        <title>Recipe 3-2:  Writing a Jakarta Server Faces Managed Bean</title>
    </h:head>
    <h:body>
        <f:view>
            <h2>Perform a Calculation</h2>
            <p>
                Use the following form to perform a calculation on two numbers.
                <br/>
                Enter
                the numbers in the two text fields below, and select a calculation to
                <br/>
                perform, then hit the Calculate button.
                <br/>
                <br/>
                <h:messages errorStyle="color: red" infoStyle="color: green"
                globalOnly="true"/>
                <br/>
                <h:form id="calculationForm">
                    Number1:
                    <h:inputText id="num1" value="#{calculationController.num1}"/>
                    <br/>
                    Number2:
                    <h:inputText id="num2" value="#{calculationController.num2}"/>
                    <br/>
                    <br/>
```

```
                    Calculation Type:
                    <h:selectOneMenu id="calculationType" value="#{calculationController.
                    calculationType}">
                        <f:selectItems value="#{calculationController.calculationList}"/>
                    </h:selectOneMenu>
                    <br/>
                    <br/>
                    Result:
                    <h:outputText id="result" value="#{calculationController.result}"/>
                    <br/>
                    <br/>
                    <h:commandButton action="#{calculationController.performCalculation()}"
                    value="Calculate"/>
                </h:form>
            </p>
        </f:view>
    </h:body>
</html>
```

The resulting Jakarta Server Faces view looks like Figure 3-3 when displayed to the user.

Figure 3-3. *Resulting Jakarta Server Faces view page*

How It Works

The Jakarta Server Faces controller class is responsible for providing the application logic for a Jakarta Server Faces–based web application. Much like the JavaBean is to a Jakarta Server Pages, the controller class is the backbone for a Jakarta Server Faces view. They are also referred to as *backing beans* or *managed beans*, because there is typically one Jakarta Server Faces controller class for each Jakarta Server Faces view. Controller classes have changed a bit since the Jakarta Server Faces technology was introduced. There used to be configuration required for each controller class in a faces-config.xml configuration file and in the

114

web.xml file for use with some application servers. Starting with the release of JSF 2.0, the controller class became easier to use, and coding powerful Jakarta Server Faces applications is easier than ever. This recipe focuses on newer controller class technology.

```
@Named(value="calculationController")
```

The example for this recipe demonstrates many of the most important features of a Jakarta Server Faces controller class. The view components refer to the controller class as calculationController. By default, a Jakarta Server Faces controller class can be referred to within a Jakarta Server Faces view using the name of the bean class with a lowercase first letter. A controller class must be annotated with @Named to mark it as an injectable CDI bean. Using the @Named annotation, the string that is used to reference the bean from within a view can be changed. In the example, calculationController is also used as the name passed to the @Named annotation, but it could have easily been some other string. The @Named annotation should be placed before the class declaration.

```
calculationList.add(new SelectItem(ADDITION));
```

The jakarta.faces.model.SelectItem class is a convenience class that encapsulates common information about a single item in a selectable component such as a drop-down list. A SelectItem is used to group a set of related items together. Here, the drop-down list component is represented by an array of SelectItem objects.

Scopes

The bean in the example will be initialized when it is first accessed by a session and destroyed when the session is destroyed. It is a controller class that "lives" with the session. The scope of the bean is configured by an annotation on the class, just before the class declaration. There are different annotations that can be used for each available scope. In this case, the annotation is @SessionScoped, denoting that the controller class is session scoped. All of the possible controller class scopes are listed in Table 3-1.

Table 3-1. *Controller Class Scopes*

Scope Annotation	Description
@ApplicationScoped	Specifies that a bean is application scoped. Initialized when the application is started up. Destroyed when the application is shut down. Controller classes with this scope are available to all application constructs within the same application
@RequestScoped	Specifies that a bean is request scoped in a web application context. Initialized when an HTTP request to the bean is made and destroyed when the request is complete
@SessionScoped	Specifies that a bean is session scoped in a web application context. Initialized when first accessed within a session. Destroyed when the session ends. Available to all servlet requests that are made within the same session
@ConversationScoped	Specifies that a bean is conversation scoped. A conversation is a series of HTTP requests and responses that occur in a step-by-step manner, in order to complete a process. This application scope is specific to web application contexts. Initialized when a conversation is started and destroyed when the conversation ends. Controllers with this scope are available throughout the life cycle of a conversation and belong to a single HTTP session. If the HTTP session ends, all conversation contexts that were created during the session are destroyed

(continued)

Table 3-1. (*continued*)

Scope Annotation	Description
@Singleton	This is a pseudoscope, meaning that it is not proxied as with other CDI scopes. This scope specifies that only one instance of the bean will exist for the entire application
@Dependent	This is a pseudoscope, meaning that it is not proxied as with other CDI scopes. Beans that use this scope behave differently than a controller class containing any of the other scopes
@TransactionScoped	Life of a bean annotated with this scope indicates that the lifespan will exist for the duration of an active transaction. The first time a CDI bean uses a controller with this annotation in a session, the same instance will be used throughout the transaction
@FlowScoped	Beans of this scope are used in the context of a Jakarta Server Faces flow. The bean will be instantiated the first time it is accessed in the scope of a flow, and it will be destroyed once the flow is complete
@ViewScoped	This scope indicates that the bean will remain available throughout the life of the Jakarta Server Faces view

The @Named annotation specifies to the application server container that the class is a CDI bean. Prior to Jakarta Server Faces 2.0, a controller class had to be declared in the faces-config.xml file, and they were annotated with @ManagedBean until Jakarta Server Faces 2.2+. The addition of annotations has made the Jakarta Server Faces controller class XML configuration-free. It is important to note that the controller class implements java.io.Serializable; all controller classes should be specified as serializable so that they can be persisted to disk by the container if necessary.

Fields declared in a controller should be specified as private to adhere to object-oriented methodology. To make a field accessible to the public and usable from Jakarta Server Faces views, accessor methods should be declared for it. Any field that has a corresponding "getter" and "setter" is known as a Jakarta Server Faces controller class *property*. Properties are available for use within Jakarta Server Faces views by utilizing lvalue Jakarta Expression Language expressions, meaning that the expression is contained in the #{ and } character sequences and that it is readable and writable. lvalue expressions can specify targets, whereas rvalue expressions cannot. For instance, to access the field num1 that is declared in the controller class, the Jakarta Server Faces view can use the #{calculationController.num1} expression, as you can see in the Jakarta Server Faces view code for the example.

Any public method contained in a Jakarta Server Faces controller class is accessible from within a Jakarta Server Faces view using the same Jakarta Expression Language expression syntax, that is, by specifying #{beanName.methodName} as the expression. In the example to this recipe, the performCalculation method of the controller class is invoked from within the Jakarta Server Faces view using an h:commandButton Jakarta Server Faces component. The component action is equal to the Jakarta Expression Language expression that will invoke the Jakarta Server Faces controller class method. To learn more about Jakarta Server Faces components and how to use them in the view, see Recipe 3-3 and Chapter 5.

```
<h:commandButton action="#{calculationController.performCalculation}" value="Calculate"/>
```

■ **Note** The input form tag for this example contains no action attribute. Jakarta Server Faces forms do not contain action attributes since Jakarta Server Faces components within the view are responsible for specifying the action method, rather than the form itself. This makes it component based with added flexibility and simplicity.

Jakarta Server Faces controller classes are a fundamental part of the Jakarta Server Faces web framework. They provide the means for developing dynamic, robust, and sophisticated web applications with the Java platform.

3-3. Building Sophisticated Jakarta Server Faces Views with Components

Problem

You want to create a sophisticated user interface composed of prebundled components.

Solution

Use the bundled Jakarta Server Faces components in your Jakarta Server Faces views. Jakarta Server Faces components contain bundled application logic and view constructs, including styles and JavaScript actions, that can be used in applications by merely adding tags to a view. In the following example, several Jakarta Server Faces components are used to create a view that displays the authors for an Apress book and allows for a new author to be added to the list. The image should be present in the folder structure as shown in Figure 3-4.

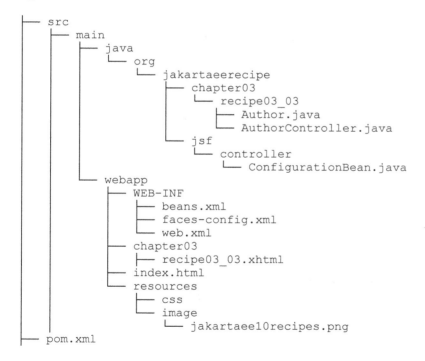

Figure 3-4. *Project folder structure*

The following code is from recipe03_03.xhtml, the XHTML for the Jakarta Server Faces view:

```
<html xmlns="http://www.w3.org/1999/xhtml"
      xmlns:f="http://java.sun.com/jsf/core"
      xmlns:h="http://xmlns.jcp.org/jsf/html">
<h:head>
    <title>Recipe 3-3: Building Sophisticated Jakarta Server Faces Views with
    Components</title>
</h:head>
    <h:body>
        <h:form id="componentForm">
            <h1>Jakarta Server Faces Components, Creating a Sophisticated Page</h1>
            <p>
                The view for this page is made up entirely of Jakarta Server Faces standard
                components.
                <br/>As you can see, there are many useful components bundled with Jakarta
                Server Faces out of the box.
                <br/>
            </p>
            <p>Book Recommendation:  Java EE to Jakarta EE 10 Recipes
                <br/>
<h:graphicImage id="jakartaee10recipes" library="image" name="jakartaee10recipes.png"
width="350px"/>
                <br/>
            <h:dataTable id="authorTable" value="#{authorController.authorList}"
                            var="author">
                <f:facet name="header">
                    Java EE to Jakarta EE 10 Recipes Authors
                </f:facet>
                <h:column>
                <h:outputText id="authorName" value="#{author.first} #{author.last}"/>
                </h:column>
            </h:dataTable>
            <br/>
            <br/>
            <p>
                Use the following form to add an author to the list.
            </p>
            <h:outputLabel for="newAuthorFirst" value="New Author First Name: "/>
            <h:inputText id="newAuthorFirst" value="#{authorController.newAuthorLast}"/>
            <br/>
            <h:outputLabel for="newAuthorLast" value="New Author Last Name: "/>
            <h:inputText id="newAuthorLast" value="#{authorController.newAuthorLast}"/>
            <br/>
            <h:inputTextarea id="bio" cols="20" rows="5"
                            value="#{authorController.bio}"/>
            <br/>
            <br/>
            <h:commandButton id="addAuthor" action="#{authorController.addAuthor}"
                            value="Add Author"/>
            <br/>
```

```
            <br/>
        </p>
    </h:form>
  </h:body>
</html>
```

This example utilizes a Jakarta Server Faces controller class named AuthorController. The controller class declares a handful of properties that are exposed in the view, and it also declares and populates a list of authors that is displayed on the page in a Jakarta Server Faces h:dataTable component:

```
package org.jakartaeerecipe.chapter03.recipe03_03;

import java.io.Serializable;

import java.util.ArrayList;
import java.util.List;

import jakarta.enterprise.context.SessionScoped;
import jakarta.inject.Named;

@Named(value = "authorController")
@SessionScoped
public class AuthorController implements Serializable {
    private String newAuthorFirst;
    private String newAuthorLast;
    private String bio;
    private List<Author> authorList;
    /**
     * Creates a new instance of RecipeController
     */
    public AuthorController() {
        populateAuthorList();
    }
    private void populateAuthorList(){
        System.out.println("initializing authors");
        authorList = new ArrayList<>();
        authorList.add(new Author("Josh", "Juneau", null));
        authorList.add(new Author("Tarun", "Telang", null));
        System.out.println("AuthorList size:" +authorList.size());
    }
    public void addAuthor() {
        getAuthorList().add(
                new Author(this.getNewAuthorFirst(),
                        this.getNewAuthorLast(),
                        this.getBio()));
    }
// getters and setters
// ...
}
```

Finally, the Author class is used to hold instances of Author objects that are loaded into the authorList instance variable. The following code is for the Author class:

```
package org.jakartaeerecipe.chapter03.recipe03_03;

public record Author ( private String getFirst,  private String getLast, private String
getBio) implements Serializable {

}
```

The resulting web page will resemble the page shown in Figure 3-5.

Jakarta Server Faces Components, Creating a Sophisticated Page

The view for this page is made up entirely of Jakarta Server Faces standard components.
As you can see, there are many useful components bundled with Jakarta Server Faces out of the box.

Book Recommendation: Java EE to Jakarta EE 10 Recipes

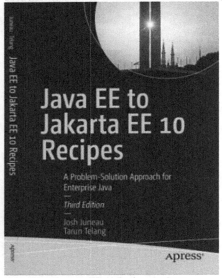

Java EE to Jakarta EE 10 Recipes Authors
Josh Juneau
Tarun Telang

Use the following form to add an author to the list.
New Author First Name: [   ]
New Author Last Name: [   ]
[   ]
[Add Author]

Figure 3-5. *Sophisticated Jakarta Server Faces view example*

How It Works

Jakarta Server Faces views consist of well-formed XML, being a mixture of HTML and Jakarta Server Faces component tags. Any well-formed HTML can be used in a Jakarta Server Faces view, but the components are the means by which Jakarta Server Faces communicates with controller class instances. There are components shipped with Jakarta Server Faces that can be used for adding images to views, text areas, buttons, check boxes, and much more. Moreover, there are several very good component libraries that include additional Jakarta Server Faces components, which can be used within your applications. This recipe is meant to give you an overall understanding of Jakarta Server Faces components and how they work. You can learn more details regarding Jakarta Server Faces components and the use of external component libraries by reading the recipes in Chapter 5.

The first step toward using a component in a Jakarta Server Faces view is to declare the tag library on the page. This is done within the HTML element at the top of the page. The example in this recipe declares both the Jakarta Server Faces core component library and the Jakarta Server Faces HTML component library within the HTML element near the top of the page. These two libraries are standard Jakarta Server Faces component libraries that should be declared in every Jakarta Server Faces view:

```
...
<html xmlns="http://www.w3.org/1999/xhtml"
      xmlns:f="http://xmlns.jcp.org/jsf/core"
      xmlns:h="http://xmlns.jcp.org/jsf/html">
...
```

Once a library is declared, a component from within that library can be used in the view by specifying the library namespace, along with the component you want to use. For instance, to specify an HTML element for displaying text, use the Jakarta Server Faces h:outputText component tag, along with the various component attributes.

Prior to JSF 2.0, it was important to enclose a Jakarta Server Faces view along with all of the components in the f:view tag. Since Jakarta Server Faces 2.0, the tag is no longer required because the underlying Facelets view technology is part of every Jakarta Server Faces view by default, so it takes care of specifying the view automatically. However, the f:view element can still be useful for specifying locale, content type, or encoding. See the online documentation for more information regarding the use of those features: https://javadoc.io/doc/jakarta.faces/jakarta.faces-api/latest/index.html.

The <h:head> and <h:body> tags can be used to specify the header and body for a Jakarta Server Faces web view. However, using the standard HTML <head> and <body> tags is fine also. Some Java IDEs will automatically use <h:head> and <h:body> in place of the standard HTML tags when writing Jakarta Server Faces views. An important note is that you must enclose any content that will be treated as an HTML input form with the <h:form> Jakarta Server Faces tag. This tag encloses a Jakarta Server Faces form and renders an HTML form using a POST method if none is specified. No action attribute is required for a Jakarta Server Faces form tag because the Jakarta Server Faces controller class action is invoked using one of the Jakarta Server Faces action components such as h:commandButton or h:commandLink.

■ **Tip** Always specify an id for the h:form tag because the form id is added as a prefix to all Jakarta Server Faces component tag ids when the page is rendered. For instance, if a form id of myform contained a component tag with an id of mytag, the component id will be rendered as myform:mytag. If you do not specify an id, then one will be generated for you automatically. If you want to use JavaScript to work with any of the page components, you will need to have an id specified for h:form, or you will never be able to access them programmatically.

■ **Note**　This recipe provides a quick overview of a handful of the standard Jakarta Server Faces components. For an in-depth explanation of Jakarta Server Faces components and their usage, see Chapter 4.

The standard Jakarta Server Faces component library contains a variety of components, and a few of them are utilized in the example. The h:graphicImage tag can be used to place an image on the page and utilize a Jakarta Server Faces controller class if needed. The h:graphicImage tag is rendered into an HTML component, and as with all of the other Jakarta Server Faces components, it accepts Jakarta Expression Language expressions in its attributes, which allows for the rendering of dynamic images. In this recipe, a static image is specified with the url attribute, but an expression could also be used, using a Jakarta Server Faces controller class field. The library attribute is used to specify the directory in which the resource, in this case an image, resides:

```
<h:graphicImage id="jakartaee10recipes" library="image" name="jakartaee10recipes.png"
width="350px"/>
```

The h:outputLabel tag is useful for reading controller class properties and displaying their values when the view is rendered. They are rendered as a label for a corresponding field within the view. The example utilizes static values for the h:outputLabel component, but they could include Jakarta Server Faces expressions if needed. The h:outputText component is also useful for reading controller class properties and displaying their values. This component renders basic text on the page. The difference between h:outputLabel and h:outputText is that they are rendered into different HTML tags. Both components can accept Jakarta Server Faces controller class expressions for their value attributes.

In the example, a couple of text fields are displayed on the page using the h:inputText component, which renders an input field. The value attribute for h:inputText can be set to a Jakarta Server Faces controller class field, which binds the text field to the corresponding controller class property. For instance, the example includes an h:inputText component with a value of #{authorController.newAuthorFirst}, which binds the component to the newAuthorFirst property in the AuthorController class. If the field contains a value, then a value will be present within a text field when the page is rendered. If a value is entered into the corresponding text field and the form is submitted, the value will be set into the newAuthorFirst field using its setter method. The h:inputText tag allows for both reading and writing of controller class properties because it uses lvalue Jakarta Expression Language expressions. The h:inputTextarea tag is very similar to h:inputText in that it works the same way, but it renders a text area rather than a text field.

The h:commandButton component is used to render a submit button on a page. Its action attribute can be set to a Jakarta Server Faces controller class method. When the button is pressed, the corresponding controller class method will be executed, and the form will be submitted. The request will be sent to the FacesServlet controller, and any properties on the page will be set. See Recipe 3-1 for more details regarding the Jakarta Server Faces life cycle. The h:commandButton used in the example has an action attribute of #{authorController.addAuthor}, which will invoke the addAuthor method within the AuthorController class. As you can see from the method, when invoked it will add a new Author object to the authorList, utilizing the values that were populated in the corresponding h:inputText components for the newAuthorFirst, newAuthorLast, and bio fields. The following excerpt from the example's Jakarta Server Faces view lists the h:commandButton component:

```
<h:commandButton id="addAuthor" action="#{authorController.addAuthor}"
                        value="Add Author"/>
```

The last component in the example that bears some explanation is the h:dataTable. This Jakarta Server Faces component is rendered into an HTML table, and it enables developers to dynamically populate tables with collections of data from a controller class. In the example, the h:dataTable value attribute is set to the controller class property of #{authorController.authorList}, which maps to an instance list that is populated with Author objects. The dataTable var attribute contains a string that will be used to reference the different objects contained in each row of the table. In the example, the var attribute is set to author, so referencing #{author.first} in the dataTable will return the value for the current Author object's first property. The dataTable in the example effectively prints out the first and last names of each Author object within the authorList. This is just a quick overview of how the Jakarta Server Faces dataTable component works. For more details, refer to Recipe 3-12.

As you work more with constructing Jakarta Server Faces views, you will become very familiar with the component library. The tags will become second nature, and you will be able to construct highly sophisticated views for your application. To learn more about each of the components, refer to this Javadoc link: https://javadoc.io/doc/jakarta.faces/jakarta.faces-api/latest/index.html. Adding external Jakarta Server Faces component libraries into the mix along with using Ajax for updating components is the real icing on the cake! You will learn more about spreading the icing on the cake and creating beautiful and user-friendly views in Chapter 5!

3-4. Displaying Messages in Jakarta Server Faces Pages

Problem

You have the requirement to display an information message on the screen for your application users.

Solution

Add the h:messages component to your Jakarta Server Faces view and create messages as needed within the view's controller class using FacesMessage objects. The following Jakarta Server Faces view is an excerpt from the file /webapp/chapter03/recipe03_04.xhtml; it contains an h:messages component tag that will render any messages that were registered with FacesContext within the corresponding page's controller class. It also includes an h:message component that is bound to an h:inputText field. The h:message component can display messages that are specific to the corresponding text field:

```
<?xml version='1.0' encoding='UTF-8' ?>
<!DOCTYPE html>
<html xmlns="http://www.w3.org/1999/xhtml"
      xmlns:h="http://xmlns.jcp.org/jsf/html">
    <h:head>
        <meta http-equiv="Content-Type" content="text/html; charset=UTF-8"/>
        <title>Recipe 3-4: Displaying Messages in Jakarta Server Faces</title>
    </h:head>
    <h:body>
        <h:form id="componentForm">
            <h1>Jakarta Server Faces Messages</h1>
            <p>
                This page contains a Jakarta Server Faces message component below.  It
                will display
                messages from a Jakarta Server Faces managed bean once the bean has been
                initialized.
            </p>
            <h:messages errorStyle="color: red" infoStyle="color: green" globalOnly="true"/>
            <br/>
            <br/>
```

```
                Enter the word Java here:
                <h:inputText id="javaText" value="#{messageController.javaText}"/>
                <h:message for="javaText"  errorStyle="color: red" infoStyle="color: green"/>
                <br/><br/>
                <h:commandButton id="addMessage" action="#{messageController.newMessage}"
                                value="New Message"/>
        </h:form>
    </h:body>
</html>
```

The controller class in this example is named `MessageController`. It will create a Jakarta Server Faces message upon initialization, and then each time the `newMessage` method is invoked, another message will be displayed. Also, if the text *java* is entered into the text field that corresponds to the `h:inputText` tag, then a success message will be displayed for that component. Otherwise, if a different value is entered into that field or if the field is left blank, then an error message will be displayed. The following listing is that of `MessageController`:

```
package org.jakartaeerecipe.chapter03.recipe03_04;

import java.util.Date;

import jakarta.enterprise.context.SessionScoped;

import jakarta.faces.application.FacesMessage;
import jakarta.faces.context.FacesContext;

import jakarta.inject.Named;

@Named
@SessionScoped
public class MessageController implements java.io.Serializable {
    int hitCounter = 0;
    private String javaText;
    /**
     * Creates a new instance of MessageController
     */
    public MessageController() {
        javaText = null;
        FacesMessage facesMsg = new FacesMessage(FacesMessage.SEVERITY_INFO, "Managed Bean
        Initialized", null);
        FacesContext.getCurrentInstance().addMessage(null, facesMsg);
    }
    public void newMessage(){
        String hitMessage;
        hitCounter++;
        if(hitCounter > 1){
            hitMessage = hitCounter + " times";
        } else {
            hitMessage = hitCounter + " time";
        }
```

```
        Date currDate = new Date();
        FacesMessage facesMsg = new FacesMessage(FacesMessage.SEVERITY_ERROR,
                "You've pressed that button " + hitMessage + "!  The current date
                and time: "
                        + currDate, null);
        FacesContext.getCurrentInstance().addMessage(null, facesMsg);
        FacesMessage javaTextMsg;
        if (getJavaText().equalsIgnoreCase("java")){
            javaTextMsg = new FacesMessage(FacesMessage.SEVERITY_INFO,
                    "Good Job, that is the correct text!", null);
        } else {
            javaTextMsg = new FacesMessage(FacesMessage.SEVERITY_ERROR,
                    "Sorry, that is NOT the correct text!", null);
        }
        FacesContext.getCurrentInstance().addMessage("componentForm:javaText", javaTextMsg);
    }
    /**
     * @return the javaText
     */
    public String getJavaText() {
        return javaText;
    }
    /**
     * @param javaText the javaText to set
     */
    public void setJavaText(String javaText) {
        this.javaText = javaText;
    }
}
```

The message will be displayed on the page in red text if it is an error message and in green text if it is an informational message. In this example, the initialization message is printed in green, and the update message is printed in red. Typing the URL `http://localhost:8080/JakartaEERecipes_Chapter03-1.0-SNAPSHOT/chapter03/recipe03_04.xhtml` in your browser will display the output as in Figure 3-6.

JSF Messages

This page contains a JSF message component below. It will display messages from a JSF managed bean once the bean has been initialized.

- You've pressed that button 1 time! The current date and time: Fri Jan 07 21:20:58 IST 2022

Enter the word Java here: [Java] Good Job, that is the correct text!

[New Message]

Figure 3-6. *Resulting Jakarta Server Faces view*

How It Works

It is always a good idea to relay messages to application users, especially in the event that some action needs to be taken by the user. The Jakarta Server Faces framework provides an easy API that allows messages to be added to a view from the Jakarta Server Faces controller class. To use the API, add the h:message component to a view for displaying messages that are bound to specific components and add the h:messages component to a view for displaying messages that are not bound to specific components. The h:message component contains a number of attributes that can be used to customize message output and other things. It can be bound to a component within the same view by specifying that component's id in the for attribute of h:message. The most important attributes for the h:message component are as follows:

- id: Specifies a unique identifier for the component
- rendered: Specifies whether the message is rendered
- errorStyle: Specifies the CSS styles to be applied to error messages
- errorClass: Indicates the CSS class to apply to error messages
- infoStyle: Specifies the CSS styles to be applied to informational messages
- infoClass: Indicates the CSS class to apply to informational messages
- for: Specifies the component for which the message belongs

For a list of all attributes available for the h:message component, refer to the online documentation. In the example for this recipe, the h:message component is bound to the h:inputText component with an id of javaText. When the page is submitted, the newMessage method in the MessageController class is invoked. That method is used in this example for generating messages to display on the page. If the text entered in the javaText property matches Java, then a successful message will be printed on the page. To create a message, an instance of the jakarta.faces.application.FacesMessage class is generated, passing three parameters that correspond to message severity, message summary, and message detail. A FacesMessage object can be created without passing any parameters, but usually it is more productive to pass the message into the constructor at the time of instantiation. The general format for creating a FacesMessage object is as follows:

```
new FacesMessage(FacesMessage.severity severity, String summary, String detail)
```

Passing a static field from the FacesMessage class specifies the message severity. Table 3-2 shows the possible message severity values along with their descriptions.

Table 3-2. *FacesMessage Severity Values*

Severity	Description
SEVERITY_ERROR	Indicates that an error has occurred
SEVERITY_FATAL	Indicates that a serious error has occurred
SEVERITY_INFO	Indicates an informational message rather than an error
SEVERITY_WARN	Indicates that an error may have occurred

In the example, if the value entered for the javaText property equals Java, then an informational message is created. Otherwise, an error message is created. In either case, once the message is created, then it needs to be passed into the current context using FacesContext.getCurrentInstance(). addMessage(String componentId, FacesMessage message). In the example, the method is called, passing a component ID of componentForm:javaText. This refers to the component within the Jakarta Server Faces view that has an ID of javaText (h:inputText component). The componentForm identifier belongs to the form (h:form component) that contains the h:inputText component, so in reality the h:inputText component is nested within the h:form component. To reference a nested component, combine component IDs using a colon as a delimiter. The following is an excerpt from the example, demonstrating how to create a message and send it to the h:message component:

```
FacesMessage javaTextMsg = new FacesMessage(FacesMessage.SEVERITY_ERROR,
            "Sorry, that is NOT the correct text!", null);
FacesContext.getCurrentInstance().addMessage("componentForm:javaText", javaTextMsg);
```

The h:messages component can be used for displaying all messages that pertain to a view, or it can be used for displaying only noncomponent-related messages by using the globalOnly attribute. All other attributes for h:messages are very similar to the h:message component. By indicating a true value for the globalOnly attribute, you are telling the component to ignore any component-specific messages. Therefore, any FacesMessage that is sent to a specific component will not be displayed by h:messages. In the example, the message that is displayed by h:messages is generated in the same manner as the component-specific message, with the exception of specifying a specific component to which the message belongs. The following excerpt demonstrates sending an error message to the h:messages component. Note that the last argument that is sent to the FacesMessage call is a null value. This argument should be the clientId specification, and by setting it to null, you are indicating that there is no specified client identifier. Therefore, the message should be a global message rather than tied to a specific component.

```
FacesMessage facesMsg = new FacesMessage(FacesMessage.SEVERITY_ERROR,
            "You've pressed that button " + hitMessage + "!  The current date
            and time: "
            + currDate, null);
FacesContext.getCurrentInstance().addMessage(null, facesMsg);
```

Displaying the appropriate message at the right time in an application is very important. By utilizing FacesMessages objects and displaying them using either the h:message or h:messages component, you can ensure that your application users will be well informed of the application state.

3-5. Updating Messages Without Recompiling

Problem

Rather than hard-coding messages into your controller classes, you want to specify the messages in a properties file so that they can be edited on the fly.

Solution

Create a resource bundle or properties file and specify your messages within it. Then retrieve the messages from the bundle and add them to the FacesMessages objects rather than hard-coding a String value. In the example that follows, a resource bundle is used to specify a message that is to be displayed on a page. If you need to change the message at any time, simply modify the resource bundle and reload the page in the browser without the need to redeploy the entire application or change any code.

The following code is an excerpt from the file (/webapp/chapter03/recipe03_05.xhtml); it is a Jakarta Server Faces view that contains the h:messages component for displaying the message from a corresponding controller class:

```
<?xml version='1.0' encoding='UTF-8' ?>
<!DOCTYPE html>
<html xmlns="http://www.w3.org/1999/xhtml"
    xmlns:f="http://xmlns.jcp.org/jsf/core"
    xmlns:h="http://xmlns.jcp.org/jsf/html">
    <h:head>
        <meta http-equiv="Content-Type" content="text/html; charset=UTF-8"/>
        <title>Recipe 3-5: Specifying Updatable Messages</title>
    </h:head>
    <h:body>
        <h:form id="componentForm">
            <h1>Utilizing a resource bundle</h1>
            <p>
                The message below is displayed from a resource bundle.  The h:outputText
                component has been added to the page only to instantiate the bean for this
                example.  To change
                the message, simply modify the corresponding message within the bundle
                and then refresh the page.
            </p>
            <h:outputText id="exampleProperty" value="#{exampleController.
            exampleProperty}"/>
            <br/>
            <h:messages errorStyle="color: red" infoStyle="color: green" globalOnly="true"/>
        </h:form>
    </h:body>
</html>
```

Next, the controller class is responsible for creating the message and sending it to the h:messages component via the FacesContext. The following source is for ExampleController, which is the controller class for the Jakarta Server Faces view in this example:

```
package org.jakartaeerecipe.chapter03.recipe03_05;

import java.util.ResourceBundle;
import jakarta.enterprise.context.RequestScoped;
import jakarta.faces.application.FacesMessage;
import jakarta.faces.context.FacesContext;
import jakarta.inject.Named;

@Named(value="exampleController")
@RequestScoped
public class ExampleController {
    private String exampleProperty;
    /**
     * Creates a new instance of ExampleController
     */
```

```java
public ExampleController() {
    exampleProperty = "Used to instantiate the bean.";
    FacesMessage facesMsg = new FacesMessage(FacesMessage.SEVERITY_INFO,
            ResourceBundle.getBundle("/org/jakartaeerecipe/chapter03/Bundle").
            getString("ExampleMessage"), null);
    FacesContext.getCurrentInstance().addMessage(null, facesMsg);
}
/**
 * @return the exampleProperty
 */
public String getExampleProperty() {
    return exampleProperty;
}
/**
 * @param exampleProperty the exampleProperty to set
 */
public void setExampleProperty(String exampleProperty) {
    this.exampleProperty = exampleProperty;
}
}
```

The location for the resource bundle is shown in Figure 3-7.

```
∨ ▣ WEB-INF
   ∨ ▣ classes
      > ▣ css
      > ▣ image
      > ▣ org
      ∨ ▣ Resource Bundle 'Bundle'
          ▣ Bundle.properties
          ▣ Bundle_en.properties
          ▣ Bundle_en_IN.properties
          ▣ Bundle_en_US.properties
       –  …
```

Figure 3-7. *Resource bundles containing messages after internationalization*

The resource bundle, which contains the message, is read by the controller class to obtain the message. If you want to update the message, you can do so without recompiling any code:

```
# This file is an example resource bundle
ExampleMessage=This message can be changed by updating the message bundle!
```

When the page is loaded, the h:outputText component instantiates ExampleController, which in turn creates the FacesMessage objects that are used to display the message on the screen.

How It Works

Oftentimes, it is useful to have the ability to update custom system or user messages rather than hard-coding them. This could be useful in the case that some custom information that is contained in a particular message may have the possibility of changing in the future. It'd be nice to simply update the message in text format rather than editing the code, recompiling, and redeploying your application. It is possible to create updatable messages using a resource bundle. A resource bundle is simply a properties file, which contains name-value pairs. When adding custom messages to a bundle, name the message appropriately and then add the custom message as the value portion of the property. An application can then look up the property by name and utilize its value. In this case, the value is a string that will be used to create a `FacesMessage` instance.

In the example, the bundle contains a property named `ExampleMessage`, along with a corresponding value. When the Jakarta Server Faces view is loaded into the browser, the `ExampleController` class is instantiated, causing its constructor to be executed. A `FacesMessage` instance is created, generating a message of type `FacesMessage.SEVERITY_INFO`, and it reads the resource bundle and obtains the value for the `ExampleMessage` property. The following excerpt demonstrates how to obtain a specified message value from the resource bundle:

```
ResourceBundle.getBundle("/org/jakartaeerecipe/chapter03/Bundle").
getString("ExampleMessage"), null);
```

After the message is created, it is added to the current instance of `FacesContext` and, subsequently, displayed on the page when it is rendered. Using a resource bundle to specify your messages can make life much easier because you'll no longer be required to recompile code to update such messages. This feature is also very useful in internationalization as it can be used to store locale-specific resources. Figure 3-8 shows the output of this recipe.

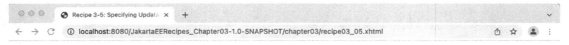

Utilizing a resource bundle

The message below is displayed from a resource bundle. The h:outputText component has been added to the page only to instantiate the bean for this example. To change the message, simply modify the corresponding message within the bundle and then refresh the page.

Used to instantiate the bean.

- This message can be changed by updating the message bundle!

Figure 3-8. Resulting Jakarta Server Faces view

3-6. Navigating Based upon Conditions

Problem

Your Jakarta Server Faces application contains multiple pages, and you want to set up navigation between them.

Solution

Utilize one of the following techniques for performing navigation within Jakarta Server Faces applications:

- Utilize explicit navigation through the use of a Jakarta Server Faces controller class method along with a corresponding `faces-config.xml` configuration file to control the navigation for your application.

- Use implicit navigation for specifying the next view to render from within the controller class, returning the name of the view in String format from an action method.

- Use implicit navigation by specifying the name of the view to render as the `action` attribute of a component tag, bypassing the controller class altogether.

The example in this recipe consists of four Jakarta Server Faces views, and each one contains `h:commandButton` components that invoke navigation to another view. The `h:commandButton` components are linked to controller class methods that are present in the view's corresponding controller class named `NavigationController`. Figure 3-9 shows a diagram depicting navigation between different Jakarta Server Faces views.

Figure 3-9. *Diagram depicting page navigation between different Jakarta Server Faces views*

The first view (recipe03_06a.xhtml) listed here contains two `h:commandButton` components, each of which invokes a method within the controller class named `NavigationController`. The first button utilizes explicit Jakarta Server Faces navigation, and the second uses implicit navigation:

```
<?xml version='1.0' encoding='UTF-8' ?>
<!DOCTYPE html>
<html xmlns="http://www.w3.org/1999/xhtml"
      xmlns:h="http://xmlns.jcp.org/jsf/html">
    <h:head>
        <meta http-equiv="Content-Type" content="text/html; charset=UTF-8"/>
        <title>Recipe 3-6</title>
    </h:head>
    <h:body>
        <h:form id="componentForm">
            <h1>Jakarta Server Faces Navigation - Page 1</h1>
            <p>
                Clicking the submit button below will take you to Page #2.
            </p>
            <br/>
```

```
            <h:commandButton id="navButton" action="#{navigationController.pageTwo}"
                             value="Go To Page 2"/>
            <br/>
            <br/>
            <h:commandButton id="navButton2" action="#{navigationController.nextPage}"
                             value="Implicitly Navigate to Page 3"/>
        </h:form>
    </h:body>
</html>
```

The source for the second Jakarta Server Faces view (recipe03_06b.xhtml) is very similar, except that a different controller class method is specified in the action attribute of the view's h:commandButton component:

```
<?xml version='1.0' encoding='UTF-8' ?>
<!DOCTYPE html>
<html xmlns="http://www.w3.org/1999/xhtml"
      xmlns:h="http://xmlns.jcp.org/jsf/html">
    <h:head>
        <meta http-equiv="Content-Type" content="text/html; charset=UTF-8"/>
        <title>Recipe 3-6 Jakarta Server Faces Navigation</title>
    </h:head>
    <h:body>
        <h:form id="componentForm">
            <h1>Jakarta Server Faces Navigation - Page 2</h1>
            <p>
                Clicking the submit button below will take you to Page #1.
            </p>
            <br/>
            <h:commandButton id="navButton" action="#{navigationController.pageOne}"
                             value="Go To Page 1"/>
        </h:form>
    </h:body>
</html>
```

The third Jakarta Server Faces view (recipe03_06c.xhtml) contains an h:commandButton component that invokes a controller class action and utilizes conditional navigation, rendering pages depending on a conditional outcome in faces-config.xml:

```
<?xml version='1.0' encoding='UTF-8' ?>
<!DOCTYPE html>
<html xmlns="http://www.w3.org/1999/xhtml"
      xmlns:h="http://xmlns.jcp.org/jsf/html">
    <h:head>
        <meta http-equiv="Content-Type" content="text/html; charset=UTF-8"/>
        <title>Recipe 3-6 Jakarta Server Faces Navigation</title>
    </h:head>
    <h:body>
        <h:form id="componentForm">
            <h1>Jakarta Server Faces Navigation - Page 3</h1>
            <p>
```

```
            The button below will utilize conditional navigation to take a user
            to the next page.  The application will use authentication to test
            conditional navigation.
        </p>
        <br/>
        <h:commandButton id="loginButton" action="#{navigationController.login}"
                         value="Login Action"/>
    </h:form>
  </h:body>
</html>
```

Lastly, the fourth Jakarta Server Faces view (recipe03_06d.xhtml) in the navigational example application contains an h:commandButton that invokes a method and uses implicit navigation to return to the third Jakarta Server Faces view, specifying the view name within the action attribute directly and bypassing the controller class altogether:

```
<?xml version='1.0' encoding='UTF-8' ?>
<!DOCTYPE html>
<html xmlns="http://www.w3.org/1999/xhtml"
      xmlns:h="http://xmlns.jcp.org/jsf/html">
    <h:head>
        <meta http-equiv="Content-Type" content="text/html; charset=UTF-8"/>
        <title>Recipe 3-6 Jakarta Server Faces Navigation</title>
    </h:head>
    <h:body>
        <h:form id="componentForm">
            <h1>Jakarta Server Faces Navigation - Page 4</h1>
            <p>
                Clicking the submit button below will take you to Page #1 using conditional
                navigation rules.
            </p>
            <br/>
            <h:commandButton id="navButton2" action="recipe03_06c"
                             value="Implicitly Navigate to Page 3"/>
        </h:form>
    </h:body>
</html>
```

Now let's look at the source listing for NavigationController. It contains the methods that are specified within each page's h:commandButton action attribute. Some of the methods return a String value, and others do not. However, after the methods are invoked, then the FacesServlet processes the request, and the faces-config.xml configuration file is traversed, if needed, to determine the next view to render:

```
package org.jakartaeerecipe.chapter03.recipe03_06;

import jakarta.inject.Named;
import jakarta.enterprise.context.RequestScoped;

@Named(value = "navigationController")
@RequestScoped
public class NavigationController implements java.io.Serializable{
```

```java
    private boolean authenticated = false;
    /**
     * Creates a new instance of NavigationController
     */
    public NavigationController() {
    }
    public String pageOne(){
        return "PAGE_1";
    }
    public String pageTwo(){
        return "PAGE_2";
    }
    /**
     * Utilizing implicit navigation, a page name can be returned from an
     * action method rather than listing a navigation-rule within faces-config.xml
     * @return the page name
     */
    public String nextPage(){
        // Perform some task, then implicitly list a page to render
        return "recipe03_06c";
    }
    /**
     * Demonstrates the use of conditional navigation
     */
    public void login(){
        // Perform some tasks, if needed, and then return boolean
        setAuthenticated(true);
        System.out.println("Here");
    }
    /**
     * @return the authenticated
     */
    public boolean isAuthenticated() {
        return authenticated;
    }
    /**
     * @param authenticated the authenticated to set
     */
    public void setAuthenticated(boolean authenticated) {
        this.authenticated = authenticated;
    }
}
```

At the heart of navigation is the /WEB-INF/faces-config.xml file. It specifies which view should be displayed after a corresponding outcome. Two of the navigation-rules use standard Jakarta Server Faces navigation, and the last navigation-rule uses conditional navigation:

```xml
<?xml version='1.0' encoding='UTF-8'?>
<faces-config version="3.0" xmlns="https://jakarta.ee/xml/ns/jakartaee"
    xmlns:xsi="http://www.w3.org/2001/XMLSchema-instance"
    xsi:schemaLocation="https://jakarta.ee/xml/ns/jakartaee
```

```
    https://jakarta.ee/xml/ns/jakartaee/web-facesconfig_3_0.xsd">
    <navigation-rule>
        <from-view-id>/chapter03/recipe03_06a.xhtml</from-view-id>
        <navigation-case>
            <from-outcome>PAGE_2/from-outcome>
            <to-view-id>/chapter03/recipe03_06b.xhtml</to-view-id>
        </navigation-case>
    </navigation-rule>
    <navigation-rule>
        <from-view-id>/chapter03/recipe03_06b.xhtml</from-view-id>
        <navigation-case>
            <from-outcome>PAGE_1</from-outcome>
            <to-view-id>/chapter03/recipe03_06a.xhtml</to-view-id>
        </navigation-case>
    </navigation-rule>
    <navigation-rule>
        <navigation-case>
            <from-action>#{navigationController.login}</from-action>
            <if>#{navigationController.authenticated}</if>
            <to-view-id>/chapter03/recipe03_06d.xhtml</to-view-id>
            <redirect/>
        </navigation-case>
    </navigation-rule>
</faces-config>
```

The project folder structure is shown in Figure 3-10.

- ∨ 📁 src
  - ∨ 📁 main
    - ∨ 📁 java
      - ∨ 📁 org.jakartaeerecipe.chapter03
        - © NavigationController
    - ❯ 📁 resources
    - ∨ 📁 webapp
      - ∨ 📁 chapter03
        - 📄 recipe03_06a.xhtml
        - 📄 recipe03_06b.xhtml
        - 📄 recipe03_06c.xhtml
        - 📄 recipe03_06d.xhtml
      - ∨ 📁 WEB-INF
        - 📄 web.xml
      - 📄 faces-config.xml

Figure 3-10. *Project folder structure*

How It Works

One of the most daunting tasks when building a web application is to determine the overall page navigation. Many web frameworks have instituted XML configuration files for organizing page navigation. This is one technique used by the Java Server Faces web framework, and the navigational XML is placed in a Jakarta Server Faces application's `faces-config.xml` configuration file. When it's using standard navigation, Jakarta Server Faces utilizes navigation rules to determine which view to render based on the outcome of page actions. If it's using standard Jakarta Server Faces navigation, when a page action occurs, the controller class method that is associated with the action can return a `String` value. That value is then evaluated using the navigational rules that are defined in the `faces-config.xml` file and used to determine which page to render next.

The standard navigation infrastructure works well in most cases, but in some instances, it makes more sense to directly list the next page to be rendered within the controller class, rather than making a navigation rule in the configuration file. When a controller class action is invoked, it can return the name of a view, without the `.xhtml` suffix. Such navigation was introduced with the release of Jakarta Server Faces 2.0, and it is known as *implicit navigation*. As shown in the fourth example for the solution, you can also perform implicit navigation by specifying the name of a view without the suffix for an `action` attribute of the component tag.

Yet another type of navigation was introduced with Jakarta Server Faces 2.0, taking navigation to the next level by allowing the use of Jakarta Expression Language expressions in the `faces-config.xml` navigation rules. Conditional navigation allows for an `<if>` element to be specified within the navigational rule, which corresponds to a Jakarta Expression Language condition. If the condition evaluates to `true`, then the specified view is rendered.

Navigation rules are constructed in XML residing within the `faces-config.xml` descriptor, and each rule has a root element of `navigation-rule`. Within each rule construct, the `from-view-id` element should contain the name of the view from which the action method was invoked. A series of `navigation-cases` should follow the `from-view-id` element. Each `navigation-case` contains a `from-outcome` element, which should be set to a `String` value corresponding to the `String` value that is returned from a subsequent action method. For instance, when the pageOne method is invoked in the example, the `String` `"PAGE_1"` is returned, and it should be specified within the `from-outcome` element within a `navigation-case` in the `faces-config.xml` file. Lastly, the `to-view-id` element should follow the `from-outcome` element within the `navigation-case`, and it should specify which view to render if the string in `from-outcome` is returned from the action method. The following excerpt shows the standard navigation rule that allows for navigation from page 1 to page 2 of the application:

```
<navigation-rule>
        <from-view-id>/chapter03/recipe03_06a.xhtml</from-view-id>
        <navigation-case>
            <from-outcome>PAGE_1</from-outcome>
            <to-view-id>/chapter03/recipe03_06b.xhtml</to-view-id>
        </navigation-case>
</navigation-rule>
```

Implicit navigation does not require any XML navigation rules to be declared. The action method that is invoked via an `h:commandButton` returns a `String` that is equal to the name of the view that should be rendered next. In the example, the second `h:commandButton` on view 1 invokes the `nextPage` controller class method, which returns the name of the next view that should be rendered:

```
public String nextPage(){
        // Perform some task, then implicitly list a page to render
        return "recipe03_06c";
}
```

If you want to use implicit navigation, you can bypass the controller class altogether and specify the name of the view that you want to render directly within the `action` attribute of `h:commandButton` or `h:commandLink`. The fourth Jakarta Server Faces view in the example demonstrates this technique.

The third view in the example, named recipe03_05c.xhtml, demonstrates conditional navigation. Its h:commandButton action invokes the login method within the NavigationController class. That method does not contain much business logic in this example, but it does set the bean's authenticated field equal to true. Imagine that someone entered an incorrect password and failed to authenticate; in such a case, the authenticated field would be set to false. After the login method is executed, the faces-config. xml file is parsed to determine the next view to render, and the conditional navigation rule utilizes Jakarta Expression Language to specify the navigation condition. The from-action element is set equal to the Jakarta Expression Language that is used to invoke the login method, and an <if> element is specified, referencing the navigationController.authenticated field via Jakarta Server Faces EL. If that field is equal to true, then the view specified within the to-view-id element will be rendered. Note that the <redirect/> is required to tell Jakarta Server Faces to redirect to the view listed in the <to-view-id> element since Jakarta Server Faces uses a redirect rather than a forward:

```
<navigation-rule>
        <navigation-case>
            <from-action>#{navigationController.login}</from-action>
            <if>#{navigationController.authenticated}</if>
            <to-view-id>/chapter03/recipe03_06d.xhtml</to-view-id>
            <redirect/>
        </navigation-case>
    </navigation-rule>
</faces-config>
```

Standard Jakarta Server Faces navigation allows enough flexibility for most cases, and its architecture is much more sophisticated than other web frameworks. However, in Jakarta Server Faces 2.0, two new navigational techniques known as *implicit* and *conditional navigation* were introduced. With the addition of the new techniques, Jakarta Server Faces navigation is more robust and easier to manage. To view the output of this recipe, navigate to the URL http://localhost:8080/JakartaEERecipes_Chapter03-1.0-SNAPSHOT/ chapter03/recipe03_06a.xhtml in your browser to see the outputs as in Figure 3-11.

Figure 3-11. *Resulting Jakarta Server Faces view*

3-7. Validating User Input

Problem

You want to add the ability for your application to validate any data that is entered into a Jakarta Server Faces form.

Solution

Register a Jakarta Server Faces validator on any text field components or other input components that need to be validated. Use predefined Jakarta Server Faces validators where applicable and create custom validator classes when needed. The example for this recipe utilizes predefined validators for two h:inputText components in order to ensure that the values entered into them are of proper length. A custom validator is added to a third text field, and it is responsible for ensuring that the text contains a specified string. The three fields make up an employee input form, and when an employee is entered and the data validates successfully, a new Employee object is created and added to a list of employees. An h:dataTable element in the view is used to display the list of employees if there are any. This is perhaps not the most true-to-life example, but you can apply the basic philosophy to validate real-world needs in your own applications.

The following listing is for the Jakarta Server Faces view (\webapp\chapter03\recipe03_07.xhtml) that constructs the employee input form, including the validation tags for each input text field:

```
<html xmlns="http://www.w3.org/1999/xhtml"
    xmlns:f="http://xmlns.jcp.org/jsf/core"
    xmlns:h="http://xmlns.jcp.org/jsf/html">
    <h:head>
        <title>Recipe 3-7: Validating Data</title>
    </h:head>
    <h:body>
        <h:form id="employeeForm">
            <h1>Java Developer Employee Information</h1>
            <br/>
            <h:messages globalOnly="true" errorStyle="color: red" infoStyle="color: green"/>
            <br/>
            <h:dataTable id="empTable" var="emp"
                        border="1" value="#{employeeController.employeeList}"
                        rendered="#{employeeController.employeeList.size() > 0}">
                <f:facet name="header">
                    Current Employees
                </f:facet>
                <h:column id="empNameCol">
                    <f:facet name="header">Employee</f:facet>
                    <h:outputText id="empName" value="#{emp.employeeFirst}
                    #{emp.employeeLast}"/>
                </h:column>
                <h:column id="titleCol">
                    <f:facet name="header">Title</f:facet>
                    <h:outputText id="title" value="#{emp.employeeTitle}"/>
                </h:column>
            </h:dataTable>
```

```
        <p>
            Please use the form below to insert employee information.
        </p>
        <h:panelGrid columns="3">
            <h:outputLabel for="employeeFirst" value="First: " />
            <h:inputText id="employeeFirst" value="#{employeeController.employeeFirst}">
                <f:validateLength minimum="3" maximum="30"/>
            </h:inputText>
            <h:message for="employeeFirst" errorStyle="color:red"/>
            <h:outputLabel for="employeeLast" value="Last: "   />
            <h:inputText id="employeeLast" value="#{employeeController.employeeLast}">
                <f:validateLength minimum="3" maximum="30"/>
            </h:inputText>
            <h:message for="employeeLast" errorStyle="color:red"/>
            <h:outputLabel for="employeeTitle" value="Title (Must be a Java
            Position): "/>
            <h:inputText id="employeeTitle" value="#{employeeController.employeeTitle}">
                <f:validator validatorId="employeeTitleValidate" />
            </h:inputText>
            <h:message for="employeeTitle" errorStyle="color:red"/>
        </h:panelGrid>
        <h:commandButton id="employeeInsert" action="#{employeeController.
        insertEmployee}"
                            value="Insert Employee"/>
    </h:form>
</h:body>
</html>
```

The third h:inputText component in the view utilizes a custom validator. The f:validator tag is used to specify a custom validator, and its validatorId attribute is used to specify a corresponding validator class. The following listing is the Java code for a class named EmployeeTitleValidate, the custom validation class for the text field:

```
package org.jakartaeerecipe.chapter03.recipe03_07;

import jakarta.faces.application.FacesMessage;
import jakarta.faces.component.UIComponent;
import jakarta.faces.context.FacesContext;
import jakarta.faces.validator.FacesValidator;
import jakarta.faces.validator.Validator;
import jakarta.faces.validator.ValidatorException;


@FacesValidator("employeeTitleValidator")
public class EmployeeTitleValidate implements Validator {
    @Override
    public void validate(FacesContext facesContext, UIComponent uiComponent, Object value)
            throws ValidatorException {
        checkTitle(value);
    }
    private void checkTitle(Object value) {
        String title = value.toString();
```

```
        if (!title.contains("Java")) {
            String messageText = "Title does not include the word Java";
            throw new ValidatorException(new FacesMessage(FacesMessage.SEVERITY_ERROR,
                    messageText, messageText));
        }
    }
}
```

■ **Note** As of Jakarta Server Faces 2.3, it is possible to inject resources into validator classes. User-generated validator classes are also injectable into other resources.

Now let's look at the Jakarta Server Faces controller class for the Jakarta Server Faces view that contains the validation tags. The controller class is named EmployeeController, and the action method, insertEmployee, is used to add new Employee objects containing valid data to an ArrayList:

```
package org.jakartaeerecipe.chapter03.recipe03_07;

import java.io.Serializable;
import java.util.ArrayList;
import java.util.List;
import jakarta.enterprise.context.SessionScoped;

import jakarta.faces.application.FacesMessage;
import jakarta.faces.context.FacesContext;
import jakarta.inject.Named;

@Named(value="employeeController")
@SessionScoped
public class EmployeeController implements Serializable {

    private String employeeFirst;
    private String employeeLast;
    private String employeeTitle;
    private List <Employee> employeeList;
    public EmployeeController(){
        employeeList = new ArrayList();
    }
    public void insertEmployee(){
        Employee emp = new Employee(employeeFirst,
                                    employeeLast,
                                    employeeTitle);
        employeeList.add(emp);
        FacesMessage facesMsg = new FacesMessage(FacesMessage.SEVERITY_INFO, "Employee
        Successfully Added", null);
        FacesContext.getCurrentInstance().addMessage(null, facesMsg);
    }
    // getters and setters
    // ....

}
```

Below is the code for the Employee class, it's a simple Plain Old Java Object (POJO) class.

```
package org.jakartaeerecipe.chapter03.recipe03_07;

public record Employee(String getEmployeeFirst, String getEmployeeLast, String
getEmployeeTitle) {
}
```

In the end, the validators will raise exceptions if a user attempts to enter an employee first or last name using an invalid length or a title that does not contain the word *Java*. When user input validation fails, error messages are displayed next to the components containing the invalid entries. The output of this recipe would be as in Figure 3-12.

Java Developer Employee Information

Please use the form below to insert employee information.

First:		employeeForm:employeeFirst: Validation Error: Length is less than allowable minimum of '3'
Last:		employeeForm:employeeLast: Validation Error: Length is less than allowable minimum of '3'
Title (Must be a Java Position):	Author	Title does not include the word Java

Insert Employee

Figure 3-12. *Resulting Jakarta Server Faces view*

How It Works

The Jakarta Server Faces framework contains many features that make it more convenient for developers to customize their applications. Validators are one of those features, because they can be used to solidify application data and ensure data is correct before storing in a database or other data store. The Jakarta Server Faces framework ships with a good deal of validators that are already implemented. To use these predefined validators, simply embed the appropriate validator tag within a component tag in a view to validate that component's data values. Sometimes, there are cases where the standard validators will not do the trick. In such cases, Jakarta Server Faces provides a means for developing custom validator classes that can be used from within a view in the same manner as the predefined validators.

In the example for this recipe, two of the h:inputText components contain standard Jakarta Server Faces validators used to validate the length of the values entered. The f:validateLength tag can be embedded into a component for string-length validation, and the tag's minimum and maximum attributes can be populated with the minimum and maximum string length, respectively. As mentioned previously, Jakarta Server Faces ships with a good number of these predefined validators. All that the developer is required to do is embed the validator tags in the components that they want to validate. Table 3-3 lists all standard validator tags and what they do. For a detailed look at each of the validator attributes, see the online documentation.

Table 3-3. *Standard Validators*

Validator Tag	Description
validateLength	Checks the length of a string
validateLongRange	Checks the range of a numeric value
validateDoubleRange	Checks the range of a floating-point value
validateRequired	Ensures the input field is not empty (also an alternative to using the required attribute on an input field component tag)
validateRegex	Validates the component against a given regular expression pattern

Oftentimes, there is a need for some other type of validation to take place for a specified component. In such cases, developing a custom validator class may be the best choice. Many developers shy away from writing their own validators because it seems to be a daunting task at first glance. However, Jakarta Server Faces 2.0 took great strides toward making custom validator classes easier to write and understand.

To create a custom validator class, implement the jakarta.faces.validator.Validator class. Annotate the validator class with the @FacesValidator annotation, specifying the string you want to use for registering your validator within the f:validator tag. In the example, the name used to reference the validator class is employeeTitleValidate. The only requirement is that the validator class overrides the validate method, which is where the custom validation takes place. The validate method contains the following signature:

```
public void validate(FacesContext facesContext, UIComponent uiComponent, Object value)
            throws ValidatorException
```

Utilizing the parameters that are passed into the method, you can obtain the current FacesContext, a handle on the component being validated, as well as the component's value. In the example, a helper method is called from within the validate method, and it is used to check the component's value and ensure that the word *Java* is contained somewhere within it. If it does not validate successfully, a ValidatorException is created and thrown. The message that is placed within the ValidatorException is what will appear next to the component being validated if the validation fails. The following excerpt from the validation class demonstrates creating and throwing a ValidatorException:

```
throw new ValidatorException(new FacesMessage(FacesMessage.SEVERITY_ERROR,
                messageText, messageText));
```

So, when does the validation occur? That is the key to the validator, isn't it? The answer is immediately, before the request is sent to the controller class action method. Any validation occurs during the *Process Validations* phase, and if one or more components being validated within a view throw a ValidatorException, then the processing stops, and the request is not sent to the action method. When the user clicks the Submit button, the validation takes place first, and if everything is okay, then the request is passed to the action method.

■ **Note** A means of validating that an input component simply contains a value is to use the required attribute. The required attribute of input component tags can be set to true in order to force a value to be entered for that component.

142

The validation of components in a Jakarta Server Faces view using standard validators can really save a developer some time and increase the usability and precision of an application's data. The ability to create custom validators allows validation to be performed for any scenario. Be constructive, use validation on all of your application's input forms, and create custom validators to perform validation using unique techniques. Your application users will appreciate it!

3-8. Evaluating Page Expressions Immediately

Problem

You want to have some of your Jakarta Server Faces component values evaluated immediately, rather than waiting until the form is submitted.

Solution

Specify true for the component tag's immediate attribute, and also specify the component's onchange attribute and set it equal to submit(). This will cause the input form to be submitted immediately when the value for the component is changed, and Jakarta Server Faces will skip the Render Response phase when doing so and execute all components that specify an immediate attribute set to true during the Apply Request Values Jakarta Server Faces life-cycle phase. The example for this recipe uses an employee form. Instead of waiting until the form is submitted, the first and last h:inputText components will be evaluated and validated during the Apply Request Values phase immediately when their values change. The following source is for the Jakarta Server Faces view named /webapp/chapter03/recipe03_08.xhtml:

```
<html xmlns="http://www.w3.org/1999/xhtml"
    xmlns:f="http://xmlns.jcp.org/jsf/core"
    xmlns:h="http://xmlns.jcp.org/jsf/html">
    <h:head>
        <title>Recipe 3-8 Immediate View Evaluation</title>
    </h:head>
    <h:body>
        <h:form id="employeeForm">
            <h1>Java Developer Employee Information</h1>
            <br/>
            <h:messages globalOnly="true" errorStyle="color: red" infoStyle="color: green"/>
            <br/>
            <h:dataTable id="empTable" var="emp"
                        border="1" value="#{employeeController.employeeList}"
                        rendered="#{employeeController.employeeList.size() > 0}">
                <f:facet name="header">
                    Current Employees
                </f:facet>
                <h:column id="empNameCol">
                    <f:facet name="header">Employee</f:facet>
                    <h:outputText id="empName" value="#{emp.employeeFirst}
                    #{emp.employeeLast}"/>
                </h:column>
                <h:column id="titleCol">
                    <f:facet name="header">Title</f:facet>
                    <h:outputText id="title" value="#{emp.employeeTitle}"/>
```

```
                    </h:column>
                </h:dataTable>
                <p style="width: 40%;">
                    Please use the form below to insert employee information. The first and
                    last text fields will result in immediate evaluation during the
                    apply request
                    values phase, whereas the text field
                    in the middle will result in standard evaluation and be validated during
                    the invoke application phase.
                    <br/><br/>
                    To test, try inserting just one character in the first text field
                    and then tab to the next field.  You should see an immediate result.
                </p>
                <h:panelGrid columns="3">
                    <h:outputLabel for="employeeFirst" value="First: " />
                    <h:inputText id="employeeFirst" immediate="true" onchange="submit()"
                    value="#{employeeController.employeeFirst}">
                        <f:validateLength minimum="3" maximum="30"/>
                    </h:inputText>
                    <h:message for="employeeFirst" errorStyle="color:red"/>
                    <h:outputLabel for="employeeLast" value="Last: "  />
                    <h:inputText id="employeeLast" value="#{employeeController.employeeLast}">
                        <f:validateLength minimum="3" maximum="30"/>
                    </h:inputText>
                    <h:message for="employeeLast" errorStyle="color:red"/>
                    <h:outputLabel for="employeeTitle" value="Title (Must be a Java
                    Position): "/>
                    <h:inputText id="employeeTitle" immediate="true"
                    value="#{employeeController.employeeTitle}">
                        <f:validator validatorId="employeeTitleValidator" />
                    </h:inputText>
                    <h:message for="employeeTitle" errorStyle="color:red"/>
                </h:panelGrid>
                <h:commandButton id="employeeInsert" action="#{employeeController.
                insertEmployee}"
                                value="Insert Employee"/>
            </h:form>
        </h:body>
</html>
```

As you can see, the h:inputText components with ids of employeeFirst and employeeTitle specify both the immediate="true" and the onchange="submit()" attributes. These two attributes cause the components to be validated immediately rather than when the h:commandButton action is invoked. The output of this recipe is shown in Figure 3-13.

Java Developer Employee Information

Please use the form below to insert employee information. The first and last text fields will result in immediate evaluation during the apply request values phase, whereas the text field in the middle will result in standard evaluation and be validated during the invoke application phase.

To test, try inserting just one character in the first text field and then tab to the next field. You should see an immediate result.

First: [s] employeeForm:employeeFirst: Validation Error: Length is less than allowable minimum of '3'

Last: [ ]

Title (Must be a Java Position): [Author] Title does not include the word Java

[Insert Employee]

Figure 3-13. *Resulting Jakarta Server Faces view*

How It Works

Event handling that occurs immediately can be useful in cases where you do not want to validate the entire form in order to process input but, rather, when you want chosen components to be validated immediately. As mentioned in Recipe 3-1, when a Jakarta Server Faces view is processed, a number of phases are executed. As such, when a form is submitted, the Invoke Application phase initiates the event handlers for view components, and validation occurs. When the immediate attribute for a component is set to true, the event handlers for that component execute during the Apply Request Values phase, which occurs before the Process Validations phase, where component validation normally occurs. This allows for an immediate validation response for the specified components, resulting in immediate error messages if needed.

As mentioned previously, specify the immediate attribute for a component and set it to true if you want to have that component evaluated immediately. This will cause the component to be evaluated and validated during the Apply Request Values phase. The real fun comes into play when you also specify the onclick attribute and set it equal to submit(), causing the form to be submitted when the value for the component changes. Specifying attributes as such will cause any component in the view that has an immediate attribute set to true to be validated when the component value changes.

■ **Note** The immediate attribute can also be useful when used on a commandButton component in such instances where you do not want any form processing to take place, such as if you want to set up a Cancel button or another button to bypass form processing.

3-9. Passing Page Parameters to Methods

Problem

You want to pass parameters (such as lastName) to controller class methods from within a Jakarta Server Faces view via the Expression Language (EL).

Solution

Use a standard Jakarta Expression Language expression to invoke a controller class method and enclose the parameters that you want to pass to the method within parentheses. In the example for this recipe, an h:dataTable component is used to display a list of Author objects in a view. Each row in the h:dataTable contains an h:commandLink component, which invokes a Jakarta Server Faces controller class method when selected. The h:commandLink displays the current row's author name and invokes the AuthorController class displayAuthor method when clicked, passing the last name for the author being displayed in the current row. In the displayAuthor method, the list of authors is traversed, finding the element that contains the same last name as the parameter, which is passed into the method. The current author is then displayed in a subsequent page, which is rendered using implicit navigation.

The following source is for the Jakarta Server Faces view entitled recipe03_09a.xhtml, which displays the list of authors using an h:dataTable component:

```
<html xmlns="http://www.w3.org/1999/xhtml"
      xmlns:h="http://xmlns.jcp.org/jsf/html">
    <h:head>
        <title>Recipe 3-9: Passing Page Parameters to Methods</title>
    </h:head>
    <h:body>
        <h:form id="componentForm">
            <h1>Author List</h1>
            <p>
                Below is the list of authors.  Click on the author's last name
                for more information regarding the author.
            </p>
            <h:graphicImage id="java9recipes" style="width: 10%; height: 20%"
            library="image" name="java9recipes.png"/>
            <br/>
            <h:dataTable id="authorTable" border="1" value="#{authorTableController.
            authorList}"
                            var="author">
                <f:facet name="header">
                    Java 9 Recipes Authors
                </f:facet>
                <h:column>
                <h:commandLink id="authorName" action="#{authorTableController.
                displayAuthor(author.last)}"
                                value="#{author.first} #{author.last}"/>
                </h:column>
            </h:dataTable>
            <br/>
            <br/>
        </h:form>
    </h:body>
</html>
```

The next listing is that of the controller class for the preceding Jakarta Server Faces view. The controller class populates an ArrayList with Author objects upon instantiation:

```
package org.jakartaeerecipes.chapter03.recipe03_09;
import java.io.Serializable;
import java.util.ArrayList;
import java.util.List;
import jakarta.enterprise.context.SessionScoped;
```

```java
import jakarta.inject.Named;
@Named(value = "authorTableController")
@SessionScoped
public class AuthorController implements Serializable {
    private List<Author> authorList = null;
    private final String juneauBio = "This is Josh Juneau's Bio";
    private final String telangBio = "This is Tarun Telang's Bio";
    private Author current;
    private String authorLast;
    /**
     * Creates a new instance of RecipeController
     */
    public AuthorController() {
        super();
        authorLast = null;
        populateAuthorList();
    }
    private void populateAuthorList() {
        if(authorList == null){
            System.out.println("initializing authors list");
            authorList = new ArrayList<>();
            authorList.add(new Author("Josh", "Juneau", juneauBio));
            authorList.add(new Author("Tarun", "Telang", telangBio));
        }
    }
    public String displayAuthor(String last){
        for(Author author:authorList){
            if(author.getLast().equals(last)){
                current = author;
                break;
            }
        }
        return "recipe03_09b";
    }
    // getters and setters
    // ....
}
```

The output of the page should be as in Figure 3-14.

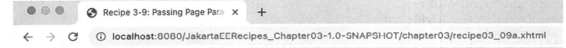

Author List

Below is the list of authors. Click on the author's last name for more information regarding the author.

Java 9 Recipes Authors
Josh Juneau
Tarun Telang

Figure 3-14. *Resulting Jakarta Server Faces view*

The Author class is the same Author Plain Old Java Object (POJO) that was utilized in Recipe 3-3. For the source of the Author class, refer to that recipe. Lastly, the following code is for a Jakarta Server Faces view entitled recipe03_09b.xhtml, the detail view for each author. When an author name is clicked from the h:dataTable component in the first view, the component's corresponding controller class method is invoked, and then this view is rendered to display the selected author's information:

```
<html xmlns="http://www.w3.org/1999/xhtml"
      xmlns:f="http://xmlns.jcp.org/jsf/core"
      xmlns:h="http://xmlns.jcp.org/jsf/html">
    <h:head>
        <meta http-equiv="Content-Type" content="text/html; charset=UTF-8"/>
        <title>Recipe 3-9: Passing Page Parameters to Methods</title>
    </h:head>
    <h:body>
        <h:form id="componentForm">
            <h1>#{authorTableController.current.first} #{authorTableController.current.
            last}</h1>
            <p>
                <h:graphicImage library="image" name="jakartaee10recipes.png"
                id="jakartaee10recipes" style="width: 10%; height: 20%"/>

                <br/>
                #{authorTableController.current.bio}
            </p>
            <h:link value="Go Back to List" outcome="recipe03_09a"/>
        </h:form>
```

```
        </h:body>
</html>
```

Clicking the author's name takes you to a page with output as shown in Figure 3-15.

← → C ⓘ localhost:8080/JakartaEERecipes_Chapter03-1.0-SNAPSHOT/chapter03/recipe03_09a.xhtml

Tarun Telang

This is Tarun Telang's Bio

Go Back to List

Figure 3-15. *Resulting Jakarta Server Faces view*

How It Works

The 2.0 release contained many enhancements that made the life of Jakarta Server Faces developers much easier than before. The ability to pass parameters to controller class methods from within Jakarta Server Faces views is one such enhancement. As you can see from the example for this recipe, it is possible to pass parameters to a method within a Jakarta Expression Language construct in the same manner that you would call any method with parameters in Java: by enclosing the argument(s) within parentheses after the method name. It cannot get much simpler than that!

Let's look at the lines of code that make this example hum. The first Jakarta Server Faces view displays a table of author names, and each name is displayed using an h:commandLink component. The value attribute for the h:commandLink component is set to the author name, and the action attribute is set to the Jakarta Server Faces EL, which invokes a controller class action method named displayAuthor. Notice that within the call to the controller class method, the Jakarta Expression Language for the author's last name is passed as a String parameter.

```
<h:dataTable id="authorTable" border="1" value="#{authorTableController.authorList}"
                    var="author">
        <f:facet name="header">
                    Java 9Recipes Authors
        </f:facet>
        <h:column>
                    <h:commandLink id="authorName" action="#{authorTableController.
                    displayAuthor(author.last)}"
                            value="#{author.first} #{author.last}"/>
        </h:column>
</h:dataTable>
```

The displayAuthor method in the controller class accepts a String parameter value, which is the author's last name, and then finds an Author object within the list of authors that contains the same last name. When it's found, a class field named current is set equal to the Author object for the matching List element. The subsequent Jakarta Server Faces view then displays content utilizing the current Author information.

Prior to Jakarta Server Faces 2.0, developers were unable to pass parameters to controller class methods from within a view. This made it a bit more difficult to perform such techniques and usually involved a bit more code.

3-10. Using Operators and Reserved Words in Expressions

Problem

You want to perform some arithmetic and combine expressions within your Jakarta Server Faces views.

Solution

Jakarta Server Faces Jakarta Expression Language expressions can contain arithmetic using standard arithmetic operators. It is also possible to combine two or more expressions utilizing some of Jakarta Server Faces EL reserved words. In the following example (recipe03_10.xhtml), some Jakarta Expression Language expressions are used to display mathematical results on a page. The usage of arithmetic and reserved words is in the expressions below:

```
<html xmlns="http://www.w3.org/1999/xhtml"
    xmlns:h="http://xmlns.jcp.org/jsf/html"
    xmlns:c="http://xmlns.jcp.org/jsp/jstl/core">
    <h:head>
        <title>Recipe 3-10: Arithmetic and Reserved Words</title>
    </h:head>
    <h:body>
        <h:form id="componentForm">
            <h1>Jakarta Server Faces Arithmetic and Reserved Words in Jakarta Expression
            Language</h1>
            <p>
                The following examples use Jakarta Expression Language to perform some
                arithmetic.
            </p>
            1 + 1 = #{1 + 1}
            <br/>
            <h:outputText value="20 / 5 = #{20 / 5}"/>
            <br/>
            <h:outputText rendered="#{1 + 1 eq 2}" value="1 + 1 DOES equal 2"/>
            <br/>
            <h:outputText rendered="#{5 * 4 != 20}" value="Is 5 * 4 equal to 20?"/>
            <br/>
            <h:outputText rendered="#{5 * 5 eq 25 and 1 + 1 eq 2}" value="Combining some
            expressions"/>
            <br/>
        </h:form>
    </h:body>
</html>
```

Some of the expressions contain controller class references for a bean named `EvaluationController`. The listing for this controller class is as follows:

```
package org.jakartaeerecipe.chapter03.recipe03_10;

import jakarta.enterprise.context.RequestScoped;
import jakarta.inject.Named;

@Named(value = "evaluationController")
@RequestScoped
public class EvaluationController {
    private boolean field1 = true;
    /**
     * Creates a new instance of EvaluationController
     */
    public EvaluationController() {
    }
    /**
     * @return the field1
     */
    public boolean isField1() {
        return field1;
    }
    /**
     * @param field1 the field1 to set
     */
    public void setField1(boolean field1) {
        this.field1 = field1;
    }
}
```

The resulting page will look like Figure 3-16.

Jakarta Server Faces Arithmetic and Reserved Words in EL

The following examples use Jakarta Server Faces EL to perform some arithmetic.

1 + 1 = 2
20 / 5 = 4.0
1 + 1 DOES equal 2

Combining some expressions

Figure 3-16. *Resulting Jakarta Server Faces view*

How It Works

It is possible to use standard arithmetic and combine expressions using reserved words within Jakarta Expression Language expressions. All standard arithmetic operators are valid in EL, but a couple of things are different. For instance, instead of writing an expression such as #{1 + 1 = 2}, you could use the eq reserved characters so that the expression reads #{1 + 1 eq 2}. Similarly, the != symbol could be used to specify that some value is not equal to another value, but rather, in this example, the new reserved word is used. Table 3-4 describes all such reserved words.

Table 3-4. *Jakarta Expression Language Reserved Words*

Reserved Word	Description
and	Combines two or more expressions
div	Used to divide
empty	Used to refer to an empty list
eq	Equal to
false	Boolean false
ge	Greater than or equal to
gt	Greater than
instanceof	Used to evaluate whether an object is an instance of another
le	Less than or equal
lt	Less than
mod	Modulus
ne	Not equal
not	Used for negation
null	Evaluates a null value
or	Combines two or more expressions
true	Boolean true

Table 3-5 lists the available operators that can be used within Jakarta Expression Language expressions, in order of precedence.

Table 3-5. *Operators for Use in Expressions*

Operator
[]
()
- (unary), not, !, empty
*, /, div, %, mod
+, - (binary)
<, >, <=, >=, lt, gt, le, ge
==, !, eq, ne
&&, and
||, or
?, :

3-11. Creating Bookmarkable URLs

Problem

You want to enable your application to allow URLs that will be linked to display specific objects. For instance, you want to use a GET URL such as `http://localhost:8080/JakartaEERecipes_Chapter03-1.0-SNAPSHOT/chapter03/recipe03_11.xhtml?authorLast=Juneau` to display a page containing information on the author with the specified last name.

Solution

Add view parameters to a Jakarta Server Faces view for which you want to create a bookmarkable URL by defining the parameter in an `f:viewParam` tag, which is a subtag of the `f:metadata` tag. Doing so will allow a page to become accessible via a URL that contains request parameters, which can be used for record identification. In this example, the view contains a view parameter, via the `f:viewParam` tag, that allows for the specification of an author's last name when the view is requested. In the following example, the controller class that was created in Recipe 3-9 has been modified to include a new property named `authorLast` in order to accommodate the new view parameter.

The sources for the view named `\webapp\chapter03\recipe03_11.xhtml` are listed next. They are very similar to the view named `recipe03_09b.xhtml`, except that they include an `f:viewParam` element, which is enclosed between opening and closing `f:metadata` elements:

```
<html xmlns="http://www.w3.org/1999/xhtml"
    xmlns:f="http://xmlns.jcp.org/jsf/core"
    xmlns:h="http://xmlns.jcp.org/jsf/html">
    <h:head>
        <title>Recipe 3-11: Creating Bookmarkable URLs</title>
    </h:head>
    <h:body>
        <f:metadata>
```

```
            <f:viewParam name="authorLast" value="#{authorTableController.authorLast}"/>
        </f:metadata>
        <h:form id="componentForm">
            <h1>#{authorTableController.current.first} #{authorTableController.current.
            last}</h1>
            <p>
                <h:graphicImage id="java9recipes" library="image" style="width: 10%; height:
                20%" name="java9recipes.png"/>
                <br/>
                #{authorTableController.current.bio}
            </p>
            <h:link value="Go Back to List" outcome="recipe03_09a"/>
        </h:form>
    </h:body>
</html>
```

The code for the AuthorController class that's pertinent to this example is listed next:

```
@Named(value = "authorController")
@SessionScoped
public class AuthorController implements Serializable {
    ...
    private String authorLast;
    ...
    /**
     * @return the authorLast
     */
    public String getAuthorLast() {
        return authorLast;
    }
    /**
     * @param authorLast the authorLast to set
     */
    public void setAuthorLast(String authorLast) {
        displayAuthor(authorLast);
    }
}
```

As mentioned previously, a property named authorLast has been included in this controller. This property makes it possible for the Jakarta Server Faces view listed in the example to accept a request parameter named authorLast via a GET URL and pass it to the bean when the page is requested. In the end, the URL for accessing the view and requesting the details for the author Josh Juneau would be as follows:

http://localhost:8080/JakartaEERecipes_Chapter03-1.0-SNAPSHOT/chapter03/recipe03_11.
xhtml?authorLast=Juneau

Figure 3-17 shows the output.

Josh Juneau

This is Josh Juneau's Bio

Go Back to List

Figure 3-17. *Resulting Jakarta Server Faces view*

How It Works

In the past, Jakarta Server Faces applications had a weakness in that they used to require a launch view, which created an entry point for accessing the application. This gave the application a view that would set up an initial state for the application session. While this concept is nice because each user session would begin with an initialized application state, it prevented the ability for records to be linked directly via a URL. Sometimes, it is very useful to have the ability to link a view to a URL that contains request parameters so that records matching the given parameters can be returned to the view without further user interaction; for instance, say a website included information regarding a book and wanted to include a URL to find out more about the book's author. It's much nicer to directly link to a view containing that author's information rather than redirecting the user to a website that requires them to perform a manual search for the author. Such URLs are also known as *bookmarkable* URLs because the URL contains all of the state that is required to make the request. Therefore, they allow the user of a web application to bookmark the URL for direct access to a specific point in an application.

Jakarta Server Faces 2.0 introduced the ability to include view parameters, adding the ability for views to accept request parameters. Utilizing a GET-based URL, a request parameter can be appended to the end along with its value, and a view containing the new view parameter can then pass the parameter to a controller class before the response is rendered. The bean can then accept the parameter value and query a database or search through some other collection of data to find a record that matches the given value before rendering the response.

To include one or more view parameters within a view, you must add an opening and closing f:metadata element to the view and embed the number of f:viewParam elements between them. The f:viewParam element includes two attributes that must have values, those being the name and value attributes. The name attribute specifies the name of the request parameter as you would like it to appear within the bookmarkable URL, and the value attribute specifies the controller class field that should be mapped to that request parameter. In the example for this recipe, the Jakarta Server Faces view contains a view parameter named `authorLast`, and the associated `authorLast` field within the controller class contains a setter method, which is invoked when the page is requested. The following excerpt from the view demonstrates the lines for adding the metadata and view parameter:

```
<f:metadata>
    <f:viewParam name="authorLast" value="#{authorTableController.authorLast}"/>
</f:metadata>
```

With the addition of the view parameter, the page can be requested with a URL containing the `authorLast` request parameter as follows:

```
http://my-server.com/JakartaEERecipes/chapter03/chapter03_11.xhtml?authorLast=Juneau
```

When the page is requested, the view parameter's value invokes the `setAuthorLast` method in the controller class, which then searches for an author record that contains a last name equal to the given request parameter value:

```
...
public void setAuthorLast(String authorLast) {
        displayAuthor(authorLast);
    }
...
```

The addition of view parameters to Jakarta Server Faces 2.0 has made it easy to create bookmarkable URLs. This allows applications to be more flexible and produce results immediately without requiring a user to navigate through several pages before producing a result.

3-12. Displaying Lists of Objects

Problem

You want to display a list of objects in your rendered Jakarta Server Faces page.

Solution

Use a Jakarta Server Faces `h:dataTable` component to display the list objects, iterating over each object in the list and displaying the specified values. The `h:dataTable` component is very customizable and can be configured to display content in a variety of layouts. The following Jakarta Server Faces view contains two `h:dataTable` components that are used to display the authors for the *Java 9 Recipes* book using controller classes developed in previous recipes. The first table in the view is straightforward and displays the names of each author. It has been formatted to display alternating row colors. The second table contains two rows for each corresponding list element, displaying the author names on the first row and their bios on the second:

```
<html xmlns="http://www.w3.org/1999/xhtml"
    xmlns:f="http://xmlns.jcp.org/jsf/core"
    xmlns:h="http://xmlns.jcp.org/jsf/html">
    <h:head>
        <title>Recipe 3-12: Displaying Lists of Objects</title>
        <link href="#{facesContext.externalContext.requestContextPath}/css/styles.css"
            rel="stylesheet" type="text/css" />
    </h:head>
    <h:body>
```

```
<h:form id="componentForm">
    <p>
        <h:graphicImage id="java9recipes" style="width: 10%; height: 20%"
        library="image" name="java9recipes.png"/>
        <br/>
        #{authorTableController.current.bio}
    </p>
    <h:dataTable id="authorTable" border="1"
                value="#{authorTableController.authorList}"
                styleClass="authorTable"
                rowClasses="authorTableOdd, authorTableEven"
                var="author">
        <f:facet name="header">
            Java 9 Recipes Authors
        </f:facet>
        <h:column>
        <h:outputText id="authorName" value="#{author.first} #{author.last}"/>
        </h:column>
    </h:dataTable>
    <br/><br/>
    <h:dataTable id="authorTable2" border="1" value="#{authorTableController.
    authorList}"
                var="author" width="500px;">
        <f:facet name="header">
            Java 9 Recipes Authors
        </f:facet>
        <h:column>
            <h:panelGrid columns="2" border="1" width="100%">
                <h:outputText id="authorFirst" value="#{author.first}"
                style="width: 50%"/>
                <h:outputText id="authorLast" value="#{author.last}"
                style="width:50%"/>
            </h:panelGrid>
            <h:outputText id="authorBio" value="#{author.bio}"/>
        </h:column>
    </h:dataTable>
</h:form>
</h:body>
</html>
```

The example utilizes a cascading style sheet to help format the colors on the table. The source for the style sheet is as follows:

```
.authorTable{
    border-collapse:collapse;
}
.authorTableOdd{
    text-align:center;
    background:none repeat scroll 0 0 #CCFFFF;
    border-top:1px solid #BBBBBB;
}
```

```
.authorTableEven{
        text-align:center;
        background:none repeat scroll 0 0 #99CCFF;
        border-top:1px solid #BBBBBB;
}
```

The resulting page should look similar to Figure 3-18.

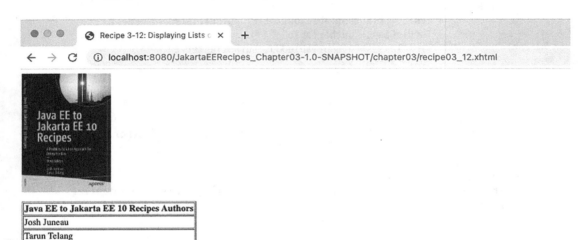

Figure 3-18. *Jakarta Server Faces dataTable component examples*

How It Works

A Jakarta Server Faces h:dataTable component can be used to display lists of objects in a page. When rendered, an HTML table is constructed, populating the cells of the table with the data for each list element or record of data. The h:dataTable can iterate over a collection of data, laying it out in a columnar format including column headers and the ability to customize the look using Cascading Style Sheets (CSS). The component contains a number of important attributes, as listed in Table 3-6. Perhaps the most important of them are the value and var attributes. The value attribute specifies the collection of data to iterate, and the var attribute lists a String that will be used to reference each individual row of the table. The collection usually comes from the controller class, such as in the example for this recipe. The legal data types for the value attribute are Array, DataModel, List, and Result. The var attribute is used in each column to reference a specific field in an object for the corresponding row.

Table 3-6. *DataTable Attributes*

Attribute	Description
id	ID for the component
border	An integer indicating border thickness; 0 is default
bgcolor	Background color of the table
cellpadding	Padding between the cell wall and its contents
cellspacing	Spacing within the cells
width	Overall width of the table, specified in pixels or percentages
first	The first entry in the collection to display
rows	Total number of rows to display
styleClass, captionClass, headerClass, footerClass, rowClasses, columnClasses	CSS attributes
rendered	Boolean value indicating whether the component will be rendered

The h:dataTable can contain any number of columns, and each is specified within the h:dataTable component in the Jakarta Server Faces view. The h:column nested element encloses the output for each column. A column can contain just about any valid component or HTML, even embedded dataTables. An h:column normally does not have any attributes specified, but it always contains an expression or hard-coded value for display:

```
<h:column>my column value</h:column>
```

or

```
<h:column>#{myTable.myColValue}</h:column>
```

Normally, columns in an HTML table contain headers. You can add headers to the h:dataTable or individual columns by embedding an f:facet element within the h:dataTable and outside of the column specifications or within each h:column by specifying the name attribute as header. The f:facet element can also specify a caption for the name attribute in order to add a caption to the table. The following excerpt from the example demonstrates an h:dataTable that includes each of these features:

```
<h:dataTable id="authorTable" border="1"
                value="#{authorTableController.authorList}"
                styleClass="authorTable"
                rowClasses="authorTableOdd, authorTableEven"
                var="author">
    <f:facet name="header">
        Java EE to Jakarta EE 10 Recipes Authors
    </f:facet>
    <h:column>
        <h:outputText id="authorName" value="#{author.first} #{author.last}"/>
    </h:column>
</h:dataTable>
```

In the example, you can see that the h:dataTable value attribute is listed as #{authorTableController. authorList}, a list of Author objects declared in the controller class. The var attribute establishes a variable named author that refers to the current author who is being processed from the author list. The author variable can then be accessed from within each h:column, displaying the data associated with the current list element.

An important piece of the puzzle to help make tables easier to read and follow is the CSS that can be used to style the table. The h:dataTable supports various attributes that allow you to apply externally defined CSS classes to your table, specifically, the styleClass, captionClass, headerClass, footerClass, rowClasses, and columnClasses attributes. Each of them can contain a CSS class specification for formatting. The example demonstrates this feature.

3-13. Creating Page Templates

Problem

You want to make each of the Jakarta Server Faces views in your application follow the same structure. Moreover, you want to have the ability to reuse the same layout for each view.

Solution

Create a page template using the Facelets view definition language. Facelets ships as part of Jakarta Server Faces, and you can use it to create highly sophisticated layouts for your views in a proficient manner. The template demonstrated in this recipe will be used to define the standard layout for all pages within an application. The demo application for this chapter is for a bookstore website. The site will display a number of book titles on the left side of the screen, a header at the top, a footer at the bottom, and a main view in the middle. When a book title is clicked in the left menu, the middle view changes, displaying the list of authors for the selected book.

To create a template, you must first develop a new XHTML view file and then add the appropriate HTML/Jakarta Server Faces/XML markup to it. Content from other views will displace the ui:insert elements in the template once the template has been applied to one or more Jakarta Server Faces views. The following source is that of a template named /webapp/chapter03/layout/custom_template.xhtml; this is the template that will be used for all views in the application:

```
<html xmlns="http://www.w3.org/1999/xhtml"
      xmlns:ui="http://xmlns.jcp.org/jsf/facelets"
      xmlns:h="http://xmlns.jcp.org/jsf/html">
    <h:head>
        <meta http-equiv="Content-Type" content="text/html; charset=UTF-8" />
        <h:outputStylesheet library="css" name="default.css"/>
        <h:outputStylesheet library="css" name="cssLayout.css"/>
        <h:outputStylesheet library="css" name="styles.css"/>
        <title>#{faceletsAuthorController.storeName}</title>
    </h:head>
    <h:body>
        <div id="top">
            <h2>#{faceletsAuthorController.storeName}</h2>
        </div>
        <div>
            <div id="left">
                <h:form id="navForm">
```

```
            <h:commandLink action="#{faceletsAuthorController.
            populateJavaRecipesAuthorList}" >Jakarta EE Fundamentals </h:commandLink>
            <br/>
            <br/>
            <h:commandLink action="#{faceletsAuthorController.populateJakarta
            EERecipesAuthorList}">Jakarta EE 10 Recipes </h:commandLink>
        </h:form>
    </div>
    <div id="content" class="left_content">
        <ui:insert name="content">Content</ui:insert>
    </div>
</div>
<div id="bottom" style="position: absolute;width: 100%;bottom: 20px;">
    Written by Josh Juneau and Tarun Telang, Apress Author
</div>
    </h:body>
</html>
```

The template defines the overall structure for the application views. However, it uses a CSS style sheet to declare the formatting for each of the <div> elements within the template. The style sheet, entitled default. css, should be contained within a resources directory in the application so that it will be accessible to the views. Refer to Recipe 3-15 for more details on the resources directory.

■ **Note**   The CSS style sheets can be automatically generated for you if you're using the NetBeans IDE.

There are also a couple of Jakarta Expression Language expressions utilized within the template. The Jakarta Expression Language references a Jakarta Server Faces controller by the name of AuthorController, which is referenced by faceletsAuthorController. While the source for this class is very important for the overall application, you'll wait to look at that code until Recipe 3-15 since it does not play a role in the application template layout.

How It Works

To create a unified application experience, all of the views should be coherent in that they look similar and function in a uniform fashion. The idea of developing web page templates has been around for a number of years, but unfortunately many template implementations contain duplicate markup on every application page. While duplicating the same layout for every separate web page works, it creates a maintenance nightmare. What happens when there is a need to update a single link within the page header? Such a conundrum would cause a developer to visit and manually update every web page of an application if the template was duplicated on every page. The Facelets view definition language provides a robust solution for the development of view templates, and it is one of the major bonuses of working with the Jakarta Server Faces technology.

Facelets provide the ability for a single template to be applied to one or more views within an application. This means a developer can create one view that constructs the header, footer, and other portions of the template, and then this view can be applied to any number of other views that are responsible for containing the main view content. This technique mitigates issues such as changing a single link within the page header, because now the template can be updated with the new link, and every other view within the application will automatically reflect the change.

To create a template using Facelets, create an XHTML view, declare the required namespaces, and then add HTML, Jakarta Server Faces, and Facelets tags accordingly to design the layout you desire. The template can be thought of as an "outer shell" for a web view, in that it can contain any number of other views within it. Likewise, any number of Jakarta Server Faces views can have the same template applied, so the overall look and feel of the application will remain constant. Figure 3-19 provides a visual demonstrating the concept of an application template.

Figure 3-19. *Visual representation of a Facelets template and client*

You may have noticed from the view listing in the solution to this recipe that there are some tags toting the `ui:` prefix. Those are the Facelets tags that are responsible for controlling the view layout. To utilize these Facelets tags, you'll need to declare the XML namespace for the Facelets tag library in the `<html>` element in the template. Note that the XML namespace for the standard Jakarta Server Faces tag libraries is also specified here:

```
<html xmlns="http://www.w3.org/1999/xhtml"
      xmlns:ui="http://xmlns.jcp.org/jsf/facelets"
      xmlns:h="http://xmlns.jcp.org/jsf/html">
...
```

■ **Note** The Facelets template must include the `<html>`, `<head>` or `<h:head>`, and `<body>` or `<h:body>` elements because they define the overall layout for each view that uses it. Each view that uses a Facelets template is known as a `composition`. One template can be used by multiple compositions or views. In actuality, everything outside of the `<ui:composition>` opening and closing tags in a composition is ignored. You'll learn more about that in the next recipe!

Facelets contain several special tags that can be used to help control page flow and layout. Table 3-7 in Recipe 3-15 lists the Facelets tags that are useful for controlling page flow and layout. The only Facelets tag that is used within the template for this recipe example is `ui:insert`. The `ui:insert` tag contains a name attribute, which is set to the name of the corresponding `ui:define` element that will be included in the view. Looking at the source for this recipe, you can see the following `ui:insert` tag:

```
<ui:insert name="content">Content</ui:insert>
```

If a view that uses the template, a.k.a. the template client, specifies a `ui:define` tag with the same name as the `ui:insert` name, then any content that is placed between the opening and closing `ui:define` tags will be inserted into the view in that location. However, if the template client does not contain a `ui:define` tag with the same name as the `ui:insert` tag, the content between the opening and closing `ui:insert` tags in the template will be displayed.

Templates can be created via an IDE, such as NetBeans, to provide a more visual representation of the layout you are trying to achieve. To create a Facelets template from within NetBeans, right-click the project folder into which you want to place the template and select New ➤ Other from the contextual menu to open the New File window. Once that's open, select JavaServer Faces from the Category menu and then Facelets Template from within the file types, as shown in Figure 3-20.

Figure 3-20. Creating a Facelets template from within NetBeans

After you've selected the Facelets Template file type, click the Next button to open the New Facelets Template window (see Figure 3-21). This window allows you to select the overall layout that you want to compose for your application views, as well as choose the location and name for the template.

Figure 3-21. *New Facelets Template window in NetBeans*

After you've selected the layout of your choice and filled in the other options, the template will be opened within the NetBeans code editor, and you can begin to apply the template to Jakarta Server Faces view clients (see Recipe 3-15). Using a wizard such as the one offered by NetBeans can help since you can choose a visual representation of the template at creation time.

In summary, a Facelets template consists of HTML and Jakarta Server Faces markup, and it is used to define a page layout. Sections of the template can specify where page content will be displayed through the ui:insert tag. Any areas in the template that contain a ui:insert tag can have content inserted into them from a template client.

3-14. Applying Templates

Problem

You have created a template for use within your Jakarta Server Faces web views, and you want to apply it to the views of your application.

Solution

Use the `ui:composition` tag in each view that will utilize the template. The `ui:composition` tag should be used to invoke the template, and `ui:define` tags should be placed where content should be inserted. The following listings demonstrate how Facelets templates are applied to various views.

View #1: recipe03_14a.xhtml

`recipe03_14a.xhtml` is the markup for a view within the bookstore application that is used to display the authors for the *Java EE to Jakarta EE 10 Recipes* book. The template is applied to the view, and individual `ui:define` tags are used in the view to specify the content that should be inserted into the page/view:

```
<html xmlns="http://www.w3.org/1999/xhtml"
      xmlns:ui="http://xmlns.jcp.org/jsf/facelets"
      xmlns:f="http://xmlns.jcp.org/jsf/core"
      xmlns:h="http://xmlns.jcp.org/jsf/html">
    <body>
        <ui:composition template="./layout/custom_template.xhtml">
            <ui:define name="top"/>
            <ui:define name="left"/>
            <ui:define name="content">
                <h:form id="componentForm">
                    <h1>Author List for Java EE to Jakarta EE 10 Recipes</h1>
                    <p>
                        Below is the list of authors. Click on the author's last name for
                        more information regarding the author.
                    </p>
                    <h:graphicImage id="javarecipes" style="width: 100px; height: 120px"
                    library="image" name="java9recipes.png"/>
                    <br/><br/>
                    <h:dataTable id="authorTable" border="1" value="#{faceletsAuthor
                    Controller.authorList}"
                                 var="author">
                        <f:facet name="header">
                            Java EE to Jakarta EE 10 Recipes Authors
                        </f:facet>
                        <h:column>
                            <h:commandLink id="authorName" action="#{faceletsAuthorControll
                            er.displayAuthor(author.last)}"
                                           value="#{author.first} #{author.last}"/>
                        </h:column>
                    </h:dataTable>
                </h:form>
            </ui:define>
        </ui:define>
```

```
        <ui:define name="bottom">bottom </ui:define>
    </ui:composition>
  </body>
</html>
```

View #2: recipe03_14b.xhtml

The following is the excerpt from the recipe03_14b.xhtml file, which contains the sources for the second view within the bookstore application. It is used to list the authors for the *Java EE to Jakarta EE 10 Recipes* book. The code within this file is mostly the same as the recipe03_15a excerpt:

...

```
            <h:form id="componentForm">
                <h1>Author List for Java EE to Jakarta EE 10 Recipes</h1>
                <p>
                    Below is the list of authors. Click on the author's last name for
                    more information regarding the author.
                </p>
                <h:graphicImage id="akartaee10recipes" library="image" style="width:
                100px; height: 120px" name="jakartaee10recipes.png"/>
                <br/><br/>
                <h:dataTable id="authorTable" border="1" value="#{faceletsAuthor
                Controller.authorList}"
                            var="author">
                <f:facet name="header">
                    Java EE to Jakarta EE 10 Recipes Authors
                </f:facet>
                <h:column>
                    <h:commandLink id="authorName" action="#{faceletsAuthor
                    Controller.displayAuthor(author.last)}"
                                value="#{author.first} #{author.last}"/>
                </h:column>
                </h:dataTable>
```

...

View #3: recipe03_14c.xhtml

Recipe03_14c.xhtml contains the sources for another view listing that is part of the bookstore application. This view is responsible for displaying the individual author detail. Again, the template is applied to this page:

```
<html xmlns="http://www.w3.org/1999/xhtml"
    xmlns:f="http://xmlns.jcp.org/jsf/core"
    xmlns:ui="http://xmlns.jcp.org/jsf/facelets"
    xmlns:h="http://xmlns.jcp.org/jsf/html">
    <h:head>
        <title>Recipe 3-14: Facelets Page Template</title>
    </h:head>
    <h:body>
```

```
    <ui:composition template="./layout/custom_template.xhtml">
        <ui:define name="top">
        </ui:define>
        <ui:define name="left">
        </ui:define>
        <ui:define name="content">
            <h:form id="componentForm">
                <h1>#{faceletsAuthorController.current.first}
                #{faceletsAuthorController.current.last}</h1>
                <p>
                    #{faceletsAuthorController.current.bio}
                </p>
            </h:form>
        </ui:define>
        <ui:define name="bottom">
            bottom
        </ui:define>
    </ui:composition>
</h:body>
</html>
```

Managed Bean Controller: AuthorController

Of course, all the business logic and navigation is occurring from within a Jakarta Server Faces controller class. AuthorController is the bean that handles all the logic for the bookstore application. Note that the @Named annotation specifies a String value of faceletsAuthorController, which is used to reference the bean from within the views:

```
package org.jakartaeerecipe.chapter03.recipe03_14;

import java.io.Serializable;
import java.util.*;
import jakarta.annotation.PostConstruct;
import jakarta.enterprise.context.SessionScoped;
import jakarta.inject.Named;

@Named(value = "faceletsAuthorController")
@SessionScoped
public class AuthorController implements Serializable {
    private List<Author> authorBookList;
    private List<Author> completeAuthorList;
    private List<Author> authorList;
    private String storeName = "Acme Bookstore";

    private Author current;
    private String authorLast;

    /**
     * Methods that are annotated with @PostConstruct are invoked when the
     * controller class is created.
     */
```

```
@PostConstruct
public void init(){
    populateJavaRecipesAuthorList();
}
public String populateJakartaFundamentalsAuthorList() {
    authorList = null;
    authorList = new ArrayList<>();
    authorList.add(new Author("Tarun", "Telang", telangBio));
    return "recipe03_14a";
}
public String populateJakarta EERecipesAuthorList() {
    System.out.println("initializing authors list");
    authorList = new ArrayList<>();
    authorList.add(new Author("Josh", "Juneau", juneauBio));
    authorList.add(new Author("Tarun", "Telang", telangBio));
    return "recipe03_14b";
}
public String displayAuthor(String last) {
    for (Author author : authorList) {
        if (author.getLast().equals(last)) current = author
    }
    return "recipe03_14c";
}
// getters and setters
// ...

}
```

In the end, the overall application will look like Figure 3-22. To run the application from the sources, deploy the WAR file distribution to your application server, and then load the following URL into your browser: http://your-server:port_number/Jakarta EERecipes/faces/chapter03/chapter03_14a.xhtml.

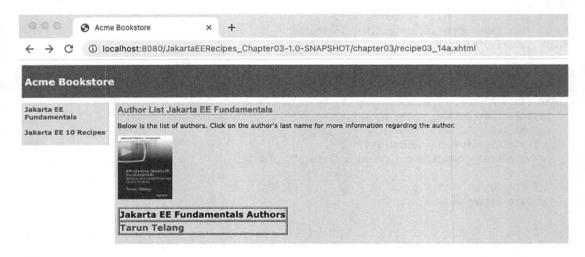

Figure 3-22. *Application using the Facelets template*

How It Works

Applying a Facelets template to individual views in a Jakarta Server Faces application is quite easy. Views that use a template are known as *template clients*. As mentioned in Recipe 3-14, a view template can specify individual ui:insert tags, along with the name attribute, in any location on the template where view content could be inserted. The name attribute within the ui:insert tag will pair up with the name attribute within the ui:define tag in the template client in order to determine what content is inserted.

▧ **Note** As noted in Recipe 3-14, each view that uses a Facelets template can be referred to as a composition. It can also be referred to as a `template client`. It is important to note that a template client, or composition, contains an opening and closing `<ui:composition>` tag. Everything outside of those tags is actually ignored at rendering time because the template body is used instead. You can also omit the `<html>` tags within a template client and just open and close the view using the `<ui:composition>` tags instead. See the "Opening/Closing Template Clients with <ui:composition>" sidebar for an example.

OPENING/CLOSING TEMPLATE CLIENTS WITH <UI:COMPOSITION>

It is common to see template client views using opening and closing `<html>` tags, as demonstrated with the example views in the solution to this recipe. However, since everything outside of the `<ui:composition>` tags is ignored at rendering time, you can omit those tags completely. It is sometimes useful to open and close a template client with the `<ui:composition>` tag. However, some page editors will be unable to work with the code or errors will be displayed because the view does not include the `<html>` element at its root. Here's an example of using `<ui:composition>` as the opening and closing elements of a template client:

```
<ui:composition xmlns="http://www.w3.org/1999/xhtml"
      xmlns:ui="http://xmlns.jcp.org/jsf/facelets"
      xmlns:f="http://xmlns.jcp.org/jsf/core"
      xmlns:h=http://xmlns.jcp.org/jsf/html
      template="./layout/custom_template.xhtml">
<<same as code per the view samples in the solution to this recipe>>
  </ui:composition>
```

Use the technique that suits your application the best! Remember, Jakarta Server Faces and Facelets will treat each view the same, and you can save a few lines of code specifying `<ui:composition>` as the root.

Applying Templates

A template can be applied to a view by specifying it within the template attribute within the view's ui:composition tag. For instance, all the views in this example specify the same template, as you can see in the following excerpt:

```
<ui:composition template="./layout/custom_template.xhtml">
```

The name of the template in the example is `custom_template.xhtml`, and the path to the template is `./layout/`. The `ui:composition` tag should encapsulate all other markup in a Facelets view. All views that are to use the template must specify the `ui:composition` tag. A number of other useful Facelets template tags come along with Facelets, as described in Table 3-7.

Table 3-7. *Facelets Page Control and Template Tags*

Tag	Description
ui:component	Defines a template component and specifies a file name for the component
ui:composition	Defines a page composition and encapsulates all other Jakarta Server Faces markup
ui:debug	Creates a debug component, which captures debugging information, namely, the state of the component tree and the scoped variables in the application, when the component is rendered
ui:define	Defines content that is inserted into a page by a template
ui:decorate	Decorates pieces of a page
ui:fragment	Defines a template fragment, much like ui:component, except that all content outside of a tag is not disregarded
ui:include	Allows another XHTML page to be encapsulated and reused within a view
ui:insert	Inserts content into a template
ui:param	Passes parameters to an included file or template
ui:repeat	Iterates over a collection of data
ui:remove	Removes content from a page

The `ui:define` tag encloses content that will be inserted into the template at the location of the template's `ui:insert` tags. The `ui:define` tag is matched to a template's `ui:insert` tag based on the value of the name attribute that is common to each tag. As you can see from the first view listing in this example, the first `ui:define` tag specifies top for the name attribute, and this will correspond to the template `ui:insert` tag with a name attribute equal to top. But the template does not specify such a tag! That is okay; there does not have to be a one-to-one match between the `ui:define` and `ui:insert` tags. A view can specify any number of `ui:define` tags, and if they do not correspond to any of the `ui:insert` tags in the template, then they are ignored. Likewise, a template can specify any number of `ui:insert` tags, and if they do not correspond to a `ui:define` tag in the template client view, then the content that is defined in the template in that location will be displayed.

Looking at the same view, another `ui:define` tag contains a name attribute value equal to content, and this tag does correspond with a `ui:insert` tag in the template that also has a name attribute value of content. The following excerpt is taken from the template, and it shows the `ui:insert` tag that corresponds to the view's `ui:define` tag with the same name attribute. You can see the full listing for the template in Recipe 3-14.

```
<div id="content" class="left_content">
        <ui:insert name="content">Content</ui:insert>
</div>
```

As you can see, it can be very powerful to define a view template that can be applied to several views in an application. Facelets templating provides a very powerful solution for defining such a template, allowing for a consistent page layout and reusable page code.

3-15. Adding Resources into the Mix

Problem

You want to include resources, such as CSS, images, and JavaScript code, within your views that are accessible for use from every view within your application. For instance, rather than hard-coding a URL to an image, you want to reference the image location and have the application dynamically create the URL to the image location at runtime.

Solution

Create a resource directory and, optionally, subfolders within the resources directory to contain the resources that your application will utilize. Any CSS files, images, and so on, that are placed within subdirectories in the resources folder can be referenced within a Jakarta Server Faces view via a Jakarta Server Faces component's library attribute, rather than specifying the full path to the resource. In the following example, a cascading style sheet is used to style the table of authors within the application. For this recipe, you will use the styles.css sheet that was applied to the h:dataTable in an earlier recipe. The style sheet declaration will reside in the custom_template.xhtml template, and you will use an h:outputStylesheet component rather than a <link> tag. As a matter of fact, all of the <link> tags will be removed and replaced with h:outputStylesheet components to take advantage of the resources folder. The directory structure should look like Figure 3-23 when set up correctly.

Figure 3-23. *Utilizing the resources directory*

The following listing is the updated custom_template.xhtml, because it now utilizes the h:outputStylesheet component rather than the <link> tag. Note that the library attribute is specified as css.

```
<html xmlns="http://www.w3.org/1999/xhtml"
      xmlns:ui="http://xmlns.jcp.org/jsf/facelets"
      xmlns:f="http://xmlns.jcp.org/jsf/core"
      xmlns:h="http://xmlns.jcp.org/jsf/html">
```

```
<body>
    <ui:composition template="./layout/custom_template.xhtml">
        <ui:define name="content">
            <h:form id="componentForm">
                <h1>Author List for Jakarta EE Fundamentals</h1>
                <p>
                    Below is the list of authors.  Click on the author's last name
                    for more information regarding the author.
                </p>
                <h:graphicImage id="javarecipes"
                                library="image" style="width: 100px; height: 120px"
                                name="java9recipes.png"/>
                <br/>
                <h:dataTable id="authorTable" border="1" value="#{faceletsAuthorControl
                ler.authorList}"
                                styleClass="authorTable"
                                rowClasses="authorTableOdd, authorTableEven"
                                var="author">
                    <f:facet name="header">
                        Java 9 Recipes Authors
                    </f:facet>
                    <h:column>
                        <h:commandLink id="authorName" action="#{faceletsAuthorControll
                        er.displayAuthor(author.last)}"
                                        value="#{author.first} #{author.last}"/>
                    </h:column>
                </h:dataTable>
                <br/>
                <br/>
            </h:form>
        </ui:define>
    </ui:composition>
</body>
</html>
```

The h:dataTable component that is used to list the authors within the views of the Acme Bookstore application can now use the styles that are listed in styles.css. The following excerpt from the XHTML document named recipe03_16.xhtml demonstrates the h:dataTable component with the styles applied:

```
<h:dataTable id="authorTable" border="1" value="#{faceletsAuthorController.authorList}"
                                styleClass="authorTable"
                                rowClasses="authorTableOdd, authorTableEven"
                                var="author">
    <f:facet name="header">
        Java 9 Recipes Authors
    </f:facet>
    <h:column>
        <h:commandLink id="authorName"
                action="#{faceletsAuthorController.displayAuthor(author.last)}"
                 value="#{author.first} #{author.last}"/>
    </h:column>
</h:dataTable>
```

The table should now look like Figure 3-24 when rendered on a page.

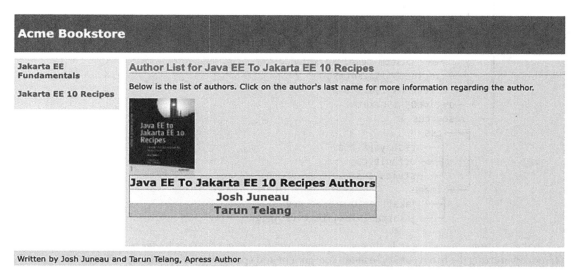

Figure 3-24. *Author table with styles applied*

How It Works

It is easy to add a resource to a Jakarta Server Faces application because there is no need to worry about referring to a static path when declaring the resources. Since the release of Jakarta Server Faces 2.0, the resources folder can be used to list subfolders, also known as *libraries*, into which the resources can be placed. The Jakarta Server Faces components that can use resources now have the library attribute baked into them. This allows a specific library to be specified for such components so that the component will know where to find the resources that it requires.

To use the new resources folder, create a folder at the root of an application's web directory and name it resources. That resources folder can then contain subfolders, which will become the libraries that can be utilized within the Jakarta Server Faces components. For instance, subfolders can be named css and images, and then those names can be specified for the library attribute of Jakarta Server Faces components that utilize such resources. The following is the project structure for your reference:

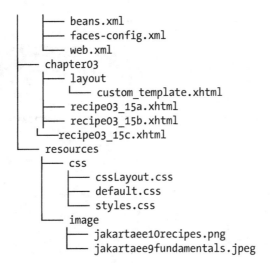

```
                        ├──── beans.xml
                        ├──── faces-config.xml
                        └──── web.xml
            ├──── chapter03
            │       ├──── layout
            │       │       └──── custom_template.xhtml
            │       ├──── recipe03_15a.xhtml
            │       ├──── recipe03_15b.xhtml
            │       └──recipe03_15c.xhtml
            └──── resources
                    ├──── css
                    │       ├──── cssLayout.css
                    │       ├──── default.css
                    │       └──── styles.css
                    └──── image
                            ├──── jakartaee10recipes.png
                            └──── jakartaee9fundamentals.jpeg
```

In the example, cascading style sheets are placed into the resources/css folder, and then they are referenced utilizing the h:outputStylesheet component and specifying the css library as follows:

```
<h:outputStylesheet library="css" name="default.css"/>
```

Other resources can be placed in such libraries. The h:graphicImage component also contains the library attribute, so the images for the books can be moved into a folder named resources/image, and then the h:graphicImage tag can reference the image as such:

```
<h:graphicImage id="jakartaee10recipes"
                            library="image" style="width: 100px; height: 120px"
                            name=" jakartaee10recipes.jpeg"/>
```

It has always been a challenge referencing resource files from the pages of a web application. To do so, a developer needs to know the exact path to the resource, and sometimes the path can be broken if folder names are changed or if the application is deployed in a different server environment. The use of the resources folder in Jakarta Server Faces 2.0 along with the new library attribute has greatly reduced the complexity of managing such resources.

CHAPTER 4

▦ ▦ ▦

Advanced Jakarta Server Faces

The Jakarta Server Faces (formerly JSF or Java Server Faces) framework allows developers to build applications utilizing a series of views, each of which has a series of components. The framework is a puzzle in that each component must fit into its proper position for the whole thing to work smoothly. Sprinkled into those pieces of the puzzle are advanced capabilities that are used to create a seamless user interface experience.

Components are just one piece of the puzzle. Components are the building blocks that make up Jakarta Server Faces views. One of the strengths of using the Jakarta Server Faces framework is the abundance of components that are available for use within views. Components are tags that can be used in XHTML views. Components are like standard HTML tags; they include a set of attributes, an opening and closing tag, and components that may often be included within other components. Components can also be written in Java code, and their tags can be bound to Java code that resides in a Jakarta Server Faces managed bean (a.k.a. controller class). The Jakarta Server Faces framework comes with several standard components.

Another important piece of the Jakarta Server Faces user interface puzzle is seamless integration with the backend business logic. A task that can be run in the background, independent of other running tasks, is known as an asynchronous task. JavaScript is the most popular modern browser language that is used to implement asynchronous tasking in web applications. Ajax is a set of technologies that allows you to perform asynchronous tasks using JavaScript in the background, sending responses from the client browser to the server and then sending a response back to the client. That response is used to update the page's Document Object Model (DOM). Enhancing an application to make use of such asynchronous requests and responses can greatly improve the overall user experience. The Jakarta Server Faces framework allows developers to create rich user experiences via the use of technologies such as Ajax and HTML5. Much of the implementation detail behind these technologies can be abstracted away from the developer using Jakarta Server Faces components. As such, the developer needs to worry only about how to use a Jakarta Server Faces component tag and relate it to a server-side property.

This chapter delves into using Ajax with the Jakarta Server Faces web framework. Along the way, you will learn how to spruce up applications and make the user interface richer and more user-friendly so that it behaves more like a desktop application. You'll also learn how to listen to different component phases and system events, allowing further customization of application functionality.

This chapter goes through the fundamental components in depth, with recipes that will allow you to put them to use right away in your applications. This chapter primarily covers the Jakarta Server Faces standard component library. Each recipe in this chapter builds on one another from beginning to end. At the conclusion of this chapter, you will have a complete full-featured newsletter page for the Acme Bookstore.

The following section gives a quick overview of the Jakarta Server Faces standard components and associated common component tags, which will come in handy as you go through the recipes.

4-1. Component and Tag Primer

Table 4-1 lists the components that are available with the Jakarta Server Faces framework.

Table 4-1. *Jakarta Server Faces HTML Components*

Component	Tag	Description
UIColumn	h:column	Represents a column of data in the dataTable component
UICommand	h:commandButton	Submits a form
	h:commandLink	Links pages or actions
	h:commandScript	Provides ability to call an arbitrary server-side method via Ajax from a Jakarta Server Faces view
UIData	h:dataTable	Represents a table used for iterating over collections of data
UIForm	h:form	Represents an input form
UIGraphic	h:graphicImage	Displays an image
UIInput	h:inputHidden	Includes a hidden variable in a form
	h:inputSecret	Allows text entry without displaying the actual text
	h:inputText	Allows text entry
	h:inputTextarea	Allows multiline text entry
UIOutcomeTarget	h:link	Links to another page or location
UIMessage	h:message	Displays a localized message
UIMessages	h:messages	Displays localized messages
UIOutput	h:outputFormat	Displays a formatted localized message
	h:outputLabel	Displays a label for a specified field
	h:outputLink	Links to another page or location
UIPanel	h:panelGrid	Displays a table
	h:panelGroup	Groups components
UISelectBoolean	h:selectBooleanCheckbox	Displays a boolean choice
UISelectItem	h:selectItem	Represents one item in a list of items for selection
UISelectItems	h:selectItems	Represents a list of items for selection
UISelectMany	h:selectManyCheckbox	Displays a group of check boxes that allow multiple user choices
	h:selectManyListbox	Allows a user to select multiple items from a list
	h:selectManyMenu	Allows a user to select multiple items from a drop-down menu
UISelectOne	h:selectOneListbox	Allows a user to select a single item from a list
	h:selectOneMenu	Allows a user to select a single item from a drop-down menu
	h:selectOneRadio	Allows a user to select one item from a set

Jakarta Server Faces provides several core tags that can be used to provide more functionality for the components. For example, these tags can be embedded inside Jakarta Server Faces component tags and specify rules that can be used to convert the values that are displayed or used as input for the component. Other uses of the core tags are to provide a list of options for a select component, validate input, and provide action and event listeners. Table 4-2 describes the Jakarta Server Faces core tags.

Table 4-2. *Jakarta Server Faces Core Tags*

Tag	Function
f:actionListener	Registers an action listener method with a component
f:phaseListener	Registers a PhaseListener to a page
f:setPropertyActionListener	Registers a special form submittal action listener
f:valueChangeListener	Registers a value change listener with a component
f:converter	Registers an arbitrary converter with a component
f:convertDateTime	Registers a DateTimeConverter instance with a component
f:convertNumber	Registers a NumberConverter with a component
f:facet	Adds a nested component to particular enclosing parents
f:metadata	Registers a particular facet with a parent component
f:selectItem	Encapsulates one item in a list
f:selectItems	Encapsulates all items of a list
f:websocket	Provides ability to receive messages into a view via WebSockets
f:validateDoubleRange	Registers a DoubleRangeValidator with a component
f:validateLength	Registers a LengthValidator with a component
f:validateLongRange	Registers a LongRangeValidator with a component
f:validator	Registers a custom validator with a component
f:validateRegex	Registers a RegExValidator with a component (JSF 2.0)
f:validateBean	Delegates validation of a local value to a BeanValidator (JSF 2.0)
f:validateWholeBean	Delegates validation of an entire bean or class
f:validateRequired	Ensures that a value is present in a parent component

■ **Note**   The common sources and the completed classes to run the application for Chapter 4 are contained in the org.jakartaeerecipe.chapter04 package, and one or more recipes throughout this chapter will utilize classes contained in that package.

Common Component Tag Attributes

Each standard Jakarta Server Faces component tag contains a set of attributes that must be specified to uniquely identify it from the others, register the component to a managed bean, and so on. There is a set of attributes that are common across each component tag, and this section lists those attributes, along with a description of each. *All attributes besides* id *can be specified using Jakarta Expression Language:*

- `binding`: A managed bean property can be specified for this attribute, and it can be used to bind the tag to a component instance within a managed bean. Doing so allows you to programmatically control the component from within the managed bean.

- `id`: This attribute can be set to uniquely identify the component. If you do not specify a value for the `id` attribute, then Jakarta Server Faces will automatically generate one. Each component within a view must have a unique `id` attribute, or an error will be generated when the page is rendered. I recommend you manually specify a value for the id attribute on each component tag, because then it will be easy to statically reference the tag from a scripting language or a managed bean if needed. If you let Jakarta Server Faces automatically populate this attribute, it may be different each time, and you will never be able to statically reference the tag from a scripting language.

- `immediate`: This attribute can be set to true for input and command components in order to force the processing of validations, conversions, and events when the request parameter values are applied.

- `rendered`: The rendered attribute can be used to specify whether the component should be rendered. This attribute is typically specified in Jakarta Expression Language that is bound to a managed bean property yielding a boolean result. The expression must be an `rvalue` expression, meaning that it is read-only and cannot set a value.

- `style`: This attribute allows a CSS style to be applied to the component. The specified style will be applied when the component is rendered as output.

- `styleClass`: This attribute allows a CSS style class to be applied to the component. The specified style will be applied when the component is rendered as output.

- `value`: This attribute identifies the value of a given component. For some components, the `value` attribute is used to bind the tag to a managed bean property. In this case, the value specified for the component will be read from, or set within, the managed bean property. Other components, such as the `commandButton` component, use the `value` attribute to specify a label for the given component.

Common JavaScript Component Tags

Table 4-3 lists several attributes that are shared by many of the components, which enable JavaScript functionality to interact with the component.

Table 4-3. *Common Component Attributes*

Attribute	Description
onblur	JavaScript code that should be executed when the component loses focus
onchange	JavaScript code that should be executed when the component loses focus and the value changes
ondblclick	JavaScript code that should be executed when the component has been clicked twice
onfocus	JavaScript code that should be executed when the component gains focus
onkeydown	JavaScript code that should be executed when the user presses a key down and the component is in focus
onkeypress	JavaScript code that should be executed when the user presses a key and the component is in focus
onkeyup	JavaScript code that should be executed when the key press is completed and the component is in focus
onmousedown	JavaScript code that should be executed when the user clicks the mouse button and the component is in focus
onmouseout	JavaScript code that should be executed when the user moves the mouse away from the component
onmouseover	JavaScript code that should be executed when the user moves the mouse onto the component
onmousemove	JavaScript code that should be executed when the user moves the mouse within the component
onmouseup	JavaScript code that should be executed when mouse button click is completed and the component is in focus
onselect	JavaScript code that should be executed when the component is selected by the user

Binding Components to Properties

All Jakarta Server Faces components can be bound to managed bean properties. Do so by declaring a property for the type of component you want to bind within the managed bean and then by referencing that property using the component's binding attribute. For instance, the following dataTable component is bound to a managed bean property and then manipulated from within the bean.

In the view:

```
<h:dataTable id="myTable" binding="#{myBean.myTable}" value="#{myBean.myTableCollection}"/>
```

In the bean:

```
// Provide getter and setter methods for this property
private jakarta.faces.component.UIData myTable;
...
myTable.setRendered(true);
...
```

179

Binding can prove to be very useful in some cases, especially when you need to manipulate the state of a component programmatically before re-rendering the view. For example, you may need to disable a button if the user has already submitted the form. Or, you may need to set the value of a text field based on the selection of a drop-down menu.

In both cases, binding would be the best way to achieve the desired result. With binding, you can programmatically manipulate the component tree before re-rendering the view.

Project Folder Structure for This Chapter

The source code containing recipes for this chapter is organized as per the following folder structure:

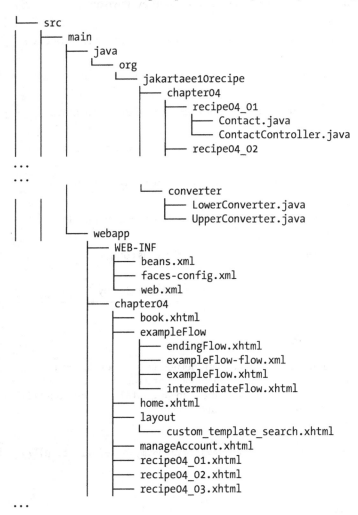

```
└── src
    ├── main
    │   ├── java
    │   │   └── org
    │   │       └── jakartaee10recipe
    │   │           ├── chapter04
    │   │               ├── recipe04_01
    │   │                   ├── Contact.java
    │   │                   └── ContactController.java
    │   │               ├── recipe04_02
...
...
    │   │                       └── converter
    │   │                           ├── LowerConverter.java
    │   │                           └── UpperConverter.java
    │   └── webapp
    │       ├── WEB-INF
    │       │   ├── beans.xml
    │       │   ├── faces-config.xml
    │       │   └── web.xml
    │       ├── chapter04
    │           ├── book.xhtml
    │           ├── exampleFlow
    │               ├── endingFlow.xhtml
    │               ├── exampleFlow-flow.xml
    │               ├── exampleFlow.xhtml
    │               └── intermediateFlow.xhtml
    │           ├── home.xhtml
    │           ├── layout
    │               └── custom_template_search.xhtml
    │           ├── manageAccount.xhtml
    │           ├── recipe04_01.xhtml
    │           ├── recipe04_02.xhtml
    │           ├── recipe04_03.xhtml
...
...
```

```
└── resources
    ├── css
    │   ├── cssLayout.css
    │   ├── default.css
    │   └── styles.css
    └── image
        ├── ajaxloading.png
        ├── book.png
        ├── jakartaeefundamentals.jpeg
```

The controller classes or backing beans are placed with their corresponding package using the following convention within the src/main/java/<package> folder structure:

`org.jakartaee10recipe.chapter04.recipe04_<xx>`

All the xhtml files are placed within the /webapp/chapter04/ folder they are named using the convention:

`recipe04_<xx>.xhtml`

Here, <xx> can be replaced by the recipe number such as 01, making the file name recipe04_01.xhtml. The \webapp\resources folder contains assets like stylesheets and images.

4-2. Creating an Input Form

Problem

You want to add input fields to a form within your application.

Solution

Create an input form by enclosing child input components within a parent form component. There are four Jakarta Server Faces components that will allow for text entry as input. Those components are inputText, inputSecret, inputHidden, and inputTextarea. Any or all these components can be placed within a form component in order to create an input form that accepts text entry.

In the example for this recipe, you will create an input form that will be used to sign up for the Acme Bookstore newsletter. The users will be able to enter their first and last names, an email address, a password, and a short description of their interests.

The View: recipe04_01.xhtml

The following code is for the view recipe04_01.xhtml, which constructs the layout for the input form:

```
<html xmlns="http://www.w3.org/1999/xhtml"
      xmlns:h="http://xmlns.jcp.org/jsf/html"
      xmlns:ui="http://xmlns.jcp.org/jsf/facelets">
    <f:view>
        <h:messages globalOnly="true"  errorStyle="color: red" infoStyle="color: green"/>
        <h:form id="contactForm">
```

```
<h1>Subscribe to Newsletter</h1>
<p>Enter your information below to be added to the Acme Bookstore newsletter.
</p><br/>
<label for="first">First: </label>
<h:inputText id="first" size="40" value="#{contactController.current.
first}"/><br/><br/>
<label for="last">Last: </label>
<h:inputText id="last" size="40" value="#{contactController.current.
last}"/><br/><br/>
<label for="email">Email: </label>
<h:inputText id="email" size="40" value="#{contactController.current.
email}"/><br/><br/>
<label for="password">Enter a password for site access:</label>
<h:inputSecret id="password" size="40" value="#{contactController.current.
password}"/><br/><br/>
<label for="description">Enter your book interests</label>
<br/><br/>
<h:inputTextarea id="description" rows="5" cols="100" value="#{contactController.
current.description}"/>
<br/><br/>
<h:commandButton id="contactSubmit" action="#{contactController.subscribe}"
value="Save"/>
</h:form>
    </f:view>
</html>
```

───

■ **Note** As you can see from the example, HTML can be mixed together with Jakarta Server Faces component tags. An HTML label tag is used to specify a label for each input component in this recipe. In Recipe 4-3, you will learn about the Jakarta Server Faces component that is used to render a label.

To learn more about how the commandButton component works, see Recipe 4-2.

───

Managed Bean: Contact.java

Each view that contains an input form needs to have an associated managed bean, right? The name of the bean class is Contact:

```
package com.jakartaeerecipe.chapter04;

import java.io.Serializable;

public class Contact implements Serializable {

    private String first;
    private String last;
    private String password;
    private String description;
```

```
    private String email;

    public String getFirst() {  return first;  }

    public String getLast() {  return last;    }

    public String getPassword() {  return password; }

    public String getEmail() { return email;  }

    public String getDescription() { return description; }

    public void setFirst(String first) { this.first = first; }

    public void setLast(String last) { this.last = last; }

    public void setPassword(String password) { this.password = password; }

    public void setDescription(String description) { this.description = description; }

    public void setEmail(String email) { this.email = email; }
}
```

Managed Bean Controller: ContactController.java

The name of the managed bean controller class is ContactController. In this case, it is **RequestScoped**. An excerpt from the listing for the ContactController class is as follows:

```
package com.jakartaeerecipe.chapter04;

import jakarta.enterprise.context.RequestScoped;
import jakarta.faces.application.FacesMessage;
import jakarta.faces.context.FacesContext;
import jakarta.inject.Named;

@RequestScoped
@Named(value = "contactController")
public class ContactController {

    private Contact current;

    /**
     * Obtain the current instance of the Contact object
     * @return Contact
     */
```

```java
    public Contact getCurrent(){
        if (current == null){
            current = new Contact();
        }
        return current;
    }

    /**
     * Adds a subscriber to the newsletter
     * @return String
     */
    public String subscribe(){
        // No implementation yet, will add to a database table in Chapter 7
        FacesMessage facesMsg = new FacesMessage(FacesMessage.SEVERITY_INFO,
                "Successfully Subscribed to Newsletter for " + getCurrent().
                getEmail(), null);
        FacesContext.getCurrentInstance().addMessage(null, facesMsg);
        return "SUBSCRIBE";
    }

    /**
     * Navigational method
     * @return String
     */
    public String add(){
        return "ADD_SUBSCRIBER";
    }
}
```

■ **Note** At this time, nothing happens when the Submit button is clicked other than a nice "Success" message being displayed on the screen. Later in the book, we will revisit the subscribe method and add the code for creating a record within an underlying database. The input screen should look like Figure 4-1 when rendered. The code can be executed by visiting the URL http://localhost:8080/JakartaEERecipes_ Chapter04-1.0-SNAPSHOT/chapter04/recipe04_01.xhtml in your browser.

Figure 4-1. *Jakarta Server Faces input form for subscribing to the Acme Bookstore newsletter*

How It Works

The Java Server Faces framework ships with a slew of standard components that can be utilized within Jakarta Server Faces views. There are four standard components that can be used for capturing text input: inputText, inputSecret, inputHidden, and inputTextarea. These component tags, as well as all the other standard Jakarta Server Faces component tags, share a common set of attributes and some attributes that are unique to each specific tag. To learn more about the common attributes, see the related section in the introduction to this chapter.

In this recipe, I go over the specifics for each of these input components. The h:view component is used to define the content of a view. It determines what will be displayed in your application and how that data should look. The form component, specified via the h:form tag, is used to create an input form within a Jakarta Server Faces view. Each component that is to be processed within the form should be enclosed between the opening and closing h:form tags. Each form typically contains at least one command component, such as a commandButton. A view can contain more than one form component, and only those components that are contained within the form will be processed when the form is submitted.

■ **Note** I recommend you always specify the `id` attribute for each component. Most importantly, specify the `id` attribute for the `form` component. If you do not specify the `id` attribute for a given Jakarta Server Faces component, then one will be automatically generated for you. The automatic generation of Jakarta Server Faces component `ids` prohibits the ability to statically reference a component from within a scripting language, such as JavaScript, or a managed bean. For instance, in the example for this recipe, the `form id` attribute is set to `contactForm`, and the first `inputText` component `id` is set to `first`. This allows you to reference the component statically by appending the `form id` to the component `id` from a scripting language or managed bean. In the case of the example, you'd reference the first component as `contactForm:first`.

Each of the input tags supports the list of attributes that is shown in Table 4-4, in addition to those already listed as common component attributes in the introduction to this chapter.

Table 4-4. *Input Component Tag Attributes*

Attribute	Description
converter	Allows a converter to be applied to the component's data
converterMessage	Specifies a message that will be displayed when a registered converter fails
dir	Specifies the direction of text displayed by the component (LTR *is used to indicate left-to-right, and* RTL *is used to indicate right-to-left)*
immediate	Flag indicating that, if this component is activated by the user, notifications should be delivered to interested listeners and actions immediately (i.e., during the Apply Request Values phase) rather than waiting until the Invoke Application phase
label	Specifies a name that can be used for component identification
lang	Allows a language code to be specified for the rendered markup
required	Accepts a boolean to indicate whether the user must enter a value for the given component
requiredMessage	Specifies an error message to be displayed if the user does not enter a value for a *required* component
validator	Allows a validator to be applied to the component
valueChangeListener	Allows a managed bean method to be bound for event handling purposes. The method will be called when there is a change made to the component

The `inputText` component is used to generate a single-line text box within a rendered page. The `inputText` component `value` attribute is most bound to a managed bean property so that the values of the property can be retrieved or set when a form is processed. In the recipe example, the first `inputText` component is bound to the managed bean property named `first`. The Jakarta Expression Language expression `#{contactController.current.first}` is specified for the component `value`, so if the managed bean's `first` property contains a value, then it will be displayed in the `inputText` component. Likewise, when the form is submitted, then any value that has been entered within the component will be saved within the `first` property in the managed bean.

The inputSecret component generates a single-line text box within a rendered page, and when text is entered into the component, then it is not displayed; rather, asterisks are displayed in place of each character typed. This component makes it possible for a user to enter private text, such as a password, without it being displayed on the screen for others to read. The inputSecret component works identically to the inputText component, other than hiding the text with asterisks. In the example, the value of the inputSecret component is bound to a managed bean property named password via the #{contactController.current. password} expression.

The inputTextarea component is used to generate a multiline text box within a rendered page. As such, this component has a couple of additional attributes that can be used to indicate how large the text area should be. The inputTextarea has the rows and cols attributes, which allow a developer to specify how many rows (height) and how many columns (wide) of space the component should take up on the page, respectively. Other than those two attributes, the inputTextarea component works in much the same manner as the inputText component. In the example, the value attribute of the inputTextarea component is specified as #{contactController.current.description}, so the description property will be populated with the contents of the component when the form is submitted.

The input component I have not yet discussed is the inputHidden component. This component is used to place a hidden input field into the form. It works in the same manner as the inputText component, except that it is not rendered on the page for the user to see. The value for an inputHidden component can be bound to a managed bean property in the same way as the other components. You can use such a component for passing a hidden token to and from a form.

Utilizing the Jakarta Server Faces standard input components, it is possible to bind values to managed bean properties using Jakarta Server Faces Jakarta Expression Language expressions. This makes it much easier for developers to submit values from an input form for processing. Rather than retrieving parameters from a page, assigning them to variables, and then processing, the Jakarta Server Faces framework takes care of that overhead for you. Although I have not covered the usage of all input component attributes within this recipe, I will cover more in the recipes that follow as I build upon the Acme Bookstore newsletter subscription page.

4-3. Invoking Actions from Within a Page

Problem

You want to trigger a server-side method to be invoked from a button or link on one of your application pages.

Solution

Utilize the commandButton or commandLink components within your view to invoke action methods within a managed bean controller. The command components allow for the user invocation of actions within managed beans. Command components bind buttons and links on a page directly to action methods, allowing developers to spend more time thinking about the development of the application and less time thinking about the Java servlet–processing life cycle.

In the example for this recipe, a button and a link are added to the newsletter page for the Acme Bookstore. The button that will be added to the page will be used to submit the input form for processing, and the link will allow users to log in to the application and manage their subscriptions and bookstore accounts.

■ **Note**   This recipe will not cover any authentication or security features; it focuses only on invoking actions within managed beans. For more information regarding authentication, see Chapter 15.

The View: manageAccount.xhtml

The following code is for the Manage Account view. This page is displayed when the user clicks the Manage Subscription link. The sources are for the file named manageAccount.xhtml:

```
<html xmlns="http://www.w3.org/1999/xhtml"
      xmlns:h="http://xmlns.jcp.org/jsf/html"
      xmlns:f="http://xmlns.jcp.org/jsf/core">
<f:view>
    <h:outputLabel value="Manage Accounts"/>
</f:view>
</html>
```

The View: recipe04_02.xhtml

Add the following code at the end of the newsletter subscription view for this new command component. The complete source is in the file named recipe04_02.xhtml.

```
...
    <h:commandLink  id="manageAccount" action="#{contactController.manage}" value="Manage
Subscription"/>
...
```

Managed Bean: Subscription.java

This managed bean contains the List implementation of Subscription; the following is the code for this class:

```
package com.jakartaeerecipe.chapter04;

import java.io.Serializable;
import java.util.*;

public class Subscription implements Serializable {
    private List<Contact> subscriptionList;

    Subscription() {
        subscriptionList = new ArrayList<>();
    }

    public List<Contact> getSubscriptionList() {
        return subscriptionList;
    }

    public void setSubscriptionList(List<Contact> subscriptionList) {
        this.subscriptionList = subscriptionList;
    }
}
```

Managed Bean Controller: ContactController.java

The managed bean that contains the action methods is named ContactController, which was created in Recipe 4-1. The following code excerpt is taken from the ContactController class, and it shows the updates that have been made to the methods for this recipe.

■ **Note** The complete implementation of ContactController resides in the org.jakartaeerecipe. chapter05 package.

```java
@RequestScoped
@Named(value= "contactController")
public class ContactController {
...
    private Subscription subscription;

  public Subscription getSubscription() {
        if (subscription == null) {
            subscription = new Subscription();
        }
        return subscription;
    }
...
    /**
     * Adds a subscriber to the newsletter
     * @return String
     */
    public String subscribe(){
        // Using a list implementation for now,
        // but will add to a database table in Chapter 7
        // Add the current contact to the subscription list
        subscription.getSubscriptionList().add(current);
        FacesMessage facesMsg = new FacesMessage(FacesMessage.SEVERITY_INFO,
                "Successfully Subscribed to Newsletter for " + getCurrent().
                getEmail(), null);
        FacesContext.getCurrentInstance().addMessage(null, facesMsg);
        return "SUBSCRIBE";
    }
...
    /**
     * This method will allow a user to navigate to the manageAccount view.
     * This method will be moved into another managed bean that focuses on
     * authentication later on.
     * @return
     */
    public String manage(){
        return "/chapter04/manageAccount.xhtml";
    }
...
```

When the view is rendered, the resulting page looks like Figure 4-2. The code can be executed by visiting the URL http://localhost:8080/JakartaEERecipes_Chapter04-1.0-SNAPSHOT/chapter04/recipe04_02.xhtml in your browser.

Figure 4-2. *Utilizing command components within a view*

How It Works

The command components make Jakarta Server Faces vastly different from using Jakarta Server Pages technology. In many of the other technologies, form actions are used to handle request parameters and perform any required business logic with them. With the Jakarta Server Faces command components, Java methods can be bound directly to a button or a link and invoked when the components are activated (button or link clicked). In the example for this recipe, both the commandButton and commandLink components are utilized. The commandButton component is used to submit the form request parameters for processing, and the commandLink component is bound to an action method that performs a redirect to another application page.

The command components have a handful of attributes that are of note. Those attributes, along with a description of each, are listed in Tables 4-5 and 4-6.

Table 4-5. *commandButton Component Additional Attributes*

Attribute	Description
action	Expression that specifies a managed bean action method that will be invoked when the user activates the component
actionListener	Expression that specifies a managed bean action method that will be notified when this component is activated. The action method should be public and accept an ActionEvent parameter, with a return type of void
class	CSS style class that can be applied to the component
dir	Direction indication for text (LTR, left-to-right; RTL, right-to-left)
disabled	A Boolean to indicate whether the component is disabled
image	Absolute or relative URL to an image that will be displayed on the button
immediate	Flag indicating that, if this component is activated by the user, notifications should be delivered to interested listeners and actions immediately (i.e., during the Apply Request Values phase) rather than waiting until the Invoke Application phase
label	Name for the component
lang	Code for the language used for generating the component markup
readonly	Boolean indicating whether the component is read-only
rendererType	Identifier of a renderer instance
tabindex	Index value indicating the number of Tab button presses it takes to bring the component into focus
title	Tooltip that will be displayed when the mouse hovers over the component
transient	Boolean indicating whether components should be included in the state of the component tree
type	Indicates the type of button to create. Values are submit (default), reset, and button

Table 4-6. *commandLink Component Additional Attributes*

Attribute	Description
action	EL that specifies a managed bean action method that will be invoked when the user activates the component
accessKey	Access key value that will transfer the focus to the component
cords	Position and shape of the hotspot on the screen
dir	Direction indication for text (LTR, left-to-right; RTL, right-to-left)
disabled	Specifies a boolean to indicate whether the component is disabled
hreflang	Language code of the resource designated by the hyperlink

(continued)

Table 4-6. (*continued*)

Attribute	Description
immediate	Flag indicating that, if this component is activated by the user, notifications should be delivered to interested listeners and actions immediately (i.e., during the Apply Request Values phase) rather than waiting until the Invoke Application phase
lang	Code for the language used for generating the component markup
rel	Relationship from the current document to the anchor specified by the hyperlink
rev	Reverse anchor specified by this hyperlink to the current document
shape	Shape of the hotspot on the screen
tabindex	Index value indicating the number of Tab button presses it takes to bring the component into focus
target	Name of a frame where the resource retrieved via the hyperlink will be displayed
title	Tooltip that will be displayed when the mouse hovers over the component
type	Indicates the type of button to create. Values are submit (default), reset, and button
charset	Character encoding of the resource designated by the hyperlink

The commandButton and commandLink components in the example to this recipe specify only a minimum number of attributes. That is, they both specify id, action, and value attributes. The id attribute is used to uniquely identify each of the components. The action attribute is set to the Jakarta Server Faces EL, which binds the components to their managed bean action methods. The commandButton component has an action attribute of #{contactController.subscribe}, which means that the ContactController class's subscribe method will be invoked when the button on the page is clicked. The commandLink has an action attribute of #{contactController.manage}, which means that the ContactController class's manage method will be invoked when the link is clicked. Each of the components also specifies a value attribute, which is set to the text that is displayed on the button or link when rendered.

As you can see, only a handful of the available attributes are used in the example. However, the components can be customized using the additional attributes that are available. For instance, an actionListener method can be specified, which will bind a managed bean method to the component, and that method will be invoked when the component is activated. JavaScript functions can be specified for each of the attributes beginning with the word on, providing the ability to produce client-side functionality.

Command components vastly changed the landscape of Jakarta EE web application development. They allow the incorporation of direct Java method access from within user pages and provide an easy means for processing request parameters.

4-4. Displaying Output

Problem

You want to display text from a managed bean property in your application pages.

Solution

Incorporate Jakarta Server Faces output components into your views. Output components are used to display static or dynamic text on a page, as well as the results of expression language arithmetic. The standard Jakarta Server Faces component library contains five components that render output: outputLabel, outputText, outputFormat, outputLink, and link. The Acme Bookstore utilizes each of these components in the bookstore newsletter application façade.

The View: recipe04_03.xhtml

In the following example, the newsletter subscription view has been rewritten to utilize some of the output components:

```
...
                <h:outputLabel for="first" value="First: "/>
                <h:inputText id="first" size="40" value="#{contactController.current.first}">
                    <f:validateRequired/>
                    <f:validateLength minimum="2" maximum="40"/>
                </h:inputText><br/><br/>
                <h:outputLabel for="last" value="Last: "/>
                <h:inputText id="last" size="40" value="#{contactController.current.last}">
                    <f:validateRequired/>
                     <f:validateLength minimum="2" maximum="40"/>
                </h:inputText><br/><br/>
                <h:outputLabel for="email" value="Email: "/>
                <h:inputText id="email" size="40" value="#{contactController.current.email}">
                        <f:validateRequired/>
                        <f:validateRegex pattern=""/>
                </h:inputText><br/>
                <h:outputLabel for="password" value="Enter a password for site access: "/>
                <h:inputSecret id="password" size="40" value="#{contactController.current.
                password}"/>
                    <f:validateRegex pattern=""/>
                </h:inputSecret>
                <br/><br/>
    <h:outputLabel  for="description" value="Enter your book interests"/>
    <br/>
    <h:inputTextarea id="description" rows="5" cols="100" value="#{contactController.
    current.description}"/>
    <br/>
    <h:commandButton id="contactSubmit" action="#{contactController.subscribe}"
    value="Save"/>
    <br/><br/>
    <h:outputFormat value="Cart contains the books {0}, {1}, {2}">
            <f:param value="Jakarta EE Fundamdenatals"/>
            <f:param value="Introducing Java 17 Fundamentals"/>
            <f:param value="Jakarta EE 10 Recipes"/>
    </h:outputFormat>
    <br/><br/>
    <h:commandLink id="manageAccount" action="#{contactController.manage}" value="Manage
    Subscription"/>
```

```
<br/><br/>
<h:outputLink id="homeLink" value="home.xhtml">
    <h:outputText value="User Home Page"/>
    <f:param name="username" value="#{contactController.current.email}"/>
    </h:outputLink>
    </h:form>
</f:view>
</html>
```

Managed Bean: ContactController.java

The ContactController managed bean has been modified throughout the recipes in this chapter to incorporate new functionality as the recipes move forward. In this recipe, a new property has been added to the ContactController that contains the description of the newsletter.

■ **Note** The hard-coded newsletter description is not a good idea for use in a production application. It is used in this example for demonstration purposes only. For a production application, the utilization of resource bundles or database storage would be a more viable approach for storing strings of text.

The following source excerpt from the ContactController class shows the code that is of interest in this example:

```
...
    private String newsletterDescription;
    public ContactController() {
        current = null;
        newsletterDescription = "Enter your information below in order to be " +
                "added to the Acme Bookstore newsletter.";
    }
...
    public String getNewsletterDescription() {
        return newsletterDescription;
    }
    public void setNewsletterDescription(String newsletterDescription) {
        this.newsletterDescription = newsletterDescription;
    }
...
```

The resulting page looks like Figure 4-3. Note that the text is the same because it is merely reading the same text from a managed bean property. Also, note that there is now an additional link added to the bottom of the page, which reads Home. The code can be executed by visiting the URL http://localhost:8080/ JakartaEERecipes_Chapter04-1.0-SNAPSHOT/chapter04/recipe04_03.xhtml in your browser.

Figure 4-3. *Utilizing output components within a view*

How It Works

Output components can be used to display output that is generated in a managed bean or to render a link to another resource. They can be useful in many cases for displaying dynamic output to a web view. The example for this recipe demonstrates three out of the five output component types: outputText, outputLink, and outputLabel. Each of the components shares a common set of attributes, which are listed in Table 4-7.

Table 4-7. *Common Output Component Attributes (Not Listed in the Introduction)*

Attribute	Description
class	CSS class for styling
converter	Converter that is registered with the component
dir	Direction of text (LTR, left-to-right; RTL, right-to-left)
escape	Boolean value to indicate whether XML- and HTML-sensitive characters are escaped
lang	Code for the language used when generating markup for the component
parent	Parent component
title	Tooltip text for the component
transient	Boolean indicating whether the component should be included in the state of the component tree

■ **Note** The outputText component has become a bit less important since the release of JSF 2.0 because the Facelets view definition language implicitly wraps inline content with a similar output component. Therefore, the use of the outputText tag within JSF 2.0 is necessary only if you want to utilize some of the tag attributes for rendering, JavaScript invocation, or the like.

The outputText component in the example contains a value of #{contactController. newsletterDescription}, which displays the contents of the newsletterDescription property within ContactController. Only the common output component attributes can be specified within the h:outputText tag. Therefore, an attribute such as class or style can be used to apply styles to the text displayed by the component. If the component contains HTML or XML, the escape attribute can be set to true to indicate that the characters should be escaped.

The outputFormat component shares the same set of attributes as the outputText component. The outputFormat component can be used to render parameterized text. Therefore, if you require the ability to alter different portions of a string of text, you can do so via the use of Jakarta Server Faces parameters (via the f:param tag). For example, suppose you wanted to list the name of books that someone has purchased from the Acme Bookstore; you could use the outputFormat component like in the following example:

```
<h:outputFormat value="Cart contains the books {0}, {1}, {2}">
            <f:param value="Jakarta EE Fundamdenatals"/>
            <f:param value="Introducing Java 17 Fundamentals"/>
            <f:param value="Jakarta EE 10 Recipes"/>
</h:outputFormat>
```

The outputLink and outputLabel components can each specify a number of other attributes that are not available to the previously discussed output components. The additional attributes are listed in Tables 4-8 (outputLink) and 4-9 (outputLabel). The outputLink component can be used to create an anchor or link that will redirect an application user to another page when the link is clicked. In the example, the outputLink component is used to redirect a user to a view named home.xhtml. The value for the outputLink component can be set to a static page name, as per the example, or it can contain an expression corresponding to a managed bean property. It is also possible to pass parameters to another page using the outputLink component by nesting f:param tags between opening and closing h:outputLink tags as follows:

```
<h:outputLink id="homeLink" value="home.xhtml">
    <h:outputText value="User Home Page"/>
    <f:param name="username" value="#{contactController.current.email}"/>
</h:outputLink>
```

Table 4-8. *outputLink Additional Attributes*

Attribute	Description
accessKey	Access key value that will transfer the focus to the component
binding	ValueExpression linking this component to a property in a backing bean
charset	The character encoding of the resource designated by this hyperlink
cords	Position and shape of the hotspot on the screen
dir	Direction indication for text (LTR, left-to-right; RTL, right-to-left)
disabled	Specifies a boolean to indicate whether the component is disabled
fragment	Identifier for the page fragment that should be brought into focus when the target page is rendered
hreflang	Language code of the resource designated by the hyperlink
lang	Code for the language used for generating the component markup
rel	Relationship from the current document to the anchor specified by the hyperlink
rev	Reverse anchor specified by this hyperlink to the current document
shape	Shape of the hotspot on the screen
tabindex	Index value indicating the number of Tab button presses it takes to bring the component into focus
target	Name of a frame where the resource retrieved via the hyperlink will be displayed
title	Tooltip that will be displayed when the mouse hovers over the component
type	Type of button to create. Values are submit (default), reset, and button

Table 4-9. *outputLabel Additional Attributes*

Attribute	Description
accessKey	Access key value that will transfer the focus to the component
binding	ValueExpression linking this component to a property in a backing bean
dir	Direction indication for text (LTR, left-to-right; RTL, right-to-left)
escape	Flag indicating that characters that are sensitive in HTML and XML markup must be escaped
for	Client identifier of the component for which this element is a label
lang	Code for the language used for generating the component markup
tabindex	Index value indicating the number of Tab button presses it takes to bring the component into focus
title	Tooltip that will be displayed when the mouse hovers over a component
type	Type of button to create. Values are submit (default), reset, and button

The previous example would produce a link with the text *User Home Page* when rendered on the page. It would produce the following HTML link, where `emailAddress` corresponds to the Jakarta Expression Language expression of `#{contactController.current.email}`:

```
<a href="home.xhtml?username=emailAddress">Home Page</a>
```

The View: home.xhtml

The following is the code for `home.xhtml`. The Jakarta Expression Language expression `#{param['username']}` could be used to read the value of the parameter passed in the previous code snippet:

```
<html xmlns="http://www.w3.org/1999/xhtml"
      xmlns:h="http://xmlns.jcp.org/jsf/html"
      xmlns:ui="http://xmlns.jcp.org/jsf/facelets"
      xmlns:f="http://xmlns.jcp.org/jsf/core">
<f:view>
    <h:outputLabel value="Hello #{param['username']}"/>
</f:view>
</html>
```

Similarly, rather than displaying a link as text on the page, an image can be used by embedding a `graphicImage` component (see Recipe 4-6 for details).

The `outputLabel` component renders an HTML `<label>` tag, and it can be used in much the same way as the `outputText` component. In the example, the `outputLabel` component values are all using static text, but they could also utilize Jakarta Expression Language expressions to use managed bean property values if that is more suitable for the application.

The last output component that I'll cover in this recipe is the link component. It was introduced to Jakarta Server Faces in release 2.0, and it makes the task of adding links to a page just a bit easier. The `outputLink` and `link` components produce similar results, but `link` has just a couple of different attributes that make it react a bit differently. The `value` attribute of the `h:link` tag specifies the label or text that should be used when the link is rendered on the page, and the `outcome` attribute specifies the page that should be linked to. The following example of the link component produces the same output as the `outputLink` component in the example for this recipe:

```
<h:link id=""homeLink"" value=""Home"" outcome=""home""/>
```

Parameters and images can also be embedded within the `h:link` tag, in the same manner as with `outputLink`. The `link` component also contains some custom attributes, as listed in Table 4-10.

Table 4-10. *link Component Additional Attributes*

Attribute	Description
charset	Character encoding of the resource that is designated by the hyperlink
cords	Position and shape of the hotspot on the screen, usually used when generating maps or images containing multiple links
disabled	Flag to indicate that the component should never receive focus
fragment	Identifier for the page fragment that should be brought into focus when the link is clicked. The identifier is appended to the # character

(continued)

Table 4-10. (*continued*)

Attribute	Description
hreflang	Language of the resource designated by this link
includeviewparams	Boolean indicating whether to include page parameters when redirecting
outcome	Logical outcome used to resolve a navigational case
rel	Relationship from the current document to the resource specified by the link
rev	Reverse link from the anchor specified from this link to the current document
shape	Shape of the hotspot on the screen
target	Name of the frame in which the resource linked to is to be displayed
type	Content type of the resource that is linked to

This recipe provided a high-level overview of the Jakarta Server Faces standard output components. In Jakarta Server Faces 2.0+, it is important to note that you can simply include a Jakarta Expression Language expression without using an output component to display text in a page. However, these components can still be quite useful under certain circumstances, making them an important set of components to have in your arsenal.

4-5. Adding Form Validation

Problem

To ensure that valid data is being submitted via your form, you need to incorporate some validation on your input fields.

Solution #1

Utilize prebuilt Jakarta Server Faces validator tags on the view's input components where possible. Jakarta Server Faces ships with a handful of prebuilt validators that can be applied to components within a view by embedding the validator tag within the component you want to validate. The following code excerpt is taken from a Jakarta Server Faces view that defines the layout for the newsletter subscription page of the Acme Bookstore application. The sources can be found in the view named recipe04_04.xhtml, and the excerpt demonstrates applying prebuilt validators to some inputText components:

```
...
<h:outputLabel for="first" value="First: "/>
<h:inputText id="first" size="40" value="#{contactController.current.first}">
    <f:validateLength minimum="1" maximum="40"/>
 </h:inputText><br/>
<h:message id="firstError" for="first" errorStyle="color:red"/><br/>
<h:outputLabel for="last" value="Last: "/>
<h:inputText id="last" size="40" value="#{contactController.current.last}">
    <f:validateLength minimum="1" maximum="40"/>
</h:inputText><br/>
<h:message id="lastError" for="last" errorStyle="color:red"/><br/>
...
```

In the preceding code excerpt, you can see that the `f:validateLength` validator tags have been embedded in different `inputText` components. When the form is submitted, these validators will be applied to the values in the `inputText` component fields and will return an error message if the constraints have not been met.

Solution #2

Utilize Jakarta Server Faces bean validation by annotating managed bean fields with validation annotations. It is possible to perform validation from within the managed bean by annotating the property field declaration with the validation annotations that are needed. When the form is submitted, the bean validation will be performed.

■ **Note** An `f:validateBean` tag can be embedded within the component in the view if you're using `validationGroups` in order to delegate the validation of the local value to the Bean Validation API. If you're using `f:validateBean`, the `validationGroups` attribute will serve as a filter that instructs which constraints should be enforced.

The following code excerpt is taken from the Jakarta Server Faces view that defines the layout for the newsletter subscription page of the Acme Bookstore application. The sources can be found in the view named `recipe04_04.xhtml`.

```
...
<h:outputLabel for="email" value="Email: "/>
<h:inputText id="email" size="40" value="#{contactController.current.email}"/><br/>
<h:message id="emailError" for="email" errorStyle="color:red"/>
...
```

Next is an excerpt from the `Contact` managed bean that demonstrates applying a validation annotation to the `email` property field declaration:

```
...
@Pattern(regexp = "[a-zA-Z0-9]+@[a-zA-Z0-9]+\\.[a-zA-Z0-9]+", message = "Email format is
invalid.")
    private String email;
...
```

When the form is submitted, the validation on the `email` field will occur. If the value entered into the `inputText` component does not validate against the regular expression noted in the annotation, the message will be displayed within the corresponding `messages` component.

Solution #3

Create a custom validator method within a managed bean and register that method with an input component by specifying the appropriate Jakarta Expression Language for the component's `validator` attribute. The following code excerpt is taken from the Jakarta Server Faces view that defines the layout for the newsletter subscription page of the Acme Bookstore application. The sources can be found in the view named recipe04_04.xhtml, and the excerpt demonstrates a custom validator method to a component by specifying it for the validator attribute:

```
...
<h:outputLabel for="password" value="Enter a password for site access: "/>
<h:inputSecret id="password" size="40" redisplay="true" value="#{contactController.current.
password}"/>
<br/>
<h:outputLabel for="passwordConfirm" value="Confirm Password: "/>
<h:inputSecret id="passwordConfirm" size="40"
redisplay="true"    validator="#{contactController.validatePassword}"/>
<br/>
<h:message id="passwordConfirmError" for="passwordConfirm"  style="color:red"/>
...
```

■ **Note**   If you are thinking outside of the box, you'll see that the previous code fragment would be an excellent choice for creating into a composite component! If a composite component is created, it would be as simple as adding a tag such as `<custom:passwordValidate>` to your form. See Recipe 4-4 for more details on developing composite components.

The validator attribute specifies the validatePassword method within the ContactController managed bean. The following excerpt is taken from ContactController, and it shows the validator method's implementation:

```
...
/**
     * Custom validator to ensure that password field contents match
     * @param context
     * @param component
     * @param value
     */
    public void validatePassword(FacesContext context,
                                 UIComponent component,
                                 Object value){
        Map <String, String> map = context.getExternalContext().getRequestParameterMap();
        String passwordText = (String) map.get(("contactForm:password"));
        String confirmPassword = value.toString();
        if (!passwordText.equals(confirmPassword)) {
            throw new ValidatorException(new FacesMessage("Passwords do not match"));
        }
    }
...
```

When the form is submitted, the validatePassword method will be invoked during the Process Validations phase. The method will read the values of both the password and passwordConfirm fields, and an exception will be thrown if they do not match. For example, if the input form for the newsletter subscription page is submitted without any values, then the page should be re-rendered and look like Figure 4-4. The code can be executed by visiting the URL http://localhost:8080/JakartaEERecipes_Chapter04-1.0-SNAPSHOT/chapter04/recipe04_04.xhtml in your browser.

Figure 4-4. *Validation errors on input fields*

How It Works

There are a few different ways to apply validation to form input fields. The easiest way to apply validation to an input component is to utilize the prebuilt validator tags that ship with Jakarta Server Faces. There are prebuilt tags for validating data for a specified length, range, and so on. See Table 4-2 in the introduction to this chapter for the complete list of validator tags. You can also choose to apply validation to input components using bean validation. Bean validation requires validation annotations to be placed on the property declaration within the managed bean. Yet another possible way to perform validation is to create a custom validation method and specify the method within the input component's `validator` attribute. This section will provide a brief overview of each prebuilt validation tag, cover the basics of bean validation, and demonstrate how to build a custom validation method.

■ **Note** It is possible to create a class that implements the `Validator` interface to perform validation. For more information, see Recipe 3-7.

No matter which validation solution you choose to implement, the validation occurs during the Process Validations phase of the Jakarta Server Faces life cycle. When a form is submitted, via a command component or an Ajax request, all validators that are registered on the components within the tree are processed. The rules that are specified within the attributes of the component are compared against the local value for the component. At this point, if any of the validations fails, the messages are returned to the corresponding message components and displayed to the user.

To utilize the prebuilt validation tags, they must be embedded between opening and closing input component tags and specify attributes according to the validation parameters you want to set in Solution #1. For this recipe, you learned how to use the f:validateLength validator tag, which allows validation of component data for a specified length. The minimum and maximum attributes are set to the minimum string length and maximum string length, respectively.

The f:validateLongRange validator can be used to check the range of a numeric value that has been entered. The minimum and maximum attributes of f:validateLongRange are used to determine whether the value entered falls within the lower and upper bounds, respectively.

Similar to f:validateLongRange is the f:validateDoubleRange validator, which is used to validate the range of a floating-point value. Again, the minimum and maximum attributes of f:validateDoubleRange are used to determine whether the value entered falls within the lower and upper bounds, respectively.

New with the release of Jakarta Server Faces 2.0 was the f:validateRequired validator, which is used to ensure that an input field is not empty. No attributes are needed with this validator; simply embed it within a component tag to ensure that the component will not contain an empty value.

Another new validator that shipped with the Jakarta Server Faces 2.0 release was the f:validateRegex validator. This validator uses a regular expression pattern to determine whether the value entered matches the specified pattern. The validator's pattern attribute is used to specify the regular expression pattern, as shown in the example for Solution #1 to this recipe.

In Solution #2, Jakarta Server Faces bean validation is demonstrated, which was also a new feature of the Jakarta Server Faces 2.0 release. Bean validation allows you to annotate a managed bean field with constraint annotations that indicate the type of validation that should be performed. The validation automatically occurs on the annotated fields when a form is submitted that contains input components referencing them. A handful of standard constraint annotations can be applied to bean fields, as listed in Table 4-11. Each annotation accepts different attributes; see the online documentation for more details.

Table 4-11. *Constraint Annotations Used for Bean Validation*

Annotation	Description
@AssertFalse	The annotated element must be false
@AssertTrue	The annotated element must be true
@DecimalMax	The annotated element must be a decimal that has a value less than or equal to the specified maximum
@DecimalMin	The annotated element must be a decimal that has a value greater than or equal to the specified minimum
@Digits	The annotated element must be a number within the accepted range
@Email	The annotated element must adhere to the format of an email address
@Future	The annotated element must be a date in the future
@Max	The annotated element must be a number that has a value less than or equal to the specified maximum

(*continued*)

Table 4-11. (*continued*)

Annotation	Description
@Min	The annotated element must be a number that has a value greater than or equal to the specified minimum
@Negative	The annotated element must be a negative number
@NotBlank	The annotated element must not be null or blank after removing any trailing or leading whitespace
@NotEmpty	The annotated element must not be null or empty
@NotNull	The annotated element must not be null
@Null	The annotated element must be null
@Past	The annotated element must be a date in the past
@Pattern	The annotated element must match the pattern specified in the regular annotation's regular expression
@Positive	The annotated element must be a positive number
@Size	The annotated element must be between the specified boundaries

When using bean validation, the input component that references an annotated bean field can contain an f:validateBean tag to customize behavior. The f:validateBean tag's validationGroups annotation can be used to specify validation groups that can be used for validating the component. For instance, such a solution may resemble something like the following:

```
<h:inputText id="email" size="40" value="#{contactController.current.email}">
    <f:validateBean/>
</h:inputText>
```

■ **Note** Validation groups define a subset of constraints that can be applied for validation. A validation group is represented by an empty Java interface. The interface name can then be applied to annotation constraints within a bean class in order to assign such constraints to a particular group. For instance, the following field that is annotated with @Size @Email validation constraints.

```
@Size(min=2, max=30)
@Email
private String email;
```

When utilizing the f:validateBean tag, any constraint annotations that are contained in the specified group will be applied to the field for validation.

When you're using bean validation, a custom error message can be displayed if the validation for a field fails. To add a custom message, include the `message` attribute in the annotation, along with the error message that you want to have displayed. As a best practice, error messages should be pulled from a message bundle so that they can be updated without the need to change code.

The example for Solution #3 demonstrates the use of a custom validator method in order to perform validation on an input component. The input component's `validator` attribute can reference a managed bean method that has no return type and accepts a `FacesContext`, a `UIComponent`, and an `Object`. The method can utilize the parameters to gain access to the current `FacesContext`, the `UIComponent` that is being validated, and the current value that is contained in the object, respectively. The validation logic can throw a `jakarta.faces.validator.ValidatorException` if the value does not pass validation and then return a message to the user via the exception. In the example, the method named `validatePassword` is used to compare the two password field contents to ensure that they match. The first two lines of code within the method are used to obtain the value of the component with the `id` of `password` and save it into a local variable. The actual validation logic compares that value against the incoming parameter's `Object` value, which is the current value of the component being validated, to determine whether there is a match. If not, then a `ValidationException` is thrown with a corresponding message. That message will then be displayed within the `messages` component that corresponds to the component being validated.

As mentioned at the beginning of this recipe, there are a few ways to validate input. None of them is any better than the other; their usage depends on the needs of your application. If you are going to be changing validation patterns often, then you may want to stick with the prebuilt validator tags so that you do not need to recompile code in order to change the validation. On the other hand, if you know that your validation will not change, then it may be easier for you to work with the bean validation technique. Whatever the case, validation can be made even easier with Ajax, and that topic is covered in Chapter 5.

4-6. Adding Select Lists to Pages

Problem

You want to provide a list of options to choose from for some of the input fields on your page.

Solution

Use the Jakarta Server Faces `selectOneMenu`, `selectManyMenu`, `selectOneListbox`, or `selectManyListbox` component, depending on the type of list your application requires. Each of these selection components allows for either one or many selections to be made from a particular set of values. The example for this recipe adds to the newsletter subscription page of the Acme Bookstore. The bookstore application will allow the customers to select their occupation from a drop-down list and to select one or more newsletters to which they would like to subscribe from a multiple-select list. Since they'll be selecting only a single option for their occupation, a `selectOneMenu` is used. However, since multiple newsletter selections can be made, a `selectManyListbox` is the best choice.

The View: recipe04_05.xhtml

The following excerpt is taken from the Jakarta Server Faces view named `recipe04_05.xhtml`, and it demonstrates the usage of these components:

```
...
<h:outputLabel for="occupation" value="Occupation: "/>
<h:selectOneMenu id="occupation" value="#{contactController.current.occupation}">
    <f:selectItem itemLabel="" itemValue=""/>
```

```
    <f:selectItems value="#{contactController.occupationList}"/>
</h:selectOneMenu>
<br/><br/>
<h:outputLabel for="newsletterList" value="Newsletters:"/>
<h:selectManyListbox id="newsletterList" value="#{contactController.current.
newsletterList}">
    <f:selectItems value="#{contactController.allNewsletters}"/>
</h:selectManyListbox>
...
```

Managed Bean Controller: ContactController.java

The components are bound to properties in the ContactController managed bean. The following excerpt, taken from ContactController, shows the declaration of the properties, along with their corresponding initialization methods:

```
@RequestScoped
@Named(value="contactController")
public class ContactController {
...
public ContactController() {
    current = null;
    newsletterDescription = "Enter your information below in order to be " +
            "added to the Acme Bookstore newsletter.";
    subscription = new Subscription();
    populateNewsletterList();
    populateOccupationList();
}
...
// Declaration of the managed bean properties
private List<String> occupationList;
private Map<String, Object> newsletterList;
...
// Example of populating the object
private void populateOccupationList(){
        occupationList = new ArrayList();
        occupationList.add("Author");
        occupationList.add("IT Professional");
}
// Example of populating the object
private void populateNewsletterList(){
    allNewsletters = new LinkedHashMap<String,Object>();
    allNewsletters = new LinkedHashMap<String,Object>();
    allNewsletters.put("Introducing Java 17 Fundamentals", "Java");
    allNewsletters.put("Jakarta EE Fundamentals", "Jakarta EE");
    allNewsletters.put("Building High Performing Java 17 Applications", "GraalVM");
    allNewsletters.put("New Books Weekly", "New Books");}
```

```
/**
    * @return the occupationList
    */
public List<String> getOccupationList() {
    return occupationList;
}
/**
    * @param occupationList the occupationList to set
    */
public void setOccupationList(List<String> occupationList) {
    this.occupationList = occupationList;
}

public Map<String, Object> getAllNewsletters() {
        return allNewsletters;
    }

public void setAllNewsletters(Map<String, Object> allNewsletters) {
        this.allNewsletters = allNewsletters;
}
```

The following excerpt, taken from Contact, shows the declaration of the properties, along with their corresponding accessor methods:

...

```
/**
    * @return the newsletterList
    */
public Map<String,Object> getNewsletterList() {
    return newsletterList;
}
/**
    * @param newsletterList the newsletterList to set
    */
public void setNewsletterList(Map<String,Object> newsletterList) {
    this.newsletterList = newsletterList;
}
...
```

The newly updated newsletter subscription page should look like Figure 4-5. The code can be executed by visiting the URL http://localhost:8080/JakartaEERecipes_Chapter04-1.0-SNAPSHOT/chapter04/recipe04_05.xhtml in your browser.

Figure 4-5. *Selection components including lists of values*

How It Works

To ensure data integrity, it is always a good idea to include input components that are prepopulated with data if possible. Doing so ensures that users are not entering free-text values of varying varieties into text boxes, and it also gives the user a convenient choice of options. Utilizing selection components provides the user with a list of values to choose from, allowing one or more selections to be made. The standard Jakarta Server Faces component library ships with four input components that accept lists of data from which a user can choose one or more selections. The selection components are selectOneListbox, selectManyListbox, selectOneMenu, and selectManyMenu. Each of these components shares a common set of attributes. Those common attributes that were not already displayed in Table 4-2 are listed in Table 4-12.

Table 4-12. *Select Component Attributes*

Attribute	Description
accesskey	Access key that, when pressed, transfers focus to the component
dir	Direction indication for text (LTR, left-to-right; RTL, right-to-left)
disabled	Boolean value to indicate whether the component is disabled
disabledClass	CSS style class to apply to the rendered label on disabled options
enabledClass	CSS style class to apply to the rendered label on enabled options
label	Localized user-presentable name for the component
lang	Code describing the language used in the generated markup for the component
size	Number of available options to be always shown (selectManyListbox)
tabindex	Index value indicating the number of Tab button presses it takes to bring the component into focus
title	Tooltip that will be displayed when the mouse hovers over a component

Populating the Select Lists

Before diving into each of the four components and a brief description of how they work, it is important to note that each component displays a collection of data, and the f:selectItem or f:selectItems tags are used to specify that set of data. If you want to list each data item separately, then the f:selectItem tag should be used. One f:selectItem tag represents one element in the collection of values. The f:selectItem tag contains several attributes, but I cover only some of the important ones in this discussion. Every f:selectItem tag should minimally contain both the itemValue and itemLabel attributes, specifying the value for the element and the label that is to be displayed, respectively. These attributes accept a Jakarta Expression Language expression or a string of text. In the example, both the itemValue and itemLabel attributes are left blank, which will render an empty selection for the first menu choice. When the user selects an option from the list, the itemValue attribute value is set into the corresponding selection component's value.

The f:selectItems tag can be used to specify a collection of data that should be used for the component. A List of SelectItem objects can be built within a managed bean and specified for the f:selectItems tag. Much like the f:selectItem tag, several attributes can be used with this tag, and I'll cover the essential ones here. Both the itemValue and itemLabel attributes can also be specified for the f:selectItems tag, corresponding to a List or Map of values and a string label, respectively. However, most often, the value attribute is specified, referencing a managed bean property that contains a Collection or array of objects. The Collection or array can contain any valid Java object, and in the example, a LinkedHashMap is used to populate the newsletterList property. It is possible to populate individual SelectItem objects and then load them into a List for use with the f:selectItems tag. The following lines of code show how to populate a collection of newsletters:

```
private void populateNewsletterList(){
        allNewsletters = new LinkedHashMap<String,Object>();
        allNewsletters.put("Introducing Java 17 Fundamentals", "Java");
        allNewsletters.put("Jakarta EE Fundamentals", "Jakarta EE");
        allNewsletters.put("Building High Performing Java 17 Applications", "GraalVM");
        allNewsletters.put("New Books Weekly", "New Books");
    }
```

Regarding Each Component Type

The selectOneMenu is probably the most commonly used selection component, and it renders a collection of data into a drop-down list. The user can select one entry from the menu, and the selected entry will be set into the managed bean property that is specified for the value attribute of the component. In the example to this recipe, the value is set to #{contactController.current.occupation}, so when an entry from the list is selected, then it will be set into the currently selected Contact object's occupation field.

The selectOneListbox allows a user to select one value from a list of data. The user can see at least a few of the entries within the list within a box on the screen and can select one of the options from the list box. The selectOneListbox contains an additional attribute named collectionType, which allows the type of collection to be specified using a literal value.

Both the selectManyMenu and selectManyListbox components allow the user to choose more than one option in the selection list. The example demonstrates how to use a selectManyListbox component, allowing the user to choose more than one newsletter from the list. The main difference when using one of these components is that the managed bean property value for the component must be able to accept more than one value. In the example, the selectManyListbox component value references the Contact class's newsletterList field. The newsletterList field is declared as a List of String objects, so when the user selects more than one value from the newsletterList, all the choices can be stored in the current Contact object.

In the example for this recipe, two components are used to display lists of options for selection. One of the components allows a user to select one value from the collection and displays the options in a drop-down list, and the other allows a user to select more than one value and displays the options within a list box.

4-7. Adding Graphics to Your Pages

Problem

You want to incorporate a graphic into your site template or other select application pages.

Solution

Place the images that you want to display into a library in your application's resources folder inside the webapp folder, and then use the graphicImage component to display them. The book.xhtml view for the Acme Bookstore application contains an image of each book in the store. To render the image, the book image name is populated from the image field of the Book managed bean. The following code excerpt taken from book.xhtml demonstrates how to use the h:graphicImage tag:

```
<h:graphicImage id="bookImage" library="image"
            style="width: 100px; height: 120px" name="#{book.image}"/>
```

How It Works

Since the inception of Jakarta Server Faces, the graphicImage component has been used to display images. Using the library attribute of the graphicImage component, a Jakarta Server Faces view can reference an image resource without needing to specify a fully qualified path to the image file. In the solution to this recipe, the value specified for the library attribute is image, meaning that the image can be found in the \webapp\resource\image folder. It also provides the convenience of accepting Jakarta Expression Language in attributes as needed so that images can be dynamically loaded based upon the current values in the corresponding managed bean properties. The graphicImage component makes it easy to display images, both dynamically and statically.

Managed Bean: Book.java

This managed bean encapsulates the book image name; the following is the code for this class:

```
package com.jakartaeerecipe.chapter04;

import jakarta.inject.Named;

@Named(value = "book")
public class Book {
    private String image;

    public Book(){
        image = "book.png";
    }

    public String getImage() {
        return image;
    }

    public void setImage(String image) {
        this.image = image;
    }
}
```

The h:graphicImage tag supports a number of attributes, above and beyond the standard Jakarta Server Faces component attributes, as listed in Table 4-13.

Table 4-13. *graphicImage Component–Specific Attributes*

Attribute	Description
alt	Alternate textual description of the element rendered by the component
dir	Direction indication for text (LTR, left-to-right; RTL, right-to-left)
height	Overrides the height of the image
ismap	Boolean indicating whether the image is to be used as a server-side image map
lang	Code describing the language used in the generated markup for the component
longdesc	URI to a long description of the image represented by the element
title	Advisory title information about the markup elements generated by the component
usemap	Name of a client-side image map for which this element provides the image
width	Overrides the width of the image

When the page is rendered in the example to this recipe, the image that resides within the application's resources/image directory that corresponds to the name attribute on the tag will be displayed. If the user selects a different book from the menu, then that book's image will be displayed using the same graphicImage component, because the name specified for the image can be changed depending on the currently selected book object in the managed bean.

By utilizing a graphicImage in your views, you enable your images to take on the dynamic characteristics of standard Jakarta Server Faces components. To see this sample code in action, refer to Recipe 4-17.

4-8. Adding Check Boxes to a View

Problem

You need to add check box fields to an application view.

Solution

Utilize the selectOneCheckbox and selectManyCheckbox components within the view. These components allow you to specify a boolean value as input by simply checking a box for a true value and deselecting the check box for a false value.

The View: recipe04_07.xhtml

The following code excerpt is taken from the view named recipe04_07.xhtml, and it demonstrates the use of these components:

```
...
<h:outputLabel for="notifyme" value="Would you like to receive other promotional email?"/>
<h:selectBooleanCheckbox id="notifyme"
value="#{contactController.current.receiveNotifications}"/>
<br/><br/>
<h:outputLabel for="notificationTypes"
                       value="What type of notifications are you interested in
                       receiving?"/>
<h:selectManyCheckbox id="notificationTypes" value="#{contactController.current.
notificationType}">
    <f:selectItems value="#{contactController.notificationTypes}"/>
</h:selectManyCheckbox>
...
```

Managed Bean Controllers

Each of the components is bound to a Contact object, so when the form is submitted, the current Contact object will receive the data if valid. The following listing contains excerpts from the updated Contact class, an object that is used to hold the contact's information. For the complete listing, see the Contact.java sources in the org.jakartaeerecipe.chapter04 packages in the sources.

```
...
private boolean receiveNotifications;
private Map<String, Object> notificationType;
...
/**
    * @return the receiveNotifications
    */
public boolean isReceiveNotifications() {
    return receiveNotifications;
}
/**
    * @param receiveNotifications the receiveNotifications to set
    */
public void setReceiveNotifications(boolean receiveNotifications) {
    this.receiveNotifications = receiveNotifications;
}
/**
     * @return the notificationTypes
     */
    public Map<String, Object> getNotificationTypes() {
        return notificationTypes;
    }
    /**
     * @param notificationTypes the notificationTypes to set
     */
    public void setNotificationTypes(Map<String, Object> notificationTypes) {
        this.notificationTypes = notificationTypes;
    }
```

The last piece of the puzzle is the list of notification types that are bound to the f:selectItems tag that is embedded within the h:selectManyCheckbox component. These are bound to a property named notificationTypes in the ContactController managed bean. The following listing contains the relevant excerpts from that class:

```
...
// Declaration
private Map<String, String> notificationTypes;
...
/**
    * Creates a new instance of ContactController
    */
public ContactController() {
    current = null;
        newsletterDescription = "Enter your information below in order to be " +
            "added to the Acme Bookstore newsletter.";
        subscription = new Subscription();
        populateOccupationList();
        populateNewsletterList();

        // Population occurs within the constructor, calling the populateNotificationTypes method
        populateNotificationTypes();
}
```

```
private void populateNotificationTypes() {
        notificationTypes = new HashMap<>();
        notificationTypes.put("Product Updates", "1");
        notificationTypes.put("Best Seller Alerts","2");
        notificationTypes.put("Spam", "3");
    }
...
```

The resulting newsletter subscription input screen for the Acme Bookstore application, including the new check box components, will look like Figure 4-6. The code can be executed by visiting the URL http://localhost:8080/JakartaEERecipes_Chapter04-1.0-SNAPSHOT/chapter04/recipe04_07.xhtml in your browser.

Figure 4-6. *Incorporating check boxes into your pages*

How It Works

Check boxes are very common in applications because they provide an easy means for users to enter boolean values. The box is either checked or not, and a checked box relates to a `true` value, leaving an unchecked box relating to a `false` value. The Jakarta Server Faces standard component library ships with a couple of different check box selection components, namely, the `selectBooleanCheckbox` and the `selectManyCheckbox`. The `selectBooleanCheckbox` renders a single HTML input element with `type="checkbox"` on the page, whereas the `selectManyCheckbox` component renders multiple HTML input elements with `type="checkbox"`. As with all Jakarta Server Faces components, the check box selection components share a standard set of attributes above and beyond the common Jakarta Server Faces component attributes, which are listed in Table 4-14.

Table 4-14. *Check Box Selection Component Attributes*

Attribute	Description
accessKey	Access key that, when pressed, transfers focus to the element
border	Width of the border to be drawn around the table containing the options list (`selectManyCheckbox`)
dir	Direction indication for text (`LTR`, left-to-right; `RTL`, right-to-left)
disabled	Boolean value indicating whether the element must receive focus or be included in a submit
label	Localized user presentable name for the component
lang	Code describing the language used in the generated markup for the component
layout	Orientation of the options list to be created (`selectManyCheckbox`)
readonly	Boolean indicating whether the component is read-only
tabindex	Index value indicating the number of Tab button presses it takes to bring the component into focus
title	Tooltip that will be displayed when the mouse hovers over a component

A `selectBooleanCheckbox` component `value` attribute Jakarta Expression Language expression should correspond to a boolean property in the managed bean. In the example to this recipe, the `selectBooleanCheckbox` value is set to `#{contactController.current.receiveNotifications}`, a boolean field in the current `Contact` object that indicates whether the contact wants to receive notifications. If the user checks the box for the component, then the value for the `receiveNotifications` field will be set to `true`; otherwise, it will be set to `false`. The `value` attribute is the only attribute that is required for use. However, oftentimes the `valueChangeListener` attribute is set to a method within a managed bean that will be invoked if the value for the component value changes. This is most useful when using an Ajax form submit so that the client can see the results of a `ValueChangeEvent` immediately, rather than after the form is re-rendered.

The `selectManyCheckbox` component displays one or more check boxes on a page. The `value` attribute for this component should correspond to a string array. Each check box contained within the component has a corresponding `String` value. Now you are probably thinking to yourself, what does a string have to do with a boolean value? In fact, each string in the array corresponds to a check box on the page, and when a box is checked, the string that corresponds to that box is added to the array. If no boxes are checked, then there are no strings added to the array. Therefore, the presence of the string signifies that the check box corresponding to that string value has been checked.

To add check boxes, individual f:selectItem tags can be used for each check box, or a collection of check boxes can be added using the f:selectItems tag. If you're using f:selectItem, then the itemValue attribute is set to the String value that corresponds to that check box, and the itemLabel attribute is set to the check box label. In the example, the f:selectItems tag is used to populate check boxes for the component. The f:selectItems tag in the example contains a value attribute that is set to #{contactController.notificationTypes}, which corresponds to the notificationTypes field in the ContactController class. If you take a look at the notificationTypes field, you will see that it is declared as a Map<String, Object>, and each element in the array will correspond to a check box. When the ContactController class is instantiated, the populateNotificationTypes method is called, which populates the map with the values for each check box. The following listing is that of the populateNotificationTypes method. Each element in the map corresponds to a check box:

```
private void populateNotificationTypes() {
    notificationTypes = new HashMap<>();
    notificationTypes.put("Product Updates", "1");
    notificationTypes.put("Best Seller Alerts","2");
    notificationTypes.put("Spam", "3");
}
```

Check boxes make it easy for users to indicate a true or false (checked or unchecked) value for a given option. The Jakarta Server Faces check box selection components help organize content on a page, and they provide a good means of ensuring data integrity since the user does not have to enter free text.

4-9. Adding Radio Buttons to a View

Problem

You want to display a set of items on a page in the form of radio buttons and allow the user to select only one of them.

Solution

Use radio buttons on your page to provide the user the option of selecting one item from a set. Radio buttons are often a nice solution when you want to display all options on the screen at once but allow only one selection. For this recipe, the Acme Bookstore wants to add a radio button on the newsletter subscription page to determine whether the subscriber is male or female.

The View: recipe04_08.xhtml

The following excerpt is taken from the Jakarta Server Faces view named recipe04_08.xhtml, and it demonstrates the selectOneRadio component:

```
...
<h:outputLabel for="gender" value="Gender: "/>
<h:selectOneRadio id="gender" value="#{contactController.current.gender}">
    <f:selectItem itemValue="M" itemLabel="Male"/>
    <f:selectItem itemValue="F" itemLabel="Female"/>
</h:selectOneRadio>
<br/><br/>
```

```
<h:message id="genderError"
           for="gender"
           errorStyle="color:red"/>
<br/>
...
```

Managed Bean

The component is bound to a managed bean property named gender that has been added to the Contact class. The following listing contains excerpts from the Contact class, which show the updates for incorporating the new field:

```
...
private String gender;
...
/**
    * @return the gender
    */
public String getGender() {
    return gender;
}
/**
    * @param gender the gender to set
    */
public void setGender(String gender) {
    this.gender = gender;
}
...
```

When the selectOneRadio component is rendered on the screen, it adds a radio button for each of the available options. The updated Acme Bookstore newsletter page looks like that in Figure 4-7. The code can be executed by visiting the URL http://localhost:8080/JakartaEERecipes_Chapter04-1.0-SNAPSHOT/chapter04/recipe04_08.xhtml in your browser.

Figure 4-7. *Using a selectOneRadio component*

How It Works

Radio buttons are very similar to check boxes in that they provide the user with an on or off value for a designated page value. The value added to using radio buttons is that they make it easy to display several options on the screen at once and allow the user to select only one of them. If a user tries to select a different option, then the currently selected item becomes unselected, forcing the user to select only one option. The Jakarta Server Faces selectOneRadio component is used to render radio buttons on a page, and the component works in much the same manner as the selectManyCheckbox (see Recipe 4-7).

The selectOneRadio shares all of the same attributes as the selectBooleanCheckbox component. See Table 4-14 for a listing of those attributes. The selectOneRadio component also contains a number of additional attributes, as listed in Table 4-15.

Table 4-15. selectOneRadio Attributes (in Addition to Those Listed in Table 4-14)

Attribute	Description
disabledClass	CSS style class to apply to the rendered label on disabled options
group	Specifies a group of radio buttons to which the component belongs
enabledClass	CSS style class to apply to the rendered label on enabled options

To use the selectOneRadio component, the value attribute should be set to a string. In the example, the value for the selectOneRadio component is set to the gender field in the current Contact object. When one of the radio buttons is selected, the String value corresponding to that button will be set into the field value. The radio buttons are populated using either the f:selectItem tag or the f:selectItems tag, much like the selectManyCheckbox component (see Recipe 4-7). In the example, two f:selectItem tags are used to add two radio buttons to the component; the itemValue attribute is the string that will be submitted for the selected button, and the itemLabel attribute is the string that is displayed next to the corresponding button.

If you want to use an f:selectItems tag to populate a collection of radio buttons, the f:selectItems value attribute should be set to a managed bean property that is declared as a string array, a map, or a list of SelectItem objects. To see an example, review the example for the selectManyCheckbox component in Recipe 4-7.

■ **Note** In Jakarta Server Faces 2.3, the group attribute was added to the component. This attribute allows radio buttons to be placed in a view individually while still having the ability to share selection with all other buttons of the same group.

Radio buttons are an easy way to display multiple options to a user and allow them to select one. If you understand how a selectManyCheckbox component works, then the selectOneRadio is very similar.

4-10. Displaying a Collection of Data

Problem

You are interested in displaying a collection of data in one of your Jakarta Server Faces application pages.

Solution

Utilize a dataTable component to display a collection of data. A dataTable component can be used
to iterate over a collection of data, providing a handle for each row object so that column data can be
interrogated if need be or simply displayed. For this example, the book page is being updated to display
the table of contents for a chosen book. The table of contents will be displayed in a dataTable component,
which has been customized for readability.

The View: recipe04_09.xhtml

The following listing is that of the view named recipe04_09.xhtml, which is an incomplete snapshot of the
book.xhtml view:

```
<html xmlns="http://www.w3.org/1999/xhtml"
      xmlns:ui="http://xmlns.jcp.org/jsf/facelets"
      xmlns:f="http://xmlns.jcp.org/jsf/core"
      xmlns:h="http://xmlns.jcp.org/jsf/html">
<h:head>
        <meta http-equiv="content-type" content="text/html; charset=UTF-8"/>
        <title>Acme Bookstore</title>
    </h:head>
    <h:body>
        <ui:composition template="./layout/custom_template_search.xhtml">
            <ui:define name="content">
                <h:form id="componentForm">
                    <h1>Author List for #{ch4AuthorController.currentBook.title}</h1>
                    <p>
                        Below is the list of authors. Click on the author's last name
                        for more information regarding the author.
                    </p>
                    <h:graphicImage id="javarecipes" library="image"
                                    style="width: 100px; height: 120px"
                                    name="#{ch4AuthorController.currentBook.image}"/>
                    <br/>
                    <h:dataTable  id="authorTable" border="1"
                          value="#{ch4AuthorController.authorList}"
                                var="author">
                        <f:facet name="header">
                            #{ch4AuthorController.currentBook.title} Authors
                        </f:facet>
                        <h:column >
                            <h:commandLink id="authorName" action="#{ch4AuthorController.
                            displayAuthor(author.last)}"
                                            value="#{author.first} #{author.last}"/>
                        </h:column>
                    </h:dataTable>
                    <br/><br/>
                    <h:dataTable id="bookDetail" border="1"
                                value="#{ch4AuthorController.currentBook.chapters}"
                                var="book" style="width:100%"
                                rowClasses="tocTableOdd, tocTableEven" columnClasses="col1">
```

```
                        <f:facet name="header">
                            #{ch4AuthorController.currentBook.title} Details
                        </f:facet>
                        <h:column >
                            <f:facet name="header">
                                Chapter
                            </f:facet>
                            <h:outputText value="#{book.chapterNumber}"/>
                        </h:column>
                        <h:column>
                            <f:facet name="header">
                                Title
                            </f:facet>
                            <h:outputText value="#{book.title}"/>
                        </h:column>
                    </h:dataTable>
                    <br/>
                    <br/>
                </h:form>
            </ui:define>
        </ui:composition>
    </h:body>
</html>
```

CSS

The dataTable utilizes some CSS style classes in order to make it easier to read. The following excerpt is taken from the Acme Bookstore application style sheet named styles.css, and it contains the styles utilized by the table. The styles.css sheet is linked to the view because it is declared as a resource within the template.

```
.tocTableOdd{
    background: #c0c0c0;
}
.tocTableEven{
    background: #e0e0e0;
}
.col1{
    text-indent: 15px;
    font-weight: bold;
}
```

■ **Note** In Jakarta Server Faces 2.3, the dataTable has a new rowClass attribute, which accepts Jakarta Expression Language to access the current row. Therefore, something like the following is possible:

```
<h:dataTable id="bookDetail" border="1"
```

```
value="#{ch4AuthorController.currentBook.chapters}"
```

```
var="book" style="width:100%"

rowClass="#{book eq 'Java EE to Jakarta EE 10 Recipes ' ? style1:style2}"

columnClasses="col1">
```

The h:column had a new styleClass attribute added in Jakarta Server Faces 2.3. This attribute allows you to apply a specified style to an individual column.

Managed Bean

To accommodate the new table, a class named Chapter has been added to the application. The Chapter class is an object that will contain the chapter number, the title, and a description of each chapter. There has to be one Chapter object instantiated for each chapter in every book. To view the listing, see the org. jakartaeerecipe.chapter04.Chapter class in the sources. To populate the Chapter objects for each book, the AuthorController managed bean has been updated. The following excerpt is taken from the AuthorController managed bean, and it shows how the chapters are populated into the Book objects.

■ **Note** The example demonstrates hard-coding of strings within Java classes. This is generally a bad idea, and the use of a database or resource bundle for obtaining strings is a better fit for enterprise applications.

```
@PostConstruct
public void init(){
    authorLast = null;
    populateAuthors();
    populateJakartaFundamentalsAuthorList();
}
...
public void populateAuthors(){
...
    Book book1 = new Book("Java EE to Jakarta EE 10 Recipes", "book.png");
    book1 = addChapters1(book1);
...
}
...
    private Book addChapters1(Book book){
        Chapter chapter1 = new Chapter(1, "What is Jakarta EE", null);
        Chapter chapter2 = new Chapter(2, "History", null);
        Chapter chapter3 = new Chapter(3, "The Need for Jakarta EE and its Guiding
        Principles", null);
        Chapter chapter4 = new Chapter(4, "Specifications", null);
        Chapter chapter5 = new Chapter(5, "Specifications Overview", null);
        Chapter chapter6 = new Chapter(6, "Testing Compatibility Kits (TCKs)", null);
        Chapter chapter7 = new Chapter(7, "Compatible Implementations", null);
```

```
    List <Chapter> chapterList = new ArrayList<>();
    chapterList.add(chapter1);
    chapterList.add(chapter2);
    chapterList.add(chapter3);
    chapterList.add(chapter4);
    chapterList.add(chapter5);
    chapterList.add(chapter6);
    chapterList.add(chapter7);
    book.setChapters(chapterList);
    return book;
}...
```

The resulting table of contents on the book page will look like Figure 4-8. The code can be executed by visiting the URL http://localhost:8080/JakartaEERecipes_Chapter04-1.0-SNAPSHOT/chapter04/recipe04_09.xhtml in your browser.

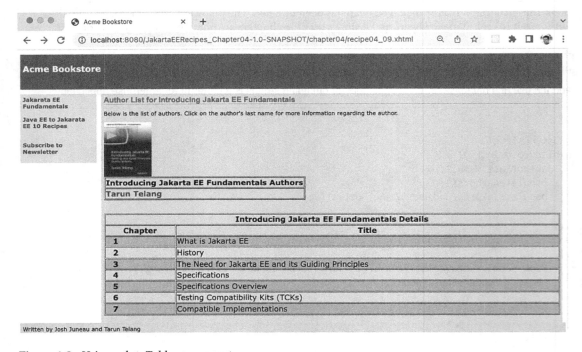

Figure 4-8. *Using a dataTable component*

How It Works

The Jakarta Server Faces dataTable component can be used to display collections of data in a uniform fashion. The dataTable component is easy to work with, and it allows the flexibility to work with each field within a data collection. There are other means of displaying collections of data, such as the ui-repeat Facelets tag or the use of a panelGrid component, but a dataTable makes a developer's life easy if the table does not need to be customized to the *n*th degree.

The dataTable component contains various attributes that can be used to customize the look and feel of the table, as well as some behavioral characteristics. Each of those attributes is listed in Table 4-16. Each dataTable also contains column components, which are declared within a dataTable component using the h:column tag. As with any other Jakarta Server Faces tag, there are many attributes that correspond to the h:column tag, as listed in Table 4-17.

Table 4-16. *dataTable Attributes*

Attribute	Description
bgcolor	Name or code of the background color for the table
bodyrows	Comma-separated list of row indices for which a new <tbody> element should be started
border	Width (pixels) of the border to be drawn around the table
captionClass	Space-separated list of CSS style classes that will be applied to any caption generated for the table
captionStyle	CSS style to be applied when the caption is rendered
cellpadding	Definition of how much space the user agent should leave between the border of each cell and its contents
cellspacing	Definition of how much space the user agent should leave between the left side of the table and the leftmost column, the top of the table and the top of the top side of the topmost row, and so on, for the right and bottom of the table. This also specifies how much space to leave between cells
columnClasses	Comma-delimited list of CSS styles that will be applied to the columns of the table. A space-separated list of classes can also be specified for any individual column
columns	Number of columns to render before starting a new row
dir	Direction indication for text (LTR, left-to-right; RTL, right-to-left)
footerClass	Space-separated list of CSS style classes that will be applied to any footer generated for the table
frame	Code specifying which sides of the frame surrounding the table will be visible
headerClass	Space-separated list of CSS style classes that will be applied to any header generated for the table
lang	Code describing the language used in the generated markup for the component
rowClass	Accepts Jakarta Expression Language to access rows and can be used to apply CSS style classes to specified rows
rowClasses	Comma-delimited list of CSS style classes that will be applied to the rows of the table. A space-separated list of classes may also be specified for each individual row
rules	Code specifying which rules will appear between the cells of the table. Valid values include none, groups, rows, cols, and all
summary	Summary of the table's purpose and structure for user agents rendering to nonvisual media
title	Advisory title information about markup elements generated for the component
width	Width of the entire table

Table 4-17. *h:column Attributes*

Attribute	Description
footerClass	CSS class that will be applied to the column footer
headerClass	CSS class that will be applied to the column header
styleClass	Allows CSS class to be applied to the individual column

The easiest way to describe the dataTable is to walk through an example. The solution to this recipe contains a Jakarta Server Faces view, in which there are two dataTable components utilized. The first dataTable has an id attribute of authorTable, and the second has an id attribute of bookTable. You are most interested in the second dataTable, whose id attribute equals bookTable, although the first dataTable functions in much the same way. The bookTable component is used to iterate over a collection of Chapter objects and display the corresponding chapter number and title for the currently selected book. The value attribute of the dataTable is set to #{ch4AuthorController.currentBook.chapters}, which corresponds to a List<String> property within the AuthorController managed bean. A dataTable can iterate over many different collection types, including a list, DataModel, and array. Beginning with the release of Jakarta Server Faces 2.2, the common Collection interface also became supported. The var attribute of the dataTable component is used to specify a handle that allows access to the collection data at the row level. This means you can hone in on a specific field of the data collection if needed. The dataTable tag does not display anything on its own; it must have column components embedded within it in order to display the content. Each h:column tag within a dataTable correlates to a single column of the resulting table when it is rendered. For instance, if you look at the first h:column tag within the dataTable that has an id of bookDetail, it has an embedded outputText component, which specifies a value of #{book.chapterNumber}. This specific column is used to display the chapter number, which is a field within the Chapter object that correlates to the currentBook object's chapters List.

A column component can contain any valid Jakarta Server Faces component, or it can contain plain Jakarta Server Faces Jakarta Expression Language correlating to a data field within the collection. If you look at the dataTable that has an id attribute of authorTable, you will see that a commandLink component is used within one of the columns. Oftentimes, such is the case, because you may want to link to the currently selected row's data from within a table cell. The dataTable with an id of authorTable contains a good example of doing just that. The commandLink in the table contains an action attribute that specifies a method within the AuthorController class, and the currently selected row's value, lastName, is passed to the method as a parameter. The underlying method uses that parameter to retrieve all the data for the selected row and display it in a different view:

```
<h:commandLink id="authorName" action="#{ch4AuthorController.displayAuthor(author.last)}"
                        value="#{author.first} #{author.last}"/>
```

To place a header or footer on the table, you must embed a facet into the table using an f:facet tag. The f:facet tag contains a number of typical Jakarta Server Faces component attributes, but one that stands out for this component is the name attribute. The name attribute is used to specify what type of facet the tag is, and in the case of the dataTable, those names are header and footer. To create the table header or footer, simply embed the f:facet tag, specifying the name of the facet (type of facet to create) inside the dataTable component.

■ **Note** A unique data type that can be used for a dataTable collection is the DataModel. To have the ability to display row numbers, use a DataModel.

The dataTable component can be extremely useful in situations when you need to display a collection of data. One of the pitfalls to using the dataTable is that it does not provide an overabundance of customizability. However, it is very possible to extend the functionality of the dataTable to suit one's need. There are plenty of third-party component libraries that do just that; they provide extended dataTables that feature sorting, row expansion, inline editing, and so forth. To learn more about using these custom dataTable components, see Chapter 7.

4-11. Implementing File Uploading

Problem

You want to add a file upload component to your application.

Solution

Use the Jakarta Server Faces file upload component to create an Ajax or non-Ajax-based file upload system for your application. To utilize the inputFile component, it must be placed within a Jakarta Server Faces form that has an enctype set to multipart/form-data and does not specify an id attribute. The h:form element contains the attributes enctype and prependId, which can be used to specify these requirements, respectively. A Jakarta Server Faces command component or the f:ajax tag should be set to an action method within the managed bean that will save the file to disk.

The following Jakarta Server Faces view demonstrates the use of the inputFile component in a non-Ajax solution:

```
<h:form prependId="false" enctype="multipart/form-data">
    Choose a file to upload to the server:    <br/>
     <h:inputFile id="uploadFile" value="#{ajaxBean.file}"/>
    <br/> <h:commandButton action="#{ajaxBean.uploadFile()}" value="Upload File"/>
</h:form>
```

The sources for the uploadFile method that is invoked via the commandButton are as follows:

```
@Named(value = "ajaxBean")
@SessionScoped
public class AjaxBean implements Serializable {

    private Part file = null;

    public AjaxBean() { }

    // getters and setters
    // ...
    public void uploadFile() {
        try(InputStream is = file.getInputStream();) {
            byte[] b = new byte[1024];
            is.read(b);
            String fileName = file.getName();
            FileOutputStream os = new FileOutputStream("/Java_Dev/" + fileName);
        } catch (IOException ex) {
```

```
            Logger.getLogger(AjaxBean.class.getName()).log(Level.SEVERE, null, ex);
    }
}}
```

Note that in the example, the path /Java_Dev/ indicates an operating system path or directory to which the uploaded file will be saved. The project file structure is shown in Figure 4-9.

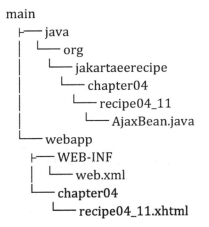

```
main
├── java
│   └── org
│       └── jakartaeerecipe
│           └── chapter04
│               └── recipe04_11
│                   └── AjaxBean.java
└── webapp
    ├── WEB-INF
    │   └── web.xml
    └── chapter04
        └── recipe04_11.xhtml
```

Figure 4-9. *Project file structure*

The code can be executed by visiting the URL http://localhost:8080/JakartaEERecipes_Chapter04-1.0-SNAPSHOT/chapter04/recipe04_10.xhtml in your browser. Figure 4-10 is how the output should look like.

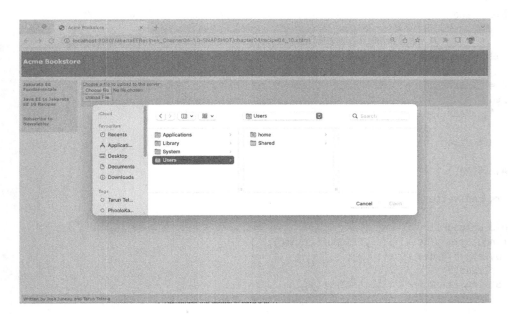

Figure 4-10. *Using a dataTable component*

How It Works

Jakarta Server Faces 2.2 included a new file upload component that relies on new Servlet 3.1 file upload support. The file upload support can be Ajax-enabled or non-Ajax-enabled. The `inputFile` component can be used with or without the `f:ajax` tag, so files can be uploaded with a page refresh (non-Ajax) or without (Ajax).

The following line of code demonstrates how to set the attributes for a form containing an `inputFile` component:

```
<h:form prependId="false" enctype="multipart/form-data">
```

The `value` attribute of the `inputFile` component is set to a variable of type `jakarta.servlet.http. Part` within the `AjaxBean` managed bean, and the `commandButton` has an action set to the managed bean's `uploadFile` method. To make the solution utilize Ajax, simply embed an `f:ajax` tag into the `commandButton`, which invokes the underlying managed bean method.

The addition of a native file upload component to Jakarta Server Faces is much welcomed. For years now, Jakarta Server Faces developers have had to rely on third-party libraries to handle file-uploading procedures. The scope of components that requires third-party integration is becoming narrower, and the default Jakarta Server Faces component toolset is becoming complete enough to be the only requirement for standard enterprise applications.

4-12. Validating Input with Ajax

Problem

You want to validate the values that are entered into text fields of a form, but you want them to be evaluated immediately, rather than after the form is submitted.

Solution

Perform validation on the field(s) by embedding the f:ajax tag within each component whose values you want to validate. Specify appropriate values for the event and render attributes so that the Ajax validation will occur when the field(s) loses focus, and any validation errors will be identified immediately. The following listing is the Jakarta Server Faces view for the newsletter subscription page of the Acme Bookstore application. It has been updated to utilize Ajax validation so that the validation occurs immediately, without the need to submit the form before corresponding errors are displayed:

```
<ui:composition xmlns="http://www.w3.org/1999/xhtml"
                xmlns:ui="http://xmlns.jcp.org/jsf/facelets"
                xmlns:f="http://xmlns.jcp.org/jsf/core"
                xmlns:h="http://xmlns.jcp.org/jsf/html"
                template="layout/custom_template_search.xhtml">
    <ui:define name="content">
        <h:messages globalOnly="true" errorStyle="color: red" infoStyle="color: green"/>
        <h:form id="contactForm">
            <h1>Subscribe to Newsletter</h1>
            <p>
                <h:outputText id="newsletterSubscriptionDesc" value="#{ch3contactController.
                newsletterDescription}"/>
            </p>
```

```
<br/>
<h:panelGrid columns="2" bgcolor="" border="0">
    <h:panelGroup>
        <h:outputLabel for="first" value="First: "/><br/>
        <h:inputText id="first" size="40" value="#{ch3contactController.current.
        first}">
            <f:validateLength minimum="1" maximum="40"/>
            <f:ajax event="blur" render="firstError"/>
        </h:inputText>
    </h:panelGroup>
    <h:panelGroup>
        <h:outputLabel for="last" value="Last: "/><br/>
        <h:inputText id="last" size="40" value="#{ch3contactController.
        current.last}">
            <f:validateLength minimum="1" maximum="40"/>
            <f:ajax event="blur" render="lastError"/>
        </h:inputText>
    </h:panelGroup>
    <h:message id="firstError"
            for="first"
            errorStyle="color:red"/>
    <h:message id="lastError"
            for="last"
            errorStyle="color:red"/>
    <h:panelGroup>
        <h:outputLabel for="email" value="Email: "/><br/>
        <h:inputText id="email" size="40" value="#{ch3contactController.current.
        email}">
            <f:ajax event="blur" render="emailError"/>
        </h:inputText>
    </h:panelGroup>
    <h:panelGroup/>
    <h:message id="emailError"
            for="email"
            errorStyle="color:red"/>
    <h:panelGroup/>
    <h:selectOneRadio title="Gender" id="gender" value="#{ch3contactController.
    current.gender}">
        <f:selectItem itemValue="M" itemLabel="Male"/>
        <f:selectItem itemValue="F" itemLabel="Female"/>
    </h:selectOneRadio>
    <h:panelGroup>
        <h:outputLabel for="occupation" value="Occupation: "/><br/>
        <h:selectOneMenu id="occupation" value="#{ch3contactController.current.
        occupation}">
            <f:selectItems value="#{ch3contactController.occupationList}"/>
        </h:selectOneMenu>
    </h:panelGroup>
    <h:message id="genderError"
            for="gender"
            errorStyle="color:red"/>
```

```
    </h:panelGrid>
    <br/>
    <h:panelGrid columns="2" bgcolor="" border="0">
        <h:panelGroup>
            <h:outputLabel for="description" value="Enter your book
            interests"/><br/>
            <h:inputTextarea id="description" rows="5" cols="75"
                            value="#{ch3contactController.current.description}"/>
            <br/>

            <h:outputLabel for="password" value="Enter a password for site
            access: "/><br/>
            <h:inputSecret id="password" size="40" value="#{ch3contactController.
            current.password}">
                <f:validateRequired/>
                <f:ajax event="blur" render="passwordError"/>
            </h:inputSecret><br/>
            <h:outputLabel for="passwordConfirm" value="Confirm Password: "/><br/>
            <h:inputSecret id="passwordConfirm" size="40"
            value="#{ch3contactController.passwordConfirm}"
                            validator="#{ch3contactController.validatePassword}">
                <f:ajax event="blur" render="passwordConfirmError"/>
            </h:inputSecret>

            <h:message id="passwordError"
                        for="password"
                        style="color:red"/>
            <br/>
            <h:message id="passwordConfirmError"
                        for="passwordConfirm"
                        style="color:red"/>
            <br/>
            <hr/>
            <br/>
        </h:panelGroup>
    </h:panelGrid>
    <h:panelGrid columns="3">
        <h:panelGroup>
            <h:outputLabel for="newsletterList" value="Newsletters:" style=" "/>
            <h:selectManyListbox id="newsletterList" value="#{ch3contactController.
            current.newsletterList}">
                <f:selectItems value="#{ch3contactController.allNewsletters}"/>
            </h:selectManyListbox>
        </h:panelGroup>
        <h:panelGroup/>
        <h:panelGroup>
            <h:panelGrid columns="1">
                <h:panelGroup>
                    <h:outputLabel for="notifyme" value="Would you like to receive
                    other promotional email?"/>
                    <h:selectBooleanCheckbox id="notifyme"
```

```
                                                value="#{ch3contactController.current.
                                                receiveNotifications}"/>
                        </h:panelGroup>
                        <h:panelGroup/>
                        <hr/>
                        <h:panelGroup/>
                        <h:panelGroup>
                            <h:outputLabel for="notificationTypes"
                                            value="What type of notifications are you
                                            interested in receiving?"/>
                            <br/>
                            <h:selectManyCheckbox id="notificationTypes"
                                                value="#{ch3contactController.current.
                                                notificationType}">
                                <f:selectItems value="#{ch3contactController.
                                notificationTypes}"/>
                            </h:selectManyCheckbox>
                        </h:panelGroup>
                    </h:panelGrid>
                </h:panelGroup>
            </h:panelGrid>
            <hr/>
            <br/>
            <h:commandButton id="contactSubmit" action="#{ch3contactController.subscribe}"
            value="Save"/>
            <h:panelGrid columns="2" width="400px;">
                <h:commandLink id="manageAccount" action="#{ch3contactController.manage}"
                value="Manage Subscription"/>
                <h:outputLink id="homeLink" value="home.xhtml">Home</h:outputLink>
            </h:panelGrid>
        </h:form>
    </ui:define>
</ui:composition>
```

Once the input components have been "Ajaxified" by embedding the f:ajax tag within them, then tabbing through the fields (causing the onBlur event to occur for each field) will result in a form that resembles Figure 4-11. The code can be executed by visiting the URL http://localhost:8080/ JakartaEERecipes_Chapter04-1.0-SNAPSHOT/chapter04/recipe04_11.xhtml in your browser.

Figure 4-11. *Ajax validation using the f:ajax tag*

In releases prior to JSF 2.0, performing immediate validation required the manual coding of JavaScript or a third-party component library. The f:ajax tag was added to the Jakarta Server Faces arsenal with the release of 2.0, bringing with it the power to easily add immediate validation (and other asynchronous processes) to Jakarta Server Faces views using standard or third-party components. The f:ajax tag can be embedded within any Jakarta Server Faces input component in order to immediately enhance the component, adding Ajax capabilities to it. This provides many benefits to the developer in that there is no longer a need to manually code JavaScript to perform client-side validation. It also allows validation to occur on the server (in Java code within a Jakarta Server Faces controller class) asynchronously, providing seamless interaction between the client and server and generating an immediate response to the client. The result is a rich modern web application that behaves in much the same manner as a native desktop application. Validation can now occur instantaneously in front of an end user's eyes without the need to perform several page submits in order to repair all of the possible issues.

To use the f:ajax tag, simply embed it within any Jakarta Server Faces component. There are a number of attributes that can be specified with f:ajax, as described in Table 4-18. If an attribute is not specified, then the default values are substituted. It is quite possible to include no attributes in an f:ajax tag, and if this is done, then the default attribute values for the component in which the f:ajax tag is embedded will take effect.

Table 4-18. *f:ajax Tag Attributes*

Attribute	Description
delay	A value that is specified in milliseconds, corresponding to the amount of delay between sending Ajax requests from the client-side queue to the server. The value none can be specified to disable this feature
disabled	Boolean value indicating the tag status. A value of true indicates that the Ajax behavior should not be rendered, and a value of false indicates that the Ajax behavior should be rendered. The default value is false
event	A String that identifies the type of event to which the Ajax action shall apply. If specified, it must be one of the supported component events. The default value is the event that triggers the Ajax request for the parent component of the Ajax behavior. The default event is action for ActionSource components and is valueChange for EditableValueHolder components
execute	A collection that identifies a list of components to be executed on the server. A space-delimited String of component identifiers can be specified as the value for this attribute, or a ValueExpression (Jakarta Expression Language) can be specified. The default value is @this, meaning the parent component of the Ajax behavior
immediate	Boolean value indicating whether the input values are processed early in the life cycle. If true, then the values are processed, and their corresponding events will be broadcast during the Apply Request Values phase; otherwise, the events will be broadcast during the Invoke Application phase
listener	Name of the listener method that is called when an AjaxBehaviorEvent has been broadcast for the listener
onevent	Name of the JavaScript function used to handle UI events
onerror	Name of the JavaScript function used to handle errors
resetValues	If true, then this particular Ajax transaction will reset the values
Render	Collection that identifies the components to be rendered on the client when the Ajax behavior is complete. A space-delimited String of component identifiers can be specified as the value for this attribute, or a ValueExpression (Jakarta Expression Language) can be specified. The default value is @none, meaning that no components will be rendered when the Ajax behavior is complete

The execute and render attributes of the f:ajax tag can specify a number of keywords to indicate which components are executed on the server for the Ajax behavior or which are rendered again after the Ajax behavior is complete, respectively. Table 4-19 lists the values that can be specified for both of these two attributes.

Table 4-19. *f:ajax Tag execute and render Attribute Values*

Attribute Value	Description
@all	All component identifiers are executed on the server, and all component identifiers are re-rendered once Ajax behavior is complete
@form	The form that encloses the component
@none	No component identifiers (default for the render attribute)
@this	The Ajax behavior parent component
@child(n)	The nth child of the base component
@composite	Closest composite component ancestor of the base component
@id(id)	All component descendants of the base component with the specified id
@namingcontainer	Closest NamingContainer ancestor of the base component
@next	Next component in view after the base component
@parent	Parent of the base component
@previous	Previous component to the base component
@root	UIViewRoot
Component IDs	Space-separated list of individual component identifiers
Jakarta Expression Language	Expression that resolves to a collection of string identifiers

In the example for this recipe, an f:ajax tag has been embedded inside many of the input components within the form. Each of those components has been Ajaxified, in that the data entered as the values for the components will now have the ability to be processed using the JavaScript resource library associated with JSF. Behind the scenes, the jsf.ajax.request() method of the JavaScript resource library will collect the data for each component that has been Ajaxified and post the request to the Java Server Faces life cycle. In effect, the data is sent to the controller class property without submitting the page in a traditional fashion. Notice that the event attribute specifies a JavaScript event that will be used to trigger the Ajax behavior. The JavaScript events that can be specified for the event attribute are those same JavaScript event attributes that are available on the parent component's tag, but the on prefix has been removed. For instance, if you want to perform an Ajax behavior on an inputText component when it loses focus, you would specify blur for the f:ajax event attribute rather than onBlur. Applying this concept to the example, when a user leaves the first or last name field, they will be validated using their associated f:validate tags immediately because the f:ajax tag has been embedded in them and the event on the f:ajax tag is specified as blur. When the Ajax behavior (the validation in this case) is complete, then the components whose identifiers are specified in the f:ajax render attribute will be re-rendered. In the case of the first and last inputText fields, their associated message components will be re-rendered, displaying any errors that may have occurred during validation.

UTILIZING AN ACTION LISTENER

It is possible to bind an action listener to an f:ajax tag so that when the invoking action occurs, the listener method is invoked. Why would you want to bind an action listener? There are any reasons to do so. For instance, suppose you wanted to capture the text that a user is typing into a text field. You could do so by binding an action method within a controller class to the listener attribute of an inputText field's corresponding f:ajax tag and then obtaining the current component's value from the AjaxBehaviorEvent object within the action method. For instance, suppose that you wanted to test a password for complexity

233

and display a corresponding message indicating whether a password was strong enough. The inputSecret component for the password could be modified to include an f:ajax tag with an event specification of keyup and a listener specified as #{ch3ContactController.passwordStrength}, as the following listing demonstrates:

Within the view:

```
<h:outputLabel for="password" value="Enter a password for site access: "/>
<h:inputSecret id="password" size="40"
        value="#{ch3ContactController.current.password}">
    <f:validateRequired/>
    <f:ajax event="keyup" listener="#{ch3ContactController.passwordStrength}"
                                    render="passwordStrengthMessage"/>
</h:inputSecret>
...
```

Within the controller:

```
. . .
private String passwordStrengthMessage;
. . .
public void passwordStrength(AjaxBehaviorEvent event){
        UIInput password = (UIInput) event.getComponent();
        boolean isStrong = false;
        String input = password.getValue().toString();
        if(input.matches("((?=.*\\d)(?=.*[a-z])(?=.*[A-Z]).{6,})")) {
            isStrong = true;
        }
        if(isStrong == true){
            setPasswordStrengthMessage("Password is strong");
        } else {
            setPasswordStrengthMessage("Password is weak");
        }
    }
}
```

The code in this example would create a listener event that, when a user types a value, would check the present entry to determine whether it met the given criteria for a secure password. A message would then be displayed to the user to let them know whether the password was secure.

Using the f:ajax tag makes it easy to add Ajax behavior to a Jakarta Server Faces component. Before the f:ajax tag, special third-party JavaScript libraries were often used to incorporate similar behaviors within Jakarta Server Faces views. f:ajax adds the benefit of allowing the developer to choose between using Ajax behaviors, without the need for coding a single line of JavaScript.

4-13. Submitting Pages Without Page Reloads
Problem

You want to enable your input form to have the ability to submit input fields for processing without reloading the page. In essence, you want your web application input form to react more like that of a desktop application rather than navigating from page to page to process data.

Solution

Embed an <f:ajax/> tag within the command component in the view so that the CDI controller class action is invoked without the page being submitted. Enable f:ajax to update the messages component in the view so that any errors or success messages that result from the processing can be displayed. In this example, the newsletter subscription page for the Acme Bookstore will be changed so that the form is submitted using Ajax, and the commandButton component is processed without submitting the form in a traditional manner. The following excerpt from the newsletter subscription form sources from recipe03_06.xhtml, which demonstrates how to add Ajax functionality to the action components within the form:

```
...
<h:commandButton id="contactSubmit" action="#{ch3ContactController.subscribe}" value="Save">
    <f:ajax event="action" execute="@form" render="@all"/>
</h:commandButton>
<h:panelGrid  columns="2" width="400px;">
...
```

When the button or link is clicked, JavaScript will be used in the background to process the request so that the results will be displayed immediately without needing to refresh the page.

How It Works

The user experience for web applications has traditionally involved a point, click, and page refresh mantra. While this type of experience is not particularly a bad one, it is not as nice as the immediate response that is often presented within a native desktop application. The use of Ajax within web applications has helped create a more unified user experience, allowing a web application the ability to produce an "immediate" response much like that of a native desktop application. Field validation (covered in Recipe 4-13) is a great candidate for immediate feedback, but another area where immediate responses work well is when forms are being submitted.

The f:ajax tag can be embedded in an action component in order to invoke the corresponding action method using JavaScript behind the scenes. The f:ajax tag contains a number of attributes, covered in Table 4-18 (see Recipe 4-13), that can be used to invoke Ajax behavior given a specified event and re-render view components when that Ajax behavior is complete. Please refer to Table 4-19 to see the values that can be specified for the execute and render attributes of the f:ajax tag.

In the example for this recipe, the commandButton component with an identifier of contactSubmit contains an f:ajax tag that specifies the event attribute as action, the execute attribute as @form, and the render attribute as @all. This means that when the button is invoked, the ch3ContactController.subscribe method will be called asynchronously using JavaScript, and it will send all the input component values from the form to the server (controller class) for processing. When the Ajax behavior (subscribe method) is complete, all of the components within the view will be re-rendered. By re-rendering all the components in the view, this allows those message components to display any messages that have been queued up as a result of failed validation or a successful form submission. It is possible to process or render only specified components during an Ajax behavior; to learn more about doing so, please see Recipe 4-15.

■ **Note** The event attribute has a default value of action when the f:ajax tag is embedded within a UICommand component. However, it is specified in the code for this example for consistency.

4-14. Making Partial-Page Updates

Problem

You want to execute only a section of a page using an Ajax event and then render the corresponding section's components when the Ajax behavior is complete.

Solution

Use the f:ajax tag to add Ajax functionality to the components that you want to execute and render when the Ajax behavior is completed. Specify only the component identifiers corresponding to those components, or @form, @this, or one of the other execute keywords, for the f:ajax tag execute attribute. Likewise, specify only the component identifiers for the corresponding message components within the render attribute.

Suppose that the Acme Bookstore wants to execute the submission of the newsletter subscription form values and update the form's global message only when the submission is complete. The following commandButton component would execute only the form in which it is placed and the component corresponding to the identifier newsletterSubscriptionMsgs:

```
...
<h:commandButton id="contactSubmit" action="#{ch3ContactController.subscribe}" value="Save">
    <f:ajax event="action" execute="@form" render="newsletterSubscriptionMsgs"/>
</h:commandButton>
...
```

When the button is clicked, the current form component values will be processed with the request, and the ContactController controller class subscribe() method will be invoked. Once the subscribe() method is complete, the component within the form that contains an identifier of newsletterSubscriptionMsgs (in this case, a messages component) will be re-rendered.

■ **Note**   In the case of the newsletter subscription form for the Acme Bookstore, a partial-page render upon completion is a bad idea. This is because the form will never be submitted if the values within the form do not validate correctly. In this case, if some of the form values do not validate correctly, then nothing will be displayed on the page when the save button is clicked because the subscribe method will never be invoked. If the f:ajax tag's render attribute is set to @all, then all of the components that failed validation will have a corresponding error message that is displayed. This example should demonstrate how important it is to process the appropriate portions of the page for the result you are trying to achieve.

How It Works

The f:ajax tag makes it simple to perform partial-page updates. To do so, specify the identifiers for those components that you want to execute for the f:ajax execute attribute. As mentioned in the example for this recipe, suppose you want to execute only a portion of a page, rather than all of the components on the given page. You could do so by identifying the components that you want to execute within the view, specifying them within the f:ajax execute attribute, and then rendering the corresponding message components when the Ajax behavior was completed. If nothing is specified for an f:ajax execute attribute, then the f:ajax tag must be embedded inside a component, in which case the parent component would be executed. Such is the default behavior for the f:ajax execute attribute. In the example, the execute attribute of the f:ajax tag specifies the @form keyword, rather than a specific component id. As mentioned previously, a number of keywords can be specified for both the execute and render attributes of the f:ajax tag. Those keywords are listed in Table 4-19, which describes that the @form keyword indicates that all components within the same form as the given f:ajax tag will be executed when the Ajax behavior occurs. Therefore, all fields within the newsletter subscription form in this example will be sent to the controller class for processing when the button is clicked.

The same holds true for the render attribute, and once the Ajax behavior has completed, any component specified for the render attribute of the f:ajax tag will be re-rendered. Thus, if a validation occurs when a component is being processed because of the result of an f:ajax method call, a corresponding validation failure message can be displayed on the page after the validation fails. Any component can be rendered again, and the same keywords that can be specified for the execute attribute can also be used for the render attribute. In the example, the newsletterSubscriptionMsgs component is rendered once the Ajax behavior is completed.

4-15. Applying Ajax Functionality to a Group of Components

Problem

You want to apply Ajax functionality to a group of input components, rather than to each component separately.

Solution

Enclose any components to which you want to apply Ajax functionality within an f:ajax tag. The f:ajax tag can be the parent to one or more Jakarta Server Faces components, in which case each of the child components inherits the given Ajax behavior. Applying Ajax functionality to multiple components is demonstrated in the following code listing. In the following example excerpt, the newsletter subscription view of the Acme Bookstore application is adjusted so that each of the inputText components that contains a validator is enclosed by a single f:ajax tag. Given that each of the inputText components is embodied within the same f:ajax tag, the f:ajax render attribute has been set to specify the message component for each of the corresponding inputText fields in the group:

```
<ui:define name="content">
    <h:form id="contactForm">
        <h1>Subscribe to Newsletter</h1>
        <p>
            <h:outputText id="newsletterSubscriptionDesc"
                        value="#{ch3ContactController.newsletterDescription}"/>
        </p>
        <br/>
        <h:messages id="newsletterSubscriptionMsgs" globalOnly="true"  errorStyle="color:
        red" infoStyle="color: green"/>
        <br/>
        <f:ajax event="blur" render="firstError lastError emailError genderError
        passwordError passwordConfirmError">
            <h:panelGrid columns="2" bgcolor="" border="0">
                <h:panelGroup>
                    <h:outputLabel for="first" value="First: "/>
```

```
        <h:inputText id="first" size="40" value="#{ch3ContactController.current.
        first}">
            <f:validateLength minimum="1" maximum="40"/>
        </h:inputText>
    </h:panelGroup>
    <h:panelGroup>
        <h:outputLabel for="last" value="Last: "/>
        <h:inputText id="last" size="40" value="#{ch3ContactController.
        current.last}">
            <f:validateLength minimum="1" maximum="40"/>
        </h:inputText>
    </h:panelGroup>
    <h:message id="firstError"
            for="first"
            errorStyle="color:red"/>
    <h:message id="lastError"
            for="last"
            errorStyle="color:red"/>
    <h:panelGroup>
        <h:outputLabel for="email" value="Email: "/>
        <h:inputText id="email" size="40" value="#{ch3ContactController.current.
        email}">
        </h:inputText>
    </h:panelGroup>
    <h:panelGroup/>
    <h:message id="emailError"
            for="email"
            errorStyle="color:red"/>
    <h:panelGroup/>
    <h:selectOneRadio title="Gender" id="gender" value="#{ch3ContactController.
    current.gender}">
        <f:selectItem  itemValue="M" itemLabel="Male"/>
        <f:selectItem itemValue="F" itemLabel="Female"/>
    </h:selectOneRadio>
    <h:panelGroup>
        <h:outputLabel for="occupation" value="Occupation: "/>
        <h:selectOneMenu id="occupation" value="#{ch3ContactController.current.
        occupation}">
            <f:selectItems value="#{ch3ContactController.occupationList}"/>
        </h:selectOneMenu>
    </h:panelGroup>
    <h:message id="genderError"
            for="gender"
            errorStyle="color:red"/>
</h:panelGrid>
<br/>
<h:outputLabel for="description" value="Enter your book interests"/>
<br/>
<h:inputTextarea id="description" rows="5" cols="75"
value="#{ch3ContactController.current.description}"/>
<br/>
```

```
<h:panelGrid columns="2">
    <h:outputLabel for="password" value="Enter a password for site access: "/>
    <h:inputSecret id="password" size="40" value="#{ch3ContactController.
    current.password}">
        <f:validateRequired/>
        <f:ajax event="keyup" listener="#{ch3ContactController.
        passwordStrength}" render="passwordStrengthMessage"/>
    </h:inputSecret>
    <h:outputLabel for="passwordConfirm" value="Confirm Password: "/>
    <h:inputSecret id="passwordConfirm" size="40" value="#{ch3ContactController.
    passwordConfirm}"
                    validator="#{ch3ContactController.validatePassword}">
    </h:inputSecret>
</h:panelGrid>
<h:panelGroup>
    <h:outputText id="passwordStrengthMessage" value="#{ch3ContactController.
    passwordStrengthMessage}"/>
    <h:message id="passwordError"
                for="password"
                style="color:red"/>
</h:panelGroup>
<br/>
<h:message id="passwordConfirmError"
            for="passwordConfirm"
            style="color:red"/>
<br/>
<hr/>
<br/>
<h:panelGrid columns="3">
    <h:panelGroup>
        <h:outputLabel for="newsletterList" value="Newsletters:" style=" "/>
        <h:selectManyListbox id="newsletterList" value="#{ch3ContactController.
        current.newsletterList}">
            <f:selectItems value="#{ch3ContactController.newsletterList}"/>
        </h:selectManyListbox>
    </h:panelGroup>
    <h:panelGroup/>
    <h:panelGroup>
        <h:panelGrid columns="1">
            <h:panelGroup>
                <h:outputLabel for="notifyme" value="Would you like to receive
                other promotional email?"/>
                <h:selectBooleanCheckbox id="notifyme"
                value="#{ch3ContactController.current.receiveNotifications}"/>
            </h:panelGroup>
            <h:panelGroup/>
            <hr/>
            <h:panelGroup/>
            <h:panelGroup>
                <h:outputLabel for="notificationTypes" value="What type of
                notifications are you interested in receiving?"/>
                <br/>
```

239

```
                    <h:selectManyCheckbox id="notifyTypes"
                    value="#{ch3ContactController.current.notificationType}">
                        <f:selectItems value="#{ch3ContactController.
                        notificationTypes}"/>
                    </h:selectManyCheckbox>
                </h:panelGroup>
            </h:panelGrid>
        </h:panelGroup>
    </h:panelGrid>
    <hr/>
    <br/>
</f:ajax>
<h:commandButton id="contactSubmit" action="#{ch3ContactController.subscribe}"
value="Save">
    <f:ajax event="action" execute="@form" render="@all"/>
</h:commandButton>
<h:panelGrid  columns="2" width="400px;">
    <h:commandLink id="manageAccount" action="#{ch3ContactController.manage}"
    value="Manage Subscription">
        <f:ajax event="action" execute="@this" render="@all"/>
    </h:commandLink>
    <h:outputLink id="homeLink" value="home.xhtml">Home</h:outputLink>
</h:panelGrid>
    </h:form>
</ui:define>
```

When the page is rendered, each component will react separately given their associated validations. That is, if validation fails for one component, only the message component that corresponds with the component failing validation will be displayed, although each component identified within the f:ajax render attribute will be re-rendered.

■ **Note** As a result of specifying a global f:ajax tag, the password component can now execute two Ajax requests. One of the Ajax requests for the field is responsible for validating to ensure that the field is not blank, and the other is responsible for ensuring that the given password String is strong.

How It Works

Grouping multiple components with the same Ajax behavior has its benefits. For one, if the behavior needs to be adjusted for any reason, one change can now be made to the Ajax behavior, and each of the components in the group can benefit from the single adjustment. However, the f:ajax tag is smart enough to enable each component to still utilize separate functionality, such as validation or actions, so each can still have their own customized Ajax behavior. To group components under a single f:ajax tag, they must be added to the view as subelements of the f:ajax tag. That is, any child components must be enclosed between the opening and closing f:ajax tags. All of the enclosed components will then use Ajax to send requests to the server using JavaScript in an asynchronous fashion.

In the example for this recipe, a handful of the inputText components within the newsletter subscription view have been embodied inside an f:ajax tag so that their values will be validated using server-side bean validation when they lose focus. The f:ajax tag that is used to group the components has an event attribute set to blur, and its render attribute contains the String-based identifier for each of the message components corresponding to the components that are included in the group. The space-separated list of component ids is used to re-render each of the message components when the Ajax behavior is complete, displaying any errors that occur as a result of the validation.

4-16. Custom Processing of Ajax Functionality

Problem

You want to customize the Ajax processing for Jakarta Server Faces components within a view in your application.

Solution

Write the JavaScript that will be used for processing your request, and utilize the jsf.ajax.request() function along with one of the standard JavaScript event handling attributes for a Jakarta Server Faces component. The following example is the Jakarta Server Faces view for the newsletter subscription page for the Acme Bookstore application. All of the f:ajax tags that were previously used for validating inputText fields (Recipe 3-1) have been removed, and the onblur attribute of each inputText component has been set to use the jsf.ajax.request() method in order to Ajaxify the component. The following excerpt is taken from the view named recipe04_15.xhtml, representing the updated newsletter subscription Jakarta Server Faces view:

...

```
<h:outputScript name="jsf.js" library="jakarta.faces" target="head"/>
<h1>Subscribe to Newsletter</h1>
<p>
    <h:outputText id="newsletterSubscriptionDesc"
                  value="#{ch3ContactController.
                  newsletterDescription}"/>
</p>
<br/>
<h:messages id="newsletterSubscriptionMsgs" globalOnly="true"
errorStyle="color: red" infoStyle="color: green"/>
<br/>
<h:panelGrid columns="2" bgcolor="" border="0">
    <h:panelGroup>
        <h:outputLabel for="first" value="First: " />
        <h:inputText id="first" size="40" value="#{ch3ContactController.
        current.first}"
                     onblur="jsf.ajax.request(this, event, {execute:
                     'first', render: 'firstError'});
     return false;">
            <f:validateLength minimum="1" maximum="40"/>
        </h:inputText>
    </h:panelGroup>
    <h:panelGroup>
        <h:outputLabel for="last" value="Last: " />
        <h:inputText id="last" size="40" value="#{ch3ContactController.
        current.last}"
                     onblur="jsf.ajax.request(this, event, {execute:
                     'last', render: 'lastError'});
```

```
                    return false;">
                        <f:validateLength minimum="1" maximum="40"/>
                    </h:inputText>
                </h:panelGroup>
                <h:message id="firstError"
                        for="first"
                        errorStyle="color:red"/>
                <h:message id="lastError"
                        for="last"
                        errorStyle="color:red"/>
                <h:panelGroup>
                    <h:outputLabel for="email" value="Email: "/>
                    <h:inputText id="email" size="40" value="#{ch3ContactController.
                    current.email}"
                            onblur="jsf.ajax.request(this, event, {execute:
                            'email', render: 'emailError'});
                    return false;"/>
                </h:panelGroup>
                <h:panelGroup/>
                <h:message id="emailError"
                        for="email"
                        errorStyle="color:red"/>
                <h:panelGroup/>
...
```

■ **Note** The <h:panelGroup/> tag is used to add a placeholder panel group to the grid for spacing purposes.

Using this technique, the inputText components that specify Ajax behavior for the onblur event will asynchronously have their values validated when they lose focus. If any custom JavaScript code needs to be used, it can be added to the same inline JavaScript call to jsf.ajax.request().

■ **Note** Method calls to CDI controllers cannot be made using the jsf.ajax.request() technique, so it is not possible to invoke a listener explicitly with the Ajax request.

How It Works

The JavaScript API method jsf.ajax.request() can be accessed directly by a Facelets application, enabling a developer to have slightly more control than using the f:ajax tag. Behind the scenes, the f:ajax tag is converted into a call to jsf.ajax.request(), sending the parameters as specified via the tag's attributes. To use this technique, you must include the jsf.js library within the view. A Jakarta Server Faces outputScript tag should be included in the view, specifying jsf.js as the script name and jakarta.faces as the library. The jsf.js script within this example will be placed in the head of the view, which is done by specifying the head for the target attribute of the outputScript tag. The following excerpt from the example demonstrates what the tag should look like:

```
<h:outputScript name="jsf.js" library="jakarta.faces" target="head"/>
```

■ **Note**   To avoid nested IDs, it is a good idea to specify the h:form attribute of prependId="false" when using jsf.ajax.request() manually. For instance, the form tag should look as follows:

```
<h:form prependId="false">
```

The jsf.ajax.request() method can be called inline, as is the case with the example for this recipe, and it can be invoked from within any of the JavaScript event attributes of a given component. The format for calling the JavaScript method is as follows:

```
jsf.ajax.request(component, event,{execute:'id or keyword', render:'id or keyword'});
```

Usually when the request is made using an inline call, the this keyword is specified for the first parameter, signifying that the current component should be passed. The event keyword is passed as the second parameter, and it passes with it the current event that is occurring against the component. Lastly, a map of name-value pairs is passed, specifying the execute and render attributes along with the component identifiers or keywords that should be executed and rendered after the execution completes, respectively.

■ **Note**   You can also utilize the jsf.ajax.request method from within a controller class by specifying the @ResourceDependency annotation (https://jakarta.ee/specifications/faces/2.3/apidocs/javax/faces/application/ResourceDependency.html) as follows:

```
@ResourceDependency(name="jsf.js" library="jakarta.faces" target="head")
```

The following code may be run by entering the URL http://localhost:8080/JakartaEERecipes_Chapter04-1.0-SNAPSHOT/chapter04/recipe04_15.xhtml in your browser. The final output of this recipe should look like Figure 4-12.

Figure 4-12. *Recipe output*

4-17. Listening for System-Level Events

Problem

You want to invoke a method within your application whenever a system-level event occurs.

Solution

Create a system event listener class by implementing the SystemEventListener interface and overriding the processEvent(SystemEvent event) and isListenerForSource(Object source) methods. Implement these methods accordingly to perform the desired event processing. The following code listing is for a class named BookstoreAppListener, and it is invoked when the application is started up or when it is shutting down:

```
public class BookstoreAppListener implements SystemEventListener {
    @Override
    public void processEvent(SystemEvent event) throws AbortProcessingException {
        if(event instanceof PostConstructApplicationEvent){
```

```
        System.out.println("The application has been constructed...");
    }
    if(event instanceof PreDestroyApplicationEvent){
        System.out.println("The application is being destroyed...");
    }
}
@Override
public boolean isListenerForSource(Object source) {
    return(source instanceof Application);
}
}
```

Next, the system event listener must be registered in the faces-config.xml file. The following excerpt is taken from the faces-config.xml file for the Acme Bookstore application:

```
...
<application>
            <system-event-listener>
                        <system-event-listener-class>
                                    org.jakartaeerecipes.chapter03.recipe03_10.
                                    BookstoreAppListener
                        </system-event-listener-class>
                        <system-event-class>
                                    jakarta.faces.event.
                                    PostConstructApplicationEvent
                        </system-event-class
            </system-event-listener>
            <system-event-listener>
                        <system-event-listener-class>
                                    org.jakartaeerecipes.chapter03.recipe03_10.
                                    BookstoreAppListener
                        </system-event-listener-class>
                        <system-event-class>
                                    jakarta.faces.event.PreDestroyApplicationEvent
                        </system-event-class>
            </system-event-listener>
    </application>
...
```

When the application is started, the message "The application has been constructed..." will be displayed in the server log. When the application is shutting down, the message "The application is being destroyed..." will be displayed in the server log.

How It Works

The ability to perform tasks when an application starts up can sometimes be useful. For instance, let's say you'd like to have an email sent to the application administrator each time the application starts. You can do this by performing the task of sending an email within a class that implements the SystemEventListener interface. A class that implements SystemEventListener must then override two methods, processEvent(SystemEvent event) and isListenerForSource(Object source). The processEvent() method is where the real action occurs, because it is the method into which your custom code should be placed.

245

Whenever a system event occurs, the processEvent() method is invoked. In this method, you will need to perform a check to determine what type of event has occurred so that you can process only those events that are pertinent. To determine the event that has occurred, perform an instanceof() check on the SystemEvent object. In the example, there are two if statements used to determine the type of event that is occurring and to print a different message for each. If the event type is of PostConstructApplicationEvent, then that means the application is being constructed. Otherwise, if the event type is of PreDestroyApplicationEvent, the application is about to be destroyed. The PostConstructApplicationEvent event is called just after the application has been constructed, and PreDestroyApplicationEvent is called just prior to the application destruction.

The other method that must be overridden within the SystemEventListener class is named isListenerForSource(). This method must return true if this listener instance is interested in receiving events from the instance referenced by the source parameter. Since the example class is built to listen for system events for the application, a true value is returned if the source parameter is an instance of Application.

After the system event listener class has been written, it needs to be registered with the application. In the example, you want to listen for both the PostConstructApplicationEvent and the PreDestroyApplicationEvent, so there needs to be a system-event-listener element added to the faces-config. xml file for each of these events. Within the system-event-listener element, specify the name of the event listener class within a system-event-listener-class element and the name of the event within a system-event-class element.

4-18. Listening for Component Events

Problem

You want to invoke a listener method when a specified component event is occurring. For instance, you want to listen for a component render event.

Solution

Embed an f:event tag within the component for which you want to listen for events. The f:event tag allows components to invoke controller class listener methods based upon the current component state. For instance, if a component is being rendered or validated, a specified listener method could be invoked. In the example for this recipe, an outputText component is added to the book view of the Acme Bookstore application to specify whether the current book is in the user's shopping cart. When the outputText component is being rendered, a component listener is invoked that checks the current state of the cart to see whether the book is contained within it. If it is in the cart, then the outputText component will render a message stating so; if not, then the outputText component will render a message stating that it is not in the cart.

The following excerpt is taken from a view named recipe04_17.xhtml, a derivative of the book view for the application. It demonstrates the use of the f:event tag within a component. Note that the outputText component contains no value attribute because the value will be set within the event listener:

```
...
<h:outputText id="isInCart" style="font-style: italic;">
    <f:event type="preRenderComponent" listener="#{ch3CartController.isBookInCart}"/>
</h:outputText>
...
```

The CartController class contains a method named isBookInCart(ComponentSystemEvent). The f:event tag in the view references this listener method via the CartController controller name ch3CartController. The listener method is responsible for constructing the text that will be displayed in the outputText component:

```java
public void isBookInCart(ComponentSystemEvent event) {
        UIOutput output = (UIOutput) event.getComponent();
        if (cart != null) {
            if (searchCart(authorController.getCurrentBook().getTitle()) > 0) {
                output.setValue("This book is currently in your cart.");
            } else {
                output.setValue("This book is not in your cart.");
            }
        } else {
            output.setValue("This book is not in your cart.");
        }
}
```

How It Works

Everything that occurs within Jakarta Server Faces applications is governed by the application life cycle. As part of the life cycle, Jakarta Server Faces components go through different phases throughout their lifetimes. Listeners can be added to Jakarta Server Faces components to perform different tasks when a given phase is beginning or ending. There are two pieces to the puzzle for creating a component listener: the tag that is embedded within the component for which your listener will perform tasks and the listener method itself. To add a listener to a component, the f:event tag should be embedded within the opening and closing tags of the component that will be interrogated. The f:event tag contains a handful of attributes, but only two of them are mandatory for use: type and listener. The type attribute specifies the type of event that will be listened for, and the listener attribute specifies the controller class listener method that will be invoked when that event occurs. The valid values that could be specified for the name attribute are preRenderComponent, postAddToView, preValidate, and postValidate. In addition to these event values, any Java class that extends jakarta.faces.event.ComponentSystemEvent can also be specified for the name attribute.

The listener method must accept a ComponentSystemEvent object. In the example, the listener checks to see whether the shopping cart is null, and if it is, then a message indicating an empty cart will be set for the outputText component's value. Otherwise, if the cart is not empty, then the method looks through the List of books in the cart to see whether the currently selected book is in the cart. A message indicating whether the book is in the cart is then added to the value of the outputText component. Via the listener, the actual value of the component was manipulated. Such a technique could be used in various ways to alter components to suit the needs of the situation.

The following code may be run by visiting the following URL in your browser: http://localhost:8080/JakartaEERecipes_Chapter04-1.0-SNAPSHOT/chapter04/recipe04_16.xhtml. The end product of this recipe should resemble Figure 4-13.

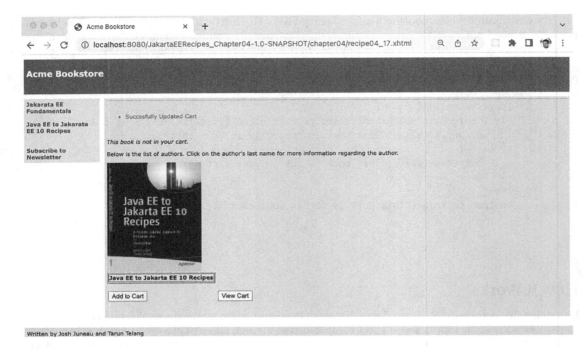

Figure 4-13. *The output of Recipe 4-17*

4-19. Developing a Page Flow

Problem

You want to develop a flow of pages within your application that share information with one another.

Solution

Define a page flow using the faces flow technology, a solution that allows a defined set of views to be interrelated with one another to share a common set of data, and views outside of the flow do not have access to the flow's data. Flows also have their own set of navigational logic, so they are almost like a subprogram within an application. To enable an application to utilize faces flow, a <flow-definition> section should be added to the faces-config.xml file. The section can be empty, because the navigational logic can instead reside in a separate configuration file for the flow. The following faces-config.xml file demonstrates how to enable faces flow for an application:

```
<faces-config version="3.0"
      xmlns="http://xmlns.jcp.org/xml/ns/javaee"
      xmlns:xsi="http://www.w3.org/2001/XMLSchema-instance"
      xsi:schemaLocation="https://jakarta.ee/xml/ns/jakartaee
      https://jakarta.ee/xml/ns/jakartaee/web-facesconfig_3_0.xsd">
  ...
```

```
<flow-definition>
    </flow-definition>
    ...
</faces-config>
```

The views belonging to a flow should be separated from the rest of the application views and placed into a folder at the root of the application's web directory. The folder containing the flow views should be named the same as the flow identifier. Navigation and configuration code is contained within a separate XML configuration file that resides within the flow view directory, and the file is named flowname-flow.xml, where flowname is the flow identifier. The following configuration file demonstrates the configuration for a very basic flow identified by exampleFlow. You can find more information regarding the different elements that can be used within the flow configuration in the "How It Works" section:

```
<faces-config version="3.0" xmlns="https://jakarta.ee/xml/ns/jakartaee"
            xmlns:xsi="http://www.w3.org/2001/XMLSchema-instance"
            xsi:schemaLocation="https://jakarta.ee/xml/ns/jakartaee
                                https://jakarta.ee/xml/ns/jakartaee/web-
                                facesconfig_3_0.xsd">
    <flow-definition id="exampleFlow">
    </flow-definition>
</faces-config>
```

The views belonging to the flow should reside within the flow folder alongside the flow configuration file. Each of the views can access a controller class that is dedicated to facilitating the flow. The flows share a context that begins when the flow is accessed and ends when the flow exits. The following view demonstrates the entry point to a flow named exampleFlow. This example view can be found in the book sources in the file recipes04_18.xhtml:

```
<ui:composition xmlns:ui="http://xmlns.jcp.org/jsf/facelets"
            xmlns:f="http://xmlns.jcp.org/jsf/core"
            xmlns:h="http://xmlns.jcp.org/jsf/html"
            template="layout/custom_template_search.xhtml">
    <ui:define name="content">
        <h:messages globalOnly="true"  errorStyle="color: red" infoStyle="color: green"/>
        <h:form id="flowForm">
            <p>
                Faces Flow Example
            </p>
            <h:commandButton value="Begin Flow" action="exampleFlow"/>
            <h:commandButton value="Stay Here" action="stay"/>
        </h:form>
    </ui:define>
</ui:composition>
```

Next, let's take a look at a view that is accessing the controller class that is dedicated to the flow. In the following view, the controller class named FlowBean is accessed to invoke a method, which will return an implicit navigational String directing the application to the next view in the flow. Notice that this view also accesses the facesContext.application.flowHandler, which I will discuss more in the "How It Works" section:

```
<h:body>
        <f:view>
            <h:form>
```

```
    <p>
        This is the first view of the flow.
        <br/><br/>
        Flow ID: #{facesContext.application.flowHandler.currentFlow.id}
        <br/>
        <h:commandLink value="Go to another view in the flow" action="#{flowBean.
        navMethod()}"/>
    </p>
        </h:form>
    </f:view>
</h:body>
```

Each subsequent view within the flow can also access the resources of the flow's controller class. Lastly, you'll look at the code that is contained within org.jakartaeerecipes.chapter03.FlowBean, which is the controller class that is dedicated to the flow:

```
import jakarta.faces.flow.FlowScoped;
import jakarta.inject.Named;
@Named
@FlowScoped("exampleFlow")
public class FlowBean implements java.io.Serializable {
    private String flowValue;
    private String parameter1;
    /**
     * Creates a new instance of FlowBean
     */
    public FlowBean() {
    }
    /**
     * Initializes the flow
     */
    public void initializeIt(){
        System.out.println("Initialize the flow...");
    }
    /**
     * Finalizes the flow
     */
    public void finalizeIt(){
        System.out.println("Finalize the flow...");
    }
    public String navMethod(){
        return "intermediateFlow";
    }
    public String testMethod(){
        return "intermediate";
    }
    public String endFlow(){
        return "endingFlow";
    }
    /**
     * @return the flowValue
     */
```

```
    public String getFlowValue() {
        return flowValue;
    }
    /**
     * @param flowValue the flowValue to set
     */
    public void setFlowValue(String flowValue) {
        this.flowValue = flowValue;
    }
    /**
     * @return the parameter1
     */
    public String getParameter1() {
        return parameter1;
    }
    /**
     * @param parameter1 the parameter1 to set
     */
    public void setParameter1(String parameter1) {
        this.parameter1 = parameter1;
    }
}
```

This solution provided a quick overview of the files that are required for creating a flow within a Jakarta Server Faces application. In the next section, I'll cover the features in more detail.

How It Works

The concept of session management has been a difficult feat to tackle since the beginning of web applications. A web flow refers to a grouping of web views that are related and must have the ability to share information with each view within the flow. Many web frameworks have attempted to tackle this issue by creating different solutions that would facilitate the sharing of data across multiple views. Oftentimes, a mixture of session variables, request parameters, and cookies are used as a patchwork solution.

Since JSF 2.2, a solution has been adopted for binding multiple Jakarta Server Faces views to each other, allowing them to share information among each other. This solution is referenced as faces flow; and it allows a group of interrelated views to belong to a flow instance, and information can be shared across all the views belonging to a flow instance. Flows contain separate navigation that pertains to the flow itself and not the entire application. As such, flow navigation can be defined in an XML format or via code. A flow contains a single point of entry, and it can be called from any point within an application.

Defining a Flow

As mentioned in the solution to this recipe, the faces-config.xml file for a Jakarta Server Faces application that will utilize the flow feature must contain a <flow-definition> section. This section of the faces-config.xml file can contain information specific to one or more flows residing within an application. However, for the purposes of this recipe, the solution utilizes a separate XML configuration file for use with the flow. Either way will work; the syntax does vary just a bit because the XML configuration file that is flow specific uses a new Jakarta Server Faces taglib for accessing the flow-specific configuration tags.

■ **Note** To learn more about using the faces-config.xml file for flow configuration, please refer to the online documentation (`https://eclipse-ee4j.github.io/jakartaee-tutorial/#navigation-model`).

Even if a flow is not using the faces-config.xml file for defining the flow configuration, the <flow-definition> section must exist to tell the Jakarta Server Faces runtime that flows are utilized within the application.

The flow-specific configuration file and all flow-related views should reside within the same folder, at the root of the application's web directory. The name of the folder should be the same as the flow identifier. As mentioned in the solution, the flow configuration file should be named flowname-flow.xml, where flowname is the same as the flow identifier.

The Flow Controller Class

A flow contains its own controller class annotated as @FlowScoped, which differs from @SessionScoped because the data can be accessed only by other views (ViewNodes) belonging to the flow. The @FlowScoped annotation relies upon Contexts and Dependency Injection (CDI), because FlowScoped is a CDI scope that causes the runtime to consider classes with the @FlowScoped annotation to be in the scope of the specified flow. A @FlowScoped bean maintains a life cycle that begins and ends with a flow instance. Multiple flow instances can exist for a single application, and if a user begins a flow within one browser tab and then opens another, a new flow instance will begin in the new tab. This solution resolves many lingering issues around sessions and standard browsers that allow users to open multiple tabs. To maintain separate flow instances, the ClientId is used by Jakarta Server Faces to differentiate among multiple instances.

Each flow can contain an initializer and a finalizer (i.e., a method that will be invoked when a flow is entered and a method that will be invoked when a flow is exited, respectively). To declare an initializer, specify a child element named <initializer> within the flow configuration <flow-definition>. The initializer element can be an EL expression that declares the controller class initializer method, as such:

```
...
<initializer>#{flowBean.initializeIt}</initializer>
...
```

Similarly, a <finalizer> element can be specified within the flow configuration to define the method that will be called when the flow is exited. The following demonstrates how to set the finalizer to an EL expression declaring the controller class finalizer method:

```
...
<finalizer>#{flowBean.finalizeIt}</finalizer>
...
```

Flows can contain method calls and variable values that are accessible only via the flow nodes. These methods and variables should be placed within the FlowScoped bean and used the same as standard controller class methods and variables. The main difference is that any method or variable that is defined within a FlowScoped bean is available only for a single flow instance.

Navigating Flow View Nodes

Flows contain their own navigational rules, which can be defined within the faces-config.xml file or the individual flow configuration files. These rules can be straightforward and produce a page-by-page navigation, or they can include conditional logic. There are a series of elements that can be specified within the navigation rules, which will facilitate conditional navigation. Table 4-20 lists the different elements, along with an explanation of what they do.

Table 4-20. *Flow Navigational Elements*

Element	Description
view	Navigates to a standard Jakarta Server Faces view
switch	Represents one or more EL expressions that conditionally evaluate to true or false. If true, then navigation occurs to the specified view node
flow-return	Outcome determined by the caller of the flow
flow-call	Represents a call to another flow; creates a nested flow
method-call	Arbitrary method call that can invoke a method that returns a navigational outcome

The following navigational sequence is an example of a flow navigation that contains conditional logic using the elements listed in Table 4-20:

```
<flow-definition>
    <start-node>exampleFlow</start-node>
    <switch id="startNode">
        <navigation-case>
            <if>#{flowBean.someCondition}</if>
                <from-outcome>newView</from-outcome>
        </navigation-case>
    </switch>
    <view id="oneFlow">
        <vdl-document>oneFlow.xhtml</vdl-document>
    </view>
    <flow-return id="exit">
        <navigation-case>
            <from-outcome>exitFlow</from-outcome>
        </navigation-case>
    </flow-return>
    <finalizer>#{flowBean.finalizeIt}</finalizer>
 </flow-definition>
```

Flow Expression Language

Flows contain a new Expression Language variable named facesFlowScope. This variable is associated with the current flow, and it is a map that can be used for storing arbitrary values for use within a flow. The key-value pairs can be stored and read via a Jakarta Server Faces view or through Java code within a controller class. For example, to display the content for a particular map key, you could use the following:

The content for the key is: #{facesFlowScope.myKey}

To execute this code, go to the following URL in your browser:

http://localhost:8080/JakartaEERecipes_Chapter04-1.0-SNAPSHOT/chapter04/recipe04_18.xhtml

Once the page is loaded the output in your browser will look similar to Figure 4-14.

Figure 4-14. *The output of Recipe 4-18*

4-20. Broadcasting Messages from the Server to All Clients

Problem

Your organization has constructed a Jakarta EE application, and it is in use by several clients. You wish to have the ability to send a message from the server and have that message distributed to all the clients at once.

Solution

Make use of the f:websocket tag, which was new with the release of JSF 2.3, to send a message to all listening clients. The following example includes a client view which contains a text box, a send button, and an f:websocket tag. The user can type a message into the text box and click the send button, and the typed message will be sent to all other clients that are currently listening on the same channel:

```
<html xmlns="http://www.w3.org/1999/xhtml"
      xmlns:ui="http://xmlns.jcp.org/jsf/facelets"
      xmlns:f="http://xmlns.jcp.org/jsf/core"
      xmlns:h="http://xmlns.jcp.org/jsf/html">
    <head>
    </head>
    <body>
        <ui:composition template="layout/custom_template_search.xhtml">
            <ui:define name="content">
```

```
                <h:messages globalOnly="true"  errorStyle="color: red" infoStyle="color:
                green"/>
                <h:form id="webSocketForm">
                    <script type="text/javascript">
                        function messageListener(message) {
                            document.getElementById("messageDiv").innerHTML += message +
                            "<br/>";
                        }
                    </script>
                    <p>
                        Websocket Integration Example
                    </p>
                    <p>
                        Enter text into the box below and press the send button.  This
                        will send
                        a message to all connected clients.
                    </p>
                    <h:inputText id="websocketMessageText" value="#{bookstoreController.
                    messageText}"/>
                    <br/>
                    <h:commandButton id="sendMessage" action="#{bookstoreController.
                    sendMessage}" value="Send">
                        <f:ajax/>
                    </h:commandButton>
                    <br/>
                    <f:websocket channel="messagePusher" onmessage="messageListener" />
                    <div id="messageDiv"/>
                </h:form>
            </ui:define>
        </ui:composition>
    </body>
</html>
```

The following code shows the server-side code behind the messagePusher channel and the bookstoreController.sendMessage() method:

```
import java.util.Date;
import jakarta.enterprise.context.ApplicationScoped;
import jakarta.faces.push.Push;
import jakarta.faces.push.PushContext;
import jakarta.inject.Inject;
import jakarta.inject.Named;
@Named("bookstoreController")
@ApplicationScoped
public class BookstoreController {
    private Date dayAndTime = null;
    private int counter;
    @Inject
    @Push(channel="messagePusher")
    private PushContext push;
    private String messageText;
. . .
```

```
/**
    * Initiates a notification to all Websocket clients.
    */
   public void sendMessage(){
       System.out.println("sending message");
       push.send(messageText);
       messageText = null;
   }
. . .
}
```

The resulting solution looks like the following. If one types and clicks send, all listening clients (on the same view) will receive the message. The code can be executed by visiting the URL http://localhost:8080/ JakartaEERecipes_Chapter04-1.0-SNAPSHOT/chapter04/recipe04_19.xhtml in your browser. The output of this recipe would look like Figure 4-15.

Figure 4-15. *Sending messages to connected clients using WebSockets in Jakarta Server Faces*

How It Works

WebSockets have become a standard protocol for client and server communication. There are a couple of different ways in which to implement WebSocket solutions. One can utilize a framework such as Atmosphere to develop WebSockets, or since the release of Java EE 7, the native WebSocket support can be utilized. Both approaches are supported by the Jakarta Server Faces WebSocket. The support in JSF 2.3 includes both implementations, so it provides some flexibility. To enable this support, one must specify the jakarta.faces. ENABLE_WEBSOCKET_ENDPOINT context parameter in the web.xml deployment descriptor with a value of true, as follows:

```
<context-param>
    <param-name>jakarta.faces.ENABLE_WEBSOCKET_ENDPOINT</param-name>
    <param-value>true</param-value>
</context-param>
```

The f:websocket tag enables support for WebSockets within Jakarta Server Faces client views. The tag includes a required channel attribute, which is a ValueExpression used to list the channel on which the WebSocket client will listen. The tag also includes a required onmessage attribute, which is also a ValueExpression, and it is used to list the name of a JavaScript function that is to be executed when the WebSocket message is received. In the example, you can see that the channel is set to messagePusher, meaning that the server must send message(s) to the channel named messagePusher in order to successfully send to this client. The message attribute is set to messageListener, and if you look at the JavaScript source that has been added to the view, you can see that it contains a function named messageListener. This function is executed when the message is received. In this example, the function merely prints a message to the div with an ID of messageDiv in the view. The signature of the JavaScript function in this example accepts the message only. However, a JavaScript function could also accept a channel name and event argument, if needed.

The f:websocket tag contains a number of other useful attributes as well. While optional, the following parameters may be of use in certain circumstances:

- onclose: Specifies a JavaScript function to invoke when the message is closed.

- scope: Used to specify a limit as to where messages are propagated. If set to session, this attribute limits the messages to all client views with the same WebSocket channel in the current session only.

- port: Specifies the TCP port number other than the HTTP port, if needed.

Now let's take a look at the server-side implementation. The solution to this recipe uses a new PushContext, which is injected into an ApplicationScoped bean. This PushContext is used to send the message to all listening clients, and it can be injected into any CDI bean by including the @Push annotation, along with the context. The name of the channel can be specified via an optional channel attribute on the @Push annotation; otherwise, it will assume the same name as the PushContext identifier. In the example, the PushContext is simply named "push." This is the channel on which all clients must listen.

To send a message, call upon the send() method of the PushContext, passing the message to be broadcast. The message will be encoded as JSON and delivered to the message argument of the JavaScript function on the client which corresponds to the function named in the f:websocket onmessage attribute. The message can be composed of any number of containers, including a plain String, List, Map, Object, and so on.

4-21. Programmatically Searching for Components

Problem

You wish to use Expression Language or Java code to find a particular component or a set of components within a Jakarta Server Faces view. There are a number of reasons why you may wish to obtain access to components, such as invoking the component programmatically or referencing them from another component within the view.

Solution #1

Make use of the Jakarta Server Faces component search framework via the use of expression language or programmatically from Java code. In the following example, a Jakarta Server Faces panelGrid component is updated via expression language using key Jakarta Server Faces search terms. The f:ajax tag contains a render attribute that specifies @parent, indicating that the parent component should be re-rendered once the Ajax process is complete:

```
<h:panelGrid columns="2">
                <h:outputLabel for="password" value="Enter a password for site access: "/>
                <h:inputSecret id="password" size="40" value="#{ch3ContactController.
                current.password}">
                    <f:validateRequired/>
                    <f:ajax event="blur" render="@parent"/>
                </h:inputSecret>
                <h:panelGroup/>
                <h:message id="passwordError"
                        for="password"
                        style="color:red"/>
                <h:outputLabel for="passwordConfirm" value="Confirm Password: "/>
                <h:inputSecret id="passwordConfirm" size="40" value="#{ch3ContactController.
                passwordConfirm}"
                                validator="#{ch3ContactController.validatePassword}">
                    <f:ajax    event="blur" render="@parent"/>
                </h:inputSecret>
                <h:panelGroup/>
                <h:message id="passwordConfirmError"
                        for="passwordConfirm"
                        style="color:red"/>
        </h:panelGrid>
```

Solution #2

Utilize the programmatic API to search for components from within a server-side CDI controller class. In the following solution, a button from a Jakarta Server Faces view is used to invoke an action method in the CDI bean. The action method merely demonstrates the programmatic search expression API. In the action method, a component is looked up by explicit ID:

```
public void findById() {
        FacesContext context = FacesContext.getCurrentInstance();
        SearchExpressionContext searchContext = SearchExpressionContext.createSearchExpressi
        onContext(context, context.getViewRoot());
        context.getApplication()
                .getSearchExpressionHandler()
                .resolveComponent(
                    searchContext,
                    "passwordConfirm",
                    (ctx, target) -> out.print(target.getId()));
}
```

How It Works

For years, Jakarta Server Faces developers had difficulty referencing Jakarta Server Faces components within a view by ID. There are a couple of problems that can be encountered if attempting to simply look up a component by ID. First, if an ID is not explicitly assigned to a Jakarta Server Faces component, then the FacesServlet assigns one automatically. In this situation, the ID is unknown until runtime, and therefore it is almost impossible to reference the component using EL or from within Java code. Second, even if a Jakarta Server Faces component is assigned a static ID, then the nesting architecture of Jakarta Server Faces views and the Jakarta Server Faces component tree causes the IDs of each parent component to be prepended to the ID of the child component. This can cause long and sometimes difficult to maintain component IDs. Moreover, even if a specified component is easy to identify by prepending parent IDs, some components, such as those nested in tables, will still have a dynamic ID assigned at runtime.

There have been a number of third-party libraries that have developed solutions to combat this problem. OmniFaces and PrimeFaces are some of the most widely used. The addition of the Jakarta Server Faces search expression API to Jakarta Server Faces proper significantly reduces the work that needs to be done in order to gain access to Jakarta Server Faces components within a view. This is especially the case in the event that a component is nested deep within other components in a view or part of a dataTable as mentioned previously. The search expression API allows one to utilize keywords to help search the component tree in a dynamic manner, rather than hard-coding static IDs that may change down the road.

Prior to JSF 2.3, there were four abstract search keywords that could be used to obtain reference to components, those being "@all", "@this", "@form", and "@none". Moreover, one could only perform EL search expressions in the f:ajax tag. This was quite a limitation, and JSF 2.3 greatly expands this functionality. Please refer to Table 4-21 for the search keywords. The following features have been added to the search expression API:

- Keywords and search expressions can be used programmatically.

- Many more keywords have been added.

- Keywords accept arguments.

- Keywords are extendible and can be chained.

Table 4-21. *Search Keywords*

Keyword	Description
@child(n)	The nth child of the base component
@composite	Nearest composite component of the base
@id(id)	Nearest descendant of the base component with an id matching a specified value
@namingcontainer	Nearest naming container of the base component
@next	Next component in view following the base component
@parent	Parent of the base component
@previous	Previous component to the base
@root	The UIViewRoot

The solution demonstrates how to find components using the @parent keyword, but any of the others can be used and strung together in order to find desired components.

Another new feature with JSF 2.3 is the programmatic search expression API. This makes it possible to gain access to components from within the controller class. The second listing in the solution demonstrates how to use the programmatic API. To use the API, first create a SearchExpressionContext, which will later be passed as a parameter to help find the component. Second, call upon the FacesContext to gain reference to the application via getApplication(), and then invoke getSearchExpressionHandler().resolveComponent(), passing the SearchExpressionContext, the search expression string, and the function to call when the component is found. This can be used to search for any component via a programmatic API.

CHAPTER 5

■ ■ ■

Jakarta MVC

Over the years, Jakarta EE has evolved from a servlet-centric platform to one that supports a variety of different approaches for creating web and enterprise applications. In the early days of enterprise Java, one would focus on developing servlets for building the front end, as well as the integration and business layers. This was because it was mainly focused on component orientation. Jakarta Server Pages made things get more dynamic. Developers could now split the workload between teams who would focus on HTML markup and Jakarta Server Pages tags to generate the front end and those who would focus on application logic. Jakarta Server Faces took it one step further by adhering to the Model-View-Controller pattern, whereby code logic was completely separated from page markup, creating three different tiers. This design pattern makes development more logical and long-term maintenance much easier. The architecture of the Model-View-Controller pattern is depicted in Figure 5-1.

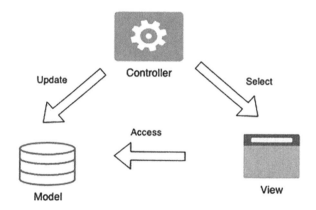

Figure 5-1. *Jakarta MVC architecture*

Jakarta Server Faces is a mature and robust technology for building enterprise applications; the framework is somewhat inflexible in that you must adhere to many philosophies. For example, Jakarta Server Faces has a life cycle that must be followed. Certain phases of the life cycle can be skipped, but ultimately there is still some level of control given to the Faces servlet. The Jakarta MVC framework takes the Model-View-Controller focus one step further. It allows developers to adhere to the three-tier architecture without forcing certain behavior. The MVC framework was originally intended to be included with Jakarta EE 8 under JSR 371, but later to minimize the number of new specifications for inclusion, it was removed from the platform. However, Oracle handed off the ownership of MVC 1.0 to the community, which later transferred the specification to the Eclipse Foundation.

Throughout this chapter, I will discuss the configuration for a Jakarta MVC application; how to develop controllers, models, and views; and how to tie it all together. The framework was built on top of Jakarta RESTful Web Services, so many of the key components are the same. Therefore, you'll learn a bit about the fundamentals of the Jakarta RESTful Web Services API in this chapter as well. As I always state, if you have more tools in the shed, you will be able to accomplish a larger variety of tasks. The same holds true about application development, and frameworks such as Jakarta Server Faces are great for development of some applications, but Jakarta MVC may be even better for developing others. After reading this chapter, you will have a better understanding of the differences that Jakarta MVC has to offer. You should be able to dive in developing with the Jakarta MVC framework as I will walk through the development of a Jakarta MVC application from start to finish, using the Apache NetBeans IDE for development.

Project Structure

The code for this chapter is organized as per the following structure:

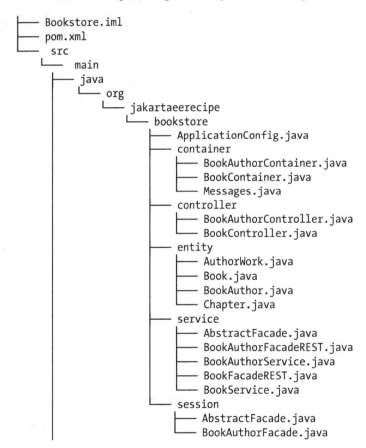

```
├── Bookstore.iml
├── pom.xml
└── src
    └── main
        ├── java
        │   └── org
        │       └── jakartaeerecipe
        │           └── bookstore
        │               ├── ApplicationConfig.java
        │               ├── container
        │               │   ├── BookAuthorContainer.java
        │               │   ├── BookContainer.java
        │               │   └── Messages.java
        │               ├── controller
        │               │   ├── BookAuthorController.java
        │               │   └── BookController.java
        │               ├── entity
        │               │   ├── AuthorWork.java
        │               │   ├── Book.java
        │               │   ├── BookAuthor.java
        │               │   └── Chapter.java
        │               ├── service
        │               │   ├── AbstractFacade.java
        │               │   ├── BookAuthorFacadeREST.java
        │               │   ├── BookAuthorService.java
        │               │   ├── BookFacadeREST.java
        │               │   └── BookService.java
        │               └── session
        │                   ├── AbstractFacade.java
        │                   └── BookAuthorFacade.java
```

```
├── resources
│   └── META-INF
│       ├── beans.xml
│       └── persistence.xml
└── webapp
    ├── WEB-INF
    │   ├── views
    │   │   ├── book.jsp
    │   │   ├── bookAuthor.jsp
    │   │   ├── bookAuthor.xhtml
    │   │   └── books.xhtml
    │   └── web.xml
    └── glassfish-web.xml
```

5-1. Configure an Application for the Jakarta MVC Framework

Problem

You wish to create a Jakarta MVC application project. Therefore, you need to configure the project to work with the Jakarta MVC API (an implementation of Jakarta MVC).

Solution

Add the appropriate configuration files to the project and configure Jakarta RESTful Web Services accordingly. In this chapter, I will cover the use of Maven as the project build system, but you could easily configure it using another build system, such as Gradle. The configuration of a Jakarta MVC application is very much like that of an application that uses the Jakarta RESTful Web Services specification. To begin, let's create a new project in Apache NetBeans. Create a Maven web application project, and name it Bookstore, as shown in Figures 5-2 and 5-3.

Figure 5-2. *New project*

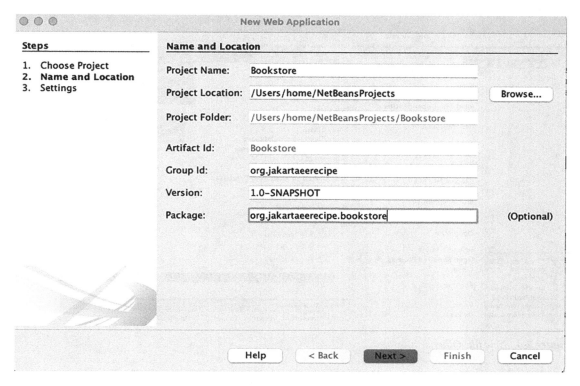

Figure 5-3. *New Maven web application: Name and Location*

Next, be sure to choose a Jakarta EE Web or Jakarta EE–compliant application server for deployment, and then select Jakarta EE version as the Jakarta EE version of your application server.

Click "Finish" to create the project. Once the project has been created, generate a beans.xml file. To do this, right-click the project, and click "New" ➤ Other.... as shown in Figure 5-4.

Then select "Contexts and Dependency Injections" from Categories and "beans.xml (CDI Configuration File)" as File Types in the dialog shown in Figure 5-5.

Next, accept the defaults to create it within WEB-INF and keep the name beans.xml, and finally click "Finish."

Figure 5-4. *New file: Other...*

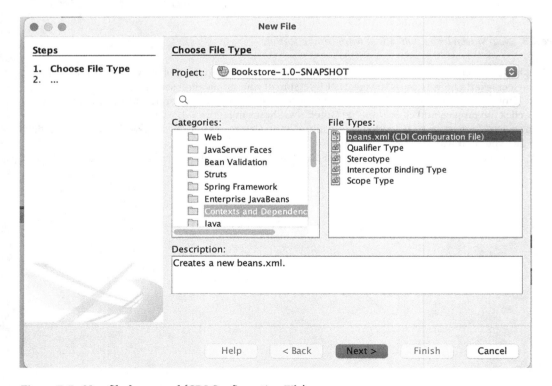

Figure 5-5. *New file: beans.xml (CDI Configuration File)*

Next, add the required dependencies to the POM file. To do so, right-click the project and choose "Open POM" from the contextual menu. Once the POM file opens, add the dependencies for the Jakarta MVC API:

```
<dependencies>
        <dependency>
            <groupId>jakarta.platform</groupId>
            <artifactId>jakarta.jakartaee-web-api</artifactId>
            <version>10.0.0-RC1</version>
            <scope>provided</scope>
        </dependency>
        <dependency>
            <groupId>jakarta.mvc</groupId>
            <artifactId>jakarta.mvc-api</artifactId>
            <version>2.0.0</version>
        </dependency>
        <dependency>
            <groupId>org.eclipse.krazo</groupId>
            <artifactId>krazo-core</artifactId>
            <version>2.0.1</version>
        </dependency>
        <dependency>
            <groupId>org.eclipse.krazo</groupId>
            <artifactId>krazo-jersey</artifactId>
            <version>2.0.1</version>
        </dependency>
    </dependencies>
```

The jakarta.mvc-api includes APIs defined in MVC spec 2.0, and the krazo-core is its implementation. For GlassFish, as the underlying RESTful Web Service provider is Jersey, you would need a krazo-jersey as an adapter to your dependency. In case your application server uses other implementations of RESTful Web Services like RESTEasy and cxf, you need to replace this dependency with an appropriate adapter.

Lastly, the application will need to be configured for use with Jakarta RESTful Web Services. To do so, create an ApplicationConfig class within the org.jakartaeerecipe.bookstore package by selecting File ➤ New ➤ "Java Class," as seen in Figure 5-6.

Figure 5-6. *Create an ApplicationConfig class*

The ApplicationConfig class is used to map the RESTful web services to a URI. The @ApplicationPath annotation is used to configure the path for URI. The following code shows the sources for this class:

```
package org.jakartaeerecipe.bookstore;

import java.util.*;
import jakarta.mvc.security.Csrf;
import jakarta.ws.rs.*;

@ApplicationPath("controller")
public class ApplicationConfig extends Application {
    @Override
    public Map<String, Object> getProperties() {
        final Map<String, Object> map = new HashMap<>();
        map.put(Csrf.CSRF_PROTECTION, Csrf.CsrfOptions.EXPLICIT);
        return map;
    }
}
```

Once these configurations are complete, you are ready to begin coding a Jakarta MVC application.

How It Works

The Jakarta MVC framework requires several easy configurations made to a project to pull in the required dependencies and to configure CDI and Jakarta RESTful Web Services properly. In this recipe, I showed how to make these configurations, so now let's see why we need to make them. As mentioned previously, the Jakarta RESTful Web Services configuration should reside within a class that extends `jakarta.ws.rs.core.Application`, which defines components and metadata for a Jakarta RESTful Web Services application. The Jakarta MVC framework builds upon the Jakarta RESTful Web Services API, so this configuration is mandatory to provide the ability to generate controller classes (see Recipe 5-3 for more details).

In the solution, I named the class which extends the `jakarta.ws.rs.core.Application` class `ApplicationConfig`. As you see from the code, by extending the `Application` class, we can override the `getProperties()` method to provide application-specific configuration. In this case, I added CSRF (Cross-Site Request Forgery) Protection, which is a standard security feature (see Recipe 5-8). The `getProperties()` method should return a `Map<String, Object>`. Lastly, the class should be annotated with `@ApplicationPath`, and the URI mapping for the controllers (or Jakarta RESTful Web Services classes) should be passed as a String. In this case, the path is "controller," and the URL for accessing controller classes should translate to `http://localhost:8080/Bookstore/controller/`.

The dependencies for Jakarta MVC must be referenced within the Maven POM file. In this case, there are dependencies, with the expectation that the Jakarta EE full or web profile is also a dependency.

■ **Note** There are different profiles available for Jakarta EE. The web profile contains a smaller number of dependencies for developing web projects, whereas the full profile contains all Jakarta EE dependencies. With Jakarta EE 10, we have a new profile known as Core Profile which is designed for small runtimes. It includes specifications geared toward microservices and ahead-of-time compilations.

The required dependencies for Jakarta MVC are `jakarta.mvc-api` and `krazo`, which is the reference implementation. Lastly, ensure that you create a `beans.xml` configuration file for Contexts and Dependency Injection. This configuration file allows one to specify how CDI beans are discovered. For the purposes of this example, accept the default discovery mode of annotated, as follows:

```xml
<?xml version="1.0" encoding="UTF-8"?>
<beans xmlns="https://jakarta.ee/xml/ns/jakartaee"
       xmlns:xsi="http://www.w3.org/2001/XMLSchema-instance"
       xsi:schemaLocation="https://jakarta.ee/xml/ns/jakartaee https://jakarta.ee/xml/ns/
       jakartaee/beans_3_0.xsd"
       bean-discovery-mode="annotated">
</beans>
```

This recipe walked through the configurations required to create a Jakarta MVC project. In the following recipes, I will cover how to build out the project into a fully functional web application.

5-2. Making Data Available for the Application

Problem

You need to obtain existing data for your application, and you'd like to easily make the data available for your web views.

Solution #1

Utilize the Jakarta Persistence API along with Jakarta Enterprise Beans to provide data to your application from a database. In this chapter, we would be using the Apache Derby database. First, create entity classes which will map each of your database tables to a corresponding Java object. Please see Chapter 8 for more details on generating entity classes.

For the purposes of the application that is being developed for this chapter, entity classes will be generated for several of the tables being used throughout this book. In this solution, only a single entity class will be generated to demonstrate. However, if you look at the sources for the example application, then you will find an entity class for each of the tables that are used within the application.

Since the application will be used for the purposes of an online bookstore, the database tables that are used along with the application pertain to authors and books. In this solution, we will generate the entity class for the BOOK_AUTHOR database table. As a brief primer, an entity class maps each column of a database table to a corresponding class member. The following code is for the BookAuthor entity class:

```
package org.jakartaeerecipe.bookstore.entity;

import java.io.Serializable;
import java.math.BigInteger;
import java.util.*;
import jakarta.persistence.*;
import jakarta.validation.constraints.*;

@Entity
@Table(name = "BOOK_AUTHOR")
public class BookAuthor implements Serializable {

    private static final long serialVersionUID = 1L;

    @Id
    @Basic(optional = false)
    @Column(name = "ID")
    private BigInteger id;

    @Size(max = 30)
    @Column(name = "LASTNAME")
    private String last;

    @Size(max = 30)
    @Column(name = "FIRSTNAME")
    private String first;

    @Lob
    @Column(name = "BIO")
    private String bio;
    @ManyToMany
    @JoinTable(name="AUTHOR_WORK",
            joinColumns=
            @JoinColumn(name="AUTHOR_ID", referencedColumnName="ID"),
            inverseJoinColumns=
            @JoinColumn(name="BOOK_ID", referencedColumnName="ID"))
```

```
    private Set<Book> books;
    public BookAuthor() {
    }
    public BookAuthor(BigDecimal id) {
        this.id = id;
    }
...
    // getters and setters
...
    @Override
    public int hashCode() {
        int hash = 0;
        hash += (id != null ? id.hashCode() : 0);
        return hash;
    }
    @Override
    public boolean equals(Object object) {
        if (!(object instanceof BookAuthor)) {
            return false;
        }
        BookAuthor other = (BookAuthor) object;
        if ((this.id == null && other.id != null) || (this.id != null && !this.
        id.equals(other.id))) {
            return false;
        }
        return true;
    }
    @Override
    public String toString() {
        return "org.jakartaeerecipe.bookstore.entity.BookAuthor[ id=" + id + " ]";
    }
}
```

Once the entity classes for each database table have been created, develop Jakarta Enterprise Beans façade (session bean) classes for each of them. To do this, first generate a package to hold all the session bean classes. In this case, create a package named org.jakartaeerecipes.bookstore.session. Next, create a session bean class for each of the entity classes that have been created. To create the session bean for the BookAuthor class, create a class within the newly created package, or if using Apache NetBeans, right-click the new package and select "New" ➤ "Session Beans from Entity Classes." Name the bean BookAuthorFacade. If using Apache NetBeans, two classes will be generated, one of them is an abstract class named AbstractFacade. This abstract class will be extended by each of the session beans that are created for the application. It contains a set of common methods that can be used throughout all of the session beans. If creating a session bean from scratch, you'll need to create these methods for each bean or use a similar technique to provide a common implementation for beans to use, similar to the AbstractFacade.

No matter which technique you choose, you will need to generate a persistence unit for your application. This is an XML configuration file that is used to contain connection configuration for your database. Typically, the persistence unit contains Java Naming and Directory Interface (JNDI) information for connecting to a data source that has been defined within an application server container. In this case, create a persistence unit by right-clicking your project and choosing "Create Persistence Unit" if using Apache NetBeans. Choose an existing data source that has been configured for your database within Apache NetBeans.

The following code is that of the `AbstractFacade`, which is automatically generated by Apache NetBeans:

```
package org.jakartaeerecipe.bookstore.session;

import jakarta.persistence.*;
import jakarta.persistence.criteria.*;
import java.util.List;

public abstract class AbstractFacade<T> {
    private final Class<T> entityClass;
    public AbstractFacade(Class<T> entityClass) {
        this.entityClass = entityClass;
    }
    protected abstract EntityManager getEntityManager();
    public void create(T entity) {
        getEntityManager().persist(entity);
    }
    public void edit(T entity) {
        getEntityManager().merge(entity);
    }
    public void remove(T entity) {
        getEntityManager().remove(getEntityManager().merge(entity));
    }
    public T find(Object id) {
        return getEntityManager().find(entityClass, id);
    }
    public List findAll() {
        CriteriaQuery<Object> cq = getEntityManager().getCriteriaBuilder().createQuery();
        cq.select(cq.from(entityClass));
        return getEntityManager().createQuery(cq).getResultList();
    }
    public List findRange(int[] range) {
        CriteriaQuery<Object> cq = getEntityManager().getCriteriaBuilder().createQuery();
        cq.select(cq.from(entityClass));
        Query q = getEntityManager().createQuery(cq);
        q.setMaxResults(range[1] - range[0] + 1);
        q.setFirstResult(range[0]);
        return q.getResultList();
    }
    public int count() {
        CriteriaQuery<Object> cq = getEntityManager().getCriteriaBuilder().createQuery();
        Root<T> rt = cq.from(entityClass);
        cq.select(getEntityManager().getCriteriaBuilder().count(rt));
        Query q = getEntityManager().createQuery(cq);
        return ((Long) q.getSingleResult()).intValue();
    }
}
```

Next, let's look at the code that is generated for the BookAuthorFacade. This code is also automatically generated by Apache NetBeans, or it could be manually created if you wish:

```
package org.jakartaeerecipes.bookstore.session;

import jakarta.ejb.Stateless;
import org.jakartaeerecipe.bookstore.entity.BookAuthor;
import jakarta.persistence.EntityManager;
import jakarta.persistence.PersistenceContext;

@Stateless
public class BookAuthorFacade extends AbstractFacade<BookAuthor> {

    @PersistenceContext(unitName = "default")
    private EntityManager em;

    public BookAuthorFacade() {
        super(BookAuthor.class);
    }

    @Override
    protected EntityManager getEntityManager() {
        return em;
    }
}
```

Solution #2

Utilize RESTful web services to obtain data for your application. As mentioned in Solution #1, create entity classes which will map each of your database tables to a corresponding Java object. Once the entity classes have been created, develop REST service classes for each of them. If using an IDE such as Apache NetBeans, it will only take a few clicks to generate these RESTful web services, as most IDEs provide an autogeneration option. Otherwise, simply create a Plain Old Java Object (POJO) and annotate it accordingly to develop a RESTful service class.

To begin, create a new package and name it org.jakartaeerecipe.bookstore.service. Next, create the RESTful class inside the newly created package. In the Apache NetBeans IDE, right-click the package and select "New…" ➤ "Web Services" ➤ "RESTful Web Services from Entity Classes" and then choose "Next." When the "New RESTful Web Services from Entity Classes" dialog is displayed, select the org. jakartaeerecipes.entity.BookAuthor class. On the next screen, change the resource package such that it is org.jakartaeerecipes.bookstore.service, as shown in Figure 5-7. Lastly, choose "Finish" to create the class.

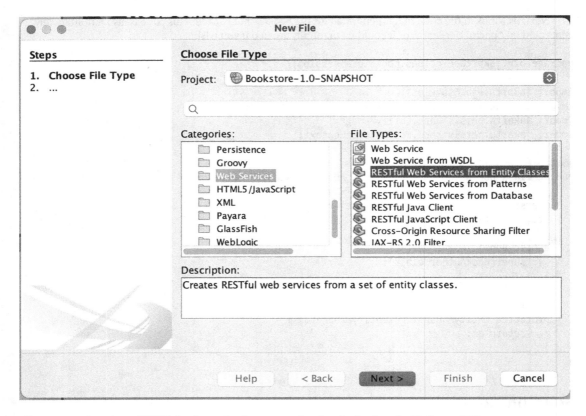

Figure 5-7. *Creating a RESTful web service from an entity class in the Apache NetBeans IDE*

Like the creation of a Jakarta Enterprise Beans, the creation of a RESTful web service provides methods that can be used to perform create, read, update, and delete actions against a database. Furthermore, since these methods are annotated as REST services, they can be invoked via a REST client. The following code shows the RESTful web service class for the BookAuthor entity. This class is named BookAuthorFacadeREST by the NetBeans IDE, or you can name it differently if generating from scratch:

```
package org.jakartaeerecipe.bookstore.service;

import java.math.BigDecimal;
import java.util.List;

import jakarta.ejb.Stateless;
import jakarta.persistence.*;
import jakarta.ws.rs.*;

import org.jakartaeerecipe.bookstore.entity.BookAuthor;
@Stateless
@Path("org.jakartaeerecipe.bookstore.entity.bookauthor")
public class BookAuthorFacadeREST extends AbstractFacade<BookAuthor> {
    @PersistenceContext(unitName = "BookStore_1.0PU")
    private EntityManager em;
```

```java
    public BookAuthorFacadeREST() {
        super(BookAuthor.class);
    }
    @POST
    @Override
    @Consumes({MediaType.APPLICATION_XML, MediaType.APPLICATION_JSON})
    public void create(BookAuthor entity) {
        super.create(entity);
    }
    @PUT
    @Path("{id}")
    @Consumes({MediaType.APPLICATION_XML, MediaType.APPLICATION_JSON})
    public void edit(@PathParam("id") BigDecimal id, BookAuthor entity) {
        super.edit(entity);
    }
    @DELETE
    @Path("{id}")
    public void remove(@PathParam("id") BigDecimal id) {
        super.remove(super.find(id));
    }
    @GET
    @Path("{id}")
    @Produces({MediaType.APPLICATION_XML, MediaType.APPLICATION_JSON})
    public BookAuthor find(@PathParam("id") BigDecimal id) {
        return super.find(id);
    }
    @GET
    @Override
    @Produces({MediaType.APPLICATION_XML, MediaType.APPLICATION_JSON})
    public List<BookAuthor> findAll() {
        return super.findAll();
    }
    @GET
    @Path("{from}/{to}")
    @Produces({MediaType.APPLICATION_XML, MediaType.APPLICATION_JSON})
    public List<BookAuthor> findRange(@PathParam("from") Integer from, @PathParam("to")
    Integer to) {
        return super.findRange(new int[]{from, to});
    }
    @GET
    @Path("count")
    @Produces(MediaType.TEXT_PLAIN)
    public String countREST() {
        return String.valueOf(super.count());
    }
    @Override
    protected EntityManager getEntityManager() {
        return em;
    }
}
```

To learn more about generating RESTful web services and the respective annotations, please see Chapter 13. Once a RESTful web service has been created, it can be called upon from other applications to obtain data in various formats, being XML, JSON, plain text, or some other medium. A Jakarta MVC application can utilize a JAX-RS client to call upon RESTful web services to obtain data for the application. This can be achieved by generating a service class that contains the Jakarta RESTful Web Services client and web service calls to obtain the data.

To begin, create a class within the org.jakartaeerecipe.bookstore.service package, and name it BookAuthorService. This will be a session-scoped CDI bean (see Chapter 11 for details on CDI), which will create a client upon bean construction, and then load data for use within the application, as needed. In the next recipe which covers Jakarta MVC controllers, I'll demonstrate how to call upon this service class from within a controller class to obtain data.

The following code shows the finished product for the BookAuthorService class:

```
package org.jakartaeerecipe.bookstore.service;

import java.util.List;
import jakarta.annotation.PostConstruct;
import jakarta.enterprise.context.SessionScoped;
import jakarta.ws.rs.client.*;
import jakarta.ws.rs.core.GenericType;
import org.jakartaeerecipe.bookstore.entity.BookAuthor;

@SessionScoped
public class BookAuthorService  implements java.io.Serializable {

    Client jaxRsClient;

    private List<BookAuthor> bookAuthorList;

    final String hostUri = "http://localhost:8080/BookStore/bookstore";
    public BookAuthorService(){
    }
    @PostConstruct
    public void init(){
        // Construct a Jakarta RESTful Web Services Client
        jaxRsClient = ClientBuilder.newClient();
        loadData();
    }
    private void loadData(){
        bookAuthorList = jaxRsClient.target(hostUri + "/org.jakartaeerecipe.bookstore.
        entity.bookauthor/findAll")
                .request("application/xml")
                .get(new GenericType<List<BookAuthor>>() {
                }
                );
    }

    /**
     * @return the bookAuthorList
     */
    public List<BookAuthor> getBookAuthorList() {
```

```
        if(bookAuthorList == null){
            loadData();
        }
        return bookAuthorList;
    }

    /**
     * @param bookAuthorList
     */
    public void setBookAuthorList(List<BookAuthor> bookAuthorList) {
        this.bookAuthorList = bookAuthorList;
    }
}
```

The service class can be used to load the data and obtain the set of data for our application. This class could be modified later to provide RESTful web service methods for creating, updating, and removing data, as needed.

How It Works

Most enterprise applications do some work with data. Jakarta MVC applications are no different, as data typically plays an important role. The way to obtain data for a Jakarta MVC application is very much the same as it would be for many other Java web applications, and RESTful web services or Jakarta Enterprise Beans are some great options. Keep in mind that these are not the only options for pulling data into a Jakarta MVC application. Since the Jakarta MVC framework provides a very fluid design pattern, it allows the developer to make many choices along the way. To that end, one could certainly use another methodology such as JDBC or a homegrown data access object (DAO) to orchestrate work with the database. This recipe shows two of the most standard approaches.

Jakarta MVC is based on the Model-View-Controller design pattern, which separates the application into three components: the Model, the View, and the Controller.

Containers are injected into the Controller. The Controller has access to all of the services. It is responsible for handling all incoming requests and mapping them to the appropriate action. It also retrieves data from the Model and passes it on to the View. The View then uses this data to generate a response that is sent back to the user.

In Solution #1, I showed how one could create entity classes based upon existing (or new) database tables and then write a Jakarta Enterprise Beans façade used in tandem with the entity classes to work with the data. This is, by far, one of the most standard approaches for coercing data into Java objects, dating back to the J2EE days. Back in the days of J2EE, developers were required to write heavyweight EJB solutions and lots of XML to pull off the same feat that can be resolved nowadays using simple POJOs with annotations.

The use of Jakarta Enterprise Beans goes hand in hand with the use of entity classes for mapping database tables to Java objects. To learn more about the use of entity classes, please refer to Chapter 6 where object-relational mapping is discussed. Once an entity class has been constructed, it is easy to create a Jakarta Enterprise Beans that can be used to work with the entity class to orchestrate the data. Since Chapter 8 is dedicated to the use of Jakarta Enterprise Beans, you can look there for more information on creating and using them. The point of this recipe is to show how to use these options within a Jakarta MVC application. One can bind the use of Jakarta Enterprise Beans with the Jakarta MVC controller classes to obtain data and manipulate it, as needed. In the next recipe, you will learn more about Jakarta MVC controller classes.

Solution #2 shows how to also make use of entity classes for mapping Java objects to database tables, but instead uses RESTful service classes to obtain the data. The solution demonstrates how to create the RESTful web services that will provide the data, and it also shows how to create a Jakarta RESTful Web Services client service class that can be used to call upon the RESTful web services to obtain data. Most likely with these two solutions, the Jakarta RESTful Web Services and web services client will not be part of the same application. Typically, one application or microservice will obtain the data from the database and provide it to other consumers via the web service, and other applications or microservices will act as consumers, using Jakarta RESTful Web Services clients to obtain the data from the web service. I only demonstrated both the web service and the client in this application for the purposes of example.

Since Chapter 13 covers RESTful web services in entirety, I will point you to that chapter for more information. Let's focus on how we can glean the data from the web services using a Jakarta RESTful Web Services client for our MVC application. Typically, an MVC controller (see the next recipe) will call upon the Jakarta RESTful Web Services client to obtain the data for the application. In Solution #2, a simple client is created to obtain the list of BookAuthor entities from the web service and load them into a local list. The BookAuthorService class is a session-scoped CDI bean, so it is annotated with @SessionScoped (jakarta. enterprise.context.SessionScoped). Since this class may need to be saved to disk to store the session data, it must be made serializable. Next, declare a jakarta.ws.rs.client.Client and a List<BookAuthor> so that the client can be created and the list of BookAuthor objects can be stored in the session. The class should create the client and load the data when the bean is created, so one of the methods should be annotated with @PostConstruct so that it is automatically invoked upon bean construction. In this case, the init() method is invoked upon construction, allowing the client to make a RESTful service call to the org. jakartaeerecipe.bookstore.entity.bookauthor web service to obtain all of the records and store them into the bookAuthorList. Figure 5-8 shows the key components of the Jakarta MVC framework and how they interact with each other.

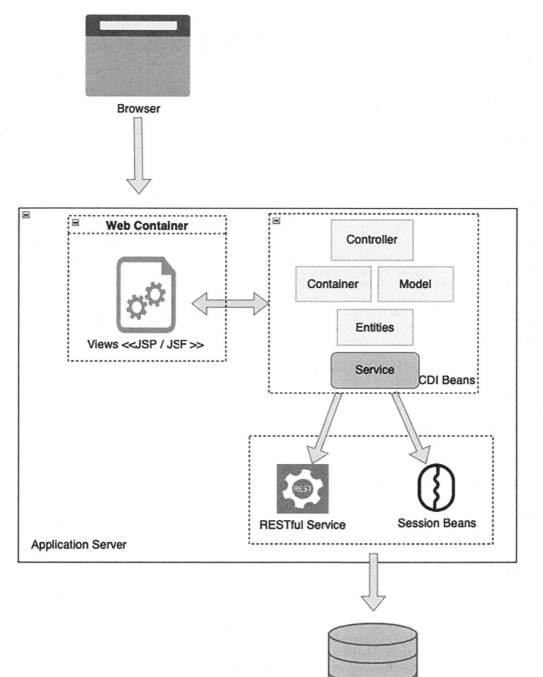

Figure 5-8. *Layers of Jakarta MVC*

Although this recipe does not directly pertain to the Jakarta MVC application methodology, it is an important piece of the puzzle for obtaining data for use with the application. In the next recipe, I will dive directly into the Jakarta MVC controller class, which is the heart of the business logic for a Jakarta MVC application.

5-3. Writing a Controller Class

Problem

You would like to orchestrate the navigation and business logic for a Jakarta MVC application.

Solution

Develop Jakarta MVC controller classes to provide the business logic and navigation logic behind the application. To get started, create a new package in which to store the controllers for the application. In this example, I've named the package org.jakartaeerecipe.bookstore.controller. Also, create a package to hold classes that will be used as objects for transporting data within the application. Name this package org.jakartaeerecipe.bookstore.container. Before the controller class can be created, a container needs to be created within the newly created org.jakartaeerecipe.bookstore.container package, and name it BookAuthorContainer. This class is merely a SessionScoped CDI bean that will be used to hold instances of the BookAuthor objects and expose them to the web views of the application. The sources for BookAuthorContainer should look as follows:

```
package org.jakartaeerecipe.bookstore.container;
import java.util.List;
import jakarta.enterprise.context.SessionScoped;
import jakarta.inject.Inject;
import jakarta.inject.Named;
import org.jakartaeerecipe.bookstore.entity.BookAuthor;
@Named
@SessionScoped
public class BookAuthorContainer implements java.io.Serializable {
    private BookAuthor bookAuthor;
    private List<BookAuthor> bookAuthorList;
    public BookAuthorContainer(){
    }
    ...
    // Getters and Setters
    ...
}
```

Next, create a class named BookAuthorController inside of the org.jakartaeerecipe.bookstore. controller package, and annotate the controller class with the @Path("/bookAuthor") and @Controller annotations. Next, create a public method with a return type of String and name it getBookAuthors, accepting no arguments. Annotate the method with @GET and within this method query data for loading the BookAuthor list, and return a String of "bookAuthor.jsp". The following sources show the code for the BookAuthorController class:

```
package org.jakartaeerecipe.bookstore.controller;
import java.util.List;
import jakarta.inject.Inject;
import jakarta.ws.rs.Path;
import jakarta.mvc.annotation.Controller;
import jakarta.ws.rs.GET;
import org.jakartaeerecipe.bookstore.entity.BookAuthor;
import org.jakartaeerecipe.bookstore.service.BookAuthorService;
@Path("/bookAuthor")
@Controller
public class BookAuthorController {
    @Inject
    private BookAuthorService bookAuthorService;
    public BookAuthorController(){
    }
    @GET
    public String getBookAuthors(){
        // obtain list of authors
        return "bookAuthor.jsp";
    }
}
```

If a URI containing the path indicated by the @Path annotation is loaded, the bookAuthor.jsp view will be loaded.

How It Works

A Jakarta MVC controller class is used to bind business logic to the view and process requests and responses. Controller classes are CDI controllers that contain several annotations, as the Jakarta MVC controller façade is based upon the Jakarta RESTful Web Services API. Every controller class is indicated as such via the jakarta.mvc.annotation.Controller annotation. The jakarta.ws.rs.Path annotation is applied at the controller class level to indicate which URI will be used to access controller class methods via the web application. For instance, this controller class can be accessible via a URI matching the following format since there is only one method:

http://localhost:8080/BookStore/controller/bookAuthor

It is important to note that the controller class is annotated like a Jakarta RESTful Web Services class. Controllers in the Jakarta MVC framework are implemented using the same annotations that are used to implement a Jakarta RESTful web service class. That said, when the preceding URI is used to access the application, the BookAuthor CDI controller is invoked due to the application path being /BookStore/ and the matching @Path annotation specifying /bookAuthor as the matching path. When invoked, the GET requests are handled by the getBookAuthors() method, as it is annotated with @GET without a specified path. The @GET annotation is used to indicate an HTTP GET method. Since this controller only has one controller method annotated with @GET, the default path is going to invoke the single method. If there were more than one method in the controller, each method would also need to be annotated with @Path to indicate the subpath to invoke each method in turn. A Jakarta MVC controller should utilize other HTTP methods such as @PUT and @POST for inserting or updating records in a database.

In the example, when the getBookAuthors() method is invoked, the BookAuthorService is called upon, invoking the getBookAuthorList() method and loading the local bookAuthors list. Next, data loaded into a list will be accessible via the view. The data loading processes are omitted from this recipe, but they are covered in greater detail in Recipe 5-5.

The last important detail to note is that the return value from the getBookAuthorList() method is the next view that will be rendered when the response is returned. The default return type for a controller method is text/html, but that can be changed via the @Produces annotation. A String returned from a controller method is the view path. In this case, the bookAuthor.jsp view is next to be loaded. It is possible to provide navigation to the next view in a number of different ways, and returning the name of the next view is the first technique.

A controller method can also have a return type of void, and in such cases the method must be annotated with @View("returnViewName"). As seen here, the String-based view name is passed as an attribute to the annotation. This technique makes it easy to separate navigational logic from business logic:

```
@GET
@View("bookAuthor.jsp")
public void getBookAuthors(){
    //obtain authors
}
```

The next technique involves returning a Viewable, which would look like the following lines of code. A Viewable provides flexibility, especially in cases where one wishes to implement a nonstandard view engine:

```
@GET
public Viewable getBookAuthors(){
    //obtain authors
    return new Viewable("bookAuthor.jsp");
}
```

The final technique for controlling navigation is to return a response object, which provides a lot of information since it can include different response codes depending upon certain situations:

```
@GET
public Response getBookAuthors(){
    // obtain authors
    return Response.status(Response.Status.OK).entity("bookAuthor.jsp").build();
}
```

As mentioned previously, Jakarta MVC controller classes are very much the same as Jakarta RESTful Web Services classes in that they use common annotations. In the example, the controller class is utilized as a Jakarta MVC controller only, but it is possible for a controller class to become a hybrid class which also contains Jakarta RESTful Web Services methods. To do this, move the @Controller annotation to each Jakarta MVC method, rather than at the class level itself. The jakarta.mvc.annotation.View annotation can also be applied at either the class or the method level. As mentioned previously, it points to the view for the controller method.

The controller method defines the business logic for a Jakarta MVC application. Controllers utilize annotations and provide plumbing for the request-response life cycle. Lastly, controllers are responsible for returning responses including data to application views.

5-4. Using a Model to Expose Data to a View

Problem

You wish to obtain data from a data source and make it available for use within an application view.

Solution

Inject and make use of the Models API from within your controller class. In the following example, the method getBookAuthors(), which is invoked when the URI path to the controller is accessed, obtains data from a web service (see Recipe 5-2 for more information) and populates data for use in a view using a model:

```
package org.jakartaeerecipe.bookstore.controller;
import java.util.List;
import jakarta.inject.Inject;
import jakarta.mvc.Models;
import jakarta.ws.rs.Path;
import jakarta.mvc.annotation.Controller;
import jakarta.ws.rs.GET;
import org.jakartaeerecipe.bookstore.entity.BookAuthor;
import org.jakartaeerecipe.bookstore.service.BookAuthorService;
@Path("/bookAuthor")
@Controller
public class BookAuthorController {
    @Inject
    private Models models;
    @Inject
    private BookAuthorService bookAuthorService;
    public BookAuthorController(){
    }
    @GET
    public String getBookAuthors(){
        List<BookAuthor> bookAuthors = bookAuthorService.getBookAuthorList();
        models.put("bookauthors", bookAuthors);
        return "bookAuthor.jsp";
    }
}
```

The JSP view markup that is contained within the bookAuthor.jsp JSP view looks like the following:

```
<%@ page contentType="text/html;charset=UTF-8" language="java" %>
<%@ taglib prefix="c" uri="http://java.sun.com/jsp/jstl/core" %>
<!DOCTYPE html>
<html>
    <head>
        <meta http-equiv="Content-Type" content="text/html; charset=UTF-8">
        <title>Example of Jakarta MVC Using JSP for View</title>
    </head>
```

```
<body>
    <h1>Book Authors</h1>
    <table class="table table-striped">
        <colgroup>
            <col style="width: 80%;" />
        </colgroup>
        <thead>
            <tr>
                <th class="text-left">Author</th>
            </tr>
        </thead>
        <tbody>
            <c:forEach var="bookAuthor" items="${bookauthors}">
                <tr>
                    <td class="text-center">
                        ${bookAuthor.last}
                    </td>
                </tr>
            </c:forEach>
        </tbody>
    </table>
</body>
</html>
```

The code can be executed by opening the URL http://localhost:8080/JakartaEE_Chapter05-1.0-SNAPSHOT/views/bookAuthor.xhtml in the browser. Given the sample dataset, the results of the simple view will look like that in Figure 5-9.

Book Authors

Author

Juneau

Dea

Gennick

Figure 5-9. *Example of bookAuthor.jsp results*

How It Works

The Models API must be included in every implementation of the Jakarta MVC framework. Essentially, the Models API provides a jakarta.mvc.Models map which is used to store a dataset with a key identifier as a key/value pair that is exposed to the next rendered view. The HashMap for the Models API adheres to the following format:

```
Map<String, Object> model = new HashMap<String, Object>();
```

In the example, the Models map is injected into the controller class using CDI @Inject. Once injected, the model can be used to store data for exposure. A List<BookAuthor> is placed into the Models map as follows:

```
models.put("bookauthors", bookAuthors);
```

The model is exposed to the view via the bookauthors key. In the example JSP view, the ${bookauthors} expression is used within a JSTL c:if tag to display the records in a table:

```
<c:forEach var="bookAuthor" items="${bookauthors}">
    <tr>
        <td class="text-center">
            ${bookAuthor.last}
        </td>
    </tr>
</c:forEach>
```

As seen in the example, the Models API is very easy to utilize. However, it is not the preferred method for exposing data, as CDI is preferred. CDI is preferred in general because it allows for more flexibility than the Models API. Recipe 5-5 delves into utilizing CDI beans for exposing data.

5-5. Utilizing CDI for Exposing Data

Problem

You are interested in exposing data from a controller into a view, but you'd like to not make use of Jakarta MVC Models to do so. Instead, you'd like to harness the power of CDI to expose data to views.

Solution

Utilize CDI models to return data to the view. The use of CDI is the preferred technique for exposing data to views. In this recipe, a CDI bean is injected into the controller, and then it is utilized to store data. This CDI bean is session scoped, so the data that is placed within the bean will last the entire web session. The following code is that of the CDI bean which is used to expose the data:

```
package org.jakartaeerecipe.bookstore.container;

import java.util.List;
import jakarta.enterprise.context.SessionScoped;
import jakarta.inject.Named;
import org.jakartaeerecipe.bookstore.entity.Book;
@Named
@SessionScoped
public class BookContainer implements java.io.Serializable {
    private Book book;
    private List<Book> bookList;
    public BookContainer(){
    }
```

```
...
// Getters and setters
...
}
```

Next, the controller class utilizes the CDI bean to store data and make it available to the view:

```
@Path("/book")
@Controller
public class BookController {
    @Inject
    private BookContainer bookContainer;
    public BookController() {
    }
    /**
     * Queries all books using the <code>BookService</code> and then
     * returns to the <code>book.jsp</code> JSP page.
     * @return
     */
    @GET
    public String getBooks(){
        Book book = new Book();
        book.setTitle("Jakarta EE Recipes");
        bookContainer.setBook(book);
        return "book.jsp";
}
```

The following markup is that of the book.jsp view. As you can see from the example, the view simply displays the name of the book that was loaded into the CDI bean:

```
<%@page contentType="text/html" pageEncoding="UTF-8"%>
<!DOCTYPE html>
<html>
    <head>
        <meta http-equiv="Content-Type" content="text/html; charset=UTF-8">
        <title>Jakarta EE Recipes: Recipe 5-5</title>
    </head>
    <body>
        <h1>Book List</h1>
        The book that was loaded in BookController:   ${bookContainer.book.title}
    </body>
</html>
```

To execute this code, open http://localhost:8080/JakartaEERecipes_Chapter05-1.0-SNAPSHOT/views/bookAuthor.jsp in your browser. Figure 5-10 shows the output of the code provided in this recipe.

Book Authors

Author

Juneau

Dea

Gennick

Figure 5-10. *Example of book.jsp results*

How It Works

The preferred technique for exposing data to the web views of a Jakarta MVC application is to utilize Contexts and Dependency Injection (CDI) beans. CDI is a specification that binds many of the Java EE and Jakarta EE technologies together. CDI is a large specification that includes many details, but in-depth explanations of the specification are out of scope for this recipe. For more details on CDI, please refer to Chapter 11. One of the functions of CDI is to wire beans together, effectively making it possible for data and scope to be shared between classes and between the backend and front-facing views of an application.

For the purposes of the Jakarta MVC framework, one of the core focuses is the ability to share contextual objects between the backend code and the frontend views. In this simple example, the CDI bean is merely a SessionScoped container named BookContainer. As seen in the code, the BookContainer class is annotated with @Named, which marks the class as a CDI bean and makes it available for injection into other classes using the class name with the first letter in lowercase. In this case, the bean will be injectable via the name bookContainer. The @Named annotation does accept a String-based alias, which can be used to call upon the class at injection time from a view. The BookContainer class is also annotated with @SessionScoped, which defines the scope of the bean. The other available scope possibilities are @RequestScoped, @ ApplicationScoped, and @ConversationScoped.

The BookController utilizes a contextual proxy to the bean by injecting an instance of it using the @ Inject annotation. The bean is used within the getBooks() method, as it accepts a Book instance for which the title and description have been populated. It is also possible to define different class fields within the CDI bean and populate them with data directly to expose it to a view or other classes. Once the data has been populated, the BookController bean can be accessed from a view using an expression language, or the same instance of the bean can be injected into another class and made accessible. In this example, the controller method getBooks() simply returns the name of the next view to be loaded, books.jsp. The books.jsp JSP view accesses the title of the book by referring to the bean via the injection name ${bookContainer.book.title}.

CDI can be very powerful for managing contextual instances of classes within a Jakarta EE application. Using CDI to expose data to a view within a Jakarta MVC application brings forth the same functionality as the use of the Models API, and it also allows data to be utilized in other classes, if needed.

5-6. Supplying Message Feedback to the User

Problem

You wish to display feedback to a user after a request is processed.

Solution

Utilize CDI beans to easily provide feedback to users in the form of messages displayed onscreen. In the following scenario, all books in a bookstore are loaded and displayed in the book.jsp view. A RequestScoped CDI bean entitled Messages is used to encapsulate the logic for storing informative or error messages. In the controller class, a message indicating the number of books that are loaded is set into the bean using the info field. This bean is then available for display within the view.

First, here is a look at the CDI bean named Messages:

```
package org.javaee8recipes.bookstore.container;
import jakarta.enterprise.context.RequestScoped;
import jakarta.inject.Named;
import java.util.ArrayList;
import java.util.Collections;
import java.util.List;
/**
 * This class encapsulates messages displayed to the users. There can be a
 * single info message and multiple error messages. Controllers can use this
 * class to queue messages for rendering. The class shows how named CDI beans
 * can be used as a model for the view. Whether to include some class like
 * this in the spec is not decided yet.
 */
@Named
@RequestScoped
public class Messages {
  private String info;
  private final List<String> errors = new ArrayList<>();
  public Messages addError(String error) {
    errors.add(error);
    return this;
  }
  public List<String> getErrors() {
    return Collections.unmodifiableList(errors);
  }
  public String getInfo() {
    return info;
  }
  public void setInfo(String info) {
    this.info = info;
  }
}
```

The code for the controller class used to load the book listing and provide the message is as follows:

```java
@Inject
private Messages messages;

...
@GET
@Path("/books")
public String displayBookListing() {
    bookList = bookService.getBookList();
    bookContainer.setBookList(bookList);
    messages.setInfo("There are " + bookList.size() + " books in the library.");
    return "book.jsp";
}
```

The subsequent book.jsp view markup is as follows:

```jsp
<%@page contentType="text/html" pageEncoding="UTF-8"%>
<!DOCTYPE html>
<html>
    <head>
        <meta http-equiv="Content-Type" content="text/html; charset=UTF-8">
        <link href="${pageContext.request.contextPath}/webjars/bootstrap/3.3.4/dist/css/
        bootstrap.css" rel="stylesheet">
        <script src="${pageContext.request.contextPath}/webjars/bootstrap/3.3.4/dist/js/
        bootstrap.js"></script>
        <title>Jakarta EE Recipes</title>
    </head>
    <body>
        <h1>Book List</h1>
        The book that was loaded in BookController:  ${bookContainer.book.title}
        <br/><br/>
        <c:if test="${messages.info != null}">
                <div class="alert alert-success" role="alert">
                    ${messages.info}
                </div>
        </c:if>
        <c:if test="${not empty messages.errors}">
                <div class="alert alert-danger" role="alert">
                    <ul class="list-unstyled">
                        <c:forEach var="error" items="${messages.errors}">
                            <li>${error}</li>
                        </c:forEach>
                    </ul>
                </div>
        </c:if>
        <br/>
        <table class="table table-striped">
                <colgroup>
                    <col style="width: 80%;" />
                </colgroup>
```

```
            <thead>
                <tr>
                    <th class="text-left">Book</th>
                </tr>
            </thead>
            <tbody>
            <c:forEach var="book" items="${bookContainer.bookList}">
                    <tr>
                        <td class="text-center">
                            ${book.title}
                        </td>
                    </tr>
                </c:forEach>
            </tbody>
        </table>
    </body>
</html>
```

How It Works

CDI beans can be leveraged to easily display messages from a controller. As seen in Recipe 5-5, the CDI bean can be injected into a controller class, data can be set into the controller, and then it can be made available in subsequent views. In the example for this recipe, a message containing the number of books within the bookList is created as a String, and then it is assigned to the info field of the Messages bean:

```
messages.setInfo("There are " + bookList.size() + " books in the library.");
```

When the book.jsp view is loaded, the message is displayed within the view using an expression language in the ${messages.info} format. In the view, a <c:if> tag is used to conditionally display the informative message if it exists, or if the error message exists, then it will be displayed instead. If users are seeing an error message, it usually helps to have that message stand out in red text or bold text. If a user is seeing helpful information within a message, it may be helpful to see that message in green text or something of the like. In such cases, the Jakarta MVC framework can leverage existing JavaScript APIs to provide nice message formatting. The example utilizes the Bootstrap JavaScript library to display messages nicely depending upon type. To run the code, open the URL http://localhost:8080/JakartaEERecipes_Chapter05-1.0-SNAPSHOT/views/book.jsp in your browser, as shown in Figure 5-11.

Book Listing

There are 2 books in the library.

Figure 5-11. Messages displayed nicely using Bootstrap

5-7. Inserting and Updating Data

Problem

You wish to utilize a form to insert or update data.

Solution

Create controller methods that are annotated with @PUT or @POST, depending upon whether the methods will be utilized for inserting or updating, respectively. The following markup, excerpted from book.jsp, contains a form that is used to create a new book record. Take note that in the following example, the action invoked upon submit will initiate the RESTful web service with the "/create" path:

```
<form action="${pageContext.request.contextPath}/bookstore/book/create" method="POST"
class="form-inline">
                <div class="panel panel-default">
                    <div class="panel-heading">
                        <h3 class="panel-title">Book Information</h3>
                    </div>
                    <div class="panel-body">
                        <div class="form-group">
                            <label for="subject">Title</label>
                            <input type="text" class="form-control" id="title" name="title"
                            placeholder="Title"
                                    value="${book.title}" autofocus>
                        </div>
                    </div>
                </div>
                <br/><br/>
                <div class="form-group">
                    <label for="description">Description:</label>
                    <br/>
                    <textarea cols="100" rows="4" class="form-control" id="description"
                    name="description" placeholder="Description">
                        ${book.description}
                    </textarea>
                </div>
                <br/><br/>
                <button type="submit" class="btn btn-primary">Create</button>
        </form>
```

The submit action in the form invokes the controller method named createItem(), which obtains data that was submitted via a form and utilizes Jakarta RESTful Web Services to insert into the database:

```
@POST
@Path("/create")
@Controller
public String createItem(@BeanParam @Valid Book form) {
    // Create new book
    // Obtain issue list to count records for ID population
    bookList = bookService.getBookList();
```

```
    form.setId(new BigDecimal(bookList.size() + 1));
    Book entity = new Book();
    entity.setId(form.getId());
    entity.setTitle(form.getTitle());
    entity.setDescription(form.getDescription());
    bookService.create(entity);
    return displayBookListing();
}
```

Once the method has been executed, the book listing is refreshed because the final line of createItem() invokes displayBookListing(), which executes the code as follows:

```
@GET
@Path("/books")
public String displayBookListing() {
    bookList = bookService.getBookList();
    bookContainer.setBookList(bookList);
    messages.setInfo("There are " + bookList.size() + " books in the library.");
    System.out.println("Issue count: " + bookList.size());
    return "book.jsp";
}
```

The resulting view, http://localhost:8080/JakartaEERecipes_Chapter05-1.0-SNAPSHOT/views/book.jsp, will display the newly created book within the listing of books, as seen in the previous recipe in Figure 5-11.

How It Works

The overall mantra of the Jakarta MVC framework is complete control and ease of use. This example demonstrates exactly those ideals, as it demonstrates how the entire request-processing life cycle is handled by the developer, and the framework makes it easy to achieve. To create or update data, an HTML form is used to submit form data to a controller method. In this case, the form is written in JSP markup, and the submit action invokes a RESTful controller method entitled createItem(). The createItem() method contains a signature that returns a String for the next view to render after completion, and it accepts a parameter of type Book. Note that the parameter is annotated with @BeanParam and @Valid. The @BeanParam annotation indicates that the Book class contains some form parameter annotations to specify for fields. Specifically, in this case the Book entity class contains the following:

```
public class Book implements Serializable {
    private static final long serialVersionUID = 1L;

    @Id
    @GeneratedValue(strategy = GenerationType.SEQUENCE,
            generator = "book_s_generator")
    @SequenceGenerator(name = "book_s_generator", sequenceName = "book_s",
    allocationSize = 1)
    @Basic(optional = false)
//  @NotNull
    @Column(name = "ID")
    private BigDecimal id;
```

```
//@Size(max = 150)
    @FormParam(value="title")
    @Column(name = "TITLE")
    protected String title;

//@Size(max = 500)
    @Column(name = "IMAGE")
    private String image;

    @FormParam(value="description")
    @Lob
    @Column(name = "DESCRIPTION")
    private String description;
```

Therefore, the @BeanParam annotation will introspect the Book object for injection annotations and set them appropriately. The @Valid annotation indicates that Bean Validation processing should be invoked for this object. At method invocation time (form submit), the bean validation will take place and help to prevent erroneous data from being submitted.

Once initiated, the book listing is obtained from the BookService, which will be used to count the number of books. This number is used to increment a number to produce the primary key for the new record being created. The new Book entity is then created, values are set accordingly, and then the create() method is called to persist the data. Once persisted, the database is queried again via the call to displayBookListing(), and then the response is returned and the book.jsp view is displayed.

CHAPTER 6

JDBC with Jakarta EE

The Java Database Connectivity (JDBC) API is a standard for accessing Relational Database Management Systems (RDBMSs) via Java. It has been in use for years and can be used when developing all types of Java applications, including desktop, stand-alone, and web. Almost every nontrivial application utilizes an RDBMS for storing and retrieving data. Therefore, it is important for application developers of all types to learn how to work with JDBC.

Enterprise application development has proven to be more productive for developers when working directly with Java objects as opposed to database access. While the JDBC API is still very mainstream for the development of enterprise applications and microservices, many developers have begun to adopt object-relational mapping programming interfaces as a standard. One of the easiest ways to map Java objects to database tables is to encapsulate JDBC logic into classes containing private methods for performing database access and exposing those methods using public methods that work with objects instead of SQL. This chapter contains recipes to demonstrate the technique of abstracting JDBC logic from ordinary business logic, sometimes referred to as creating data access objects.

For a full list of the new features and enhancements with the latest JDBC release, please visit the online documentation: https://docs.oracle.com/en/database/oracle/oracle-database/21/jjdbc/index.html. After reviewing the recipes included in this chapter, you should be comfortable using JDBC within your Java web applications.

Note   The Acme Bookstore application has been completely rewritten for this chapter in order to utilize an Oracle database rather than simple Java lists of data. Please run the `create_database.sql` script within your database prior to working with the examples from this chapter. Also, you will need to provide the necessary database connection properties for your database within the `db_props.properties` file and/or within the code examples for this chapter. If you are utilizing another database vendor, you should be able to adjust the SQL accordingly to work with that database. To access the Acme Bookstore application utilizing the database, be sure to deploy the `JakartaEERecipes_Chapter06` web application to your Eclipse GlassFish or Payara application server, and visit the URL `http://localhost:8080/JakartaEERecipes_Chapter06-1.0-SNAPSHOT/faces/chapter06/home.xhtml`. This chapter will typically reference the Eclipse GlassFish server (a.k.a. GlassFish), although most of the references will be the same for the Payara server.

6-1. Project Structure

The entity relationship (ER) diagram representing the database model used in this chapter is shown in Figure 6-1.

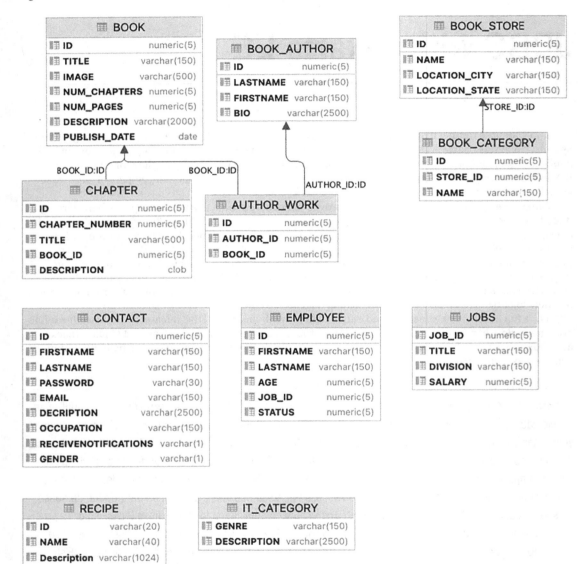

Figure 6-1. *ER diagram for the database model*

The following is the code structure for the project containing the recipes for this chapter. The SQL scripts for creating tables and inserting records in the database tables are provided in the *sql* folder.

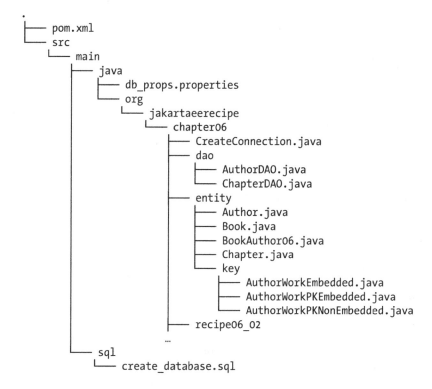

```
.
├── pom.xml
└── src
    └── main
        ├── java
        │   ├── db_props.properties
        │   └── org
        │       └── jakartaeerecipe
        │           └── chapter06
        │               ├── CreateConnection.java
        │               ├── dao
        │               │   ├── AuthorDAO.java
        │               │   └── ChapterDAO.java
        │               ├── entity
        │               │   ├── Author.java
        │               │   ├── Book.java
        │               │   ├── BookAuthor06.java
        │               │   ├── Chapter.java
        │               │   └── key
        │               │       ├── AuthorWorkEmbedded.java
        │               │       ├── AuthorWorkPKEmbedded.java
        │               │       └── AuthorWorkPKNonEmbedded.java
        │               ├── recipe06_02
        │               ...
        └── sql
            └── create_database.sql
```

6-2. Obtaining Database Drivers and Adding Them to the CLASSPATH

Problem

You need to have the ability to utilize a database from your application, so you need to obtain drivers and configure the databases for your application.

Solution

Download the appropriate drivers for the database that you will be working with, and add them to the CLASSPATH for your application. In this solution, I will assume you are going to develop an enterprise-level web application and deploy it to the GlassFish application server. The application will utilize the Oracle database for persistence. In this case, it is recommended to download the most current Oracle database driver for Java Database Connectivity (JDBC). At the time of this writing, the driver is ojdbc8.jar, but you can find the latest online at www.oracle.com/database/technologies/appdev/jdbc-ucp-21-4c-patched-downloads.html. Optionally, it can be used as a Maven dependency via the following coordinates:

```
<!-- https://mvnrepository.com/artifact/com.oracle.database.jdbc/ojdbc11 -->
<dependency>
    <groupId>com.oracle.database.jdbc</groupId>
    <artifactId>ojdbc11</artifactId>
    <version>21.4.0.0.1</version>
</dependency>
```

The driver for your application may be different, depending upon which database you plan to use. For instance, to work with a PostgreSQL database, you would need to download the driver from the location https://jdbc.postgresql.org/.

Once you have downloaded the required drivers for your database, add them to the application CLASSPATH. If using an IDE, you can adjust the project properties for your application project accordingly to include the JAR that contains your database driver. If you are working from the command line or terminal, you can add the driver to your CLASSPATH by issuing one of the following commands, depending upon the OS platform you are using.

Use the following on Unix-based systems or OS X:

```
export CLASSPATH=/<path to jar>/ojdbc11.jar
```

Use the following on Windows:

```
set CLASSPATH=C:\<path to jar>\ojdbc11.jar
```

Replace <path to jar> with the actual path to the ojdbc jar file in your computer.

You should now be able to work with the database from your application, but to deploy to the GlassFish application server, you will need to make the database driver available for GlassFish. You can do this by copying the JAR containing the database driver into the GlassFish lib directory. Restart the application server instance, and you are ready to deploy your database application.

How It Works

The first step to working with any database from an application is to configure the database driver for the specific vendor of your choice. Whether you decide to use Apache Derby, MySQL, PostgreSQL, Oracle, Microsoft SQL, or another database, most databases have a JDBC driver available. This driver must be added to the application CLASSPATH and integrated development environment (IDE) project CLASSPATH if using one. If working from the command line or terminal, you will need to set the CLASSPATH each time you open a new session. If using an IDE, your settings can usually be saved so that you need to configure them only one time. After the driver for your database has been added to the application or project CLASSPATH, you are ready to begin working with the database.

When it comes time to deploy the application to a server, you will need to ensure that the server has access to the database driver. You can simply add the driver JAR for your database to the lib directory and restart the server. Once you've done this, then you can either deploy your JDBC-based application or set up a database connection pool for your database. Please see Recipe 6-2 for more information on how to connect to your database from within an application using standard JDBC connectivity or how to set up a JDBC connection pool via the GlassFish or Payara application server.

6-3. Connecting to a Database

Problem

You need to connect to a database so that your application can perform database transactions.

Solution #1

Perform a JDBC connection to the database from within your application. Do this by creating a new Connection object, and then load the driver that you need to use for your particular database. Once the Connection object is ready, call its getConnection() method. The following code demonstrates how to obtain a connection to an Oracle database:

```
public class OracleConnection {

    private final String HOST = "myHost";            // hostname of database
    private final String PORT = "1521";              // port for database
    private final String DB = "myDatabase";          // database name
    private final String USER = "user";              // username for database
    private final String PASSWORD = "password";      // password for the database

    public static Connection getConnection() throws SQLException {
        Connection conn = null;
        String jdbcUrl = "jdbc:oracle:thin:@" + HOST + ":"
                + PORT + ":" + DB;
        conn = DriverManager.getConnection(jdbcUrl, USER, PASSWORD);
        System.out.println("Successfully connected");
        return conn;
    }
    public static void main(String[] args) throws SQLException {
        getConnection();
    }
}
```

The method portrayed in this example returns a Connection object that is ready to be used for database access. On compiling and executing the preceding Java class, it should print the message "Successfully connected" in the console.

Solution #2

Configure a database connection pool within an application server, and connect to it from your application. Use a DataSource object to create a connection pool. The DataSource object must have been properly implemented and deployed to an application server environment. After a DataSource object has been implemented and deployed, it can be used by an application to obtain a connection to a database.

■ **Note** A connection pool is a cluster of identical database connections that are allocated by the application server (container-managed connection pool) to be utilized by applications for individual client sessions.

To create a connection pool using the GlassFish administrative console, first log in to the console using the credentials that were specified upon installation, by visiting http://localhost:4848 (assuming you are on the same machine as the server and that your GlassFish installation is using the default port numbers). Once successfully logged in to the console, click the JDBC menu under Resources, and then expand the JDBC Connection Pools menu, as shown in Figure 6-2.

Figure 6-2. *Displaying the JDBC connection pools within the GlassFish administrative console*

Click the New button on the JDBC Connection Pools screen, and it will then navigate you to the New JDBC Connection Pool (Step 1 of 2) screen. There, you can name the pool, select a resource type, and select a database driver vendor. For this example, I am using Oracle Database 12c. Therefore, the entries should be specified like those shown in Figure 6-3, although you could change the pool name to something you like better.

New JDBC Connection Pool (Step 1 of 2)

Next   Cancel

Identify the general settings for the connection pool.

* Indicates required field

General Settings

Pool Name: *   OraclePool

Resource Type: ⌄

Must be specified if the datasource class implements more than 1 of the interface.

Database Driver Vendor: ⌄

Oracle

Select or enter a database driver vendor

Introspect: ☐

If enabled, data source or driver implementation class names will enable introspection.

Figure 6-3. *Creating a GlassFish JDBC connection pool*

When the next screen opens, it should automatically contain the mappings for your Oracle database DataSource Classname as oracle.jdbc.pool.OracleDataSource. If it does not look like Figure 6-4, then you may not yet have the ojdbc8.jar database driver in the application server **lib** directory. Be sure to check the Enabled check box next to the Ping option.

New JDBC Connection Pool (Step 2 of 2)

Previous   Finish   Cancel

Identify the general settings for the connection pool. Datasource Classname or Driver Classname must be specified for the connection pool.

* Indicates required field

General Settings

Pool Name: OraclePool

Resource Type: java.sql.Driver

Database Driver
Vendor: Oracle

Datasource   ⌄
Classname:

Select or enter vendor-specific classname that implements the DataSource and/or XADataSource APIs

Driver Classname: oracle.jdbc.OracleDriver   ⌄

Select or enter vendor-specific classname that implements the java.sql.Driver interface.

Ping: ☐

When enabled, the pool is pinged during creation or reconfiguration to identify and warn of any erroneous values for its attributes

Description:

Figure 6-4. *Data source class name automatically populates*

Lastly, go down to the bottom of the second screen, and check all the properties within the Additional Properties table with the exception of User, Password, and URL. Please specify the information for these properties according to the database you will be connecting against, as shown in Figure 6-5. Once you populated them accordingly, click the Finish button.

Transaction

Non Transactional Connections: ☐
Returns non-transactional connections

Transaction Isolation: [⌄]
If unspecified, use default level for JDBC Driver

Isolation Level: ☑ **Guaranteed**
All connections use same isolation level; requires Transaction Isolation

Additional Properties (3)

Select	Name		Value		Description	
☐	password		myuser			
☐	user		mypass			
☐	URL		jdbc:oracle:thin:@myserver:1521:mydatabase			

[Previous] [Finish] [Cancel]

Figure 6-5. *Populating the additional properties for your database*

After clicking Finish, you should see a message indicating that the "ping" has succeeded. Now you can set up your JDBC resource by clicking the JDBC Resources menu within the left tree menu. When the JDBC Resources screen appears, click the New… button. Enter a JNDI name for your resource, beginning with jdbc/, and then select the pool name for the database connection pool you just created. The screen should resemble Figure 6-6. Once you've populated it accordingly, click the OK button to complete the creation of the resource.

■ **Note** JNDI is the communication technology that allows applications to communicate with services by name within an application server container (https://docs.oracle.com/javase/jndi/tutorial/getStarted/overview/index.html).

New JDBC Resource　　　　　　　　　　　　　　　　　　　　　　　　[OK] [Cancel]

Specify a unique JNDI name that identifies the JDBC resource you want to create. The name must contain only alphanumeric, underscore, dash, or dot characters.

JNDI Name: * [jdbc/OracleConnection]
Pool Name: [OraclePool ∨]
　　　　　　Use the JDBC Connection Pools page to create new pools
Description: [   ]
Status: ☑

Additional Properties (0)
[Add Property] Delete Properties

Select	Name	Value	Description
No items found.			

Figure 6-6. *Creating a JDBC resource*

You can use the following code to obtain a database connection via a DataSource object:

```
public static Connection getDSConnection() {
    Connection conn = null;
    try {
        Context ctx = new InitialContext();
        DataSource ds = (DataSource)ctx.lookup("jdbc/OracleConnection");
        conn = ds.getConnection();
    } catch (NamingException | SQLException ex) {
        ex.printStackTrace();
    }
        return conn;
}
```

Notice that the only information required in the DataSource implementation is the name of a valid DataSource object. All the information that is required to obtain a connection with the database is managed within the application server.

How It Works

You have a couple of options for creating database connections for use within Java applications. If you are writing a stand-alone or desktop application, usually a standard JDBC connection is the best choice. However, if working with an enterprise-level or web-based application, DataSource objects may be the right choice. Solution #1 for this recipe covers the former option, and it is the easiest way to create a database connection in a stand-alone environment. I will cover the creation of a JDBC Connection via Solution #1 first.

Once you've determined which database you are going to use, you will need to obtain the correct driver for the database vendor and release of your choice. Please see Recipe 6-1 for more information on obtaining a driver and placing it into your CLASSPATH for use. Once you have the JAR file in your CLASSPATH, you can use a JDBC DriverManager to obtain a connection to the database.

■ **Note** As of JDBC version 4.0, drivers that are contained within the CLASSPATH are automatically loaded into the DriverManager object. If you are using a JDBC version prior to 4.0, the driver will have to be manually loaded.

To obtain a connection to your database using the DriverManager, you need to pass a String containing the JDBC URL to it. The JDBC URL consists of the database vendor name, along with the name of the server that hosts the database, the name of the database, the database port number, and a valid database username and password that has access to the schema you want to work with. Many times, the values used to create the JDBC URL can be obtained from a properties file so that the values can be easily changed if needed. To learn more about using a properties file to store connection values, please see Recipe 6-4. The code that is used to create the JDBC URL for Solution #1 looks like the following:

```
String jdbcUrl = "jdbc:oracle:thin:@" + this.hostname + ":" +
this.port + ":" + this.database;
```

Once all the variables have been substituted into the String, it will look something like the following:

```
jdbc:oracle:thin:@hostname:1521:database
```

Once the JDBC URL has been created, it can be passed to the DriverManager.getConnection() method to obtain a java.sql.Connection object. If incorrect information has been passed to the getConnection() method, a java.sql.SQLException will be thrown; otherwise, a valid Connection object will be returned.

■ **Note** The prefix of the jdbcUrl connection string in the example, jdbc:oracle:thin, indicates that you will be using the Oracle drivers, which are located within the ojdbc11.jar. DriverManager makes the association.

If running on an application server, such as GlassFish, the preferred way to obtain a connection is to use a DataSource. To work with a DataSource object, you need to have an application server to deploy it to. Any compliant application server such as Apache TomEE, GlassFish, Oracle WebLogic, or Open Liberty will work. Microservices containers such as Payara Micro will also work with the DataSource. Most of the application servers contain an administrative web interface that can be used to easily deploy a DataSource object, such as demonstrated via GlassFish in Solution #2 to this recipe. However, you can manually deploy a DataSource object by using code that will look like the following:

```
org.jakartaeerecipes.chapter5.recipe05_02.FakeDataSourceDriver ds =
new org.jakartaeerecipes.chapter5.recipe05_02.FakeDataSourceDriver();
ds.setServerName("my-server");
ds.setDatabaseName("JakartaEERecipes");
ds.setDescription("Database connection for Jakarta EE 8 Recipes");
```

This code instantiates a class that represents a new DataSource driver class, and then it sets properties based upon the database you want to register. DataSource code such as that demonstrated here is typically used when registering a DataSource in an application server or with access to a JNDI server. Application servers usually do this work behind the scenes if you are using a web-based administration tool to deploy a DataSource. Most database vendors will supply a DataSource driver along with their JDBC drivers, so if the correct JAR resides within the application or server CLASSPATH, it should be recognized and available for use. Once a DataSource has been instantiated and configured, the next step is to register the DataSource with a JNDI naming service.

The following code demonstrates the registration of a DataSource with JNDI:

```
try {
    Context ctx = new InitialContext();
    DataSource ds =
    (DataSource) ctx.bind("jdbc/OracleConnection");
} catch (NamingException ex) {
    ex.printStackTrace();
}
```

Once the DataSource has been deployed, any application that has been deployed to the same application server will have access to it. The beauty of working with a DataSource object is that your application code doesn't need to know any connection information, such as user credentials, for the database; it needs to know only the name of the DataSource. By convention, the name of the DataSource begins with a jdbc/prefix, followed by an identifier. To look up the DataSource object, an InitialContext object is used. The InitialContext looks at all the DataSources available within the application server, and it returns a valid DataSource if it is found; otherwise, it will throw a java.naming.NamingException exception. In Solution #2, you can see that the InitialContext returns an object that must be cast as a DataSource:

```
Context ctx = new InitialContext();
DataSource ds = (DataSource)ctx.lookup("jdbc/OracleConnection");
```

If the DataSource is a connection pool cache, the application server will send one of the available connections within the pool when an application requests it. The following line of code returns a Connection object from the DataSource:

```
Connection conn = ds.getConnection();
```

Of course, if no valid connection can be obtained, a java.sql.SQLException is thrown. The DataSource technique is preferred over manually specifying all details and passing to the DriverManager because database connection information is stored in only one place: the application server or microservices container, not within each application. Once a valid DataSource is deployed, it can be used by many applications.

After a valid connection has been obtained by your application, it can be used to work with the database. To learn more about working with the database using a Connection object, please see the recipes within this chapter regarding working with the database.

6-4. Handling Database Connection Exceptions

Problem

A database activity in your application has thrown an exception. You need to handle that SQL exception so your application does not crash.

Solution

Use a try-catch block to capture and handle any SQL exceptions that are thrown by your JDBC connection or SQL queries. The following code demonstrates how to implement a try-catch block in order to capture SQL exceptions:

```
try {
    // perform database tasks
} catch (java.sql.SQLException){
    // perform exception handling
}
```

How It Works

A standard try-catch block can be used to catch java.sql.SQLException exceptions. Your code will not compile if these exceptions are not handled, and it is a good idea to handle them in order to prevent your application from crashing if one of these exceptions is thrown. Almost any work that is performed against a java.sql.Connection object will need to perform error handling to ensure that database exceptions are handled correctly. You need to ensure that connections are closed once work has been performed and the Connection object is no longer used. Similarly, it is a good idea to close java.sql.Statement objects for memory allocation cleanup.

   Because Statement and Connection objects need to be closed, it is common to see try-with-resource used to ensure that all resources have been tended to as needed. It is not unlikely that you will see JDBC code that resembles the following style:

```
try (Connection conn = DirverManager.getConnection(jdbcUrl)) {
    // perform database tasks
} catch (java.sql.SQLException ex) {
    // perform exception handling
}
```

   Proper exception handling sometimes makes JDBC code rather laborious to write, but it will also ensure that an application requiring database access will not fail, causing data to be lost.

6-5. Simplifying Connection Management

Problem

Your application requires the use of a database. To work with the database, you need to open a connection. Rather than code the logic to open a database connection every time you need to access the database, you want to simplify the connection process.

Solution

Write a class to handle all the connection management within your application. Doing so will allow you to call that class in order to obtain a connection, rather than setting up a new Connection object each time you need access to the database. Perform the following steps to set up a connection management environment for your JDBC application:

1. Create a class named CreateConnection.java that will encapsulate all the connection logic for your application.

2. Create a properties file to store your connection information. Place the file in a designated location so that the CreateConnection class can load it.

3. Use the CreateConnection class to obtain your database connections.

▓ **Note**   If utilizing an application server, you can handle a similar solution via a container-managed connection pool. However, if the application is not deployed to an application server container, then building a connection management utility such as the one in this solution is a good alternative.

The following code is the org.jakartaeerecipes.chapter06.CreateConnection class that can be used for centralized connection management:

```
package org.jakartaeerecipes.chapter06;

import java.io.File;
import java.io.FileInputStream;
import java.io.FileNotFoundException;
import java.io.IOException;
import java.io.InputStream;
import java.nio.file.FileSystems;
import java.nio.file.Files;
import java.sql.Connection;
import javax.sql.DataSource;import java.sql.DriverManager;
import java.sql.SQLException;
import java.util.Properties;
import javax.naming.Context;
import javax.naming.InitialContext;
import javax.naming.NamingException;

public final class CreateConnection {
    static Properties props = new Properties();
    static String hostname = null;
    static String port = null;
    static String database = null;
    static String username = null;
    static String password = null;
    static String jndi = null;
    public CreateConnection() {
    }
    public static void loadProperties() {
        // Return if the host has already been loaded
        if(hostname != null){
            return;
        }
```

```
        try(InputStream in = Files.newInputStream(FileSystems.getDefault().getPath(System.
        getProperty("user.dir")
                    + File.separator + "db_props.properties"));) {
            // Looks for properties file in the root of the src directory in project
            System.out.println(FileSystems.getDefault().getPath(System.
            getProperty("user.dir")
                    + File.separator + "db_props.properties"));
            props.load(in);
        } catch (IOException ex) {
            ex.printStackTrace();
        }
        hostname = props.getProperty("host_name");
        port = props.getProperty("port_number");
        database = props.getProperty("db_name");
        username = props.getProperty("username");
        password = props.getProperty("password");
        jndi = props.getProperty("jndi");
        System.out.println(hostname);
    }
    public static Connection getConnection() throws SQLException {
        Connection conn = null;
        String jdbcUrl = "jdbc:oracle:thin:@" + hostname + ":"
                    + port + ":" + database;
        conn = DriverManager.getConnection(jdbcUrl, username, password);
        System.out.println("Successfully connected");
        return conn;
    }
    public static Connection getDSConnection() {
        Connection conn = null;
        try {
            Context ctx = new InitialContext();
            DataSource ds = (DataSource) ctx.lookup(jndi);
            conn = ds.getConnection();
        } catch (NamingException | SQLException ex) {
            ex.printStackTrace();
        }
        return conn;
    }
    public static void main(String[] args) {
        Connection conn = null;
        try {
            CreateConnection.loadProperties();
            System.out.println("Beginning connection..");
            conn = CreateConnection.getConnection();
            //performDbTask();
        } catch (java.sql.SQLException ex) {
            ex.printStackTrace();
        } finally {
            if (conn != null) {
                try {
                    conn.close();
```

```
                } catch (SQLException ex) {
                    ex.printStackTrace();
                }
            }
        }
    }
}
```

Next, the following lines of code are an example of what should be contained in the properties file that is used for obtaining a connection to the database. For this example, the properties file is named db_props. properties:

```
host_name=your_db_server_name
db_name=your_db_name
username=db_username
password=db_username_password
port_number=db_port_number
jndi=jndi_connection_string
```

Finally, use the CreateConnection class to obtain connections for your application. The following code demonstrates this concept:

```
Connection conn = null;
try {
    CreateConnection.loadProperties();
    System.out.println("Beginning connection..");
    conn = CreateConnection.getConnection();
    //performDbTask();
} catch (java.sql.SQLException ex) {
    System.out.println(ex);
} finally {
    if (conn != null) {
        try {
            conn.close();
        } catch (SQLException ex) {
            ex.printStackTrace();
        }
    }
}
```

■ **Note** You could update this code to use the try-with-resources syntax to get rid of the finally block requirement. However, I'm showing this syntax to demonstrate how to ensure that a Connection object is closed, if you're not using try-with-resources.

To run the code for testing, execute the class org.jakartaeerecipes.chapter06.CreateConnection. java because it contains a main method for testing purposes.

How It Works

Obtaining a connection within a database application can be code intensive. Moreover, the process can be prone to error if you retype the code each time you need to obtain a connection. By encapsulating database connection logic within a single class, you can reuse the same connection code each time you require a connection to the database. This increases your productivity, reduces the chances of typing errors, and also enhances manageability because if you have to make a change, it can occur in one place rather than in several different locations.

Creating a strategic connection methodology is beneficial to you and others who might need to maintain your code in the future. Although data sources are the preferred technique for managing database connections when using an application server or JNDI, the solution to this recipe demonstrates how to use standard JDBC DriverManager connections. One of the security implications of using the DriverManager is that you will need to store the database credentials somewhere for use by the application. It is not safe to store those credentials in plain text anywhere, and it is also not safe to embed them in application code, which might be decompiled at some point in the future. As seen in the solution, a properties file that resides on disk is used to store the database credentials. Assume that this properties file will be encrypted at some point before deployment to a server.

As shown in the solution, the code reads the database credentials, hostname, database name, and port number from the properties file. That information is then pieced together to form a JDBC URL that can be used by DriverManager to obtain a connection to the database. Once obtained, that connection can be used anywhere and then closed. Similarly, if using a DataSource that has been deployed to an application server, the properties file can be used to store the JNDI connection. That is the only piece of information that is needed to obtain a connection to the database using the DataSource. To the developer, the only difference between the two types of connections would be the method name that is called in order to obtain the Connection object, those being getDSConnection() or getConnection() in the example.

You could develop a JDBC application so that the code that is used to obtain a connection needs to be hard-coded throughout. Instead, this solution enables all the code for obtaining a connection to be encapsulated by a single class so that the developer does not need to worry about it. Such a technique also allows the code to be more maintainable. For instance, if the application was originally deployed using the DriverManager but then later had the ability to use a DataSource, very little code would need to be changed.

6-6. Querying a Database

Problem

You have a table that contains authors within the company database, and you want to query that table to retrieve the records.

Solution

Obtain a JDBC connection using one of the techniques covered in Recipe 6-2 or 6-4; then use the java.sql. Connection object to create a Statement object. A java.sql.Statement object contains the executeQuery method, which can be used to parse a String of text and use it to query a database. Once you've executed the query, you can retrieve the results of the query into a ResultSet object. The following example, excerpted from the org.jakartaeerecipes.chapter06.dao.AuthorDAO class, queries a database table named BOOK_AUTHOR and prints the results to the server log:

```
public void queryBookAuthor() {

    final String qry = "select id, first, last, bio from book_author";

    CreateConnection.loadProperties();

    try (Connection conn = CreateConnection.getConnection();
         Statement stmt = conn.createStatement();
         ResultSet rs = stmt.executeQuery(qry)) {
        while (rs.next()) {
            int author_id = rs.getInt("ID");
            String first_name = rs.getString("FIRSTNAME");
            String last_name = rs.getString("LASTNAME");
            String bio = rs.getString("BIO");
            System.out.println(author_id + "\t" + first_name
                    + " " + last_name + "\t" + bio);
        }
    } catch (SQLException e) {
        e.printStackTrace();
    }
}
```

Executing this method against the database schema that ships with this book will produce the results shown in Figure 6-7, considering that the BIO column is null for each author record.

```
Successfully connected
2    Josh Juneau Author of Apress Books
3    Tarun Telang    Author of Apress Books

Process finished with exit code 0
```

Figure 6-7. *Output from queryBookAuthor() of the AuthorDAO class*

How It Works

One of the most commonly performed operations against a database is a query. Performing database queries using JDBC is quite easy, although there is a bit of boilerplate code that needs to be used each time a query is executed. First, you need to obtain a Connection object for the database and schema that you want to run the query against. You can do this by using one of the solutions in Recipe 6-2. Next, you need to form a query and store it in String format. The CreateConnection properties are then loaded via a call to the loadProperties() method, which ensures that the db_props.properties file is used to populate database connection information. Next, a try-with-resources clause is used to create the objects that are necessary for querying the database. Since the objects are instantiated within the try-with-resources, then they will be closed automatically once they are no longer being used. The Connection object is then used to create a Statement. Your query String will be passed to the Statement object's executeQuery method in order to actually query the database:

```
String qry = "select ID, FIRSTNAME, LASTNAME, BIO from book_author";
        CreateConnection.loadProperties();
        try (Connection conn = CreateConnection.getConnection();
                Statement stmt = conn.createStatement();
                ResultSet rs = stmt.executeQuery(qry);) {
. . .
```

As you can see, the Statement object's executeQuery method accepts a String and returns a ResultSet object. The ResultSet object makes it easy to work with the query results so that you can obtain the information you need in any order. If you take a look at the next line of code, a while loop is created on the ResultSet object. This loop will continue to call the ResultSet object's next method, obtaining the next row that is returned from the query with each iteration. In this case, the ResultSet object is named rs, so while rs.next() returns true, the loop will continue to be processed. Once all the returned rows have been processed, rs.next() will return a false to indicate that there are no more rows to be processed.

Within the while loop, each returned row is processed. The ResultSet object is parsed to obtain the values of the given column names with each pass. Notice that if the column is expected to return a String, you must call the ResultSet getString() method, passing the column name in String format. Similarly, if the column is expected to return an int, you'd call the ResultSet getInt() method, passing the column name in String format. The same holds true for the other data types. These methods will return the corresponding column values. In the example in the solution to this recipe, those values are stored into local variables:

```
int author_id = rs.getInt("ID");
String first_name = rs.getString("FIRSTNAME");
String last_name = rs.getString("LASTNAME");
String bio = rs.getString("BIO");
```

Once the column value has been obtained, you can do what you want to do with the values you have stored within local variables. In this case, they are printed out using the System.out.println() method. Notice that there is a try-catch-finally block used in this example. A java.sql.SQLException could be thrown when attempting to query a database (for instance, if the Connection object has not been properly obtained or if the database tables that you are trying to query do not exist). You must provide exception handling to handle errors in these situations. Therefore, all database-processing code should be placed within a try block. The catch block then handles a SQLException, so if it is thrown, the exception will be handled using the code within the catch block. Sounds easy enough, right? It is, but you must do it each time you perform a database query. That means lots of boilerplate code. Inside the finally block, you will see that the Statement and Connection objects are closed if they are not equal to null.

■ **Note** Performing these tasks also incurs the overhead of handling java.sql.SQLException when it is thrown. They might occur if an attempt is made to close a null object. It is always a good idea to close statements and connections if they are open. This will help ensure that the system can reallocate resources as needed and act respectfully on the database. It is important to close connections as soon as possible so that other processes can reuse them.

6-7. Performing CRUD Operations

Problem

You need to have the ability to perform standard database operations from within your enterprise application. That is, you need to have the ability to create, retrieve, update, and delete (CRUD) database records.

Solution

Create a Connection object and obtain a database connection using one of the solutions provided in Recipe 6-2; then perform the CRUD operation using a java.sql.Statement object that is obtained from the java.sql.Connection object. The following code, taken from org.jakartaeerecipes.chapter06.recipe05_06.AuthorDAOStandard.java, demonstrates how to perform each of the CRUD operations against the BOOK_AUTHORS table using JDBC, with the exception of the query (retrieve) since that is already covered in Recipe 6-5.

■ **Note** This recipe demonstrates the use of String concatenation for creating SQL statements rather than substitution variables with PreparedStatements. This is not a safe practice because the variables could potentially contain malicious values that may compromise your database. The solution to this recipe demonstrates the practice of creating SQL statements using String concatenation so that you can see the different options that are available. For information on using PreparedStatement objects and a safer alternative to String concatenation, please see Recipe 6-7.

```java
private void performCreate(String first, String last, String bio) {
        String sql = "INSERT INTO BOOK_AUTHOR VALUES("
                + "BOOK_AUTHOR_S.NEXTVAL, "
                + "'" + last + "', "
                + "'" + first + "', "
                + "'" + bio + "')";
        try (Connection conn = CreateConnection.getConnection();
                PreparedStatement stmt = conn.prepareStatement(sql)) {
            // Returns row-count or 0 if not successful
            int result = stmt.executeUpdate();
            if (result > 0) {
                System.out.println("-- Record created --");
            } else {
                System.out.println("!! Record NOT Created !!");
            }
        } catch (SQLException e) {
            e.printStackTrace();
        }
    }
    private void performUpdate(String first, String last, String bio) {
        String sql = "UPDATE BOOK_AUTHOR "
                + "SET BIO = '" + bio + "' "
                + "WHERE LASTNAME = '" + last + "' "
                + "AND FIRSTNAME = '" + first + "'";
```

```
    try (Connection conn = CreateConnection.getConnection();
            PreparedStatement stmt = conn.prepareStatement(sql)) {
        int result = stmt.executeUpdate();
        if (result > 0) {
            System.out.println("-- Record Updated --");
        } else {
            System.out.println("!! Record NOT Updated !!");
        }
    } catch (SQLException e) {
        e.printStackTrace();
    }
}
private void performDelete(String first, String last) {
    String sql = "DELETE FROM BOOK_AUTHOR WHERE LASTNAME = '" + last + "' "
            + "AND FIRSTNAME = '" + first + "'";
    try (Connection conn = CreateConnection.getConnection();
            PreparedStatement stmt = conn.prepareStatement(sql)) {
        int result = stmt.executeUpdate();
        if (result > 0) {
            System.out.println("-- Record Deleted --");
        } else {
            System.out.println("!! Record NOT Deleted!!");
        }
    } catch (SQLException e) {
        e.printStackTrace();
    }
}
```

■ **Note** If you follow the code, you will notice that whenever a `String` of data is passed to the database, it is first changed to uppercase by calling the `toUpperCase` method on it. This is to help maintain a standard uppercase format for all data within the database.

Executing the following main method will produce the results that follow:

```
public static void main(String[] args) {
        AuthorDAO authorDao = new AuthorDAO();
        authorDao.queryBookAuthor();
        authorDao.performCreate("Nikita", "Goswami", "N/A");
        authorDao.performUpdate("Nikita", "Goswami", "Nikita's Bio");
        authorDao.queryBookAuthor();
        authorDao.performDelete("Nikita", "Goswami");
}
```

The results from running the main method of the class should be like Figure 6-8.

```
Successfully connected
2    Josh Juneau Author of Apress Books
3    Tarun Telang    Author of Apress Books
Successfully connected
-- Record created --
Successfully connected
-- Record Updated --
Successfully connected
2    Josh Juneau Author of Apress Books
3    Tarun Telang    Author of Apress Books
8    Nikita Goswami  Nikita's Bio
Successfully connected
-- Record Deleted --

Process finished with exit code 0
```

Figure 6-8. *Output from the AuthorDAO class*

How It Works

The same basic code format is used for performing just about every database task. The format is as follows:

1. Obtain a connection to the database within the try clause.

2. Create a statement from the connection within the try clause.

3. Perform a database task with the statement.

4. Do something with the results of the database task.

5. Close the statement (and database connection if finished using it).

This step is done automatically for you if using the try-with-resources clause, as demonstrated in the solution to this recipe.

The main difference between performing a query using JDBC and using Data Manipulation Language (DML) is that you will call different methods on the Statement object, depending on which operation you want to perform. To perform a query, you need to call the Statement executeQuery method. To perform DML tasks, such as insert, update, and delete, call the executeUpdate method.

The performCreate method in the solution to this recipe demonstrates the operation of inserting a record into a database. To insert a record in the database, you will construct a SQL insert statement in String format. To perform the insert, pass the SQL string to the Statement object's executeUpdate method. If the insert is performed, an int value will be returned that specifies the number of rows that have been inserted. If the insert operation is not performed successfully, either a zero will be returned or a SQLException will be thrown, indicating a problem with the statement or database connection.

The performUpdate method in the solution to this recipe demonstrates the operation of updating record(s) within a database table. First, you will construct a SQL update statement in String format. Next, to perform the update operation, you will pass the SQL string to the Statement object's executeUpdate method. If the update is successfully performed, an int value will be returned, which specifies the number of records that were updated. If the update operation is not performed successfully, either a zero will be returned or a SQLException will be thrown, indicating a problem with the statement or database connection.

The last database operation that is covered in the solution is the delete operation. The performDelete method in the solution to this recipe demonstrates how to delete records from the database. First, you will construct a SQL delete statement in String format. Next, to execute the deletion, you will pass the SQL string to the Statement object's executeUpdate method. If the deletion is successful, an int value specifying the number of rows deleted will be returned. Otherwise, if the deletion fails, a zero will be returned, or a SQLException will be thrown, indicating a problem with the statement or database connection.

Almost every database application uses at least one of the CRUD operations at some point. This is a fundamental JDBC that you need to know if you are working with databases within Java applications. Even if you will not work directly with the JDBC API, it is good to know these basics.

6-8. Preventing SQL Injection

Problem

Your application performs database tasks. To reduce the chances of a SQL injection attack, you need to ensure that no unfiltered Strings of text are being appended to SQL statements and executed against the database.

■ **Tip** Prepared statements provide more than just protection against SQL injection attacks. They also provide a way to centralize and better control the SQL used within an application, and performance benefits. Instead of creating multiple and possibly different versions of the same query, you can create the query once as a prepared statement and invoke it from many different places within your code. Any change to the query logic needs to happen only at the point that you prepare the statement.

■ **Note** There have been data access objects (DAOs) created for each database table used by the Acme Bookstore application for this recipe. The DAO classes are used to perform CRUD operations against each of the tables for the Acme Bookstore application. The CRUD operations utilize PreparedStatements in order to add security and enhance the performance of the application.

Solution

Utilize PreparedStatements for performing the database tasks. PreparedStatements send a precompiled SQL statement to the DBMS rather than a clear-text String. The following code demonstrates how to perform a database query and a database update using a java.sql.PreparedStatement object. The following code excerpts are taken from a new data access object named org.jakartaeerecipes.chapter06. dao.AuthorDAO, which utilizes PreparedStatement objects rather than String concatenation for executing SQL statements:

```
. . .
    public Author performFind(int id) {
        String qry = "SELECT ID, LASTNAME, FIRSTNAME, BIO "
                + "FROM BOOK_AUTHOR "
                + "WHERE ID = ?";
        Author author = null;
        CreateConnection.loadProperties();
        try (Connection conn = CreateConnection.getConnection();
                PreparedStatement stmt = conn.prepareStatement(qry)) {
            stmt.setInt(1, id);
            try (ResultSet rs = stmt.executeQuery();) {
                if (rs.next()) {
                    int author_id = rs.getInt("ID");
                    String first_name = rs.getString("FIRSTNAME");
                    String last_name = rs.getString("LASTNAME");
                    String bio = rs.getString("BIO");
                    author = new Author(author_id,
                            first_name,
                            last_name,
                            bio);
                }
            }
        } catch (SQLException e) {
            e.printStackTrace();
        }
        return author;
    }
    public List<Author> performFind(String first, String last) {
        String qry = "SELECT ID, LASTNAME, FIRSTNAME, BIO "
                + "FROM BOOK_AUTHOR "
                + "WHERE LASTNAME = ? "
                + "AND FIRSTNAME = ?";
        List authorList = new ArrayList();
        try (Connection conn = CreateConnection.getConnection();
                PreparedStatement stmt = conn.prepareStatement(qry)) {
            stmt.setString(1, last);
            stmt.setString(2, first);
            try (ResultSet rs = stmt.executeQuery();) {
                while (rs.next()) {
                    int author_id = rs.getInt("ID");
                    String first_name = rs.getString("FIRST");
                    String last_name = rs.getString("LAST");
                    String bio = rs.getString("BIO");
                    Author author = new Author(author_id,
                            firstName,
                            lastName,
                            bio);
                    authorList.add(author);
                }
            }
```

```
        } catch (SQLException e) {
            e.printStackTrace();
        }
        return authorList;
    }
    private void performCreate(String first, String last, String bio) {
        String sql = "INSERT INTO BOOK_AUTHOR VALUES("
                + "BOOK_AUTHOR_S.NEXTVAL, ?, ?, ?)";
        try (Connection conn = CreateConnection.getConnection();
                PreparedStatement stmt = conn.prepareStatement(sql)) {
            stmt.setString(1, last);
            stmt.setString(2, first);
            stmt.setString(3, bio);
                // Returns row-count or 0 if not successful
                int result = stmt.executeUpdate();
                if (result > 0) {
                    System.out.println("-- Record created --");
                } else {
                    System.out.println("!! Record NOT Created !!");
                }
        } catch (SQLException e) {
            e.printStackTrace();
        }
    }
    private void performUpdate(int id, String first, String last, String bio) {
        String sql = "UPDATE BOOK_AUTHOR "
                + "SET bio = ?,"
                + "    last = ?,"
                + "    first = ? "
                + "WHERE ID = ?";
        try (Connection conn = CreateConnection.getConnection();
                PreparedStatement stmt = conn.prepareStatement(sql)) {
            stmt.setString(1, bio);
            stmt.setString(2, last);
            stmt.setString(3, first);
            stmt.setInt(4, id);
                int result = stmt.executeUpdate();
                if (result > 0) {
                    System.out.println("-- Record Updated --");
                } else {
                    System.out.println("!! Record NOT Updated !!");
                }
        } catch (SQLException e) {
            e.printStackTrace();
        }
    }
    private void performDelete(int id) {
        String sql = "DELETE FROM BOOK_AUTHOR WHERE ID = ?";
        try (Connection conn = CreateConnection.getConnection();
                PreparedStatement stmt = conn.prepareStatement(sql)) {
            stmt.setInt(1, id);
```

```
            int result = stmt.executeUpdate();
            if (result > 0) {
                System.out.println("-- Record Deleted --");
            } else {
                System.out.println("!! Record NOT Deleted!!");
            }
        } catch (SQLException e) {
            e.printStackTrace();
        }
    }
...
```

The methods displayed previously exhibit the use of PreparedStatement objects rather than using standard JDBC Statement objects and String concatenation for appending variables into SQL statements.

How It Works

While standard JDBC statements will get the job done, the harsh reality is that they can be insecure and difficult to work with. For instance, bad things can occur if a dynamic SQL statement is used to query a database and a user-accepted String is assigned to a variable and concatenated with the intended SQL String. In most ordinary cases, the user-accepted String would be concatenated, and the SQL String would be used to query the database as expected. However, an attacker could decide to place malicious code inside the String (a.k.a. *SQL injection*), which would then be inadvertently sent to the database using a standard Statement object. Using PreparedStatements prevents malicious Strings from being concatenated into a SQL string and passed to the DBMS. PreparedStatements use substitution variables rather than concatenation to make SQL strings dynamic. They are also precompiled, which means that a valid SQL string is formed prior to the SQL being sent to the DBMS. Moreover, PreparedStatements can help your application perform better because if the same SQL has to be run more than one time, it has to be compiled only once per session. After that, the substitution variables are interchangeable, but the PreparedStatement can execute the SQL very quickly.

Let's take a look at how a PreparedStatement works in practice. If you look at the example in the solution to this recipe, you can see that the database table BOOK_AUTHOR is being queried in the performFind() method, sending the author's ID as a substitution variable and retrieving the results for the matching record. The SQL string looks like the following:

```
String qry = "SELECT ID, LASTNAME, FIRSTNAME, BIO "
                + "FROM BOOK_AUTHOR "
                + "WHERE ID = ?";
```

Everything looks standard with the SQL text except for the question mark (?) at the end of the string. Placing a question mark within a string of SQL signifies that a substitution variable will be used in place of that question mark when the SQL is executed.

The next step for using a PreparedStatement is to declare a variable of type PreparedStatement. You can see this with the following line of code:

```
PreparedStatement stmt = null;
```

Now that a PreparedStatement has been declared, it can be put to use. However, using a PreparedStatement may or may not cause an exception to be thrown. Therefore, any use of a PreparedStatement should occur within a try-catch block so that any exceptions can be handled gracefully. For instance, exceptions can occur if the database connection is unavailable for some reason or if the SQL string is invalid. Rather than crashing an application because of such issues, it is best to handle the exceptions wisely within a catch block. The following try-catch block includes the code that is necessary to send the SQL string to the database and retrieve results:

```
try (Connection conn = CreateConnection.getConnection();
        PreparedStatement stmt = conn.prepareStatement(qry)) {
    stmt.setInt(1, id);
    try (ResultSet rs = stmt.executeQuery();) {
    if (rs.next()) {
        int author_id = rs.getInt("ID");
        String first_name = rs.getString("FIRST");
        String last_name = rs.getString("LAST");
        String bio = rs.getString("BIO");
        author = new Author(author_id,
                                first_name,
                                last_name,
                                bio);
    }
  }
} catch (SQLException e) {
    e.printStackTrace();
}
```

First, you can see that the Connection object is used to instantiate a PreparedStatement object. The SQL string is passed to the PreparedStatement object's constructor upon creation. Next, the PreparedStatement object is used to set values for any substitution variables that have been placed into the SQL string. As you can see, the PreparedStatement setString() method is used in the example to set the substitution variable at position 1 equal to the contents of the id variable. The positioning of the substitution variable is associated with the placement of the question mark (?) within the SQL string. The first question mark within the string is assigned to the first position, the second one is assigned to the second position, and so forth. The number of question marks must be equal to the number of substitution variables, or an error will be thrown. If there were more than one substitution variable to be assigned, there would be more than one call to the PreparedStatement setter methods, assigning each of the variables until each one has been accounted for. PreparedStatements can accept substitution variables of many different data types. For instance, if a Date value were being assigned to a substitution variable, a call to the setDate(position, variable) method would be in order. Please see the online documentation or your IDE's code completion for a complete set of methods that can be used for assigning substitution variables using PreparedStatement objects.

It is also possible to utilize named parameters, rather than indexes. To use this technique, provide a name prefixed with a colon for each substitution variable, rather than a question mark. The following lines of code demonstrate named parameters:

```
String qry = "SELECT ID, LAST, FIRST, BIO "
                + "FROM BOOK_AUTHOR "
                + "WHERE LAST = :last "
                + "AND FIRST = :first";
        List authorList = new ArrayList();
        try (Connection conn = CreateConnection.getConnection();
                PreparedStatement stmt = conn.prepareStatement(qry)) {
            stmt.setString("last", last);
            stmt.setString("first", first);
            try (ResultSet rs = stmt.executeQuery();) {
. . .
```

Once all the variables have been assigned, the SQL string can be executed. The PreparedStatement object contains an executeQuery() method that is used to execute a SQL string that represents a query.

The executeQuery() method returns a ResultSet object, which contains the results that have been fetched from the database for the particular SQL query. Next, the ResultSet can be traversed to obtain the values retrieved from the database. There are two different ways to retrieve the results from the ResultSet. Positional assignments can be used to retrieve the results by calling the ResultSet object's corresponding getter methods and passing the position of the column value, or the String identifier of the column value that you want to obtain can be passed to the getter methods. If passing the position, it is determined by the order in which the column names appear within the SQL string. In the example, String-based column identifiers are used to obtain the values. As you can see from the example, passing the column identifier to the appropriate getter method will retrieve the value. When the record values from the ResultSet are obtained, they are stored into local variables. Once all the variables have been collected for a particular author, they are stored into an Author object, which will eventually be returned from the method. Of course, if the substitution variable is not set correctly or if there is an issue with the SQL string, an exception will be thrown. This would cause the code that is contained within the catch block to be executed.

If you do not use the try-with-resources clause, as demonstrated in the solution, you should be sure to clean up after using PreparedStatements by closing the statement when you are finished using it. It is a good practice to put all the cleanup code within a finally block to be sure that it is executed even if an exception is thrown. For example, a finally block that is used to clean up unused Statement and Connection objects may look like the following:

```
finally {
    if (stmt != null) {
        try {
            stmt.close();
        } catch (SQLException ex) {
            ex.printStackTrace();
        }
    }
    if (conn != null) {
        try {
            conn.close();
            conn = null;
        } catch (SQLException ex) {
            ex.printStackTrace();
        }
    }
    return author;
}
```

You can see that the PreparedStatement object that was instantiated, stmt, is checked to see whether it is NULL. If not, it is closed by calling the close() method. Working through the code in the solution to this recipe, you can see that similar code is used to process database insert, update, and delete statements. The only difference in those cases is that the PreparedStatement executeUpdate() method is called rather than the executeQuery() method. The executeUpdate() method will return an int value representing the number of rows affected by the SQL statement.

The use of PreparedStatement objects is preferred over JDBC Statement objects. This is because they are more secure and perform better. They can also make your code easier to follow and easier to maintain.

6-9. Utilizing Java Objects for Database Access

Problem

Your application works with an underlying database for storing and retrieving data. You would prefer to code your business logic using Java objects, rather than working directly with JDBC and SQL for performing database activities.

Solution

Create a data access object (DAO) for each database table that will be used to perform the mundane JDBC and SQL work. Within the DAO, create façade methods that accept Java objects to represent a single record of data for the database table for which the DAO has been created. Use the Java objects to pass record data to and from the DAO, while the DAO breaks the objects apart and utilizes the data fields within standard SQL statements.

The following class excerpts demonstrate a data access object for the AUTHOR database table, which is used for storing book author data (a main method has been included merely for testing purposes within this DAO):

■ **Note** For the full source listing, please refer to the `org.jakartaeerecipes.chapter06.dao.` `AuthorDAO` class, located in the JakartaEERecipes NetBeans project.

```
...
public class AuthorDAO {
    public AuthorDAO() {
    }
    public void queryBookAuthor() {
        String qry = "select id, first, last, bio from book_author";
        CreateConnection.loadProperties();
        try (Connection conn = CreateConnection.getConnection();
                Statement stmt = conn.createStatement();
                ResultSet rs = stmt.executeQuery(qry);) {
            while (rs.next()) {
                int author_id = rs.getInt("ID");
                String first_name = rs.getString("FIRST");
                String last_name = rs.getString("LAST");
                String bio = rs.getString("BIO");
                System.out.println(author_id + "\t" + first_name
                        + " " + last_name + "\t" + bio);
            }
        } catch (SQLException e) {
            e.printStackTrace();
        }
    }
    public List<Author> obtainCompleteAuthorList() {
        String qry = "select id, first, last, bio from book_author";
        List<Author> authors = new ArrayList();
        CreateConnection.loadProperties();
        try (Connection conn = CreateConnection.getConnection();
```

```
            Statement stmt = conn.createStatement();
            ResultSet rs = stmt.executeQuery(qry);) {
        while (rs.next()) {
            int author_id = rs.getInt("ID");
            String first_name = rs.getString("FIRST");
            String last_name = rs.getString("LAST");
            String bio = rs.getString("BIO");
            Author author = new Author(author_id, first_name,
                    last_name, bio);
            authors.add(author);
        }
    } catch (SQLException e) {
        e.printStackTrace();
    }
    return authors;
}
public Author performFind(int id) {
    String qry = "SELECT ID, LAST, FIRST, BIO "
            + "FROM BOOK_AUTHOR "
            + "WHERE ID = ?";
    Author author = null;
    CreateConnection.loadProperties();
    try (Connection conn = CreateConnection.getConnection();
            PreparedStatement stmt = conn.prepareStatement(qry)) {
        stmt.setInt(1, id);
        try (ResultSet rs = stmt.executeQuery();) {
            if (rs.next()) {
                int author_id = rs.getInt("ID");
                String first_name = rs.getString("FIRST");
                String last_name = rs.getString("LAST");
                String bio = rs.getString("BIO");
                author = new Author(author_id,
                        first_name,
                        last_name,
                        bio);
            }
        }
    } catch (SQLException e) {
        e.printStackTrace();
    }
    return author;
}
 public List<Author> performFind(String first, String last) {
    String qry = "SELECT ID, LAST, FIRST, BIO "
            + "FROM BOOK_AUTHOR "
            + "WHERE LAST = ? "
            + "AND FIRST = ?";
    List authorList = new ArrayList();
    try (Connection conn = CreateConnection.getConnection();
            PreparedStatement stmt = conn.prepareStatement(qry)) {
        stmt.setString(1, last);
```

```
                stmt.setString(2, first);
                try (ResultSet rs = stmt.executeQuery();) {
                    while (rs.next()) {
                        int author_id = rs.getInt("ID");
                        String first_name = rs.getString("FIRST");
                        String last_name = rs.getString("LAST");
                        String bio = rs.getString("BIO");
                        Author author = new Author(author_id,
                                first_name,
                                last_name,
                                bio);
                        authorList.add(author);
                    }
                }
            } catch (SQLException e) {
                e.printStackTrace();
            }
        return authorList;
    }
    private void performCreate(String first, String last, String bio) {
        String sql = "INSERT INTO BOOK_AUTHOR VALUES("
                + "BOOK_AUTHOR_S.NEXTVAL, ?, ?, ?)";
        try (Connection conn = CreateConnection.getConnection();
                PreparedStatement stmt = conn.prepareStatement(sql)) {
            stmt.setString(1, last);
            stmt.setString(2, first);
            stmt.setString(3, bio);
                // Returns row-count or 0 if not successful
                int result = stmt.executeUpdate();
                if (result > 0) {
                    System.out.println("-- Record created --");
                } else {
                    System.out.println("!! Record NOT Created !!");
                }
        } catch (SQLException e) {
            e.printStackTrace();
        }
    }
    private void performUpdate(int id, String first, String last, String bio) {
        String sql = "UPDATE BOOK_AUTHOR "
                + "SET bio = ?,"
                + "    last = ?,"
                + "    first = ? "
                + "WHERE ID = ?";
        try (Connection conn = CreateConnection.getConnection();
                PreparedStatement stmt = conn.prepareStatement(sql)) {
            stmt.setString(1, bio);
            stmt.setString(2, last);
            stmt.setString(3, first);
            stmt.setInt(4, id);
                int result = stmt.executeUpdate();
```

```java
                if (result > 0) {
                    System.out.println("-- Record Updated --");
                } else {
                    System.out.println("!! Record NOT Updated !!");
                }

        } catch (SQLException e) {
            e.printStackTrace();
        }
    }
    private void performDelete(int id) {
        String sql = "DELETE FROM BOOK_AUTHOR WHERE ID = ?";
        try (Connection conn = CreateConnection.getConnection();
                PreparedStatement stmt = conn.prepareStatement(sql)) {
            stmt.setInt(1, id);
                int result = stmt.executeUpdate();
                if (result > 0) {
                    System.out.println("-- Record Deleted --");
                } else {
                    System.out.println("!! Record NOT Deleted!!");
                }
        } catch (SQLException e) {
            e.printStackTrace();
        }
    }
    /**
     * Returns the next ID in the BOOK_AUTHOR_S sequence
     *
     * @return
     */
    public int getNextId() {
        String qry = "select book_author_s.currval as ID from dual";
        int returnId = -1;
        CreateConnection.loadProperties();
        try (Connection conn = CreateConnection.getConnection();
                Statement stmt = conn.createStatement();
                ResultSet rs = stmt.executeQuery(qry);) {
            while (rs.next()) {
                int author_id = rs.getInt("ID");
                returnId = author_id + 1;
            }
        } catch (SQLException e) {
            e.printStackTrace();
        }
        return returnId;
    }
    /**
     * Facade method for inserting Author objects into the BOOK_AUTHOR table
     *
     * @param author
     */
```

```java
    public void insert(Author author) {
        performCreate(author.getFirst(),
                author.getLast(),
                author.getBio());
    }
    /**
     * Facade method for updating Author objects in the BOOK_AUTHOR table
     *
     * @param author
     */
    public void update(Author author) {
        this.performUpdate(author.getId(), author.getFirst(), author.getLast(), author.
        getBio());
    }
    /**
     * Facade method for deleting Author objects from the BOOK_AUTHOR table
     *
     * @param args
     */
    public void delete(Author author) {
        performDelete(author.getId());
    }
    public static void main(String[] args) {
        AuthorDAO authorDao = new AuthorDAO();
        authorDao.queryBookAuthor();
        authorDao.performCreate("Joe", "Blow", "N/A");
        // Find any author named Joe Blow and store in authList
        List<Author> authList = authorDao.performFind("Joe", "Blow");
        // Update the BIO for any author named Joe Blow
        for (Author auth : authList) {
            auth.setBio("New Bio");
            authorDao.update(auth);
        }
        authorDao.queryBookAuthor();
        // Delete any author named Joe Blow
        for (Author auth : authList) {
            authorDao.delete(auth);
        }
    }
}
```

How It Works

It can be advantageous for developers to separate different types of work into different classes within an application code base. In the same way that you separate web views from Java code within a Java web application, you should also separate JDBC from classes that are used to perform business logic. Have you ever had to maintain or debug a class that was riddled with business logic and SQL statements? It can be a nightmare! Simplifying code by breaking it down into smaller, more manageable pieces can oftentimes make maintenance and debugging much easier on a developer. The idea of separating JDBC and database-specific code from other business logic within an application falls within this same concept. Creating data access objects that are used solely for accessing the database can allow developers to code against Java objects rather than database tables.

A DAO is not a standard Java enterprise object. There is no framework that is used for creating DAOs. A DAO is simply a class that contains all of the JDBC code that is relevant for working with a single database table for your application. If there are 20 database tables that are required for use, then there should be that same number of DAOs. A DAO should contain minimally eight different methods. There should be at least one method for each of the four possible database transactions that could take place, those being CREATE, READ, UPDATE, and DELETE. These methods would contain specific JDBC code for connecting to the database, performing JDBC calls, and then closing the connection. The DAO should also contain four façade methods that will be used directly by classes containing the business logic. These methods should accept Java objects that correspond to the database table for which the DAO was written, and they should break down the object into separate fields and pass them to the JDBC methods to perform the actual database transaction.

In the solution to this recipe, the AuthorDAO class contains more than eight methods. This is because there is more than one way to search for author records within the database, and, therefore, there is more than one find method within the class. A couple of different performFind() methods are available, each with a different method signature. These methods allow one to find an author based upon ID or by name. Once a matching author record is found in the database, the values for that record are retrieved using standard JDBC methods, and they are stored into the corresponding fields within a new Author object. In the end, either a list of Author objects or a single Author object is returned to the caller. These finder methods contain public modifiers, so a managed bean can call them directly to retrieve a list of Author objects or a single Author object.

The performCreate(), performUpdate(), and performDelete() methods are private, and therefore they can be accessed only by other methods within the same class. The insert, update, and delete methods accept Author objects, and they perform the task of breaking down the Author object by field and passing the appropriate fields to their corresponding private methods in order to perform database activities. For instance, a bean can call the AuthorDAO insert method, passing an Author object. The insert method then calls the performCreate method, passing the fields of the Author object in their respective positions. Each of the CRUD operations can be performed in the same manner, allowing the business logic to interact directly with Author objects rather than deal with SQL.

6-10. Querying and Storing Large Objects

Problem

The application you are developing requires the storage of Strings of text that can include an unlimited number of characters.

Solution

Because the size of the Strings that need to be stored is unlimited, it is best to use a character large object (CLOB) data type to store the data. The following is the SQL script to create the CHAPTER table:

```
create table CHAPTER
(
    ID              NUMERIC(5) not null
        primary key,
    CHAPTER_NUMBER NUMERIC(5),
    TITLE           VARCHAR(500),
    BOOK_ID         NUMERIC(5)
```

```
        constraint FK_CHAPTER_BOOK_ID
            references BOOK,
    DESCRIPTION     CLOB
);
```

The code in the following example demonstrates how to load a CLOB into the database and how to query it. The following excerpts are two methods from the org.jakartaeerecipes.chapter06.dao. ChapterDAO class.

Let's take a look at how to read a CLOB column value from the database. The readClob() method queries the database, reading the CHAPTER_NUMBER, TITLE, and DESCRIPTION columns from the CHAPTER database table. The length of the DESCRIPTION, which is the CLOB column, is printed to the command line along with the chapter number, title, and description:

```
public void readClob() {
        String qry = "select chapter_number, title, description from chapter";
        Clob theClob = null;

        try (Connection conn = CreateConnection.getConnection();
                PreparedStatement stmt = conn.prepareStatement(qry)) {
            try (ResultSet rs = stmt.executeQuery()) {
                while (rs.next()) {
                    int chapterNumber = rs.getInt(1);
                    String title = rs.getString(2);
                    theClob = rs.getClob(3);
                    System.out.println("Clob length: " + theClob.length());
                    System.out.println(chapterNumber + " - " + title + ": ");
                    java.io.InputStream in =
                            theClob.getAsciiStream();
                    int i;
                    while ((i = in.read()) > -1) {
                        System.out.print((char) i);
                    }
                    System.out.println();
                }
            }
        } catch (IOException | SQLException ex) {
            ex.printStackTrace();
        }
}
```

The code can be executed by running it as a stand-alone application. The resulting output from running the method would look similar to Figure 6-9, depending upon which records are stored in the database.

```
Successfully connected
Clob length: 11
1 - Getting Started with Java 17:
description
Clob length: 11
2 - Strings:
description
Clob length: 11
3 - Numbers and Dates:
description
Clob length: 11
4 - Data Types, Conditionals, and Iterations:
description
Clob length: 11
5 - Input and Output:
description
Clob length: 11
6 - Exceptions and Logging:
description
Clob length: 11
7 - Object-Oriented Java:
description
Clob length: 11
8 - Concurrency:
description
Clob length: 11
9 - Debugging and Unit Testing:
description
Clob length: 11
10 - Unicode, Internationalization, and Currency Codes:
description

Process finished with exit code 0
```

Figure 6-9. *Output from the ChapterDAO class*

What about inserting CLOB values into the database? The next method accepts values for each field within a record of the CHAPTER table, and it constructs the CLOB contents and lastly performs the insert:

```
private void performCreate(int chapterNumber, int bookId, String title, String
description) {
        String sql = "INSERT INTO CHAPTER VALUES("
                + "CHAPTER_S.NEXTVAL, ?, ?, ?, ?)";
        Clob textClob = null;
        CreateConnection.loadProperties();
```

```java
    try (Connection conn = CreateConnection.getConnection();
            PreparedStatement stmt = conn.prepareStatement(sql)) {
        textClob = conn.createClob();
        textClob.setString(1, description);
        stmt.setInt(1, chapterNumber);
        stmt.setString(2, title);
        stmt.setClob(3, textClob);
        stmt.setInt(4, bookId);
        // Returns row-count or 0 if not successful
        int result = stmt.executeUpdate();
        if (result > 0) {
            System.out.println("-- Record created --");
        } else {
            System.out.println("!! Record NOT Created !!");
        }
    } catch (SQLException e) {
        e.printStackTrace();
    }
}
```

How It Works

If your application requires the storage of String values, you need to know how large those Strings might possibly become. Most databases have an upper boundary when it comes to the storage size of VARCHAR fields. For instance, the Oracle database has an upper boundary of 4000 bytes, and anything exceeding that length will be cut off. If you have large amounts of text that need to be stored, use a CLOB field in the database.

A CLOB is handled a bit differently from a String within Java code. In fact, it is actually a bit odd to work with the first couple of times you use it because you have to create a CLOB from a Connection.

■ **Note** In reality, CLOBs and BLOBs (binary large objects) are not stored in the Oracle table where they are defined. Instead, a large object (LOB) locator is stored in the table column. Oracle might place the CLOB in a separate file on the database server. When Java creates the Clob object, it can be used to hold data for update to a specific LOB location in the database or to retrieve the data from a specific LOB location within the database.

Let's take a look at the performCreate() method that is contained in the solution to this recipe. As you can see, a Clob object is created using the Connection object's createClob() method. Once the Clob has been created, you set its contents using the setString() method by passing the position, which indicates where to place the String, and the String of text itself:

```java
textClob = conn.createClob();
textClob.setString(1, "This will be the recipe text in clob format");
```

Once you have created and populated the Clob, you simply pass it to the database using the PreparedStatement setClob() method. In the case of this example, the PreparedStatement performs a database insert into the CHAPTER table by calling the executeUpdate() method as usual. Querying a Clob is fairly straightforward as well. As you can see in the readClob() method that is contained within the solution to this recipe, a PreparedStatement query is set up, and the results are retrieved into a ResultSet. The only difference between using a Clob and a String is that you must load the Clob into a Clob type. Calling the Clob object's getString() method will pass you a strange-looking String of text that denotes a Clob object. Therefore, calling the Clob object's getAsciiStream() method will return the actual data that is stored in the Clob. This technique is used in the solution to this recipe.

Although Clobs are fairly easy to use, they take a couple of extra steps to prepare. It is best to plan your applications accordingly and try to estimate whether the database fields you are using might need to be CLOBs because of size restrictions. Proper planning will prevent you from going back and changing standard String-based code to work with Clobs later.

CHAPTER 7

▦ ▦ ▦

Object-Relational Mapping

For years, the Java Database Connectivity (JDBC) API was the standard for working with databases of both web and desktop Java applications alike. Over the years, techniques for obtaining access to data stores and working with data within applications have evolved, and many organizations began to develop their own strategies for working with data in a more convenient way. Developers often find it easier to work with Java objects rather than Structured Query Language (SQL) for relational data. This chapter discusses some techniques that have been used in order to encapsulate SQL into separate utility classes and abstract it from developers so that they can work with Java objects rather than the SQL. Such strategies are known as *object-relational mapping* (ORM) strategies, and there are several well-known ORM strategies available from a multitude of organizations today.

Object-relational mapping (ORM) tools help developers to work with Java objects rather than with SQL for relational data. There are many different ORM tools available. Among the most well-known ORM strategies are Hibernate, Oracle TopLink (`www.oracle.com/middleware/technologies/top-link.html`), and EclipseLink.

To standardize the industry, the Jakarta Persistence has been deemed the strategy to use for moving forward with Java and Jakarta EE. Jakarta Persistence includes many features that were first introduced in ORM strategies such as Hibernate and TopLink. In fact, some of the top representatives from many of the different ORM projects formulated the Java Specification Requests (JSRs) for producing the Jakarta Persistence API, providing Java enterprise developers with a standard, efficient, and highly productive way to work with an underlying RDBMS from within Java applications. The Jakarta Persistence API allows developers to choose from a variety of Java persistence providers to utilize the configuration with which they are most comfortable, without the need to include multiple third-party libraries or customizations within the application. Some of the possible providers are as follows:

- *EclipseLink* (`www.eclipse.org/eclipselink/`): The default Jakarta Persistence API implementation

- *Hibernate* (`https://hibernate.org`): A popular ORM tool for Java

- *OpenJPA* (`https://openjpa.apache.org/`): An open source implementation of Jakarta Persistence

- *MyBatis* (`https://mybatis.org`): A simple-to-use SQL mapper framework

- *Oracle TopLink* (`www.oracle.com/middleware/technologies/top-link.html`): An advanced ORM tool created by Oracle

Object-relational mapping is the process of mapping a Java object to a database table, such that each column of the database table maps to a single field or property within the Java object. Java objects that are used to map against database tables are referred to as *entity classes*, and this chapter will focus on the creation and use of entity classes. Recipes will cover areas such as creating classes and performing standard

© Josh Juneau and Tarun Telang 2022
J. Juneau and T. Telang, *Java EE to Jakarta EE 10 Recipes*, https://doi.org/10.1007/978-1-4842-8079-9_7

database transactions. You will learn how to configure a connection against a database, how to utilize the Jakarta Persistence API to persist and retrieve objects without using SQL, and how to relate objects to one another in a meaningful and productive manner.

Not only does ORM programming abstract the implementation details of working directly with a database from a developer, but it also provides a standard mechanism for deploying applications on databases from multiple vendors. The Jakarta Persistence API takes care of translating code into SQL statements, so once an application is written using the Jakarta Persistence API, it can be deployed using almost any underlying database.

■ **Note** The recipes within this chapter may or may not be available for your use depending upon which Jakarta Persistence API provider you choose. For instance, providers may include a different set of metadata annotations to use. Rather than list each annotation that is available for use in each recipe, I will direct you to very good resources for learning about all of the possible annotations that can be used along with each of the most widely used providers. While most of the annotations are common among all providers, there are a handful of custom annotations for each.

EclipseLink: `www.eclipse.org/eclipselink/documentation/`
Hibernate: `https://docs.jboss.org/hibernate/orm/6.0/javadocs/`
TopLink: `www.oracle.com/middleware/technologies/top-link.html`
The sources for this chapter reside within the `org.jakartaeerecipe.chapter07` package.

To run the examples from this chapter, deploy the application to the application server, and then visit the URL `http://localhost:8080/JakartaEERecipes/faces/chapter07/home.xhtml`. It should be noted that the examples for this chapter cannot be run within a web application without the use of other technologies such as Enterprise JavaBean, which will be covered in Chapter 8. For that reason, many of the examples in this chapter utilize stand-alone Java classes for testing purposes.

7-1. Creating an Entity

Problem

You want to create a Java object that can be mapped to a database table such that the class can be used for persistence, rather than using JDBC.

Solution

Create an entity class against a particular database table. Declare persistent fields or properties for each of the columns in the underlying data table and use annotations to map the fields to a given column. Provide getters and setters for each of the persistent fields or properties that are declared within the entity so that other classes can access the contents.

The following code is an entity class named BookAuthor, which maps the BOOK_AUTHOR database table to a standard Java object for use within the application:

```
package org.jakartaeerecipe.chapter07.entity;

import java.io.Serializable;
import java.math.BigDecimal;
import jakarta.persistence.*;
```

```java
import jakarta.validation.constraints.NotNull;
import jakarta.validation.constraints.Size;

@Entity
@Table (name = "BOOK_AUTHOR")
public class BookAuthor implements Serializable {

    private static final long serialVersionUID = 1L;

    @Id
    @Basic(optional = false)
    @NotNull
    @Column(name = "ID")
    private BigDecimal id;

    @Size(max = 30)
    @Column(name = "LAST")
    private String last;

   @Size(max = 30)
    @Column(name = "FIRST")
    private String first;

    @Lob
    @Column(name = "BIO")
    private String bio;
    public BookAuthor() {
    }

    public BookAuthor(BigDecimal id) {
        this.id = id;
    }
    ...
    // getters and setters
    ...
    @Override
    public int hashCode() {
        int hash = 0;
        hash += (id != null ? id.hashCode() : 0);         return hash;
    }

  @Override
   public boolean equals(Object object) {

       if (!(object instanceof BookAuthor)) return false;

       BookAuthor other = (BookAuthor) object;
```

```
        if ((this.id == null && other.id != null) || (this.id != null && !this.
        id.equals(other.id))) return false;

        return true;
    }

    @Override
    public String toString() {
        return "BookAuthor[ id=" + id + " ]";
    }
}

public static void main(String[] args) {
        EntityManagerFactory emf = Persistence.createEntityManagerFactory("JakartaEE
        Recipes_LOCAL");
        EntityManager em = emf.createEntityManager();

        try {
            EntityTransaction transaction = em.getTransaction();
            transaction.begin();
            Query query = em.createQuery("SELECT b FROM BookAuthor b");
            List<BookAuthor> authorList = (List<BookAuthor>) query.getResultList();
            for (BookAuthor author : authorList) {
                System.out.print("Name:" + author.getFirstname() + " " + author.
                getLastname());
                System.out.println();
            }
            transaction.commit();

        }catch (Exception e) {
            e.printStackTrace();
        }
    }

}
```

The entity itself cannot be used alone to access the database. Minimally, a persistence unit is required in order to connect with a database and perform transactions with the entity classes. To learn more about creating a persistence unit, please refer to Recipe 7-3.

Figure 7-1 shows the output of the preceding code.

```
[EL Info]: 2022-01-28 20:18:37.821--ServerSession(386163331)--EclipseLink, version: Eclipse Persistence Services - 3.0.2.v202107160933
Name:Josh Juneau
Name:Tarun Telang

Process finished with exit code 0
```

Figure 7-1. *Output from the execution of the BookAuthor.main() method*

How It Works

As an object-oriented developer, it sometimes makes more sense to work with objects that represent data, rather than working with variables of data and writing SQL to work directly with the underlying data store. The concept of mapping objects to database tables is better known as *object-relational mapping*. The Java Persistence API utilizes ORM for storing and retrieving data from a database via the usage of object classes known as *entity classes*. An entity class is a Java object that represents an underlying database table.

■ **Note** Prior to EJB 3.0, XML files were used instead of annotations in order to manage metadata for entity classes. You can still use XML descriptors to manage metadata today, but I will not cover how to do so in this book. Most annotations can be used to selectively override default values within a class.

The entity class is usually named the same as the underlying database table, using camel-case lettering (capitalized first letters for all words) to separate different words within the table name. For instance, the BOOK_AUTHOR database table has a Java entity class named BookAuthor. The name of the entity can differ from the name of the underlying database table. However, it is a standard practice to name the entity class the same. In such cases where the name of the entity class has to differ from the database table, the @Table annotation can be used to annotate the entity class, providing the name of the underlying data table. Every entity class must be annotated as such by specifying the jakarta.persistence.Entity annotation. In the example, the BookAuthor entity class specifies only those annotations that are required. If the entity were to be named differently than the database table, the @Table annotation could be utilized as follows:

```
...
@Entity
@Table(name = "BOOK_AUTHOR")
...
```

An entity class must have a public or protected no-argument constructor. It is always a good idea to make an entity class Serializable by implementing the java.io.Serializable interface because doing so ensures that the entity class may be passed by value and persisted to disk, if needed. All entity classes must contain private or protected instance variables for each of the columns within the underlying database table, as well as variables for each relationship that the entity may have with other entities. (To read more about entity relationships, look at Recipes 7-6, 7-7, and 7-8.) All database tables that will be mapped to Java entity classes must contain a primary key field, and the corresponding instance variable within the entity class that maps to the primary key column must be annotated with @Id. Each of the instance variables that maps to a database column can be annotated with @Column, specifying the name of the underlying database column. However, if no @Column annotation is specified, the name of the variable should match the database column name exactly, using camel-case lettering to separate words within the column name. To signify that a particular database column and its mapped instance variable cannot contain a NULL value, the variable can be annotated with @NotNull.

Another annotation worth mentioning that is used within the example for this recipe is @Size, which is used to specify the maximum size for a String variable. The size value should correspond to the database column size for the corresponding column. In addition, the @Lob annotation can be used to signify that the underlying database data type is a large object. There are other annotations that can be used to further customize an entity class; please see the link within the introduction to this chapter for the Jakarta Persistence API provider that you are using in order to learn more about all of the annotations that can be used. Table 7-1 summarizes the most used annotations when creating an entity class. Those annotations are covered within the solution to this recipe.

Table 7-1. *Commonly Used Annotations for Creating Entity Classes*

Annotation	Description
@Entity	Designates a Plain Old Java Object (POJO) class as an entity so that it can be used with Persistence services. This annotation is a must for a class that needs to be stored in a relational database
@Table	Specifies the name of the primary table associated with an entity (optional)
@Id	Designates one or more persistent fields or properties of the entity's primary key. @Entity without an @Id field results in an error
@Basic	Indicates that a field should be mapped to a table column without any additional processing. Its fetch attribute configures the fetch type of the field to EAGER by default. When the entity is loaded, the data in fields is eagerly fetched, meaning it is retrieved from the database and stored in memory
	It can also be set as LAZY for lazy loading. The data in the field will not be retrieved from the database until it is needed. This can help to improve performance by avoiding unnecessary database queries
@Column	Associates a persistent attribute with a different name if the column name is awkward, incompatible with a preexisting data model, or invalid as a column name in your database

As mentioned in the solution for this recipe, an entity class cannot be used by itself. It is part of an overall solution for working with an underlying data source. Entity classes make it easy to map Java objects to database tables. They should be used in tandem with Jakarta Enterprise Beans classes (Chapter 8) and Contexts and Dependency Injection (CDI) or stand-alone with a persistence unit (Recipe 7-3) to perform database operations. A full Java EE solution utilizing the Jakarta Server Faces framework can also use managed beans to work directly with Jakarta Enterprise Beans, or Jakarta RESTful Web Services clients, which in turn conduct work via the entity classes.

■ **Note** You may be wondering why the hashCode() and equals() methods are overridden in the example. The equals() method is present in every Java object, and it is used to determine the object identity. Every entity class needs to contain an implementation of these methods in order to differentiate objects from one another. It is very possible for two entity objects to point to the same row in a database table. The equals() method can determine whether two entities both point to the same row. Moreover, all Java objects that are equal to one another should contain the same hashCode. In entity classes, it is important to override these methods to determine whether objects represent the same database table row.

7-2. Mapping Data Types

Problem

You are interested in mapping database table columns with entity class fields, but you are unsure which data types to declare for the fields within the class.

■ **Note** Transient fields or properties cannot contain mapping annotations. A transient field or property is not persisted to the database.

Solution

Map database table column data types with their equivalent data types in the Java language specification when declaring instance variables for the columns within an entity class. The Jakarta EE container will convert the database value accordingly so long as the database column data type matches up to a Java data type that will contain the specified column's value. To demonstrate data type mapping, an entity class will be written for the Acme Bookstore's CONTACT database table. The CONTACT table has the description shown in Figure 7-2.

Table:

CONTACT			

Columns (9)	Keys (1)	Indexes (1)	Foreign Keys

+	−	▲	▼

```
ID                    NUMERIC(5) -- part of primary key
FIRSTNAME             VARCHAR(150)
LASTNAME              VARCHAR(150)
PASSWORD              VARCHAR(30)
EMAIL                 VARCHAR(150)
OCCUPATION            VARCHAR(150)
RECEIVE_NOTIFICATIONS VARCHAR(1)
GENDER                VARCHAR(1)
DESCRIPTION           CLOB
```

Figure 7-2. *Contact table schema definition*

The corresponding entity class is named Contact, and its class listing, shown next, demonstrates how to match each database column type to an appropriate Java data type:

```
package org.jakartaeerecipe.chapter07.recipe07_02;
...
@Entity
@Table(name = "CONTACT")
public class Contact implements Serializable {
    private static final long serialVersionUID = 1L;

    @Id
    @Basic(optional = false)
    @NotNull
```

```java
 @Column(name = "ID")
 private BigDecimal id;

@Size(max = 50)
 @Column(name = "FIRSTNAME")
 private String first;

 @Size(max = 50)
 @Column(name = "LASTNAME")
 private String last;

@Size(max = 150)
 @Column(name = "EMAIL")
 private String email;

 @Size(max = 30)
 @Column(name = "PASSWORD")
 private String password;

 @Lob
 @Column(name = "DESCRIPTION")
 private String description;

 @Size(max = 150)
 @Column(name = "OCCUPATION")
 private String occupation;

 @Size(max = 1)
 @Column(name = "RECEIVE_NOTIFICATIONS")
 private String receivenotifications;

 @Size(max = 1)
 @Column(name = "GENDER")
 private String gender;

 public Contact() {  } // default constructor
 ...
 // getters and setters
 ...
 @Override
 public int hashCode() {
     ...
 }
 @Override
 public boolean equals(Object object) {
     ...
 }
 @Override
 public String toString() {
     return "org.jakartaeerecipe.chapter07.entity.Contact[ id=" + id + " ]";
 }
```

```
public static void main(String[] args) {
    EntityManagerFactory emf = Persistence.createEntityManagerFactory("JakartaEERecip
    es_LOCAL");
    EntityManager em = emf.createEntityManager();
    queryAllContacts(em);
}

private static void queryAllContacts(EntityManager em) {
    try {
        EntityTransaction transaction = em.getTransaction();
        transaction.begin();
        Query query = em.createQuery("SELECT c FROM Contact c");
        List<Contact> contactList = (List<Contact>) query.getResultList();
        for (Contact contact : contactList) {
            System.out.print("Name:" + contact.getFirst() + " " + contact.getLast());
            System.out.println();
        }
        transaction.commit();

    }catch (Exception e) {
        e.printStackTrace();
    }
}

}
```

It is important to specify the correct mapping data types because errors can occur down the line if not done correctly. Such is often the case with numerical data types.

The output of the preceding program would be as shown in Figure 7-3.

```
[EL Info]: 2022-02-04 01:50:10.73--ServerSession(1949298838)--EclipseLink, version: Eclipse Persistence Services - 3.0.2.v202107160933
Name:Josh Juneau
Name:Tarun Telang

Process finished with exit code 0
```

Figure 7-3. *Output for Recipe07_02*

How It Works

To create a Java class that will be used to represent a database table, you must map each of the table's columns to a class instance variable. In doing so, the variable must be assigned a data type that corresponds to that database column's data type. In some cases, more than one Java data type will map to a single database column's data type. In other cases, however, a database column's data type must match up to a specific Java data type. Table 7-2 lists the different Java data types and their associated database data types. If you are using another database for your work besides Oracle, please see the documentation for the database to rectify any discrepancies between the data types from those used by Oracle.

MySQL Data Mapping Documentation: https://dev.mysql.com/doc/connector-j/8.0/en/connector-j-reference-type-conversions.html

Table 7-2. *Oracle Database and Java Data Type Mapping*

Oracle Data Type	Java Data Type
BINARY_INTEGER, NATURAL, NATURALN, PLS_INTEGER, POSITIVE, POSITIVEN, SIGNTYPE, INT, INTEGER	int
CHAR, CHARACTER, VARCHAR2 LONG, STRING, VARCHAR	java.lang.String
RAW, LONG RAW	byte[]
DEC, DECIMAL, NUMBER	java.math.BigDecimal
DOUBLE PRECISION, FLOAT	double
SMALLINT	int
REAL	float
DATE	java.sql.Timestamp java.sql.Date
TIMESTAMP (or derivative)	java.sql.Timestamp
BOOLEAN	boolean
CLOB	java.sql.Clob
BLOB	java.sql.Blob
VARRAY	java.sql.Array
REF CURSOR	java.sql.ResultSet

Mapping data types correctly is a very important step in the creation of an entity class because an incorrect mapping can result in incorrect precision for numerical values and so forth. Utilizing the correct data types when mapping entity classes to the database table may vary depending upon the database vendor, but Table 7-2 should be easily translated from Oracle data types to the data types for the RDBMS of your choice.

7-3. Creating a Persistence Unit

Problem

You want to use an entity class to perform database transactions. Therefore, you need to configure your application's database connectivity.

Solution

Create a persistence unit to configure a database connection, and then use the persistence unit to perform transactions with a given entity class. A persistence unit can use a database connection pool configured within an application server, or it can utilize a local JDBC configuration in order to obtain a database connection. In this example, I will demonstrate the use of the local JDBC configuration since the example will be run as a stand-alone application, rather than being deployed to an application server.

The following persistence unit is configured to create local JDBC connections, rather than using the Jakarta Persistence API for connections. However, you can learn more about configuring a persistence unit to work with database connection pools that are configured within an application server in the "How It Works" section of this recipe. The following code is from a file named persistence.xml, which is located in the src/main/resource/META-INF directory for this chapter:

```xml
<?xml version="1.0" encoding="UTF-8"?>
<persistence xmlns="https://jakarta.ee/xml/ns/persistence"
             xmlns:xsi="http://www.w3.org/2001/XMLSchema-instance"
             xsi:schemaLocation="https://jakarta.ee/xml/ns/persistence https://jakarta.ee/
             xml/ns/persistence/persistence_3_0.xsd"
             version="3.0">
  <persistence-unit name="JakartaEERecipesLOCAL" transaction-type="RESOURCE_LOCAL">
      <class>org.jakartaeerecipe.entity.BookAuthor</class>
      <properties>
          <property name="jakarta.persistence.jdbc.user" value="username"/>
          <property name="jakarta.persistence.jdbc.password" value="password"/>
          <property name="jakarta.persistence.jdbc.url" value="jdbc:derby://<hostname>:
          <port>/<database>"/>
          <!-- JDBC driver class ->
          <property name="jakarta.persistence.jdbc.driver" value="org.apache.derby.jdbc.
          ClientDriver"/>
      </properties>
  </persistence-unit>
</persistence>
```

How It Works

To work with a database, an application needs to have the ability to connect to it. Usually, a database connection pertains to a single username/password within a database. The persistence context XML file is where the connection information for the Java Persistence API resides, in our case a persistence.xml file. A persistence context can contain configuration for more than one connection to the database. Each connection configuration is referred to as a *persistence unit*, and each has a unique name that is used to identify the connection from within the application classes. The persistence.xml file can be packaged as part of a web archive (WAR) or enterprise archive (EAR) file, or it can be packed into a JAR file, which is, in turn, packaged with a WAR or EAR. If packaged with an EAR file, it should reside within the META-INF directory. If using a WAR file, the persistence.xml file should be packaged within the resources/META-INF directory. Lastly, if packaging into a JAR file, the JAR should reside within the WEB-INF/lib directory of a WAR or the library directory of an EAR.

As mentioned previously, each persistence.xml file can contain more than one database configuration, or persistence unit. Each persistence unit contains the type of Jakarta Persistence provider that will be used for the connection, the transaction type (JTA or RESOURCE_LOCAL), classes to be used for persistence (entity classes), and database connection specifics. In this section, I will break down the persistence unit that is configured for the recipe solution and describe each piece.

At the root of each persistence unit is the persistence-unit element, which contains the name and transaction-type attributes. Each persistence unit has a name; in the case of the example, it is JakartaEERecipesLOCAL, and this name is used to obtain a reference to the persistence unit from within application code. The transaction-type attribute of a persistence unit indicates whether Java Transaction API entity managers will be created (for use within an application server) or Resource-Local entity managers will be created (for use with stand-alone applications).

Next, in the example, you will see a series of classes listed within separate class elements. Within the persistence-unit element, zero or more classes can be identified for use with the persistence unit. These classes are the entity classes that will be mapped to the underlying database table. If using the RESOURCE_ LOCAL transaction type, each entity class must be listed within the persistence unit. If using JTA (deployed to an application server within a WAR or EAR file), then the container takes care of identifying the entity classes, and they do not need to be listed in the persistence unit. If an entity class is not identified in the persistence unit and the transaction type is RESOURCE_LOCAL, then that entity class will not be available for use within the application.

■ **Note** A persistence unit may also include an <exclude-unlisted-classes> element, which should be set to a Boolean value. This element is used to indicate whether classes must be listed using a <class> element within the persistence unit when using JTA, and it is FALSE by default. It may make sense to set this element to TRUE if two or more data sources are being used within an application, and only specified entity classes should be used for each.

The properties element should contain subelements that define the connection to the database. Specifically, the user, password, and database URL are identified within subproperties of the properties element. For RESOURCE_LOCAL persistence units, the following points are true:

- The property jakarta.persistence.jdbc.username should be used to identify the database username for the connection.

- The property jakarta.persistence.jdbc.password should identify the database user password for the connection.

- The property jakarta.persistence.jdbc.url should identify the database URL for the connection.

The properties for a Java Transaction API connection are different. In fact, for JTA, there can be no properties specified. Instead, an element named jta-data-source can be used to specify a JNDI name of a database connection that has been configured within the application server for use. For example, let's say the database connection is configured as jdbc/DBConnection within the application server. Furthermore, let's assume you are deploying a WAR file to the GlassFish application server, and you will use JTA instead of RESOURCE_LOCAL. If this is the case, the persistence unit may look like the following:

```
<persistence-unit name="JakartaEERecipesJTA" transaction-type="JTA">
    <jta-data-source>jdbc/DBConnection</jta-data-source>
    <properties/>
</persistence-unit>
```

■ **Note** There are no classes listed in the JTA example because the application server automatically identifies the entity classes for use with the persistence unit. However, there are circumstances for which it may be useful to list classes, as mentioned in the preceding note.

To use a persistence unit, an EntityManagerFactory object must first be obtained. An EntityManagerFactory object can be obtained by calling the Persistence.createEntityManagerFactory method and passing the string-based name of the persistence unit for which you want to obtain a connection. Once an `EntityManagerFactory` object has been obtained, an `EntityManager` object can be created and used to begin a database transaction. Obtaining a connection via a persistence unit would look similar to the following:

```
...
EntityManagerFactory emf = Persistence.createEntityManagerFactory("JakartaEERecipesLOCAL");
EntityManager em = emf.createEntityManager();
try {
    EntityTransaction entr = em.getTransaction();
    entr.begin();
    Query query = em.createNamedQuery("BookAuthor.findAll");
...
```

■ **Note** The preceding example uses the `createNamedQuery` method to substitute a named query rather than writing the Java Persistence Query Language (JPQL) inline. For more information, please see Recipe 7-9.

The `persistence.xml` configuration file contains the database connection information that will be utilized by an application to work with database(s). If you are working with the Jakarta Persistence API, you will become very familiar with creating a persistence unit, whether using local JDBC connections or an application server connection pool.

7-4. Using Database Sequences to Create Primary Key Values

Problem

Your database contains sequences that are used to generate primary key values for your database table records. Your application needs to use those database sequences in order to assign primary key values when creating and persisting objects.

Solution

Annotate an entity class's primary key field with a `SequenceGenerator` and then associate it with an entity generator in order to utilize a database sequence for populating a database table column value. In the following example, the BookAuthor entity has been updated to utilize the BOOK_AUTHOR_S database sequence for creating primary key values. As such, the id field has been annotated accordingly:

```
package org.jakartaeerecipe.chapter07.entity;

...
@Entity
@Table(name = "BOOK_AUTHOR")
// Named queries are covered in Recipe 7-9
@NamedQuery(name = "BookAuthor08.findAll", query = "SELECT b FROM BookAuthor08 b")
@NamedQuery(name = "BookAuthor08.findById", query = "SELECT b FROM BookAuthor08 b WHERE
b.id = :id")
```

```
@NamedQuery(name = "BookAuthor08.findByLast", query = "SELECT b FROM BookAuthor08 b WHERE
b.last = :last"),
@NamedQuery(name = "BookAuthor08.findByFirst", query = "SELECT b FROM BookAuthor08 b WHERE
b.first = :first")
public class BookAuthor implements Serializable {

    private static final long serialVersionUID = 1L;

    @Id
    @Basic(optional = false)@SequenceGenerator(name="book_author_s_
generator",sequenceName="book_author_s",initialValue=1, allocationSize=1)
    @GeneratedValue(strategy=GenerationType.SEQUENCE,
    generator="book_author_s_generator")
    @NotNull
    @Column(name = "ID")
    private BigDecimal id;
    ...
```

When a new BookAuthor object is persisted to the database, the next sequence value for BOOK_AUTHOR_S
will be used as the primary key value for the new database record. The class org.jakartaeerecipe.
chapter07.recipe07_04.SequenceTest.java can be run to test the sequence-generated primary key once
the persistence context has been configured for the local JDBC database connection (see Recipe 7-3 for
details). The following excerpt is taken from the SequenceTest class, and it demonstrates how to add a new
BookAuthor object to the database:

```
...
EntityManagerFactory emf = Persistence.createEntityManagerFactory("JakartaEERecipesLOCAL");
EntityManager em = emf.createEntityManager();
try {
    EntityTransaction entr = em.getTransaction();
    entr.begin();
    BookAuthor author = new BookAuthor();
    author.setFirst("JOE");
    author.setLast("TESTER");
    author.setBio("An author test account.");
    boolean successful = false;
    try {
        em.persist(author);
        successful = true;
    } finally {
        if (successful){
            entr.commit();
        } else {
            entr.rollback();
        }
    }
    Query query = em.createNamedQuery("BookAuthor.findAll");
    List authorList = query.getResultList();
    Iterator authorIterator = authorList.iterator();
    while (authorIterator.hasNext()) {
        author = (BookAuthor) authorIterator.next();
```

```
        System.out.print("Name:" + author.getFirstname() + " " + author.getLastname());
        System.out.println();
    }
} catch (Exception ex){
    ex.printStackTrace();;
} finally {
    em.close();
}
...
```

■ **Note** This example demonstrates the use of database transactions. Transactions allow for an entire sequence of processes to be performed at once. If a failure occurs in one of the processes, then all processes in the transaction fail, and changes to the database are rolled back. Otherwise, if all processes in the transaction complete successfully, then they are committed to the database. Transactions are very useful in situations where multiple database events depend upon one another.

Executing the preceding code will generate the output shown in Figure 7-4.

```
[EL Info]: 2022-01-28 22:44:45.523--ServerSession(2075809815)--EclipseLink, version: Eclipse Persistence Services - 3.0.2.v202107160933
Name:Josh Juneau
Name:Tarun Telang
Name:JOE TESTER

Process finished with exit code 0
```

Figure 7-4. *Output for Recipe07_04*

How It Works

In many cases, it makes sense to generate primary key values for database table records via a database sequence. Utilizing the Jakarta Persistence API allows you to do so by incorporating the use of the @ SequenceGenerator and @GeneratedValue annotations into an entity class. Every database table that is mapped to an entity class must have a primary key value, and using database sequences to obtain those values makes sense for many reasons. For instance, in some cases an application administrator will need to know what the next number, current number, or last number used for a primary key value might be. By using a database sequence, gathering information regarding the next, current, or last numbers is just a query away.

The @SequenceGenerator annotation should be placed directly before the declaration of the primary key field or property within the entity class, or it can be placed before the entity class declaration. Note that other annotations may be placed between the @SequenceGenerator annotation and the actual variable declaration. The @SequenceGenerator annotation accepts values regarding the database sequence that is to be used for primary key generation. More specifically, the annotation accepts the following attributes:

- name (required): The name of the generator (this name can be an arbitrary value)
- sequenceName (optional): The name of the database sequence from which to obtain the primary key value
- initialValue (optional): The initial value of the sequence object
- allocationSize (optional): The amount of increment when allocating numbers from the sequence

347

The @GeneratedValue annotation provides for the specification of the primary key generation strategy for the entity. Like the @SequenceGenerator attribute, it can be placed before the declaration of the primary key field or property within the entity class, or it can be placed before the entity class declaration. It is used to specify the means for which the entity class primary key will be generated. The three options are as follows:

- The entity class will generate its own primary key value before inserting a new record.

- The entity class will use a database sequence for the key generation.

- The entity class will generate keys via some other means.

The attributes that can be specified for the @GeneratedValue annotation are as follows:

- generator (optional): This is the name of the primary key generator to use as specified by the @SequenceGenerator annotation. This must match the name attribute that was supplied for the @SequenceGenerator annotation unless using a @TableGenerator. This defaults to the ID generator supplied by the persistence provider.

- strategy (optional): This is the primary key generation strategy that will be used by the persistence provider to generate the primary key for the annotated field or entity class. This defaults to AUTO if not supplied.

The strategy attribute of @GeneratedValue can accept four different jakarta.persistence. GenerationType Enum values:

- AUTO: Indicates that the persistence provider should choose an appropriate strategy for a particular database

- IDENTITY: Indicates that the persistence provider must assign primary keys for the entity using the database identity column

- SEQUENCE: Indicates that the persistence provider must assign primary keys for the entity using the database sequence column

- TABLE: Indicates that the persistence provider must assign primary keys for the entity using an underlying database table to ensure unique values are provided

In the example for this recipe, the BOOK_AUTHOR_S database sequence is specified for the sequenceName attribute of the @SequenceGenerator annotation, and the name of the generator is book_author_s_ generator. Note that the @GeneratedValue name attribute matches that of the @SequenceGenerator annotation; this is very important! Once specified, the entity class will automatically obtain the next value from the database sequence when a new object is persisted.

■ **Note** There are other options for generating key values, such as AUTO, IDENTITY, and TABLE. These strategies can be valid in different situations. For more information on using other options, please refer to the online Jakarta EE documentation at https://javaee.github.io/.

7-5. Generating Primary Keys Using More Than One Attribute

Problem

A particular database table does not contain a primary key. Since the use of the Java Persistence API requires a primary key for mapping entity classes to database tables, you need to join the values of two or more of the table columns to create a primary key for each record.

Solution #1

Create a composite primary key by developing an embedded composite primary key class and denoting the composite key field within an entity using the jakarta.persistence.EmbeddedId and jakarta.persistence.Id class annotations. Consider the AUTHOR_WORK database table that is used for the Acme Bookstore application. Suppose that the AUTHOR_WORK database table did not contain a primary key column. It would be possible to generate a primary key for each record based upon its BOOK_ID and AUTHOR_ID columns. The following entity class is for the AuthorWork entity. Instead of using the ID column as a primary key, it uses both the bookId and authorId columns together to formulate a composite primary key:

```
package org.jakartaeerecipe.chapter07.entity;

import java.io.Serializable;
import java.math.BigInteger;
import jakarta.persistence.*;
import jakarta.validation.constraints.NotNull;
import org.jakartaeerecipe.chapter07.entity.key.AuthorWorkPKEmbedded;

@Entity
@Table(name = "AUTHOR_WORK")
@NamedQuery(name = "AuthorWork.findAll", query = "SELECT a FROM AuthorWork a")
public class AuthorWorkEmbedded implements Serializable {

    private static final long serialVersionUID = 1L;

    // You can use an embedded ID in-place of a standard Id if a table
    // contains more than one column to compose a primary key.  Comment
    // out along with the getters and setters to use a non-embeddable primary key.
    @EmbeddedId
    private AuthorWorkPKEmbedded embeddedId;

    public AuthorWorkEmbedded(BigInteger bookId, BigInteger authorId) {
        this.embeddedId = new AuthorWorkPKEmbedded(bookId, authorId);
    }

    /**
     * @return the embeddedId
     */
    public AuthorWorkPKEmbedded getEmbeddedId() {
        return embeddedId;
    }
```

```
    /**
     * @param embeddedId the embeddedId to set
     */
    public void setEmbeddedId(AuthorWorkPKEmbedded embeddedId) {
        this.embeddedId = embeddedId;
    }
}
```

To utilize an embedded primary key, you must create a class that contains the logic for mapping the primary key ID to the columns that are used to compose it. For this example, the AuthorWorkPKEmbedded class serves this purpose, which is shown here:

```
package org.jakartaeerecipe.chapter07.entity.key;

import java.io.Serializable;
import java.math.BigInteger;
import jakarta.persistence.Embeddable;

/**
 * Embeddable Primary Key class for AuthorWork
 */
@Embeddable
public class AuthorWorkPKEmbedded implements Serializable {

    private static final long serialVersionUID = 1L;

    @Column(name = "AUTHOR_ID")
    private BigInteger authorId;

    @Column(name = "BOOK_ID")
    private BigInteger bookId;

    public AuthorWorkPKEmbedded() { }

    public AuthorWorkPKEmbedded(BigInteger bookId, BigInteger authorId){
        this.bookId = bookId;
        this.authorId = authorId;
    }
...
    // getters and setters
...
    public int hashCode() {
        return bookId.hashCode() + authorId.hashCode();
    }
    public boolean equals(Object obj) {
        if (obj == this) {
            return true;
        }
        if (!(obj instanceof AuthorWorkPKEmbedded)) {
            return false;
        }
```

```
        AuthorWorkPKEmbedded pk = (AuthorWorkPKEmbedded) obj;

        return ((((Objects.equals(bookId, ((AuthorWorkPKEmbedded) obj).getBookId())))
                && ((Objects.equals(authorId, ((AuthorWorkPKEmbedded) obj).
                getAuthorId())))));
}
```

■ **Note**   Although the preceding example is not an entity class, its member values are persisted. Even if the members are not designated as @Basic, they are still persisted.

Both the hashCode() and equals() methods must be present in composite key classes.

Solution #2

Create a composite primary key by developing a non-embedded composite primary key class, and denote two or more of the columns within the entity class with the @Id annotation. Also, if using a non-embedded primary key class, the entity class must be designated as such by utilizing the @IdClass annotation and specifying the non-embedded primary key class.

Consider the AUTHOR_WORK database table that is used for the Acme Bookstore application. Suppose that the AUTHOR_WORK database table did not contain a primary key column. It would be possible to generate a primary key for each record based upon its BOOK_ID and AUTHOR_ID columns since together they would formulate a unique value for each record. The following entity class is that for the AuthorWork entity. Instead of using the ID column as a primary key, it uses both the bookId and authorId columns together to formulate a composite primary key:

```
package org.jakartaeerecipe.chapter07.entity;

import java.io.Serializable;
import java.math.BigInteger;
import jakarta.persistence.*;
import org.jakartaeerecipe.chapter07.entity.key.AuthorWorkPKNonEmbedded;

@IdClass(AuthorWorkPKNonEmbedded.class)
@Entity
@Table(name = "AUTHOR_WORK_LEGACY")
@NamedQuery(name = "AuthorWork.findAll", query = "SELECT a FROM AuthorWork a")
public class AuthorWorkNonEmbedded implements Serializable {

    private static final long serialVersionUID = 1L;

    @Id
    @Column(name = "BOOK_ID")
    private BigInteger bookId;

    @Id
    @Column(name= "AUTHOR_ID")
    private BigInteger authorId;
```

```
    public AuthorWorkNonEmbedded() {
    }
    public AuthorWorkNonEmbedded(BigInteger bookId, BigInteger authorId) {
        this.bookId = bookId;
        this.authorId = authorId;
    }
...
// getters and setters
...
}
```

The associated non-embeddable primary key class is named AuthorWorkPKNonEmbedded. The code for this class is as follows:

```
package org.jakartaeerecipe.chapter07.entity.key;

import java.io.Serializable;
import java.math.BigInteger;
public class AuthorWorkPKNonEmbedded implements Serializable {
    private BigInteger bookId;
    private BigInteger authorId;
    public AuthorWorkPKNonEmbedded() {
    }
...
// getters and setters
...
    public int hashCode() {
        return bookId.hashCode() + authorId.hashCode();
    }
    public boolean equals(Object obj) {
        if (obj == this) {
            return true;
        }
        if (!(obj instanceof AuthorWorkPKEmbedded)) {
            return false;
        }
        if (obj == null) {
            return false;
        }
        AuthorWorkPKEmbedded pk = (AuthorWorkPKEmbedded) obj;
        return ((((bookId == ((AuthorWorkPKEmbedded) obj).getBookId()))
                && ((authorId == ((AuthorWorkPKEmbedded) obj).getAuthorId()))));
    }
}
```

■ **Note** Although the AuthorWorkPKNonEmbedded class is not an entity, its member values are persisted.

How It Works

There can be situations in which a database table may not contain a single primary key value to uniquely identify each row. Oftentimes, this can be the case when working with legacy databases. In the Java Persistence API, all entity classes must contain a primary key that can be used to uniquely identify an object. To get around this obstacle when working with tables that do not contain a single primary key value, a composite primary key can be used to uniquely identify an object.

A composite primary key is composed of two or more fields or properties within an entity class that can be combined to create a unique identifier. Think in terms of performing a database query and attempting to return a record that matches only certain criteria. In such a case, you often need to include multiple relationships within the SQL WHERE clause. Creating a composite primary key within an entity class is basically the same concept in that you are telling Jakarta Persistence to use all the fields or properties designated within the composite key in order to uniquely identify an object.

There are a couple of different techniques, embeddable and non-embeddable, that can be used to develop a composite primary key. The two techniques are similar in that they each require the creation of a separate class to compose the primary key, but they differ by the way in which the primary key is denoted within the entity class. In fact, the separate primary key class in both techniques can be created almost identically, except that an embeddable primary key class must be annotated using @Embeddable, as demonstrated in Solution #1 to this recipe. An entity with an embeddable primary key class should contain only a single primary key, and the data type for the primary key should be the same as the embeddable primary key class. That is, the primary key class should be declared within the entity using a private modifier, along with all of the other persistent properties and fields, and it should be annotated with @Id to indicate that it is the primary key. The following excerpt from Solution #1 shows how this is done:

```
@EmbeddedId
private AuthorWorkPKEmbedded embeddedId;
```

The entity class containing an embedded primary key should contain a constructor that accepts one parameter for each of the persistent fields or properties used for the primary key. Within the constructor, a new instance of the embeddable primary key class should then be instantiated using the passed-in arguments. The entity class using an embeddable primary key should contain accessor methods for the primary key field or property. However, unlike most entity classes, the hashCode() and equals() methods are not present because they are within the primary key class instead. Now that I've gone over the logistics of an entity class that uses an embeddable primary key, let's take a look at the embeddable primary key class itself to see how it works.

A primary key class that is used for creating an embeddable primary key should contain declarations for each of the persistent fields or properties that will be used to compose the primary key for the associated entity class. Of course, these fields or properties should be made private, and there should be corresponding getters and setters for accessing the fields. The embeddable primary key class should be annotated with @Embeddable. It can contain two constructors: one that accepts no arguments and another optional constructor that accepts an argument for each of the persistent fields or properties that compose the primary key. Remember how the entity class that uses the embeddable primary key contains no hashCode() method? That is because it resides within the primary key class, and it simply adds together the hashCodes for each of the fields used to compose the primary key, and it returns the sum.

The most important piece of the primary key class is the equals() method since it is used to determine whether an object or database record uniquely matches the associated primary key. The equals() method should accept an argument of type Object, which will be the object that is being compared against the current primary key object. The object is then compared to determine whether it is equal to the current primary key object, and if so, a true is returned. If not equal, then the object is compared to determine whether it is the same type of class as the embeddable primary key class, and a false is returned if it is not the same type. A false is also returned if the object is NULL. Finally, if a Boolean has not yet been returned based upon the conditionals that have been tested, then the object is casted into the same type of object as the primary key class, and each of its fields or properties is compared against those in the current primary key class. If equal, then a true is returned; if not equal, then a false is returned. The following lines of code demonstrate the equals() method:

```
public boolean equals(Object obj) {
    if (obj == this) {
        return true;
    }
    if (!(obj instanceof AuthorWorkPKEmbedded)) {
        return false;
    }
    if (obj == null) {
        return false;
    }
    AuthorWorkPKEmbedded pk = (AuthorWorkPKEmbedded) obj;
    return (((bookId == ((AuthorWorkPKEmbedded) obj).getBookId()))
            && ((authorId == ((AuthorWorkPKEmbedded) obj).getAuthorId()))));
}
```

Solution #2 covers the use of a non-embedded primary key. The generation of a non-embeddable primary key is sometimes preferred over the use of an embedded primary key because some believe that the resulting entity class is easier to read. The overall construction of a non-embeddable primary key is basically the same, although there are a few subtle differences. For instance, when developing the primary key class for the non-embedded primary key, there is no @Embeddable annotation on the class. Another difference that you may notice from the code in Solution #2 is that there is only one constructor used. Of course, an optional second constructor can still be created, accepting an argument for each of the persistent fields or properties that are used to compose the primary key.

Most differences take place within the entity class itself. To use a non-embedded composite primary key, the entity class must be annotated with @IdClass, naming the class that is used to construct the composite primary key. In the case of Solution #2, the @IdClass is as follows:

```
@IdClass(AuthorWorkPKNonEmbedded.class)
```

Another big difference in an entity class that uses a non-embeddable composite primary key is that instead of declaring one persistent field or property as an ID using the @Id annotation, the two or more fields or properties that are used to compose the primary key for the entity are declared directly within the entity, and each of them is annotated accordingly. The rest of the implementation is the same as an entity that uses an embedded composite primary key.

Which type of composite key you decide to use is completely a personal preference. Many people use a non-embeddable primary key to make the entity class easier to follow, in that it resembles a standard entity class more closely than an entity class using an embeddable composite primary key. In the end, both will produce the same result and allow entity classes to be created for those database tables that do not contain a single primary key field.

7-6. Defining a One-to-One Relationship

Problem

A database table that is used by your application contains data that has a one-to-one reference with data records from another table. As such, you want to create a one-to-one relationship between two entity objects within your application.

Solution

Create an association between the two tables that have a one-to-one relationship by declaring each of the entity classes themselves as persistent fields or properties within each other using an "owned" relationship, and annotate those fields with @OneToOne. For instance, let's say that each record within the AUTHOR database table can be associated to a record in another table named AUTHOR_DETAIL and vice versa. The AUTHOR_DETAIL table contains contact information for the author, so, in fact, these tables have a one-to-one relationship. To correlate them to each other from within the entity classes, specify the @OneToOne annotation on the field or property that is associated with the corresponding entity class. To have the ability to obtain the full author information from either table, a bidirectional one-to-one relationship needs to be created.

■ **Note**   A one-to-one mapping could be unidirectional or bidirectional. A unidirectional mapping contains only a @OneToOne annotation on the owning entity for the corresponding entity class, whereas a bidirectional mapping contains a @ManyToOne, @OneToMany, or @ManyToMany annotation, depending upon the association.

A relationship is referred to as *owned* if one entity contains a reference to another entity object referring to the entity itself. On the other hand, a relationship where an entity refers to another entity by primary key value is known as an *unowned* relationship.

In this solution, the Author entity would contain a @OneToOne reference for the AuthorDetail entity to create a bidirectional one-to-one mapping. In this code excerpt from the Author entity, the Author entity is the owning entity:

```
...
@Entity
@Table(name = "AUTHOR")
public class Author implements Serializable {

    private static final long serialVersionUID = 1L;

    @Id
    @Basic(optional = false)
    @SequenceGenerator(name="author_s_generator",
sequenceName="author_s", initialValue=1, allocationSize=1)
    @GeneratedValue(strategy=GenerationType.SEQUENCE,
    generator="author_s_generator")
    @NotNull
    @Column(name = "ID")
    private BigDecimal id;
```

```
@Size(max = 30)
@Column(name = "LAST")
private String last;

@Size(max = 30)
@Column(name = "FIRST")
private String first;

@Lob
@Column(name = "BIO")
private String bio;

@OneToOne
private AuthorDetail authorId;

public Author() { }
...
```

An excerpt for the entity class for the AUTHOR_DETAIL table is shown next. Of course, it has the name of AuthorDetail, and it contains a reference to the Author entity class:

```
...
@Entity
@Table(name = "AUTHOR_DETAIL")
public class AuthorDetail implements Serializable {

    private static final long serialVersionUID = 1L;

    @Id
    @Basic(optional = false)
    @SequenceGenerator(name="author_detail_s_generator",sequenceName="author__detail_s",
    initialValue=1, allocationSize=1)
    @GeneratedValue(strategy=GenerationType.SEQUENCE,
    generator="author_detail_s_generator")
    @NotNull
    @Column(name = "ID")
    private BigDecimal id;

    @Size(max = 200)
    @Column(name = "ADDRESS1")
    private String address1;

    @Size(max = 200)
    @Column(name = "ADDRESS2")
    private String address2;

    @Size(max = 250)
    @Column(name = "CITY")
    private String city;
```

```
@Size(max = 2)
@Column(name = "STATE")
private String state;

@Size(max = 10)
@Column(name = "ZIP")
private String zip;

@Column(name = "START_DATE")
@Temporal(TemporalType.DATE)
private Date startDate;

@Lob
@Column(name = "NOTES")
private String notes;

@OneToOne(optional=false, mappedBy="authorDetail")
private Author authorId;

public AuthorDetail() {
}
...
```

How It Works

It is not uncommon in the world of relational databases to have one table that depends upon another table. In the case where a record from a table has a one-to-one correspondence to a record from another table, an entity class for one table should be configured to have a one-to-one correspondence with the entity class for the other table. Working with objects is a bit different from working with database records, but the concept is basically the same. Within the database, a unique identifier is used to correlate one table to another. For instance, in the case of this example, the AUTHOR_DETAIL table contains a field named AUTHOR_ID, and it must contain an ID from the AUTHOR database table in order to map the two records together. Owned entity relationships work a bit differently in that the entity object itself is used to map to another entity, rather than an ID number.

When creating a bidirectional one-to-one relationship between entity classes, each entity class must declare the other entity class as a persistent field or property and then designate the type of relationship using the @OneToOne annotation. The @OneToOne annotation is used to designate a one-to-one relationship between the entities. The @OneToOne annotation contains the following optional attributes:

- cascade: The operations (e.g., delete) that must be cascaded to the target of the association. Default: No operations.

- fetch: Whether the association should be lazily loaded or must be eagerly fetched. Default: EAGER.

- optional: Whether the association is optional. For instance, can the entity be persisted without the association? Default: true.

- mappedBy: The field that owns the relationship. Default: " ".

In the solution to this recipe, the AuthorDetail entity specifies the @OneToOne annotation prior to the declaration of the Author field specifying the mappedBy and optional attributes. The mappedBy attribute is set to authorDetail, because this will be the mapping field, and the optional attribute is set to false.

On the other hand, the Author entity specifies the @OneToOne annotation prior to the declaration of the AuthorDetail field, and there are no attributes specified. In practice, when these entities are used, a bidirectional mapping will be enforced. This means that an AuthorDetail object cannot exist without a corresponding Author object.

7-7. Defining One-to-Many and Many-to-One Relationships

Problem

You want to associate two entity classes to each other, such that one entity object can contain a reference to many of the other entity objects.

Solution

Define a relationship between the two entities by specifying the @OneToMany annotation on a field or property referencing the other entity class within the owning object and by specifying the @ManyToOne annotation on a field or property referencing the owning object within the non-owning entity. For instance, let's say you allow an Author object to contain many different addresses or AuthorDetail objects. In fact, an Author can contain as many addresses as needed. That being the case, there would be one Author object for every AuthorDetail object. Likewise, there could be many AuthorDetail objects for every Author object.

In the following code listings, I will demonstrate the one-to-many relationship between the Author and AuthorDetail objects. First, let's take a look at the Author object, which is otherwise referred to as the *owning* object. This entity class can contain a reference to many different AuthorDetail objects:

```
@Entity
@Table(name = "AUTHOR")
public class Author implements Serializable {

    private static final long serialVersionUID = 1L;

    @Id
    @Basic(optional = false)
    @SequenceGenerator(name="author_s_generator",sequenceName="author_s", initialValue=1,
    allocationSize=1)
    @GeneratedValue(strategy=GenerationType.SEQUENCE,
    generator="author_s_generator")
    @NotNull
    @Column(name = "ID")
    private BigDecimal id;

    @Size(max = 30)
    @Column(name = "LAST")
    private String last;

    @Size(max = 30)
    @Column(name = "FIRST")
    private String first;
```

```
    @Lob
    @Column(name = "BIO")
    private String bio;

    @OneToMany(mappedBy="author")
    private Set<AuthorDetail> authorDetail;
    public Author() { }
```
...

Next, I'll show the non-owning object, also known as the AuthorDetail class. There may be many AuthorDetail objects within a single Author object:

```
public class AuthorDetail implements Serializable {
    private static final long serialVersionUID = 1L;
    @Id
    @Basic(optional = false)
    @SequenceGenerator(name="author_detail_s_generator",sequenceName="author__detail_s",
    initialValue=1, allocationSize=1)
    @GeneratedValue(strategy=GenerationType.SEQUENCE,
    generator="author_detail_s_generator")
    @NotNull
    @Column(name = "ID")
    private BigDecimal id;

    @Size(max = 200)
    @Column(name = "ADDRESS1")
    private String address1;

    @Size(max = 200)
    @Column(name = "ADDRESS2")
    private String address2;

    @Size(max = 250)
    @Column(name = "CITY")
    private String city;

    @Size(max = 2)
    @Column(name = "STATE")
    private String state;

    @Size(max = 10)
    @Column(name = "ZIP")
    private String zip;

    @Column(name = "START_DATE")
    @Temporal(TemporalType.DATE)
    private Date startDate;

    @Lob
    @Column(name = "NOTES")
    private String notes;
```

```
@ManyToOne
  private Author author;
  public AuthorDetail() {  }
...
```

■ **Note**　To run the `org.jakartaeerecipe.chapter07.recipe07_07.RecipeTest.java` example, please be sure to add both entity classes for this example to the `persistence.xml` context file. Also, be sure to comment out any other entities within the persistence context by the same name, because there cannot be duplicate entities within a single persistence context.

How It Works

The most common database table relationship is the one-to-many or many-to-one relationship, whereby a record in one table may relate to one or more records within another table. Consider the scenario from the solution to this recipe, being that a single AUTHOR table record may have one or more address records within the AUTHOR_DETAIL table. Defining this relationship within the entity classes is easy, because annotations are used to indicate the relationship.

When creating a one-to-many relationship within an entity, the entity that corresponds to the table where one record can correlate to many in another table is known as the *owning* entity. The entity that correlates to the database table that may contain more than one record relating to the single record in the other table is known as the *non-owning* entity. The owning entity class should declare a persistent field or property for the entity to which it relates and may have more than one related object. Since there may be more than one non-owning entity object, the owning entity must declare a Set of the non-owning objects and indicate as such using the @OneToMany annotation. The mappedBy attribute of the @OneToMany annotation should be set to the name, which is used within the non-owning entity for declaration of the many-to-one relationship. In the example, the Author entity contains a one-to-many relationship with AuthorDetail. Therefore, the Author entity declares the relationship as follows:

```
@OneToMany(mappedBy="author")
private Set<AuthorDetail> authorDetail;
```

On the other end of the spectrum is the many-to-one relationship. In the example, more than one AuthorDetail object may relate to one Author object. Therefore, a many-to-one relationship should be defined within the AuthorDetail entity class for the Author entity. This is done by declaring a persistent field or property for the Author entity and signifying the relationship with the @ManyToOne annotation as follows:

```
@ManyToOne
private Author author;
```

When working with the entities, a Set containing one or more AuthorDetail objects should be persisted within a single Author object. The following code demonstrates how to use a one-to-many relationship within an application:

```
EntityManagerFactory emf = Persistence.createEntityManagerFactory("JakartaEERecipesLOCAL");
EntityManager em = emf.createEntityManager();
try {
    em.getTransaction().begin();
```

```
    Author author = new Author();
    author.setFirst("JOE");
    author.setLast("TESTER");
    author.setBio("An author test account.");

    Set detailSet = new HashSet<AuthorDetail>();
    AuthorDetail detail = new AuthorDetail();
    detail.setAddress1("Address 1");
    detail.setAddress2("Address 2");
    detail.setCity("NoMansLand");
    detail.setState("ZZ");
    detail.setZip("12345");
    detail.setNotes("This is a test detail");
    detailSet.add(detail);

    AuthorDetail detail2 = new AuthorDetail();
    detail.setAddress1("Address 1");
    detail.setAddress2("Address 2");
    detail.setCity("NoMansLand");
    detail.setState("ZZ");
    detail.setZip("12345");
    detail.setNotes("This is a test detail");
    detailSet.add(detail2);

    em.persist(author);
    em.getTransaction().commit();

} catch (Exception ex){
    ex.printStackTrace();
} finally{
            if (em != null){
                em.close();
            }
}
```

The @OneToMany annotation contains the following optional attributes:

- cascade: The operations (e.g., delete) that must be cascaded to the target of the association. Default: No operations

- fetch: Whether the association should be lazily loaded or must be eagerly fetched. Default: EAGER

- orphanRemoval: Whether to apply the remove operation to entities that have been removed from the relationship and to cascade the remove operation to those entities. Default: False

- targetedEntity: The entity class that is the target of the association. Default: ""

The @ManyToMany annotation contains the following optional attributes:

- cascade: The operations (e.g., delete) that must be cascaded to the target of the association. Default: No operations

- fetch: Whether the association should be lazily loaded or must be eagerly fetched. Default: EAGER

- targetedEntity: The entity class that is the target of the association. Default: ""

7-8. Defining a Many-to-Many Relationship

Problem

There are tables within your database that contain cases where multiple records from one table may correlate to multiple records from another. You want to define entity relationships for these tables.

Solution

Create a many-to-many association between the two tables by declaring a field or property within each entity class for a Set of objects corresponding to the entity class on the opposite end. Utilize the @ManyToMany annotation to specify the relationship, and mark the owning side of the relationship by specifying a mappedBy attribute on the non-owning entity's @ManyToMany annotation. Therefore, the class org.jakartaeerecipe. chapter07.recipe07_08.Book is the entity class corresponding to the BOOK database table, and it will contain the @ManyToMany annotation on a declaration for a Set of BookAuthor objects. A mapping table in the database will be "automagically" populated with the associated mappings from the entities. Shown next is the partial code for the Book class, the "owning" entity:

```
@Entity
@Table(name = "BOOK")
@NamedQuery(name = "Book.findAll", query = "SELECT b FROM Book b")
public class Book implements Serializable {

    private static final long serialVersionUID = 1L;

    @Id
    @Basic(optional = false)
    @SequenceGenerator(name="book_s_generator",sequenceName="book_s", initialValue=1,
    allocationSize=1)
    @GeneratedValue(strategy=GenerationType.SEQUENCE,
    generator="book_s_generator")
    @NotNull
    @Column(name = "ID")
    private BigDecimal id;
    @Size(max = 150)
    @Column(name = "TITLE")
    private String title;

    @Size(max = 500)
    @Column(name = "IMAGE")
    private String image;
```

```
@Lob
@Column(name = "DESCRIPTION")
private String description;

@ManyToMany
private Set<BookAuthorMany> bookAuthors;
```

The BookAuthor class is mapped to the Book class using the same concept. The only difference is that it contains a mappedBy attribute within the @ManyToOne annotation to signify the owning table relation:

```
@Entity
@Table(name = "BOOK_AUTHOR")
@NamedQueries({
    @NamedQuery(name = "BookAuthor.findAll", query = "SELECT b FROM BookAuthor b"),
    @NamedQuery(name = "BookAuthor.findById", query = "SELECT b FROM BookAuthor b WHERE
    b.id = :id"),
    @NamedQuery(name = "BookAuthor.findByLast", query = "SELECT b FROM BookAuthor b WHERE
    b.last = :last"),
    @NamedQuery(name = "BookAuthor.findByFirst", query = "SELECT b FROM BookAuthor b WHERE
    b.first = :first")})
public class BookAuthorMany implements Serializable {

    private static final long serialVersionUID = 1L;

    @Id
    @Basic(optional = false)
    @SequenceGenerator(name="book_author_s_generator",sequenceName="book_author_s",
    initialValue=1, allocationSize=1)
    @GeneratedValue(strategy=GenerationType.SEQUENCE,
    generator="book_author_s_generator")
    @NotNull
    @Column(name = "ID")
    private BigDecimal id;

    @Size(max = 30)
    @Column(name = "LAST")
    private String last;

    @Size(max = 30)
    @Column(name = "FIRST")
    private String first;

    @Lob
    @Column(name = "BIO")
    private String bio;

    @ManyToMany(mappedBy="bookAuthors")
    private Set<Book> books;
```

■ **Note** The BookAuthor entity has been named BookAuthorMany so that there are no conflicting entity classes within the JakartaEERecipes sources. No entities with duplicate names can exist within the same application.

How It Works

It is possible for databases to contain a many-to-many relationship between two or more different tables. In the case of the example in this recipe, a book may have many authors, and an author may have written many books. On that note, both the database table containing books and the database table containing authors are associated to each other via a many-to-many relationship. It is easy to associate entity classes to one another to form a many-to-many relationship via the use of the @ManyToMany annotation. The @ManyToMany annotation is used to signify that an entity contains a many-to-many association with the annotated persistent field or property.

To create the association, each entity within the many-to-many relationship should declare a field or property for a Set of the associated entity objects. In the case of the example, the Book entity should declare a Set of BookAuthor objects and vice versa. That declaration is then annotated with @ManyToMany, using any attributes that are deemed necessary to make the association. The @ManyToMany annotation contains the following optional attributes:

- targetEntity: The entity class that is the target of the association. This is necessary only if the collection-valued relationship property is not defined using Java generics.

- cascade: The operations that must be cascaded to the target of the association.

- fetch: Whether the association should be lazily loaded or eagerly fetched. The default is jakarta.persistence.FetchType.LAZY.

- mappedBy: The field that owns the relationship. This is not required if the relationship is unidirectional.

As such, when creating an object of either type, one may persist a Set of the associated entity objects using the persistent field or property that has been annotated with @ManyToMany. The following example demonstrates how to create an entity with a many-to-many relationship (excerpt from the org. jakartaeerecipe.chapter07.recipe07_08.RecipeTest class):

```
EntityManagerFactory emf = Persistence.createEntityManagerFactory("JakartaEERecipesLOCAL");
EntityManager em = emf.createEntityManager();
try {
    em.getTransaction().begin();
    Book book1 = new Book();
    book1.setTitle("New Book 1");
    Book book2 = new Book();
    book2.setTitle("New Book 2");
    BookAuthorMany author1 = new BookAuthorMany();
    author1.setFirst("JOE");
    author1.setLast("AUTHOR 1");
    BookAuthorMany author2 = new BookAuthorMany();
    author2.setFirst("MARYJJOE");
    author2.setLast("AUTHOR 2");
    Set authors = new HashSet();
    authors.add(author1);
```

```
    authors.add(author2);
    Set books = new HashSet();
    books.add(book1);
    books.add(book2);
    book1.setBookAuthor(authors);
    author1.setBooks(books);
    em.persist(author1);
    em.persist(book1);
    em.getTransaction().commit();
} catch (Exception ex){
    // Please use a logging framework, such as log4j in production
    System.err.println(ex);
} finally{
            if (em != null){
                em.close();
            }
}
```

When an entity object that contains a many-to-many association with another is created, a record is populated into a mapping table that contains the primary key from each associated table record. You can optionally specify the name of the mapping table by using the annotation @JoinTable and specifying the name of the table. If no @JoinTable annotation is used, then the mapping table name is derived from a concatenation of the two entity classes, beginning with the owning entity. Therefore, in the example, the mapping table name is BOOK_BOOK_AUTHOR, and it contains a field for storing the primary key from the associated records of each table.

7-9. Querying with Named Queries

Problem

Rather than issue SQL or Jakarta Persistence Queries to a persistence unit, you want to define one or more predefined queries for an entity class that can be called by name.

Solution

Specify a single named query or a group of named queries for an entity class. Provide a name for each of the named queries so that they can be called by that name. In this example, a group of named queries will be added to the BookAuthor entity class, and then a separate class may be used to query the entity class using the named queries. We will create an EntityManagerFactory and database connection based upon a persistence.xml file that obtains a local JDBC connection to the database. The following excerpt is taken from the BookAuthor entity, and it demonstrates how to associate named queries with an entity class:

```
@Entity
@Table(name = "BOOK_AUTHOR")

@NamedQuery(name = "BookAuthor.findAll", query = "SELECT b FROM BookAuthor b")
@NamedQuery(name = "BookAuthor.findById", query = "SELECT b FROM BookAuthor b WHERE
b.id = :id")
@NamedQuery(name = "BookAuthor.findByLast", query = "SELECT b FROM BookAuthor b WHERE b.last
= :last")
```

```
@NamedQuery(name = "BookAuthor.findByFirst", query = "SELECT b FROM BookAuthor b WHERE
b.first = :first")
public class BookAuthor implements Serializable {

    private static final long serialVersionUID = 1L;

    @Id
    @Basic(optional = false)
    @SequenceGenerator(name="book_author_s_generator",sequenceName="book_author_s",
    initialValue=1, allocationSize=1)
    @GeneratedValue(strategy=GenerationType.SEQUENCE,
    generator="book_author_s_generator")
    @NotNull
    @Column(name = "ID")
    private BigDecimal id;

    @Size(max = 30)
    @Column(name = "LAST")
    private String last;

    @Size(max = 30)
    @Column(name = "FIRST")
    private String first;

    @Lob
    @Column(name = "BIO")
    private String bio;
    public BookAuthor() {   }
...
```

In another class, the named queries that have been registered with the BookAuthor entity can be called
by name. The following excerpt from the org.jakartaeerecipe.chapter07.recipe07_09.RecipeTest class
demonstrates how to invoke a named query:

```
EntityManagerFactory emf = Persistence.createEntityManagerFactory("JakartaEERecipesLOCAL");
EntityManager em = emf.createEntityManager();
try {
    EntityTransaction entr = em.getTransaction();
    entr.begin();
    Query query = em.createNamedQuery("BookAuthor.findAll");
    List authorList = query.getResultList();
    Iterator authorIterator = authorList.iterator();
    while (authorIterator.hasNext()) {
        BookAuthor author = (BookAuthor) authorIterator.next();
        System.out.print("Name:" + author.getFirst() + " " + author.getLast());
        System.out.println();
    }
} catch (Exception ex){
    System.err.println(ex);
}
```

Figure 7-5 will be the output of this recipe.

```
[EL Info]: 2022-02-04 01:50:10.73--ServerSession(1949298838)--EclipseLink, version: Eclipse Persistence Services - 3.0.2.v202107160933
Name:Josh Juneau
Name:Tarun Telang

Process finished with exit code 0
```

Figure 7-5. *Output of Recipe 7-9*

How It Works

A named query is contained within an entity class, and it consists of a static Jakarta Persistence query that is specified via metadata. A given entity class can include zero or more named queries. A named query is expressed via the @NamedQuery annotation, which contains two attributes: name and query. The name attribute of the @NamedQuery annotation is used to specify a String-based name for the query, and the query attribute is used to specify the static query against the entity. If an entity contains a group of named query annotations, then @NamedQuery annotation can be repeated for each of the query.

The Jakarta Persistence Query Language within a named query can contain zero or more bind variables that can have values substituted when the named query is called. To utilize a named query, you must first obtain an active connection to the database. To learn more about obtaining an active connection to the database via an EntityManagerFactory, please refer to Recipe 7-3. Once an active database connection has been obtained, the EntityManager object's createNamedQuery method can be called, passing the string-based name of the named query that you would like to issue. A Query object is returned from the call, and it can be used to obtain the query results.

In the example for this recipe, you can see that the BookAuthor entity is queried, returning a List of BookAuthor objects. A simple while loop is used to iterate through the List of objects, printing the first and last names from each BookAuthor object to System.out.

7-10. Performing Validation on Entity Fields

Problem

You want to specify validation rules for specific fields within an entity class to prevent invalid data from being inserted into the database.

Solution

Include bean validation constraints within an entity class. Bean validation constraints are annotations that are applied to persistent fields or properties of an entity class. The bean validation mechanism provides a number of annotations that can be placed on fields or properties in order to validate data in different ways. In the following example, the AuthorWork entity has been enhanced to include bean validation for the id, address1, state, and zip fields:

```
...
@Entity
@Table(name = "AUTHOR_DETAIL")
public class AuthorDetailBeanValidation implements Serializable {

    private static final long serialVersionUID = 1L;
```

```
@Id
@Basic(optional = false)
@SequenceGenerator(name="author_detail_s_generator",sequenceName="author__detail_s",
initialValue=1, allocationSize=1)
@GeneratedValue(strategy=GenerationType.SEQUENCE,
generator="author_detail_s_generator")
@NotNull
@Column(name = "ID")
private BigDecimal id;

@Size(max = 200)
@Pattern(regexp="", message="Invalid Address")
@Column(name = "ADDRESS1")
private String address1;

@Size(max = 200)
@Column(name = "ADDRESS2")
private String address2;

@Size(max = 250)
@Column(name = "CITY")
private String city;

@Size(max = 2)
@Column(name = "STATE")
@Pattern(regexp="^(?-i:A[LKSZRAEP]|C[AOT]|D[EC]|F[LM]|G[AU]|HI|I[ADLN]|K[SY]|LA|M[ADEHIN
OPST]|N[CDEHJMVY]|O[HKR]|P[ARW]|RI|S[CD]|T[NX]|UT|V[AIT]|W[AIVY])$",
        message="Invalid State")
private String state;

@Size(max = 10)
@Column(name = "ZIP")
@Pattern(regexp="^\\d{5}\\p{Punct}?\\s?(?:\\d{4})?$",
        message="Invalid Zip Code")
private String zip;

@Column(name = "START_DATE")
@Temporal(TemporalType.DATE)
private Date startDate;

@Lob
@Column(name = "NOTES")
private String notes;

@ManyToOne
private AuthorBeanValidation author;
...
```

To insert a value that does not conform to the validation rules, the object will not be persisted, and the message correlating to the bean validation annotation will be displayed.

How It Works

It is always a good idea to utilize a data validation strategy when working with user input, especially if the data will be persisted into a database or other data stores for later use. The Java Persistence API allows bean validation to occur within an entity class, whereby a developer can place validation rules directly on a persistent field or property. By default, the persistence provider automatically invokes validation processes on entities containing bean validation annotation constraints after the PrePersist, PreUpdate, and PreRemove life-cycle events occur. At that time, any value that does not adhere to the given validation constraint will cause the entity to stop persistence and display an associated message.

The details of bean validation are the same, whether it be on a Plain Old Java Object (POJO) or an entity class. In the case of an entity class, either the persistent field or property can be annotated with the desired bean validation constraint. To see a list of possible bean validation constraint annotations, please refer to Chapter 10.

In the example for this recipe, the @NotNull and @Pattern annotations are specified on persistent properties of the AuthorDetail entity. Specifically, the id field is annotated with @NotNull, and validation will fail in an attempt to enter a NULL value for that field. The state and zip fields contain a @Pattern annotation, along with a corresponding regular expression and failure message. If the values for those fields do not adhere to the regular expression that has been specified, then the message that is assigned to the message attribute of the @Pattern annotation will be displayed via a Jakarta Server Faces view by the h:message component corresponding to the validated field. What if you want to apply a set of regular expression patterns to a given field or property? Such a feat can be done using the @Pattern.List syntax, whereby the list would contain a comma-separated list of @Pattern annotations. The following lines of code demonstrate this technique:

```
@Pattern.List({
    @Pattern(regexp="regex-pattern", message="Error Message"),
    @Pattern(regexp="another regex-pattern", message("Error Message 2")
})
```

Bean validation is a good way to ensure that invalid data is not submitted to a data store. However, most advanced desktop or web applications today use a couple tiers of validation to make the user experience more convenient. Many times, web applications use JavaScript field validation first so that users do not have to submit a page in order to see their validation errors displayed on the screen. If using Jakarta Server Faces or other web frameworks, some components allow direct access to bean validation, in which cases an Ajax submission of a given field or property will occur behind the scenes, allowing the bean validation to take place without page submission. Whatever tact you take, bean validation within entity classes is important and should become a handy tool to add to your arsenal.

7-11. Generating Database Schema Objects Automatically

Problem

You are developing an application and want to automatically have your entity classes generated into tables within the underlying database.

Solution

Use the automatic schema generation that was introduced in EJB 3.2. Schema generation is determined by the object-relational metadata of the persistence.xml unit, unless custom scripts are provided for the generation. The application developer can package scripts as part of the persistence unit or can supply URLs to the location of the scripts for schema generation. The execution of such scripts can be carried out by the container itself, or the container may direct the persistence provider to take care of script execution. Table 7-3 in the "How It Works" section of this recipe lists the different `persistence.xml` or `EntityManagerFactory` properties that are used to configure schema generation. These properties are passed as a `Map` argument from the container to the `PersistenceProvider generateSchema` method or the `createContainerEntityManagerFactory` method.

Table 7-3. *Schema Generation Properties*

Property	Purpose
`schema-generation-action`	Controls the action to be taken by the persistence provider with regard to object generation and destruction. **Values**: none, `create`, `drop-and-create`, and `drop`
`schema-generation-target`	Controls whether schema is to be created within the database, whether Data Definition Language (DDL) scripts are to be created, or both. **Values**: `database`, `scripts`, and `database-and-scripts`
`ddl-create-script-target,` `ddl-drop-script-target`	Controls target locations for writing scripts if the schema-generation-target specifies script generation. Writers are preconfigured for the persistence provider. **Values**: `java.io.Writer` (e.g., `MyWriter.class`) or URL strings
`ddl-create-script-source,` `ddl-drop-script-source`	Specifies locations from which DDL scripts are to be read. Readers are preconfigured for the persistence provider. **Values**: `java.io.Reader` (e.g., `MyReader.class`) or URL strings
`sql-load-script-source`	Specifies the file location of the SQL bulk load script. **Values**: `java.io.Reader` (e.g., `MyReader.class`) or URL string
`schema-generation-connection`	JDBC connection to be used for performing schema generation
`database-product-name,` `database-major-version,` `database-minor-version`	Needed if scripts are to be generated. Values are those obtained from JDBC `DatabaseMetaData`
`create-database-schemas`	Whether the persistence provider needs to create schema in addition to creating database objects such as tables, sequences, constraints, and so on. **Values**: `true` and `false`

To define the different objects that need to be generated, annotate entity classes accordingly. The standard entity class annotations (`@Table`, `@Id`, etc.) determine what objects are created and how they are structured. For more information regarding the specification of annotations within entity classes to generate schema objects, please refer to the annotations listed in Table 7-4 within the "How It Works" section of this recipe.

Table 7-4. *Schema Generation Annotations*

Annotation	Description	Elements
@Table	Used for generating tables. By default, the table name is generated from the entity name, and the entity name is defaulted from the class name	
@SecondaryTable	A secondary table is created to partition the mapping of entity state across multiple tables	
@CollectionTable	A collection table is created for mapping of an element collection. The Column, AttributeOverride, and AssociationOverride annotations may be used to override CollectionTable mappings	
@JoinTable	Used in mapping of associations. By default, join tables are created for the mapping of many-to-many relationships and unidirectional one-to-many relationships	
@TableGenerator	Used to store generated primary key values	
@Column	Determines the name and configuration for a column within a table	unique, nullable, columnDefinition, table, length, precision, scale, name
@MapKeyColumn	Specifies the mapping name of a key column of a map when the key is of basic type	unique, nullable, columnDefinition, table, length, precision, scale
@Enumerated, @MapKeyEnumerated	Controls whether string- or integer-valued columns are generated for basic attributes of enumerated types and therefore impact the default column mapping of these types	
@Temporal, @MapKeyTemporal	Controls whether date-, time-, or timestamp-valued columns are generated for basic attributes of temporal types and therefore impact the default column mappings for these types	
@Lob	Specifies that a persistent attribute is to be mapped to a database large object type	
@OrderColumn	Specifies the generation of a column that is used to maintain the persistent ordering of a list that is represented in an element collection, one-to-many, or many-to-many relationship	name, nullable, columnDefinition

(continued)

371

Table 7-4. (*continued*)

Annotation	Description	Elements
@DiscriminatorColumn	Generated for the SINGLE_TABLE mapping strategy and may optionally be generated by the provider for use with the JOINED inheritance strategy	
@Version	Specifies the generation of a column to serve as an entity's optimistic lock	
@Id	Specifies a database primary key column. Use of the @Id annotation results in the creation of a primary key which consists of the corresponding column or columns	
@EmbeddedId	Specifies an embedded attribute whose corresponding columns formulate a database primary key. Use of the @EmbeddedId annotation results in the creation of a primary key consisting of the corresponding columns	
@GeneratedValue	Indicates a primary key that should have an automatically generated value. If a strategy is indicated, the provider must use it if it is supported by the target database	
@JoinColumn	The @JoinColumn annotation is typically used for specifying a foreign key mapping	name, referencedColumnName, unique, nullable, columnDefinition, table, foreignKey
@MapKeyJoinColumn	Specifies foreign key mappings to entities that are map keys in element collections or relationships that consist of map values	name, referencedColumnName, unique, nullable, columnDefinition, table, foreignKey
@PrimaryJoinKeyColumn	Specifies that a primary key column is to be used as a foreign key. This annotation is used in the specification of the JOINED mapping strategy and for joining a secondary table to a primary table in a one-to-one relationship mapping	
@ForeignKey	Used within the JoinColumn, JoinColumns, MapKeyJoinColumn, MapKeyJoinColumns, PrimaryKeyJoinColumn, and PrimaryKeyJoinColumns annotations to specify or override a foreign key constraint	
@SequenceGenerator	Creates a database sequence to be used for ID generation	
@Index	Generates an index consisting of the specified columns	
@UniqueConstraint	Generates a unique constraint for the given table	

How It Works

Schema generation refers to the creation of underlying database tables, views, constraints, and other database artifacts. Prior to the Java EE 7 release, schema generation had been automated only via the use of an IDE such as NetBeans or Eclipse. However, the EE 7 release took a step toward breaking this dependency on an IDE by allowing schema generation to become automated by configuring an appropriate persistence.xml file for an application.

Schema generation can be applied directly to the database, or it can generate SQL scripts that can be manually applied to the database (or both), depending upon which options are configured for the application. Schema generation may occur prior to application deployment or when an EntityManagerFactory is created as part of the application deployment and initialization. To perform schema generation, the container may call the PersistenceProvider generateSchema method separately from and/or prior to the entity manager factory for the persistence unit. The createContainerEntityManagerFactory call can accept additional information to cause the generation of schema constructs to occur as part of the entity manager factory creation or initialization process. Furthermore, this information can determine whether the database is manipulated directly or whether SQL scripts are created, or both.

■ **Note** Schema generation is also available outside of a managed container (e.g., web application server) in Java SE environments. To perform schema generation in a Java SE environment, the application may call the Persistence generateSchema method separately from and/or prior to the creation of the entity manager factory or may pass information to the createEntityManagerFactory method to cause schema generation to occur as part of the entity manager factory creation.

Table 7-3 lists the different schema generation properties that can be specified in the persistence.xml file to automate schema generation.

Programmatically, schema generation is determined by a series of annotations that are placed in entity classes. The @Table annotation denotes an entity mapping to an underlying database table. By default, a table is generated for each top-level entity and includes columns based upon the specified attributes for that entity. Therefore, the @Column and @JoinColumn annotations are used for generating such columns for a table. Column ordering is not determined based upon the ordering of @Column or @JoinColumn annotations. If column ordering is important, then a Data Definition Language (DDL) script must be supplied for generating the table. Other annotations and annotation attributes, such as @Id, also play important roles in schema generation. Table 7-4 lists the different annotations that are involved in schema generation, along with a brief description and the elements that can be populated for further control over the generated schema.

As per Table 7-4, there are a couple of annotations that have been created specifically to facilitate schema generation. The new annotations are @Index and @ForeignKey, where @Index is responsible for generating an index of the specified columns. @ForeignKey is used to define a foreign key on a table.

The following is the excerpt from *persistence.xml* to enable table creation as part of schema generation:

```
<property name="jakarta.persistence.schema-generation.database.action" value="create"/>
<property name="jakarta.persistence.schema-generation.create-source" value="metadata"/>
```

Adding the preceding property will result in autogeneration of database schema objects.

7-12. Mapping Date-Time Values

Problem

You wish to utilize the Date-Time API to persist Java LocalDate values to the database.

Solution

Use JPA 2.2 support for the Date-Time API to work with the LocalDate. Since the JPA 2.2 maintenance release supports the Java Date-Time API, it is possible to make use of the date and time objects that were introduced in Java 8 to persist without the need for the @Temporal annotation. The following entity class demonstrates how to achieve this feat:

```
public class Book implements Serializable {
    private static final long serialVersionUID = 1L;
    @Id
    @Basic(optional = false)
    @Column(name = "ID")
    private BigDecimal id;

    @Size(max = 150)
    @Column(name = "TITLE")
    protected String title;

    @Size(max = 500)
    @Column(name = "IMAGE")
    private String image;

    @Lob
    @Column(name = "DESCRIPTION")
    private String description;

    @Column(name = "PUBLISH_DATE")
    private LocalDate publishDate;

    @ManyToMany(mappedBy="books")
    private Set<BookAuthor> authors;

    @OneToMany(mappedBy="book", cascade=CascadeType.ALL)
    private List<Chapter> chapters = null;

    public Book() { }
...
}
```

As you can see, the entity class contains a LocalDate field that includes no special annotations.

How It Works

When Java 8 was initially released, Java EE and JPA did not have support for the updated Date-Time API. Therefore, in order to utilize the newer date and time objects, one had to develop a converter to perform automatic conversion between the new date and time objects and `java.util.Date`. Since JPA maintenance release 2.2, this issue has been mitigated, as the Java Date-Time API is officially supported, making it easier than ever before to persist fields that contain date and time values.

To map a database column that contains a date to a Java object, simply annotate the column with the `@Column` annotation, specifying the column name if you wish. The `@Temporal` annotation is no longer required. Apply one of the following data types to the class field:

- java.time.LocalDate
- java.time.LocalTime
- java.time.LocalDateTime
- java.time.OffsetTime
- java.time.OffsetDateTime

It is as simple as that! The Jakarta Persistence API Date-Time support has provided the ability to utilize the API within Java EE applications without the requirement of a converter. It is also cut down on code because `@Temporal` is no longer required.

7-13. Using the Same Annotation Many Times

Problem

You wish to utilize the same annotation a number of different times within a given class. For instance, suppose that you would like to use more than one `@PersistenceContext` annotation within a single class.

Solution

Take advantage of the Java 8 repeatable annotation support that has been provided with JPA 2.2. This added support provides the ability to use repeatable annotations for a number of situations. In the following example, the `@NamedQuery` annotation is utilized more than one time in the same class. Prior to JPA 2.2, this would not work without first grouping the annotations together into a single container annotation:

```
@Entity
@Table(name = "EMPLOYEE")
@XmlRootElement
@NamedQuery(name = "Employee.findAll", query = "SELECT e FROM Employee e")
@NamedQuery(name = "Employee.findById", query = "SELECT e FROM Employee e WHERE e.id = :id")
@NamedQuery(name = "Employee.findByFirst", query = "SELECT e FROM Employee e WHERE e.first =
:first")
@NamedQuery(name = "Employee.findByLast", query = "SELECT e FROM Employee e WHERE e.last
= :last")
@NamedQuery(name = "Employee.findByAge", query = "SELECT e FROM Employee e WHERE e.age
= :age")
@NamedStoredProcedureQuery(name = "createEmp", procedureName = "CREATE_EMP")
```

```java
public class Employee implements Serializable {

    private static final long serialVersionUID = 1L;
    // @Max(value=?)  @Min(value=?)//if you know range of your decimal fields consider using
        these annotations to enforce field validation
    @Id
    @Basic(optional = false)
    //@NotNull
    @Column(name = "ID")
    private BigDecimal id;

    @Size(max = 30)
    @Column(name = "FIRSTNAME")
    private String first;

    @Size(max = 30)
    @Column(name = "LASTNAME")
    private String last;

    @Column(name = "AGE")
    private BigInteger age;

    @ManyToOne(optional = false)

    @JoinColumn(name = "JOB_ID", nullable = false)
    private Jobs job;

    @Column(name = "STATUS")
    private String status;

    public Employee() { }
...
}
```

How It Works

Repeatable annotation support came to the Java platform with the release of Java 8. This enables one to utilize the same annotation more than once within a portion of code. Annotations are not repeatable by default; the annotation class must be designated as such with the @Repeatable annotation. Therefore, not all annotations will be usable more than once within a class. The following annotations were made repeatable for the Java EE 8 release:

- AssociationOverride

- AttributeOverride

- Convert

- JoinColumn

- MapKeyJoinColumn

- NamedEntityGraph

- NamedNativeQuery

- NamedQuery

- NamedStoredProcedureQuery

- PersistenceContext

- PersistenceUnit

- PrimaryKeyJoinColumn

- SecondaryTable

- SqlResultSetMapping

As mentioned previously, annotations must be designated as repeatable by marking them with the @Repeatable annotation. Therefore, if you have created a custom annotation and you would like to make it repeatable, then you can do so.

CHAPTER 8

■ ■ ■

Jakarta Enterprise Beans

Jakarta Enterprise Beans were created to separate the view layer from the database access and business layers. Jakarta Enterprise Beans are where all the database (EntityManager) access and business logic can take place within a Jakarta EE application, and they have become significantly easier to use over the past few releases. Jakarta Enterprise Beans are used to coordinate database tasks with entities, and Jakarta Server Faces CDI controllers (a.k.a. controller classes) are used to interact directly with the Jakarta Server Faces views or web pages. CDI beans are used to provide a façade between the view layer and the business layer.

Jakarta Enterprise Beans are deployed to an application server container, which manages the bean life cycle. The container also provides features such as transaction management and security for Jakarta Enterprise Beans. Jakarta Enterprise Beans are portable, meaning that they can be deployed to different application server containers. This adds benefit for Jakarta Enterprise Beans developers because a single Jakarta Enterprise Beans can be utilized across multiple applications. Jakarta Enterprise Beans also alleviate the issue of modifying applications to work with multiple databases due to the use of Java Persistence Query Language (covered in Chapter 9) rather than routine SQL is used to perform database operations. Therefore, if an application is developed on one database, it can be ported to another without the need to rewrite any SQL.

There are three types of Jakarta Enterprise Beans that can be used: stateless, stateful, and message driven. This chapter will cover the first two, and message-driven beans (MDBs) will be covered in Chapter 12 where the Jakarta Message Service is covered. Stateless session beans are used most often, because they are used for quick transactions and do not maintain any conversational state. Stateful beans, on the other hand, are to be used in situations where a conversational state across multiple client requests is required.

This chapter includes recipes to familiarize you with stateful and stateless session beans. You will learn how to access Jakarta Enterprise Beans from a Jakarta Server Faces CDI controller client and display content within a Jakarta Server Faces view or web page that the Jakarta Enterprise Beans has queried from the database. There are also recipes covering useful tactics such as using bean Timers and creating singleton session beans.

■ **Note** In recent times, Jakarta Enterprise Beans may be considered older technology because CDI beans can now be used in their place.

8-1. Obtaining an Entity Manager

Problem

You have created a persistence unit for your database connection, and you want to use it to obtain a connection for working with the database.

Solution #1

Create an EntityManagerFactory object utilizing a local JDBC connection by calling the jakarta.persistence. Persistence createEntityManagerFactory method and passing the name of the JakartaEERecipesLOCAL persistence unit. Obtain an EntityManager object from the factory object that has been created, and then utilize the EntityManager object as needed to work with the database entities. The following lines of code demonstrate how to accomplish the creation of an EntityManager object using a local JDBC connection:

```
EntityManagerFactory emf = Persistence.createEntityManagerFactory("JakartaEERecipesLOCAL");
 EntityManager em = emf.createEntityManager();
```

■ **Note**   For further reference regarding the creation of a persistence unit, please see Recipe 8-3.

Solution #2

Inject EntityManager into EJB when using a database connection within an environment utilizing Java Naming and Directory Interface (JNDI), such as an application server. To do so, declare a private field of the EntityManager type, and annotate it using @PersistenceContext. Pass the name of the relevant persistence unit to the @PersistenceContext annotation. The following lines of code demonstrate how this technique is performed. In an application, these lines of code would reside within an EJB for an entity class:

```
@PersistenceContext(unitName = "JakartaEERecipes")
 private EntityManager em;
```

How It Works

Before an entity class can be used to persist an object or obtain query results, an entity manager must be created from the persistence unit database connection configuration. The way in which you achieve the creation of an entity manager will differ depending upon the type of database connection you are using. For instance, if you are creating an entity manager from a local JDBC connection, then there is a little more work to be done because an EntityManagerFactory must be used to obtain the EntityManager object. On the other hand, if you are creating a container-managed entity manager from a database connection that is registered with an application server via JNDI, then much of the work is done for you behind the scenes via metadata annotations. This is the preferred approach as configuration is easy to manage centrally from the application server.

In the first solution to this recipe, a persistence unit pertaining to a local JDBC connection is used to obtain an EntityManager object. As mentioned previously, within a Jakarta Enterprise Beans, an EntityManagerFactory object must first be obtained by calling the jakarta.persistence.Persistence class's createEntityManagerFactory method and passing the string-based persistence unit name to the method. From there, an EntityManager object can be instantiated by invoking the EntityManagerFactory's createEntityManager method.

In the second solution to this recipe, a container-managed EntityManager object instance is obtained. If an application is deployed to an enterprise application server container such as Eclipse GlassFish, this is the preferred way to obtain an EntityManager. Utilizing container-managed entity managers makes Jakarta Persistence development easier because a Jakarta EE container manages the life cycle of container-managed entity managers. Moreover, container-managed entity managers are automatically propagated to all application components within a single Jakarta Transaction API transaction. To obtain a container-managed entity manager, declare an EntityManager field within a Jakarta Enterprise Beans and simply annotate it with @PersistenceContext, passing the string-based name of the persistence unit to the annotation. Doing so injects the entity manager into the application component.

After performing either of these solutions, the newly obtained EntityManager object is ready to be utilized. The most often used EntityManager methods are createQuery, createNamedQuery, find, and persist. You will learn more about utilizing the EntityManager in the following recipes.

The Maven dependencies for the project are as follows:

```xml
<dependency>
    <groupId>jakarta.ejb</groupId>
    <artifactId>jakarta.ejb-api</artifactId>
    <version>4.0.0</version>
    <scope>provided</scope>
</dependency>

<dependency>
    <groupId>jakarta.persistence</groupId>
    <artifactId>jakarta.persistence-api</artifactId>
    <version>3.1.0</version>
</dependency>

<dependency>
    <groupId>org.eclipse.persistence</groupId>
    <artifactId>eclipselink</artifactId>
    <version>4.0.0-M3</version>
</dependency>

<dependency>
    <groupId>org.apache.derby</groupId>
    <artifactId>derbyclient</artifactId>
    <version>10.15.2.0</version>
    <scope>runtime</scope>
</dependency>

<dependency>
    <groupId>org.apache.derby</groupId>
    <artifactId>derbynet</artifactId>
    <version>10.15.2.0</version>
    <scope>runtime</scope>
</dependency>

<dependency>
    <groupId>jakarta.platform</groupId>
    <artifactId>jakarta.jakartaee-web-api</artifactId>
    <version>10.0.0-RC1</version>
</dependency>
```

8-2. Developing a Stateless Session Bean

Problem

You want to create a class that can be used to perform tasks for a client, but the application does not require the bean to retain any state between transactions. Additionally, you want to have the ability to interact with a database from within the class.

Solution #1

Create a stateless session bean for the entity class for which you'd like to perform tasks. Create an EntityManager object from a persistence unit, and initiate tasks against the database using the entity classes. In the following solution, a stateless session bean is created for working with the Book entity:

```
package org.jakartaeerecipe.chapter08.session;

import jakarta.ejb.Stateless;
import jakarta.persistence.EntityManager;
import jakarta.persistence.PersistenceContext;
import org.jakartaeerecipe.chapter08.entity.Book;

@Stateless
public class BookFacade {
    @PersistenceContext(unitName = "JakartaEERecipes")
    private EntityManager em;
    protected EntityManager getEntityManager() {
        return em;
    }
    public BookFacade() {
    }
    /**
     * Create a book object
     * @param book
     */
    public void create(Book book){
        em.persist(book);
    }
    /**
     * Update a book object
     * @param book
     */
    public void edit(Book book){
        em.merge(book);
    }
    /**
     * Remove a book object
     * @param book
     */
    public void remove(Book book){
        em.remove(book);
```

```
    }
    /**
     * Return a Book object based upon a given title.  This assumes that there are no
       duplicate titles in the database.
     * @param title
     * @return
     */
    public Book findByTitle(String title){
        Book returnValue = null;
        try{
        returnValue = (Book) em.createQuery("select object(o) from Book o " +
                              "where o.title = :title")
                              .setParameter("title", title.toUpperCase())
                              .getSingleResult();
        } catch (NoResultException ex){
            ex.printStackTrace();
        }
        return returnValue;
    }
}
```

In the example session bean, the create, edit, and remove methods can be called via a client to perform CRUD operations with the database. The findByTitle() method can be called via a client to obtain a Book object from the database.

Solution #2

Create a stateless session bean for the entity class for which you'd like to perform tasks, and extend an abstract class that encapsulates standard operations from the session bean. Create an EntityManager object from a persistence unit, and initiate tasks against the database using the entity classes. In the following solution, a stateless session bean is created for working with the Book entity. It extends a class named AbstractFacade, which contains implementations for most of the commonly used tasks within EJBs.

First, let's look at the BookFacade class, the stateless session bean:

```
package org.jakartaeerecipe.chapter08.session;

import jakarta.ejb.Stateless;
import jakarta.persistence.EntityManager;
import jakarta.persistence.PersistenceContext;
import org.jakartaeerecipe.chapter08.entity.Book;

@Stateless
public class BookFacade extends AbstractFacade<Book> {
    @PersistenceContext(unitName = "JakartaEERecipes")
    private EntityManager em;
    @Override
    protected EntityManager getEntityManager() {
        return em;
    }
    public BookFacade() {
        super(Book.class);
```

```
}
/**
 * Return a Book object based upon a given title.  This assumes that there
 * are no duplicate titles in the database.
 * @param title
 * @return
 */
public Book findByTitle(String title){
    return (Book) em.createQuery("select object(o) from Book o " +
                        "where o.title = :title")
                    .setParameter("title", title.toUpperCase())
                    .getSingleResult();
}
}
```

As you can see, there is only a single method implemented within the Jakarta Enterprise Beans, which is the findByTitle() method. However, other CRUD functionality such as create, update, and remove for the Book entity can also be performed via the BookFacade session bean because it extends AbstractFacade. The AbstractFacade class is an abstract class that implements the most used Jakarta Enterprise Beans methods. It accepts an entity class type specified as a generic, and its implementation is as follows.

■ **Note**   The following code was automatically generated via the Apache NetBeans IDE along with the BookFacade session bean after creating a stateless session bean for the Book entity class. If you are using other IDEs like Eclipse or IntelliJ, you might need to code it manually.

```
package org.jakartaeerecipe.chapter08.session;

import java.util.List;
import jakarta.persistence.EntityManager;
/**
 * Abstract Facade for Session Beans
 */
public abstract class AbstractFacade<T> {
    private Class<T> entityClass;
    public AbstractFacade(Class<T> entityClass) {
        this.entityClass = entityClass;
    }
    protected abstract EntityManager getEntityManager();
    public void create(T entity) {
        getEntityManager().persist(entity);
    }
    public void edit(T entity) {
        getEntityManager().merge(entity);
    }
    public void remove(T entity) {
        getEntityManager().remove(getEntityManager().merge(entity));
    }
    public T find(Object id) {
        return getEntityManager().find(entityClass, id);
```

```
    }
    public List<T> findAll() {
        jakarta.persistence.criteria.CriteriaQuery cq = getEntityManager().
        getCriteriaBuilder().createQuery();
        cq.select(cq.from(entityClass));
        return getEntityManager().createQuery(cq).getResultList();
    }
    public List<T> findRange(int[] range) {
        jakarta.persistence.criteria.CriteriaQuery cq = getEntityManager().
        getCriteriaBuilder().createQuery();
        cq.select(cq.from(entityClass));
        jakarta.persistence.Query q = getEntityManager().createQuery(cq);
        q.setMaxResults(range[1] - range[0]);
        q.setFirstResult(range[0]);
        return q.getResultList();
    }
    public int count() {
        jakarta.persistence.criteria.CriteriaQuery cq = getEntityManager().
        getCriteriaBuilder().createQuery();
        jakarta.persistence.criteria.Root<T> rt = cq.from(entityClass);
        cq.select(getEntityManager().getCriteriaBuilder().count(rt));
        jakarta.persistence.Query q = getEntityManager().createQuery(cq);
        return ((Long) q.getSingleResult()).intValue();
    }
}
```

All the methods declared in the AbstractFacade are available to the BookFacade since it extends the class. One of the biggest benefits of using an abstract class to implement the standard CRUD functionality is that it can be applied across many different Jakarta Enterprise Beans, rather than written from scratch each time.

How It Works

A Java class that is used to encapsulate the business logic and data access for an application is also known as a *session bean*. More specifically, session beans typically correspond to entity classes, whereas there is usually one bean per entity, although this is not a requirement and there are instances in which such an implementation does not work well. Any database transactions for an application should be encapsulated within a session bean class that is responsible for business process implementations, and clients should then make calls to the session beans in order to invoke those business processes. A stateless session bean does not retain any state, meaning that variables within the bean are not guaranteed to retain their values across invocations. An application server container maintains a pool of session beans for use by its clients, and when a client invokes a bean, then one is taken from the pool for use. Beans are returned to the pool immediately after the client is finished with the invoking task. Therefore, stateless session beans are thread-safe, and they work very well within a concurrent user environment.

Stateless session beans should contain a no-argument constructor, and they are instantiated by an application server container at application startup. To signify that a session bean is stateless, the class should be annotated with @Stateless, optionally passing a String-based name parameter for the bean. If no name parameter is specified within the @Stateless annotation, then the name of the bean is used. A stateless session bean should not be final or abstract; therefore, all methods within the bean should contain an implementation. They can extend other session beans or POJOs in order to extend functionality. In pre–EJB 3.1 environments, there was a requirement for session beans to implement business interfaces that contained method signatures for those methods that were to be made public for client use. However, it is no longer a requirement for a session bean to implement a business interface, and indeed the solutions to this recipe do not demonstrate the use of business interfaces (see Recipe 8-4 for a concrete example).

Zero or more variables can be declared within a stateless session bean, although the contents of those variables are not guaranteed for retention across client calls. It is typical for a stateless session bean to contain at least one EntityManager connection, although it is possible for a bean to contain zero or more connections. For instance, in some cases session beans do not have a need to persist data, and in such cases no database connection would be needed. In other instances, there may be a need for a session bean to have the ability to work with multiple databases, in which case multiple database connections would be necessary. In the example for this recipe, a single database connection is declared as an EntityManager object, corresponding to the JakartaEERecipes persistence unit. It is possible to make use of standard JDBC persistence units, as well as standard JDBC DataSource objects within a session bean. The use of a standard JDBC DataSource declaration may look like the following:

```
@Resource(name="jdbc/MyDataSource")
private DataSource dataSource;
```

As mentioned previously, stateless session beans can implement business interfaces, although it is not required. The business interfaces that can be implemented via a stateless session bean can be local, remote, or web service endpoints. A local business interface is designed for clients of stateless session beans that exist within the same container instance as the session bean itself. Designating a business interface with the @Local annotation specifies a local interface. Remote business interfaces are designed for use by clients that reside outside of the session bean's container instance. A remote business interface is denoted by the @Remote annotation.

Stateless session beans contain "callback methods" that will be invoked by the container automatically when certain life-cycle events occur. Specifically, stateless session beans can make use of two callbacks: PostConstruct and PreDestroy. After the container constructs a stateless session bean and resources have been injected, any method within the bean that is denoted with a @PostConstruct annotation will be invoked. Similarly, when the container decides that a bean should be removed from the pool or destroyed, then any method denoted with a @PreDestroy annotation will be invoked before the bean is destroyed. Callback methods can be very useful for instantiating database connections and so forth.

LIFE CYCLE OF A STATELESS SESSION BEAN

Stateless session beans have the following life cycle:

1. A container creates a stateless session bean using the default no-argument constructor.

2. Resources are injected as necessary (i.e., database connections).

3. A managed pool of beans is generated, and multiple instances of the session bean are placed into the pool.

4. An idle bean is taken from the pool when the invocation request is received from a client. If all beans in a pool are currently in use, more beans are instantiated until the maximum specified amount of beans has been reached.

5. The business method invoked by the client is executed.

6. The bean is returned to the pool after the business method process is complete.

7. The bean is destroyed from the pool on an as-needed basis.

In the first solution to this recipe, a stateless session bean is listed that does not implement any interfaces or extend any other classes. Such a stateless session bean is very typical, and it is not uncommon to see it in EJB 3.1+ applications. The bean in the solution declares an `EntityManager` object, and the application server container performs the creation of the `EntityManager` automatically and injects it into the bean since the `@PersistenceContext` annotation is specified. The annotation must designate a persistence unit name to tell the container the type of `EntityManager` to inject. In the case where a bean needs access to multiple database connections, then more than one `EntityManager` object may be declared, specifying different names for each persistence unit corresponding to the different connections that are required by the bean. A no-argument constructor is specified as per the guidelines for stateless session beans. The solution also contains one business method implementation, `findByTitle()`, which accepts a `String` argument and queries the `Book` entity for the specified book title. If found, the matching `Book` object is returned to the caller. The `findByTitle()` method demonstrates the typical usage of an `EntityManager` object for working with a database from within a session bean.

In the second solution to the recipe, the `BookFacade` stateless session bean extends a class named `AbstractFacade`. The `AbstractFacade` class contains a number of method implementations that are commonly used within session bean classes. For instance, the `create` method within `AbstractClass` can be used to persist an object (insert into the database), and the `edit` method can be used to update an object. Solution #2 demonstrates a good technique that can be used to encapsulate commonly used business logic into a separate class so that it can be extended to multiple different beans. Consider that the application may contain several different stateless session beans that corresponded to several different entity classes, and each of those beans would need to contain `create`, `edit`, and `remove` methods. It is much easier to simply extend a single class that contains this functionality, rather than rewriting in each separate session bean class.

Stateless session beans are highly performant objects that are used to encapsulate the business logic and data access corresponding to an application entity. While most times a single session bean is written for each entity class, this is not a mandatory rule. Stateless session beans should be considered first when deciding upon which type of bean to use for encapsulating the logic for a particular application process. If a conversational state between the client and the bean is not required (no state needs to be maintained), then stateless session beans are the best choice since they provide the most concurrency and best performance. If, however, a state is required, then consider the use of stateful session beans.

8-3. Developing a Stateful Session Bean

Problem

You want to develop a session bean that has the capability of maintaining a conversational state with the client. For instance, you want the client to have the ability to perform a multistep process without the state of the session bean being lost between requests.

Solution

Create a stateful session bean and implement the business logic pertaining to the entity class of your choice. Consider that a customer is browsing the pages of the Acme Bookstore application and wants to add a book to a shopping cart. The cart would need to be maintained within a stateful session bean since it would be required to maintain the state until the customer decides to make a purchase, cancel an order, or close the browser.

The following class is that of OrderFacade, the stateful session bean that maintains a visitor's shopping cart and purchases:

```java
package org.jakartaeerecipe.chapter08.session;

import java.util.concurrent.TimeUnit;
import jakarta.ejb.PostActivate;
import jakarta.ejb.PrePassivate;
import jakarta.ejb.Remove;
import jakarta.ejb.Stateful;
import jakarta.ejb.StatefulTimeout;
import org.jakartaeerecipe.chapter08.object.Cart;
@Stateful
@StatefulTimeout(unit = TimeUnit.MINUTES, value = 30)
public class OrderFacade {
    private Cart cart;
    @SuppressWarnings("unused")
    @PrePassivate
    private void prePassivate() {
        System.out.println("In PrePassivate method");
    }
    @SuppressWarnings("unused")
    @PostActivate
    private void postActivate() {
        System.out.println("In PostActivate method");
    }
    public Cart getCart() {
        if(cart == null)
            cart = new Cart();
        return cart;
    }
    public void setCart(Cart cart) {
        this.cart = cart;
    }
    public void completePurchase() {
        System.out.println("Not yet implemented..");
    }
    @Remove
    public void destroy() {
        System.out.println("Destroying OrderFacade...");
    }
}
```

A client can make calls to a stateful session bean in the same manner as with a stateless session bean (see Recipe 8-2). That is, a client can access the methods of the stateful session bean via a business interface or controller class/CDI bean. In this example, the CartController bean will access the stateful session bean. The following code for CartController demonstrates how to access the OrderFacade. The main point of access to the EJB takes place within the getCart() method:

```java
@Named(name = "cartController")    // Specifies a CDI bean
@SessionScoped                     // Specifies a session scoped bean
public class CartController implements Serializable {
    private Item currentBook = null;
    @EJB         // Injects EJB
    OrderFacade orderFacade;
    @Inject      // Injects specified CDI bean controller
    private AuthorController authorController;
    /**
     * Creates a new instance of CartController
     */
    public CartController() {
    }
    public String addToCart() {
        if (getCart().getBooks() == null) {
            getCart().addBook(getAuthorController().getCurrentBook(), 1);
        } else {
            getCart().addBook(getAuthorController().getCurrentBook(),
                    searchCart(getAuthorController().getCurrentBook().getTitle()) + 1);
        }
        FacesMessage facesMsg = new FacesMessage(FacesMessage.SEVERITY_INFO,
                "Succesfully Updated Cart", null);
        FacesContext.getCurrentInstance().addMessage(null, facesMsg);
        return null;
    }
    /**
     * Determines if a book is already in the shopping cart
     * If no book with the specified title is present, then
     * 0 is returned.
     *
     * @param title
     * @return
     */
    public int searchCart(String title) {
        int count = 0;
        for (Item item : getCart().getBooks()) {
            if (item.getBook().getTitle().equals(title)) {
                count++;
            }
        }
        return count;
    }
    public String viewCart() {
        if (getCart() == null) {
            FacesMessage facesMsg = new FacesMessage(FacesMessage.SEVERITY_INFO,
                    "No books in cart...", null);
            FacesContext.getCurrentInstance().addMessage(null, facesMsg);
        }
        return "/chapter08/cart";
    }
```

```java
    public String continueShopping() {
        return "/chapter08/book";
    }
    public String editItem(String title) {
        for (Item item : getCart().getBooks()) {
            if (item.getBook().getTitle().equals(title)) {
                currentBook = item;
            }
        }
        return "/chapter08/reviewItem";
    }
    public String updateCart(String title) {
        Item foundItem = null;
        if (currentBook.getQuantity() == 0) {
            for (Item item : getCart().getBooks()) {
                if (item.getBook().getTitle().equals(title)) {
                    foundItem = item;
                }
            }
        }
        getCart().getBooks().remove(foundItem);
        FacesMessage facesMsg = new FacesMessage(FacesMessage.SEVERITY_INFO,
                "Succesfully Updated Cart", null);
        FacesContext.getCurrentInstance().addMessage(null, facesMsg);
        return "/chapter08/cart";
    }
    /**
     * @return the cart
     */
    public Cart getCart() {
        return orderFacade.getCart();
    }
    /**
     * @return the currentBook
     */
    public Item getCurrentBook() {
        return currentBook;
    }
    /**
     * @param currentBook the currentBook to set
     */
    public void setCurrentBook(Item currentBook) {
        this.currentBook = currentBook;
    }
    public void isBookInCart(ComponentSystemEvent event) {
        UIOutput output = (UIOutput) event.getComponent();
        if (getCart() != null) {
            if (searchCart(getAuthorController().getCurrentBook().getTitle()) > 0) {
                output.setValue("This book is currently in your cart.");
            } else {
                output.setValue("This book is not in your cart.");
            }
```

```
        } else {
            output.setValue("This book is not in your cart.");
        }
    }
    public void updateRowData(RowEditEvent e) {
        System.out.println("Perform editing logic here...");
        currentBook = (Item)e.getObject();
        // Call the updateCart method, passing the title of the current book.
        updateCart(((Item)e.getObject()).getBook().getTitle());
    }
    /**
     * @return the authorController
     */
    public AuthorController getAuthorController() {
        return authorController;
    }
    /**
     * @param authorController the authorController to set
     */
    public void setAuthorController(AuthorController authorController) {
        this.authorController = authorController;
    }
}
```

How It Works

A stateful session bean is a Java class that is used to encapsulate business logic for an application. In most cases, a stateful bean has a one-to-one correspondence with an entity class, in that the bean handles all of the database calls regarding one particular entity. Programmatically, a stateful session bean is very similar to a stateless session bean in that regard. However, stateful session beans are guaranteed to maintain a conversational state with a client, whereas a stateless session bean is not. That said, the application server container handles stateful session beans differently, and they have a much different life cycle than stateless session beans. The application server container maintains a pool of the stateful session beans for client use, but there is a one-to-one mapping between a client and a bean in that when a client invokes a stateful bean, it will not release that bean back to the pool while it is still active. Therefore, stateful session beans can be less efficient than stateless, and they can take up a larger memory footprint than stateless session beans because if there are a large number of active sessions using a stateful bean, then there will be a large number of stateful beans retained in memory remaining active for those sessions.

To make a stateful session bean, the class must be designated as such by annotating it with @Stateful. The optional name parameter of the @Stateful annotation can be used to specify a string-based name for the bean. Similar to stateless session beans, a stateful session bean can implement a business interface, but as of EJB 3.1, it is not mandatory. In the example for this recipe, no business interface is used; therefore, any method within the bean that has a public modifier will be available for use by a client. Any variables that are used to store conversational state must be Java primitive types or Serializable. When an instance variable is used to store data, it will be maintained throughout the life cycle of the conversation.

Every stateful session bean must also contain a method that will be called when the bean client removes it. The state of the bean will be maintained until the @Remove method is called. The container will invoke the method annotated with @Remove when this occurs, and the bean will be removed after the @Remove method completes.

LIFE CYCLE OF STATEFUL SESSION BEANS

Stateful session beans have the following life cycle:

1. The container creates new bean instances utilizing the default constructor whenever a new client session is started.

2. Resources are injected into the bean.

3. The bean instance is stored in memory.

4. The method invoked by the client is executed.

5. The bean waits and executes any subsequent requests.

6. The bean is *passivated* or removed from active memory into temporary storage if the client remains idle for a period of time.

7. The client invocation of a passivated bean will bring it back into memory from temporary storage.

8. Failure of the client to invoke a passivated bean instance for a period of time will cause the bean to be destroyed.

9. If a client requests the removal of a bean instance, then it is activated if necessary and then destroyed.

Stateful session beans are stored in memory for a period. If the client does not request a stateful bean for use again after a period of time, then the container passivates it. Passivation is the process of taking a stateful session bean out of active memory and storing it into a temporary location on disk. The container does this by serializing the entire bean instance and moving it into permanent storage on disk. A bean is then activated later if a client invokes it, and activation is the opposite of passivation.

Another way to passivate a stateful session bean on a timed basis is by annotating the class using @StatefulTimeout. This annotation allows the developer to choose how long to maintain the state of the bean. In the case of the example for this recipe, the state is maintained for 30 minutes before the bean is passivated:

```
@StatefulTimeout(unit = TimeUnit.MINUTES, value = 30)
```

Stateful session beans have more callback methods than stateless session beans. Callback methods can be used to perform operations at a certain point in the bean's life cycle. Specifically, the following annotations can be placed before method signatures in order to mark them for execution when the given bean life-cycle event occurs: @PostConstruct, @PrePassivate, @PostActivate, and @PreDestroy. The @PostConstruct annotation denotes that the annotated method will be executed by the container as an instance is created. @PrePassivate denotes that the annotated method will be executed by the container before passivation occurs. @PostActivate denotes that the annotated method should be executed after activation or, in other words, once a bean becomes active again. Lastly, methods annotated with @PreDestroy will be executed by the container just before the bean is destroyed.

If your session bean needs the ability to retain state throughout a conversation, then you will need to make use of a stateful session bean. However, it is important to make use of stateful session beans sparingly since they are less efficient than stateless session beans and they require a larger memory footprint on the application server.

8-4. Utilizing Session Beans with Jakarta Server Faces

Problem

You want to develop a web-based client for a session bean that resides within the same container as the session bean itself.

Solution

Write a Java client and work directly with the session bean of your choice. The following code demonstrates a CDI controller that interacts directly with a stateless session bean. The Jakarta Server Faces CDI bean, named BookController, is the client class for the BookFacade session bean. You will see from the code that the bean is able to interact directly with the session bean public methods via the declaration of a property pertaining to the BookFacade class:

```
package org.jakartaeerecipe.chapter08.jsf;

import java.math.BigDecimal;
import java.util.List;
import java.util.Map;
import jakarta.ejb.EJB;
import jakarta.enterprise.context.SessionScoped;
import jakarta.inject.Inject;
import jakarta.inject.Named;
import org.jakartaeerecipe.chapter08.entity.Book;
import org.jakartaeerecipe.chapter08.entity.BookAuthor;
import org.jakartaeerecipe.chapter08.session.BookFacade;
@Named(value="bookController")
@SessionScoped
public class BookController implements java.io.Serializable {
    @EJB
    BookFacade ejbFacade;
    private List<Book> completeBookList = null;
    private List<Map> customBookList = null;
    private List<Book> booksByAuthor = null;
    private List<Book> nativeBookList = null;
    private List<Book> namedNativeBookList = null;
    @Inject
    private AuthorController authorController;
    public BookController(){
    }
    public List<Book> getCompleteBookList() {
        completeBookList = ejbFacade.findAll();
        return completeBookList;
    }
    public List<Map> getCustomBookList(){
        customBookList = ejbFacade.obtainCustomList();
        return customBookList;
    }
    public void setCompleteBookList(List<Book> completeBookList) {
        this.completeBookList = completeBookList;
    }
```

393

```java
    public String populateBookList(BigDecimal bookId){
        String returnValue = authorController.populateAuthorList(bookId);
        return returnValue;
    }
    public String findBooksByAuthor(BookAuthor author){
        setBooksByAuthor(ejbFacade.findBooksByAuthor(author));
        return "/chapter08/recipe08_2b.xhtml";
    }
    /**
     * @return the booksByAuthor
     */
    public List<Book> getBooksByAuthor() {
        return booksByAuthor;
    }
    /**
     * @param booksByAuthor the booksByAuthor to set
     */
    public void setBooksByAuthor(List<Book> booksByAuthor) {
        this.booksByAuthor = booksByAuthor;
    }
    public List<Book> getNativeBookList() {
        nativeBookList = ejbFacade.obtainNativeList();
        return nativeBookList;
    }
    /**
     * @param nativeBookList the nativeBookList to set
     */
    public void setNativeBookList(List<Book> nativeBookList) {
        this.nativeBookList = nativeBookList;
    }
    /**
     * @return the namedNativeBookList
     */
    public List<Book> getNamedNativeBookList() {
        namedNativeBookList = ejbFacade.obtainNamedNativeList();
        return namedNativeBookList;
    }
    /**
     * @param namedNativeBookList the namedNativeBookList to set
     */
    public void setNamedNativeBookList(List<Book> namedNativeBookList) {
        this.namedNativeBookList = namedNativeBookList;
    }
}
```

As you can see from the example, it is also possible for one Jakarta Server Faces CDI controller client to work with another Jakarta Server Faces CDI controller client because the BookController class declares a variable for the AuthorController CDI controller and injects it into the class. The Jakarta Server Faces view can interact directly with the methods within the bean, making it easy to form the complete cycle for a web view utilizing information from a database.

How It Works

Jakarta Enterprise Beans is the class within an application that is used to work directly with database objects. Jakarta Server Faces web views and desktop Java clients cannot work directly with Jakarta Enterprise Beans methods since they reside on the application server. For this reason, Jakarta Enterprise Beans must provide a way for clients to communicate with their methods, whether that client resides within the same container as the Jakarta Enterprise Beans itself or in a remote location.

In most Jakarta EE applications that are developed, a web framework such as Jakarta Server Faces is used to work with the Jakarta Enterprise Beans to manipulate or read data from data sources. Such clients are local to the container in which the Jakarta Enterprise Beans pools reside, and therefore they would access the Jakarta Enterprise Beans via a local business interface.

■ **Note**   At first, the concept of a local client may be difficult to understand, so I will try to explain in a bit more detail. A typical Jakarta Server Faces application utilizes local clients, those being Contexts and Dependency Injection (CDI) controller classes, to work directly with the Jakarta Enterprise Beans. Although the user of the web application is sitting in a remote location from the Jakarta Enterprise Beans server container, they are working with HTML pages that are generated by Jakarta Server Faces views within a browser, and those views interact directly with the controllers. It is almost as if the views are bound directly to the controllers, which usually reside within the same container as the Jakarta Enterprise Beans. Figure 8-1 shows how this relationship works.

Figure 8-1. *HTML client (Jakarta Server Faces view) to Jakarta Enterprise Beans relationship*

Since EJB 3.1+, it has been possible for local clients to utilize "no-interface" business views for access to public Jakarta Enterprise Beans methods, thereby alleviating the need for the Jakarta Enterprise Beans to implement an interface. Using the no-interface view technique enables developers to be more productive because there is one less Java file to maintain (no interface needed), and the workflow becomes easier to understand since the local client can interact directly with the Jakarta Enterprise Beans, rather than via an interface. Remote clients, such as Java classes running in a remote application server container, cannot use the no-interface view, and therefore a @Remote business interface is still needed in such situations.

The solution demonstrates the use of the no-interface view to allow Jakarta Server Faces CDI controllers to work with publicly declared Jakarta Enterprise Beans methods. To obtain a reference to the no-interface view of an EJB through dependency injection, use the jakarta.naming.EJB annotation, along with a declaration of the enterprise bean's implementation class. The following code excerpt taken from the CDI controller in the solution demonstrates the dependency injection technique:

```
@EJB
BookFacade ejbFacade;
```

It is possible to use JNDI to perform a lookup on the Jakarta Enterprise Beans rather than using dependency injection, although such situations are rarely required. To do so, use the `jakarta.naming.` `InitialContext` interface's lookup method in order to perform the JNDI lookup as follows:

```
BookFacade ejbFacade = (BookFacade)
        InitialContext.lookup("java:module/BookFacade");
```

■ **Note** Enterprise Jakarta Beans allows developers to focus on application features rather than worry about life-cycle and resource handling. The container manages the life cycle and resources.

8-5. Persisting an Object

Problem

You want to persist an object in your Java enterprise application. In other words, you want to create a new database record within one of the database tables used by your application.

Solution

Create an `EntityManager` object using one of the solutions provided in Recipe 8-1, and then call its `persist()` method, passing the object you want to persist. The following lines of code demonstrate how to persist an object to the database using an `EntityManager`. In this case, a `Book` object is being persisted into the `BOOK` database table. This excerpt is taken from the `BookFacade` session bean:

```
...
@PersistenceContext(unitName = "JakartaEERecipes")
    private EntityManager em;
...
em.persist(book);
...
```

How It Works

The persistence of entity objects takes place within Jakarta Enterprise Beans classes. To persist an object to the underlying data store and manage it, call the `EntityManager` object's `persist()` method. You must pass a valid entity object to the `persist()` method, and the object should not yet exist in the database, meaning that it must have a unique primary key.

A few different exceptions may be thrown when working with the `persist()` method that will help you determine what issues are occurring. The `EntityExistsException` is self-explanatory, and it is thrown if the primary key for the entity that you are persisting already exists. However, in some cases a `PersistenceException` will be thrown instead at flush or commit time, so you should catch each of these exceptions when issuing a call to persist. If the object that you are trying to persist is not an entity, then the `IllegalArgumentException` will be thrown. Lastly, the `TransactionRequiredException` will be thrown if invoked on a container-managed entity manager of type `PersistenceContextType.TRANSACTION` and there is no transaction made.

8-6. Updating an Object

Problem

The contents of an entity object have been changed, and you want to persist the updates to the underlying data source.

Solution

Create an EntityManager object using one of the solutions provided in Recipe 8-1, and then call the EntityManager object's merge() method, passing a populated entity object that you want to update. The following lines of code demonstrate how to persist an object to the database using an EntityManager. In this case, a Book object is being updated in the BOOK database table. This excerpt is taken from the BookFacade session bean:

```
...
@PersistenceContext(unitName = "JakartaEERecipes")
    private EntityManager em;
...
em.merge(book);
...
```

▓ **Note** If the entity object (database record) being persisted does not already exist within the table, it will be stored as a newly persisted object rather than updated.

How It Works

The code implementation that is responsible for updating entity objects within the underlying data store resides within Jakarta Enterprise Beans classes. A valid EntityManager object must be available for use, and then the EntityManager's merge() method can be called, passing a valid entity object for update within the underlying data store. When this is done, the state of the entity object will be merged into the data store, and the underlying data will be updated accordingly.

Two possible exceptions may be thrown when attempting to merge data. An IllegalArgumentException may be thrown if the instance being merged is not an entity (the database table does not exist) or is a removed entity. A TransactionRequiredException may be thrown if the merge() method is invoked on a container-managed entity manager of type PersistenceContextType.TRANSACTION and there is no transaction.

8-7. Returning Data to Display in a Table

Problem

You want to display the contents of a database table via a Jakarta Server Faces dataTable.

Solution #1

Return a List of entity objects from the underlying table containing the contents you want to display. Map a Jakarta Server Faces dataTable component value to a Contexts and Dependency Injection (CDI) controller property that contains a List of objects. In this case, the controller property would be the List of the entity objects corresponding to the database table. Within the CDI controller, the List of entity objects can be obtained via a Jakarta Enterprise Beans call.

The following code excerpt is taken from the controller named BookController. The CDI controller property named completeBookList will be referenced from a dataTable component within a Jakarta Server Faces view, displaying the data from the underlying table:

```
@Named(value="bookController")
@SessionScoped
public class BookController implements java.io.Serializable {
    @EJB
    BookFacade ejbFacade;
    private List<Book> completeBookList;
    @Inject
    private AuthorController authorController;
...
    public List<Book> getCompleteBookList() {
        completeBookList = ejbFacade.findAll();
        return completeBookList;
    }
    public void setCompleteBookList(List<Book> completeBookList) {
        this.completeBookList = completeBookList;
    }
...
}
```

Next, let's look at an excerpt from the Jakarta Enterprise Beans named BookFacade. It is a stateless session bean that contains the method, which is invoked by the BookController in order to obtain the List of entity objects.

■ **Note** The findAll() method that is called by BookController is inherited from the AbstractFacade class.

```
...
@Stateless
public class BookFacade extends AbstractFacade<Book> {
    @PersistenceContext(unitName = "JakartaEERecipes")
    private EntityManager em;
    @Override
    protected EntityManager getEntityManager() {
        return em;
    }
    public BookFacade() {
        super(Book.class);
    }
...
```

In the AbstractFacade, the findAll() method is implemented in a generic manner:

```
public abstract class AbstractFacade<T> {
    private Class<T> entityClass;
    public AbstractFacade(Class<T> entityClass) {
        this.entityClass = entityClass;
    }
    protected abstract EntityManager getEntityManager();
    public List<T> findAll() {
        jakarta.persistence.criteria.CriteriaQuery cq = getEntityManager().
        getCriteriaBuilder().createQuery();
        Root<T> root = cq.from(entityClass);
        cq.select(root);
        return getEntityManager().createQuery(cq).getResultList();
    }
...
}
```

The List<Book> is returned from the findAll() method in the Jakarta Enterprise Beans, which is contained within the AbstractFacade abstract class. This list is used to populate the completeBookList property within the BookController. Since the BookController communicates directly with the view layer, the Jakarta Server Faces view will be able to utilize the completeBookList property to display the data.

Solution #2

Return a List of Map objects containing the results of a native SQL query against the underlying table. The Jakarta Server Faces CDI controller can contain a property that is a List of Map objects, and it can be referenced from within a Jakarta Server Faces dataTable component. In this case, the Jakarta Enterprise Beans method that is invoked by the controller will make a native SQL query against the database, returning certain columns of data from the table and populating map objects with those column values.

In the following excerpt, the BookController.getCustomBookList() method populates a CDI controller property named customBookList via a call to the Jakarta Enterprise Beans method named obtainCustomList. Excerpts including both of these methods are shown next.

Here's the excerpt from org.jakartaeerecipe.chapter08.BookController:

```
...
public List<Map> getCustomBookList(){
        customBookList = ejbFacade.obtainCustomList();
        return customBookList;
    }
...
```

Here are the excerpts from org.jakartaeerecipe.chapter08.session.BookFacade:

```
...
    protected EntityManager getEntityManager() {
        return em;
    }
...
public List<Map> obtainCustomList(){
        List<Object[]> results = em.createNativeQuery(
```

```
                "select id, title, description " +
                "FROM BOOK " +
                " ORDER BY id").getResultList();
        List data = new ArrayList<HashMap>();
        if (!results.isEmpty()) {
            for (Object[] result : results) {
                HashMap resultMap = new HashMap();
                resultMap.put("id", result[0]);
                resultMap.put("title", result[1]);
                resultMap.put("description", result[2]);
                data.add(resultMap);
            }
        }
        return data;
    }
```

The `customBookList` property of the `BookController` class is populated by the EJB method, making the data available to the view.

How It Works

One of the most often required tasks of a web application is to display content. What's more, displaying database content is key to just about every enterprise application. Displaying content in table format provides the user with the ability to see the data because it is stored within the underlying table, in columnar format. The Jakarta Server Faces `dataTable` component provides Jakarta EE applications utilizing the Jakarta Server Faces framework with an efficient and powerful way to display entity data in a table format.

The Jakarta Server Faces `dataTable` component can take a `List`, `DataModel`, or `Collection` of objects and display them to the user. This recipe covers two different variations of retrieving data and storing it within a `List` for use in a `dataTable` component. The first solution is the most common situation. In both solutions, a CDI controller property is used to store the `List` of entity objects. However, the first solution stores a `List` of entity objects themselves, whereas the second solution stores a `List` of `Map` objects. Let's walk through each a little more closely.

In Solution #1 to this recipe, the `completeBookList` field within the `BookController` CDI controller class is used to store the `List` of Book entities. The `getCompleteBookList()` method populates the `List` by invoking the `BookFacade` session bean's `findAll()` method to return all of the rows within the BOOK database table. Each database row is stored in a separate Book entity object, and, in turn, each Book entity object is stored in the `List`. Finally, that list is returned to the `BookController` and assigned to the `completeBookList` field. In the end, the Jakarta Server Faces `dataTable` component references the `completeBookList` to display the content.

In Solution #2, the `BookController` field named `customBookList` is used to populate a Jakarta Server Faces `dataTable`. The `customBookList` field is a `List` of `Map` objects. As far as the `BookController` method of population goes, the `customBookList` field is populated in much the same manner as the `completeBookList` in Solution #1. A Jakarta Enterprise Beans method is called, which returns the populated `List` of objects. In this case, the Jakarta Enterprise Beans named `BookFacade` returns a `List` of `Map` objects from a native SQL query. The `BookFacade` session bean class method `obtainCustomList` is responsible for creating the native SQL query and then storing the results within `Map` objects. In this case, the native query returns only a subset of the columns that are present within the BOOK database table in each row as a `resultList` and stores them into a `List<Object[]>`. A new `ArrayList` of `HashMaps` is then created and populated with the contents of the List from the database query. To populate the `ArrayList`, the `List<Object[]>` is traversed using a for loop. A `HashMap` object is created for each object that is returned from the database. The `HashMap` object is populated with name-value pairs, with the name of the column being the first part and the value from the entity object being the second part in each element. Each column that was retrieved via the query is stored into the HashMap, and the HashMap itself is then added to a List. In the end, the List of HashMap objects is returned to the CDI controller and stored into the customBookList field. In the Jakarta Server Faces view, the names that were associated with each of the database columns in the HashMap are used to reference the values for display within the dataTable.

Both solutions showcased in this recipe offer valid options for displaying data from the database, which uses Jakarta Persistence within a Jakarta Server Faces dataTable component. I recommend using the first solution where possible because it is less error-prone than Solution #2, which will require manual mapping of the database columns to Map indices. There is also native SQL hard-coded into the Jakarta Enterprise Beans for Solution #2, which is OK when necessary but never the best option. It is always much better when you can utilize a Jakarta Enterprise Beans method, such as the findAll() method that is available in AbstractFacade (Recipe 8-2), because if the underlying database table changes, then there is no need to alter the application code.

8-8. Creating a Singleton Bean

Problem

You want to develop a session bean in which all application clients will use the same. Only one instance of the bean should be allowed per application so that there is always a single site visitor counter for the number of visitors.

■ **Note** In this recipe, the counter is not cumulative. That is, it is not persisted across application startups. To create a cumulative counter, the current count must be persisted to the database before the application or server is restarted and restored when the application is resumed.

Solution

Develop a singleton session bean that allows concurrent access by all application clients. The bean will keep track of the number of visitors who have been to the bookstore and display the number within the footer of the Acme Bookstore application. The following bean named BookstoreSessionCounter is a singleton session bean for the Acme Bookstore that is responsible for keeping track of an active session count:

```
package org.jakartaeerecipe.chapter08.session;
import jakarta.ejb.Singleton;
import jakarta.ejb.ConcurrencyManagement;
import static jakarta.ejb.ConcurrencyManagementType.CONTAINER;
@Singleton
@ConcurrencyManagement(CONTAINER)
public class BookstoreSessionCounter {
    private int numberOfSessions;
    /**
     * Initialize the Bean
     */
    @PostConstruct
    public void init(){
        // Initialize bean here
        System.out.println("Initalizing bean...");
    }
```

```
    // Resets the counter on application startup
    public BookstoreSessionCounter(){
        numberOfSessions = 0;
    }
    /**
     * @return the numberOfSessions
     */
    public int getNumberOfSessions() {
        numberOfSessions++;
        return numberOfSessions;
    }
    /**
     * @param numberOfSessions the numberOfSessions to set.  This could be set
 *  from the database if the current counter were persisted before the application
 *  was shutdown
     */
    public void setNumberOfSessions(int numberOfSessions) {
        this.numberOfSessions = numberOfSessions;
    }
}
```

Next, let's look at the Jakarta Server Faces CDI controller that invokes the singleton session bean method for updating the site counter. The following excerpt is taken from a session-scoped CDI controller named BookstoreSessionController, and the counter property is used to update the number of visitors within the Jakarta Enterprise Beans:

```
...
@Named("bookstoreSessionController")
@SessionScoped
public class BookstoreSessionController {
    @EJB
    BookstoreSessionCounter bookstoreSessionCounter;
    private int counter;
    private boolean flag = false;
    /**
     * @return the counter
     */
    public int getCounter() {
        if (!flag) {
            counter = bookstoreSessionCounter.getNumberOfSessions();
            flag = true;
        }
        return counter;
    }
    /**
     * @param counter the counter to set
     */
    public void setCounter(int counter) {
        this.counter = counter;
    }
}
```

Lastly, the counter is bound to a Jakarta expression within the Acme Bookstore Facelets template. The following line of code is excerpted from the template named `custom_template_search.xhtml`, which resides in the `chapter08/layout` directory of the book sources:

```
Number of Visitors: #{bookstoreSessionController.counter}
```

How It Works

A class that is specified as a singleton is created once per application. There is only one instance of a singleton class at any given time, and all client sessions interact with that same instance. To generate a singleton session bean, denote a bean as such by specifying the `jakarta.ejb.Singleton` annotation. Programmatically, the annotation specification is one of the main differences between the coding of a standard stateless session bean and a singleton session bean. However, functionally, the bean is treated much different by the container than a standard stateless session bean.

Singleton session beans are instantiated by the container at an arbitrary point in time. To force the instantiation of a singleton instance at application startup, the `jakarta.ejb.Startup` annotation can be specified. In the case of the example, there is no `@Startup` annotation specified, so the singleton instance could be instantiated by the container at any given point. However, a singleton will be started up before any of the application Jakarta Enterprise Beans begin to receive requests. In the example, you can see that the `@PostConstruct` callback annotation is being used. This causes the method on which the annotation is specified to be executed directly after instantiation of the bean. Singletons share the same callback methodology as standard stateless session beans. To read more about callback methods, please refer to Recipe 8-2.

■ **Note** If one or more singleton beans depend upon other singleton beans for initialization, the `@DependsOn` annotation can be specified for the bean to denote which bean it depends upon. A chain of dependencies can be set up using this annotation if needed.

By default, singletons are concurrent, meaning that multiple clients can access them at the same time (also known as *thread-safe*). There are two different ways in which to control concurrent access to singleton beans. The `@ConcurrencyManagement` annotation can be specified along with a given `ConcurrentManagementType` in order to tell the bean which type of concurrency to use. The two types of concurrency are `CONTAINER`, which is the default type if nothing is specified, and `BEAN`. In the example, the bean is annotated to specify container-managed concurrency. When container-managed concurrency is specified, the Jakarta Enterprise Beans container manages the concurrency. The `@Lock` annotation can be specified on methods of the singleton to tell the container how client access should be managed on the method. To use the `@Lock` annotation, specify a lock type of `LockType.READ` or `LockType.WRITE` (default) within the annotation to tell the container that many clients can access the annotated method concurrently or that the method should become locked to others when a client is accessing it. The entire class can also be annotated with @Lock, in which case the designated lock type will be used for each of the methods within the class unless they contain their own lock type designation. For example, the following lines specify a method within a singleton class that should be locked when accessed by a client so that only one client at a time has access:

```
@Lock(LockType.WRITE)
public void setCounter(int counter){
    this.counter = counter;
}
```

Bean concurrency is different in that it allows full concurrent, thread-safe locking access to all clients on all methods within the class. The developer can use Java synchronization techniques such as synchronized and volatile to help manage the state of concurrency within those singletons designated with bean-managed concurrency.

8-9. Scheduling a Timer Service

Problem

You want to schedule a task that performs database transactions on a recurring interval.

Solution #1

Use the Timer service to schedule a task within a bean using an automatic timer. The timer will specify a required interval of time, and the method used to perform the task will be invoked each time the interval of time expires. The following session bean is set up to create an automatic timer, which will begin upon application deployment. The following code is contained within the Java file named org.jakartaeerecipe. chapter08.timer.TimerBean:

```
import jakarta.ejb.Singleton;
import jakarta.ejb.Schedule;

@Singleton
public class TimerBean {
@Schedule(minute="*/5", hour="*")
    public void automaticTimer(){
        System.out.println("*** Automatic Timeout Occurred ***");
    }
}
```

The automatic timer will begin when the class is deployed to the application server and the application server starts. Every five minutes, the automaticTimer() method will be invoked as will any processes that are performed within that method.

Solution #2

Create a programmatic timer and specify it to start when it is deployed to the application server. Configure an initialization method within the timer bean that will create the timer automatically when the bean is initialized. The following example class is named org.jakartaeerecipe.chapter08.timer. ProgrammaticTimerExample, and it will be automatically started when the application is deployed:

```
package org.jakartaeerecipe.chapter08.timer;
import jakarta.annotation.PostConstruct;
import jakarta.annotation.Resource;
import jakarta.ejb.Singleton;
import jakarta.ejb.Timer;
import jakarta.ejb.Timeout;
import jakarta.ejb.TimerService;
@Singleton
@Startup
```

```
public class ProgrammaticTimerExample {
    @Resource
    TimerService timerService;
    @PostConstruct
    public void createTimer(){
        System.out.println("Creating Timer...");
        Timer timer = timerService.createTimer(100000, "Timer has been created...");
    }
    @Timeout
    public void timeout(Timer timer){
        System.out.println("Timeout of Programmatic Timer Example...");
    }
}
```

After deployment, you should see a message in the server log indicating Creating Timer..., and then once the timer expires, the Timeout of Programmatic Timer Example... message will be displayed in the logs.

How It Works

Timer solutions make it easy to incorporate scheduled or timed tasks into an application process. The Timer service helps make such solutions possible because it offers applications a method for scheduling tasks that will be performed by the application over a specified interval of time. There are two different types of timers: programmatic and automatic. In Solution #1 to this recipe, an automatic timer is demonstrated. Although the solution does not perform any actual work, the method annotated with the @Schedule annotation is where the work takes place. An automatic timer is created when a Jakarta Enterprise Beans contains one or more methods that are annotated with @Schedule or @Schedules. The @Schedule takes a calendar-based timer expression to indicate when the annotated method should be executed.

■ **Note**   One or more @Schedule annotations can be grouped within @Scheduled{ ... }, separating each @Schedule with a comma.

Calendar-based timer expressions can contain one or more calendar attributes paired with values to indicate a point in time for invocation of the method. Table 8-1 lists the different calendar-based timer expressions, along with a description of each.

Table 8-1. *Calendar-Based Timer Expressions*

Attribute	Description
dayOfWeek	One or more days in a week: (0–7) or (Sun, Mon, Tue, Wed, Thu, Fri, Sat)
dayOfMonth	One or more days in a month: (1–31) or (Last) or (1st, 2nd, 3rd, 4th, 5th, Last) along with any of the dayOfWeek values
month	One or more months in a year: (1–12) or month abbreviation
year	Four-digit calendar year
hour	One or more hours within a day: (0–23)
minute	One or more minutes within an hour: (0–59)
second	One or more seconds within a minute: (0–59)

When creating a calendar-based timer expression, the asterisk (*) can be specified as a wildcard. The forward slash (/) can be used to indicate an interval in time. An interval in time follows this pattern:

```
beginning time (larger unit) / frequency
```

Therefore, specifying /5 in the example (minute="*/5" hour="*") indicates that you want the timer to be executed every five minutes within the hour because the wildcard indicates which hour to begin the timer and the 5 indicates how often.

Timer expression attributes can contain more than one value, and a comma should separate each value. To indicate that you want to execute a timer at 3:00 a.m. and again at 6:00 a.m., you could write the following:

```
@Schedule(hour="3,6")
```

A range of values can also be specified for timer attributes. To indicate that you want to have the timer executed every hour between the hours of 4:00 and 7:00 a.m., you could specify the following:

```
@Schedule(hour"4-7")
```

Multiple timer expressions can be combined to tune the timer in a more fine-grained fashion. For instance, to specify a timer schedule that will execute at 1:00 a.m. every Sunday morning, you could write the following:

```
@Schedule(dayOfWeek="Sun", hour="1")
```

Programmatic timers are the second option that can be used when developing a timed process, as demonstrated in Solution #2. A programmatic timer is different from an automatic timer because there is no schedule involved. Rather, a client can invoke a timer, or it can be initialized with the construction of a bean. A programmatic timer contains one method that is denoted using the @Timeout annotation. The @Timeout method will be executed when the timer expires. The timeout method must return void, and it can optionally accept a jakarta.ejb.Timer object. A timeout method must not throw an application exception.

To create a programmatic timer, invoke one of the create methods of the TimerService interface. Table 8-2 indicates the different create methods that can be used.

Table 8-2. *Programmatic Timer Create Methods*

Method	Description
createTimer	Standard timer creation
createSingleActionTimer	Creates a timer that expires once
createIntervalTimer	Creates a timer that expires based upon a given time interval
createCalendarTimer	Creates a timer based upon a calendar

In Solution #2 of this recipe, a standard timer is created, passing an interval of 100,000 milliseconds. This means that the method annotated with @Timeout will be executed once after 100,000 milliseconds has passed. The following is another syntax that could be used to create a timer that has the same schedule:

```
long duration = 100000;
Timer timer = timerService.createSingleActionTimer(duration, new TimerConfig());
```

Similarly, a date can be passed to the create method in order to specify a given date and time when the timer should expire. The following timer will expire 30 days from the date on which the application is deployed:

```
Calendar cal = Calendar.getInstance();
cal.add(Calendar.DATE, 30);
Timer timer = timerService.createSingleActionTimer(cal.getTime(), new TimerConfig());
```

To create a programmatic calendar-based timer, you must create a new schedule using the ScheduleExpression helper class. Doing so will allow you to utilize the calendar-based expressions that are listed in Table 8-1 to specify the timer expiration date. The following example demonstrates a timer that will expire every Sunday at 1:00 a.m. by the application server clock:

```
ScheduleExpression schedule = new ScheduleExpression();
schedule.dayOfWeek("Sun");
schedule.hour("1");
Timer timer = timerService.createCalendarTimer(schedule);
```

Timers do not need to be created in singleton session beans; they can be used in stateless session beans as well.

▪ **Note**   Timers cannot be specified in stateful session beans.

Timers are a topic that cannot be discussed within the boundaries of a single recipe. However, this brief introduction to timers should give you enough to get started using this technology within your applications. To learn more about timers, please refer to the online documentation at https://eclipse-ee4j.github. io/jakartaee-tutorial/#using-the-timer-service.

▪ **Note**   All timers are persistent by default, meaning that if the server is shut down for some reason, the timer will become active again when the server is restarted. If a timer should expire while the server is down, the timer will expire (or the @Timeout method will be called) once the server is functioning normally again. To indicate that a timer should not be persistent, call TimerConfig.setPersistent(false), and pass it to a timer creation method.

8-10. Performing Optional Transaction Life-Cycle Callbacks

Problem

You are interested in beginning a transaction when a bean is instantiated and ending the transaction when it is destroyed.

Solution

Choose to utilize the optional transaction life-cycle callbacks built into Jakarta Enterprise Beans. To begin a transaction during the @PostConstruct or @PreDestroy callbacks, annotate the methods accordingly with @TransactionAttribute, passing the TransactionAttributeType.REQUIRES_NEW attribute. In the following example, a transaction is started when the bean named AcmeFacade is created. Another transaction is started when the bean is being destroyed:

```
import jakarta.annotation.PostConstruct;
import jakarta.annotation.PreDestroy;
import jakarta.ejb.Stateful;
import jakarta.ejb.TransactionAttribute;
import jakarta.ejb.TransactionAttributeType;
import jakarta.persistence.EntityManager;
import jakarta.persistence.PersistenceContext;
import jakarta.persistence.PersistenceContextType;
@Stateful
public class AcmeFacade {
    @PersistenceContext(unitName = "JakartaEERecipesPU", type = PersistenceContextType.
    EXTENDED)
    private EntityManager em;
    @TransactionAttribute(TransactionAttributeType.REQUIRES_NEW)
    @PostConstruct
    public void init() {
        System.out.println("The Acme Bean has been created");
    }
    @TransactionAttribute(TransactionAttributeType.REQUIRES_NEW)
    @PreDestroy
    public void destroy() {
        System.out.println("The Acme Bean is being destroyed...");
        em.flush();
    }
}
```

How It Works

Session beans can contain callback methods that are invoked when certain stages of a bean's life cycle occur. For instance, a method can be registered within a session bean via annotation to invoke after the bean is constructed (@PostConstruct), before it is destroyed (@PreDestroy), and so on. Sometimes, it makes sense to start a new transaction when one of these events occurs. It is possible to specify the transactional status of an annotated life-cycle callback method within a session bean when using container-managed transactions.

The annotation accepts a transaction type as per the values listed in Table 8-3.

Table 8-3. *Container-Managed Transaction Demarcation*

Attribute	Description
MANDATORY	The container must invoke an enterprise bean method whose transaction is set to this attribute in the client's transaction context. The client is required to call with a transaction context
REQUIRED	The container must invoke an enterprise bean method whose transaction is set to this attribute in the client's transaction context. The client is required to call with a transaction context. If the client invokes the enterprise bean's method while the client is not associated with a transaction context, the container automatically starts a new transaction before delegating the method call to the enterprise bean method
REQUIRES_NEW	The container must invoke an enterprise bean method whose transaction is set to this attribute value with a new transaction context
SUPPORTS	If the client calls with a transaction context, then the container treats it as REQUIRED. If the client calls without a transaction context, the container treats it as NOT_SUPPORTED
NOT_SUPPORTED	The container invokes an enterprise bean method whose transaction attribute is set to this value with an unspecified transaction context
NEVER	The container invokes an enterprise bean method whose transaction is set to this value without a transaction context defined by the Jakarta Enterprise Beans specification

By default, the life-cycle callback methods are not transactional to maintain backward compatibility. By annotating the callback method with the @TransactionAttribute and the preferred demarcation type, the callback method has opted in to be transactional.

8-11. Ensuring a Stateful Session Bean Is Not Passivated

Problem

Rather than have your inactive stateful session bean passivated, you want to keep it in memory.

Solution

Specify to the container that the bean is not to be passivated by indicating as such within the @Stateful annotation. To opt out of passivation, set the passivationCapable attribute of the @Stateful annotation to false, as demonstrated in the following excerpt:

```
@Stateful(passivationCapable=false)
public class AcmeFacade {
    ...
}
```

How It Works

When a stateful session bean has been inactive for a period of time, the container may choose to passivate the bean in an effort to conserve memory and resources. Typically, the Jakarta Enterprise Beans container will passivate stateful session beans using a least recently used algorithm. When passivation occurs, the bean is moved to secondary storage and removed from memory. Prior to the passivation of a stateful session bean, any methods annotated with @PrePassivate will be invoked. When a stateful session bean that has been passivated needs to be made active again, the container activates the bean, then calls any methods annotated with @PostActivate, and finally moves the bean to the ready stage.

The stateful session beans can opt out of passivation so that they will remain in memory instead of being transferred to secondary storage if inactive. This may be helpful in situations where a bean needs to remain active for application processes or if the bean contains a nonserializable field, since these fields cannot be passivated and are made null upon passivation. To indicate that a bean is not to be passivated, set the passivationCapable attribute of the @Stateful annotation to false, as per the solution to this recipe.

8-12. Denoting Local and Remote Interfaces

Problem

You want to explicitly designate a local or remote interface for an EJB.

Solution

A business interface cannot be declared as both a local and remote business interface for a bean. Therefore, the Jakarta Enterprise Beans specification contains an API to specify whether a business interface is intended as local or remote. The following rules pertain to business interfaces implemented by enterprise bean classes:

The java.io.Serializable, java.io.Externalizable, and interfaces defined by the package are always excluded when determination of local or remote business interfaces is declared for a bean.

If a bean class contains the @Remote annotation, then all implemented interfaces are assumed to be remote.

If a bean class contains no annotation or if the @Local annotation is specified, then all implemented interfaces are assumed to be local.

Any business interface that is explicitly defined for a bean that contains the no-interface view must be designated as @Local.

Any business interface must be explicitly designated as local or remote if the bean class explicitly specifies the @Local or @Remote annotation with a nonempty value.

Any business interface must be explicitly designated as local or remote if the deployment descriptor specifies as such.

How It Works

The no-interface view greatly simplified development because it made the making of the local business interfaces optional. The no-interface view automatically exposes all public methods of a bean to the caller. By default, a no-interface view is automatically exposed by any session bean that does not include an implements clause and has no local or remote client views defined. Through Jakarta Enterprise Beans, you can provide further granularity for those situations where local and remote interfaces need to be explicitly specified.

Let's break down the rules that were defined within the solution to this recipe. First, if an EJB exposes local interfaces, then there is no need to explicitly denote a bean as such. For instance, the following bean contains a local interface, although it is not explicitly denoted:

```
@Stateless
public class AcmeSession implements interfaceA {
    ...
}
public interfaceA { ... }
```

If a bean class is annotated with @Remote, then any interfaces that it implements are assumed to be remote. For instance, the following bean class implements two interfaces, and both are assumed to be remote, although they do not contain any annotation to indicate as such:

```
@Remote
@Stateless
public class AcmeSession implements interfaceA, interfaceB {
    ...
}
```

If a bean class contains the @Local annotation, then any interfaces that it implements are assumed to be local. For instance, the following bean class implements two interfaces, and both are assumed to be local although they do not contain any annotation to indicate as such:

```
@Local
@Stateless
public class AcmeSession implements interfaceA, interfaceB {
    ...
}
```

If a bean class contains the @Local or @Remote annotation and specifies an interface name within the annotation, then the same designation is applied as the annotation specifies. For instance, the following bean is annotated to include a local business interface, and the name of the interface is specified in the annotation, thereby making the interface local:

```
@Local(interfaceA.class)
@Stateless
public class AcmeSession implements interfaceA {
    ...
}
```

These new designation rules make it easier to designate and determine the type of business interface that is implemented by a bean.

8-13. Processing Messages Asynchronously from Enterprise Beans

Problem

You want to have the ability to process messages from session beans in an asynchronous manner.

Solution

Develop a message-driven bean to perform the message processing for your application. To develop a message bean, create a Jakarta Enterprise Beans that is annotated with @MessageDriven, passing the appropriate configuration options. In the bean, code a method named onMessage that will perform all of the message processing. The following example, org.jakartaeerecipe.chapter08.jsf.AcmeMessageBean, demonstrates how to code a message-driven bean that processes messages from a jakarta.jms.Queue that has been configured within the application server container:

■ **Note**   Prior to running these examples, you must create the JMS resources within GlassFish. Please refer to Recipe 12-1 for more details.

```
@MessageDriven(mappedName="jms/Queue", activationConfig = {
    @ActivationConfigProperty(propertyName = "destinationType",
                              propertyValue = "jakarta.jms.Queue")
})
public class AcmeMessageBean implements MessageListener {
    public AcmeMessageBean(){
    }
    @Override
    public void onMessage(Message msg) {
        if(msg != null){
            performExtraProcessing();
            System.out.println("Message has been received: " + msg);
        } else {
            System.out.println("No message received");
        }
    }
    public void performExtraProcessing(){
        System.out.println("This method could perform extra processing");
    }
}
```

How It Works

Message-driven beans are Enterprise Jakarta Beans that are utilized for processing messages in an asynchronous manner. Most often, message-driven beans are Jakarta Messaging listeners, receiving messages and processing accordingly. A message-driven bean is created by annotating a bean with the @MessageDriven annotation and optionally implementing the MessageListener interface. When a message is received in the container queue, the container invokes the bean's onMessage() method, which contains the business logic that is responsible for processing the message accordingly.

■ **Note** Any session bean can be used for processing messages, but only message-driven beans can do so in an asynchronous manner.

Message-driven beans must be made public, and not static or final. A message-driven bean must contain a public, no-argument constructor, and it must contain a method named onMessage that accepts a jakarta.jms.Message argument. The onMessage method is responsible for performing all message processing, and it can utilize other methods within the bean to help out, where needed.

Bean providers may provide special configurations for message-driven beans to the deployers, such as information regarding message selectors, acknowledgment modes, and so on, by means of the activationConfig element of the @MessageDriven annotation. A standard list of activationConfig properties exists to provide JMS 2.0 alignment. Table 8-4 lists the new properties along with a description of what they do.

Table 8-4. *Jakarta Messaging Aligned activationConfig Properties*

Property	Description ·
destinationLookup	Provides advice to the deployer regarding whether the message-driven bean is intended to be associated with a Queue or Topic. Values for this property are jakarta.jms.Queue and jakarta.jms.Topic
connectionFactoryLookup	Specifies the lookup name of an administratively defined ConnectionFactory object that will be used for a connection to the Jakarta Messaging provider from which a message-driven bean will send messages
clientId	Specifies the client identifier that will be used for a connection to the Jakarta Messaging provider from which a message-driven bean will send messages
subscriptionName	If the message-driven bean is intended to be used with a Topic, then the bean provider can specify the name of a durable subscription with this property and set the subscriptionDurability property to Durable
shareSubscriptions	This property is only to be used when a message-driven bean is deployed to a clustered application server, and the value for this property can be either true or false. A value of true means that the same durable subscription name or nondurable subscription will be used for each instance in the cluster. A value of false means that a different durable subscription name or nondurable subscription will be used for each instance in the cluster

To execute the code in the recipe, visit the page `http://localhost:8080/JakartaEERecipes_Chapter08-1.0-SNAPSHOT/chapter08/recipe08_13.xhtml`. Clicking the "Send Message" button should show the output as in Figure 8-2, and log messages would also appear in the GlassFish server log.

Figure 8-2. *Output of Recipe 8-13*

CHAPTER 9

Jakarta Persistence Query Language

The Jakarta Persistence API utilizes a query language for communicating with underlying data stores. Although Jakarta EE uses entities rather than SQL for database access, it provides a query language so that developers can obtain the required information via the entities. The Jakarta Persistence Query Language does just that because it provides a facility for querying and working with Jakarta EE entity objects. Although it is very similar to SQL, it is an object-relational query language, so there are some minor differences of which developers should be aware. Using the Jakarta Persistence Query Language along with Jakarta EE entities allows developers to create versatile applications because it is not database specific, and applications can be written once and deployed to run on top of a myriad of databases.

The recipes in this chapter will not attempt to cover all the features that the Jakarta Persistence Query Language has to offer because there are many. However, the recipes contain enough information to introduce beginners to the world of the Jakarta Persistence Query Language and to get intermediate developers up to date with the latest that the Jakarta Persistence Query Language has to offer. To review the entire set of documentation for using the Jakarta Persistence Query Language, please see the online resources available at `https://projects.eclipse.org/projects/ee4j.jpa`.

9-1. Querying All Instances of an Entity

Problem

You want to retrieve all the instances for a particular entity. That is, you want to query the underlying database table associated with the entity and retrieve all rows.

Solution

Call the `EntityManager`'s `createQuery` method and use the Jakarta Persistence Query Language to formulate a query that will return all instances of a given entity. In the following example, a Jakarta Persistence Query Language query is used to return all objects within the `BookAuthor` entity:

```
public List<BookAuthor> findAuthor(){
        return em.createQuery("select object(o) from BookAuthor o").getResultList();
}
```

© Josh Juneau and Tarun Telang 2022
J. Juneau and T. Telang, *Java EE to Jakarta EE 10 Recipes*, https://doi.org/10.1007/978-1-4842-8079-9_9

When the findAuthor() method is called, a List containing all of the BookAuthor entity instances in the entity (all records in the underlying database table) will be returned. The code for this recipe can be executed by visiting the URL http://localhost:8080/JakartaEERecipes_Chapter08-1.0-SNAPSHOT/chapter09/recipe09_01.xhtml, and the output would be as shown in Figure 9-1.

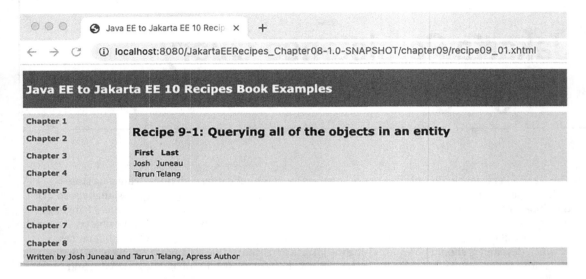

Figure 9-1. *Output of Recipe 9-1*

How It Works

An entity instance can be referred to as a *record* in the underlying data store. That is, there is an entity instance for each record within a given database table. That said, sometimes it is handy to retrieve all of the instances for a given entity. Some applications may require all objects in order to perform a particular task against each, or perhaps your application needs to simply display all of the instances of an entity for the user. Whatever the case, there are a couple of ways to retrieve all of the instances for a given entity. Each of the techniques can take place within a Jakarta Enterprise Beans or RESTful service class.

The Jakarta Persistence Query Language can be used to query an entity for all instances. To create a dynamic query, call the EntityManager's createQuery method, to which you can pass a string-based query that consists of Jakarta Persistence Query Language syntax, or a jakarta.persistence.Query instance. The Query interface has a sizable number of methods that can be used to work with the query object. Table 9-1 describes what these methods do.

Table 9-1. *jakarta.persistence.Query Interface Methods*

Method	Description
executeUpdate	Executes an update or delete statement (returns: int)
getFirstResult	Specifies the position of the first result the query object was set to retrieve (returns: int)
getFlushMode	Gets the flush mode in effect for the query execution (returns: FlushModeType)

(continued)

Table 9-1. (*continued*)

Method	Description
getHints	Gets the properties and hints and associated values that are in effect for the query instance (returns: `java.util.Map<String, Object>`)
getLockMode	Gets the current lock mode for the query (returns: `LockModeType`)
getMaxResults	Specifies the maximum number of results the query object was set to retrieve (returns: `int`)
getParameter	Gets the parameter object corresponding to the declared positional parameter (returns: `Parameter<?>`)
getParameters	Gets the parameter objects corresponding to the declared parameters of the query (returns: `java.util.Set<Parameter<?>>`)
getParameterValue(int)	Returns the value bound to the positional parameter (returns: `Object`)
getResultList	Executes a `SELECT` query and then returns the query results as an untyped `List` (returns: `java.util.List`)
getSingleResult	Executes a `SELECT` query and then returns a single untyped result (returns: `java.lang.Object`)
isBound	Returns a Boolean indicating whether a value has been bound to the parameter

In the example, a query string is passed to the method, and it reads as follows:

```
select object(o) from BookAuthor o
```

To break this down, the query is selecting all objects from the BookAuthor entity. Any letter could have been used in place of the o character within the query, but o is a bit of a standard since the Jakarta Persistence Query Language is referring to objects. All queries contain a SELECT clause, which is used to define the types of entity instances that you want to obtain. In the example, the entire instance is selected from the BookAuthor entity, as opposed to single fields that are contained within the instance. Since Jakarta Persistence works with objects, queries should always return the entire object; if you want to use only a subset of fields from the object, then you can call upon those fields from the instance(s) returned from the query. The object keyword is optional and is purposeful mainly for readability. The same Jakarta Persistence Query Language could be written as follows:

```
select o from BookAuthor o
```

The FROM clause can reference one or more identification variables that can refer to the name of an entity, an element of a single-valued relationship, an element of a collection relationship, or a member of a collection that is the multiple side of a one-to-many relationship. In the example, the BookAuthor variable refers to the entity itself.

■ **Note** For more information regarding the full query language syntax, please refer to the online documentation: `https://eclipse-ee4j.github.io/jakartaee-tutorial/#the-jakarta-persistence-query-language`.

417

9-2. Setting Parameters to Filter Query Results

Problem

You want to query an entity and retrieve only a subset of its instances that match specified criteria.

Solution #1

Write a dynamic query and specify parameters that can be bound to the query using bind variables. Call the query object's setParameter() method to assign a parameter value to each bind variable. In the following example, a query is written to search the Book entity for all Book instances that were written by a specified author. The BookAuthor object in this example is a named parameter that will be bound to the query using a bind variable:

```
public List<Book> findBooksByAuthor(BookAuthor authorId){
        return em.createQuery("select o from Book o " +
                "where :bookAuthor MEMBER OF o.authors")
                .setParameter("bookAuthor", authorId)
                .getResultList();
    }
```

The matching Book instances for the given author will be returned. To view the output of the preceding code, open the URL in your browser. The page as shown in Figure 9-2 should open in your browser.

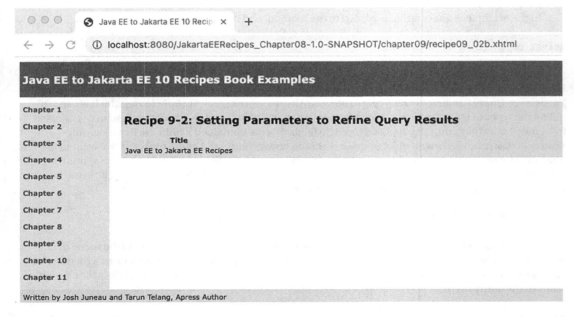

Figure 9-2. *Output from Solution #1 of Recipe 9-2*

How It Works

It is often desirable to return a refined list of results from a query, rather than returning the entire list of records within a database table. In standard SQL, the WHERE clause allows one or more expressions to be specified, which will ultimately refine the results of the query. Using the Jakarta Persistence Query Language, the WHERE clause works in the same manner, and the process of refining results of a query is almost identical to doing so with standard JDBC.

In the solution for this recipe, the Jakarta Persistence Query Language technique is used to refine the results of a query against the Book entity such that only instances pertaining to books written by a specified author will be returned. The findBooksByAuthor() method within the org.jakartaeerecipes. chapter09.session.BookFacade class accepts a BookAuthor object as an argument, and the argument will then be specified to refine the results of the query. As you'll see in the code, a single line of code (using the effective Java builder pattern) within the findBooksByAuthor() method performs the entire task. The EntityManager's createQuery() method is called, passing a string-based Jakarta Persistence Query Language query that includes a bind variable named :bookAuthor. The MEMBER OF construct in the following query tests to see if the value of the bind variable is contained within the o.authors list. The Jakarta Persistence Query Language string is as follows:

```
select o from Book o where :bookAuthor MEMBER OF o.authors
```

■ **Note**   The Java builder pattern is explained in the following reference: https://en.wikipedia.org/ wiki/Builder_pattern.

After creating the query object, the Query interface's setParameter method can be called, passing the name of the bind variable for which you want to substitute a value, along with the value you want to substitute it with. In this case, the String bookAuthor is passed along with the Author object you want to match against for obtaining Book instances. If more than one parameter needs to be specified, more than one call to setParameter() can be strung together so that each bind variable has a matching substitute. Finally, once all of the parameters have been set, the getResultList() method can be called against the Query, returning the matching objects.

■ **Note**   Two types of parameters can be used with the Jakarta Persistence Query Language: named and positional. The example in this recipe, along with many of the others in this book, uses named parameters. Positional parameters are written a bit differently in that they are denoted within the Jakarta Persistence Query Language using a question mark (?) character, and a positional number is used instead of passing the variable name to the setParameter() method. The same query that is used in this recipe can be rewritten as follows to make use of positional parameters:

```
return em.createQuery("select o from Book o " +
                "where ? MEMBER OF o.authors")
            .setParameter(1, authorId)
            .getResultList();
```

Both named and positional parameters achieve the same results. However, I recommend against using positional parameters because it makes code harder to manage, especially if there are more than a handful of parameters in use. It is also easier to mistype the setParameter() calls, and if the wrong positional number is passed with an incorrect parameter value, then issues can arise. To execute the code in this recipe, visit the URL `http://localhost:8080/JakartaEERecipes_Chapter08-1.0-SNAPSHOT/chapter09/recipe09_02b.xhtml` using your browser. The output would be similar to Figure 9-3.

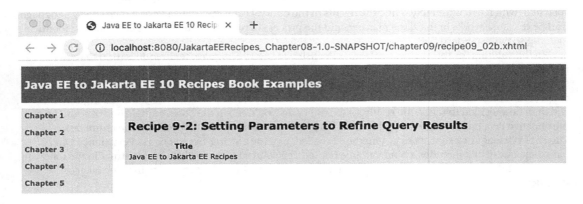

Figure 9-3. *Output from Solution #2 of Recipe 9-2*

9-3. Returning a Single Object

Problem

You have specified the Jakarta Persistence Query Language for a given query that will return exactly one matching entity instance, and you want to store it within a local object so that tasks can be performed against it.

Solution

Create a dynamic query, specifying the Jakarta Persistence Query Language that is necessary for obtaining the entity instance that matches the given criteria. The Jakarta Persistence Query Language will include a bind variable that will bind the parameter to the query in order to obtain the desired instance. The method in the following code excerpt can be found in the `org.jakartaeerecipe.jpa.session.chapter09.BookFacade` class within the sources:

```
public Book findByTitle(String title){
        return (Book) em.createQuery("select object(o) from Book o " +
                             "where o.title = :title")
                        .setParameter("title", title)
                        .getSingleResult();
}
```

To invoke the method and return results, the previous method, which resides within a Jakarta Enterprise Beans, can be invoked from within a CDI controller. The method that is defined within the controller can subsequently be referenced from within a Jakarta Server Faces view to display the results.

How It Works

A single entity instance can be retrieved by specifying a query, along with the necessary parameters to refine the possible matches to a single object. The jakarta.persistence.Query interface's getSingleResult() method allows just one instance to be returned, given that there is only one instance that matches the given query specification. In the example for this recipe, assume that each Book instance has a unique name to identify it. Therefore, you can be sure that when a name is bound to the query, it will return a single result.

Problems can arise if more than one instance matches the criteria. An attempt to call getSingleQuery() using a query that returns more than one instance will result in a NonUniqueResultException being thrown. It is a good idea to catch this exception within your applications to avoid ugly error messages being displayed to the user if more than one matching instance exists. Another case to watch out for is when a query returns no result at all. If no result is returned, then a NoResultException will be thrown.

9-4. Creating Native Queries

Problem

The query you want to use against an entity contains some SQL functionality that pertains to the specific database vendor that your application is using, or you are more comfortable working with standard SQL than using the Jakarta Persistence Query Language. That said, you want to use standard SQL to query one of your entity objects.

■ **Note**   When using native queries, you will be forced to work against database records, rather than Java objects. For this reason, it is recommended to use the Jakarta Persistence Query Language unless necessary.

Solution #1

Create a native query by calling the EntityManager object's createNativeQuery() method, and pass a SQL query as the first parameter and pass the entity class that you want to return the results of the query into as the second parameter. Once the query has been created, call one of the corresponding jakarta.persistence.Query methods (see Table 9-1) to return the results. The following example taken from the org.jakartaeerecipe.jpa.session.BookFacade Jakarta Enterprise Beans demonstrates the use of a native query on the Book entity:

```
public List<Book> obtainNativeList(){
        Query query = em.createNativeQuery(
                "select id, title, description " +
                "FROM BOOK " +
                " ORDER BY id", org.jakartaeerecipes.jpa.entity.Book.class);
        return query.getResultList();
}
```

In the preceding example, each of the database attributes will map to a field within the Book class.

Solution #2

Specify a @NamedNativeQuery within the entity class for the entity class that you want to query. Provide a name, query, and mapping class for the @NamedNativeQuery via the annotation. Within the EJB method, call the EntityManager object's createNativeQuery() method, and provide the name that was specified as a named native query rather than a SQL string. The following code excerpt demonstrates the creation of a named native query for the org.jakartaeerecipes.jpa.entity.Book entity:

```
...
@Entity
@Table(name="BOOK")
@NamedNativeQuery(
    name="allBooks",
    query = "select id, title, description " +
            "FROM BOOK " +
            "ORDER BY id",
    resultClass=Book.class)
...
```

Next, let's take a look at how the named native query is invoked from within the EJB. The following excerpt of code is taken from the org.jakartaeerecipes.jpa.session.BookFacade bean, and it demonstrates the invocation of the allBooks named native query:

```
public List<Book> obtainNamedNativeList(){
        Query query = em.createNamedQuery(
                "allBooks", org.jakartaeerecipes.jpa.entity.Book.class);
        return query.getResultList();
}
```

Figure 9-4 shows the output from the query. Solutions #1 and #2 could be executed by opening the files recipe09_04a.xhtml and recipe09_04b.xhtml, respectively.

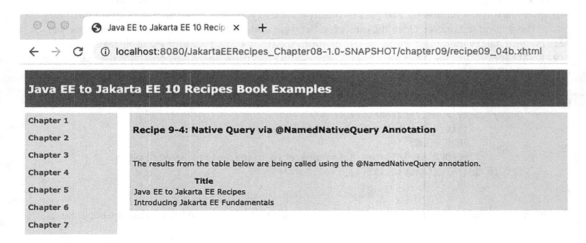

Figure 9-4. *Output of the recipe*

How It Works

Native queries provide a way to utilize native SQL code for retrieving data from an underlying data store. Not only do they allow an inexperienced Jakarta Persistence Query Language developer to write in native SQL, but they also allow native SQL syntax, such as Oracle-specific PL/SQL functions, or stored procedure calls to be made. On the downside, however, native queries do not return results in an entity-oriented manner, but rather as plain old objects. For this reason, the named native query provides the option to specify an entity class into which the results should be returned.

There are a handful of ways to work with native queries, and I've covered a couple of the most commonly used tactics in this recipe. A jakarta.persistence.Query is generated either by calling the EntityManager's createNativeQuery() method or by calling the EntityManager's createNamedQuery() method and passing a named native query.

In Solution #1, a String-based SQL query is used to retrieve results into an entity class. For starters, the createNativeQuery() method accepts a query in String format or a named native query for the first parameter. In Solution #1, a query is used to obtain all the records from the BOOK database table. The second argument to the createNativeQuery() method is an optional mapping class into which the results of the query will be stored. Solution #1 specifies Book.class as the second parameter, which will map the columns of the database table to their corresponding fields within the Book entity. Once the Query instance is created, then its methods can be invoked in order to execute the query. In this case, the getResultSet() method is invoked, which will return a List of the matching records and bind each of them to a Book entity class instance.

In Solution #2, a named native query is demonstrated. Named native queries allow the SQL string to be specified once within the corresponding entity class, and then they can be executed by simply passing the String-based name that has been assigned to the named native query. To utilize a named native query, add the @NamedNativeQuery annotation to the entity class that you want to query, and then specify values for the three parameters of the annotation: name, query, and resultClass. For the name parameter of the @NamedNativeQuery annotation, a String-based name that will be used to reference the query must be specified, the query parameter must be the native SQL string, and the resultClass must be the entity class that the query results will be stored into. The @NamedNativeQuery also includes the resultSetMapping parameter that can be optionally used to specify a SqlResultSetMapping for those queries involving more than one table. To execute the named native query, use the same technique as demonstrated in Solution #1, but instead call the EntityManager object's createNamedQuery() method. Instead of specifying a SQL String, pass the name that was specified within the @NamedNativeQuery annotation for the respective query.

▪ **Note** If the named query involves more than one database table, then a SqlResultSetMapping must be defined. Please see Recipe 9-5 for more details.

In some cases, using a native SQL query is the only solution for retrieving the data that your application requires. In all cases, it is recommended that the Jakarta Persistence Query Language be used, rather than native SQL, if possible. However, for those cases where native SQL is the only solution, then creating a native query using one of the techniques provided in this recipe is definitely the way to go. Which technique is better? Well, that depends on what you need to do. If you are trying to create a dynamic query, whereas the actual SQL String for the query may change dynamically, then the standard native query is the solution for you. However, if the SQL query that you are specifying will not change in a dynamic manner, then perhaps the named native query is the best choice for two reasons. First, the named native query allows SQL to be organized and stored within a single location, which is the entity class on which the SQL is querying. Second, named native queries can achieve better performance because they are cached after the first execution. Therefore, the next time the named native query is called, the SQL does not have to be recompiled. Such is not the case with a standard native query. Each time a standard native query is called, the SQL must be recompiled, which ultimately means that it will not be executed as fast.

9-5. Querying More Than One Entity

Problem

The Jakarta Persistence Query Language or native SQL query being used references more than one entity or underlying database table. Since there are attributes from more than one table, the results cannot be stored into a single entity object.

Solution #1

Use a SqlResultSetMapping, which allows the specification of more than one entity class for returning query results. The @SqlResultSetMapping annotation can be specified in order to map a result set to one or more entities, allowing the joining of database tables to become a nonissue. In the following example, the BOOK and BOOK_AUTHOR database tables are joined together using a native SQL query, and the results are returned using a SqlResultSetMapping. The following @SqlResultSetMapping can be found within the org.jakartaeerecipe.entity.BookAuthor entity class:

```
@SqlResultSetMapping(name="authorBooks",
        entities= {
            @EntityResult(entityClass=org.jakartaeerecipe.entity.Book.class, fields={
                @FieldResult(name="id", column="BOOK_ID"),
                @FieldResult(name="title", column="TITLE")
            }),
            @EntityResult(entityClass=org.jakartaeerecipe.entity.BookAuthor.class, fields={
                @FieldResult(name="id", column="AUTHOR_ID"),
                @FieldResult(name="firstname", column="FIRSTNAME"),
                @FieldResult(name="lastname", column="LASTNAME")
            })
        })
```

Next, let's look at how the SqlResultSetMapping is used. The following method is taken from the org.jakartaeerecipe.session.BookAuthorFacade session bean:

```
public List findAuthorBooksMapping(){
    Query qry = em.createNativeQuery(
            "select b.id as BOOK_ID, b.title as TITLE, " +
            "ba.id AS AUTHOR_ID, ba.firstname as FIRSTNAME, ba.lastname as LASTNAME " +
            "from book_author ba, book b, author_work aw " +
            "where aw.author_id = ba.id " +
            "and b.id = aw.book_id", "authorBooks");
    return qry.getResultList();
}
```

The resulting List can then be referenced from within a Jakarta Server Faces dataTable or another client data iteration device to display the results of the query.

Solution #2

Utilize a native query to return the necessary fields from more than one database table, and return the results to a HashMap, rather than to an entity class. In the following method taken from the org.jakartaeerecipe. session.BookAuthorFacade session bean, this technique is demonstrated:

```
public List<Map> findAuthorBooks(){
        Query qry = em.createNativeQuery(
            "select ba.id, ba.lastname, ba.firstname, ba.bio, b.id, b.title, b.image,
            b.description " +
            "from book_author ba, book b, author_work aw " +
            "where aw.author_id = ba.id " +
            "and b.id = aw.book_id");
        List<Object[]> results = qry.getResultList();
        List data = new ArrayList<Map>();
        if (!results.isEmpty()) {
            for (Object[] result : results) {
                Map resultMap = new HashMap<String, Object>();
                resultMap.put("authorId", result[0]);
                resultMap.put("authorLast", result[1]);
                resultMap.put("authorFirst", result[2]);
                resultMap.put("authorBio", result[3]);
                resultMap.put("bookId", result[4]);
                resultMap.put("bookTitle", result[5]);
                resultMap.put("bookImage", result[6]);
                resultMap.put("bookDescription", result[7]);
                data.add(resultMap);
            }
        }
        return data;
}
```

Using this solution, no SqlResultSetMapping is required, and the results are manually stored into a Map that can be referenced from a client, such as a Jakarta Server Faces view.

How It Works

The SqlResultSetMapping can come in handy when you need to map your ResultSet to two or more entity classes. As demonstrated in the first solution to this recipe, configure the mapping by specifying a @SqlResultSetMapping annotation on the entity class of which you are querying. SqlResultSetMapping is useful when working with native queries and joining underlying database tables.

In the example, the @SqlResultSetMapping annotation is used to create a mapping between the Book and BookAuthor entity classes. The @SqlResultSetMapping annotation accepts a few different parameters, as described in Table 9-2.

Table 9-2. *SqlResultSetMapping Parameters*

Parameter	Description
name	String-based name for the SqlResultSetMapping
entities	One or more @EntityResult annotations, denoting entity classes for the mapping
columns	One or more columns against which to map a resultSet, designated by @FieldResult or @ColumnResult annotations

To use a SqlResultSetMapping, simply specify its name rather than an entity class when creating the native query. In the following excerpt taken from the solution, the query results are mapped to the authorBooks SqlResultSetMapping:

```
Query qry = em.createNativeQuery(
                "select b.id as BOOK_ID, b.title as TITLE, " +
                "ba.id AS AUTHOR_ID, ba.firstname as FIRSTNAME, ba.lastname as LASTNAME" +
                "from book_author ba, book b, author_work aw " +
                "where aw.author_id = ba.id " +
                "and b.id = aw.book_id", "authorBooks");
```

The List of results that is returned from this query can be utilized within a client, such as a JSF view, in the same manner as any List containing a single entity's results. The SqlResultSetMapping allows fields of an entity class to be mapped to a given name so that the name can then be specified to obtain the value for the mapped field. For instance, the following Jakarta Server Faces dataTable source is taken from the chapter09/recipe09_05a.xhtml view, and it displays the List of results from the query in the solution:

```
<h:dataTable id="table" value="#{authorController.authorBooks}"
                                var="authorBook">
    <h:column>
        <f:facet name="header">
            <h:outputText value="Book ID"/>
        </f:facet>
        <h:outputText value="#{authorBook.id}"/>
    </h:column>
    <h:column>
        <f:facet name="header">
            <h:outputText value="Title"/>
        </f:facet>
        <h:outputText value="#{authorBook.title}"/>
    </h:column>
    <h:column>
        <f:facet name="header">
            <h:outputText value="Author"/>
        </f:facet>
        <h:outputText value="#{authorBook.firstname} #{authorBook.lastname}"/>
    </h:column>
</h:dataTable>
```

As mentioned previously, entity fields can be mapped to a specified field returned from the database within the native SQL query. You can do so by specifying either the @FieldResult or @ColumnResult annotation for the columns parameter of a @SqlResultSetMapping annotation. For instance, in the example, you return only the TITLE and BOOK_ID columns from the BOOK database table, as well as the AUTHOR_ID, FIRSTNAME, and LASTNAME columns from the BOOK_AUTHOR table. You include the SQL in the native query to join the tables and retrieve the values from these columns and return a SqlResultSetMapping that corresponds to the following:

```
@SqlResultSetMapping(name="authorBooks",
        entities= {
                @EntityResult(entityClass=org.jakartaeerecipe.entity.Book.class, fields={
                        @FieldResult(name="id", column="BOOK_ID"),
                        @FieldResult(name="title", column="TITLE")
                }),
                @EntityResult(entityClass=org.jakartaeerecipe.entity.BookAuthor.class, fields={
                        @FieldResult(name="id", column="AUTHOR_ID"),
                        @FieldResult(name="first", column="FIRSTNAME"),
                        @FieldResult(name="last", column="LASTNAME")
                })
        })
```

In Solution #2, no SqlResultSetMapping is used, and instead the results of the query are returned into a List of HashMap objects, rather than entity objects. The query returns a list of Object[], which can then be iterated over in order to make the data accessible to the client. As shown in the example, after the list of Object[] is obtained, a for loop can be used to iterate over each Object in the list obtaining the data for each returned database record field and storing it into a HashMap. To access the field data, specify a positional index that corresponds to the position of the database field data that you want to obtain. The positional indices correlate to the ordering of the returned fields within the SQL query, beginning with an index of zero. Therefore, to obtain the data for the first field returned in the query, specify an index of zero on the Object for each row. As the Object[] is traversed, each database record can be parsed, in turn obtaining the data for each field in that row. The resulting data is then stored into the HashMap, and a String-based key that corresponds to the name of the returned field is specified so that the data can be made accessible to the client.

When accessing a HashMap of results from a client, such as a JSF view, the data can be accessed in the same manner as if a standard entity list were being used. This is because each HashMap element contains a key field that corresponds to the name of the data field. The following excerpt, taken from chapter09/recipe09_05b.xhtml, demonstrates how to use the results of a native query that have been stored into a HashMap using this technique:

```
<h:dataTable id="table" value="#{authorController.authorBooks}"
                                var="authorBook">
    <h:column>
        <f:facet name="header">
            <h:outputText value="Title"/>
        </f:facet>
        <h:outputText value="#{authorBook.bookTitle}"/>
    </h:column>
    <h:column>
        <f:facet name="header">
            <h:outputText value="Author"/>
        </f:facet>
        <h:outputText value="#{authorBook.authorFirst} #{authorBook.authorLast}"/>
    </h:column>
</h:dataTable>
```

427

The SqlResultSetMapping is a repeatable annotation, so you may use more than one of them in the same entity class without encapsulating it within a container annotation. The SqlResultSetMapping makes it possible to use customized queries and joins into returning results via entity class objects. It is one more of the techniques that help complete the object-relational mapping (ORM) experience when using JPA.

9-6. Calling Jakarta Persistence Query Language Aggregate Functions

Problem

You want to return the total number of records from a database table that match the specified filtering criteria. For example, you want to return the total count of BookAuthor instances for a specified book.

Solution

Use the Jakarta Persistence Query Language aggregate function COUNT to return the total number of objects that match the given query. The following method, which resides within the org.jakartaeerecipes. session.AuthorWorkFacade class, uses the COUNT aggregate function:

```
public Long findAuthorCount(Book book){
        Query qry = em.createQuery("select COUNT(o.authorId) from AuthorWork o " +
                "where o.bookId = :book")
                .setParameter("book", book.getId());
        return (Long) qry.getSingleResult();
}
```

The function will return a Long result, which will be the count of matching AuthorWork results.

How It Works

Aggregate functions are those that can group values of multiple rows together on certain criteria to form a single value. Native SQL contains aggregate functions that can be useful for calculating the sum of all rows in a particular table, maximum values of a column, first values within a column, and so on. The Jakarta Persistence Query Language contains several aggregate functions that can be used within queries.

In this recipe, the example demonstrates the use of the COUNT function, which returns the total number of rows in an underlying data store table. The value is calculated and returned as a Long data type, which can be cast from a call to the jakarta.persistence.Query object's getSingleResult method. However, there are a number of other functions at your disposal. Table 9-3 lists those functions and their return type.

Table 9-3. Aggregate Functions

Function	Description	Return Type
COUNT	Total number of records	Long
MAX	Record with the largest numeric value	Same as the field to which applied
MIN	Record with the lowest numeric value	Same as the field to which applied
AVG	Average of all numeric values in a column	Double
SUM	Sum of all values in a column	Long when applied to integral types Double when applied to floating-point BigInteger when applied to BigInteger BigDecimal when applied to BigDecimal

If a particular database record contains a NULL value for a column to which an aggregate function is being applied, then that NULL value is eliminated before the function is applied. The DISTINCT keyword can be used to specify that any duplicate values should be eliminated before the function is applied. The following line of code demonstrates the use of DISTINCT:

```
Query qry = em.createQuery("select DISTINCT(COUNT(o.title)) from Book o");
```

The important thing to remember when using aggregate functions is that they are applied to the same field within all objects that satisfy the query. This is analogous to the function being applied to all values returned for a single column's results within a query.

9-7. Invoking Database Stored Procedures Natively

Problem

The application you are writing uses the Jakarta Persistence Query Language and relies on one or more database stored procedures to perform tasks on the data. You need to have the ability to call those stored procedures from within the business logic of your Java application code.

Solution

Create a native query, and write a SQL String that executes the database stored procedure. Suppose you have a database procedure named CREATE_USER and it accepts two arguments: username and password. You can invoke the CREATE_USER procedure by calling it via a native SQL query. The following method, named createUser, accepts a username and password as arguments and passes them to the underlying database procedure and executes it:

```
public void createUser(String user, String pass){
        Query qry = (Query) em.createNativeQuery(
        "select CREATE_USER('" + user + "','" + pass + "') from dual");
        qry.getSingleResult();
}
```

How It Works

Historically, the only way to work with database stored procedures from JPA was to utilize a native query. The solution to this recipe demonstrates this tactic because a native query is used to invoke a database stored procedure. In the example, a method named createUser accepts two parameters, username and password, which are both passed to the database stored procedure named CREATE_USER via the native query. The EntityManager's createNativeQuery() method is called, and a SQL String that performs a SELECT on the stored procedure is passed to the method. In SQL, performing a SELECT on a stored procedure will cause the procedure to be executed. Notice that the DUAL table is being referenced in the SQL. The DUAL is a dummy table that can be used when you need to apply SELECT statements to different database constructs, such as a stored procedure.

The execution of native SQL is an acceptable solution for invoking stored procedures that have no return values or when you have only a limited number of SQL statements to maintain. However, in most enterprise situations that require an application with multiple stored procedure calls or calls that require a return value, the @NamedStoredProcedure solution in Recipe 9-10 can be advantageous.

9-8. Joining to Retrieve Instances from Multiple Entities

Problem

You want to create joins between entities to return fields from more than one underlying database table.

Solution

Use the Jakarta Persistence Query Language to create a join between two entities that share a one-to-many and many-to-one relationship with each other. In this example, a one-to-many relationship is set up against the Book and Chapter entities such that one book can contain many chapters. The following excerpt from the org.jakartaeerecipe.entity.Book class demonstrates the one-to-many relationship declaration:

```
@OneToMany(mappedBy="book", cascade=CascadeType.ALL)
private List<Chapter> chapters = null;
```

The Chapter entity contains a many-to-one relationship with the Book entity, such that many chapters can be related to one book. The following excerpt from the org.jakartaeerecipe.entity.Chapter class demonstrates the many-to-one relationship:

```
@ManyToOne
@JoinColumn(name = "BOOK_ID", insertable = false, updatable = false)
private Book book;
```

Please note, the relationship is declared as read-only, by marking the join column as insertable=false and updatable=false. Ultimately, the join query is contained within a method named findBookByChapterTitle(), which resides in the org.jakartaeerecipe.session.Chapter session bean. The following code excerpt contains the lines of code that make up that method:

```
public List<Book> findBookByChapterTitle(String chapterTitle){
    return em.createQuery("select b from Book b INNER JOIN b.chapters c " +
        "where c.title = :title")
        .setParameter("title", chapterTitle)
        .getResultList();
}
```

■ **Note** To return several different properties within the SELECT clause, rather than an object, the result will be returned in an Object[ ]. To find out more about working with such a solution, please refer to Solution #2 of Recipe 9-5.

How It Works

The most common type of database table join operation is known as an *inner join*. When performing an inner join, all the columns from each table will be available to be returned as if it were a single, combined table. To create a join between two entities, they must be related to each other via a one-to-many relationship. This means that one of the entities could contain an instance that possibly contains many references to the other entity, whereas the other entity could have many instances that would reference only one instance of the former entity. In the example for this recipe, the Book entity has a one-to-many relationship with the Chapter entity. This means that a single book may contain many chapters.

The example for this recipe demonstrates a join between the Book and Chapter entities. The method findBookByChapterTitle( ) contains a Jakarta Persistence query that will return any Book objects that contain a matching chapter title. To generate an inner join query, invoke the EntityManager object's createQuery( ) method, passing the String-based Jakarta Persistence query that contains the join syntax. A Jakarta Persistence Query Language string for performing an inner join should be written in the following format, where INNER is an optional (default) keyword:

```
SELECT a.col1, a.col2 from Entity1 a [INNER] JOIN a.collectionColumn b WHERE expressions
```

In the example, an entire Book instance will be returned for each Book entity that contains a Chapter instance, which has a title matching the parameter. Typically, the join occurs over a foreign key, and in the case of the one-to-many relationship, it occurs on the field that is a collection of the related entity's instances.

9-9. Joining to Retrieve All Rows Regardless of Match

Problem

You want to create joins between entities to produce results that will include all objects of the left entity listed and matching results or NULL values when there is no match from the right entity listed.

Solution

In this example, a one-to-many relationship is set up against the Book and Chapter entities such that one book can contain many chapters. The following excerpt from the org.jakartaeerecipes.entity.Book class demonstrates the one-to-many relationship declaration:

```
@OneToMany(mappedBy="book", cascade=CascadeType.ALL)
private List<Chapter> chapters = null;
```

The Chapter entity has a many-to-one relationship with the Book entity, such that many chapters can be related to one book. The following excerpt from the org.jakartaeerecipes.entity.Chapter class demonstrates the many-to-one relationship:

```
@ManyToOne
@JoinColumn(name = "BOOK_ID")
private Book book;
```

The code that contains the left outer join query resides within the findAllBooksByChapterNumber() method, which is contained within the org.jakartaeerecipes.session.ChapterFacade class. The following excerpt taken from the class lists the method implementation:

```
public List<Book> findAllBooksByChapterNumber(BigDecimal chapterNumber){
        return em.createQuery("select b from Book b LEFT OUTER JOIN b.chapters c " +
                "where c.chapterNumber = :num")
                .setParameter("num", chapterNumber)
                .getResultList();
    }
```

How It Works

An outer join, otherwise known as a LEFT OUTER JOIN or LEFT JOIN, is not as common of an occurrence as an inner join. To explain an outer join in database terminology, all rows of the table listed on the left side of the JOIN keyword are returned in a LEFT SQL join, and only those matching rows from the table listed to the right of the keyword will be returned in a "Left Outer" SQL join. In other words, an outer join enables the retrieval of a set of database records where a matching value within the join may not be present. In JPA terminology, all instances of the entity class to the left of the JOIN keyword will be returned.

Outer joins on entities usually occur between two related entities in which there is a one-to-many relationship or vice versa. To form an outer join Jakarta Persistence Query Language query, use the following format, where the [OUTER] keyword is optional:

```
SELECT a.col1, a.col2 FROM Entity1 a LEFT [OUTER] JOIN a.collectionColumn b WHERE expression
```

In the example, all Book objects are returned, but only those Chapter objects that match the specified criteria would be included in the ResultSet.

9-10. Applying Jakarta Persistence Query Language Functional Expressions

Problem

You want to apply functions within your Jakarta Persistence Query Language Strings to alter the results of the execution. For example, you are interested in altering Strings that will be used within the WHERE clause of your Jakarta Persistence Query Language query.

Solution

Utilize any of the built-in Jakarta Persistence Query Language functions to apply functional expressions to your Jakarta Persistence Query Language. To alter Strings that are utilized within a Jakarta Persistence Query Language query, develop the query containing String functions that will be applied within the WHERE clause of the query. In the following example, the UPPER function is utilized in order to change the case of the given text into all uppercase letters. In this case, a search page has been set up for users to enter an author's last name and search the database for a match. The String that the user enters is converted to uppercase and used to query the database.

The following lines of code are taken from the search view, which resides within the Jakarta Server Faces view that is composed within the chapter09/recipe09_10.xhtml file:

```
<ui:composition template="layout/custom_template_search.xhtml">
    <ui:define name="content">
        <h:form>
        <h2>Recipe 9-10: Using Jakarta Persistence Query Language String Functions</h2>
            <br/>
            <p>Enter an author's last name below to search the author database.</p>
        <br/>
            <h:outputLabel value="Last Name:"/>
            <h:inputText id="last" value="#{authorController.authorLast}" size="75"/>
            <br/>
            <br/>
            <h:commandButton value="Search" action="#{authorController.findAuthorByLast}"/>
        </h:form>
    </ui:define>
</ui:composition>
```

Next, the code for the CDI bean controller method, findAuthorByLast(), is listed. This method resides within the org.jakartaeerecipes.jsf.AuthorController class. This code is responsible for populating the authorList and then directing navigation to the recipe09_10b.xhtml view:

```
public String findAuthorByLast(){
    authorList = ejbFacade.findAuthorByLast(authorLast);
    return "/chapter09/recipe09_10b.xhtml";
}
```

Lastly, the EJB method named findAuthorByLast(String) is contained within the org.jakartaeerecipes.session.BookAuthorFacade class. The method accepts the String value that the user entered into the web search form and uses it to query the database for a matching author, converting the text to uppercase before performing the comparison:

```
public List<BookAuthor> findAuthorByLast(String authorLast){
    return em.createQuery("select o from BookAuthor o " +
    "where o.last = UPPER(:authorLast)")
    .setParameter("authorLast", authorLast).getResultList();
}
```

The resulting page will display any author names that match the text that was entered by the user.

How It Works

The JPA query language contains a handful of functions that can be used to manipulate Strings, perform arithmetic, and make dates easier to work with. The functions can be specified within the WHERE or HAVING clause of query Strings. The Jakarta Persistence Query Language contains several String functions. Table 9-4 lists the different String functions that are available, along with a description of what they do.

Table 9-4. *String Functions*

Function	Description
CONCAT(string1, string2)	Returns a concatenated String composed of the two arguments
SUBSTRING(string, expr1, expr2)	Returns a substring of the specified String. The first position within the substring is denoted by expr1, and the length of the substring is denoted by expr2
TRIM([[spec][char]FROM] str)	Trims a specified character (spec) from a string (str)
LOWER(string)	Returns the given String in all lowercase letters
UPPER(string)	Returns the given String in all uppercase letters

There are also several functions within the Jakarta Persistence Query Language to help perform arithmetic within queries. Table 9-5 lists the different arithmetic functions that are available, along with a description of what they do.

Table 9-5. *Arithmetic Functions*

Function	Description
ABS(expr)	Returns the absolute value. Takes a numeric argument and returns a number of the same type
SQRT(expr)	Returns the square root value. Takes a numeric argument and returns a double
MOD(expr1, expr2)	Returns the modulus value in integer format
SIZE(collection)	Returns the total number of elements in the given collection in integer format. If the collection contains no elements, it evaluates to zero

Working with dates from any programming language can sometimes be a bit tough. The Jakarta Persistence Query Language contains a handful of helpful datetime functions to make it a bit easier. Table 9-6 lists the different datetime functions that are available, along with a description of what they do.

Table 9-6. *Datetime Functions*

Function	Description
CURRENT_DATE	Returns the current date
CURRENT_TIME	Returns the current time
CURRENT_TIMESTAMP	Returns the current timestamp

9-11. Forcing Query Execution Rather Than Cache Use

Problem

The default EntityManager is using cached results from a database query, and you want to force a query to be executed each time a table is loaded, rather than allowing the results of the cache to be displayed.

Solution

After the jakarta.persistence.Query instance is created, set a hint, jakarta.persistence.cache.
retrieveMode, to bypass the cache and force the query to be executed. In the following lines of code, the
Book entity is queried, and the cache is bypassed by setting the hint:

```
public List<Book> findAllBooks(){
    Query qry = em.createQuery("select o from Book o");
    qry.setHint("jakarta.persistence.cache.retrieveMode", CacheRetrieveMode.BYPASS);
    return qry.getResultList();
}
```

Upon execution, the query will be forced to execute, returning the most current results from the
underlying database table as shown in Figure 9-5.

Figure 9-5. *The output of the recipe*

■ **Note**   By default, results from Jakarta Persistence API queries are cached to provide peak performance. This
enables the cache data to be returned in the event that the same query is used multiple times.

How It Works

There are often occasions when an application requires the most current table data to be displayed or used
for performing a given task. For instance, if you were to write a stock market application, it would not make
sense to cache the current market results since stale data would not be very useful to investors. In such
cases, it is imperative to force queries to be executed and bypass any caching. This is possible via the use of
hints that can be registered with jakarta.persistence.Query instances.

By setting the jakarta.persistence.cache.retrieveMode hint to CacheRetrieveMode.BYPASS, the
Jakarta Persistence API is told to always force the execution of a query. When the query is executed, it will
always return the most current results from the database.

9-12. Performing Bulk Updates and Deletes

Problem

You want to update or delete a group of entity objects.

Solution

Perform a bulk update or deletion using the Criteria API. The Criteria API allows the use of the builder pattern for specifying entity operations. In the following example, a bulk update is performed on the Employee entity. The following example method resides in a session bean class for the org. jakartaeerecipes.entity.Employee entity. The session bean class name is org.jakartaeerecipes. session.EmployeeSession.java, and the following excerpt from that class shows how to perform a bulk update:

```
...
public String updateEmployeeStatusInactive() {
        String returnMessage = null;
        CriteriaBuilder builder = em.getCriteriaBuilder();
        CriteriaUpdate<Employee> q = builder.createCriteriaUpdate(Employee.class);
        Root<Employee> e = q.from(Employee.class);
        q.set(e.get("status"), "ACTIVE")
                .where(builder.equal(e.get("status"), "INACTIVE"));
        Query criteriaUpdate = em.createQuery(q);
        int result = criteriaUpdate.executeUpdate();
        if (result > 0){
            returnMessage = result + " records updated";
        } else {
            returnMessage = "No records updated";
        }
        return returnMessage;
    }
...
```

Similarly, the Criteria API can be used to perform a bulk deletion. The following method, also within the EmployeeSession bean, demonstrates how to do so:

```
...
    public String deleteEmployeeOnStatus(String condition) {
        CriteriaBuilder builder = em.getCriteriaBuilder();
        CriteriaDelete<Employee> q = builder.createCriteriaDelete(Employee.class);
        Root<Employee> e = q.from(Employee.class);
        q.where(builder.equal(e.get("status"), condition));
        return null;
    }
...
```

How It Works

The Criteria API supports bulk updates and deletions. The Criteria API allows developers to utilize
Java language syntax to perform database queries and manipulations, instead of Jakarta Persistence or
SQL. A jakarta.persistence.criteria.CriteriaUpdate object can be used to perform bulk update
operations, and a jakarta.persistence.criteria.CriteriaDelete object can be used to perform bulk
deletion operations. How do we obtain such objects? The Criteria API is dependent upon the jakarta.
persistence.criteria.CriteriaBuilder interface, which is used to return objects that can be used to
work with specified Entity classes. The CriteriaBuilder include methods createCriteriaUpdate() and
createCriteriaDelete(), which will return the CriteriaUpdate or CriteriaDelete object, respectively.

To use the CriteriaBuilder, you first need to obtain a CriteriaBuilder from the EntityManager.
You can then use the CriteriaBuilder to obtain the CriteriaUpdate or CriteriaDelete object of your
choosing. In the following lines of code, a CriteriaUpdate object is obtained for use with an Employee entity:

```
CriteriaBuilder builder = em.getCriteriaBuilder();
CriteriaUpdate<Employee> q = builder.createCriteriaUpdate(Employee.class);
```

Once obtained, the CriteriaUpdate can be used to build a query and set values, as desired, for making
the necessary updates or deletions. In the following excerpt, the CriteriaUpdate object is used to update all
Employee objects that have a status of INACTIVE, changing that status to ACTIVE:

```
Root<Employee> e = q.from(Employee.class);
q.set(e.get("status"), "ACTIVE")
        .where(builder.equal(e.get("status"), "INACTIVE"));
```

Let's break this down a bit to explain what exactly is going on. First, the query root is set by calling
the q.from method and passing the entity class for which you want to obtain the root, where q is the
CriteriaUpdate object. Next, the q.set method is invoked, passing the Path to the Employee status
attribute, along with the ACTIVE string. The q.set method is performing the bulk update. To further refine
the query, a WHERE clause is added using a chained call to the .where method and passing the Employee
objects that have a status of INACTIVE. The entire criteria can be seen in the solution for this recipe.

Finally, to complete the transaction, you must create the Query object and then execute it using the
following lines of code:

```
Query criteriaUpd = em.createQuery(q);
criteriaUpd.executeUpdate();
```

The bulk deletion is very similar, except instead of using the CriteriaBuilder to obtain a
CriteriaUpdate object, use it to obtain a CriteriaDelete object instead. To obtain a CriteriaDelete
object, call the CriteriaBuilder createCriteriaDelete method, as follows:

```
CriteriaBuilder builder = em.getCriteriaBuilder();
CriteriaDelete<Employee> q = builder.createCriteriaDelete(Employee.class);
```

Once a CriteriaDelete object has been obtained, then the conditions for deletion need to be specified
by filtering the results using a call (or chain of calls) to the .where method. When using the bulk delete,
all objects that match the specified condition will be deleted. For example, the following lines of code
demonstrate how to delete all Employee objects that have the status attribute equal to INACTIVE:

```
Root<Employee> e = q.from(Employee.class);
q.where(builder.equal(e.get("status"), "INACTIVE"));
```

■ **Note**   Both the `CriteriaUpdate` and `CriteriaDelete` examples demonstrated can be made more type-safe by using the MetaModel API. For each entity class in a particular persistence unit, a metamodel class is created with a trailing underscore, along with the attributes that correspond to the persistent fields of the entity class. This metamodel can be used to manage entity classes and their persistent state and relationships. Therefore, instead of specifying an error-prone `String` in the `Path` to obtain a particular attribute, you could specify the metamodel attribute instead, as follows: `e.get(Employee_.status)`.

For more information on using the MetaModel API to create type-safe queries, please refer to the online documentation.

The Criteria API can be very detailed, and it is also very powerful. To learn more about the Criteria API, please see the documentation online at `https://eclipse-ee4j.github.io/jakartaee-tutorial/#using-the-criteria-api-to-create-queries`.

9-13. Retrieving Entity Subclasses

Problem

You want to obtain the data for an entity, along with all the data from that entity's subclasses.

Solution

Utilize the downcasting feature of the Jakarta Persistence API. To do so, specify the TREAT keyword within the FROM and/or WHERE clause of a Jakarta Persistence query in order to filter the specified types and subtypes that you want to retrieve. In the following example, the query will return all BookStore entities that are from the IT books. The assumption is that the ItCategory entity is a subtype of the BookCategory entity. The method in the example, named getBookCategories(), resides within the org.jakartaeerecipes.session. BookCategoryFacade session bean:

```
public List getBookCategories(){
        TypedQuery<Object[]> qry = em.createQuery("select a.name, a.genre, a.description " +
                "from BookStore s JOIN TREAT(s.categories as ItCategory) a", Object[].class);
        List data = new ArrayList();
        if (!qry.getResultList().isEmpty()) {
            List<Object[]> tdata = qry.getResultList();
            for (Object[] t : tdata) {
                HashMap resultMap = new HashMap();
                resultMap.put("name", t[0]);
                resultMap.put("genre", t[1]);
                resultMap.put("categoryDesc", t[2]);
                data.add(resultMap);
            }
        }
        return data;
    }
```

When invoked, this query will return data from the ItCategory entity, which is a subclass of the BookCategory entity, as per the previous description. To better understand how to relate the entities, please refer to the entire source code within the two entities, located within the org.jakartaeerecipe.entity.BookCategory.java and org.jakartaeerecipe.entity.ItCategory.java files in the sources for this book.

How It Works

The act of *downcasting* is defined as the casting of a base type or class reference to one of its derived types or classes. The Jakarta EE platform introduced the concept of downcasting in the Jakarta Persistence API by providing the ability to obtain a reference to a subclass of a specified entity within a query. In other words, you can explicitly query one or more entities and retrieve the attributes from each of the entities as well as any attributes from entities that are subclasses of those that are explicitly declared. To provide this ability, the TREAT keyword was added to Jakarta Persistence.

The use of the TREAT operator is supported for downcasting within path expressions in the FROM and WHERE clauses. The first argument to the TREAT operator should be a subtype of the target type; otherwise, the path is considered to have no value, attributing nothing to the end result. The TREAT operator can filter on the specified types and subtypes, as well as perform a downcast.

The syntax for use of the TREAT operator is as follows:

```
SELECT b.attr1, b.attr2
FROM EntityA a JOIN TREAT(a.referenceToEntityB as EntityBSubType) b
```

In the preceding query, the TREAT operation contains an attribute from the specified entity (EntityA) that relates to a joined entity (EntityB). The TREAT operation tells the container to treat the referenced entity (EntityB) as the type of EntityBSubtype. Therefore, the downcast takes place and allows access to those subtype entities. The following lines of code demonstrate this technique in action:

```
SELECT a.name, a.genre, a.description
FROM BookStore s JOIN TREAT(s.categories AS ItCategory) a
```

As mentioned previously, the TREAT operator can also be used within the WHERE clause to filter a query based upon subtype attribute values. Downcasting support allows Jakarta Persistence to be even more flexible for developers to use, making more complex queries possible. This technique makes it easier to obtain values from related entities or subtypes, without the need to issue an extra query.

9-14. Joining with ON Conditions

Problem

You want to retrieve all the entities that match the specified criteria for joining two entities, along with each entity that does not match on the left side of an OUTER join.

Solution

Utilize the ON condition to specify a join of two or more entity classes based upon the specified filtering criteria. The following method includes the Jakarta Persistence Query Language for retrieving all Jobs entities, along with a count of the number of Employee entities that belong to those Jobs. This method, named obtainActiveEmployeeCount(), utilizes the ON condition to filter the join based upon the Employee status:

```
public List obtainActiveEmployeeCount() {
        TypedQuery<Object[]> qry = em.createQuery("SELECT j.title, count(e) "
                + "FROM Jobs j LEFT JOIN j.employees e "
                + "ON e.status = 'ACTIVE' "
                + "WHERE j.salary >= 50000 "
                + "GROUP BY j.title", Object[].class);
        List data = new ArrayList();
         if (!qry.getResultList().isEmpty()) {
             List<Object[]> tdata = qry.getResultList();
            for (Object[] t : tdata) {
                HashMap resultMap = new HashMap();
                resultMap.put("title", t[0]);
                resultMap.put("count", t[1]);
                data.add(resultMap);
            }
        }
        return data;
    }
```

How It Works

When writing Jakarta Persistence Query Language queries, it is sometimes beneficial to join two or more database tables to acquire related information. Furthermore, it is usually helpful to filter information based upon certain specified criteria so that the number of records returned can be manageable. Jakarta Persistence Query Language joins typically include INNER, OUTER, and FETCH joins. To review, an INNER join allows retrieval from two tables such that records being returned contain at least one match in both tables. For instance, you may want to query an Employee entity and join it to the Jobs entity to return only those employees who have a specific job title. An OUTER join allows retrieval from two tables such that all the records from one of the entities (left entity) are returned, regardless of whether they match with a record in the other entity. Lastly, a FETCH join enables the fetching of an association as a side effect of the query execution. The Jakarta Persistence Query Language includes the ON condition, which allows you to perform an OUTER join and include a specified condition with the join. This capability has always been available with the WHERE clause of the Jakarta Persistence Query Language query, but what about the cases when you want to return all matching records along with those that may not match, like with an OUTER join? Jakarta Persistence provides this functionality in a concise manner using ON conditions. Simply put, an ON condition modifies a join query such that it will incorporate better control over the data that is returned in a concise manner.

To demonstrate this new syntax, let's look at a SQL query, and then you will compare it to its Jakarta Persistence Query Language counterpart. The following SQL will join the EMPLOYEE table with the JOBS table on the JOB_ID field. It will also limit the returned records to those that include a salary of greater than or equal to 50,000 with the specification in the WHERE clause:

```
SELECT J.TITLE, COUNT(E.ID)
FROM JOBS J LEFT JOIN EMPLOYEE E
    ON J.JOB_ID = E.JOB_ID and E.STATUS 'ACTIVE'
WHERE J.SALARY >= 50000
GROUP BY J.TITLE;
```

This SQL will return all the JOB records and include a count of each job that contains an Employee whose status is ACTIVE. The method in the solution of this recipe contains the Jakarta Persistence Query

Language equivalent for this SQL, using the ON condition to perform the join. In the end, the ON condition helps make Jakarta Persistence Query Language outer joins more concise and easier to use. Although the same capability has been available in previous versions of the Jakarta Persistence Query Language, the ON clause helps make record filtering with joins much easier.

9-15. Processing Query Results with Streams

Problem

You wish to process the results of a Jakarta Persistence query using a concise functional style.

Solution

Utilize streams to process the results of a Jakarta Persistence query. In the following example, a Stream is returned from a Jakarta Persistence query. The Stream is then processed using the Stream API to retrieve the desired results. This example demonstrates a Stream being used to process author works by author:

```
public List<AuthorWork> performFindByAuthorStream(BookAuthor author){
    Stream<AuthorWork> awStream = em.createQuery("select object(o) from AuthorWork o")
        .getResultStream();
    return awStream.filter(
        ba -> author.equals(ba.getAuthorId()))
        .collect(Collectors.toList());
}
```

■ **Note** This example demonstrates filtering the results of a SQL query using streams, which may not be the most effective approach. A very large result set may significantly increase the time it takes to process. Please be sure to weigh the performance benefits of using the standard Jakarta Persistence Query Language vs. using Streams to ensure you choose the best option for your situation.

How It Works

Streams offer a powerful alternative to processing SQL result sets. The Jakarta Persistence API is aligned with the Stream API of Java SE, allowing developers to benefit from the use of the Stream API while processing results. The Stream API allows one to apply filters and functions to data in a functional way, making processing much more concise and easy to follow. The getResultStream() method of the *Query* and TypeQuery interfaces, allows one to return a Stream of results, rather than a List or single object result. Once the Stream has been returned, it can be processed accordingly.

Breaking down the recipe example, first the AuthorWork entity is queried without any filters. Note that instead of calling upon getResultList(), the getResultStream() is called upon. This will return a Stream of the objects that are being queried. Once the Stream has been returned, it is processed by filtering the data to return only those records that have an authorId matching what was passed into the method. Note the notation which is used for processing is as follows:

```
ba -> authorId.equals(ba.getAuthorId())
```

First, note that the syntax is very much like that of the lambda processing syntax. The `ba -> ` portion is simply a local variable that is declared to represent the current object in the `Stream`, and the arrow characters are used to note that the processing expression follows. Each object in the stream is iterated, and `ba` changes for each one. Next, the filter is applied, only retaining those records that have `authorId` equal to the one that is passed into the method. Next, we wish to return a `List` of the results from that filtering process, so the `Collectors` utility is used to collect the filtered results into a list:

```
.collect(Collectors.toList())
```

It is important to keep in mind that if it is possible to filter queries in the traditional manner, via the SQL `where` clause, that may perform better than the `Stream` alternative. The reason is that the default `Stream toResultStream()` implementation will fetch all of the data from the query into an in-memory list and then process accordingly. This could be very bad if the result set is large. It is possible for different implementations of this process to be created. At the time of the Jakarta EE 8 release, Hibernate provides something similar in the `stream()` method, whereby a scrollable `ResultSet` is returned, rather than the entire list of results. Such an implementation would perform much better in a large dataset scenario.

9-16. Converting Attribute Data Types

Problem

You wish to convert the data type of a particular entity class attribute when it is retrieved from the database. In turn, you wish to convert back to the original data type when persisting data back to the database column.

Solution

Create an attribute converter to convert to/from different data types when retrieving and persisting data. Suppose that you would like to convert between a Boolean-based full employee status within a Java entity and a String-based ACTIVE or INACTIVE value within the database. Each time the attribute is accessed, the converter is used to automatically convert the values to/from the desired data types:

```java
package org.jakartaeerecipes.converter;
import jakarta.persistence.AttributeConverter;
import jakarta.persistence.Converter;
@Converter
public class EmployeeStatusConverter implements AttributeConverter<Boolean, String> {
    @Override
    public String convertToDatabaseColumn(Boolean entityValue) {
        if(entityValue){
            return "ACTIVE";
        } else {
            return "INACTIVE";
        }
    }
    @Override
    public Boolean convertToEntityAttribute(String databaseValue) {
        return databaseValue.equals("ACTIVE");
    }
}
```

The converter can be applied to a single entity class attribute, as follows:

```
@Column(name= "STATUS")
@Convert(converter=org.jakartaeerecipe.converter.EmployeeStatusConverter.class)
private boolean status;
```

In this example, when the Employee object is persisted to the database, a true would be converted to "ACTIVE". Likewise, when an Employee object is retrieved, then an "INACTIVE" status value is converted to false.

How It Works

Attribute converters allow for data type conversion to occur between the database column and an entity class attribute. Attribute converters can be created by annotating a class with @Converter and implementing the AttributeConverter interface. The AttributeConverter type takes two arguments, those being the type of the entity class attribute and the type of the database column. When implementing AttributeConverter, two methods must be overridden. The convertToDatabaseColumn() method should provide the implementation for conversion from the entity class attribute to the database column type. Similarly, the convertToEntityAttribute() method should provide the opposite implementation, conversion from the database column type to the entity class attribute.

In the example for this recipe, the attribute converter is applied to a single entity class attribute. To do so, the @Convert annotation is applied to the attribute, passing the converter class as an argument. The converter could also be applied to all entity class attributes pertaining to the entity data type by changing the @Converter annotation on the attribute converter to the following: @Converter(autoApply=true).

CHAPTER 10

■ ■ ■

Jakarta Bean Validation

One of the most important pieces of any data-driven application is data validation. It is imperative that one validates data before it is inserted into a database to maintain integrity. There are many reasons to validate, the most important being security purposes, data consistency, and proper formatting. Many web applications use validation in the presentation layer via JavaScript for validation of form data and in the persistence layer. However, sometimes JavaScript can become problematic in that the code can become unwieldy, and there is also no guarantee that it will execute. It is oftentimes found to be a good idea to perform validation within the domain model, although this can cause code clutter.

In this chapter, we will look at the Jakarta Bean Validation API, which is used to apply validation to a JavaBean. In the context of Jakarta EE, since Jakarta Persistence entity classes are Plain Old Java Objects (POJOs), this allows developers to make use of Jakarta Bean Validation on entity classes and entity class attributes. A Java controller class may have validation logic to ensure that only specific data passes through to the database. The Jakarta Bean Validation API is another means of performing data validation in either the domain model or presentation layer via metadata, using an annotation-based approach. To validate with this API, one simply applies validation constraint annotations on the entity class attribute(s), as needed, and the constraint validators will automatically enforce the validation. Jakarta Bean Validation was first introduced into the Jakarta EE platform with Java EE 6, and it had been given a face-lift in Java EE 8, introducing several new features for the Bean Validation 2.0 release. In Jakarta Bean Validation 3.0, only changes are made to support migration of javax to jakarta package namespace in Jakarta EE. Although this chapter will focus on the use of Jakarta Bean Validation with Jakarta EE, it can be used across all different flavors of Java, be it Java FX, previous Java EE releases, or Java SE. Jakarta Bean validation contains an API that can be used to manually invoke validation, but in most cases the validation occurs automatically because of the integration that has been made across the various Jakarta EE specifications.

Jakarta Bean Validation annotation constraints can be applied on types, fields, methods, constructors, parameters, container elements, and other container annotations. Validation is applied not only to the object level, but it can also be inherited from super classes. Entire object graphs can be validated, meaning that if a class declares a field which has the type of a separate class containing validation, cascading validation can occur.

This chapter will demonstrate examples of each validation type, explaining the strongholds for each of the different methodologies. In the end, you will have a good understanding of how the Jakarta Bean Validation API works, and you should be able to apply Jakarta Bean Validation strategies to your applications.

■ **Note**   Jakarta Bean Validation also allows declaring constraints via XML, rather than annotations. For the purposes of brevity, this chapter will not cover this feature. For more information, please see the Bean Validation 3.0 specification (https://jakarta.ee/specifications/bean-validation/3.0/jakarta-bean-validation-spec-3.0.html).

© Josh Juneau and Tarun Telang 2022
J. Juneau and T. Telang, *Java EE to Jakarta EE 10 Recipes*, https://doi.org/10.1007/978-1-4842-8079-9_10

10-1. Validating Fields with Built-In Constraints

Problem

Imagine that you create a Chapter entity class, which will be used to store the contents regarding a book chapter. In doing so, you wish to apply validation to specified fields of the entity class such that only compliant data is allowed to be inserted or updated in the database. In this case, suppose that there are several fields that must contain values, and you also want to be certain that Strings of text are within the size limits of the underlying database field.

Solution #1

Apply the pertinent Jakarta Bean Validation constraints to field(s) that you wish to validate. In this example, the standard @NotNull and @Size constraint annotations are placed on specific fields of the Chapter entity. Namely, the id attribute is marked as @NotNull so that it must contain a value, and the title attribute is marked to have a maximum size of 150 characters:

```
import jakarta.persistence.*;
import jakarta.validation.constraints.NotNull;
import jakarta.validation.constraints.Size;

import java.math.BigDecimal;

@Entity
@Table(name="CHAPTER")
public class Chapter {

    @Id
    @Basic(optional = false)
    @NotNull
    @Column(name = "ID")
    private BigDecimal id;

    @Column(name="CHAPTER_NUMBER")
    private short chapterNumber;

    @Size(max = 150)
    @Column(name="TITLE")
    private String title;

    @Lob
    @Column(name = "DESCRIPTION")
    private String description;

...
```

Solution #2

Apply the pertinent Jakarta Bean Validation constraint annotations to the getter methods (accessor methods) of the field(s) you wish to validate. In this case, the following example shows the getId() and getTitle() methods. Each of these accessor methods is annotated accordingly:

```
@NotNull
private BigDecimal getId(){
    return this.id;
}

...
@Size(max=150)
private String getTitle(){
    return this.title;
}
```

How It Works

The Jakarta Bean Validation API provides several built-in constraint definitions that are ready to use. These standard constraints span the array of common use cases for data validation. Table 10-1 lists each of the standard validation constraint annotations along with a description of each.

Table 10-1. *Standard Built-In Constraints*

Annotation	Description
@Null	The annotated element must be null
@NotNull	The annotated element must not be null
@AssertTrue	The annotated element must be true
@AssertFalse	The annotated element must be false
@Min	The annotated element must be a number with a value that is higher or equal to the specified minimum
@Max	The annotated element must be a number with a value that is lower or equal to the specified maximum
@DecimalMin	The annotated element must be a decimal with a value that is higher or equal to the specified minimum
@DecimalMax	The annotated element must be a decimal with a value that is lower or equal to the specified maximum
@Negative	The annotated element must be a strictly negative number
@NegativeOrZero	The annotated element must be a negative number or zero
@Positive	The annotated element must be a strictly positive number
@PositiveOrZero	The annotated element must be strictly positive or zero
@Size	The annotated element size must fall within the specified boundaries
@Digits	The annotated element must be a number in the accepted range

(*continued*)

447

Table 10-1. (*continued*)

Annotation	Description
@Past	The annotated element must be an instant, date, or time in the past
@PastOrPresent	The annotated element must be an instant, date, or time in the past or present
@Future	The annotated element must be an instant, date, or time in the future
@FutureOrPresent	The annotated element must be an instant, date, or time in the future or present
@Pattern	The annotated element must fall within the constraints of the specified regular expression
@NotEmpty	The annotated element must not be empty or null
@NotBlank	The annotated element must not be null and must contain at least one character
@Email	The annotated string must be a well-formed email address

To apply validation to a field, simply specify the built-in or custom Jakarta Bean `Validation` annotation to the field declaration, along with the appropriate constraint attribute(s). You also have the option of annotating a field's corresponding getter method, rather than the field declaration itself. Any single field may have more than one annotation constraint applied to it. You are welcome to combine constraints to suit the requirement. If an annotated class extends another class that contains Jakarta Bean Validation constraints, then those constraints are applied to all annotated fields, whether the field belongs to the extended class or the class that extends.

Attributes are used to associate metadata with the annotations for specifying information such as the error message that is to be displayed should the validation fail or the number of characters to be validated. Table 10-2 lists the common constraint annotation attributes that you'll find across each of the different constraints. These are all considered reserved names.

Table 10-2. *Common Constraint Annotation Attributes*

Attribute	Description
message	Allows a String for specifying an error message to display
groups	Specifies processing groups with which the constraint declaration is associated
payload	Specifies the payload with which the constraint declaration is associated
validationAppliesTo	Used to specify which constraint targets a validation constraint will apply to

Most of the constraint attributes are optional. However, in some cases, an attribute should be specified. For instance, when applying the @Size constraint, if the max attribute is not specified, the default is 2147483647. Therefore, given that someone will likely never enter a value that large, one should specify a maximum size using the max attribute. The groups attribute is used to specify if a particular annotation constraint is part of a processing group. A validation group defines a subset of constraints, and a group can simply be an empty interface. Groups are used to control the order of evaluation for constraints or to perform partial state validation for a JavaBean. To learn more about applying groups, please refer to Recipe 10-8. The payload attribute is used to assign a payload to a validation annotation. Payloads are typically used by bean validation clients to associate some kind of metadata information. A payload is usually defined as a class that implements the Payload interface. Payloads can be seen in more detail with Recipe 10-2.

10-2. Writing Custom Constraint Validators

Problem

Your application requires a specific validation that is not provided among the built-in Jakarta Bean Validation constraints. For example, you wish to validate that a book title includes the word "Java" in the title.

Solution

Implement a custom constraint validator for the application. A custom constraint can be created by developing a constraint annotation along with a validator implementation class and a default error message. The example that follows demonstrates a custom constraint that is used to compare whether a String contains the text "Java." The annotation class for such a constraint may resemble the following:

```
import jakarta.validation.Payload;

import java.lang.annotation.*;
import static java.lang.annotation.ElementType.*;
import static java.lang.annotation.RetentionPolicy.RUNTIME;

@Target({FIELD, ANNOTATION_TYPE})
@Retention(RUNTIME)
@Documented
public @interface JavaBookTitle {
    String message() default "{org.jakartaeerecipe.annotation.message}";
    Class<?>[] groups() default { };
    Class<? extends Payload>[] payload() default { };
}
```

The implementation for the validator should look like that of the BookTitleValidator class:

```
import jakarta.validation.*;

public class BookTitleValidator implements ConstraintValidator<JavaBookTitle, String> {
    @Override
    public void initialize(JavaBookTitle constraintAnnotation) {
    }

    @Override
    public boolean isValid(String title, ConstraintValidatorContext
    constraintValidatorContext) {
     return title.toUpperCase().contains("JAVA");
    }
}
```

Now that the constraint annotation has been created, it can be applied to a field as follows:

```
@JavaBookTitle(message = "Book Title Should Contain The Word Java")
@Column(name = "TITLE")
protected String title;
```

How It Works

Creating a custom validation constraint annotation is quite easy, although the implementation may look a bit daunting at first glance. A validation constraint consists of the following pieces:

- Constraint annotation
- Validator implementation class
- Default error message

The constraint annotation is created just like any standard Java annotation. The annotation declaration is a standard Java interface. The interface must be annotated with @Target, passing a list in curly brackets, which specifies the types that the annotation can be applied to. The @Retention annotation can also be specified on the declaration, passing a value to specify how long the annotation will be retained. Valid values include SOURCE, CLASS, and RUNTIME. An annotation declaration may also include the @Documented annotation, which indicates whether an annotation declaration will be documented by Javadoc by default.

Annotation declaration interfaces can contain elements to associate metadata to a validation constraint. A constraint annotation must contain three elements: a message element of type String, a groups() method, and a payload() method. Each of the elements can be declared within the annotation constraint with a default value, as seen in the example. The message element is used to create a default error message for the validator. The message may include String interpolation, and it may also be loaded from a resource bundle to take advantage of features such as internationalization. The groups() method is used to specify any processing groups to which the constraint will belong. The Default group is declared if no group is specified and the array is empty. The payload() method is typically used to associate metadata with a given validation constraint.

A validationAppliesTo element can be used to specify which targets the constraint associates against. Lastly, one may choose to declare a custom element to assist in the validation of values.

The next piece of required code is the constraint implementation class. This class should implement CustomValidator<AnnotationType, Type>. In doing so, this class must override the initialize() and isValid() methods. If there is any data that needs to be initialized prior to validation, then it should be done within the initialize method. The isValid() method should accept the data to be validated, along with ConstraintValidatorContext as arguments. The implementation of the method should validate the data and return a boolean to indicate whether the data complies with the constraint.

Once these pieces of code are in place, the annotation can be specified on the targets for validation. The annotation should specify additional elements to associate metadata, if needed. In the example, the annotation specifies the message element, which allows a default error message to be declared.

10-3. Validating at the Class Level

Problem

You wish to validate some or all the fields within an object to ensure that those fields of the object contain valid data. For instance, you must validate that a field declared as numChapters contains the same number of chapters as those in a field of type List<Chapter>.

Solution

Specify class-level constraints to perform the validation. In the example for this recipe, the Book entity contains several fields that must validate against one another in order to constitute a valid object:

```
@ValidNumChapters
public class Book implements Serializable {

    private static final long serialVersionUID = 1L;

    @Id
    @Basic(optional = false)
    @NotNull
    @Column(name = "ID")
    private BigDecimal id;

    @Size(max = 150)
    @Column(name = "TITLE")
    protected String title;

    @Size(max = 500)
    @Column(name = "IMAGE")
    private String image;

    @Column(name = "NUM_CHAPTERS")
    private int numChapters;

    @Column(name = "NUM_PAGES")
    private int numPages;

    @Lob
    @Column(name = "DESCRIPTION")
    private String description;

    @Column(name = "PUBLISH_DATE")
    private LocalDate publishDate;

    @ManyToMany(mappedBy="books")
    private Set<BookAuthor> authors;

    @OneToMany(mappedBy="book", cascade=CascadeType.ALL)
    private List<Chapter> chapters = null;
    ...
}
```

The @ValidateNumChapters annotation is used to validate that the numChapters value is greater than or equal to the chapters List. Following this logic, a Book may be in progress and more Chapter objects can be added to the list as completed, but there cannot be more Chapter objects than the numChapters value. As covered in Recipe 10-2, to create the @ValidateNumChapters annotation, there must be an annotation declaration class and a constraint implementation class. The following class is used to declare the annotation:

```
import java.lang.annotation.Documented;
import static java.lang.annotation.ElementType.ANNOTATION_TYPE;
import static java.lang.annotation.ElementType.TYPE;
import java.lang.annotation.Retention;
```

```
import static java.lang.annotation.RetentionPolicy.RUNTIME;
import java.lang.annotation.Target;

import jakarta.validation.Payload;

@Target({ TYPE, ANNOTATION_TYPE})
@Retention(RUNTIME)
@Documented
public @interface ValidNumChapters {
    String message() default "{org.jakartaeerecipe.annotation." +
            "message}";
    Class<?>[] groups() default { };
    Class<? extends Payload>[] payload() default { };
}
```

The annotation class contains the default error message as well as the declaration for the annotation itself. The following class is the constraint validation implementation for validating the number of chapters in the book:

```
public class NumChaptersValidator implements ConstraintValidator<ValidNumChapters, Book> {
    @Override
    public void initialize(ValidNumChapters constraintAnnotation) {
    }
    @Override
    public boolean isValid(Book book, ConstraintValidatorContext cvc) {
        return book == null ? true: book.getChapters().size() <= book.getNumChapters();     }
}
```

Once these classes have been created, the annotation can be placed onto the class(es) accordingly.

How It Works

The class-level validation constraint may be sometimes more useful, since it can validate one or more fields of the class. Applying a validation constraint to the class level means all the fields must adhere to the validation constraint.

If a built-in validation constraint is applied at the class level, all fields of the class must adhere to the constraint. For instance, if @NotNull were applied, then each field within the class must be filled for each instance. If a class contains fields of a type other than String, applying a constraint such as @Size at the class level will not work. Class-level constraints are mostly custom created and apply only to a specified subset of the class fields.

In the recipe example, the @ValidNumChapters constraint is placed at the class level, which means that this constraint has access to each of the fields within the class. However, the constraint implementation only actually validates the numChapters and chapters fields to determine if the number of Chapter objects within the List<Chapter> is less than or equal to the numChapters value. Recipe 10-2 covers the declaration of an annotation in detail, so I won't cover that here.

The important piece of the puzzle for this recipe is to look closely at the annotation implementation within the NumChaptersValidator class. To create this implementation, the class must implement ConstraintValidator<A extends Annotation, T>. The ConstraintValidator interface utilizes generics to specify the constraint along with an object which will be validated. In the signature of the interface, A must be the name of an annotation declaration class, so in this case ValidNumChapters. T is any given object that must resolve to a nonparameterized type, or generic parameters of T must be unbounded wildcard types. In the example, the Book entity class is specified as T.

The interface enforces the implementation of the `initialize (A constraintAnnotation)` and `isValid(T value, ConstraintValidatorContext context)` methods. Many times, the initialize method can be empty, but, if needed, it should contain code to initialize the validator in preparation for a call to `isValid`. The `isValid` method contains the actual validation logic. The Book object that is passed into the method is first checked to ensure that it is not null. If it is null, then true is returned; otherwise, the number of Chapter objects in the chapters List is compared against the numChapters value to return a boolean result.

Class-level validation can be very powerful, as it allows validation of class fields in a custom manner. It is also very easy to implement, making it even more powerful when validating complex objects such as those that contain Lists of other objects.

10-4. Validating Parameters

Problem

You want to specify some preconditions on a method such that the parameters adhere to a specified constraint.

Solution

Apply validation constraint annotations to method parameter(s) such that the parameter(s) will be validated by either built-in or custom constraints. This will enforce constraint logic at the time of a method call such that only arguments that meet the specified constraints will be acceptable as parameters to a given method. In the following example, a method that accepts a parameter is demonstrated including a validation constraint:

```
public void submitEmailAddress(@Email String emailAddress){
    System.out.println("Do something with the address: " + emailAddress);
}
```

In this example, a single parameter is being validated. However, it is possible to include more than one parameter containing a validation constraint. It is also possible to include a cross-parameter constraint at the method level, which can be used to apply validation across all the method parameters.

How It Works

Jakarta Bean Validation makes it possible to include validation constraint method parameters for the purposes of applying preconditions that will ensure invalid data cannot be passed into the method. Either built-in or custom validation constraints can be applied to method parameters. If an invalid value is passed into a method that contains a parameter constraint, a validation error will be thrown, and the method will not be executed.

In the example, the submitEmailAddress method accepts a single parameter, emailAddress. If the emailAddress parameter does not adhere to a valid email format, as specified via the @Email validation constraint, the method call will fail. It is also possible to validate more than one method parameter by applying a constraint validation on the method itself. Doing so is much the same as applying a class-level constraint (Recipe 10-3) in that the constraint can be either built-in or custom. Built-in constraints applied at the method level, such as @NotNull, would be applied to each of the parameters of the method. Custom constraints can be created in the same manner as previously shown in Recipe 10-3 whereby one or more parameters can be validated. Constraints that are placed at the method level must be configured within the

ConstraintValidator implementation using the @SupportedValidationTarget annotation to indicate that the constraint is to be placed on the method level. This is because return type constraints are also placed at the method level, so the @SupportedValidationTarget helps to distinguish which validation type shall occur. The following code example demonstrates how to write a constraint validation implementation targeted for use at the method level:

```
@SupportedValidationTarget(value = ValidationTarget.PARAMETERS)
public class ValidEmployeeEmailValidator implements ConstraintValidator<ValidEmployeeEmail,
Object[]> {
    @Override
    public void initialize(final ValidEmployeeEmail constraintAnnotation) {
        // no-op
    }
    @Override
    public boolean isValid(final Object[] parameters, final ConstraintValidatorContext
    context) {
        // Ensure employee email is from our organization
        return parameters == null || parameters[0].toString().contains("@acme.com");
    }
}
```

10-5. Constructor Validation

Problem

You wish to validate the instantiation of a class through the validation of constructor parameters.

Solution

Apply validation constraint annotations to the individual constructor parameters or at the constructor level itself to perform validation. In the following example, a constructor is annotated with @NotNull at the constructor level. Therefore, the @NotNull validation constraint is applied across each of the constructor parameters:

```
@NotNull
public ConstructorValidationController(String parameterOne,
                                       String parameterTwo){
    this.p1 = parameterOne;
    this.p2 = parameterTwo;
}
```

How It Works

In some cases, it makes sense to validate parameters that are passed into a class at the time of instantiation. Jakarta Bean Validation makes this easy by allowing one to apply constraint annotations to parameters of a class constructor or to the constructor itself. When an annotation is placed on the parameters of a class constructor, the class cannot be instantiated if the validations fail. Similarly, if a constraint annotation is placed on the constructor declaration itself, then it will be applied across all of the constructor parameters. Such a constraint that is applied at the constructor level is called a cross-parameter constraint.

In the example, a cross-parameter @NotNull annotation is applied to the constructor of a class. Each of the parameters of the constructor must contain a value; otherwise, the validation will fail, and the class will not be instantiated. As mentioned previously, if a custom annotation were placed on the constructor, it could validate one or more of the parameters, just like a method-level constraint.

■ **Note** Take special care to ensure that unintended behavior does not occur because of subtype constructor constraints. It is important to keep the class hierarchy in mind when applying validation constraints on a class or class constructor.

10-6. Validating Return Values

Problem

You wish to validate the return value of a method, such that the returning value must adhere to a constraint. If the return value does not adhere, then a validation exception shall be thrown.

Solution

Place a validation constraint on the return type of a method signature to ensure that the result will conform to the validation constraint. In the following example, the return type of the method is validated by the annotation which is placed at the method level. In this case, the returned value must be in an email address format:

```
@Email
public String getEmailAddress(){
    return emailAddress;
}
```

How It Works

Validation constraint annotations that are placed at the method level can be targeted toward return value validation. In doing so, a method must return a valid value per the constraint; otherwise, a bean validation exception is thrown. To ensure that the constraint being placed at the method level is targeted toward a return type validation, the validator implementation must contain the @SupportedValidationTarget annotation, which specifies whether the validator applies to parameters or to the method itself. If a validation constraint implementation does not include this specification, there is no way for the Jakarta Bean Validation API to determine where the validation should be applied. In this case, the implementation would specify the following:

```
@SupportedValidationTarget(value = ValidationTarget.ANNOTATED_ELEMENT)
```

As with many of the other validation types, return type validation can utilize both standard and custom constraints.

10-7. Defining a Dynamic Validation Error Message

Problem

You wish to supply a dynamic error message containing information that is pertinent to the validated value for a constraint.

Solution

Utilize String interpolation within the Jakarta Bean Validation message attribute. String interpolation allows one to place message parameters and message expressions into a message String, thereby creating a dynamic String-based message. In the following example, the actual length of the String value will be substituted into the message to provide more feedback:

```
@Size(max = 150, message="The title cannot exceed {max} characters, current title is
$'{validatedValue}'")
@Column(name = "TITLE")
protected String title;
```

How It Works

Providing a clear error message for the user can make or break the success of an application. Utilizing String interpolation within an error message can help one to provide a specific message to the user to help indicate the cause of the validation failure. In much the same way that substitution variables work, an error message can contain zero or more variables that can be substituted.

■ **Note**   String interpolation requires Jakarta Expression Language libraries to be available within your project. If the Expression Language API and an implementation library are not added to the project, errors will be thrown at runtime. The following Maven dependencies can be added to fulfill this requirement:

```
<dependency>
    <groupId>jakarta.el</groupId>
    <artifactId>jakarta.el-api</artifactId>
    <version>5.0.0</version>
</dependency>
<dependency>
    <groupId>org.glassfish.web</groupId>
    <artifactId>jakarta.el</artifactId>
    <version>2.2.6</version>
</dependency>
```

To utilize String interpolation, curly braces can be used to surround the variable that will be substituted with dynamic values. Constraint attributes can be interpolated by placing the attribute inside of curly braces. In the example, the max attribute will be substituted for the {max} String interpolation. The validated value or custom expression variables can be specified to substitute values within a message by utilizing the EL notation, thereby enclosing within curly braces and preceded with a $. In the example, the $'{validatedValue}' variable is one such example. When the error message is produced, $'{validatedValue}' is replaced with the current validated value.

Message interpolation occurs in phases, outlined in the following order:

1) Resolve any message parameters using them as a key for a resource bundle named ValidationMessages.properties.

2) Resolve any message parameters using them as a key for a resource bundle that contains the standard error messages for built-in constraints.

3) Utilize a value constraint annotation member to substitute the message parameter. As such, the message parameters will simply be replaced by the value constraint annotation member of the same name.

4) Resolve any message parameters using evaluations as expressions of the Unified Expression Language. This allows us to formulate error messages based upon conditional logic and enables us to achieve advanced formatting.

The characters {,} and $ are special characters for message descriptors. Therefore, if one wishes to utilize one of these characters within a validation error message, it must be escaped by preceding it with a \. Therefore, to escape a $, one would use \$.

It is possible to define a custom message interpolation algorithm, if needed, by plugging in a custom MessageInterpolator implementation. To develop a custom interpolator, implement the jakarta.validation.MessageInterpolator interface. The interpolator must be thread-safe, and it is recommended to delegate the final implementation to the default interpolator. The default interpolator is available by calling upon Configuration.getDefaultMessageInterpolator(). For more information, please refer to the Jakarta Bean Validation specification (https://jakarta.ee/specifications/bean-validation/3.0/jakarta-bean-validation-spec-3.0.html).

10-8. Manually Invoking the Validator Engine

Problem

You wish to call upon the Jakarta Bean Validation validator engine programmatically, rather than relying upon automatic invocation.

Solution

Utilize the Validator API to perform validation. The Validator API allows one to create an executable validator from several different validation types, those being parameter, return, class, and so on. The following example demonstrates how to manually validate the data for a given entity class. In the following example, a Book entity class that is annotated with Jakarta Bean Validation constraints is manually instantiated and validated using the Validator API:

```
ValidatorFactory factory = Validation.buildDefaultValidatorFactory();
Validator validator = factory.getValidator();
Book book = new Book();
book.setId(BigDecimal.ONE);
book.setTitle("The Best Java Book");
Set<ConstraintViolation<Book>> violations = validator.validate(book);
for(ConstraintViolation<Book> violation: violations){
    System.out.println(violation.getMessage());
}
```

How It Works

Jakarta Bean Validation is typically automatically invoked within a Jakarta EE environment. For instance, if using Jakarta Server Faces, the validation occurs during the "Process Validations" phase automatically when a form is submitted either synchronously or asynchronously via Ajax. In some cases, it is useful to have the option to call upon the Validator API manually. This can be useful in a Java SE environment or perhaps when writing unit tests.

To invoke the Validator API, first create a ValidatorFactory by calling upon Validation.buildDef aultValidatorFactory(). Next, use the factory to generate a Validator. Lastly, validate a bean by calling upon the validator's validate() method, passing the bean to be validated. This method will return a Set of ConstraintViolation<T> objects. You can then iterate over each of the returned validation errors, obtaining each by calling upon the ConstraintViolation.getMessage() method.

After adding the following Maven dependencies, the recipe can be executed in the command line as a Java stand-alone application for testing:

```
<dependency>
<groupId>org.hibernate.validator</groupId>
<artifactId>hibernate-validator</artifactId>
<version>7.0.4.Final</version>
</dependency>
```

10-9. Grouping Validation Constraints

Problem

You wish to group several validation constraints together, such that an entire group of validations can occur at the same time.

Solution

Groups can be applied to constraint annotations by specifying the group(s) to which the annotation belongs via the group's annotation attribute. Groups themselves are generated via Java interfaces. The following interface defines the BookGroup:

```
public interface BookGroup {
}
```

The BookGroup group can be applied to one or more constraint annotations by specifying the interface within the groups annotation attribute, as seen in the following example:

```
...
@Entity
@Table(name = "BOOK")
@NamedNativeQuery(
    name="allBooks",
    query = "select id, title, description " +
                "FROM BOOK " +
                "ORDER BY id",
    resultClass=Book.class)
@NamedQueries({
    @NamedQuery(name = "Book.findAll", query = "SELECT b FROM Book b")})
@XmlRootElement
@ValidNumChapters
public class Book implements Serializable {
    private static final long serialVersionUID = 1L;
    @Id
    @Basic(optional = false)
    @NotNull
    @Column(name = "ID")
    private BigDecimal id;

    @JavaBookTitle(message = "Book Title Should Contain The Word Java")
    @Size(max = 150, message="The title cannot exceed {max} characters, current title is
    $'{validatedValue}'",  groups={BookGroup.class})
    @Column(name = "TITLE")
    protected String title;

    @Size(max = 500)
    @Column(name = "IMAGE")
    private String image;

    @NotNull(groups={BookGroup.class})
    @Column(name = "NUM_CHAPTERS")
    private int numChapters;
    @Column(name = "NUM_PAGES")
    private int numPages;

    @Lob
    @NotNull(groups={BookGroup.class})
    @Column(name = "DESCRIPTION")
    private String description;

    @Column(name = "PUBLISH_DATE")
    private LocalDate publishDate;

    @ManyToMany(mappedBy="books")
    private Set<BookAuthor> authors;
```

459

```
@OneToMany(mappedBy="book", cascade=CascadeType.ALL)
private List<Chapter> chapters = null;
public Book() {
}
```
...

Once the group has been put into place, validation can occur against a group, which would cause every constraint annotation that is assigned to that group to be validated. The following is a brief example of how one could utilize the Validation API to validate on a group basis:

```
ValidatorFactory factory = Validation.buildDefaultValidatorFactory();
Validator validator = factory.getValidator();
...
Set<ConstraintViolation<Book>> violations = validator.validate(book, "bookGroup");
for(ConstraintViolation<Book> violation: violations){
    System.out.println(violation.getMessage());
}
```

How It Works

Applying a group to a constraint annotation allows that annotation to become part of a grouping with other annotations to which the same group is applied. Formulating groups of annotations can be beneficial when performing tasks in which a specified set of constraints should always be validated. Validation can occur at the group level, thereby validating constraint groups as needed.

To create a group, one must utilize an interface. The Java interface should be empty and acts as a placeholder for the group. The group can be applied to a constraint annotation by specifying the annotation's groups attribute and passing a list of groups to it. The group attribute accepts one or more groups in the list. The example demonstrates a single group, named BookGroup, being applied to the annotation constraint:

```
@NotNull(groups={BookGroup.class})
@Column(name = "NUM_CHAPTERS")
```

To validate a group of constraints, pass the group or groups for validation to the Validator validate() method. In the example, the single BookGroup group is validated, but if there were more groups to be validated, the following syntax would come into play:

```
validator.validate(book, "group1", "group2");
```

Similar to Recipe 10-8, the code in this recipe can also be executed in the command line as a standalone application. Just make sure you have added in the Maven dependency the hibernate-validator or any other reference implementation of Jakarta Bean Validator.

CHAPTER 11

Jakarta Contexts and Dependency Injection

One of the most important specifications in the Jakarta EE platform is Jakarta Contexts and Dependency Injection. As stated on the cdi-spec.org site, it is a suite of complementary services that can improve the overall structure and design of code. The specification provides the following features for Jakarta EE and Java SE applications, as per the cdi-spec.org:

- Contextual objects with a well-defined life cycle providing multiple scopes of availability

- Ability to bind directly between contextual objects and the Unified Expression Language (EL)

- Dependency injection utilizing a type-safe system that is easy to use

- Binding of interceptors to contextual objects

- Event notification model

- Portable extension SPI

As mentioned in the list, perhaps one of the most widely used features of Jakarta CDI is the ability to bind the web tier and the business logic or transactional tier of the Jakarta EE platform together. Jakarta CDI makes it easy to expose business objects for use within web views via EL so that developers can directly bind Jakarta Server Faces view components to public JavaBean members and methods. Another widely used feature is the injection of contextual classes and resources into other Java objects in a type-safe and efficient manner.

Note Jakarta Faces (`https://github.com/jakartaee/faces`) is the Jakarta EE open source specification that was previously Java Server Faces.

Jakarta CDI is architected from two methodologies: contexts and dependency injection. *Contexts* provide the ability to bind the life cycle and interactions of stateful components to well-defined but extensive contexts. In the Jakarta EE tutorial, *dependency injection* is defined as the ability to inject components into an application in a type-safe way, including the ability to choose at deployment time which implementation of a particular interface to inject. To make use of Jakarta CDI, a developer should become familiar with a series of annotations that can be used to decorate objects and injected components. This chapter covers recipes that will demonstrate such annotations and where they should be used.

© Josh Juneau and Tarun Telang 2022
J. Juneau and T. Telang, *Java EE to Jakarta EE 10 Recipes*, https://doi.org/10.1007/978-1-4842-8079-9_11

461

Since Jakarta CDI provides a high level of loose coupling, it is an important piece of any Java enterprise application. Those applications that make use of Jakarta CDI in the correct manner can become very efficient because Jakarta CDI provides a decoupling of resources, as well as strong typing, which eliminates the requirement to use `String`-based names for managed resources by using declarative Java. This chapter will cover widely used features of this important specification, touching upon a few new features, including asynchronous events, and an API for booting Jakarta CDI in Java SE environments.

11-1. Injecting a Contextual Bean or Other Objects

Problem

You would like to utilize a contextual bean or other objects from within another class to take advantage of the bean's state.

Solution

Utilize dependency injection to make the bean or object available from within another class. The following class represents an object that can be injected into another class:

```
package org.jakartaeerecipe.chapter11;
import jakarta.inject.Named;

@Named("myBean")
@RequestScoped
public class CalculationBean implements java.io.Serializable{

    private int num1 = 0;
        private int num2 = 1;
        private int sum;

    public CalculationBean() { }

    // getters and setters
    // ...
    public int addNumbers(int[] numArray) {
        System.out.println("addNumbers() called...");
            setSum(getNum1() + getNum2());
 }
}
```

As you can see, the `CalculationBean` class represents a standard Java object. This object can be injected into another class by using the `@Inject` annotation. The following class, located in the same package as `CalculationBean` within the sources, demonstrates how to inject an object. Note that `CalculationBean` is never specifically instantiated; rather, it is injected:

```
package org.jakartaeerecipe.chapter11;

import jakarta.inject.Inject;

@Named
```

```
public class Calculator {
    @Inject
    CalculationBean calcBean;

    public void performCalculation(){
        calcBean.addNumbers();
    }
}
```

In the example, `CalculationBean` is injected into the bean. Once the bean or resource is injected into another Java class, it can be referenced as if it were local to the class into which it was injected. The @Inject annotation can be used to mark fields, methods, and constructors as injectable.

How It Works

The concept of dependency injection greatly reduces the amount of overhead that is necessary for a developer to gain reference to a contextual Java object from within another Java class. The Jakarta EE stack makes it very easy to gain reference to just about any Java object from within another class. Dependency injection refers to the ability to inject components into an application in a type-safe manner, including the ability to choose at deployment time which implementation of a particular interface to inject. Jakarta CDI allows almost any Java object to be injected into another with very little configuration. This ability increases the usability of resources since such resources can be referenced from any number of different classes and maintain the same state wherever they are being used. Just about any object can be injected anywhere with Jakarta CDI.

The following are some Java objects that can be injected:

- Almost any Java class

- Session beans

- Jakarta EE resources: data sources, JMS topics, queues, connection factories

- Persistence contexts

- Producer fields

- Objects returned by producer methods

- Web service references

- Remote EJB references

To inject a resource into another, the application module or JAR file must contain a `META-INF` directory that includes a `beans.xml` configuration file. The `beans.xml` file may be empty, or it can contain a descriptor to customize the way in which component scanning will occur within the application. As such, configuration within `beans.xml` may be slightly different depending upon the bean discovery mode for the application. However, for the purposes of this example (and for most general Jakarta CDI use cases), the `beans.xml` file specifies that bean discovery should occur for all classes within the application:

```
<?xml version="1.0" encoding="UTF-8"?>
<beans xmlns="https://jakarta.ee/xml/ns/jakartaee"
    xmlns:xsi="http://www.w3.org/2001/XMLSchema-instance"
    xsi:schemaLocation="https://jakarta.ee/xml/ns/jakartaee https://jakarta.ee/xml/ns/
    jakartaee/beans_4_0.xsd"
```

```
        version="4.0"
        bean-discovery-mode="all">
</beans>
```

The bean-discovery-mode attribute indicates how scanning shall occur. A value of all indicates that all components are processed, annotated indicates that only those components containing a class-level annotation are processed, and none effectively disables Jakarta CDI.

Next, the jakarta.inject.Inject annotation (@Inject) must be used to denote the class being injected by annotating a class member of the object type. For instance, if you want to inject a Java object of TypeA, you will declare a class variable of type TypeA and annotate it with @Inject, as follows:

```
@Inject
TypeA myTypeVar;
```

Note that the object used for injection (CalculationBean) contains a @Named annotation at the class level. This annotation doesn't need to be present to make the object available for injection unless the bean-discovery-mode="annotated". The @Named annotation allows one to provide a custom name for the object, and it also makes the object available for reference from within the Unified Expression Language.

Once said injection is performed, the declared field can be utilized throughout the class because it is a direct reference to the original class of the specified Java type. By defining a specific scope to the injection bean (Recipe 11-5), you can indicate whether an injected object will cause the instantiation of a new object of that type or whether it will look up an existing object of that type and reuse it. By far, one of the most convenient and useful cases for using Jakarta CDI is the ability to inject a managed bean into another object and make use of its current state, as if its contents existed everywhere.

Jakarta CDI provides type-safe injection because there is no need to specify a String-based name to instantiate or refer to another object. By maintaining declared variables that are used as points of injection, the variable name itself provides for strong typing and thus reduces the number of errors that may arise.

11-2. Binding a Bean to a Web View

Problem

You want to bind a JavaBean to a Jakarta Server Faces view using the Unified Expression Language (EL).

Solution

Annotate a class with the @Named annotation, and optionally specify a name for the class in String format. The String that is specified within the @Named annotation can be used to gain reference to the bean from within a Jakarta Server Faces view. If no optional String is specified, then the class name with a lowercase first letter is used to gain reference. The following example demonstrates the binding of a bean field and method to a Jakarta Server Faces view. The following Java class, named CalculationBean, is a Jakarta CDI managed bean that contains the @Named annotation, specifying myBean as the bean reference name:

```
import jakarta.enterprise.context.RequestScoped;
import jakarta.inject.Named;
@Named("myBean")
@RequestScoped
public class CalculationBean implements java.io.Serializable{
    private int num1 = 1;
    private int num2 = 0;
```

```
    private int sum;
    public CalculationBean(){
    }
    public void addNumbers(){
        System.out.println("Called");
        setSum(getNum1() + getNum2());
    }
    //getters and setters ...
}
```

The bean is bound to the Jakarta Server Faces view via the String-based name myBean, making a seamless binding between the web view and the backend business logic. The following Jakarta Server Faces view contains three fields and a Jakarta Server Faces commandButton component with an action that is bound to myBean via the Jakarta Server Faces EL:

```
<html xmlns="http://www.w3.org/1999/xhtml"
    xmlns:f="http://xmlns.jcp.org/jsf/core"
    xmlns:h="http://xmlns.jcp.org/jsf/html">
    <h:head>
        <meta http-equiv="Content-Type" content="text/html; charset=UTF-8"/>
        <title>Recipe 11-2: Binding a Bean to Jakarta Server Faces Views</title>
    </h:head>
    <h:body>
        <p>
            <h:form>
            <h:inputText value="#{myBean.num1}"/>
            <br/>
            <h:inputText value="#{myBean.num2}"/>
            <br/><br/>
            Sum: <h:outputText id="sum" value="#{myBean.sum}"/>
            <br/><br/>
            <h:commandButton value="Calculate" type="submit" action="#{myBean.addNumbers}">
            </h:commandButton>
            </h:form>
        </p>
    </h:body>
</html>
```

As mentioned previously, when the @Named annotation is specified without providing a String-based name designation, a binding name will be derived from the class name, converting the first letter of the class name to lowercase. For the following example, assume that the class CalculationBean that was referenced in the preceding example is going to be referenced from within a Jakarta Server Faces view via EL, except there will be no String-based identifier specified within the @Named annotation. Since the @Named annotation does not specify a name, the EL would refer to the class name as such:

```
<html xmlns="http://www.w3.org/1999/xhtml"
    xmlns:f="http://xmlns.jcp.org/jsf/core"
    xmlns:h="http://xmlns.jcp.org/jsf/html">
    <h:head>
        <meta http-equiv="Content-Type" content="text/html; charset=UTF-8"/>
        <title>Recipe 11-2: Binding a Bean to Jakarta Server Faces Views</title>
    </h:head>
```

```
<h:body>
    <p>
        <h:form>
        <h:inputText value="#{calculationBean.num1}"/>
        <br/>
        <h:inputText value="#{ calculationBean.num2}"/>
        <br/><br/>
        Sum: <h:outputText id="sum" value="#{ calculationBean.sum}"/>
        <br/><br/>
        <h:commandButton value="Calculate" type="submit" action="#{ calculationBean.
        addNumbers()}">
        </h:commandButton>
        </h:form>
    </p>
</h:body>
</html>
```

@MANAGEDBEAN VS. @NAMED?

If the @Named annotation can be used to specify a binding name for a Jakarta CDI bean, then what is the point of using the @ManagedBean annotation at all? The fact is the @ManagedBean annotation has been carried over from previous versions of Jakarta Server Faces. While it is still a capable mechanism of marking a bean as managed and providing a binding identifier to Jakarta Server Faces, it is suggested for use only when Jakarta CDI is not available for an application. If an application has full access to the entire Jakarta EE stack, including Jakarta CDI, then the @ManagedBean annotation is not a requirement.

The Jakarta CDI technology is much more powerful than the use of @ManagedBean, which was a customized solution for Jakarta Server Faces, and therefore Jakarta CDI is the preferred technique to use. This is the preferred technique because Jakarta CDI allows for a broader base of classes to be categorized as managed resources. Jakarta CDI also carries with it many other bonuses such as transaction management and type-safe dependency injection, of which @ManagedBean is not capable. As of Jakarta Server Faces 2.3, there are also certain capabilities that are only available when using Jakarta CDI, and @ManagedBean has become a deprecated technology.

To run the preceding code, launch this URL in your browser: `http://localhost:8080/JakartaEERecipes_Chapter08-1.0-SNAPSHOT/chapter11/recipe11_01.xhtml`.

You should see the output as shown in Figure 11-1.

```
4
1
```

Sum: 5

Calculate

Figure 11-1. *Output of Recipe 11-2*

How It Works

One of the most widely used features of Jakarta CDI is that it helps provide a seamless integration between the web views and the backend business logic for an application. Utilizing Jakarta CDI, public bean members and methods can be made accessible to Jakarta Server Faces views very easily. The jakarta. inject.Named annotation provides a facility for referencing a JavaBean class from within a Jakarta Server Faces view, either by accepting a String that will be used to make the reference or by simply utilizing the JavaBean class name with a lowercase first letter. The solutions provided within this recipe demonstrate both techniques. From a technical standpoint, the example of not using a String to provide the reference is the most type-safe solution. However, sometimes it is necessary to provide a String for reference, as demonstrated in the first example, but that solution is recommended only on an as-needed basis.

■ **Note**   Notice that the bean in the example, CalculationBean, contains a @RequestScoped annotation. This annotation specifies the scope for the bean state. For a fun trick, try to remove the @RequestScoped annotation and see what happens. As it turns out, the bean will still work as prescribed, but it will not return any results. This is because the bean will be reinitialized after each request. Therefore, the view will call the getSum method to read the current contents of the sum field, and it will have been reinitialized to a value of 0 before the request has been made. To learn more about bean scope, please see Recipe 11-4.

By annotating a class with @Named, it becomes available for use by Jakarta Server Faces views within the same application. Any public class member or method can be called upon from within a Jakarta Server Faces view by specifying the name of the class with a lowercase first letter, along with the public member or method that is needed. For instance, the following Jakarta Server Faces EL expression calls upon a method named myMethod that is contained within a class named MyClass. Note that this EL expression works if the class is named MyClass and includes an empty @Named annotation and if the class is named something different and includes the @Named("myClass") annotation:

```
#{myClass.myMethod}
```

As mentioned in the sidebar for this recipe, the @ManagedBean and @Named annotations play similar roles in that they both make Java classes available for use within a web view. However, it is safe to acknowledge that the @Named annotation is preferred over using @ManagedBean; please read the preceding sidebar for more information.

11-3. Allocating a Specific Bean for Injection

Problem

You have more than one JavaBean that implements a particular API, and you want to specify which of the beans you wish to inject.

Solution

Utilize a qualifier for the injection. To alleviate the issues of referencing a duplicate class, add a qualifier to each of the classes to differentiate them from one another. In the following code example, two classes, named PaperbackController and EbookController, each implement the Book interface. To allow client bean developers the ability to specify which of the bean classes should be injected, qualifiers are used. In the first listing, let's look at the IBook interface, which is being implemented by at least two JavaBean in the example:

```
Public interface IBook {
    String title = null;
    String description = null;
    String getTitle();
    String getDescription();

}
```

The class PaperbackController uses a qualifier @Paperback to differentiate it from other beans that implement the Book interface. The following listing is that of the PaperbackController class. Note that the Paperback interface (source shown next) must already exist to utilize the @Paperback annotation in this example:

```
package org.jakartaeerecipe.chapter11.recipe11_03;
import jakarta.inject.Named;
import jakarta.enterprise.context.SessionScoped;
import java.io.Serializable;
@Named(value = "paperbackController")
@SessionScoped
@Paperback
public class PaperbackController implements Serializable, IBook{
    /**
     * Creates a new instance of PaperbackController
     */
    public PaperbackController() {
    }
...
}
```

Another JavaBean, named EbookController, also implements the IBook interface. It contains a different qualifier, @Ebook, to differentiate it from other classes implementing the IBook interface. The EbookController class looks like the following:

```
package org.jakartaeerecipe.chapter11.recipe11_03;
import jakarta.inject.Named;
import jakarta.enterprise.context.SessionScoped;
@Named(value = "ebookController")
@SessionScoped
@Ebook
public class EbookController implements java.io.Serializable, IBook {
    /**
     * Creates a new instance of EbookController
     */
```

```
    public EbookController() {
    }
...
}
```

Lastly, let's see what the @Paperback and @Ebook binding annotations look like. The following two code listings show the contents of the org.jakartaeerecipe.chapter11.recipe11_03.Paperback and org.jakartaeerecipe.chapter11.recipe11_03.Ebook interfaces, which are used to create the two annotations:

```
import java.lang.annotation.*;

import jakarta.inject.Qualifier;

@Qualifier
@Retention(RetentionPolicy.RUNTIME)
@Target({ElementType.TYPE, ElementType.METHOD, ElementType.FIELD, ElementType.PARAMETER})
public @interface Paperback {}
```

```
import java.lang.annotation.*;

import jakarta.inject.Qualifier;

@Qualifier
@Retention(RetentionPolicy.RUNTIME)
@Target({ElementType.TYPE, ElementType.METHOD, ElementType.FIELD, ElementType.PARAMETER})
public @interface Ebook {}
```

When a client wants to make use of one or the other, it simply needs to call upon the qualifier as follows:

```
@Paperback PaperbackController paperback;
@Ebook EbookController ebook;
```

How It Works

When there are two or more classes that implement the same Java interface, Jakarta CDI needs some help to determine which of them is going to be used at an injection point. If an application that uses Jakarta CDI is deployed and an attempt is made to perform injection on a class that implements the same interface as another class, then Weld will throw an ambiguous dependency error. This means that it cannot determine what bean to use for the given injection point. When Jakarta CDI attempts to determine which bean should be used at an injection point, it takes all class types into account, and it also uses qualifiers. A qualifier is an annotation that can be applied at the class level to indicate the type of a bean. Qualifiers can also be used to annotate methods, or other areas of code, to help Jakarta CDI determine what kind of bean needs to be injected.

■ **Note** Weld is the reference implementation for Jakarta CDI. Therefore, you will see references to Weld within the server logs when utilizing Jakarta CDI within a Jakarta EE application. For more information regarding Weld, please see the online documentation at http://weld.cdi-spec.org/.

Every bean without an explicit qualifier automatically becomes annotated with the @Default qualifier. This qualifier is not needed when another qualifier type is used. In the solution to this recipe, two qualifiers are created to mark two different beans of the IBook type: the @Paperback and @Ebook qualifiers. To create a qualifier, generate a Java interface, and annotate that interface with @Qualifier, Retention(RetentionPolicy.RUNTIME), and @Target({ElementType.TYPE, ElementType.METHOD, ElementType.FIELD, ElementType.PARAMETER}). All qualifiers are created in the same manner, and once created, they can be used to annotate beans for differentiation. As you can see from the example, both the PaperbackController and EbookController classes have been annotated with their respective qualifiers. This makes for an easy way to allow Jakarta CDI to determine which bean to inject since each of the two beans is a different implementation of the Book type.

The Jakarta CDI API provides a handful of qualifiers out of the box that can be used within your bean classes. I have already discussed the @Default qualifier, which is added to any bean that does not explicitly contain a qualifier. Other qualifiers that are provided by Jakarta CDI include @Named and @Any. The @Named qualifier is used to mark a bean as EL injectable. If a bean contains a @Named qualifier, then it can be referenced within a Jakarta Server Faces view. The @Any qualifier is also included on all beans, and it allows an injection point to refer to all beans or events of a certain bean type. For instance, to refer to all the beans of type IBook, you could declare a member as follows:

```
@Inject @Any Instance<IBook> anyBook;
```

Qualifiers are not used in everyday code, but they are a feature of Jakarta EE that comes in handy on occasions where ambiguous bean injection is possible.

11-4. Determining Scope of a Bean

Problem

You want to ensure that the scope of a particular bean within your application will be available for a user's entire session.

Solution

Define the scope of the bean that you want to make available by annotating the bean accordingly. The org.jakartaeerecipe.chapter11.recipe11_03.PaperbackController and org.jakartaeerecipe.chapter11.recipe11_03.EbookController that are listed in Recipe 11-3 are examples of request-scoped beans since they are annotated as such. To make a bean available within a different scope, annotate using one of the other scope-based annotations. For example, let's create a bean that has a session scope, meaning that it will retain its state for multiple HTTP requests for the life of a web session. To create a session-scoped bean, annotate the class using @SessionScoped. The following class, named CartBean, is a Jakarta CDI session-scoped JavaBean that contains an integer field, which will be adjusted when a user invokes either the addItem or removeItem method:

```
package org.jakartaeerecipe.chapter11.recipe11_04;
// Import and change to @RequestScoped to see a functional difference
//import jakarta.enterprise.context.RequestScoped;
import jakarta.enterprise.context.SessionScoped;
import jakarta.inject.Named;
@Named
@SessionScoped
public class CartBean implements java.io.Serializable {
```

```
        private int orderList = 0;
        public CartBean(){}
        public void addItem(){
            setOrderList(getOrderList() + 1);
        }
        public void removeItem(){
            setOrderList(getOrderList() - 1);
        }
        /**
         * @return the orderList
         */
        public int getOrderList() {
            return orderList;
        }
        /**
         * @param orderList the orderList to set
         */
        public void setOrderList(int orderList) {
            this.orderList = orderList;
        }
}
```

■ **Note** The comment within the CartBean class indicates that if you change the scope to @RequestScoped, you will see a functional difference. The difference is that the orderList field will retain its state for only one HTTP request. Therefore, the number will never increase more than 1, and it will never decrease below -1.

What fun would this bean be if you did not use it within a Jakarta Server Faces view? Well, let's look at a Jakarta Server Faces view, named recipe11_04.xhtml, which utilizes the CartBean class to display the orderList field. The view contains two buttons, each of which is bound to different methods that reside within the CartBean class. One button will increase the size of the orderList int, and the other button will decrease it:

```
<html xmlns="http://www.w3.org/1999/xhtml"
    xmlns:f="http://xmlns.jcp.org/jsf/core"
    xmlns:h="http://xmlns.jcp.org/jsf/html">
    <h:head>
        <meta http-equiv="Content-Type" content="text/html; charset=UTF-8"/>
        <title>Recipe 11-4: Determining Scope of a Bean</title>
    </h:head>
    <h:body>
        <p>
            <h:form>
            <h:outputText value="#{cartBean.orderList}"/>
            <br/>
            <br/><br/>
            <h:commandButton value="Add Order" type="submit" action="#{cartBean.
            addItem()}"/>
```

```
        <h:commandButton value="Remove Order" type="submit" action="#{cartBean.
        removeItem()}"/>
        </h:form>
    </p>
  </h:body>
</html>
```

To see the result as in Figure 11-2, deploy the project in your GlassFish server and visit http://localhost:8080/JakartaEERecipes_Chapter08-1.0-SNAPSHOT/chapter11/recipe11_04.xhtml through your browser.

1

| Add Order | Remove Order |

Figure 11-2. *Output for Recipe 11-4*

How It Works

Depending upon an application's requirement, some beans may need to retain state longer than others. Sometimes, it makes sense for each user of an application to have its own version of a particular bean, whereas the state of the bean lives and dies with the user's session. Other times, it makes more sense for a bean to share its state among all users of an application, and still other times it makes sense for a bean's state to live and die with each user request. To specify the amount of time that a bean will retain its state, annotate the bean class with one of the Jakarta CDI scope annotations. Table 11-1 describes the different scope annotations.

Table 11-1. *Jakarta CDI Bean State Annotations*

Annotation	Description
@RequestScoped	Per user and retains state for a single HTTP request
@SessionScoped	Per user and retains state across multiple HTTP requests
@ApplicationScoped	Shared state across all user interactions within an application
@Dependent	Object exists to serve one client bean and contains the same life cycle as the bean (this is the default scope if none is specified)
@ConversationScoped	Per user scope and is utilized within a servlet-based application, such as one that utilizes Jakarta Server Faces. Boundaries of the scope are controlled via a developer and extend the scope across multiple invocations of the servlet life cycle. All long-running conversations are scoped to a particular servlet session and may not cross session boundaries

While it is easy to define a particular scope for a bean, sometimes it takes some practice and testing to determine the correct scope for a particular application requirement. Moreover, as an application evolves, it makes sense to review the different scopes that have been applied to various beans to ensure that the assigned scope is still desirable.

■ **Note**   One of the most common mistakes when working with the scope annotations is importing the wrong annotation for use within the bean. Remember that Jakarta Server Faces has its own set of scope-based annotations for use within managed beans (only available for backward compatibility as of Jakarta Server Faces 2.3). Always be sure to import from the `jakarta.enterprise.context.*` package when working with Jakarta CDI scope, or you will achieve erroneous results.

11-5. Injecting Non-bean Objects

Problem

You want to inject an object that is not a bean into another Java class.

Solution

Use producer fields to inject objects that are not beans, objects that require custom initialization, or objects that may have varying values at runtime. To create a `Producer` field, annotate a public class field with the `jakarta.injection.Produces` annotation, and return the field you want to inject. In most cases, you will also need to annotate a producer method with a Jakarta CDI qualifier so that Jakarta CDI will know what to inject when called upon.

In this example, a JavaBean named `InitialValueController` contains a producer field that will be called upon to assign an initial value to Jakarta CDI bean fields. The following source listing is that of the `InitialValueController` class, which contains the producer field declaration:

```
package org.jakartaeerecipe.chapter11.recipe11_05;

import jakarta.enterprise.inject.Produces;
public class InitialValueController implements java.io.Serializable {
        @Produces
        @InitValue
        public int initialValue = 1000;
}
```

The producer field in the class listing contains a qualifier annotation of `@InitValue`. The qualifier implementation is as follows:

```
package org.jakartaeerecipe.chapter11.recipe11_05;

import java.lang.annotation.*;
import jakarta.inject.Qualifier;

@Retention(RetentionPolicy.RUNTIME)
@Target({ElementType.TYPE, ElementType.METHOD, ElementType.FIELD, ElementType.PARAMETER})
@Qualifier
public @interface InitValue {}
```

The producer field can be called upon from anywhere. In this case, it is injected into a Jakarta CDI bean to initialize a bean field value. In the following listing, the Jakarta CDI bean field named ProducerExample demonstrates how to inject the producer field and make use of it:

```
package org.jakartaeerecipe.chapter11.recipe11_05;

import jakarta.enterprise.context.SessionScoped;
import jakarta.inject.Inject;
import jakarta.inject.Named;

@Named
@SessionScoped
public class ProducerExample implements java.io.Serializable {

    @Inject
    @InitValue
    private int initial;

    private int orderList = -1;

    public ProducerExample(){ }

    public void addItem(){
        setOrderList(getOrderList() + 1);
    }

    public void removeItem(){
        setOrderList(getOrderList() - 1);
    }
    /**
     * @return the orderList
     */
    public int getOrderList() {
        return orderList == -1 ? initial : orderList;
    }
    /*
     * @param orderList the orderList to set
     */
    public void setOrderList(int orderList) {
        this.orderList = orderList;
    }
}
```

When the orderList field is added to a Jakarta Server Faces view, the getOrderList() method will be invoked upon the loading of the view because the orderList property is called upon from the view. This will, in turn, cause the orderList field value to become initialized the first time the Jakarta Server Faces view is loaded. The following code demonstrates the use of the field within a Jakarta Server Faces view. To see the sources, please look at the chapter11/recipe11_05.xhtml file:

```
<html xmlns="http://www.w3.org/1999/xhtml"
      xmlns:f="http://xmlns.jcp.org/jsf/core"
```

```
    xmlns:h="http://xmlns.jcp.org/jsf/html">
<h:head>
    <meta http-equiv="Content-Type" content="text/html; charset=UTF-8"/>
    <title>Recipe 11-5: Injecting Non-Bean Objects</title>
</h:head>
<h:body>
    <p>
        <h:form>
        <h:outputText value="#{producerExample.orderList}"/>
        <br/>
        <br/><br/>
        <h:commandButton value="Add Order" type="submit" action="#{producerExample.
        addItem()}"/>
        <h:commandButton value="Remove Order" type="submit" action="#{producerExample.
        removeItem()}"/>
        </h:form>
    </p>
</h:body>
</html>
```

To execute the code in this recipe, open the page at http://localhost:8080/JakartaEERecipes_ Chapter08-1.0-SNAPSHOT/chapter11/recipe11_05.xhtml to view the output as in Figure 11-3.

1000

| Add Order | Remove Order |

Figure 11-3. *Output of Recipe 11-5*

How It Works

Situations may arise when it makes sense to inject an object other than a Jakarta CDI managed bean or resource. Objects such as fields, methods, and the like can become injection targets if they are declared as producers. In some cases, it may make sense to declare a class field as an injectable object. To do so, annotate the field with the jakarta.enterprise.inject.Produces annotation (@Produces), and the EE container will then treat the field as a getter method for the field. In most cases, a Jakarta CDI qualifier annotation should also be created and used to annotate the field so that the field can be referenced via the qualifier at the injection point.

In the solution to this recipe, a field that will be used to initialize values is declared within a Java class named InitialValueController. The field name is initialValue, and it will return an int type, being the number that will be used for initialization. Looking at the code, you can see that a qualifier named @InitValue is also placed at the field declaration. This will allow the injection point to simply refer to the qualifier to gain a handle on the injection target. To use the initialValue field, it is injected into a Jakarta CDI managed bean as follows:

```
@Inject
@InitValue
private int initial;
```

Once injected, the field can be utilized as if it were part of the class into which it was injected. In the case of this example, it is used to initialize the value of the orderList field, which is then displayed via a Jakarta Server Faces view named chapter11/recipe11_05.xhtml.

It is also possible to create producer methods, which can return values that are injectable to a bean or non-Java (Jakarta Server Faces) context. In doing so, the @Produces annotation is used to annotate the method in the same manner that a field producer is declared. For example, the following method demonstrates the declaration of a producer method that would be used to inject an object of the Book type. The method can be called upon to return the desired Book object type, depending upon the type that is passed to it:

```
@Produces @BookQualifier public Book getBook(Book book){
        if(book.equals(EbookController.class))
            return new EbookController();
        else
            return new PaperbackController();
}
```

In this case, the method also uses a qualifier named @BookQualifier. The producer method result can then be injected into a bean or non-Java context. The injection point references the qualifier to make the injection possible, and the producer method is called by the container to obtain the desired instance object as follows:

```
@Inject
@BookQualifier
Book getBook(ebookController);
```

Producers can be a great way to develop injectable objects. With a bit of practice, they can also become valuable for creating sophisticated object factories via the use of a producer method.

11-6. Ignoring Classes

Problem

You want to mark a class as ignored by Jakarta CDI. This can be useful if you want to avoid certain classes or methods from being used in your application.

Solution #1

Denote the class with the @Vetoed annotation. Any class containing the @Vetoed annotation will be ignored by Jakarta CDI. The following example demonstrates the use of @Vetoed:

```
import jakarta.enterprise.inject.Vetoed;

@Vetoed
public class OrderBean implements java.io.Serializable {

    public OrderBean(){ }

    // class implementation
}
```

Solution #2

Denote the class with the @Requires annotation to mark the class as ignored by Jakarta CDI if it does not meet the specified requirements. The following example demonstrates how to utilize the @Requires annotation:

```
@Requires("jakarta.persistence.EntityManager")
public class EmployeeFacade {
    ...
    @Produces
    public EntityManager getEntityManager(){
        ...
    }
    ...
}
```

In this example, the @Requires annotation has a String containing jakarta.persistence. EntityManager passed to it. As such, if the specified class is not available and/or the class is unable to fulfill the specified dependency, then it will be ignored by Jakarta CDI.

How It Works

To veto a bean means to mark it as ignored by Jakarta CDI. Therefore, if a bean contains the @Vetoed annotation, it cannot be processed by Jakarta CDI. A vetoed class will not contain the life cycle of a contextual instance, and it cannot be injected into other classes. In fact, if a session bean contains the @Vetoed annotation, it cannot be considered a session bean at all. In some cases, it makes sense to mark a bean as such to ensure that it cannot become managed by Jakarta CDI. The following code demonstrates how to apply the @Vetoed annotation to a class.

The @Vetoed annotation can also be placed on a package declaration, which will prevent all the beans that are contained within that package from being processed via Jakarta CDI:

```
@Vetoed
package org.jakartaeerecipe.chapter11.*;
...
```

Any of the following definitions on a vetoed type will not be processed:

- Managed beans, session beans, interceptors, decorators
- Observer methods, producer methods, producer fields

The @Requires annotation can be used to conditionally mark a class to be ignored by Jakarta CDI if it does not meet the specified required criteria. The @Requires annotation accepts a String-based fully qualified class name of the dependency or dependencies. If the object can fulfill its dependencies, then it will be managed by Jakarta CDI. Like @Vetoed, the @Requires annotation can be placed on a package as well. If that package is unable to fulfill the dependency that is denoted by @Requires, then all classes contained within that package will not be managed by Jakarta CDI.

11-7. Disposing of Producer Fields

Problem

Your application uses a producer field, and you want the producer field to be destroyed once it is no longer required for use.

Solution

The following code excerpt demonstrates a producer field:

```
...
    @Produces
    List<Book> books;
...
```

How It Works

A producer method can be used to generate an object that needs to be removed once it is no longer needed. Much like a finalizer for a class, an object that has been injected via a producer method can contain a method that is invoked when the injected instance is being destroyed. Such a method is known as a *disposer method*. To declare a method as a disposer method, create a method defined within the same class as the producer method. The disposer method must have at least one parameter, with the same type and qualifiers as the producer method. That parameter should be annotated with @Disposes.

11-8. Specifying an Alternative Implementation at Deployment Time

Problem

You want to have the ability to code different implementations of an interface and then choose which implementation to utilize when an application is deployed.

Solution

Create a default implementation for an interface, and then create any alternative implementations for that interface and denote them with the @Alternative annotation. Specifying the jakarta.enterprise.inject. Alternative annotation flags a class as an alternate, and if that class is noted in the beans.xml file, then it will be loaded at deployment time, rather than the default interface implementation.

The following code excerpt demonstrates the use of an alternative class implementation. For the purposes of this demonstration, let's assume that there is already a default implementation for the OrderType interface named BookstoreOrderBean:

```
@Alternative
public class WarehouseOrderBean implements OrderType {
...
}
```

To specify the use of the alternative implementation rather than the default, modify the beans.xml file by listing the alternative class. The following is an example excerpt from the beans.xml file that designates the use of the WarehouseOrderBean:

```
<beans ... >
    <alternatives>
        <class>org.jakartaeerecipe.chapter11.WarehouseOrderBean</class>
    </alternatives>
</beans>
```

How It Works

Sometimes, it makes sense to create two or more implementations of a class for use in different environments. However, it can become a cumbersome nightmare to remove or rename classes to build and distribute the correct implementation for each environment. The use of the jakarta.enterprise.inject.Alternative annotation allows more than one implementation of an interface to be used, and the appropriate implementation can be specified by altering the file before deployment.

11-9. Injecting a Bean and Obtaining Metadata

Problem

You want to acquire metadata information about a bean from within your application classes.

Solution

Inject the interface of a bean into the classes that need to utilize the metadata. Once it's injected, call upon the bean methods to retrieve the required metadata. In the following example, a bean named OtherBean has its metadata injected and retrieved:

```
import jakarta.enterprise.inject.spi.Bean;

@Named("OtherBean")
public class OtherBean {
    @Inject Bean<Order> bean;
    public String getBeanName(){
        return bean.getName();
    }
    public Class<? extends Annotation> getBeanScope(){
        return bean.getScope();
    }
}
```

How It Works

If you need to use bean metadata, you can easily obtain it by injecting the target bean's metadata. To do so, specify the @Inject annotation, followed by the bean class of the target bean type. Once the bean interface has been injected, methods can be called upon it to obtain the desired information. Table 11-2 describes the different methods that can be called upon the Bean class to obtain metadata.

Table 11-2. *Bean Metadata*

Method	Description
getName	Returns the name of the bean
getBeanClass	Returns the bean class
getInjectionPoints	Returns a set of InjectionPoint objects for the bean
getQualifiers	Returns a set of qualifier annotations for the bean
getScope	Returns the scope of the bean
getStereotypes	Returns a set of stereotype data (common metadata) for a bean
getTypes	Returns a set of the bean types
isAlternative	Returns a Boolean to specify whether the bean is an alternative
isNullable	Returns a Boolean to specify whether a bean can be nullable

11-10. Invoking and Processing Events

Problem

You wish to invoke an action when a particular event occurs within your application.

Solution

Process the event in a synchronous or asynchronous manner by creating a Jakarta CDI event, an optional qualifier, observer, and event handling method. In this scenario, a bookstore wishes to send an alert to the book publisher each time a sale occurs. If an online sale occurs, the publisher will receive an alert to indicate as such. Similarly, if an in-store sale occurs, the publisher will receive a different alert to indicate a store sale has occurred. First, create a book event object to contain data elements that need to be made available at event invocation. In this case, some simple data regarding the book, store of sale, number of books, and price will be included in the event object. The source of the BookEvent class is as follows:

```
package org.jakartaeerecipe.chapter11.event;
import java.math.BigDecimal;
import java.time.LocalDate;
import java.util.List;
public class BookEvent {
    private BigDecimal book;
    private String storeName;
    private BigDecimal price;
    private int numBooks;
    private LocalDate date;
    private List<String> notifyList;
    // accessor methods (getters and setters)
}
```

Next, create a qualifier for each type of book event that can occur. The qualifier is an optional step, as it is only necessary when there will be more than one event of the same type. In this case, an online sale event or a store sale event can occur. The qualifier source for the `OnlineSale` is as follows, with the qualifier for the `StoreSale` being the same with only a different name:

```
package org.jakartaeerecipe.chapter11.qualifier;

import static java.lang.annotation.ElementType.TYPE;
import static java.lang.annotation.ElementType.FIELD;
import static java.lang.annotation.ElementType.METHOD;
import static java.lang.annotation.ElementType.PARAMETER;
import java.lang.annotation.Retention;
import static java.lang.annotation.RetentionPolicy.RUNTIME;
import java.lang.annotation.Target;
import jakarta.inject.Qualifier;

@Qualifier
@Retention(RUNTIME)
@Target({METHOD, FIELD, PARAMETER, TYPE})
public @interface OnlineSale {
}
```

Next, an observer needs to be used to listen for the event invocation and act upon it once made. In this case, two observers will need to be generated, one for the `@OnlineSale` and another for `@StoreSale`. The observers reside within a class named `BookEventHandler`:

```
public class BookEventHandler {
    @Inject
    private BookController bookController;
    public BookEventHandler(){
    }
    public void  notifyPublisherOnline (@Observes @OnlineSale BookEvent event) {
        for (String s : event.getNotifyList()) {
            System.out.println("Sending Notification to Publisher: " + s + " purchase of
            book online: "
                    + bookController.findById(event.getBook()).getTitle() + " from store: "
                    + event.getStoreName()
                    + " purchase price: $" + event.getPrice()
                    + " on: " + event.getDate());
        }
    }
    public void notifyPublisherInStore (@Observes @StoreSale BookEvent event) {
        for (String s : event.getNotifyList()) {
            System.out.println("Sending Notification to Publisher: " + s + " purchase of
            book in store: "
                    + bookController.findById(event.getBook()).getTitle() + " from store: "
                    + event.getStoreName()
                    + " purchase price: $" + event.getPrice()
                    + " on: " + event.getDate());
        }
    }
}
```

Lastly, create an event handling method that will invoke the Jakarta CDI event when a sale is made. For this example, a simple Jakarta Server Faces user interface will be used to invoke a sale event, so the event handling method will be placed into a Jakarta Server Faces controller class:

```
@Named
@RequestScoped
public class BookstoreSaleController {
    @Inject
    @OnlineSale
    private Event<BookEvent> onlineSaleEvent;
    private BookEvent currentEvent;
    public BookstoreSaleController() {
    }
    /**
     * Fires synchronous Jakarta CDI event BookEvent.
     */
    public void onlineSaleAction() {
        onlineSaleEvent.fire(currentEvent);
    }
    /**
     * Fires asynchronous Jakarta CDI event BookEvent.
     */
    public void storeSaleAction() {
        onlineSaleEvent.fireAsync(currentEvent)
                .whenComplete((event, throwable) -> {
                    if (throwable != null) {
                        FacesContext.getCurrentInstance().addMessage(null, new FacesMessage(
                                FacesMessage.SEVERITY_ERROR, "FAIL", "Error has occurred " +
                                throwable.getMessage()));
                    } else {
                        FacesContext.getCurrentInstance().addMessage(null, new FacesMessage(
                                FacesMessage.SEVERITY_INFO, "SUCCESS", "Successful Brick-
                                and-Mortar Store Sale Processing..."));
                    }
                });
    }
    /**
     * @return the currentEvent
     */
    public BookEvent getCurrentEvent() {
        return currentEvent;
    }
}
```

When a sale is invoked, either an online or in-store sale type is chosen. Given the selected sale type, the corresponding Jakarta Server Faces controller method is invoked.

How It Works

Jakarta CDI events allow for decoupled event handling to occur among several beans. The bean classes do not have any binding to one another, but context can be passed between them, allowing beans to invoke contextual events without explicit binding. To orchestrate events, only a few annotations need to be placed, as there is no additional configuration. In the example, a bookstore can complete two types of sales, those being online and in-store. Therefore, when a book is sold, an event is to be invoked to notify the publisher and indicate which type of sale has been made.

To begin, a contextual object is used to contain data about each event. Therefore, a bean named BookEvent is generated as a simple Plain Old Java Object (POJO). Next, event qualifiers are coded for differentiation between the two types of possible events. An event qualifier is simply an annotation that can be placed on an event handler, and it is also used to create an event of the specified type. In the example, both online and in-store event qualifiers are created. As seen in the code for the qualifier, the annotation declaration is marked with the jakarta.inject.Qualifier annotation, and it is targeted for use with the following: METHOD, FIELD, PARAMETER, TYPE.

When an event is fired, an event handler is used to process the event. Event handlers are also known as observers, and they are simply classes that contain at least one method that can be used to contain the processing for the event. In the example, the BookEventHandler class contains two methods that are used to perform the actions of the events. Event handling methods must accept an event (simply an object) that is annotated with an optional qualifier and the @Observes annotation. The @Observes annotation signifies that the method is observing events of the type that is passed into the method. In the example, the BookEvent object is used as a parameter, and it is annotated with the qualifier annotation for each of the respective methods. Therefore, the method named notifyPublisherOnline() observes events of type @OnlineSale, and notifyPublisherInStore() observes @StoreSale event types.

Lastly, the event initiation occurs within a Jakarta CDI controller class in this example, although some other class type could also invoke an action. In the example, the BookstoreSalesController contains an injected Event<BookEvent> object, which is used for firing events of type BookEvent. The controller contains methods for firing online sales and also in-store sales. The online sale action method fires a synchronous event by calling upon the injected Event fire() method and passing the current BookEvent object. The fire() method initiates a synchronous event call, so once the event processing is completed, control is returned to the caller.

The in-store sale action method fires an asynchronous event by calling upon the injected Event fireAsync() method and passing the current BookEvent object. However, in this scenario, once the fireAsync() method is initiated, control is passed back to the caller, and the event is processed in the background. The fireAsync() method was introduced with the release of Jakarta CDI 2.0 in Jakarta EE 8.

The Jakarta CDI event model can be harnessed to provide superpowerful solutions for applications of all kinds. Since events can be called upon with a loosely coupled architecture, it makes event invocation easy to achieve in new applications and easy to add into existing applications.

To execute the code, open the URL http://localhost:8080/JakartaEERecipes_Chapter08-1.0-SNAPSHOT/chapter11/recipe11_10.xhtml in your browser. The output should be as shown in Figure 11-4.

Book Title:	Introducing Jakarta EE Fundamentals ∨
Price:	39.99
Number of Books:	1 ∨

Place Online Order   Place In-Store Order

Figure 11-4. *Output of Recipe 11-10*

11-11. Intercepting Method Invocations

Problem

You wish to intercept a method invocation in an application, such that each time the method is called upon, special functionality will occur.

Solution

Utilize a Jakarta CDI interceptor to invoke special functionality each time a specified method, or all methods within a specified class, is called upon. In the following scenario, an interceptor will be utilized to send an email to an administrator each time certain methods of an application are called upon. In this example, each time a book order is canceled, then the email is invoked.

To begin, an annotation must be generated for the interceptor. The interceptor annotation in this case is named `Notified`, and the sources are as follows:

```
package org.jakartaeerecipe.chapter11.interceptor;

import static java.lang.annotation.ElementType.*;
import java.lang.annotation.*;
import jakarta.interceptor.InterceptorBinding;
@Inherited
@InterceptorBinding
@Retention(RUNTIME)
@Target({METHOD,TYPE})
public @interface Notified {
}
```

Next, the interceptor class can be created. The interceptor class is annotated with `@Interceptor`, and it contains a method which is annotated with `@AroundInvoke`. This annotated method will be invoked whenever some method that is annotated with `@Notified` or a method contained within a class that is annotated with `@Notified` is invoked. In this case, the interceptor class is named `NotificationInterceptor`, and its implementation is as follows:

```
package org.jakartaeerecipe.chapter11.interceptor;

import java.util.Date;
import java.util.Properties;
import jakarta.interceptor.AroundInvoke;
import jakarta.interceptor.Interceptor;
import jakarta.interceptor.InvocationContext;
import jakarta.mail.Message;
import jakarta.mail.Session;
import jakarta.mail.Transport;
import jakarta.mail.internet.InternetAddress;
import jakarta.mail.internet.MimeMessage;
@Interceptor
@Notified
public class NotificationInterceptor {
    @AroundInvoke
```

```java
    public Object emailNotification(InvocationContext ctx) throws Exception {
        String smtpServer = "mysmtpserver.com";
        String email = "publisherEmail@publisher.com";
        Properties props = System.getProperties();
        props.put("mail.smtp.host", smtpServer);
        Session session = Session.getInstance(props, null);
        sendEmail(session,
                    email,
                    "Method invocation",
                    "Entering method: " + ctx.getMethod().getName());
        return ctx.proceed();
    }
    protected void sendEmail(Session session, String toEmail, String subject, String body) {
        try {
            MimeMessage msg = new MimeMessage(session);
            //set message headers
            msg.addHeader("Content-type", "text/HTML; charset=UTF-8");
            msg.addHeader("format", "flowed");
            msg.addHeader("Content-Transfer-Encoding", "8bit");
            msg.setFrom(new InternetAddress("no_reply@jakartaeerecipe.com", "NoReply"));
            msg.setReplyTo(InternetAddress.parse("no_reply@jakartaeerecipe.com", false));
            msg.setSubject(subject, "UTF-8");
            msg.setText(body, "UTF-8");
            msg.setSentDate(new Date());
            msg.setRecipients(Message.RecipientType.TO, InternetAddress.parse(toEmail,
            false));
            Transport.send(msg);
        } catch (Exception e) {
            e.printStackTrace();
        }
    }
}
```

Lastly, a class or method(s) must be designated for interception. In this example, we wish to notify the administrator each time someone logs in to the administrative console:

```java
@Notified
@Named
@RequestScoped
public class AdminConsoleController {
    public AdminConsoleController(){
    }
    public void login(){
        System.out.println("This is an action method which would allow one to log into an"
                + "administrative console");
    }
}
```

In the preceding example code, the login() method would actually be used to authenticate an individual to the administrative console for the bookstore. However, since this is for demo purposes only, it merely displays a message in the system log. To enable this interceptor, the following lines must be added to the beans.xml configuration:

```
<interceptors>
    <class>org.jakartaeerecipe.chapter11.interceptor.NotificationInterceptor
    </class>
</interceptors>
```

How It Works

Interceptors allow cross-cutting functionality to be introduced into a new or existing application without explicitly modifying the code of specified classes or methods. An interceptor allows the functionality to be executed due to an invocation of the specified methods or due to invocation of a method within a specified class. As such, interceptors are very similar to Jakarta CDI events, except they do not require an explicit call to fire() or fireAsync() for invocation.

An interceptor solution requires an interceptor binding type annotation and an implementation class. The interceptor binding type annotation is a standard annotation declaration containing the @Inherited and @InterceptorBinding annotations. The @Inherited annotation denotes that the annotation can be inherited from superclasses. The interceptor binding type annotation should contain a target of METHOD and TYPE.

The interceptor implementation class can contain methods annotated with @AroundInvoke, @PostConstruct, @PreDestroy, @PrePassivate, @PostActivate, and @AroundTimeout. These annotations are used to specify when the interceptor method will be invoked. When a class or a method is annotated with the interceptor binding, then the interceptor implementation will be invoked based upon the specified implementation. @AroundInvoke specifies that the implementation will be executed when the intercepted method is being invoked. The life-cycle callback annotations (@PostConstruct, @PreDestroy, @PrePassivate, and @PostActivate) specify that the interceptor implementation will be invoked when the intercepted method or class enters the specified state. Lastly, the @AroundTimeout annotation is used to indicate that the implementation will be invoked when the intercepted method has an EJB timeout occur.

The @AroundInvoke annotation carries with it a couple of requirements. If an implementation method is annotated as such, it must accept a jakarta.interceptor.InvocationContext argument, and it must call upon that argument's proceed() method. The invocation of the proceed() method causes the target to be invoked.

An interceptor implementation class can contain one or more methods annotated with the annotations. However, only one of each type can be specified within a given implementation class. To enable an interceptor, it must be specified within the beans.xml, as indicated in the example.

Interceptors can be a great way to add additional functionality to a process without modifying the existing code. They work well for performing actions such as logging each time a method is accessed. Typically, an interceptor can be reused in multiple circumstances because the functionality is generic and not bound to a specific line of business logic. To learn more about adding more specific business logic functionality to existing methods, please refer to Recipe 11-13 covering decorators.

11-12. Bootstrapping Java SE Environments

Problem

You wish to utilize the capabilities of Jakarta CDI in a Java SE environment, outside of a Jakarta EE container. With this approach you can use all the features of CDI, including dependency injection, contextual life-cycle management, and interceptors in a stand-alone Java application.

Solution

Bootstrap the Java SE application using the SeContainerInitializer. In this example, a standard Java SE application named BootstrapExample has been created. A beans.xml is added to the application's META-INF folder using the Jakarta CDI references:

```java
public class BootstrapExample {
    public static void main(String[] args) {
        SeContainerInitializer initializer = SeContainerInitializer.newInstance();
        try (SeContainer container = initializer.initialize()) {
            /**
             * work with Jakarta CDI
             */
            Calculator calculator = container.select(Calculator.class).get();
            System.out.println(calculator.addNumbers(new int[]{1, 2, 3, 4}));
        }
    }
}
```

When this block of code is executed, the SeContainer can be used to work with Jakarta CDI capabilities. Figure 11-5 shows the output from the execution of the main() method.

```
BootstrapExample
/Library/Java/JavaVirtualMachines/graalvm-ee-java17-21.3.0/Contents/Home/bin/java -javaagent:/Applications/IntelliJ IDEA.app/Contents/lib/idea_rt
.jar=61011:/Applications/IntelliJ IDEA.app/Contents/bin -Dfile.encoding=UTF-8 -classpath /Users/home/Downloads/JavaSE_CDI/target/classes:/Users/home/
.m2/repository/org/jboss/weld/se/weld-se-shaded/5.0.0.CR1/weld-se-shaded-5.0.0.CR1.jar BootstrapExample
Apr 13, 2022 3:38:56 PM org.jboss.weld.bootstrap.WeldStartup <clinit>
INFO: WELD-000900: 5.0.0 (CR1)
Apr 13, 2022 3:38:57 PM org.jboss.weld.bootstrap.WeldStartup startContainer
INFO: WELD-000101: Transactional services not available. Injection of @Inject UserTransaction not available. Transactional observers will be invoked synchronou
Apr 13, 2022 3:38:58 PM org.jboss.weld.environment.se.WeldContainer fireContainerInitializedEvent
INFO: WELD-ENV-002003: Weld SE container 5f4ceff8-c8ac-420c-b406-9cb5f78e6dd9 initialized
10
Apr 13, 2022 3:38:58 PM org.jboss.weld.environment.se.WeldContainer shutdown
INFO: WELD-ENV-002001: Weld SE container 5f4ceff8-c8ac-420c-b406-9cb5f78e6dd9 shut down

Process finished with exit code 0
```

***Figure 11-5.** Output of Recipe 11-12*

How It Works

There are oftentimes situations where a standard Java SE application would benefit from using the utilities which Jakarta CDI has to offer. The Jakarta CDI release has made this possible with the addition of the Bootstrapping API. To bootstrap, you must include the Jakarta CDI dependencies in the application. One must also include a beans.xml file to indicate that Jakarta CDI will be utilized. If using a Maven project, use coordinates for the cdi-core dependency as seen in the following (update version as needed):

```xml
<dependency>
    <groupId>org.jboss.weld.se</groupId>
    <artifactId>weld-se-shaded</artifactId>
    <version>5.0.0.CR1</version>
</dependency>
```

The beans.xml file should contain the Jakarta CDI configuration information. The following beans.xml source provides the minimum configuration:

```
<?xml version="1.0" encoding="UTF-8"?>
<beans xmlns="http://xmlns.jcp.org/xml/ns/javaee" xmlns:xsi="http://www.w3.org/2001/
XMLSchema-instance"
    xsi:schemaLocation="http://xmlns.jcp.org/xml/ns/javaee http://xmlns.jcp.org/xml/ns/
    javaee/beans_4_0.xsd"
    bean-discovery-mode="all" version="4.0">
</beans>
```

The SeContainerInitializer class can be used to return an instance of itself. It can be used to configure the Jakarta CDI container for your application by calling upon its many customization methods.

■ **Note**   Please see the online documentation for full details (`https://docs.jboss.org/weld/ reference/latest/en-US/html_single/`).

The SeContainerInitializer class should be utilized following the builder pattern for configuring options, and the last method to call upon should be its initialize(), as seen in the example. The SeContainerInitializer is auto-closable, so it works well within a try-with-resources block. All the Jakarta CDI usage can occur within the try block. In the example, a contextual bean is obtained and used.

While this example is brief, it shows how easy it is to bootstrap a Jakarta CDI configuration for a Java SE application.

11-13. Enhancing Business Logic of a Method

Problem

You would like to enhance the functionality of an existing method, including the ability to integrate with a bean's business logic.

Solution

Utilize a decorator to implement an enhancement of functionality for an existing method. In the following example, a decorator is generated for an existing method to enhance functionality by logging to a database. In this example, a registration form is used to register for a bookstore event. The decorator will be used to enhance the registration process by adding the registrant into a different database table for entry into a drawing.

To begin, each registrant must enter their first name, last name, and email address. This information will go into a Registration object. The object code is as follows:

```
public class Registration {
    private String first;
    private String last;
    private String email;
    public Registration(){
    }
// ... Getters and Setters
}
```

Next, an interface must be generated for the registration type. In this case, each registration type must contain a method register() that accepts a Registration object:

```
public interface BookstoreRegistration {
    public String register(Registration registration);
}
```

Now create a decorator, which is a public abstract class that takes the interface that was created earlier as an injection point:

```
package org.jakartaeerecipe.chapter11.decorator;
import jakarta.decorator.Decorator;
import jakarta.decorator.Delegate;
import jakarta.enterprise.inject.Any;
import jakarta.inject.Inject;
import org.jakartaeerecipe.chapter11.recipe11_13.BookstoreRegistration;
import org.jakartaeerecipe.chapter11.recipe11_13.Registration;
@Decorator
public abstract class RegistrationDecorator implements BookstoreRegistration {
    @Inject
    @Delegate
    @Any
    private BookstoreRegistration bookstoreRegistration;
    @Override
    public String register(Registration registration){
        // Submit to registration database table
        // Submit to promotional database table
        return registration.getEmail() + " has been entered into the giveaway";
    }
}
```

Lastly, we need to invoke the register method to initiate the decorator functionality. In this example, we invoke via a Jakarta Server Faces controller class method:

```
@Named
@ViewScoped
public class BookstoreRegistrationController implements BookstoreRegistration,
Serializable {
    @Inject
    private Registration current;
    public BookstoreRegistrationController(){
    }
// Getters and Setters
    public String register(){
        return register(current);
    }
    @Override
    public String register(Registration registration) {
        // Persist current registration
        return "chapter11/recipe11_13.xhtml";
    }
}
```

When the `register()` method is invoked, the enhanced decorator functionality will also be invoked to add the registrant to the giveaway database table. To execute the preceding code, open the URL `http://localhost:8080/JakartaEERecipes_Chapter08-1.0-SNAPSHOT/chapter11/recipe11_13.xhtml` in your browser. The output should be as shown in Figure 11-6.

Figure 11-6. *Output of Recipe 11-13*

On clicking the Register button, the following log message is printed on the GlassFish server log:

```
[2022-04-13T16:00:25.872+0530] [glassfish 7.0] [INFO] [] [] [tid: _ThreadID=42 _
ThreadName=Thread-7] [timeMillis: 1649845825872] [levelValue: 800] [[
  Executing Registration]]
```

How It Works

Decorators are another powerful component of Jakarta CDI. Much like interceptors, decorators add enhanced functionality to existing methods. These two constructs differ from each other in that decorators enhance functionality and have access to bean fields and methods for which the enhanced functionality is occurring. Interceptors, on the other hand, do not have access to bean fields and methods and therefore provide a more generic functionality in addition to the standard functionality of an existing method.

To create a decorator, one must utilize an interface as an injection point, and one or more of the interface methods will be enhanced via implementation that is added to the decorator class. In the example, a standard bookstore account registration is enhanced by adding the registrant into a sweepstakes giveaway. Although the example does not actually demonstrate the database persistence and others, if the code is executed, then you can see the decorator being invoked.

The decorator class must be denoted with a `@Decorator` annotation, and it must implement an interface and contain at least one method implementation. However, the decorator class can be made abstract so that it does not have to implement each of the methods contained within the interface. A decorator must contain a delegate injection point, which is annotated with `jakarta.decorator.Delegate`. This injection point can be a field, constructor parameter, or initializer method parameter of the decorator class.

To enable a decorator, it must be added to the `beans.xml` file. The following beans.xml demonstrates the addition of `RegistrationDecorator`:

```
<decorators>
    <class>org.jakartaeerecipe.chapter11.decorator.RegistrationDecorator</class>
</decorators>
```

An application can contain more than one decorator, of course. To manage the order in which the decorators are fired, use the `beans.xml` and list in the order of priority. Another way to manage priority is to annotate a decorator with the `@Priority` annotation. Interceptors take precedence over decorators, so if a method contains both an interceptor and a decorator, the interceptor will be fired first.

CHAPTER 12

■ ■ ■

Jakarta Messaging

The Jakarta Messaging API (formerly Java Message Service or JMS) is an API that allows software applications to create, edit, read, and send messages between other software applications or components. The API will enable resources to be created within an application server that facilitates messaging capability in various contexts. The application server houses connection factories and destination resources, and these resources are created and maintained by the application server.

In addition to the basic messaging facilities, Jakarta Messaging also allows to send messages to destinations and publish messages to subscriptions. This chapter contains recipes that focus on basic concepts of Jakarta Messaging and some advanced techniques available to the Jakarta EE platform with the release of Jakarta EE 10. When following along with the examples in this chapter, please note that you could use Jakarta Messaging in various situations for creating many different types of messages. For brevity, this chapter will cover essential concepts and use TextMessage objects only. The examples will be invoked using Jakarta Server Faces view actions, although there are many ways to implement the sending and receiving of messages in real-life applications. You can utilize Jakarta Messaging in many different contexts, from internal message invocation to scheduled tasks via a Jakarta Enterprise Beans timer or ManagedExecutorService and even messaging with message-driven beans. After reading through the recipes, you should be able to apply the recipes' strategies to create the messaging system of your needs.

Jakarta Messaging 3.1 revamped the API with a simplified technique for sending and receiving messages. In this chapter, you will see both the legacy standard API and the simplified API so that the differences can be compared. The updated API also included enhancements to message subscriptions, delivery delay, and more. The breadth of Jakarta Messaging is far too large for complete coverage in this single chapter. To learn about all the features, please refer to the Jakarta Messaging 3.1 specification (https://jakarta.ee/specifications/messaging/3.0/jakarta-messaging-spec-3.0.html).

■ **Note** The examples in this chapter focus on working with Jakarta Messaging resources within a GlassFish application server environment. However, although the focus is on GlassFish 7.0, the main concepts and techniques can be carried forth for just about every Jakarta EE–compliant application server environment. For more specific details on working with another application server or IDE, please see the documentation that is specific to the corresponding environment.

© Josh Juneau and Tarun Telang 2022
J. Juneau and T. Telang, *Java EE to Jakarta EE 10 Recipes*, https://doi.org/10.1007/978-1-4842-8079-9_12

12-1. Creating Jakarta Messaging Resources

Problem

You would like to provide the ability to create a Jakarta Messaging resource to deploy within a GlassFish 7.0+ application server environment.

Solution

Create a new JMS resource from within the GlassFish administrative console. In this recipe example, we will create a Jakarta Messaging destination resource. Specifically, we will walk through the creation of a jakarta. jms.Queue resource. Follow these steps to create the resource:

1. Log in to the GlassFish administrative console by navigating to https://localhost:4848. Expand the **Resources ➤ JMS Resources** menu in the navigation tree to expose the Destination Resources menu option (see Figure 12-1).

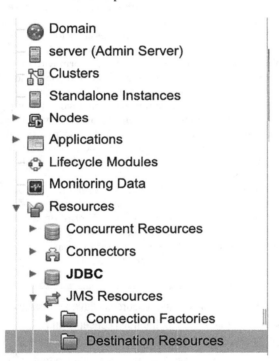

Figure 12-1. GlassFish administration console Destination Resources menu

2. Click the New button within the JMS Destination Resource window to open the New JMS Destination Resource window. Enter a JNDI name (beginning with jms/), followed by a unique name for the Physical Destination Name field (see Figure 12-2). Finally, choose the resource type that you wish to create.

New JMS Destination Resource
OK   Cancel

The creation of a new Java Message Service (JMS) destination resource also creates an admin object resource.

JNDI Name: *	jms/jakartaEERecipeQueue
Physical Destination Name *	PhysicalQueue
	Destination name in the Message Queue broker. If the destination does not exist, it will be created automatically when needed.
Resource Type: *	jakarta.jms.Topic ∨
Description:	A Queue for demo purpose
Status:	☑

Additional Properties (0)

Add Property   Delete Properties

Select	Name	Value	Description
No items found.			

OK   Cancel

Figure 12-2. *New JMS Destination Resource*

3.   Click OK to create the destination.

■ **Note**   The GlassFish `asadmin` `create-jms-resource` command can also be used to create JMS-administered objects from the command line. The `asadmin` tool can also be used to perform other tasks. For more information, please refer to the documentation at `https://glassfish.org/docs/latest/ application-development-guide/jms.html#beaop`.

How It Works

The Jakarta Messaging API utilizes administrative resources to create and consume messages. We refer to these resources as JMS resources. There are a couple of different types of JMS resources that can be created – connection resources and destination resources. The connection resources are used to create connections to a provider. There are three types of connection resources that can be created:

- `ConnectionFactory`: Instance of the `jakarta.jms.ConnectionFactory` interface. Can be used to create Topics and Queue types

- `TopicConnectionFactory`: Instance of the `jakarta.jms.TopicConnectionFactory` interface

- `QueueConnectionFactory`: Instance of the `jakarta.jms.QueueConnectionFactory` interface

493

JMS connection factory resources are very similar to JDBC connection factories in that they provide a pool of connections that an application can use to connect and produce a session. There are many attributes that can be provided when creating connection factory resources:

- *Initial and minimum pool size*: The initial and minimum number of connections that will be created and maintained by the connection pool.

- *Maximum pool size*: The maximum number of connections that can be created within the pool.

- *Pool resize quantity*: The number of connections that will be removed when the pool idle timeout expires.

- *Idle timeout*: The maximum amount of time that connections can remain in the pool if they are idle (seconds).

- *Max wait time*: The maximum amount of time that a caller will wait before a connection timeout is sent (milliseconds).

- *On any failure*: If set to true (checked), all connections would be closed and reconnected on failure.

- *Transaction support*: The level of transaction support (XATransaction, LocalTransaction, NoTransaction). The default is empty.

- *Connection validation*: If set to true, then connections will need to be validated.

■ **Note**   XATransaction always deals with a coordinating transaction manager, including one or more databases, all within a single global transaction. Non-XA transactions always involve a single resource.

You can create connection factory objects using the GlassFish administrative console by following the steps that are provided in the solution to this recipe and choosing the Connection Factories submenu rather than the Destination Resources submenu in step 1. ConnectionFactory objects are registered automatically with JNDI once created, and they can then be injected into Java classes and used. The following lines of code demonstrate how to inject a ConnectionFactory resource into a class:

```
@Resource(name = "jms/MyConnectionFactory")
private static ConnectionFactory connectionFactory;
```

Destination resources can also be created in a similar fashion to connection resources. They act as targets that receive or consume messages that are produced. They can be one of two types: jakarta.jms.Queue (Queue) or jakarta.jms.Topic (Topic). A Queue is a destination resource that consumes messages in a point-to-point (PTP) manner, much like a one-way line of traffic. When a producer sends a message to a queue, the message will stay in the queue until it is consumed. A Topic is a destination that is used in a publisher/subscriber scenario, whereas messages sent to a Topic may be consumed by multiple receivers. One or more receivers can subscribe to a Topic.

This solution demonstrates how to create a destination resource within a GlassFish application server, using the administration console. The console provides a wizard that can be used to easily create a destination resource. The most important piece of information to provide when creating a destination is the name. As with any JMS resource, the JNDI name should begin with the jms/ prefix. When creating a destination resource, a unique name must also be provided for the Destination Resource Name, although other Jakarta EE–compliant containers may or may not make this a mandatory specification. Destination resources can be injected into Java classes in the same manner as ConnectionFactory resources. The following lines of code demonstrate the injection of a Topic resource:

```
@Resource(name="jms/myTopic")
private Topic myTopic;
```

12-2. Creating a Session

Problem

You would like to create a Jakarta Messaging session so that you can send or consume messages.

Solution

Create a connection so that you can subsequently create one or more sessions, which in turn can send messages to destinations or consume messages. In order to create a connection, obtain a ConnectionFactory object by injection via the @Resource annotation, and call its createConnection method as demonstrated in the following line of code:

```
Connection connection = connectionFactory.createConnection();
```

After you have created a connection, you need to start a session. In order to do so, call the connection object's createSession method as follows:

```
Session session = connection.createSession(false,
Session.AUTO_ACKNOWLEDGE);
```

▪ **Note** If you are using the simplified Jakarta Messaging API, which is covered in more detail in Recipe 12-3, you do not need to manually create a Jakarta Messaging session. The creation of a Jakarta Messaging session is only required when utilizing the standard API.

Running the Example

If you take a look at the sources that can be found in the JakartaEERecipes project within the org. jakartaeerecipe.chapter12 package, you can see a full demonstration for creating a Jakarta Messaging session.

To see the example in action, deploy the JakartaEERecipes project to your application server after setting up a JMS connection factory (see Recipe 12-1), and visit the following URL:

http://localhost:8080/JMSDemo-1.0-SNAPSHOT/recipe12_02.xhtml

You would see the output as shown in Figure 12-3.

Connection: Session successfully created

Figure 12-3. *Output of Recipe 12-2*

495

How It Works

Before you can begin to send or consume messages, you must obtain a JMS connection so that you can start a session. A session can be used to create JMS resources such as message consumers, message producers, messages, queue browsers, and temporary queues and topics. A session can be created using a Connection object. To create a session, call a Connection object's createSession method, and pass the appropriate arguments depending upon your application's needs. The createSession syntax is as follows:

```
createSession(boolean isTransacted, int acknowledgementType)
```

The first argument to the createSession method is a Boolean value to indicate if transactions should take place within the session. If a session is created as transacted (set to true for the first argument to createSession), acknowledgment occurs once the entire transaction is successfully committed. If for some reason the transaction is not committed, the entire transaction is rolled back, and all messages are redelivered. However, if a session is not transacted, one must indicate which type of acknowledgment must be received to consider a message successfully sent. The second argument to the createSession method indicates the acknowledgment type. Table 12-1 lists the different acknowledgment types along with a description of each.

Table 12-1. *Session Message Acknowledgment*

Acknowledgment	TypeDescription
Session.AUTO_ ACKNOWLEDGE	The session automatically acknowledges a client's receipt of a message, either when the client has successfully returned from a call to receive or when the MessageListener it has called to process the message has successfully returned
Session.CLIENT_ ACKNOWLEDGE	The client acknowledges the receipt of a message by calling the message's acknowledge method
Session.DUPS_OK_ ACKNOWLEDGE	Lazy acknowledgment of messages, allowing duplicates to be received

In the solution to this recipe, the session that is created is nontransactional, and the receipt type is Session.AUTO_ACKNOWLEDGE. This is the most common type of Jakarta Messaging session that is created. Once the session has been created, then it can be used to create JMS resources.

12-3. Creating and Sending a Message

Problem

You wish to create and send a message.

Solution #1

Make use of the standard API to create and send a message. To do so, create a Message object with respect to the type of message you wish to send, and then create and use a message producer in order to send messages to a destination. To create a message, first decide upon the type of message that you wish to send. Once decided, create the appropriate message object from the JMS session. In this example, we'll demonstrate the creation of a text message. The following lines of code demonstrate how to create a text message including a String:

```
TextMessage message  = session.createTextMessage();
message.setText("Jakarta EE 10 Is the Best!");
```

Next, to create a `MessageProducer` and send the message, call a Jakarta Messaging session's `createProducer` method, and pass the object type of the destination to which you wish to send a message. The following lines of code demonstrate how to create a message producer and send the text message that was created in the previous lines. The first lines of code demonstrate how to inject the destination resource, and then the actual creation of the message producer and sending of the message follow:

```
public void sendMessage() {
        if (connection != null) {
            System.out.println("Creating Session");
            try(Session session = connection.createSession(false, Session.AUTO_ACKNOWLEDGE);
            ) {
                myQueue = (Queue) getContext().lookup("jms/jakartaEERecipeQueue");
                MessageProducer producer = session.createProducer(myQueue);
                TextMessage message = session.createTextMessage();
                message.setText("Jakarta EE 10 Is the Best!");
                producer.send(message);
                producer.close();
                setConnectionString("Message Successfully Sent to Queue");
            } catch (NamingException | JMSException e) {
                Logger.getLogger(org.jakartaeerecipe.chapter12.recipe12_02.Recipe12_02.
                class.getName())
                        .log(Level.SEVERE, null, e);
                setConnectionString("Session not created and message not sent");
            }
        } else {
            setConnectionString("No connection available");
        }
    }
```

Solution #2

Make use of the simplified API to create and send a message. To utilize the simplified API, create a `JMSContext` object, and then utilize it to create a `MessageProducer` and send the message to the appropriate destination. In the following example, a simple String-based message is sent to a `Queue` using the simplified API. This technique provides the same result as Solution #1:

```
public String sendMessageNew() {
        String response = "Message Not Sent...";
        try (JMSContext context = connectionFactory.createContext()) {
            inboundQueue = (Queue) getContext().lookup("jms/jakartaEERecipeQueue");
            StringBuilder message = new StringBuilder();
            message.append("Jakarta EE 10 Is the Best!");
            context.createProducer().send(inboundQueue, message.toString());
            response = "Message Sent...";
```

```
    } catch (NamingException e) {
        Logger.getLogger(org.jakartaeerecipe.chapter12.recipe12_02.Recipe12_02.class.
        getName())
                .log(Level.SEVERE, null, e);
    }
    return response;
}
```

Running the Examples

An example that can be run from within a Jakarta Server Faces view has been created for this recipe. The code found at org.jakartaeerecipes.chapter12.Example12_03.java contains a managed bean that includes a sendMessage method that utilizes the standard API implementation and a sendMessageNew method that utilizes the simplified API. Both methods are responsible for creating a message and sending it to a destination Queue. By running the example, you can look at the server log to see the output from the method. Deploy the JakartaEERecipes project and visit the following URL to run the example:

http://localhost:8080/JMSDemo -1.0-SNAPSHOT/recipe12_03.xhtml

You would see the output as shown in Figure 12-4.

Standard API: Message Successfully Sent to Queue

Simplified API: Message Sent...

Figure 12-4. *Output of Recipe 12-3*

How It Works

The reason that any application makes use of Jakarta Messaging is to incorporate the ability to send or receive messages. Therefore, it is no surprise that the Jakarta Messaging API has been developed to make these tasks very easy for the developer. In Java EE 7, things were made even easier using the simplified Jakarta Messaging API.

Let's begin by discussing the steps that are needed to utilize the standard API for sending a message. To send a message using the standard API, you need to create a resource destination for your message and obtain a connection and a session, as seen in Recipes 12-1 and 12-2. Once you have obtained a session, the next step is to create a MessageProducer using the Session createProducer method, passing the destination as an argument. After this legwork has been completed, the message can be constructed. You can create a message by calling the jakarta.jms.Session method that corresponds to the type of message that you wish to create.

■ **Note**   To see all of the available methods, please refer to the online documentation at https://jakarta. ee/specifications/messaging/3.0/jakarta-messaging-spec-3.0.html#sessions.

In the example for this recipe, a text message is created by calling the session.createTextMessage() method. The text is then set by calling the TextMessage object's setText method.

Once a message has been created, a MessageProducer must be created in order to facilitate the sending of the message. Again, jakarta.jms.Session comes to the rescue here as we can call its createProducer method, passing the destination resource for which we'd like to create the MessageProducer. Once created, the producer's sendMessage method can be invoked, passing the message that you wish to send.

As mentioned previously, the jakarta.jms.Session can be used to generate different message types. Table 12-2 lists the different message types that can be created, along with a description.

Table 12-2. *Message Types*

Message	TypeCreation Method
StreamMessage	The message body contains a stream of primitive values in the Java programming language. Filled and read sequentially
MapMessage	The message body contains a set of name/value pairs that are formed from String objects and Java primitives. May be accessed sequentially or randomly by name, and the order of entries is undefined
TextMessage	The message body contains a String object. Able to be used for plain text as well as XML messages
ObjectMessage	The message body contains a serializable Java object
BytesMessage	The message body contains a stream of uninterpreted bytes

When utilizing the simplified API, there are a few shortcuts that can be made. To compare Solution #1 with Solution #2, you can see that there are fewer lines of code in the second solution. The simplified API enables developers to produce the same results as the standard API with much less code. A JMSContext object is obtained via a call to the ConnectionFactory's createContext method, and it can be used to begin a chain of method invocations that will result in the sending of a message in just one line of code. To break it down a bit, after the JMSContext has been obtained, its createProducer method can be called, chaining a call to the send method, passing the Queue and the message to be sent.

Message implementations may vary between the different application server products. However, all JMS message types share some common characteristics. For instance, all messages implement the jakarta.jms.Message interface. Messages are composed of a header, properties, and a body. The header of a message contains values that are utilized by clients and providers for routing and identification purposes, properties provide message filtering, and the body portion of the message carries the actual message content or payload. The message header is used for linking messages to one another, and a field named JMSCorrelationID contains this content. Message objects contain the ability to support application-defined property values. The properties can be set via a construct known as message selectors, and they are responsible for filtering messages. For more detailed information regarding the Message interface, please see the online documentation at https://jakarta.ee/specifications/messaging/3.0/jakarta-messaging-spec-3.0.html. The body varies across the different message types, as listed in Table 12-2.

It can be useful to add properties and headers to a particular message to allow message consumers to have filtering capabilities via message selectors. To learn more about using message selectors, please refer to Recipe 12-5.

12-4. Receiving Messages

Problem

You would like to receive messages that have just been sent by a Jakarta Messaging producer.

Solution #1

Make use of the standard Jakarta Messaging API to create a message consumer. Using the Jakarta Messaging session, create the message consumer by calling the createConsumer method, passing the type of message consumer that you would like to create. Once the message consumer object has been created, invoke the start method on the connection object, and then call the consumer object's receive method to receive a message. In the following example controller class, a message consumer will be created and set up to receive the message that was sent by the producer in Recipe 12-3.

The following code excerpt is taken from the org.jakartaeerecipes.chapter12.recipe12_04. Example12_04.java source file. The method named receiveMessage is responsible for consuming messages from a specified destination point Queue. Note that the code assumes that the messages within the queue would eventually end and that there would not be a continuous stream of incoming messages:

```java
public void receiveMessage() {
    boolean stopReceivingMessages = false;
    if (connection == null) {
        createConnection();
    }
    try (Session session = connection.createSession(false, Session.AUTO_ACKNOWLEDGE)) {
        createConnection();
        System.out.println("Creating session to receive message");

        myQueue = (Queue) getContext().lookup("jms/jakartaEERecipeQueue");
        System.out.println("Setting up consumer");
        try (MessageConsumer consumer = session.createConsumer(myQueue)) {
            connection.start();

            while (!stopReceivingMessages) {
                System.out.println("Receiving message");
                Message inMessage = consumer.receive();
                if (inMessage != null) {
                    System.out.println(inMessage);
                    if (inMessage instanceof TextMessage) {
                        String messageStr = ((TextMessage) inMessage).getText();
                        System.out.println(messageStr);
                        setDisplayMessage(messageStr);
                    } else {
                        System.out.println("Message was of another type");
                        setDisplayMessage("Message was of another type");
                    }
                } else {
                    stopReceivingMessages = true;
                }
            }
            connection.stop();
        }
```

Solution #2

Utilize the simplified API to create a message consumer. Utilize a JMSContext object to create the JMSConsumer in an efficient and simplified manner. The following example method resides within a managed bean controller. The message consumer in this example will be created and set up to receive the message that was sent by the producer in Recipe 12-3:

```
public String receiveMessageNew() {
    try (JMSContext context = connectionFactory.createContext()) {
        JMSConsumer consumer = context.createConsumer(myQueue);
        return consumer.receiveBody(String.class);
    }
}
```

Running the Example

The JakartaEERecipes project contains a working example for this recipe that demonstrates the sending and receiving of messages. To view the example, you will need to deploy the project to your application server and then visit the following URL:

`http://localhost:8080/JMSDemo-1.0-SNAPSHOT/chapter12/recipe12_03.xhtml`

You would see the output as shown in Figure 12-5.

| Turn on Receiver | Send Message |

Jakarta EE 10 Is the Best!

Figure 12-5. *Output of Recipe 12-4*

How It Works

The receiving client of a message is also known as the message consumer. Message consumers can be created using the standard or the simplified Jakarta Messaging API. We will compare these two approaches in this section to give you an idea of the differences between the two.

Using the standard API, a consumer is created from session objects in the same manner that producers are created (see Recipe 12-3), calling the createConsumer method of the session and passing the destination object from which the consumer will listen for and accept messages. Message consumers have the ability to consume messages that are waiting within a queue, and they listen indefinitely for new incoming messages.

To set up a consumer, call the session object's createConsumer method, and pass the destination object that you wish to consume from. The next step is to call the connection start method. This will tell Jakarta Messaging that the consumer is ready to begin receiving messages. After invoking the connection.start() method, a consumer can receive a message by calling the Consumer object's receive method, optionally passing time in milliseconds for the consumer to listen for messages. If no time limit is specified, the consumer will listen indefinitely.

As you can see from the example in this recipe, once the receive method is called, a Message object is retrieved. Once the message is received, the application can glean whatever it needs by calling the Message object's getter methods accordingly.

Now let's look at using the simplified API. As you can see from Solution #2, there are fewer lines of code required to produce the same result achieved from Solution #1. The JMSContext object aids in producing less code by calling its createConsumer method and passing the resource from which the application will need to consume messages. This method call will return a JMSConsumer, which has a similar API to MessageConsumer, with the ability to receive messages both synchronously and asynchronously. In the example, a String message is consumed synchronously:

■ **Note** It is possible to create an asynchronous consumer by registering a MessageListener with the MessageConsumer. After a listener has been registered for the consumer, the listener's onMessage() method will be called each time a message has been delivered. For instance, the following code could be used to register a listener to the consumer that was created within the example for this recipe.

```
jakarta.jms.MessageListener jakartaEERecipesListener = new MyMessageListener();
consumer.setMessageListener(jakaratEERecipesListener);
```

12-5. Filtering Messages

Problem

You would like to provide properties for your messages that will make it easier for consumers to filter through and find messages of their choice.

Solution

Utilize message selectors in order to filter the messages that are being consumed. Message selectors are String-based expressions that can be assigned to consumers upon creation, and they are generally used to filter the types of messages that a consumer will receive. In the following example, both the sendMessage1 and sendMessage2 methods create messages. The sendMessage1 method sets a property named TYPE with a value of JAKARTAEE on the message. After setting this property, a MessageProducer is created, and the message is sent. The sendMessage2 method sets a property named TYPE with a value of JAVASE on the message. Just like sendMessage1, the sendMessage2 method then creates a MessageProducer and sends the message. The receiveMessage method sets up a MessageConsumer with a selector specified to only consume messages with a property of TYPE that includes a value of JAKARTAEE.

The following excerpt has been taken from the class named org.jakartaeerecipes.chapter12. recipe12_05.Example12_05.java:

```java
public void sendMessage1() {
    if (connection != null) {
        try (Session session = connection.createSession(false, Session.AUTO_ACKNOWLEDGE);
            MessageProducer producer = session.createProducer(myQueue);) {
            TextMessage message = session.createTextMessage();
            message.setText("Jakarta EE 10 Is the Best!");
            message.setStringProperty("TYPE", "JAKARTAEE");
            producer.send(message);
        } catch (JMSException ex) {
            System.out.println(ex);
        }
```

```
        }
    }
    public void sendMessage2() {
        if (connection != null) {
            try (Session session = connection.createSession(false, Session.AUTO_ACKNOWLEDGE);
                    MessageProducer producer = session.createProducer(myQueue);) {
                System.out.println("Creating message");
                TextMessage message2 = session.createTextMessage();
                message2.setText("Java SE 9 Is Great!");
                message2.setStringProperty("TYPE", "JAVASE");
                producer.send(message2);
            } catch (JMSException ex) {
                System.out.println(ex);
            }
        }
    }
    public void receiveMessage() {
        boolean stopReceivingMessages = false;
        String selector = "TYPE = 'JAKARTAEE'";
        try(Connection connection = connectionFactory.createConnection();
            Session session = connection.createSession(false, Session.AUTO_ACKNOWLEDGE);
            MessageConsumer consumer = session.createConsumer(myQueue, selector);) {
            connection.start();
            while (!stopReceivingMessages) {
                Message inMessage = consumer.receive();
                if (inMessage != null) {
                    if (inMessage instanceof TextMessage) {
                        String messageStr = ((TextMessage) inMessage).getText();
                        setDisplayMessage(messageStr);
                    } else {
                        setDisplayMessage("Message was of another type");
                    }
                } else {
                    stopReceivingMessages = true;
                }
            }
            connection.stop();
        } catch (JMSException ex) {
            System.out.println(ex);
        }
    }
}
```

Running the Example

If you deploy the JakartaEERecipes project, you can run the example by pointing your browser to the following URL:

```
http://localhost:8080/JMSDemo-1.0-SNAPSHOT/chapter12/recipe12_05.xhtml
```

You can click the Receive Messages button to start the consumer. Then click the Send EE Message and Send SE Message buttons to send messages, which contain different property values. Watch the server log to see output pertaining to the browsed messages.

You would see the output as shown in Figure 12-6.

The following button will turn on a receiver that filters messages based upon a selector where TYPE = 'JAKARTAEE', any messages that have a different TYPE property will not be consumed. Watch the output in the server log or at the command line.

| Turn on Receiver | Send EE Message | Send SE Message |

No messages as yet...

Figure 12-6. *Output of Recipe 12-5*

How It Works

Message selectors are String-based expressions that can be assigned to consumers upon creation. To create a selector, form a String that contains an expression with syntax based on a subset of the SQL 92 conditional expression syntax. The expression String should formulate the filter that you wish to use when consuming messages. An expression will look very much like the WHERE clause of a database query. In the example for this recipe, the selector is set to the following String:

```
TYPE = 'JAKARTAEE'
```

This selector causes the consumer to filter all messages that are received and only consume those messages containing a property named TYPE that is assigned a value of JAKARTAEE. Standard SQL 92 can be used to combine filters and build an expression that will provide the filtering capability that is required by the consumer.

To assign the selector to a consumer, pass it to the JMS session createConsumer method. After doing so, any messages received by the created consumer will be filtered based upon the selector expression.

12-6. Inspecting Message Queues

Problem

Your application makes use of a Jakarta Messaging queue, and you would like to browse through each of the messages within the queue without removing them.

Solution

Create a QueueBrowser object and use it to browse through each of the messages that are contained within the queue.

In the following excerpt from Java class org.jakartaeerecipes.chapter12.recipe12_06. Example12_06.java, the browseMessages method connects to a session, creates a browser queue, and traverses the messages within the queue:

```java
public void browseMessages() {
    try(Connection connection = connectionFactory.createConnection();
        Session session = connection.createSession(false, Session.AUTO_ACKNOWLEDGE);
        QueueBrowser browser = session.createBrowser(myQueue);) {
        Enumeration msgs = browser.getEnumeration();
        if(!msgs.hasMoreElements()){
            System.out.println("No more messages within the queue...");
```

```
        } else {
            while(msgs.hasMoreElements()){
                Message currMsg = (Message)msgs.nextElement();
                System.out.println("Message ID: " + currMsg.getJMSMessageID());
            }
        }
    } catch (JMSException ex) {
        System.out.println(ex);
    }
}
```

Running the Example

If you deploy the JakartaEERecipes project, you can run the example by pointing your browser to the following URL: http://localhost:8080/JMSDemo-1.0-SNAPSHOT/chapter12/recipe12_06.xhtml. You can click the Send Message button within the view several times and then click the Browse Through Messages button and watch the server log to see output pertaining to the browsed messages.

You would see the output as shown in Figure 12-7.

Press the "Send Message" button a few times to send some messages to the queue, then click the "Browse Through Messages" button to list the different message types at the command prompt.

| Send Message | Browse Through Messages |

No messages as yet...

Figure 12-7. *Output of Recipe 12-6*

How It Works

There are times when it is important to have the ability to search through messages in order to find the one that you would like to read. In circumstances such as these, message queue browsers come to the rescue. A QueueBrowser object provides the ability for an application to search through each message within a queue and display the header values for each of them. This capability can be important if the message header contains important information that helps to differentiate each type of message that is sent by a particular application. The QueueBrowser object makes it easy to sift through messages in order to find the one you would like, using similar semantics as those that are used to create other Jakarta Messaging objects.

To create a QueueBrowser, you must first have an open session object. You can then call the Session object's createBrowser method, passing the destination type as an argument. Therefore, if you wish to browse messages in a queue that is named jms/myQueue, you would pass the injected resource for jms/myQueue to the createBrowser method. Once you have created a browser object, simply iterate over the messages and browse through them using the Enumeration that is returned from the call to the browser.getEnumeration() method.

12-7. Creating Durable Message Subscribers
Problem

You would like to ensure that an application receives all published messages, even when the subscriber is not active.

Solution

Create a durable subscriber for the Topic destination that will be used to send and receive messages. Once created, messages can be published to the Topic using the standard message publishing techniques, as demonstrated within Recipe 12-3, sending to the Topic destination that contains the subscription. The messages can then be consumed via a message consumer that has been created using the Topic and subscription.

In this example, a durable message subscriber is created, the message is created and published to the Topic destination, and, finally, the message is consumed.

The Topic Connection

Topic connections are a bit different than Queue connections in that they utilize an object named `TopicConnection`, rather than a standard `Connection` object. Moreover, a `TopicConnectionFactory` must be injected into an object in order to create a `TopicConnection`. The following lines of code demonstrate how to create a connection factory to generate `TopicConnections` for working with subscriptions:

```
@Resource(name = "jms/jakartaEERecipesConnectionFactory")
    private TopicConnectionFactory connectionFactory;
TopicConnection connection = (TopicConnection) connectionFactory.createConnection();
connection.setClientID("durable");
```

Creating the Initial Durable Subscriber

When creating a durable subscriber, an initial durable subscriber must be created prior to sending any messages to the Topic. This initial subscriber will initialize the subscription and make it available for publishing and receiving purposes. The following code excerpt, taken from `org.jakartaeerecipes.chapter12.recipe12_07.Example12_07.java`, demonstrates the creation of a durable subscriber:

```
public void createTopicSubscriber(){
        try {
            createConnection();
            TopicSession session = connection.createTopicSession(false, Session.AUTO_
            ACKNOWLEDGE);
            myTopic = (Topic) getContext().lookup("jms/jakartaEERecipesTopic");
            TopicSubscriber subscriber = session.createDurableSubscriber(myTopic,
            "jakartaEERecipesSub");
            connection.close();
        } catch (javax.naming.NamingException | JMSException ex) {
            Logger.getLogger(Example12_07.class.getName()).log(Level.SEVERE, null, ex);
        }
    }
```

For the demonstration application, a JSF `h:commandButton` component invokes this method so that you can watch the output occurring within the server log.

Creating and Publishing a Message

Creating and publishing a message to a Topic is much like publishing messages to a Queue. However, instead of creating a producer, a publisher is generated. The following code excerpt, taken from org. jakartaeerecipes.chapter12.recipe12_07.Example12_07.java, demonstrates the creation of a Message, and then it is published to the durable subscriber:

```java
public void sendMessage() {
    try {
        createConnection();
            System.out.println("Creating session");
            TopicSession session = connection.createTopicSession(false, Session.
            AUTO_ACKNOWLEDGE);
            System.out.println("Creating message");
            TextMessage message  = session.createTextMessage();
            message.setText("Jakarta EE 8 Is the Best!");
            message.setStringProperty("TYPE", "JAKARTAEE");
            System.out.println("Creating producer");
            myTopic = (Topic) getContext().lookup("jms/jakartaEERecipesTopic");
            TopicPublisher publisher = session.createPublisher(myTopic);
            System.out.println("Sending message");
            publisher.publish(message);
            System.out.println("Message sent, closing session");
            publisher.close();
            session.close();
            connection.close();
    } catch (NamingException | JMSException ex) {
        Logger.getLogger(Example12_07.class.getName()).log(Level.SEVERE, null, ex);
    }
```

This method is also bound to an h:commandButton component for our example view, and you can see more output generated from the actions that take place within the method.

Receiving the Message

Each message created and published to the Topic is later consumed by the subscriber(s) to the Topic. The following method demonstrates how to create a durable subscriber and receive messages from it:

```java
public void receiveMessage() {
    boolean stopReceivingMessages = false;
    try {
        createConnection();
            System.out.println("Creating session to receive messages");
            TopicSession session = connection.createTopicSession(false, Session.
            AUTO_ACKNOWLEDGE);
            myTopic = (Topic) getContext().lookup("jms/jakartaEERecipesTopic");
            System.out.println("Setting up consumer");
            String selector = "TYPE = 'JAKARTAEE'";
            TopicSubscriber subscriber = session.createDurableSubscriber(myTopic,
            "jakartaEERecipesSub");
            connection.start();
```

507

```
            while (!stopReceivingMessages) {
                System.out.println("Receiving message");
                Message inMessage = subscriber.receive();
                if (inMessage != null) {
                    System.out.println(inMessage);
                    if (inMessage instanceof TextMessage) {
                        String messageStr = ((TextMessage) inMessage).getText();
                        System.out.println(messageStr);
                        setDisplayMessage(messageStr);
                    } else {
                        System.out.println("Message was of another type");
                        setDisplayMessage("Message was of another type");
                    }
                } else {
                    stopReceivingMessages = true;
                }
            }
            connection.stop();
            subscriber.close();
            session.close();
            closeConnection();
        } catch (NamingException | JMSException ex) {
            Logger.getLogger(Example12_07.class.getName()).log(Level.SEVERE, null, ex);
        }
    }
```

The receiveMessage method is bound to an h:commandButton component within the JSF view in the example program, and you can follow along with the output that can be seen in the server log.

Unsubscribing from the Subscription

It is important to unsubscribe from a subscriber when finished using it because subscribers use up additional resources, as discussed in the "How It Works" section. The following method demonstrates how to unsubscribe:

```
public void unsubscribe(){
    try {
        createConnection();
        TopicSession session = connection.createTopicSession(false, Session.
        AUTO_ACKNOWLEDGE);
        // close subscriber if open, then unsubscribe
        session.unsubscribe("jakartaEERecipesSub");
        connection.close();
    } catch (JMSException ex) {
        Logger.getLogger(Example12_07.class.getName()).log(Level.SEVERE, null, ex);
    }
}
```

Running the Example

An example that binds all the methods shown in this recipe to Jakarta Server Faces views can be executed by deploying the JakartaEERecipes project to your GlassFish server and visiting the following URL:

http://localhost:8080/JakartaEERecipes/chapter12/recipe12_7.xhtml

You would see the output as shown in Figure 12-8.

Press the "Send Message" button a few times to send some messages to the topic, then click the "Create Subscriber" button to create a subscriber and "ReciveMessages" button to recieve messages.

| Create Subscriber | Send Message | Receive Messages |

Figure 12-8. *Output of Recipe 12-7*

How It Works

A message subscription is a Jakarta Messaging consumer that retains a durable connection to a specified Topic destination. Message subscriptions cannot be made for Queue destinations, only for Topics because they utilize publish/subscribe messaging. By default, a durable subscriber remains persistent, because the delivery mode is PERSISTENT by default. Subscriptions are stored in a server cache so that they can be retrieved in the event of a server failure. Because durable message subscribers retain messages in a cache, they take up a larger memory footprint. Therefore, it is important that subscribers remain subscribed only as long as necessary, and then unsubscribe to release the memory.

■ **Note** Durable subscriptions can only have one subscriber at a time.

To work with message subscribers, a special set of connection and session objects must be used. To start, you must inject a TopicConnectionFactory into any object that will make use of Topics. A TopicConnection can be created by calling the createTopicConnection method. A TopicSession must be created which is, in turn, from the TopicConnection. The TopicSession object can be used to create durable message subscribers and message publishers.

When creating a subscriber, one must invoke the Jakarta Messaging session method, createDurableSubscriber, and pass the Topic destination, along with a String that is used to identify the subscriber. The String identifier is important because this is the identifier that will be used by consumers to subscribe to the messages being published to the Topic. A TopicSubscriber object is generated from the createDurableSubscriber method, and it is important to create the initial durable subscriber in order to create the Topic subscription. Once the initial durable subscriber has been created, messages can be sent to the subscription, and consumers can subscribe to it.

To create a message and send it to a subscription, the Jakarta Messaging session createPublisher method must be invoked, passing the Topic destination object as an argument. The call to createPublisher will generate a TopicPublisher object, which can be utilized for publishing messages to a Topic subscription. Any type of message can be sent to a Topic. To learn more about the different types of messages that can be sent, please refer to Recipe 12-3. Any number of messages can be sent to a topic, and if a consumer has subscribed to the subscriber, it will receive the messages. New subscribers will begin receiving messages that are sent to the subscription after the time when they've subscribed.

To subscribe to a Topic, a `TopicSubscriber` object should be created by calling the session `createDurableSubscriber` method, passing the Topic destination object and the String-based identifier that was originally used to establish the subscriber. Once the `TopicSubscriber` has been created, messages can be consumed as usual, invoking the `TopicSubscriber` receive method for each message that will be consumed. Typically, an application will set a boundary limit to the number of messages that will be consumed and perform a loop to receive that number of messages from a subscribed Topic.

Since a durable subscription creates a memory footprint, it is essential for consumers to unsubscribe when finished with the Topic. If a consumer does not unsubscribe, the application server will starve other subscriber resources and will eventually run out of usable memory. To unsubscribe a consumer, invoke the session unsubscribe method, passing the String-based name of the subscriber. I told you that the String you use for identifying the subscriber was important!

It is sometimes useful to create message subscriptions for certain circumstances. Pertinent situations for using a subscriber may include a subscription for client consumers to receive messages regarding application errors or for an alert system so that administrators can subscribe to alerts that they wish to receive. In any case, durable subscriptions can be useful, so long as they are used sparingly and maintained in an appropriate manner.

12-8. Delaying Message Delivery

Problem

You would like to delay a message that is being sent.

Solution

Set the time of delay in milliseconds by calling the producer's `setDeliveryDelay(long)` method. In the following example, the message sending will be delayed by 1000 milliseconds:

```
TopicPublisher publisher = session.createPublisher(myTopic);
publisher.setDeliveryDelay(1000);
```

How It Works

It is possible to delay the delivery of a message. The Jakarta Messaging API provides a method, `setDeliveryDelay`, for producers. This method can be called, passing the delay time in milliseconds, prior to sending the message. Once the delay has been set, this will cause all subsequent message deliveries by that producer to be delayed.

CHAPTER 13

RESTful Web Services

A web service can be described as a client and server application that communicates over HTTP, which provides a standard means for communication and interoperability between different applications. There are many different web service implementations available across different programming platforms. A web service is made accessible via an endpoint implementation. Entire applications can be implemented using web services that transmit messages and data to and from each other. Jakarta RESTful Web Services (formerly known as JAX-RS) play a vital role in enterprise application development.

Jakarta RESTful Web Services is the API for Representational State Transfer (REST) web services. REST services are useful for performing operations via HTTP. REST service implementations are stateless, and they provide a smaller footprint for bandwidth, making them ideal for HTTP even on mobile devices. They utilize a predefined state of stateless operations.

REST supports SSL. Newer security APIs such as JSON Web Tokens (JWT) have been introduced, providing Jakarta RESTful Web Services with levels of security required for enterprise applications.

Over the next several recipes, you will be shown how to develop Jakarta RESTful web services. You'll learn how to configure your environment to work with Jakarta RESTful Web Services and how to code a client to make use of the services.

SETTING UP A REST ENVIRONMENT

In this chapter, we focus on making use of the Jakarta RESTful Web Services implementation for REST services, which is based upon Jersey. If you are using GlassFish 7.0.0, the API jars are provided with the distribution, so you do not need to download any additional libraries to add REST functionality to your applications.

For Jakarta RESTful Web Services to handle REST requests, you will have to configure a REST servlet dispatcher within the application's web.xml configuration file or within a Java class. The following excerpt from the web.xml configuration file demonstrates how to set up Jakarta RESTful Web Services for an application:

```
<servlet>
        <servlet-name>jakarta.ws.rs.core.Application</servlet-name>
        <load-on-startup>1</load-on-startup>
    </servlet>
    <servlet-mapping>
        <servlet-name>jakarta.ws.rs.core.Application</servlet-name>
        <url-pattern>/rest/*</url-pattern>
    </servlet-mapping>
    ...
```

© Josh Juneau and Tarun Telang 2022

J. Juneau and T. Telang, *Java EE to Jakarta EE 10 Recipes*, https://doi.org/10.1007/978-1-4842-8079-9_13

One can also make use of an annotation within a Java class to configure Jakarta RESTful Web Services and forget about the web.xml configuration. To do so, add the @ApplicationPath annotation to a class which extends jakarta.ws.rs.core.Application, as follows:

```
@jakarta.ws.rs.ApplicationPath("rest")
public class ApplicationConfig extends Application {
}
```

13-1. Developing a RESTful Web Service

Problem

You would like to create a Jakarta RESTful web service that will be exposed over the Internet to handle operations on data.

Solution #1

Create a RESTful (Representational State Transfer) web service by creating a root resource class (POJO) and adding resource methods to the class. To designate a class as a root resource class, annotate it with @Path or create at least one method within the class that is annotated with @Path and a request method designator (@GET, @PUT, @POST, or @DELETE). The following example demonstrates how to create a RESTful web service that simply displays a String or HTML to a client. The sources for this code can be found in the JakartaEERecipes_Chapter13 project within the org.jakartaeerecipe.chapter13.SimpleRest.java file:

```
package org.jakartaeerecipe.chapter13.rest;

import jakarta.ws.rs.GET;
import jakarta.ws.rs.Produces;
import jakarta.ws.rs.Path;
// Set the PATH to http://host:port/<application>/rest/simplerest/
@Path("/simplerest")
public class SimpleRest {
    @GET
    // Produces plain text message
    @Produces("text/plain")
    public String getPlainMessage() {
        return "Hello from a simple rest service";
    }
    @GET
    // Produces plain text message
    @Produces("text/html")
    public String getHTMLMessage() {
        return "<P>Hello from a <b>simple</b> rest service</P>";
    }
}
```

You can deploy the JakartaEERecipes application and then visit the following URL to see the results produced from the REST service: http://localhost:8080/JakartaEERecipes_Chapter13-1.0-SNAPSHOT/ rest/simplerest. The output will be as shown in Figure 13-1.

Hello from a **simple** rest service

Figure 13-1. *Output of the SimpleRest service*

Solution #2

Utilize an IDE, such as NetBeans, to create a RESTful web service. The NetBeans IDE includes wizards for developing web services of different types. By right-clicking a project and choosing the New ➤ Other... option from the contextual menu, the New File dialog will open, and Web Services can be chosen from the selection list. Proceed with the following directions to generate a REST web service from an entity class:

1) Choose the RESTful Web Service from the Entity Classes option from the New File menu.

2) Select one or more classes from the Available Entity Classes list and click the Add button. In this example, we'll choose the org.jakartaeerecipe.entity.Book entity, as shown in Figure 13-2. Choose Next.

Figure 13-2. *Select entity classes for RESTful web services within NetBeans*

3) List the package into which the REST service class will be generated, along with a package location (see Figure 13-3). Click Finish.

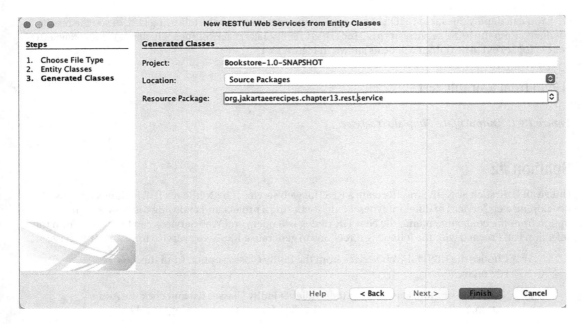

Figure 13-3. *Choose a resource package for the REST service class within NetBeans*

A REST service class that is like the following class would be generated after performing these steps:

```
// ....
@Stateless
@Path("org.jakartaeerecipe.entity.book")
public class BookFacadeREST extends AbstractFacade<Book> {
    @PersistenceContext(unitName = "JakartaEERecipesPU")
    private EntityManager em;
    public BookFacadeREST() {
        super(Book.class);
    }
    @POST
    @Override
    @Consumes({"application/xml", "application/json"})
    public void create(Book entity) {
        super.create(entity);
    }
    @PUT
    @Override
    @Consumes({"application/xml", "application/json"})
    public void edit(Book entity) {
        super.edit(entity);
    }
    @DELETE
    @Path("{id}")
    public void remove(@PathParam("id") BigDecimal id) {
        super.remove(super.find(id));
    }
```

```
@GET
@Path("{id}")
@Produces({"application/xml", "application/json"})
public Book find(@PathParam("id") BigDecimal id) {
    return super.find(id);
}
@GET
@Override
@Produces({"application/xml", "application/json"})
public List<Book> findAll() {
    return super.findAll();
}
@GET
@Path("{from}/{to}")
@Produces({"application/xml", "application/json"})
public List<Book> findRange(@PathParam("from") Integer from, @PathParam("to")
Integer to) {
    return super.findRange(new int[]{from, to});
}
@GET
@Path("count")
@Produces("text/plain")
public String countREST() {
    return String.valueOf(super.count());
}
@Override
protected EntityManager getEntityManager() {
    return em;
}
}
```

How It Works

RESTful web services are easy to develop, and they can produce and consume many different types of media. In most cases, REST web services are encouraged for services that will be sending and receiving information over the Internet. Before an application can support REST services, it must be properly configured to do so. In this book, the Jakarta RESTful Web Services implementation is utilized, which is based upon Jersey, the standard REST implementation for the industry. Please see the introduction to this chapter for more information on configuring Jakarta RESTful Web Services within your application.

A Java class that is a REST service implementation contains a myriad of annotations. Table 13-1 lists the possible annotations that may be used to create a REST service.

Table 13-1. *REST Service Annotations*

Annotation	Description
@POST	Request method designator that processes HTTP POST requests
@GET	Request method designator that processes HTTP GET requests
@PUT	Request method designator that processes HTTP PUT requests
@DELETE	Request method designator that processes HTTP DELETE requests
@HEAD	Request method designator that corresponds to the HTTP HEAD method. Processes HTTP HEAD requests
@Path	The value of this annotation should correlate to the relative URI path that indicates where the Java class will be hosted. Variables can be embedded in the URIs to make a URI path template
@PathParam	A type of parameter that can be extracted for use in the resource class. URI path parameters are extracted from the request URI, and the parameter names correspond to the URI path template variable names specified in the @Path class-level annotation
@QueryParam	A type of parameter that can be extracted for use in the resource class. Query parameters are extracted from the request
@Consumes	Used to specify the MIME media types of representations that a resource can consume
@Produces	Used to specify the MIME media types of representations that a resource can produce
@Provider	Used for anything that is of interest to the Jakarta RESTful Web Services runtime, such as a MessageBodyHeader and MessageBodyWriter

To designate a class as a REST service, the @Path annotation must be placed prior to the class or before at least one of the class method signatures. The @Path annotation is used to indicate the URI that should correspond to the service. The full URI includes the hostname, port number, application name, and REST servlet name, followed by the path designated with the @Path annotation. In the example, the @Path annotation specifies /simplerest as the service path, so the URL http://localhost:8080/ JakartaEERecipes_Chapter08-1.0-SNAPSHOT/rest/simplerest will invoke the web service. It is possible to include variables within a URL by enclosing them within brackets using the syntax {var}. For example, if each user had their own profile for a particular site, the @Path annotation could be as follows:

```
...
@Path("/simplerest/{user}")
...
```

In such a case, the URL could look like the following: http://localhost:8080/JakartaEERecipes_ Chapter08-1.0-SNAPSHOT/rest/simplerest/Juneau.

The @Path annotation can also be specified before any methods that are marked with @GET, @POST, @PUT, or @DELETE to specify a URI for invoking the denoted method. Moreover, variables can be placed within the path to accept a more dynamic URL. For instance, suppose a method was added to the class in Solution #1 that would return a greeting for the user that is specified as a parameter within the URL. You may do something like the following to make the URL unique:

```
@Path("{user}")
@GET
```

```
@Produces("text/html")
public String getUserMessage(@PathParam("user") String user){
    return "Greetings " + "<b>" + user + "</b>";
}
```

In this case, the getUserMessage method would be invoked if a URL like the following were placed into the browser: http://localhost:8080/JakartaEERecipes_Chapter08-1.0-SNAPSHOT/rest/simplerest/josh. If this URL were specified, then the method would be invoked, passing "josh" as the user variable value, and the message would be displayed as in Figure 13-4.

Greetings **josh**

Figure 13-4. *Output from the /rest/simplerest/{user} service*

■ **Note**   It is very important to create URIs that are readable and also provide intuitive information about your web service. URIs that are based upon these standards help to reduce errors within client applications and make the web service more functional.

Designate methods with the @GET, @POST, @PUT, or @DELETE designator to process the type of web service request that is desired. Doing so will generate web service functionality. If more than one method exists within a REST web service implementation and @Path is only specified at the class level and not at the method level, then the method that returns the MIME type the client requires will be invoked. If you wish your method to display content, designate a method with @GET. If you wish to create a method for creating a new object, designate the method as @POST. If you are creating a method for inserting or replacing an object that already exists, then designate it with @PUT. Finally, if you are creating a method for removing objects, then designate it with @DELETE. For more information regarding these annotations, please refer to Recipe 13-3.

REST services can become complex if they constitute many different methods and paths. Entire applications exist based upon REST services, where all CRUD (create, retrieve, update, delete) manipulations are invoked via web service calls. This recipe provides only the foundation for developing with Jakarta RESTful Web Services, as the topic is far too involved for a handful of recipes or a chapter in itself.

13-2. Consuming and Producing with REST

Problem

You would like to produce different types of content with a RESTful web service. Moreover, you would like the web service to consume content as well.

Solution

Create methods within the web service implementation class that are annotated with @GET for generating output and optionally along with @Produces for specifying the type of output. Annotate methods with @POST or @PUT for updating or inserting data. The following sections provide examples utilizing these solutions.

Add the Maven dependencies for Jakarta XML Binding library in your pom.xml file as follows:

```
<dependency>
    <groupId>jakarta.xml.bind</groupId>
    <artifactId>jakarta.xml.bind-api</artifactId>
    <version>4.0.0</version>
</dependency>
```

Producing Output

Make use of the @Produces annotation to specify the type of content you wish to produce from a decorated method. The following excerpt, taken from the JakartaEERecipes project source at org.jakartaeerecipe. chapter13.rest.SimpleRest, demonstrates the use of @Produces:

```
@GET
// Produces an XML message
@Produces("application/xml")
public MessageWrapperList getXMLMessage() {
    // Pass string to MessageWrapper class, which marshals the String as XML
    return new MessageWrapper("Hello from a simple rest service");
}
```

Producing List Output

Make use of the @Produces annotation to specify the type of content you wish to produce from a decorated method. The following excerpt, taken from the JakartaEERecipes project source at org.jakartaeerecipe. chapter13.rest.SimpleRest, demonstrates the use of @Produces and returns an object that contains a List of results:

```
@GET
// Produces an XML message
@Path("all")
@Produces("application/xml")
public MessageWrapperList getXMLMessageList() {
    ArrayList<String> messageList = new ArrayList<>();
    messageList.add("String 1");
    messageList.add("String 2");
    return new MessageWrapperList(messageList);
}
```

In this case, the MessageWrapperList object sources are as follows, but this example could be changed to accept Lists of any object type, not just Strings:

```
package org.jakartaeerecipe.chapter13.recipe13_02;
import java.util.ArrayList;
import java.util.Collection;
import java.util.List;
import jakarta.xml.bind.annotation.XmlElement;
import jakarta.xml.bind.annotation.XmlRootElement;
import jakarta.xml.bind.annotation.XmlSeeAlso;
```

```
@XmlRootElement(name="messageWrapperList")
@XmlSeeAlso(String.class)
public class MessageWrapperList extends ArrayList<String> {
    private static final long serialVersionUID = 1L;
    public MessageWrapperList(){
        super();
    }
    public MessageWrapperList(Collection<? extends String> message){
        super(message);
    }
    @XmlElement(name="messageList")
    public List<String> getMessageList() {
        return this;
    }
    public void setMessageList(List<String> messages) {
        this.addAll(messages);
    }
}
```

Accepting Input

Annotate methods within a web service class with @PUT to indicate that some content is being passed to the method. To specify the type of content being passed, annotate the same method with @Consumes(content-type). The following excerpt, taken from the JakartaEERecipes project source at org.jakartaeerecipe. chapter13.rest.SimpleRest.java, demonstrates the use of @Consumes:

```
@PUT
@Path("add")
@Consumes("text/plain")
public String add(@QueryParam("text") String text){
    this.message = text;
    return message;
}
```

To input a new message stating JakartaEERecipes, you should make the following request:
PUT http://localhost:8080/JakartaEERecipes/rest/simplerest/add?text=JakartaEERecipes
Figure 13-5 shows a screenshot from POSTMAN of the request/response used.

Figure 13-5. *Output from Recipe 13-2*

How It Works

Create a web service class by following the procedures outlined in Recipe 13-2, and then designate methods within the web service as producers or consumers by annotating them appropriately. Methods that will be generating some type of output should be annotated with @Produces, which should subsequently specify the type of output generated. Moreover, the methods that are generating output should also be annotated with @GET, which indicates that the method is a reading resource. Methods that will be accepting input should be annotated with @PUT or @POST. The @PUT annotation indicates that a new resource will be created, and the @POST annotation indicates that an existing resource will be updated or a new resource will be created. Incidentally, the methods that accept input should also be annotated with @Consumes, which should subsequently specify the type of content that is being consumed. Overall, @Produces annotations should coincide with the @GET annotated methods. That is, a method that is decorated with @GET will return some content to the client. @Consumes annotations should coincide with either @PUT or @POST annotated methods.

In the solution to this recipe, two types of methods are demonstrated. The first example demonstrates a REST method that produces XML content, and the @Produces("application/xml") annotation indicates it as such. Within the method, a String is passed to a class named MessageWrapper. The MessageWrapper class is responsible for marshaling the String as XML using Jakarta XML Binding. For more information, please refer to the sources located at org.jakartaeerecipe.chapter13.recipe13_02.MessageWrapper.java and see the Jakarta XML Binding documentation online at https://eclipse-ee4j.github.io/jakartaee-tutorial/#using-jakarta-rest-with-jakarta-xml-binding. The beauty of Jakarta RESTful Web Services is that just about any content type can be produced. A client application can visit the URL that corresponds to a web service's @GET method, and content will be returned in a format that will work for that client. For instance, if a client is a web browser, it will look for a method that produces text/html content within the web service and then invoke that method.

The other example in the solution to this recipe demonstrates a REST method that consumes String content. The @PUT annotation indicates that either a new object will be generated or an existing object will be updated with the request. In this case, the String-based message field is updated to the content that is passed into the web service via the text variable. The @Path annotation has been placed above the method signature to indicate a path following the format /add should be used to access this method. Lastly, the @Consumes annotation indicates that the method will consume plain text.

If one were interested in returning a List of values, then a wrapper class for consuming the list of returned entity objects and storing into a local List is likely one of the best approaches. In the example, a List<String> is returned from the getXMLMessageList() service. This is facilitated by utilizing a wrapper object named MessageWrapperList, which extends ArrayList<String>, therefore accepting a List of Strings, and returns that list when the getMessageList() method is called upon. Using a wrapper object such as this makes it easy to send lists of data to and from a web service.

The REST service in this example is very brief, and in real-world scenarios, many methods producing and consuming different types of content are utilized within REST service implementations. It is usually considered as bad practice to use query parameters in POST/PUT. The code snippet in this recipe is simply to demonstrate the API capabilities; hence, in production scenario, it needs to be used with a pinch of salt.

13-3. Filtering Requests and Responses

Problem

You wish to perform some activity against a web service request before it has been delivered to the network, or to a web service response before it has been sent back to the client.

Solution

Apply a filter or interceptor to the web service request or response to perform the desired activity. The following example filter is used to write alerts to the system log before an incoming request has been processed and before a response is sent back to the client:

```
import java.io.BufferedReader;
import java.io.IOException;
import java.io.InputStream;
import java.io.InputStreamReader;
import jakarta.annotation.Priority;
import jakarta.ws.rs.Priorities;
import jakarta.ws.rs.container.ContainerRequestContext;
import jakarta.ws.rs.container.ContainerRequestFilter;
import jakarta.ws.rs.container.ContainerResponseContext;
import jakarta.ws.rs.container.ContainerResponseFilter;
import jakarta.ws.rs.ext.Provider;
import org.jakartaeerecipe.chapter13.rest.interfaces.Alerter;
@Provider
@Alerter
public class AlertFilter implements ContainerRequestFilter,
        ContainerResponseFilter {
    @Override
    public void filter(ContainerRequestContext requestContext)
            throws IOException {
        alert(requestContext);
    }
    @Override
    public void filter(ContainerRequestContext crc, ContainerResponseContext crc1) throws
    IOException {
        alert(crc);
    }
```

```java
    public void alert(ContainerRequestContext context) {
        try(InputStream in = context.getEntityStream();) {
            if (in != null) {
                InputStreamReader inreader = new InputStreamReader(in);
                BufferedReader reader = new BufferedReader(inreader);
                String text = "";
                while ((text = reader.readLine()) != null) {
                    System.out.println(text);
                }
            }
        } catch (IOException ex) {
            // Error handling
        }
    }
}
```

How It Works

The concept of filters and interceptors is analogous to the post office processing your mail before it comes to your address. Rather than a message being delivered directly from point A to point B, it is first routed to one or more postal offices, where it is further processed before reaching point B. Web resource filters and interceptors apply that same concept to requests or responses that are being processed via a web service. If a filter or interceptor is bound to a web resource, then it will be invoked at some point in the life cycle of a request or response to that web resource. The type of filter or interceptor determines at what point in the life cycle it is applied. Interceptors (otherwise known as entity interceptors) wrap around a method invocation at a specified extension point. Filters, on the other hand, execute code at a specified extension point, but they are not wrapped around methods. In the next few sections, you will take a closer look at each and how they are used.

Filters

An extension point is an interface that includes a method, which is responsible for filtering or intercepting the request or response. Filters have four such extension point interfaces, those being ClientRequestFilter, ClientResponseFilter, ContainerRequestFilter, and ContainerResponseFilter. The name of the extension point helps to describe what filter is applied and at what point. ClientRequestFilter and ClientResponseFilter are for use with the Jakarta RESTful Web Services Client API. ClientRequestFilter is applied before an HTTP request is delivered to the network. A ClientResponseFilter is applied when a server response is received and before control is returned to the application. ContainerRequestFilter and ContainerResponseFilter classes are for use with the Jakarta RESTful Web Services Server API. Similar to the client-side filters, a ContainerRequestFilter is applied upon receiving a request from a client, and a ContainerResponseFilter is applied before the HTTP response is delivered.

Entity Interceptors

As mentioned in the previous section, an extension point is an interface that includes a method, which is responsible for filtering or intercepting the request or response. Entity interceptors have two such extension points, those being ReaderInterceptor and WriterInterceptor. An entity interceptor class must implement one or both of these extension points. Also mentioned previously, entity interceptors wrap calls to methods. More specifically, MessageBodyWriter implementations wrap calls to the writeTo method, whereas MessageBodyReader implementations wrap calls to the readFrom method.

Binding Filters and Interceptors

Filters and interceptors must be associated with application classes or methods, and this process is also known as *binding*. The default type of binding is global binding, and any filter or interceptor that does not include annotations is bound globally. Global binding associates the filter or interceptor with all resource methods in an application. That said, any time a resource method is invoked, all globally bound filters and interceptors are processed as well.

Filters and interceptors can be registered manually via Application or Configuration, or they can be registered dynamically. To indicate that a filter or interceptor should be registered dynamically, it should be annotated with @Provider. If a filter or interceptor is not annotated as such, it must be registered manually.

To manually bind a filter or interceptor to a resource method, the filter or interceptor class must be denoted with a @NameBinding annotation. A @NameBinding annotation can be coded just as a standard annotation would, but it should also include the @NameBinding annotation in its interface. The following annotation code could be used to create a @NameBinding annotation that might be placed on a filter that is responsible for firing alerts:

```
// ...
@NameBinding
@Target({ ElementType.TYPE, ElementType.METHOD })
@Retention(value = RetentionPolicy.RUNTIME)
public @interface Alerter { }
```

To associate the @NameBinding with a filter or interceptor, simply annotate the filter or interceptor class with it. The following AlertFilter class is a filter implementation that is denoted with the @Alerter annotation:

```
@Provider
@Alerter
class AlertFilter implements ContainerRequestFilter,
        ContainerResponseFilter {
...
}
```

That filter can now be bound to a resource method by annotating the resource method with the same @NameBinding as the filter class, as demonstrated in the following example:

```
@GET
@Produces("text/html")
@Alerter
public String  getJobs(){
    ...
}
```

■ **Note**   This same concept can be applied to Application subclasses to globally bind the filter or interceptor.

Setting Priorities

As mentioned in previous sections, filters and interceptors can be chained. Chains of filters or interceptors invoke individual filters or interceptors based upon a given priority. To assign priority to a filter or interceptor, denote the implementation class with the @BindingPriority annotation. Integer numbers are used to associate priorities. The higher the integer, the higher the priority. Therefore, the filter or interceptor that has the highest-priority integer assigned to it will be invoked first, and the lowest-priority integer will be invoked last.

13-4. Processing Long-Running Operations Asynchronously

Problem

Your server-side Jakarta RESTful Web Services method contains a long-running operation, and you would like to avoid blocking while waiting for the event to complete.

Solution

Perform asynchronous processing so that the resource method containing the long-running operation can inform Jakarta RESTful Web Services that a response is not yet readily available, but will be produced at some point in the future. In the following example, a Jakarta RESTful Web Services service named AsyncResource contains a resource method named asyncOperation. The asyncOperation method contains a long-running task, which is handed off to a ManagedExecutorService for processing:

```
import jakarta.annotation.Resource;
import jakarta.enterprise.concurrent.ManagedExecutorService;
import jakarta.ws.rs.GET;
import jakarta.ws.rs.Path;
import jakarta.ws.rs.container.AsyncResponse;
import jakarta.ws.rs.container.Suspended;
/**
 * Recipe 13-5:  Asynchronous Processing
 * @author Juneau
 */
@Path("/asynchronous/asyncResource")
public class AsyncResource {
    @Resource(name = "concurrent/__defaultManagedExecutorService")
    ManagedExecutorService mes;
    @GET
    public void asyncOperation(@Suspended final AsyncResponse ar){
        mes.submit(
                new Runnable() {
                    public void run(){
                        // Perform long running operation
                        longRunningOperation();
                        ar.resume("Performing asynchronous operation");
                    }
                });
    }
}
```

```
    public void longRunningOperation(){
        // This is a method that contains a long-running operation
        System.out.println( "Performing long running task..." );
    }
}
```

■ **Note**   To learn more about ManagedExecutorService, please see Chapter 16.

How It Works

The Jakarta RESTful Web Services API can handle long-running tasks off to a ManagedExecutorService for processing. This allows a server-side resource to return control back to a client and avoid problematic blocks. The API also includes a way to register a timeout handler in case the asynchronous process does not return within a specified amount of time, along with client-side asynchronous capabilities. To begin, the server-side asynchronous implementation will be described, followed by the others.

To perform asynchronous processing within a Jakarta RESTful Web Services resource, the resource method that contains long-running operations must accept an instance of AsyncResponse via the utilization of the @Suspended annotation. The AsyncResponse class provides a means for resuming operations and returning control to the client. A ManagedExecutorService (see Chapter 16 for more information) must be made available within the class, and it must be called upon to submit a new Runnable containing the long-running operation and a call to AsyncResponse.resume() to return control back to the client once the long-running process is completed. When the ManagedExecutorService submit method is called, the Runnable is passed to the server for further processing, forking a thread to execute the task and returning immediately. When the long-running task has completed, it will be passed back to the application, invoking the AsyncResponse resume method.

To avoid long-running operations that never return and cause a suspended connection to wait indefinitely, it is possible to specify a timeout value. The timeout value can be specified by setting a timeout handler via the AsyncResponse.setTimeoutHandler() method, passing a new instance of TimeoutHandler. After the setTimeoutHandler has been invoked, the timeout can be set by calling the AsyncResponse. setTimeout() method, passing any unit of type java.util.concurrent.TimeUnit. For instance, the following lines demonstrate how to set a timeout of 30 seconds for the long-running operation contained in the resource shown in the solution to this recipe:

```
...
@GET
    public void asyncOperation(@Suspended final AsyncResponse ar){
        ar.setTimeoutHandler(new TimeoutHandler() {
            public void handleTimeout(AsyncResponse ar){
                ar.resume("Timed out");
            }
        });
        ar.setTimeout(30, SECONDS);
        mes.submit(
                new Runnable() {
                    public void run(){
                        // Perform long running operation
                        longRunningOperation();
```

```
                    ar.resume("Performing asynchronous operation");
            }
        });
    }
...
```

Note   Jakarta RESTful Web Services implementations will generate a `ServiceUnavailableException` with a status of 503 when a timeout value is reached and no timeout handler is present.

As mentioned at the top of this section, the asynchronous Jakarta RESTful Web Services API has been extended to the client API as well. By default, invocations from a client to a target are executed in a synchronous fashion, but they can be changed to asynchronous by calling the `async` method and optionally registering an instance of `InvocationCallback`. For example, the following lines of code demonstrate a client call to the web service resource that was presented in the solution to this recipe:

```
Client client = ClientBuilder.newClient();
Target target = client.target("http://localhost:8080/JakartaEERecipes_Chapter08-1.0-
SNAPSHOT/rest/asynchronous/asyncResource");
Target.request().async().get();
```

For more information regarding the client API and asynchronous operations, please refer to the Jakarta RESTful Web Services documentation online.

13-5. Pushing One-Way Asynchronous Updates from Servers

Problem

You wish to push one-way messages from a server to one or more clients.

Solution

Utilize Server-Sent Events (SSE) to push messages from a server to one or more clients. The Jakarta RESTful Web Services 2.1 API introduced the concept of SSE, which allows one to push messages from a server to subscribed clients. It also allows for subscription events to perform server actions. The following example contains sources for a Jakarta RESTful Web Services class. The class contains a `send` method, which allows a client to connect to the server and obtain messages from the server that have been broadcast via Server-Sent Events:

```
package org.jakartaeerecipe.chapter13.rest.service;
import jakarta.ws.rs.GET;
import jakarta.ws.rs.Path;
import jakarta.ws.rs.Produces;
import jakarta.ws.rs.core.Context;
import jakarta.ws.rs.core.MediaType;
import jakarta.ws.rs.sse.Sse;
```

```
import jakarta.ws.rs.sse.SseEventSink;
@Path("sse")
public class SSEEventResource {
    @Resource(name = "DefaultManagedExecutorService")
    ManagedExecutorService executor;
    public SSEEventResource() {
    }
    @GET
    @Path("send")
    @Produces(MediaType.SERVER_SENT_EVENTS)
    public void send(@Context SseEventSink eventSink,
            @Context Sse sse) {
        executor.execute(() -> {
            try (SseEventSink sink = eventSink) {
                eventSink.send(sse.newEvent("Welcome to the List!"));
                eventSink.send(sse.newEvent("Message One!"));
                eventSink.send(sse.newEvent("SERVER-NOTIFICATION", "Message Two!"));
                eventSink.send(sse.newEventBuilder()
                        .comment("Nice Test")
                        .name("SERVER-TEST")
                        .data("Some data...could be an object")
                        .build());
                eventSink.close();
            }
        });
    }
}
```

One can visit the following URL and see the resulting messages broadcast:
http://localhost:8080/JakartaEERecipes_Chapter08-1.0-SNAPSHOT/rest/sse/send.

To broadcast to multiple clients simultaneously, one can use the SseBroadcaster to register multiple
SseEventSink instances and send messages. The following example demonstrates how to construct a
Jakarta RESTful Web Services class that allows clients to register and the server to broadcast events to those
registered clients:

```
package org.jakartaeerecipe.chapter13.rest.service;
import java.util.UUID;
import jakarta.annotation.PostConstruct;
import jakarta.ejb.Singleton;
import jakarta.ws.rs.GET;
import jakarta.ws.rs.POST;
import jakarta.ws.rs.Path;
import jakarta.ws.rs.PathParam;
import jakarta.ws.rs.Produces;
import jakarta.ws.rs.core.Context;
import jakarta.ws.rs.core.MediaType;
import jakarta.ws.rs.sse.Sse;
import jakarta.ws.rs.sse.SseBroadcaster;
import jakarta.ws.rs.sse.SseEventSink;
@Path("/")
@Singleton
```

```
public class SSEEventBroadcaster {
    @Context
    private Sse sse;
    private volatile SseBroadcaster sseBroadcaster;
    public SSEEventBroadcaster() {
    }
    @PostConstruct
    public void init() {
        sseBroadcaster = sse.newBroadcaster();
    }
    @GET
    @Path("register")
    @Produces(MediaType.SERVER_SENT_EVENTS)
    public void register(@Context SseEventSink eventSink) {
        eventSink.send(sse.newEvent("Thanks for registering!"));
        sseBroadcaster.register(eventSink);
    }
    @POST
    @Path("send/{message}")
    public void broadcast(@PathParam("message") String message) {
        sseBroadcaster.broadcast(sse.newEventBuilder()
                .mediaType(MediaType.APPLICATION_JSON_TYPE)
                .id(UUID.randomUUID().toString())
                .name("SSEEventBroadcaster Message")
                .data(message)
                .build()
        );
    }
}
```

How It Works

The Jakarta RESTful Web Services (https://jakarta.ee/specifications/restful-ws/) supports Server-Sent Events (SSE) . Server-Sent Events make it possible to push messages from a server to multiple clients at a time over HTTP or HTTPS. The connection from the client to the server can remain open, and messages can continue to be sent until the client disconnects. The API contains several interfaces that are used for sending messages to clients, registering connections, and so on, and each of them resides within the jakarta.ws.rs.sse package. The Sse interface is the server-side entry point for creating OutboundSseEvent and SseBroadcaster. It can be injected into a field or used as a parameter to a method or constructor. The SseEventSink interface is used to send a stream of messages, and it can be acquired by injecting as a resource method parameter. SseEvent is the base event class, which defines properties such as Id, Name, and Comment. The OutboundSseEvent is used by the server to package an SseEvent, and SseBroadcaster is used to manage multiple SseEventSink objects. The SseBroadcaster enables the server to send events to all registered clients and provides facilities for handling exceptions.

In the first example, a simple Jakarta RESTful Web Services class is used to demonstrate how a server can use a single method to register a client and send one or more events. In the example, the class is registered as a RESTful web service at the path "sse," and the method send() is registered at the path "sse/send." The send() method produces the type MediaType.SERVER_SENT_EVENTS. It accepts @Context parameters of type SseEventSink and Sse, which are used to register a client and push events. The class also injects a ManagedExecutorService instance, which is a server-side concurrency utility that is used to perform concurrent processes. You can learn more about the ManagedExecutorService in Chapter 16. Inside the method, a try-with-resources clause is used to open up an SseEventSink identified as eventSink. The eventSink is used to send a number of SseEvent instances. Once completed, the eventSink is closed. The entire process is sent to the ManagedExecutorService so that it can be queued up in the server and executed in a concurrent manner.

The next example demonstrates how to construct a Jakarta RESTful Web Services class that can be used to register clients and broadcast events. The class is registered as a singleton, meaning that only one instance of the class will be constructed and utilized by all sessions. An Sse context is registered with the class, as it can be used to create new SseBroadcaster objects, new SseEvent objects, and new event builder objects. An SseBroadcaster is declared as volatile, meaning that it will be stored in main Java memory and not in a cache. There is an init() method which is annotated with @PostConstruct so that it will be executed immediately after construction. The init() method contains a call to sse.newBroadcaster(), thereby obtaining a new SseBroadcaster instance. Clients can register by calling upon the register web service method, which produces MediaType.SERVER_SENT_EVENTS. An SseEventSink Context parameter is passed in as a parameter to the register method, and in the implementation a new SseEvent is sent via the eventSink. The SseEventSink is then registered to the SseBroadcaster instance. The broadcast method accepts a String as a path parameter, and inside the method the SseBroadcaster broadcast() is used to send an event. The method demonstrates the use of the SseEvent builder. As you can see, calling upon sse.newEventBuilder() allows for the construction of an SseEvent utilizing the builder pattern. In the example, the media type is set as MediaType.APPLICATION_JSON_TYPE, which indicates JSON:

```
sseBroadcaster.broadcast(sse.newEventBuilder()
    .mediaType(MediaType.APPLICATION_JSON_TYPE)
    .id(UUID.randomUUID().toString())
    .name("SSEEventBroadcaster Message")
    .data(message)
    .build()
);
```

In the next recipe, I will demonstrate how to register a client to an SseBroadcaster and also how to listen for events on the client.

13-6. Receiving Server-Sent Events As a Client

Problem

You wish to create a client which subscribes to an SseBroadcaster on which messages are pushed from a server, and you'd like to have the client perform an action when a message is received.

Solution

Utilize Server-Sent Events (SSE) to push messages from a server to one or more clients. The Jakarta RESTful Web Services 2.1 API introduced the concept of SSE, which allows a server to broadcast messages to registered clients. In the following example, a Jakarta Server Faces client is used to call upon a Jakarta RESTful Web Services SSE broadcaster and register. The client then listens to broadcast messages for 1000 milliseconds:

```
package org.jakartaeerecipe.chapter13.rest.jsf;
import jakarta.annotation.PostConstruct;
import jakarta.enterprise.context.RequestScoped;
import jakarta.inject.Named;
```

```
import jakarta.ws.rs.client.Client;
import jakarta.ws.rs.client.ClientBuilder;
import jakarta.ws.rs.client.WebTarget;
import jakarta.ws.rs.sse.SseEventSource;
@Named
@RequestScoped
public class SseClient {
    private Client client;
    @PostConstruct
    public void init() {
        client = ClientBuilder.newClient();
    }
    public void listen() {
        WebTarget target = client.target("http://localhost:8080/ http://localhost:8080/
        JakartaEERecipes_Chapter08-1.0-SNAPSHOT/rest/ ssebroadcaster/register");
        try (SseEventSource source = SseEventSource.target(target).build()) {
            source.register(System.out::println);
            source.open();
            Thread.sleep(1000); // Consume events for 1000 ms
            source.close();
        } catch (InterruptedException e) {
        }
    }
}
```

A Jakarta Server Faces commandButton could be linked to the #{sseClient.listen} method, which would then invoke the client when clicked.

How It Works

A Jakarta RESTful Web Services client can be used to register to an SSE broadcaster by simply calling upon the broadcaster's registration method. Once registered, the SseEventSource can be opened for a defined amount of time (one should not leave an SseEventSource open without bound), and then it can be closed when finished listening for messages.

In the example, the SseEventSource is set to the target of the broadcaster URL. Next, it registers the output from the incoming message to be written to System.out.println(). Therefore, each message received will be written to the system log. After the registration, the source is opened for incoming messages. In the example, a thread is hard-coded to sleep for 1000 milliseconds. This is simply to keep the client open for messages for 1000 milliseconds and would likely not be coded this way for a production application. Lastly, the SseEventSource is closed, which ends the client session.

CHAPTER 14

■ ■ ■

WebSockets and JSON

The Jakarta EE platform aims to provide a common ground for developing Java enterprise solutions that incorporate HTML5 and other modern web technologies. WebSockets are a full-duplex communication mechanism that allows both textual and binary messages to be sent between clients and servers, without the HTTP request/response life cycle. WebSockets allow either the client or the server to send a message at any time, providing an asynchronous solution for working with data while the user is performing a task.

HTML5 has become the mainstream markup language for developing content that can be presented via the World Wide Web. It defines a standard, which can be used to produce both HTML and XHTML documents. Along with standardization, HTML5 also brings forth semantic features that were previously only possible on desktop application platforms. For example, elements such as `<video>` and `<audio>` allow media content to be embedded directly in web pages, without the need to embed a media player solution. There is no doubt that HTML5, the fifth revision of the HTML standard, has opened the doors to new possibilities in web application development.

The universally supported JSON (JavaScript Object Notation) object has become a widely adopted solution for sending data between points. HTML5-based web applications can utilize JSON to transport data, using WebSockets, Ajax, or other transport technologies. The Jakarta EE platform provides the JSON Processing (JSON-P) API, which introduces utilities that make it easier to build and work with JSON objects within the Java language. Jakarta EE added enhancements to JSON-P, allowing the abilities to point to a specific location within a JSON document and patch existing JSON documents. The JSON Binding (JSON-B) API was also introduced in Jakarta EE, providing a convenient API for mapping JSON to Java objects.

This chapter will focus on recipes that demonstrate these APIs. You will learn how to make use of WebSockets, JSON-P, and JSON-B so that your application's client-server communication can become seamless, whether the user interface is written with HTML5, JSF, or another markup language.

14-1. Creating a WebSocket Endpoint

Problem

You wish to create a WebSocket endpoint that can be used to receive messages asynchronously.

© Josh Juneau and Tarun Telang 2022
J. Juneau and T. Telang, *Java EE to Jakarta EE 10 Recipes*, https://doi.org/10.1007/978-1-4842-8079-9_14

Solution

Create a WebSocket endpoint by annotating a server-side POJO (Plain Old Java Object) class and a method within that class accordingly. In the following example, a simple POJO class, named `org.jakartaeerecipe.chapter14.recipe14_01.BookChatEndpoint`, is annotated to indicate that it should be accessible via the Web as a WebSocket endpoint. The class contains a method named `messageReceiver`, which is annotated to make it accessible to a client as a callable message consumer:

```
package org.jakartaeerecipe.chapter14;
import jakarta.websocket.OnMessage;
import jakarta.websocket.server.ServerEndpoint;

@ServerEndpoint(value="/chat")
public class BookChatEndpoint {
 @OnMessage
 public String messageReceiver(String message) {
     return "Message Received: " + message;
   }
}
```

Deploy this application in the GlassFish server. The WebSocket endpoint will be accessible to clients at the URL `ws://localhost:8080/JakartaEERecipes_Chapter14-1.0-SNAPSHOT/chat`. When a message is sent from a client to the endpoint, it is sent to the `messageReceiver` method, where it is processed accordingly. In this case, a `String` message containing the message passed to the endpoint is returned to the client.

How It Works

A server-side class can accept messages from clients by configuring it as a WebSocket endpoint. To develop a WebSocket endpoint, create a Java POJO, and annotate it with `@ServerEndpoint`. The `@ServerEndpoint` annotation accepts a String-based path attribute, which is used to indicate the URI at which the server is available to accept client messages. Therefore, when the server is started, the value of the path attribute would be appended to the end of the context path and application name in which the WebSocket resides. By initiating a call to that URL, one method, annotated with `@OnMessage`, will be invoked to process the message that is sent.

In the example, a class named `BookChatEndpoint` is annotated as a WebSocket, so it is accessible to clients as an endpoint for receiving messages and returning a response. When initiating communication with the WebSocket endpoint, the client must utilize a URL that contains a URI scheme of "ws," rather than "http." The "ws" URI scheme was introduced by the WebSocket protocol and, as such, indicates that the URL is used for communication with a WebSocket. In this example, a client can send a message to the server via the `BookChatEndpoint` WebSocket, and the server can send a message back at the same time, because WebSockets allow for full-duplex communication. *Full-duplex communication* is an HTML5 standard, rather than standard HTTP, which utilizes a request-response communication.

14-2. Sending Messages to a WebSocket Endpoint

Problem

You would like to send a message from a client to a WebSocket endpoint that is available on a server.

Solution

Engineer a JavaScript solution that can be used to send messages from a client browser to a WebSocket endpoint. Invoke the JavaScript function via an action event that is bound to an HTML input tag within the view. In the following example, a button contains an onclick attribute that will invoke a JavaScript function named bookChatRelay. The bookChatRelay function is responsible for opening a session with a WebSocket endpoint so that messages can be sent. The following listing is an excerpt from the file recipe14_02.html, which is located within the /webapp/chapter14 directory of the JakartaEERecipes_Chapter14 source bundle:

```html
<html>
    <head>
        <script type="text/javascript">
            var ws;
            function bookChatRelay()
            {
                if ("WebSocket" in window)
                {
                    alert("WebSocket is supported by your Browser!");
                    if (ws == null){
                        alert("Creating new websocket connection");
                        ws = new WebSocket("ws://localhost:8080/JakartaEERecipes/chat");
                    } else {
                        ws.send("Another message");
                    }
                    ws.onopen = function()
                    {
                        // Web Socket is connected, send data using send()
                        ws.send("Message to send");
                        alert("Message is sent...");
                    };
                    ws.onmessage = function (evt)
                    {
                        var received_msg = evt.data;
                        alert("Message from server: " + received_msg);
                    };
                    ws.onclose = function()
                    {
                        // websocket is closed.
                        alert("Connection is closed...");
                    };
                }
                else
                {
                    // The browser doesn't support WebSocket
                    alert("WebSocket NOT supported by your Browser!");
                }
            }
            function closeConnection(){
                if (ws !== null){
                    ws.close();
                    ws = null;
```

```
                }
            }
        </script>
    </head>
    <body>
        <input id="wsRelay" type="button" value="WebSocket Test Message"
                onclick="bookChatRelay();"/>
        <input id="closeConn" type="button" value="Close Connection"
                onclick="closeConnection();"/>
    </body>
</html>
```

When the button is clicked, the message will be sent from the browser client to the WebSocket endpoint, and a message will be returned from the endpoint to the client.

■ **Note** The JavaScript code in this test creates a new WebSocket connection each time the button on the page is clicked. This is okay for testing purposes, but in a real-life scenario, you will want to retain and reuse the connection, if possible.

How It Works

The ability to asynchronously send messages (text or binary) from a client to a server defines the foundation of Ajax and HTML5 capability. The WebSockets API allows developers to send messages to the server via JavaScript calls to a WebSocket endpoint. Conversely, the API allows clients to receive messages and process them accordingly via a series of JavaScript functions. The example for this recipe demonstrates how to send a message to a WebSocket endpoint by clicking a button on a web page. When the button is clicked, a JavaScript function named bookChatRelay is invoked, which embodies the processing implementation.

To send a message to a WebSocket endpoint via a JavaScript function, the first task is to confirm whether the user's browser can work with WebSockets (HTML5 compliant). This confirmation can be performed using a conditional statement to verify if the "WebSocket" object is available within the client via the following if statement:

```
if("WebSocket" in window){
...
} else {
...
}
```

Figure 14-1 shows a browser message confirming WebSocket support.

Figure 14-1. *Confirmation of WebSocket support in your browser*

If the client browser can work with WebSockets, then the implementation inside the `if` block is invoked; otherwise, the implementation within the `else` block is invoked. To process the WebSocket message, a new WebSocket object must be instantiated to establish the server connection, which is done by passing the URL to the WebSocket endpoint to a new WebSocket object:

```
var ws = new WebSocket("ws://localhost:8080/JakartaEERecipes_Chapter14-1.0-SNAPSHOT/chat");
```

The constructor for creating a WebSocket takes either one or two parameters. The first parameter is the URL of the server to which the WebSocket will connect, and the optional second parameter is a `String` of protocols that can be used for message transmission. The WebSocket object contains a handful of events that are utilized to help implement message processing. The confirmation dialog for the new WebSocket connection will be as in Figure 14-2.

Figure 14-2. *Confirmation of a new WebSocket connection*

Table 14-1 lists the different events that can occur in the life cycle of a WebSocket object, along with a description of what they do.

Table 14-1. *JavaScript WebSocket Object Events*

Event	Handler Method	Description
open	onOpen	Occurs when the WebSocket connection is established
close	onClose	Occurs when the WebSocket connection is closed
error	onError	Occurs when there is a communication error
message	onMessage	Occurs when data is received from the server

After the WebSocket object has been instantiated successfully, a connection to the server will be established, which will cause the open event to occur. To process this event, assign a function to the onOpen handler, and process events accordingly within that function. Messages are usually sent to the server when the open event occurs, and this is demonstrated within the example:

```
ws.onopen = function()
{
    // Web Socket is connected, send data using send()
    ws.send("Message to send");
    alert("Message is sent...");
};
```

The corresponding output for this is as in Figure 14-3.

Figure 14-3. *WebSocket message sent confirmation prompt*

Similarly, you can listen for any other events to occur and then process tasks accordingly when they do. In the example, when a message is received from the server, it is printed within an alert dialog. Also in the example, when the WebSocket is closed, an alert dialog is presented to the user.

The example does not demonstrate all the possible ways that the WebSocket object in JavaScript can be utilized. For instance, you could send messages to the server by invoking the send() method and passing the data that you wish to send as a parameter. The close() method can be called on a WebSocket to manually terminate the existing connection. Figure 14-4 illustrates this.

Figure 14-4. *Prompt confirming the closing of WebSocket connection*

WebSocket objects also contain the helpful attributes `readyState` and `bufferedAmount`, which can be used for obtaining information about a connection. The `readyState` attribute will advise the current state of the WebSocket connection via a returned number, and the bufferedAmount attribute value represents the number of bytes of UTF-8 text that have been queued using the `send()` method. Table 14-2 displays the different possible values for the `readyState` attribute, along with a description of each.

Table 14-2. *JavaScript WebSocket* `readyState` *Values*

Value	Description
0	Connection not yet established `WebSocket.CONNECTING`
1	Connection established and communication is possible `WebSocket.OPEN`
2	Connection going through closing handshake `WebSocket.CLOSING`
3	Connection closed and cannot be opened `WebSocket.CLOSED`

14-3. Building a JSON Object

Problem

You would like to build a JSON object that can be passed from a client to a server or vice versa.

Solution

Make use of the `JsonObjectBuilder` to build a JSON object using Java code. The following example demonstrates how to utilize a `JsonObjectBuilder()` instance to create a new `JsonObject`. In this example class, multiple `JsonObjects` are created from reading the contents of a database table. Once the object is built, the sections of the object are assigned to a String that will eventually be displayed or persisted:

```java
package org.jakartaeerecipe.chapter14.recipe14_03;
import java.io.IOException;
import java.io.StringWriter;
import java.util.List;
import jakarta.ejb.EJB;
import jakarta.inject.Named;
import jakarta.json.Json;
import jakarta.json.JsonObject;
import jakarta.json.JsonObjectBuilder;
import jakarta.json.JsonWriter;
import org.jakartaeerecipes.jpa.entity.BookAuthor;
import org.jakartaeerecipes.jpa.session.BookAuthorFacade;
@Named("jsonController")
public class JsonController {
    @EJB
    BookAuthorFacade bookAuthorFacade;
    private String authorJson;
    public void buildAuthors() {
        List<BookAuthor> authors = bookAuthorFacade.findAll();
        JsonObjectBuilder builder = Json.createObjectBuilder();
        StringBuilder json = new StringBuilder();
        try (StringWriter sw = new StringWriter();) {
            for (BookAuthor author : authors) {
                System.out.println("author" + author.getLast());
                builder.add("author", Json.createObjectBuilder()
                        .add("authorId", author.getId())
                        .add("first", author.getFirst())
                        .add("last", author.getLast())
                        .add("bio", author.getBio()));
            }
            JsonObject result = builder.build();
            try (JsonWriter writer = Json.createWriter(sw)) {
                writer.writeObject(result);
            }
            json.append(sw.toString());
            authorJson = json.toString();
        } catch (IOException ex) {
            System.out.println(ex);
        }
    }
...
```

Once created, the `JsonObject` can be passed to a client for processing, or in this case, it can be persisted to disk. The code can be executed by visiting the URL http://localhost:8080/JakartaEERecipes_Chapter08-1.0-SNAPSHOT/recipe14_03.xhtml. The output would be as shown in Figure 14-5.

Figure 14-5. *The output of Recipe 14-3*

How It Works

The JavaScript Object Notation Processing (JSON-P) API was added to the Java Enterprise platform as of the release of Java EE 7. JSON-P, also referred to as "JSON with padding," has become the standard way to build JSON objects using Java. The JSON-P API includes a helper class that can be used to create JSON objects using the builder pattern. Using the `JsonObjectBuilder` class, JSON objects can be built using a series of method calls, each building upon each other – hence the builder pattern. Once the JSON object has been built, the `JsonObjectBuilder build` method can be called to return a `JsonObject`.

In the example for this recipe, you construct a JSON object that provides details regarding book authors. The `JsonObjectBuilder.beginObject()` method is used to denote that a new object is being created. The add method is used to add more name/value properties, much like that of a `Map`. Therefore, the following line adds a property named `authorId` with a value of `author.getId()`:

```
.add("authorId", author.getId())
```

Objects can be embedded inside of each other, creating a hierarchy of different sections within one `JsonObject`. In the example, after the first call to `add()`, another object named `author` is embedded inside the initial `JsonObject` by calling `beginObject()` and passing the name of the embedded object. Embedded objects can also contain properties; so to add properties to the embedded object, call the `add()` method within the embedded object. `JsonObjects` can embody as many embedded objects as needed. The following lines of code demonstrate the beginning and end of an embedded object definition:

```
.beginObject("author")
.add("first", "Josh")
.add("last", "Juneau")
.endObject()
```

It is also possible that a `JsonObject` may have an array of related subobjects. To add an array of subobjects, call the `beginArray()` method, passing the name of the array as an argument. Arrays can consist of objects and even hierarchies of objects, arrays, and so forth. In the example for this recipe, the book object has a couple of arrays defined, one being an array of `editor` objects and the other being an array of `technicalReviewer` objects.

Once a JsonObject has been created, it can be passed to a client. WebSockets work well for passing JsonObjects back to a client, but there are a bevy of different technologies available for communicating with JSON.

14-4. Writing a JSON Object to Disk

Problem

You would like to write a JSON object to the file system.

Solution

Utilize the JSON-P API to build a JSON object, and then store it to the file system. The JsonWriter class makes it possible to create a file on disk and then write the JSON to that file. In the following example, the JsonObject that was generated in Recipe 14-3 is written to disk using this technique:

```
public void writeJson() {
    try {
        JsonObject jsonObject = jsonController.buildAuthorsJson();
        javax.json.JsonWriter jsonWriter = Json.createWriter(new FileWriter
        ("Authors.json"));
        jsonWriter.writeObject(jsonObject);
        jsonWriter.close();
        FacesContext.getCurrentInstance().addMessage(null, new FacesMessage(
            FacesMessage.SEVERITY_INFO, "JSON Built",
            "JSON Built"));
    } catch (IOException ex) {
        System.out.println(ex);
    }
}
```

The code can be executed by visiting the URL http://localhost:8080/JakartaEERecipes_Chapter08-1.0-SNAPSHOT/recipe14_04.xhtml. The output would be as shown in Figure 14-6.

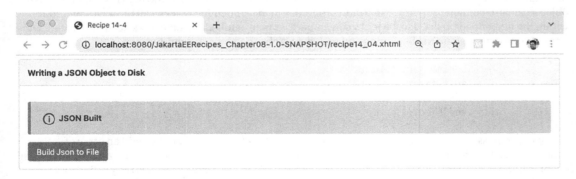

Figure 14-6. *The output of Recipe 14-4*

After a successful execution, the Authors.json file would be created at //JAVA_DEV/glassfish7/glassfish/domain/domain/config.

How It Works

The `JsonWriter` class can be utilized to write a `JsonObject` to a Java writer object. A `JsonWriter` is instantiated by passing a `Writer` object as an argument. Instantiating a `JsonWriter` will write to the `Writer` object that had been passed as an argument, using JSON format. After that `Writer` has been created, the `JsonWriter` `writeObject()` method can be invoked, passing the `JsonObject` that is to be written. Once the `JsonObject` has been written, the `JsonWriter` can be closed by calling its `close()` method. These are the only steps that are necessary for writing a JSON object to a Java `Writer` class type.

14-5. Reading JSON from an Input Source

Problem

You would like to read a JSON object that has been built or persisted to a file.

Solution

Obtain a JSON object that you would like to read, and then read it using the `jakarta.json.Json` `createReader` utility. In the following example, a JSON file is read from disk and then parsed to determine the hierarchy of events within. Each of the events is printed to the server log as the JSON is being parsed:

```
public String readObject() {
        InputStream in = new ByteArrayInputStream(controller.buildAndReturnAuthors().
        getBytes());
         // or
        //Reader fileReader = new InputStreamReader(getClass().getResourceAsStream
        ("AuthorObject.json"));
        //JsonReader reader = Json.createReader(fileReader);
        JsonReader reader = Json.createReader(in);
        JsonObject obj = reader.readObject();
        return obj.toString();
    }
```

The preceding code could be executed by visiting the URL http://localhost:8080/
JakartaEERecipes_Chapter08-1.0-SNAPSHOT/recipe14_05.xhtml. The output would be as shown in
Figure 14-7.

JSON Builder and Reader Example

The JSON below is created from reading the authors data from the database or from a JSON file.

{"author":{"authorId":2,"first":"Tarun","last":"Telang","bio":"Author of Apress Books"}}

Figure 14-7. *The output of Recipe 14-5*

How It Works

Once a JSON object has been persisted to disk, it will later need to be read back in for utilization. The
JsonReader object takes care of this task. To create a JsonReader object, call the Json.createReader()
method, passing either an InputStream or a Reader object. Once a JsonReader object has been created, it
can produce a JsonObject by calling its readObject method.

Parsing Content

To perform some tasks, a JSON object must be searched to find only the content that is desired and useful
for the current task. Utilizing a JSON parser can make jobs such as these easier, as a parser is able to
break the object down into pieces so that each different piece can be examined as needed, to produce the
desired result.

The jakarta.json.Json class contains a static factory method, createParser(), that accepts a bevy
of input and returns an Iterable JsonParser. Table 14-3 lists the different possible input types that are
accepted via the createParser() method.

Table 14-3. *createParser Method Input Types*

Input Type	Method Call
InputStream	createParser(InputStream in)
JsonArray	createParser(JsonArray arr)
JsonObject	createParser(JsonObject obj)
Reader	createParser(Reader reader)

Once a JsonParser has been created, it can be made into an Iterator of Event objects. Each Event
correlates to a different structure within the JSON object. For instance, when the JSON object is created, a
START_OBJECT event occurs, adding a name/value pair that will trigger both KEY_NAME and VALUE_STRING

events. These events can be utilized to obtain the desired information from a JSON object. In the example, the event names are merely printed to a server log. However, in a real-life application, a conditional would most likely test each iteration to find a particular event and then perform some processing. Table 14-4 lists the different JSON events, along with a description of when each occurs.

Table 14-4. *JSON Object Events*

Event	Occurrence
START_OBJECT	Start of an object
END_OBJECT	End of an object
START_ARRAY	Start of an array
END_ARRAY	End of an array
KEY_NAME	Name of a key
VALUE_STRING	Value of a name/value pair in String format
VALUE_NUMBER	Value of a name/value pair in numeric format
VALUE_TRUE	Value of a name/value pair in Boolean format
VALUE_FALSE	Value of a name/value pair in Boolean format
VALUE_NULL	Value of a name/value pair as NULL

14-6. Converting Between JSON and Java Objects

Problem

You have obtained a list of Java objects in a response from a web service, and you wish to convert it to JSON.

Solution

Utilize the JSON Binding (JSON-B) API to bind the Java object elements to JSON format. In the following example, an XML response is received from a web service, converted into Java objects, and the JSON-B API is used to convert the objects into JSON. A Jakarta RESTful Web Services client is used to obtain a response that will include several Employee objects, and each of them will be converted into a Java Employee object:

```
...
List<Employee> employees;
...
public String fetchJson(){
    WebTarget target = ClientBuilder.newClient().target("http://localhost:8080/
    JakartaEERecipes_Chapter08-1.0-SNAPSHOT/rest/org.jakartaeerecipes.entity.employee");
        employees = (target.request(javax.ws.rs.core.MediaType.APPLICATION_XML)
                .get(
                new GenericType<List<Employee>>() {
```

```
            }));
        System.out.println("Items: " + employees);
        Jsonb jsonb = JsonbBuilder.create();
        String result = null;
        result = jsonb.toJson(employees);
        return result;
    }
```

Similarly, the JSON-B API can be used to convert from JSON to Java. In the following method, a JSON string is returned from a web service call, and it is converted into a Java collection:

```
public List<Employee> fetchJavaFromJson(){
    WebTarget target = ClientBuilder.newClient().target("http://localhost:8080/
    JakartaEERecipes/rest/org.jakartaeerecipes.entity.employee");
        String employeesJson = (target.request(jakarta.ws.rs.core.MediaType.
        APPLICATION_JSON)
                .get(
                new GenericType<String>() {
        }));
    System.out.println("Items: " + employeesJson);
    Jsonb jsonb = JsonbBuilder.create();
    List<Employee> employees = new ArrayList();
    employees = jsonb.fromJson(employeesJson, ArrayList.class);
    return employees;
}
```

In the example, a Jakarta Server Faces view is used to display the contents of the Employee JSON. The view markup sources are as follows:

```
<h:body>
    <p:panel header="JSON Representation of Employees">
        <h:outputText value="#{employeeJsonController.fetchJson()}"/>
    </p:panel>
    <p:panel header="Java Representation of Employees JSON">
        <p:dataTable value="#{employeeJsonController.fetchJavaFromJson()}" var="emp">
            <p:column>
                #{emp.last}
            </p:column>
        </p:dataTable>
    </p:panel>
</h:body>
```

The recipe code can be executed by visiting the URL http://localhost:8080/JakartaEERecipes_Chapter08-1.0-SNAPSHOT/recipe14_06.xhtml.

The output would look like Figure 14-8.

JSON Representation of Customers
[{"age":32,"first":"JANE","id":1,"job":{"division":"IT","jobId":1,"salary":60000,"title":"IT TITLE A"},"last":"DEVELOPER","status":true},{"age":25,"first":"BOB","id":2,"job": {"division":"HR","jobId":4,"salary":50000,"title":"HR TITLE A"},"last":"SMITH","status":true},{"age":25,"first":"JOE","id":3,"job":{"division":"IT","jobId":3,"salary":40000,"title":"IT TITLE C"},"last":"DEVELOPER","status":true}]

JSON Representation of Employees
DEVELOPER
SMITH
DEVELOPER

Figure 14-8. *The output of Recipe 14-6*

How It Works

The JSON-B API can be used to convert between JSON and Java seamlessly.

■ **Note**   To visit the JSON-B website and view all documentation, please visit `https://javaee.github.io/jsonb-spec/`.

The key piece of the JSON-B API is the `Jsonb` interface, which provides an abstraction over the JSON binding operations. The `JsonbBuilder` can be used to obtain a `Jsonb` object, which in turn is used to convert between Java and JSON. To create the `Jsonb` object, call upon the `JsonBuilder create()` method. Once the `Jsonb` object has been obtained, it can be used to convert to JSON and serialize by passing the Java object to the `toJson()` method:

```
Jsonb jsonb = JsonbBuilder.create();
    String result = null;
    result = jsonb.toJson(employees);
```

To go in the opposite direction and deserialize from JSON back to Java, use the `Jsonb fromJson()` method, passing the JSON string as the first argument and the Java type to which the JSON will be converted as the second argument:

```
Jsonb jsonb = JsonbBuilder.create();
List<Employee> employees = new ArrayList<>();
employees = jsonb.fromJson(employeesJson, ArrayList.class);
```

The technique shown in the preceding text is only one way to convert back to a `Collection` type. If you wish to convert in a type-safe manner, back to the generic type `List<Employee>`, it can be done as follows:

```
employees = jsonb.fromJson(employeesJson, new ArrayList<Employee>(){}
                                .getClass().getGenericSuperclass());
```

The `Jsonb` object can also convert back to a single Java object by passing the Java object type as the second argument to the `fromJson()` utility method, as follows:

```
Jsonb jsonb = JsonbBuilder.create();
Employee employee = new Employee;
employee = jsonb.fromJson(singleEmployeeJson, Employee.class);
```

545

This recipe covers the basics of converting JSON to Java and vice versa. For more information regarding customizations, please see Recipe 14-7.

14-7 Custom Mapping with JSON-B

Problem

You wish to change the JSON property names when converting to a Java class or perform custom mapping for circumstances such as converting specific date formats or marking specified fields as transient.

Solution

Utilize a `JsonbConfig` to create a custom runtime configuration for the JSON mapping. There are also a handful of annotations that can be applied at the Java class level, field level, or getters/setters to customize some configurations. In the following scenario, a custom configuration is used to create a property naming strategy that includes lowercase with underscores:

```
JsonbConfig config = new JsonbConfig()
    .withPropertyNamingStrategy(PropertyNamingStragegy.LOWER_CASE_WITH_UNDERSCORES);
Jsonb jsonb = JsonbBuilder.create(config);
```

As mentioned previously, there are also a handful of annotations that can be applied to customize mapping. In the following scenario, the dog color property is marked as transient. This means that the color property will not be serialized into JSON when converting:

```
public class Dog {
    private String name;
    private int age;
    private String gender;
    @JsonbTransient
    private String color;
}
```

How It Works

The `JsonbConfig` class makes it easy to create a custom runtime configuration for your JSON mapping and formatting. Annotations can be used to create a custom compile time configuration. Such customizations can include things like changing from the default property naming convention or specifying a particular property ordering. To create a new configuration, simply create a new `JsonbConfig` class and pass the configuration to the `JsonbBuilder.create()` method, as such:

```
JsonbConfig config = new JsonbConfig();
Jsonb jsonb = JsonbBuilder.create(config);
```

The JsonbConfig class can be used to specify the runtime configurations contained in Table 14-5. In the example for this recipe, the .withPropertyNamingStrategy() option was specified to configure a property naming strategy that is lowercase with underscores.

Table 14-5. *JsonbConfig Options*

Option	Description
.withFormatting(boolean)	Creates custom configuration with formatting
.withPropertyNamingStrategy (strategy)	Provides a strategy for constructing property names. Accepts a strategy of type PropertyNamingStrategy (IDENTITY, LOWER_CASE_WITH_ DASHES, LOWER_CASE_WITH_UNDERSCORES, UPPER_CAMEL_ CASE, UPPER_CAMEL_CASE_WITH_SPACES, CASE_INSENSITIVE)
.withPropertyOrderStrategy (strategy)	Provides a strategy for ordering properties. Accepts a strategy of type PropertyOrderStrategy (LEXICOGRAPHICAL, ANY, REVERSE)
.withNullValues(boolean)	Changes the default NULL handling. Global configuration
.withDateFormat("format")	Changes the default date format. Global configuration
.withBinaryDataStrategy (strategy)	Provides a strategy for binary data encoding. Default is BYTE encoding. Accepts BinaryDataStrategy (BYTE, BASE_64, BASE_64_URL)
.withAdapters(CustomAdapter)	Assigns a CustomAdapter to a Jsonb configuration. (See JSON-B documentation for more on adapters)
.withSerializers (JsonbSerializer)	Assigns a JsonbSerializer to a Jsonb configuration
.withDeserializers (JsonbDeserializer)	Assigns a JsonbDeserializer to a Jsonb configuration
.withStrictIJSON(boolean)	Provides support for the I-JSON restricted profile of JSON

As previously mentioned, configurations can also be made at compile time by specifying annotations on Java classes, fields, or getters and setters. Table 14-6 lists the annotations that can be placed on a Java class, field, or accessor method.

Table 14-6. Annotation Configurations

Annotation	Description
@JsonbProperty("name")	Field and getter/setter level. Changes the name of a particular property. Placed on a getter: the new name will be serialized when writing to JSON. Placed on a setter: the new name will be expected when reading during deserialization. Placed on a field: the new name will be applied on both serialization and deserialization
@JsonbPropertyOrder(strategy)	Class level. Customizes the order of serialized properties. Accepts a PropertyOrderStrategy (LEXICOGRAPHICAL, ANY, REVERSE)
@JsonbTransient	Field and getter/setter level. Indicates that an annotated field should be ignored by the JSON binding engine. Placed on a field: property is ignored during serialization and deserialization. Getter: property ignored during serialization. Setter: property ignored during deserialization
@JsonbNillable(boolean)	Class and field level. Indicates if NULL values are to be serialized. Default is false
@JsonbCreator	Constructor level. Allows one to annotate a custom constructor with parameters or a static factory method used to create a class instance
@JsonbDateFormat("format")	Field level. Customizes date format for a specified property
@JsonbNumberFormat("format")	Field level. Customizes number format for a specified property

14-8. Replacing a Specified Element in a JSON Document

Problem

You wish to replace values of a JSON document that match a given pattern.

Solution

Utilize the JSON-P patch capability to replace the values within the JSON document. In the following example, a string of text is taken in from a JSF form and used to create a JSON pointer to the matching last name in the JSON String. The JSON Replace functionality is then used to replace the matching JSON String value with the String value of "JsonMaster":

```
public void findEmployeeByLast() {
    setSearchResult(null);
    String text = "/" + this.lastSearchText;
    JsonObject json = Json.createObjectBuilder().build();
    JsonValue object = json.getJsonObject(fetchJson());
    if (lastSearchText != null && object != null) {
        JsonPointer pointer = Json.createPointer(text);
        System.out.println("text: " + text + pointer);
        System.out.println("json: " + object);
        JsonValue result = pointer.getValue(object.asJsonArray());
```

```
        // Replace a value
        JsonArray array = (JsonArray) pointer.replace(object.asJsonArray(),
                            Json.createValue("JsonMaster"));
        setSearchResult(array.toString());
    }
}
```

The following markup shows the Jakarta Server Faces form that is used to send the search text and display the resulting output:

```
<h:form id="jsonPointerForm">
    <p:panel header="Employee Search By Address">
        <p:outputLabel for="lastSearchText" value="Pointer String:"/>
        <p:inputText id="lastSearchText" value="#{employeeJsonController.lastSearchText}"/>
        <br/><br/>
        <p:commandButton id="searchButton"
                        action="#{employeeJsonController.findEmployeeByLast}"
                        update="searchResult" value="Find Value"/>
    </p:panel>
    <br/>
    <h:outputText id="searchResult" value="#{customerController.searchResult}"/>
</h:form>
```

The recipe code can be executed by visiting the URL http://localhost:8080/JakartaEERecipes_Chapter08-1.0-SNAPSHOT/recipe14_08.xhtml.

The output would look like Figure 14-9.

Figure 14-9. The output of Recipe 14-8

How It Works

The JSON-P 1.1 API added the ability to point to a specified JSON value and also to replace values of a JSON document. The JSON Pointer ability allows one to identify a specific value within a JSON document. To utilize the JSON Pointer functionality, one must first obtain a `JsonObject` by calling upon the appropriate `Json` interface method for working with the JSON that is to be used. In the solution to this recipe, the `Json.createObjectBuilder().build()` methods are called upon to return a `JsonObject`. The `JsonObject` can then be used to perform a JSON Patch operation. The `fetchJson()` method in the example returns a JSON String:

```
JsonObject json = Json.createObjectBuilder().build();
JsonValue object = json.getJsonObject(fetchJson());
```

The `JsonPointer` object is obtained by calling upon the `Json` interface `createPointer()` method, passing the String of text to find in the JSON. The following excerpt from the solution shows the process of obtaining the JSON pointer:

```
JsonPointer pointer = Json.createPointer(text);
```

The JSON Patch functionality provides the ability to add, remove, or replace a portion of a JSON document or String that has been obtained via a JSON pointer. In the solution, the Replace functionality is used to replace the last name that is pointed to with the string "JsonMaster." This is done by calling upon the `JsonPointer` `replace()` method and passing the JSON object as the first argument and the `Json` that will replace the original JSON as the second argument:

```
JsonArray array = (JsonArray) pointer.replace(object.asJsonArray(),
                                    Json.createValue("JsonMaster"));
```

The `JsonPointer` object also contains the methods `add()` and `replace()`. The `add()` method can be used to add a value into a JSON object or insert a value into an array. The `add()` method accepts a `JsonObject` as the first argument and the `Json` value to add as the second argument. The `remove()` method allows one to remove a `JsonPointer` value from a JSON document.

■ ■ ■

CHAPTER 15

Jakarta Security

One of the most important components to an enterprise-level application is security. It is a fact that enterprise applications must be rock solid and secure so that data and application functionality cannot fall into the wrong hands. Utilizing a combination of application container security and application-level security can help secure applications from thugs who are targeting enterprise data.

Jakarta Security provides a standard API that can be used for securing applications in the Jakarta EE platform. In previous releases, security was certainly possible, but there was no standard API, so there were variations of homegrown authentication solutions and third-party APIs that were used throughout the applications that used the platform. In this chapter, I will touch upon techniques that may have been used in previous releases for securing applications, and I'll also outline similar solutions utilizing the standard security API that is part of the Jakarta EE platform.

Three different types of security can be applied to enterprise-level applications: declarative, programmatic, and transport security. *Declarative* security occurs within an application's deployment descriptor or via annotations that are added to classes and methods within the application. Declarative security is used to provide the application server container with the ability to guard access to certain application features via the use of user authentication and roles. *Programmatic* security occurs when the developer manually codes the authentication methods, customizing the requirements for authentication into an application. *Transport* security occurs between the client and the server, and it is responsible for securing information as it is passed between the two.

This chapter will touch upon each of these three levels of security. It contains recipes that cover application server configurations utilizing the GlassFish server for setting up database and LDAP (Lightweight Directory Access Protocol) authentication for applications that are deployed within the container. You will also learn how to utilize XML configuration, annotations, and the Jakarta Expression Language to secure portions of your applications. Lastly, it'll touch upon how to secure transport via SSL and certificates. This chapter will also touch upon the Jakarta EE Security API, which provides a standardized solution that enables developers to produce portable applications and package security implementations within the application, rather than in the container.

15-1. Setting Up Application Users and Groups in GlassFish

Problem

You want to create users, groups, and roles within your application server container for use with applications that are deployed to the container.

© Josh Juneau and Tarun Telang 2022
J. Juneau and T. Telang, *Java EE to Jakarta EE 10 Recipes*, https://doi.org/10.1007/978-1-4842-8079-9_15

Solution

Log in to the GlassFish administrative console to add users to the File security realm. You can then add the users to groups by specifying the group names when creating the users. This example will walk you through the configuration of a new user within the GlassFish application server.

Log in to the administrative console by navigating to `http://localhost:4848` and then logging in as an administrative user.

Use the tree menu on the left side of the screen to navigate to the Configurations ➤ server-config ➤ Security ➤ Realms menu. Once you click the Realms menu option, the Realms form will appear (Figure 15-1).

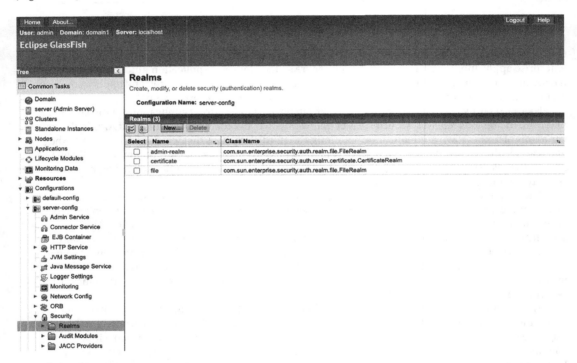

Figure 15-1. *GlassFish Realms form*

1. Click the "file" realm link to enter the Edit Realm form, as shown in Figure 15-2.

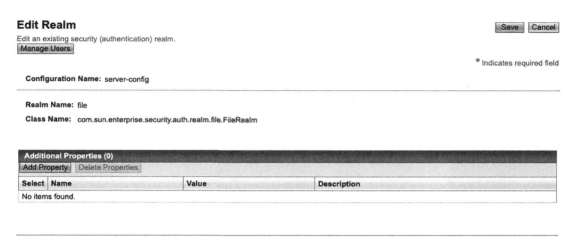

Figure 15-2. GlassFish Edit Realm form

2. Click the Manage Users button within the Edit Realm form to open the File Users form, and then click the New button within the File Users form (Figure 15-3) to enter the New File Realm User form (Figure 15-4).

Figure 15-3. GlassFish File Users form

New File Realm User

OK   Cancel

Create new user accounts for the currently selected security realm.

* Indicates required field

Configuration Name: server-config

Realm Name:	file
User ID: *	
	Name can be up to 255 characters, must contain only letters, digits, underscore, dash, or dot characters
Group List:	
	Separate multiple groups with colon
New Password:	
Confirm New Password:	

Figure 15-4. GlassFish New File Realm User form

3. Fill in a user ID and the password information to complete the New File Realm User form, and optionally add a group name to the Group List field. Click the Save button to add the user to the File Users list (Figure 15-5).

File Users

Back

Manage user accounts for the currently selected security realm.

Configuration Name: server-config

Realm Name: file

File Users (2)

New...   Delete

Select	User ID	Group List:
☐	Tarun	standard
☐	Juneau	standard

Figure 15-5. File Users list

Once they're created, users within GlassFish realms can be used for application authentication purposes. To learn more about configuring your applications to utilize application server container user authentication, please refer to Recipe 15-2.

How It Works

Adding an authentication prompt to allow user access to secured areas can be one of the best forms of protection for any application. Fortunately, the Java platform makes authentication easy for you to add to your applications. Most application servers have some mechanism for adding user accounts that can be used to access applications that are deployed in one of the server domains. GlassFish provides the ability to add users and groups to different security realms, which can then be applied to applications for authentication purposes.

■ **Note**   Most application server containers also allow for connectivity with LDAP servers or databases, which enables authentication to occur against user accounts within the LDAP server or stored within a database table, rather than within the container itself. For an example of LDAP authentication, please read Recipe 15-6.

When adding users to GlassFish, they must be incorporated with a security realm. The File security realm is available for use with the default installation, although more security realms can be created if desired. Adding users to realms is a fairly simple process, and individual users can be added by following the steps noted in the solution to this recipe. When creating a user, one of the options that can be specified is a *group*. You can think of a GlassFish user group as a role, in that more than one user can belong to a group. GlassFish does not contain a mechanism for managing the groups themselves; in fact, a group is merely a String value to GlassFish. However, if you follow through the steps in Recipe 15-2, you will see that groups can be mapped to roles at the application level. Therefore, if UserA belongs to a group named standard, then UserA can also belong to a group named admin. The application can then grant access to UserA for different portions of the application, depending upon which groups or roles the user belongs to.

Users in GlassFish are simplistic in that they are used for authentication and access purposes within the deployed applications only. Users can be managed only on a per-server installation basis, so they are a bit cumbersome since they cannot be shared across servers to provide a single sign-on solution. For that reason, it is recommended that GlassFish users be used for smaller applications/environments or testing purposes only. For a more substantial and enterprise authentication solution, either database or LDAP user accounts would be a better choice.

■ **Note**   To learn about configuring form-based authentication within the GlassFish application server and utilizing a database to store user credentials, see Recipe 15-4.

15-2. Performing Basic Web Application Authorization

Problem

You have established users and associated them with groups within the application server container. Now you want to assign users to particular roles based upon the access levels that they require for the application and apply a basic authentication mechanism for access to specified application views.

Solution #1

Configure form-based security using basic authentication within the web application deployment descriptor. Map roles to groups within the glassfish-web.xml deployment descriptor, if needed. The following excerpt was taken from the web.xml deployment descriptor of the JakartaEERecipes NetBeans project sources. It demonstrates how to secure all of the views that reside within the chapter15 folder (determined by the url-pattern element within web.xml) such that a username and password combination is required for access. The auth-method tag within web.xml specifies the type of authentication that will be used for the application. In the example, you'll use BASIC authentication. Only those usernames and passwords that have been configured in the GlassFish file realm with the appropriate group will be granted access; in this case, it is the users role:

```
<security-constraint>
      <web-resource-collection>
          <web-resource-name>secured</web-resource-name>
          <url-pattern>/faces/chapter15/*</url-pattern>
          <http-method>GET</http-method>
          <http-method>POST</http-method>
      </web-resource-collection>
      <auth-constraint>
          <role-name>users</role-name>
      </auth-constraint>
      <user-data-constraint>
          <transport-guarantee>CONFIDENTIAL</transport-guarantee>
      </user-data-constraint>
  </security-constraint>
  <login-config>
      <auth-method>BASIC</auth-method>
      <realm-name>file</realm-name>
  </login-config>
  <security-role>
      <role-name>users</role-name>
  </security-role>
</web-app>
```

If role names specified in the /webapp/WEB-INF/web.xml deployment descriptor are the same as the group names that have been associated with users in GlassFish, then you are done. Users will be granted access to those areas of the application that have been secured, based upon the group association. However, if a role name differs from those groups that have been associated to users, you can manually map role names to group names by specifying a security-role-mapping in the /webapp/WEB-INF/glassfish-web.xml file for the application. The following excerpt, taken from the glassfish-web.xml configuration file for the JakartaEERecipes application, demonstrates how to map roles to GlassFish users. In this case, the role standard that was specified for the account in Recipe 15-1 is mapped to the user's role. The user's role has access to the /faces/chapter15/* url-pattern:

```
<?xml version="1.0" encoding="UTF-8"?>
<!DOCTYPE glassfish-web-app PUBLIC "-//GlassFish.org//DTD GlassFish Application Server 3.1
Servlet 3.0//EN"
      "http://glassfish.org/dtds/glassfish-web-app_3_0-1.dtd">
<glassfish-web-app>
    <security-role-mapping>
        <role-name>users</role-name>
        <group-name>standard</group-name>
    </security-role-mapping>
</glassfish-web-app>
```

Once everything has been configured, then access will be granted according to the configurations that have been placed within the web.xml deployment descriptor. To test the authentication mechanism, deploy the JakartaEERecipes WAR file to your GlassFish application server, and visit the following URL:

`https://localhost:8080/JakartaEERecipes_Chapter15-1.0-SNAPSHOT/chapter15/index.xhtml`

You will see your request is now getting redirected to HTTPS port 8181 as we have the transport-guarantee set to CONFIDENTIAL in the web.xml:

```
<user-data-constraint>
        <transport-guarantee>CONFIDENTIAL</transport-guarantee>
</user-data-constraint>
```

You will also see a prompt for the username and password (Figure 15-6), to authenticate the user.

Figure 15-6. *Login prompt for the page /chapter15/index.xhtml*

Solution #2

Use annotations on classes and class methods to declare roles within an application for access to secured pages as deemed necessary. To implement access control on a particular class or method, annotate using `@DeclareRoles` and/or `@RolesAllowed`, specifying the roles that can be used to access them. Those users who are authenticated belonging to one of the specified roles will be granted access to the content.

In the example corresponding to this recipe, the `chapter15/recipe15_02.xhtml` Jakarta Server Faces view contains two command buttons that invoke actions within a managed bean. Figure 15-7 shows this view running inside a browser.

Figure 15-7. *Content of the page /chapter15/recipe15_02.xhtml*

Each of the buttons invokes a different action in the bean. One of the buttons invokes a method that is secured via the @RolesAllowed annotation, and the other does not. Figure 15-8 shows the view after the user has clicked "Secured Content."

Figure 15-8. *Output on click of the "Secured Content" button in /chapter15/recipe15_02.xhtml*

The following excerpt is taken from the class org.jakartaeerecipe.chapter15.recipe15_02. Recipe15_02b, which is the managed bean controller that contains the two methods being called from the command buttons:

```java
public class Recipe15_02b implements Serializable {
    public String unsecuredProcess(){
        return "recipe15_02_1.xhtml";
    }
    @RolesAllowed("users")
    public String securedProcess(){
        return "recipe15_02_2.xhtml";
    }
}
```

When the commandButton that invokes the securedProcess() method is clicked, the user will be prompted to authenticate if they have not already done so. The authentication prompt is shown in Figure 15-9.

Figure 15-9. *Login prompt from Solution #2 of Recipe 15-2*

How It Works

There are a couple of ways to secure an application using basic application server authentication. Commonly, applications provide basic authentication security via the use of XML configuration within the web.xml deployment descriptor along with optional configuration within the glassfish-web.xml deployment descriptor. It is also possible to add basic authentication security into an application using code only, via declarative security. Declarative security is based on the use of annotations for declaring roles for access to application classes and methods. While both techniques are very similar in concept, each of them has its own set of bonuses in certain situations.

In Solution #1 to this recipe, XML configuration is used to secure access to all web views that reside within a specific folder in the application. To add security via XML configuration files, the web.xml deployment descriptor needs to have the security-constraint, login-config, and security-role elements added to it for mapping application roles to GlassFish users and groups. The security-constraint element encompasses a handful of subelements that are used to tell the application server container which areas of the application to secure and which accounts are able to access those secured areas. First, a web-resource-collection element is used to declare the locations of the application to secure and which HTTP methods to secure. The following elements should be embedded within a web-resource-collection element:

- web-resource-name: This is an optional name that can be specified for the secured location. In the recipe solution, the name secured is specified.

- url-pattern: This is the URL pattern that will be used to determine which areas of the application are to be secured. An asterisk (*) is to be used as a wildcard. In the recipe solution, chapter15/* specifies that all views contained within the chapter15 folder should be secured. If you want to secure a specific page, then utilize the URL pattern to that page, including the page name.

- http-method: This is used to specify which HTTP methods should be secured for access to the locations specified by the url-pattern element.

Another subelement that can be declared within the security-constraint element is the auth-constraint element. This element lists the different security roles that are used to secure the locations specified by the url-pattern via adding role-name subelements. In the recipe solution, the users role is declared for the application. A user-data-constraint element can also be included as a subelement to the security-constraint element in order to specify the type of protection that will be applied when data is transported between the client and the server. In the example, this has been set to CONFIDENTIAL. The values that can be specified for the transport guarantee are as follows:

- NONE: Data requires no transport security.

- INTEGRAL: Data cannot be changed in transit between the client and the server.

- CONFIDENTIAL: Outside entities are unable to observe the contents of the transmission. Secure Sockets Layer (SSL) will be used in this case, and it must be configured within the web server.

The security-role XML element lists the different roles that can be used for securing access to the application pages. Add the role-name subelement to the security-role for each role specification. The login-config XML element is used to specify the method of authentication that is to be used for securing the application. The auth-method should be set to BASIC for most cases, but all possible values are BASIC, DIGEST, FORM, and CLIENT-CERT.

Adding the designated elements to the web.xml deployment descriptor, as described in this section, provides sufficient ability for applications to be secured via user credentials to specified secure locations. In some cases, it makes sense to use annotations to declare roles from within the application code itself. For such cases, the @DeclareRoles and @RolesAllowed annotations can be specified on a class or method. The following annotations can be used to specify security within a class. For each of the annotations, either a single role or a list of roles can be specified:

- @DeclareRoles: This is specified at the class or method level, and each role that is allowed to access the class should be indicated within the annotation. For instance, one or more roles can be specified for access to the class using the following syntax:

```
Class level:
@DeclareRoles("users")
public class MyClass {
  ...
}
    Method level:

public class MyClass {
  ...
    @DeclareRoles({"role1", "role2"})
    public void calculatePay(){
        ...
    }
  ...
}
```

- @RolesAllowed: This is specified at either the class or method level. A list of roles that are allowed to access the class or method should be indicated within the annotation. The syntax is the same as with that of @DeclareRoles.

- @PermitAll: This is specified at the class or method level. It indicates that all roles are allowed access.

- @DenyAll: This is specified at the class or method level. It indicates that no roles are allowed access.

When both the @DeclareRoles and @RolesAllowed annotations are used within the same class, the roles listed within each are allowed to access that class. The roles specified for access on a particular method using @RolesAllowed override the roles that are listed to access the entire class.

It is possible to programmatically check to see which roles an authenticated user belongs to by calling the SessionContext isUserInRole() method. This allows you to permit access to features of an application using conditional logic, as demonstrated by the following lines of code:

```
@DeclareRoles({"role1", "role2, "role3"}
public class MyClass {
    ...
    @RolesAllowed("role2")
    public void calculatePay(){
        ...
    }
    @PermitAll
    public void calculatePay(){
```

```
        if (ctx.isUserInRole("role1")) {
            ...
        } else if (ctx.isUserInRole("role3")){
            ...
        }
    }
    ...
}
```

15-3. Developing a Programmatic Login Form with Custom Authentication Validation

Problem

You want to secure your Jakarta Server Faces application to a specified group of users. Furthermore, you want to create a custom login view, which will be used to pass user credentials to the appropriate business objects for authentication.

Solution

Develop a login form that consists of username and password inputText fields, along with a commandButton to invoke a programmatic login action that resides within a managed bean controller. Develop logic within the managed bean controller to authenticate users. In the following example, a login form is generated using Jakarta Server Faces and Facelets, utilizing a managed bean for authentication control.

Creating the Login Form

A login form is basically the same as any other form, except it accepts a username and a password as arguments and passes them to a JavaBean that utilizes the information to accept or deny the authentication request. The login form also utilizes a standard HTML form element that passes the username (j_username) and password (j_password) field values to an action named j_security_check. The following code is used to comprise the login.xhtml form for a Jakarta Server Faces authentication mechanism:

```
<?xml version="1.0" encoding="UTF-8" ?>
<!DOCTYPE html PUBLIC "-//W3C//DTD XHTML 1.0 Transitional//EN" "http://www.w3.org/TR/xhtml1/
DTD/xhtml1-transitional.dtd">
<html xmlns="http://www.w3.org/1999/xhtml"
    xmlns:ui="http://xmlns.jcp.org/jsf/facelets"
    xmlns:h="http://xmlns.jcp.org/jsf/html"
    xmlns:f="http://xmlns.jcp.org/jsf/core"
    xmlns:p="http://primefaces.org/ui">
    <ui:composition template="/layout/custom_template.xhtml">
        <ui:define name="title">
            <h:outputText value="Welcome to the Acme Bookstore"></h:outputText>
        </ui:define>
        <ui:define name="content">
                <h:form id="login">
                    <center>
```

561

```
                    <p align="center" class="sub_head_sub"><br />
                        <strong>Acme Bookstore Application</strong>
                    </p>
                    <span class="normal">
                        You must authenticate to gain access to this application.
                    </span>
                    <br/>
                    <span class="error">
                        <h:messages errorStyle="color: red" infoStyle="color: green"
                        globalOnly="true"/>
                    </span>
                    <div>
                        <p:panel rendered="#{authenticationController.
                        authenticated}">
                            <a href="/index.xhtml">Authenticated successfully...go
                            to Application</a>
                        </p:panel>
                        <p:panel rendered="#{!authenticationController.
                        authenticated}">
                            Username: <h:inputText id="j_username"
                                                   value="#{authentication
                                                   Controller.username}"/>
                            <br/><br/>
                            Password: <h:inputSecret id="j_password"
                                                     value="#{authentication
                                                     Controller.password}"/>
                            <br/>
                            <br/>
                            <h:commandButton id="login" action="#{authenticationCon
                            troller.login}"
                                                     value="Login"/>
                        </p:panel>
                        <br/>
                    </div>
                </center>
            </h:form>
        </ui:define>
    </ui:composition>
</html>
```

___

■ **Note**   The inputSecret component used in this example will display a series of asterisks, rather than plain text, when input is typed into the text box.

___

Once loaded, the login form will resemble Figure 15-10 when using the Acme Bookstore template.

Figure 15-10. *Login form example*

Coding the Authentication Backend

The authentication backend is responsible for performing the authentication and maintaining state for a user session. The backend logic consists of a Jakarta Enterprise Beans for maintaining the authentication logic and a Jakarta Servlet Faces controller that is used for binding view methods and fields to backend logic. The controller should be session scoped so that the user state can be maintained for an entire session. Lastly, if you're using a database table to contain all of the usernames that have access to the application, then an entity class will be required for that database table.

In this section, I will introduce a custom technique as a nonstandard solution, which utilizes an EJB to authenticate an individual's credentials. The authentication occurs by calling upon the HttpServletRequest login(), passing authentication off to the application server container. This is container specific, meaning that it will only work if the application has been configured, as has been done with the first recipe in this chapter.

The second approach makes use of the Jakarta Security API, using servlet-based authentication within an HttpAuthenticationMechanism (HAM). To see more specifics regarding Jakarta Security, please see Recipe 15-4.

Jakarta Enterprise Beans (Custom Solution)

The Jakarta Enterprise Beans that is used for this custom authentication backend is a stateless session bean that contains a login method, which makes calls to the application server container authentication mechanism. The following code is from the class org.jakartaeerecipe.chapter15.recipe15_03. AutheticationBean.java file in the JakartaEERecipes project:

```
package org.jakartaeerecipe.chapter15.recipe15_03;

import java.io.Serializable;
import jakarta.ejb.Remove;
import jakarta.ejb.Stateless;
import jakarta.faces.application.FacesMessage;

import jakarta.persistence.CacheRetrieveMode;

import jakarta.faces.context.FacesContext;
import jakarta.persistence.EntityManager;
import jakarta.persistence.NoResultException;
import jakarta.persistence.PersistenceContext;
```

```
import jakarta.persistence.Query;
import jakarta.servlet.ServletException;
import jakarta.servlet.http.HttpServletRequest;
import jakarta.servlet.http.HttpSession;

@Stateless
public class AuthenticationBean implements Serializable  {

    @PersistenceContext(unitName = "JakartaEERecipesPU")
    private EntityManager em;
    private boolean authenticated = false;
    private String username = null;
    private String password = null;
    HttpSession session = null;
    User user;
    public AuthenticationBean() {
    }
    public void findUser() {
        try {
            em.flush();
            getUser();
            Query userQry = em.createQuery(
                    "select object(u) from User u "
                    + "where u.username = :username").setParameter ("username", getUser().
                    getUsername().toUpperCase());
        // Enable forced database query
            userQry.setHint("jakarta.persistence.cache.retrieveMode", CacheRetrieveMode.BYPASS);
            setUser((User) userQry.getSingleResult());
            FacesContext.getCurrentInstance().addMessage(null, new
            FacesMessage(FacesMessage.SEVERITY_INFO, "Successfully Authenticated", ""));
        } catch (Exception e) {
            FacesContext.getCurrentInstance().addMessage(null, new
            FacesMessage(FacesMessage.SEVERITY_ERROR, "Invalid username/password", ""));
            setUser(null);
        }
    }
    public HttpSession getSession() {
        FacesContext context = FacesContext.getCurrentInstance();
        HttpServletRequest request = (HttpServletRequest) context.getExternalContext().
        getRequest();
        session = request.getSession(false);
        return session;
    }
    public boolean login() {
        HttpSession session = getSession();
        HttpServletRequest request = null;
        Query userQry = null;
        System.out.println("In the login method..." + getUser().getUsername());
        try {
            FacesContext context = FacesContext.getCurrentInstance();
            request = (HttpServletRequest) context.getExternalContext().getRequest();
            request.login(getUser().getUsername(), this.password);
```

564

```
            session.setMaxInactiveInterval(1800);
            session.setAttribute("authenticated", new Boolean(true));
            em.flush();
            userQry = em.createQuery(
                    "select count(u) from User u "
                    + "where u.username = :username").setParameter("username", getUser().
                    getUsername().toUpperCase());
            userQry.setHint("jakarta.persistence.cache.retrieveMode", CacheRetrieveMode.
            BYPASS);
            Long count = (Long)userQry.getSingleResult();
            if (count > 0){
                userQry = em.createQuery(
                        "select object(u) from User u "
                        + "where u.username = :username").setParameter("username",
                        getUser().getUsername().toUpperCase());
                // Enable forced database query
                userQry.setHint("jakarta.persistence.cache.retrieveMode", CacheRetrieveMode.
                BYPASS);
                setUser((User) userQry.getSingleResult());
                System.out.println("Setting  User, user exists in database with role ->" +
                user.getSecurityRole());
                setAuthenticated(true);
            } else {
                // User cannot authenticate successfully...do something
            }

            FacesContext.getCurrentInstance().addMessage(null, new
            FacesMessage(FacesMessage.SEVERITY_INFO, "Successfully Authenticated", ""));
            return authenticated;
    } catch (NoResultException| ServletException ex) {
            setUser(null);
            setAuthenticated(false);
            session = getSession();
            session.setAttribute("authenticated", new Boolean(false));
            if(request != null){
                try {
                    request.logout();
                } catch (ServletException ex1) {
                    System.out.println("AuthBean#login Error: " + ex);
                }
            }
            FacesContext.getCurrentInstance().addMessage(null, new
            FacesMessage(FacesMessage.SEVERITY_ERROR, "Invalid username/password", ""));
            return false;
    } finally {
            setPassword(null);
    }
}
/**
 * @return the isAuthenticated
 */
```

```java
    public boolean isAuthenticated() {
        if (getSession().getAttribute("authenticated") != null) {
            boolean auth = (Boolean) getSession().getAttribute("authenticated");
            if (auth) {
                authenticated = true;
            }
        } else {
            authenticated = false;
        }
        return authenticated;
    }
    /**
     * @param isAuthenticated the isAuthenticated to set
     */
    public void setAuthenticated(boolean isAuthenticated) {
        this.authenticated = isAuthenticated;
    }
    @Remove
    public void remove() {
        System.out.println("Being removed from session...");
        setUser(null);
    }
    /**
     * @return the username
     */
    public String getUsername() {
        try {
            System.out.println("The current username is: " + user.getUsername());
            username = getUser().getUsername();
        } catch (NullPointerException ex) {
        }
        return username;
    }
    /**
     * @param username the username to set
     */
    public void setUsername(String username) {
        getUser().setUsername(username);
        System.out.println("Just set the username to : " + getUser().getUsername());
        this.username = null;
    }
    /**
     * @return the user
     */
    public User getUser(){
        if (this.user == null) {
            user = new User();
        }
        return user;
    }
    /**
```

```
     * @param user the user to set
     */
    public void setUser(User user) {
        this.user = user;
    }
    ...
    // setters and getters
    ...
}
```

Jakarta Server Faces Controller

The controller is responsible for coordinating authentication efforts between the Jakarta Server Faces view and the Jakarta Enterprise Beans. It also has a session scope so that the user's state can be maintained throughout the life of the application session. The following code is taken from the org.jakartaeerecipe.chapter15.recipe15_03.AuthenticationController.java file that is contained within the JakartaEERecipes project:

```
import jakarta.servlet.http.HttpSession;
@Named("authenticationController")
@SessionScoped
public class AuthenticationController implements Serializable {
    @EJB
    private AuthenticationBean authenticationFacade;
    private String username;
    private User user;
    private boolean authenticated = false;
    private HttpSession session = null;
    private String userAgent;
    /**
     * Creates a new instance of AuthenticationController
     */
    public AuthenticationController() {
    }
    public HttpSession getSession() {
        // if(session == null){
        FacesContext context = FacesContext.getCurrentInstance();
        HttpServletRequest request = (HttpServletRequest) context.getExternalContext().
        getRequest();
        session = request.getSession();
        return session;
    }
    /**
     * @return the username
     */
    public String getUsername() {
        this.username = getUser().getUsername();
        return this.username;
    }
    /**
     * @param username the username to set
     */
```

567

```java
    public void setUsername(String username) {
        this.username = username;
        getUser().setUsername(username);
    }
    /**
     * @return the password
     */
    public String getPassword() {
        return authenticationFacade.getPassword();
    }
    /**
     * @param password the password to set
     */
    public void setPassword(String password) {
        authenticationFacade.setPassword(password);
    }
    public User getUser() {
        if (this.user == null) {
            user = new User();
            setUser(authenticationFacade.getUser());
        }
        return user;
    }
    public void setUser(User user) {
        this.user = user;
    }
    public String login() {
        authenticationFacade.setUser(getUser());
        boolean authResult = authenticationFacade.login();
        if (authResult) {
            this.authenticated = true;
            setUser(authenticationFacade.getUser());
            return "SUCCESS_LOGIN";
        } else {
            this.authenticated = false;
            setUser(null);
            return "BAD_LOGIN";
        }
    }
    public String logout() {
        user = null;
        this.authenticated = false;
        FacesContext facesContext = FacesContext.getCurrentInstance();
        ExternalContext externalContext = facesContext.getExternalContext();
        externalContext.invalidateSession();
        return "SUCCESS_LOGOUT";
    }
    /**
     * @return the authenticated
     */
    public boolean isAuthenticated() {
```

```
    try {
        boolean auth = (Boolean) getSession().getAttribute("authenticated");
        if (auth) {
            this.authenticated = true;
        } else {
            authenticated = false;
        }
    } catch (Exception e) {
        this.authenticated = false;
    }
    return authenticated;
}
    public void setAuthenticated(boolean authenticated) {
        this.authenticated = authenticated;
    }
}
```

User Entity

For any application, it is a good idea to maintain a list of users who can access the application pages. Furthermore, if an application requires fine-grained access control, it is important to assign roles to each user to indicate which privilege level each user should have for the application. A database table can be used for this purpose, and the table should contain a field for the username of each person who has access to the application, as well as a field for the user role. The following SQL is used for creating the USER database table in an Oracle database, although similar SQL could be used to create a table in a different RDMS:

```
create table user(
user_id number,
username varchar(150) not null,
password varchar(50) not null,
primary key (id));
```

The following class listing is that for the org.jakartaeerecipe.chapter15.recipe15_03.User.java file, which is an entity class within the JakartaEERecipes_Chapter15 project:

```
import java.io.Serializable;
import java.math.BigDecimal;
import jakarta.persistence.Column;
import jakarta.persistence.Entity;
import jakarta.persistence.Id;
import jakarta.persistence.Table;
/**
 * Entity class User
 */
@Entity
@Table(name = "USER")
public class User implements Serializable {
    @Id
    @Column(name = "USER_ID", nullable = false)
    private BigDecimal userId;
    @Column(name = "USERNAME")
```

```
private String username;
@Column(name = "SECURITY_ROLE")
private String securityRole;
/** Creates a new instance of User */
public User() {
}
/**
 * Creates a new instance of User with the specified values.
 * @param userId the userId of the User
 */
public User(BigDecimal userId) {
    this.userId = userId;
}
/**
 * Gets the userId of this User.
 * @return the userId
 */
public BigDecimal getUserId() {
    return this.userId;
}
/**
 * Sets the userId of this User to the specified value.
 * @param userId the new userId
 */
public void setUserId(BigDecimal userId) {
    this.userId = userId;
}
/**
 * Gets the username of this User.
 * @return the username
 */
public String getUsername() {
    return this.username;
}
/**
 * Sets the username of this User to the specified value.
 * @param username the new username
 */
public void setUsername(String username) {
    this.username = username;
}
/**
 * Gets the securityRole of this User.
 * @return the securityRole
 */
public String getSecurityRole() {
    return this.securityRole;
}
/**
 * Sets the securityRole of this User to the specified value.
 * @param securityRole the new securityRole
```

```
    */
    public void setSecurityRole(String securityRole) {
        this.securityRole = securityRole;
    }
    /**
     * Returns a hash code value for the object.  This implementation computes
     * a hash code value based on the id fields in this object.
     * @return a hash code value for this object.
     */
    @Override
    public int hashCode() {
        int hash = 0;
        hash += (this.userId != null ? this.userId.hashCode() : 0);
        return hash;
    }
    /**
     * Determines whether another object is equal to this User.  The result is
     * <code>true</code> if and only if the argument is not null and is a User object that
     * has the same id field values as this object.
     * @param object the reference object with which to compare
     * @return <code>true</code> if this object is the same as the argument;
     * <code>false</code> otherwise.
     */
    @Override
    public boolean equals(Object object) {
        return false;
        }
        User other = (User)object;
        if (this.userId != other.userId && (this.userId == null ||!this.userId.equals(other.
        userId))) return false;
        return true;
    }

}
```

How It Works

The HTTP request login method can be used to programmatically authenticate users for an application when the application server form-based authentication has been configured. A JSF form can pass parameters to a managed bean controller, which can pass them to the HTTP request login method to perform programmatic authentication using the credentials.

As demonstrated in the login form that is listed in the solution to this recipe, a standard JSF view can be coded that passes values from the inputText components to a corresponding managed bean controller. The corresponding fields, username and password, are bound to properties within the managed bean controller. The username is then set into the username property of a new User entity object, and the password value is passed directly into the EJB for later use. The password is not stored in the managed bean controller at all, and, therefore, it is not stored into the session.

Let's take a moment to discuss the methods within the managed bean controller. In the example, a commandButton is contained within the view, which is bound to the managed bean controller's login method. Once invoked, the login method invokes a method within the EJB, which is responsible for performing the actual authentication against the application server container and JPA data store user table.

In this case, the EJB method is also named login, and when it is invoked, then the User entity object is passed to the EJB so that the username property that is stored in the object can be used for authentication purposes. The login method within the managed bean controller invokes the EJB login method, which passes back a Boolean value to indicate whether the credentials have successfully authenticated the user. Depending upon the outcome, the user is then granted or denied access to the application. Also within the managed bean controller is a logout method. This method invalidates the current session by obtaining the external context, which is the application server context, and then by invoking its invalidate() method.

The login method within the EJB is where the real activity occurs because it is where the application server HTTP request login method is invoked to verify the credentials. First, the HttpServletRequest object is obtained from the external context, and then its login method is called. This method accepts the username and password values, initiates the application server authentication mechanism, and raises an exception if the credentials are invalid. Otherwise, if the credentials are valid, then a time limit is set on the HttpSession object. The value passed to the session.setMaxInactiveInterval method indicates how long a user session can be inactive before the application server automatically invalidates the session. The remainder of this method is used for performing application-specific authentication using the User entity object. In the example, the entity manager is flushed, and then a query is issued that counts the number of User entity objects matching the username that has been entered via the login form. When querying the entity, a hint is set that forces the database to be queried each time the request is initiated. The following line of code is an excerpt from the login method of the AuthenticationBean class that demonstrates how to set this hint:

```
user.setHint("jakarta.persistence.cache.retrieveMode", CacheRetrieveMode.BYPASS);
```

If there are zero matching entity objects for a given username, then the user is not authenticated to the application, and a false value is returned to the managed bean controller to indicate invalid credentials. Otherwise, if there is a matching entity object for the given username, then the matching entity object is obtained, and a session attribute is set to indicate that the user was successfully authenticated.

■ **Note** Applications can contain their own set of users, one that is separate from those users who are managed by the GlassFish application server or database. One way of doing so is to create a separate database table for each application, which will be used to store usernames and roles for those users who may access the application. The login logic that is contained within the managed bean controller can then perform a query on the application-specific table to see whether the username specified within the login view is contained within the table. If the username is in the table, then the user can be granted access to the application; otherwise, no access will be granted. This approach adds two steps into the authentication process: application server form-based authentication and authentication at the database table level.

15-4. Authentication with the Security API Using Database Credentials

Problem

You are interested in utilizing a standard solution for integrating form-based authentication into your application, using a database to store credentials.

Solution

Utilize Jakarta Security to authenticate a user using the same form authentication as demonstrated in Recipe 15-3. However, this solution will utilize credentials saved in a database, although one could also utilize LDAP authentication or another custom means via the Security API. Configuration for the database takes place via an annotation within the application, so no application server configuration is necessary.

To configure the application, annotate an @ApplicationScoped bean to indicate the authentication identity store that will be used for the application. In this case, the @DatabaseIdentityStoreDefinition annotation is used to configure the database as an identity store for the application:

```
package org.jakartaeerecipe.chapter15;

import jakarta.enterprise.context.ApplicationScoped;
import jakarta.inject.Named;
import jakarta.security.enterprise.identitystore.DatabaseIdentityStoreDefinition;
import jakarta.security.enterprise.identitystore.Pbkdf2PasswordHash;
@DatabaseIdentityStoreDefinition(
        dataSourceLookup = "${'jdbc/acmedb'}",
        callerQuery = "#{'select password from caller_store where name = ?'}",
        groupsQuery = "select group_name from caller_groups where caller_name = ?",
        hashAlgorithm = Pbkdf2PasswordHash.class,
        priorityExpression = "#{100}",
        hashAlgorithmParameters = {
            "Pbkdf2PasswordHash.Iterations=3072",
            "${applicationConfig.hash}"
        } // just for test / example
)
@ApplicationScoped
@Named
public class ApplicationConfig {
    public String[] getHash() {
        return new String[]{"Pbkdf2PasswordHash.Algorithm=PBKDF2WithHmacSHA512",
        "Pbkdf2PasswordHash.SaltSizeBytes=64"};
    }
}
```

A singleton can be used to configure a database connection. This code will be run once each time the application is started up, and it will load the database configuration and populate the security database for testing purposes. In real life, this class would only be used to configure the data source, as the security database would likely be populated by an administrator. The following excerpt is from the sources of the singleton EJB:

```
import java.sql.Connection;
import java.sql.PreparedStatement;
import java.sql.SQLException;
import java.util.HashMap;
import java.util.Map;
import jakarta.annotation.PostConstruct;
import jakarta.annotation.PreDestroy;
import jakarta.annotation.Resource;
import jakarta.annotation.sql.DataSourceDefinition;
```

```
import jakarta.ejb.Singleton;
import jakarta.ejb.Startup;
import jakarta.inject.Inject;
import jakarta.sql.DataSource;
import jakarta.security.enterprise.identitystore.Pbkdf2PasswordHash;
@DataSourceDefinition(
    name = "java:global/JakartaEERecipes/acmedb",
    className = "org.apache.derby.jdbc.ClientDataSource",
    serverName="localhost",
    databaseName="acme",
    user = "acmeuser",
    password = "databasepassword"
)
@Singleton
@Startup
public class LoadDatabase {
    @Resource(lookup="java:global/JakartaEERecipes/acmedb")
    private DataSource dataSource;
    @Inject
    private Pbkdf2PasswordHash passwordHash;
    @PostConstruct
    public void init() {
        Map<String, String> parameters= new HashMap<>();
        parameters.put("Pbkdf2PasswordHash.Iterations", "3072");
        parameters.put("Pbkdf2PasswordHash.Algorithm", "PBKDF2WithHmacSHA512");
        parameters.put("Pbkdf2PasswordHash.SaltSizeBytes", "64");
        passwordHash.initialize(parameters);
        executeUpdate(dataSource, "CREATE TABLE caller_store(name VARCHAR(64) PRIMARY KEY,
        password VARCHAR(255))");
        executeUpdate(dataSource, "CREATE TABLE caller_groups(caller_name VARCHAR(64),
        group_name VARCHAR(64))");
        executeUpdate(dataSource, "INSERT INTO caller_store VALUES('juneau', '" +
        passwordHash.generate("eerecipes".toCharArray()) + "')");
        executeUpdate(dataSource, "INSERT INTO caller_groups VALUES('juneau', 'group1')");
        executeUpdate(dataSource, "INSERT INTO caller_groups VALUES('juneau', 'group2')");
    }
    @PreDestroy
    public void destroy() {
      try {
            executeUpdate(dataSource, "DROP TABLE IF EXISTS caller_store");
            executeUpdate(dataSource, "DROP TABLE IF EXISTS caller_groups");
      } catch (Exception e) {
            // silently ignore, concerns in-memory database
      }
    }
    private void executeUpdate(DataSource dataSource, String query) {
        try (Connection connection = dataSource.getConnection()) {
            try (PreparedStatement statement = connection.prepareStatement(query)) {
                statement.executeUpdate();
            }
        } catch (SQLException e) {
```

```
              // do nothing
          }
      }
}
```

The same Jakarta Server Faces login form from Recipe 15-3 (/webapp/chapter15/login.xhtml) can be used for the authentication UI in this case, with the exception of passing credentials and invoking `SecurityContext.authenticate()`. This is a different form-based scenario which utilizes the `@CustomFormAuthenticationMechanismDefinition` annotation. The following excerpt is taken from the Jakarta Server Faces login form, containing a PrimeFaces `commandButton` component which binds to a CDI controller action to perform the validation:

```
<html xmlns="http://www.w3.org/1999/xhtml"
    xmlns:f="http://xmlns.jcp.org/jsf/core"
    xmlns:h="http://xmlns.jcp.org/jsf/html"
    xmlns:ui="http://xmlns.jcp.org/jsf/facelets"
    xmlns:p="http://primefaces.org/ui">
  <h:head>
      <meta http-equiv="Content-Type" content="text/html; charset=UTF-8"/>
      <title>Jakarta Recipes = Chapter 15 Examples</title>
  </h:head>
  <h:body>
      <ui:composition template="layout/custom_template_search.xhtml">
          <ui:define name="content">
              <h1>Login Form for Jakarta EE Recipes Application</h1>
              <h:form id="loginForm">
                  <p:messages id="messages"/>
                  <p:panelGrid columns="2">
                      <p:outputLabel for="username" value="Username: "/>
                      <p:inputText id="username" value="#{standardizedAuthentication
                      Controller.username}"/>
                      <p:outputLabel for="password" value="Password "/>
                      <p:password id="password" value="#{standardizedAuthentication
                      Controller.password}"/>
                  </p:panelGrid>
                  <br/>
                  <p:commandButton id="loginAction" action="#{standardizedAuthentication
                  Controller.login}"
                                    value="Login"
                                    update="messages"/>
              </h:form>
          </ui:define>
      </ui:composition>
  </h:body>
</html>
```

Lastly, the code for the authentication CDI controller bean is as follows. The `@RequestScoped` controller contains properties for passing the username and password, along with the logic for authenticating the credentials that have been supplied by the user:

```
import jakarta.enterprise.context.RequestScoped;
import jakarta.faces.application.FacesMessage;
import jakarta.faces.context.FacesContext;
```

```
import jakarta.inject.Inject;
import jakarta.inject.Named;
import jakarta.security.enterprise.credential.Credential;
import jakarta.security.enterprise.credential.Password;
import jakarta.security.enterprise.credential.UsernamePasswordCredential;
import jakarta.security.enterprise.identitystore.CredentialValidationResult;
import jakarta.security.enterprise.identitystore.IdentityStoreHandler;
import jakarta.servlet.http.HttpServletRequest;
import jakarta.servlet.http.HttpServletResponse;
import jakarta.validation.constraints.NotNull;
/**
 *
 * @author Juneau
 */
@Named
@RequestScoped
public class StandardizedAuthenticationController {
    @Inject
    private IdentityStoreHandler identityStoreHandler;
    @NotNull
    private String username;
    @NotNull
    private String password;
    public void login() {
        FacesContext context = FacesContext.getCurrentInstance();
        Credential credential = new UsernamePasswordCredential(username, new
        Password(password));
        CredentialValidationResult cres = identityStoreHandler.validate(credential);
        if (cres.getStatus().equals(CredentialValidationResult.Status.VALID)) {
            context.responseComplete();
            context.addMessage(null, new FacesMessage(FacesMessage.SEVERITY_INFO,
            "Authentication Successful", null));
        } else if (cres.getStatus().equals(CredentialValidationResult.Status.INVALID)) {
            context.addMessage(null,
                    new FacesMessage(FacesMessage.SEVERITY_ERROR, "Authentication
                    Failure", null));
        }
    }
    private static HttpServletResponse getResponse(FacesContext context) {
        return (HttpServletResponse) context
            .getExternalContext()
            .getResponse();
    }
    private static HttpServletRequest getRequest(FacesContext context) {
        return (HttpServletRequest) context
            .getExternalContext()
            .getRequest();
    }
    /**
```

```
 * @return the username
 */
public String getUsername() {
    return username;
}
/**
 * @param username the username to set
 */
public void setUsername(String username) {
    this.username = username;
}
/**
 * @return the password
 */
public String getPassword() {
    return password;
}
/**
 * @param password the password to set
 */
public void setPassword(String password) {
    this.password = password;
}
}
```

How It Works

Jakarta Security defines a set of annotations that can be used to configure an application identity store and HttpAuthenticationMechanism for an application, among other security configurations. These standardized annotations are available as part of Jakarta Security across all Jakarta EE 10–compliant containers, allowing security configuration to be packaged as part of an application without additional XML configuration requirements. This makes it possible to create portable applications that contain security in which the same security configuration can be used across a number of containers.

An identity store typically holds a list of callers and caller groups, as well as security credentials for authenticating the caller. The API defines the following set of standard identity store annotations, which supply an abstraction of an identity store:

- @LdapIdentityStoreDefinition: Supports a caller that is stored in an external LDAP server

- @DatabaseIdentityStoreDefinition: Supports a caller that is stored in an external database, which is accessible via a JNDI-bound Data Source

The identity store annotations must be defined within a CDI bean that is marked as @ApplicationScoped, so that they are configured one time per application startup. An identity store is stateless, and it should include the information required to authenticate a caller into an application. The caller should not interact directly with an identity store. Instead, an HttpAuthenticationMechanism, which will be explained in the following, should perform the interaction. An identity store contains two methods that can be implemented by an authentication mechanism in order to validate a caller's credentials and return a caller's security groups. Those methods are validate() and getCallerGroups(), respectively. An identity store can implement one or both of these methods, and calling upon the identity store's validationTypes() method returns a set of values that indicate which methods are implemented via the following values: VALIDATE, PROVIDE_GROUPS.

The validate() method takes a Credential object, which is a portable object that contains a username/password that has been supplied by a caller. The validate() method returns a CredentialValidationResult, indicating the validation status. The CredentialValidationResult can be used to obtain information such as the resulting validation status, and if successful, then it also contains the identity store ID, caller principal, caller's unique ID within the identity store, and the caller's groups. The getStatus() method of CredentialValidationResult will return one of the following status values:

- VALID: Validation succeeded and caller groups can be obtained, if any are available.

- INVALID: Validation failed.

- NOT_VALIDATED: Validation was not attempted due to an invalid credential type.

More than one identity store can be configured for an application by setting a priority. Identity stores can also be programmed by implementing the IdentityStore interface, or they can be injected via the use of the identity store annotations outlined previously. These topics, as well as more in-depth analysis of the identity store concept, are covered in detail within the JSR 375 specification, available on javaee.github.io: https://javaee.github.io/security-spec/.

The HttpAuthenticationMechanism is used by the Security API to validate a user's credentials. There must be three HttpAuthenticationMechanisms supplied by a Jakarta EE–compliant application server container, which are the following:

- *Basic* (@BasicAuthenticationMechanismDefinition): Authenticates according to the HTTP basic authentication semantics.

- *Form* (@FormAuthenticationMechanismDefinition): Authenticates according to the form-based authentication semantics.

- *Custom form* (authenticate): Authenticates according to the form-based authentication semantics; however, it does not occur via posting back to j_security_check. Instead, SecurityContext.authenticate() is invoked with passed-in credentials.

An HttpAuthenticationMechanism can be coded by implementing the HttpAuthenticationMechanism interface, or it can be injected using one of the annotations. To implement, one must code the validateRequest() method, which is invoked before the doFilter() method of a servlet filter or service() method of any servlet. The validateRequest() method is also called upon in response to code calling the HttpServletRequest authenticate() method. There are two methods that are part of the HttpAuthenticationMechanism which are not required for implementation: secureResponse() and cleanSubject().

The validateRequest() method is used to allow the caller to authenticate. The secureResponse() method is provided to allow for postprocessing on the response that is generated by a servlet or servlet filter. The cleanSubject() method is provided to allow for cleanup after the caller is logged out.

Since a compliant container must provide default implementations of the HttpAuthenticationMechanism, it is possible for an application to simply use the mechanism without coding or supplying an annotation. The example in this recipe does just that; to validate this, you can visit this URL in a browser: http://localhost:8080/JakartaEERecipes_Chapter15-1.0-SNAPSHOT/chapter15/login.xhtml. When the caller inserts credentials into the login screen and clicks the button, the StandardizedAuthenticationController login() method is called. This controller class contains an injected IdentityStoreHandler, which is used to hook into the HttpAuthenticationMechanism that is provided by the container. In the login() method, the caller's username and password are passed into a UsernamePasswordCredential object to return a Credential. The Credential is then passed into the

IdentityStoreHandler.validate() method, returning a CredentialValidationResult object. This object can be used to glean the success or failure of the authentication attempt. The resulting success or failure can be tested by calling upon the CredentialValidationResult.getStatus() method.

The Jakarta Security API helps to bring standardization to an area of the platform that has been very nonstandardized in the past. While many containers will likely still retain their proprietary security APIs and techniques, any Jakarta EE 10–compliant container must also adhere to the standards of Jakarta Security.

■ **Note** There are dozens of examples that can be found on the Jakarta EE Security API (Soteria) GitHub project page at https://github.com/eclipse-ee4j/soteria. It is also a great idea to read through the specification, which is less than 50 pages, and it can be found at https://jakarta.ee/specifications/security/3.0/.

15-5. Managing Page Access Within a Jakarta Server Faces Application

Problem

You have set up authentication for your JSF application, specifying access to a limited user base via a username and password combination. You want to limit certain views within your application such that only members of a particular role will be granted permission access.

Solution

Authenticate a user to an application and store a Boolean indicating that the user has been successfully authenticated. Utilize that Boolean to perform conditional logic within Jakarta Server Faces views to render forms that should be accessed only via authenticated users. If a user is successfully authenticated, then the form is rendered, and if the user is not successfully authenticated, then the form will provide an error message indicating that authentication is required for access.

The following Jakarta Server Faces view (/webapp/chapter15/recipe15_04.xhtml) demonstrates the use of conditional logic for displaying portions of the page that require controlled access:

```
<?xml version="1.0" encoding="UTF-8" ?>
<!DOCTYPE html PUBLIC "-//W3C//DTD XHTML 1.0 Transitional//EN" "http://www.w3.org/TR/xhtml1/
DTD/xhtml1-transitional.dtd">
<html xmlns="http://www.w3.org/1999/xhtml"
    xmlns:ui="http://xmlns.jcp.org/jsf/facelets"
    xmlns:h="http://xmlns.jcp.org/jsf/html"
    xmlns:f="http://xmlns.jcp.org/jsf/core"
    xmlns:p="http://primefaces.org/ui">
    <ui:composition template="/layout/fess_template.xhtml">
        <ui:define name="title">
            <h:outputText value="Jakarta EE 10 Recipes Controlled Access"></h:outputText>
        </ui:define>
        <ui:define name="body">
            <h:panelGroup id="messagePanel" layout="block">
                <h:messages errorStyle="color: red" infoStyle="color: green" layout="table"/>
```

```
        </h:panelGroup>
        <p:panel rendered="#{authenticationController.authenticated}">
            <h:form>
                This portion of the view contains secret content!
            </h:form>
        </p:panel>
        <p:panel rendered="#{!authenticationController.authenticated}">
            Please <a href="#{request.contextPath}/ chapter15/recipe15_03.xhtml">
            authenticate</a> to use this form.
        </p:panel>
    </ui:define>
</ui:composition>
</html>
```

How It Works

The rendered attribute of Jakarta Server Faces components can be used to perform conditional rendering. If you bind the rendered attribute to a managed bean property that returns a Boolean indicating whether a user is authenticated, then this technique can be used to control access to certain components. In this example, this technique is demonstrated using a PrimeFaces panel component. The panel contains information that should be secured, and it is rendered only if the authenticated property returns a true value. If the authenticated property contains a false value, then a different panel component is rendered, which displays a message to the user indicating that authentication is required.

The controller that is used for programmatic authentication within a Jakarta Server Faces application should contain a Boolean value that can be bound to the conditional logic within the Jakarta Server Faces view to indicate whether the current user has successfully authenticated. For this example, the managed bean controller, org.jakartaeerecipe.chapter15.recipe15_03.AuthenticationController, contains a Boolean field named authenticated. The following excerpt from the class shows the isAuthenticated() method, which is called when the authenticated property is accessed from a Jakarta Server Faces view:

```
public boolean isAuthenticated() {
    try {
        boolean auth = (Boolean) getSession().getAttribute("authenticated");
        if (auth) {
            this.authenticated = true;
        } else {
            authenticated = false;
        }
    } catch (Exception e) {
        this.authenticated = false;
    }
    return authenticated;
}
```

This same technique can be used to hide or show individual components based upon a user's authentication. Furthermore, fine-grained access control can be used to provide Boolean values to the rendered attribute by utilizing Jakarta Expression Language conditional expressions. For instance, if some components should be accessed only by users who belong in certain security roles, then a conditional expression can be used to render a component if the user belongs to a specified role. The following line of code demonstrates how to render an `outputText` component if a user belongs to the `ADMIN` security role:

```
<h:outputLink rendered="${authenticationController.user.securityRole eq 'ADMIN'}" value="#"
onclick="dialog.show()">Delete Property</h:outputLink>
```

Although the `rendered` attribute may not allow you to secure every part of an application, when used along with other security measures such as annotating methods (Recipe 15-2), it can help provide a very secure environment.

15-6. Configuring LDAP Authentication Within GlassFish

Problem

You want to authenticate users to your application based upon a centrally located LDAP server for your organization's enterprise.

Solution

Create an LDAP security realm for GlassFish from within the administrative console utility, and set it up as a `com.sun.enterprise.security.auth.realm.ldap.LDAPRealm`. To create an LDAP security realm within GlassFish, use the following procedure:

- Log in to the GlassFish administrative console.

- Traverse to the Realms form by expanding the left tree menu Configurations ➤ server-config ➤ Security ➤ Realms.

- Click the New... button within the Realms form to create a new security realm.

- Within the New Realm form, provide a name for the security realm. Next, select `com.sun.enterprise.security.auth.realm.ldap.LDAPRealm` from the Class Name pull-down menu. This will open the configurations for setting up an LDAP realm (Figure 15-11).

New Realm

OK   Cancel

Create a new security (authentication) realm. Valid realm types are PAM, OSGI, File, Certificate, LDAP, JDBC, Digest, Oracle Solaris, and Custom.

* Indicates required field

Configuration Name: server-config

Name: *

Class Name: ● com.sun.enterprise.security.auth.realm.ldap.LDAPRealm

○

Choose a realm class name from the drop-down list or specify a custom class

Properties specific to this Class

JAAS Context: *

Identifier for the login module to use for this realm

Directory: *

LDAP URL for your server

Base DN: *

LDAP base DN for the location of user data

Assign Groups:

Comma-separated list of group names

Additional Properties (0)

Add Property   Delete Properties

Select	Name	Value	Description
No items found.			

Figure 15-11. *New LDAP security realm*

Complete the properties specific to the class in order to connect to an LDAP server of your choice.

1. Add the following additional properties by clicking the **Add Property** button and providing the name-value information for each:

    - search-bind-dn: Enter the fully qualified DN for your LDAP host, the directory, and the LDAP account to which you will authenticate. For example:

        CN=account-name,OU=AccountGroup,DC=dc1,DC=dc2,DC=dc3

    - search-bind-password: Enter the password for the account name you specified previously.

    - search-filter: Type the following as the value for this property: (sAMAccountName=%s).

2. Restart the application server.

How It Works

Perhaps one of the most efficient ways to authenticate to applications is to utilize an LDAP account. Using an LDAP account for authentication can provide a single sign-on solution across all of an organization's servers and applications. LDAP authentication also provides a single point of maintenance for account information and still allows individual applications to maintain their own fine-grained security via roles. The solution to this recipe enumerates the steps that are involved in setting up an LDAP security realm within the GlassFish application servers. However, you can follow similar procedures for setting up an LDAP security realm in other application server containers.

Once you have LDAP authentication set up within the application server, you can configure your applications to use it. To configure an application to use LDAP authentication, add the following configurations to the web.xml deployment descriptor:

```
<login-config>
      <auth-method>FORM</auth-method>
      <realm-name>REALM-NAME</realm-name>
      <form-login-config>
          <form-login-page>/faces/login.xhtml</form-login-page>
          <form-error-page>/faces/loginError.xhtml</form-error-page>
      </form-login-config>
</login-config>
```

In the previous excerpt from web.xml, the realm-name element should be the same as the name given to the LDAP security realm you created within GlassFish. The form-login-page and form-error-page values should reference the views that are to be used for logging in to an application and the view that is displayed when there is a login error, respectively. Authenticating into an LDAP security realm is the same as that covered in Recipe 15-3. Simply call the HttpRequest object's login method to authenticate using the credentials provided by the user via the login view.

15-7. Configuring Custom Security Certificates Within GlassFish

Problem

You want to utilize custom certificates for securing access via SSL within your GlassFish environment.

Solution

Obtain a certificate from a certified certificate authority, and then install it into the GlassFish application server container. Once installed, route requests via a secured port that utilizes SSL and force users to accept the security certificate to proceed. To install a certificate that has been obtained from a valid certificate authority, follow these steps:

1. Copy the trusted root certificate from your certified authority to your server. Issue the following command from the command line or terminal:

    ```
    keytool -import -alias root -keystore keystore_name.keystore -trustcacerts -file
    trustedcarootcertificate.crt
    ```

2. Next, import the trusted certificate:

    ```
    keytool -import -alias cert_alias -keystore keystore_name.keystore -trustcacerts
    -file certificate.crt
    ```

3. Adjust SSL settings from within the GlassFish administrative console. To adjust the settings, go to Configuration ➤ Network Config ➤ Network Listeners ➤ http-listener-2 in order to open the secured HTTP listener page. Once it's open, select the SSL tab, and enter the certificate nickname and keystore that match the ones you used in step 2. See Figure 15-12.

Figure 15-12. *Modify SSL settings*

4. Restart your server, and then access your applications securely using this URL:

    ```
    https://localhost:8181/your_application_context.
    ```

■ **Note**   In the previous numbered list, keystore_name.keystore represents the name of a keystore, and trustedcarootcertificate.crt and certificate.crt represent the names of certificates.

How It Works

GlassFish comes with a self-signed security certificate that is suitable for test environments. However, when utilizing GlassFish as a production application server solution, it is imperative that a certificate from a verified authority be put in place in order to secure application transport. This recipe demonstrates how to install a security certificate for use with SSL in order to achieve secure transport.

Before you can install a verified certificate, you need to obtain it. You will need to choose from one of the many certificate authorities and then send a certificate request, which includes the key from your application server. A keystore will need to be created in order to generate a certificate request. Issue the following command from the command line or terminal to create the keystore:

```
keytool -keysize 2048 -genkey -alias -keyalg RSA -dname "CN=yourdomain.org,O=company_
name,L=city,S=state,C=country" - keypass glassfish_master_password -storepass glassfish_
master_password -keystore choose_keystore_name.keystore
```

Once the keystore has been created, a certificate signing request (CSR) that will be sent to the certificate authority can be generated. To generate the certificate signing request (CSR), issue the following command from your server:

```
keytool -certreq -alias -keystore chosen_keystore_name.keystore -storepass glassfish_master_
password -keypass glassfish_master_password -file csrname.csr
```

■ **Note**　To change the GlassFish master password, issue the following command when your GlassFish domain is stopped: `asadmin change-master-password -savemasterpassword=true`.

Once you submit your CSR to the certificate authority, the certificate authority will send back a valid security certificate that can be installed into your server. Follow the steps in the solution to this recipe to install the certificate into GlassFish. Once the certificate is installed, your server will be verified secure via the certificate authority, and users should see a message indicating as such (usually a lock) in their browsers when visiting your secured sites.

CHAPTER 16

Concurrency and Batch

Jakarta Concurrency Utilities and Batch Processing APIs included standard techniques for processing tasks concurrently and standardization for batch application processing.

Each of the two APIs is quite large, and they include proven solutions that have been used by various enterprise projects for years. Using Java SE concurrency utilities such as java.util.concurrent and java.lang.Thread in Java EE applications has been problematic in the past, since the application server container was unable to work with such resources. Extensions of the java.util.concurrent API enabled application servers and other containers to become aware of these concurrency resources. The extensions allow enterprise applications to appropriately utilize asynchronous operations via the use of java.util.concurrent.ExecutorService resources that are made available within the enterprise environment.

The API for batch processing provides a fine-grained experience for developers, which enables them to produce and process batch applications in a variety of different ways. Enterprise applications no longer need to utilize customized classes for performing batch processing, allowing enterprise applications to adhere to an adopted standard.

As mentioned previously, the scope of these additional APIs is quite large, and this chapter will not attempt to cover each feature. However, the recipes contained within should provide enough information to get a developer up and running using some of the most frequently required pieces of each API. For more in-depth information regarding the details of Jakarta Concurrency, please refer to the JavaDoc located at https://jakarta.ee/specifications/concurrency/. The recipes for this chapter work in Eclipse GlassFish. Other Jakarta EE–compliant application servers such as Open Liberty and WildFly also contain similar solutions for the problems.

16-1. Creating Resources for Processing Tasks Asynchronously in an Application Server

Problem

You would like to register a ManagedExecutorService resource within your application server environment.

© Josh Juneau and Tarun Telang 2022
J. Juneau and T. Telang, *Java EE to Jakarta EE 10 Recipes*, https://doi.org/10.1007/978-1-4842-8079-9_16

Solution #1

Create a new ManagedExecutorService using the GlassFish asadmin create-managed-executor-service utility. To utilize concurrent utilities such as reporter tasks, the application server must be configured to utilize a ManagedExecutorService. To create a ManagedExecutorService in GlassFish, run the following command at the command prompt:

```
<path-to-glassfish>/bin/asadmin create-managed-executor-service concurrent/BatchExecutor
```

You should see the output as shown in Figure 16-1.

```
$ ./asadmin create-managed-executor-service concurrent/BatchExecutor
Enter admin user name>  admin
Enter admin password for user "admin">
Managed executor service concurrent/BatchExecutor created successfully.
Command create-managed-executor-service executed successfully.
$
```

Figure 16-1. *Creating ManagedExecutorService in GlassFish*

In the preceding command-line action, the name of the ManagedExecutorService that is being created is concurrent/BatchExecutor. However, this could be changed to better suit the application. To see all the options available for the create-managed-executor-service command, issue the --help flag. Figure 16-2 shows the results of doing so.

```
NAME
        create-managed-executor-service - creates a managed executor service
        resource

SYNOPSIS
            create-managed-executor-service [--help]
            [--enabled={false|true}]
            [--contextinfoenabled={false|true}]
            [--contextinfo={Classloader|JNDI|Security|WorkArea}]
            [--threadpriority threadpriority]
            [--longrunningtasks={false|true}]
            [--hungafterseconds hungafterseconds]
            [--corepoolsize corepoolsize]
            [--maximumpoolsize maximumpoolsize]
            [--keepaliveseconds keepaliveseconds]
            [--threadlifetimeseconds threadlifetimeseconds]
            [--taskqueuecapacity taskqueuecapacity]
            [--description description]
            [--property property]
            [--target target]
            jndi_name

DESCRIPTION
        The create-managed-executor-service subcommand creates a managed
        executor service resource.

        This subcommand is supported in remote mode only.

OPTIONS
        --help, -?
            Displays the help text for the subcommand.

        --enabled
            Determines whether the resource is enabled at runtime. The default
            value is true.
```

Figure 16-2. *Result of the --help option with the create-managed-executor-service command*

Solution #2

Create a ManagedExecutorService using the GlassFish administration console. To do so, authenticate successfully into the administrative console, and navigate to the Concurrent Resources ➤ Managed Executor Services administration panel using the left-hand tree menu (see Figure 16-3).

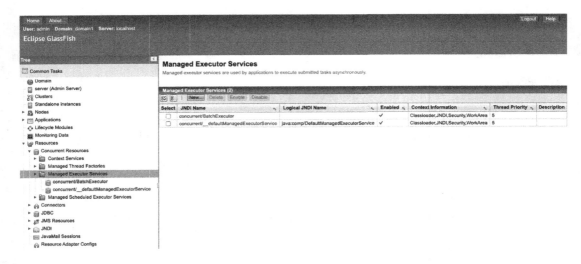

Figure 16-3. *GlassFish Managed Executor Services panel*

Once you've opened the panel, click the New button to create a new service. This will open the New Managed Executor Service panel, in which you will be required to populate a JNDI name for your new service (see Figure 16-4).

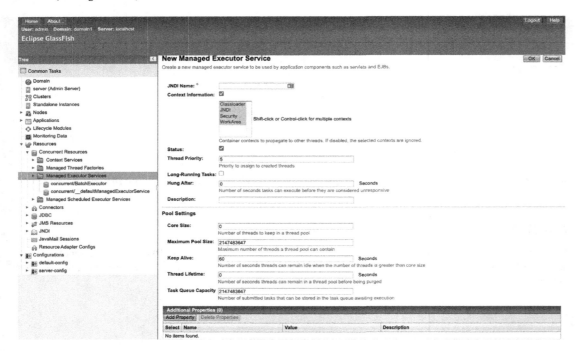

Figure 16-4. *New Managed Executor Service panel*

This panel offers quite a few options for creation of the service. However, the only option that is required is the JNDI name, as all others are populated with default values. The JNDI name that is specified should follow the format of `concurrent/YourExecutorServiceName`, where `YourExecutorServiceName` is a custom name of your choice.

How It Works

The `ManagedExecutorService` provides the ability to produce asynchronous tasks that are managed by an application server. Although there is a default `ManagedExecutorService` available for use, application server administrators can create `ManagedExecutorService` resources within an application server that can be utilized by one or more applications, much like a Java Message Service (JMS) `Topic` or `Queue`. To create a service, issue the `asadmin create-managed-executor-service` command at the command prompt, passing the name that you would like to use to identify the service. There are a bevy of options that can be used to customize the service in different ways. For instance, the service can be configured to let tasks run for a specified amount of time, pools can be configured, and so forth, allowing you to generate a `ManagedExecutorService` that will best suit the application requirements.

For those who would prefer to work within the GlassFish administration console, there are a few administration panels to make creation and management of concurrent resources easier. The Managed Executor Service panel can be used to create new application server `ManagedExecutorService` resources, as well as manage those that already exist.

■ **Note**   GlassFish and other Jakarta EE–compliant application servers come with a preconfigured default `ManagedExecutorService` resource that is named `java:comp/DefaultManagedExecutorService`.

16-2. Configuring and Creating a Reporter Task

Problem

You would like to create a long-running task that will communicate with a database and generate a report in the end.

Solution

Once the application server has been configured and the `ManagedExecutorService` has been created, an application can be written to utilize the newly created service. Within an application, you can choose to configure the application to make use of the `ManagedExecutorService` via XML, or a `@Resource` annotation can be used to inject the resource. To configure via XML, add a `<resource-env-ref>` element to the `web.xml` deployment descriptor. In this case, you need to configure a resource of type *jakarta.enterprise.concurrent.ManagedExecutorService*, as shown in the following excerpt from the /webapp/WEB-INF/web.xml:

```
<resource-env-ref>
 <description>
This executor is used for the application's reporter task. This executor has the following
requirements:
Run Location: NA
```

```
Context Info: Local Namespace
 </description>
    <resource-env-ref-name>
        concurrent/BatchExecutor
    </resource-env-ref-name>
    <resource-env-ref-type>
        jakarta.enterprise.concurrent.ManagedExecutorService
    </resource-env-ref-type>
</resource-env-ref>
```

In the XML configuration, the resource has been assigned to a reference name of concurrent/
BatchExecutor, but you could name the reference to best suit your application. If you would rather utilize an
annotation, then the following @Resource annotation can be specified to inject a ManagedExecutorService
into a class for use. You will see an example of this in use later:

```
@Resource(name = "concurrent/BatchExecutor")
ManagedExecutorService mes;
```

Once the configuration is complete, you can create a report task class, which is a class that implements
Runnable and is responsible for running the actual reports. The following class, org.jakartaeerecipe.
chapter16.recipe16_02.ReporterTask, is an example of such a class:

```
package org.jakartaeerecipe.chapter16.recipe16_02;

import java.util.List;
import jakarta.ejb.EJB;
import org.jakartaeerecipe.jpa.entity.Book;
import org.jakartaeerecipe.jpa.entity.BookAuthor;
import org.jakartaeerecipe.jpa.session.BookAuthorFacade;
import org.jakartaeerecipe.jpa.session.BookFacade;

public class ReporterTask implements Runnable {
    String reportName;
    @EJB
    private BookAuthorFacade bookAuthorFacade;
    @EJB
    private BookFacade bookFacade;
    public ReporterTask(String reportName) {
        this.reportName = reportName;
    }
    public void run() {
// Run the named report
        if ("AuthorReport".equals(reportName)) {
            runAuthorReport();
        } else if ("BookReport".equals(reportName)) {
            runBookReport();
        }
    }
    /**
     * Prints a list of authors to the system log.
     */
```

```java
    public void runAuthorReport() {
        List<BookAuthor> authors = bookAuthorFacade.findAuthor();
        System.out.println("Author Listing Report");
        System.out.println("=====================");
        for (BookAuthor author : authors) {
            System.out.println(author.getFirst() + " " + author.getLast());
        }
    }
    /**
     * Prints a list of books to a file
     */
    void runBookReport() {
        System.out.println("Querying the database");
        Path reportFile = Paths.get("BookReport.txt");
        try (BufferedWriter writer = Files.newBufferedWriter(
                reportFile, Charset.defaultCharset())) {
            Files.deleteIfExists(reportFile);
            reportFile = Files.createFile(reportFile);
            writer.append("Book Listing Report");
            writer.newLine();
            writer.append("===================");
            writer.newLine();
            List<Book> books = bookFacade.findAllBooks();
            for (Book book : books) {
                writer.append(book.getTitle());
                writer.newLine();
            }
            writer.flush();
        } catch (IOException exception) {
            System.out.println("Error writing to file");
        }
    }
}
```

Lastly, the report needs to be invoked by the ManagedExecutorService that was configured within the web.xml. In this example, the ManagedExecutorService is injected into a servlet, which is then used to invoke the report, as seen in the following code:

```java
@WebServlet(name = "BookReportServlet", urlPatterns = {"/BookReportServlet"})
public class ReportServlet extends HttpServlet implements Servlet { // Cache our executor
instance
    @Resource(name = "concurrent/BatchExecutor")
    ManagedExecutorService mes;
    protected void processRequest(HttpServletRequest request, HttpServletResponse response)
            throws ServletException, IOException {
        response.setContentType("text/html;charset=UTF-8");
```

```
    try (PrintWriter out = response.getWriter()){
        out.println("""
                    <html>
                                <head>
                                    <title>Book Report Invoker</title>
                                </head>
                                <body>
                                <h2>This servlet initiates the book report task.  Please
                                look in the server log to see the results.</h2> <br />
                        Updating the web page is not run asynchronously, however, the
                        report generation will process independently.
                            <br/><br/> """);
        ReporterTask reporterTask = new ReporterTask("BookReport");
        Future reportFuture = mes.submit(reporterTask);
        while( !reportFuture.isDone() )
            out.println("Running...<BR>");
        if (reportFuture.isDone()){
            out.println("Report Complete");
        }
        out.println("</body>");
        out.println("</html>");
    }
  }
...
```

When the servlet is visited, the reporter task will be initiated, and it will begin to produce results.

How It Works

After the ManagedExecutorService has been created, it can be utilized by one or more applications
to perform concurrent operations. An application must be configured via XML to allow access to the
ManagedExecutorService resource in the application server container, or the resource can be injected via
the use of the @Resource annotation. In the example for this recipe, each of these options is demonstrated.
For the purposes of the example, it is assumed that the @Resource annotation is utilized to inject the service
into the servlet.

To run a task concurrently using the service, you must create the task in a separate class that
implements java.util.Runnable so that it can be invoked as a separate process, much like a standard Java
Thread. In the example, a class named ReporterTask implements Runnable, and within the run() method,
the reporter task performs the tasks that we wish to run in an asynchronous manner. In this example, a
couple of methods are invoked from within the run method. The Runnable class that has been generated
can then be passed to the ManagedExecutorService to be run concurrently while other tasks are being
performed by the application. To make use of the ManagedExecutorService, register it with the application
via XML or by resource injection. In the example for this recipe, resource injection is utilized, making the
ManagedExecutorService available from within the Java servlet. To inject the resource, specify the name of it
to the @Resource annotation:

```
@Resource(name = "concurrent/BatchExecutor")
ManagedExecutorService mes;
```

The ManagedExecutorService can then be invoked by calling the submit() method and passing an instance of the Runnable task that we'd like to submit for processing. In this case, the ReporterTask class is instantiated, and an instance of it is then passed to the service, returning a java.util.concurrent. Future object:

```
ReporterTask reporterTask = new ReporterTask("BookReport");
Future reportFuture = mes.submit(reporterTask);
```

Once submitted, the Future object that was returned can be periodically checked to see if it is still running or if it has been completed by calling its isDone() method. It can be canceled by calling the cancel() method, and a canceled task can be checked by calling its isCanceled() method.

The reporter task is a long-running task that queries the database to obtain data for generation of a report.

16-3. Running More Than One Task Concurrently

Problem

You require the ability to run two or more tasks concurrently within your application. For instance, the application you are writing needs the ability to connect a database and retrieve data from two or more tables to obtain results at the same time. You wish to have the results aggregated before returning them to the user.

Solution

Create a builder task that can be used to run two different tasks in parallel. Each of the tasks can retrieve the data from the different sources, and in the end, the data will be merged and aggregated to formulate the result. To utilize a builder task, the application server environment must first be configured with a ManagedExecutorService, as per Recipe 16-1. Once the resource has been configured, an application can be configured to make use of the resource via XML or annotation. To utilize XML configuration, add a <resource-env-ref> element to the web.xml deployment descriptor. In this case, you need to configure a resource of type jakarta.enterprise.concurrent.ManagedExecutorService, as shown in the excerpt from the web.xml in Recipe 16-2 and repeated as follows:

```
<resource-env-ref>
 <description>
This executor is used for the application's builder tasks. This executor has the following
requirements:
Run Location: Local
Context Info: Local Namespace, Security
 </description>
    <resource-env-ref-name>
        concurrent/BuilderExecutor
    </resource-env-ref-name>
    <resource-env-ref-type>
        jakarta.enterprise.concurrent.ManagedExecutorService
    </resource-env-ref-type>
</resource-env-ref>
```

In this example, the ManagedExecutorService resource in the application is configured to work with a resource that has been registered with the application server container and identified by the JNDI name of concurrent/BuilderExecutor. If you would rather utilize an annotation, then the following @Resource annotation can be specified to inject a ManagedExecutorService into a class for use within the Runnable:

```
@Resource(name = "concurrent/BuilderExecutor")
ManagedExecutorService mes;
```

Once the application has been configured to work with the ManagedExecutorService resource, you can create task classes for each of the different tasks that you wish to run. Each task class must implement the jakarta.enterprise.concurrent.ManagedTask interface. The following code is from the file org.jakartaeerecipe.chapter16.recipe16_03.AuthorTask.java, and it shows what a task class should look like:

```
public class AuthorTask implements Callable<AuthorInfo>, ManagedTask {
    // The ID of the request to report on demand.
    BigDecimal authorId;
    AuthorInfo authorInfo;
    Map<String, String> execProps;
    public AuthorTask(BigDecimal id) {
        this.authorId = id;
        execProps = new HashMap<>();
        execProps.put(ManagedTask.IDENTITY_NAME, getIdentityName());
    }
    public AuthorInfo call() {
// Find the entity bean and return it to the client.
        return authorInfo;
    }
    public String getIdentityName() {
        return "AuthorTask: AuthorID=" + authorId;
    }
    public Map<String, String> getExecutionProperties() {
        return execProps;
    }
    public String getIdentityDescription(Locale locale) {
        // Use a resource bundle...
        return "AuthorTask asynchronous EJB invoker";
    }
    @Override
    public ManagedTaskListener getManagedTaskListener() {
        return new CustomManagedTaskListener();
    }
}
```

One or more of such task classes can be implemented, and then they can be processed via the builder task using the ManagedExecutorService resource that has been registered with the application server container. The following servlet makes use of a ManagedExecutorService to coordinate the invocation of two task classes. In this case, the task class names are AuthorTask and AuthorTaskTwo:

```
@WebServlet(name = "BuilderServlet", urlPatterns = {"/builderServlet"})
public class BuilderServlet extends HttpServlet implements Servlet {
```

```
// Retrieve our executor instance.
@Resource(name = "concurrent/BuilderExecutor")
ManagedExecutorService mes;
AuthorInfo authorInfoHome;
BookInfo bookInfoHome;
protected void processRequest(HttpServletRequest req, HttpServletResponse resp) throws
ServletException, IOException {
    try {
        PrintWriter out = resp.getWriter();
        // Create the task instances
        ArrayList<Callable<AuthorInfo>> builderTasks = new ArrayList<Callable
        <AuthorInfo>>();
        builderTasks.add(new AuthorTask(BigDecimal.ONE));
        builderTasks.add(new AuthorTaskTwo(BigDecimal.ONE));
        // Submit the tasks and wait.
        List<Future<AuthorInfo>> taskResults = mes.invokeAll(builderTasks);
        ArrayList<AuthorInfo> results = new ArrayList<AuthorInfo>();
        for(Future<AuthorInfo> result: taskResults){
            results.add(result.get());
            out.write("Processing Results...");
        }
    } catch (InterruptedException|ExecutionException ex) {
        Logger.getLogger(BuilderServlet.class.getName()).log(Level.SEVERE, null, ex);
    }
}
...
}
```

How It Works

After the ManagedExecutorService has been created, it can be utilized by one or more applications
to perform concurrent operations. An application must be configured via XML to allow access to the
ManagedExecutorService resource in the application server container, or the resource can be injected via
the use of the @Resource annotation. In the example for this recipe, each of these options is demonstrated.
For the purposes of the example using the servlet, it is assumed that the @Resource annotation is utilized to
inject the service into the servlet and no XML configuration has been made.

To coordinate the processing of tasks in an asynchronous manner via a ManagedExecutorService,
the tasks that need to be processed should be contained in separate classes or multiple instances of the
same task class. Each of the task classes should implement the java.util.concurrent.Callable<V> and
jakarta.enterprise.concurrent.ManagedTask interfaces. A task class should include a constructor that
enables a caller to pass arguments that are required to instantiate the object and should implement a call()
method, which returns the information that is needed to construct the report to the client. Two or more such
task classes can then be invoked via the ManagedExecutorService in order to process all results into the
required format.

To assemble the tasks for processing, create an ArrayList<Callable>, and add instances of each task
to the array. In the example, the array is named builderTasks, and instances of two different task types are
added to that array:

```
ArrayList<Callable<AuthorInfo>> builderTasks = new ArrayList<Callable<AuthorInfo>>();
builderTasks.add(new AuthorTask(BigDecimal.ONE));
builderTasks.add(new AuthorTaskTwo(BigDecimal.ONE));
```

Next, pass the array that has been constructed to the ManagedExecutorService, returning a List<Future<Object>>, which can then be used to process the results:

```
List<Future<AuthorInfo>> results = mes.invokeAll(builderTasks);
AuthorInfo authorInfo = (AuthorInfo) results.get(0).get();
// Process the results
```

Utilizing this technique, a series of tasks can be concurrently processed, returning results that can be later used to formulate a response. In this example, a report is constructed by calling two task classes and returning the results of queried information. This same technique can be applied to an array of different tasks, allowing an application to process the results of multiple task invocations in one central location.

16-4. Utilizing Transactions Within a Task

Problem

You would like to manage a transaction within an application task that will be processed using a ManagedExecutorService resource.

Solution

Make use of the jakarta.transaction.UserTransaction to create and manage a transaction. The following example demonstrates how to make use of the UserTransaction interface to demarcate transactions within a task class that will be processed by a ManagedExecutorService:

```
public class UserTransactionTask implements Runnable {
    @Resource
    SessionContext ctx;
    @EJB
    private BookAuthorFacade bookAuthorFacade;
    UserTransaction ut = ctx.getUserTransaction();
    public void run() {
        try {
            // Start a transaction
            ut.begin();
            List<BookAuthor> authors = bookAuthorFacade.findAuthor();
            for (BookAuthor author : authors) {
                // do something
            }
            ut.commit();
        } catch (NotSupportedException | SystemException | RollbackException
                | HeuristicMixedException | HeuristicRollbackException ex) {
            Logger.getLogger(UserTransactionTask.class.getName()).log(Level.SEVERE,
                null, ex);
        }
    }
}
```

The previous class can then be processed by the ManagedExecutorService by implementing a solution like the following:

```
@WebServlet(name = "UserTransactionServlet", urlPatterns = {"/userTransactionServlet"})
public class UserTransactionServlet extends HttpServlet implements Servlet {
    @Resource(name = "concurrent/BatchExecutor")
    ManagedExecutorService mes;
    protected void processRequest(HttpServletRequest request, HttpServletResponse response)
            throws ServletException, IOException {
        response.setContentType("text/html;charset=UTF-8");
        PrintWriter out = response.getWriter();
        try {
            // servlet output...
            UserTransactionTask utTask = new UserTransactionTask();
            Future utFuture = mes.submit(utTask);
            while( !utFuture.isDone() )
                out.println("Running...<BR>");
            if (utFuture.isDone()){
                out.println("Report Complete");
            }
            out.println("</body>");
            out.println("</html>");
        } finally {
            out.close();
        }
    }
}
```

How It Works

In some cases, an application may require transaction coordination within a task that will be processed via a ManagedExecutorService. Transactions can be carried out within these tasks via utilization of the jakarta.transaction.UserTransaction interface. The UserTransaction can be obtained by calling the SessionContext.getUserTransaction() method. The SessionContext resource can be injected into a bean using the @Resource annotation.

Once the UserTransaction has been obtained, the transaction can begin by calling the UserTransaction begin method. The transaction can be ended by calling the UserTransaction commit() method. The transaction encompasses any tasks that are performed after the call to begin and before the call to commit. If one of the tasks within the transaction fails, then all work performed within the transaction is halted, and values go back to what they were prior to the beginning of the transaction. This helps to ensure that all processes required for a task are completed if successful or rolled back in the event of a failure.

16-5. Running Concurrent Tasks at Scheduled Times

Problem

The application that you are utilizing needs to have the ability to periodically perform a task on a timed interval.

Solution

Use the ManagedScheduledExecutorService to create a scheduled task within your application. Before an application can use the service, it must be created within the application server container. To create a ManagedScheduledExecutorService instance within GlassFish, issue the following command from the command line:

```
bin/asadmin create-managed-scheduled-executor-service concurrent/name-of-service
```

In this command, name-of-service can be whatever name you choose. The create-managed-scheduled-executor-service command has many options that can be specified. To see and learn more about each option, invoke the command help by issuing the --help flag after the command, rather than providing the name of the service to create. Optionally, you could create the service using an application server resource, such as the GlassFish administration console.

Once the service has been created within the container, it can be utilized by an application. To utilize this type of service, the environment must be configured via XML or annotation. To utilize XML configuration, add a <resource-env-ref> element to the web.xml deployment descriptor. In this case, you need to configure a resource of type jakarta.enterprise.concurrent.ManagedScheduledExecutorService, as shown in the excerpt from the following web.xml:

```
<resource-env-ref>
 <description>Prints alerts to server log, if warranted, on a periodic basis</description>
<resource-env-ref-name>
concurrent/__defaultScheduledManagedExecutorService
</resource-env-ref-name>
 <resource-env-ref-type>
jakarta.enterprise.concurrent.ManagedScheduledExecutorService
 </resource-env-ref-type>
</resource-env-ref>
```

If you wish to use annotations rather than XML, the @Resource annotation can be used in client code to inject the ManagedScheduledExecutorService, as shown in the following lines. In this case, the injected resource references a ManagedScheduledExecutorService that is identified by the name concurrent/__defaultManagedScheduledExecutorService:

```
@Resource(name="concurrent/ScheduledAlertExecutor")
ManagedScheduledExecutorService mes;
```

To write the task that you wish to have scheduled, create a Java class that implements Runnable. As such, the class will contain a run method, which will be invoked each time the scheduled task is initiated. The following example demonstrates how to construct a task that can be used for logging. In this example, the BookAuthor entity is queried on a periodic basis to determine if new authors have been added to the database:

```
public class ScheduledLoggerExample implements Runnable {
    CreateConnection createConn = null;
    @Override
    public void run() {
        queryAuthors();
    }
}
```

```
public void queryAuthors(){
    createConn = new CreateConnection();
    String qry = "select object(o) from BookAuthor o";
    createConn.loadProperties();
    try (Connection conn = createConn.getConnection();
            Statement stmt = conn.createStatement();
            ResultSet rs = stmt.executeQuery(qry);) {
        while (rs.next()) {
        // if new author, then alert
        }
    } catch (SQLException e) {
        e.printStackTrace();
    }
    }
}
```

To periodically invoke the task, utilize the ManagedScheduledExecutorService resource. The following JSF managed bean class demonstrates how to invoke this type of service:

```
@Named
public class ScheduledTaskClient {
    Future alertHandle = null;
    @Resource(name="concurrent/__defaultManagedScheduledExecutorService")
    ManagedScheduledExecutorService mes;
    public void alertScheduler() {
        ScheduledAuthorAlert ae = new ScheduledAuthorAlert();
        alertHandle = mes.scheduleAtFixedRate(
                ae, 5L, 5L, TimeUnit.MINUTES);
        FacesMessage facesMsg = new FacesMessage(FacesMessage.SEVERITY_INFO,
                "Task Scheduled", "Task Scheduled");
                FacesContext.getCurrentInstance().addMessage(null, facesMsg);
    }
}
```

How It Works

To schedule a task to run at specific times, utilize the jakarta.concurrent. ManagedScheduledExecutorService interface. This interface extends the java.util.concurrent. ScheduledExecutorService and jakarta.enterprise.concurrent.ManagedExecutorService interfaces. The ManagedScheduledExecutorService can be used to execute a Runnable task according to a specified schedule.

As mentioned previously, a ManagedScheduledExecutorService can be used to schedule Runnable tasks. That is, any class that implements java.lang.Runnable can be invoked via the service. The code that is contained within the task class's run method is invoked each time the task is initiated. In the example for this recipe, the run method executes another method within the class that is used to query an entity and perform some work against the results.

To make use of a ManagedScheduledExecutorService, one can be created within the application server container. This can be done by issuing the asadmin create-managed-scheduled-executor-service command, as demonstrated in the example for this recipe. However, any Jakarta EE 8–compliant application server should contain a default ManagedScheduledExecutorService for use. Once the resource has been created in the application server, an application can make use of it. To enable an application to access the service, XML configuration within the web.xml deployment descriptor can be used, or a @ Resource annotation can be used to inject the resource. In the example for this recipe, both techniques are demonstrated. However, in the class that is used to initiate the example task, the @Resource annotation is used to inject the application server's default ManagedScheduledExecutorService that can be identified by the name concurrent/__defaultManagedScheduledExecutorService:

```
@Resource(name=" concurrent/__defaultManagedScheduledExecutorService ")
    ManagedScheduledExecutorService mes;
```

To schedule the task, create an instance of the task class, and then pass the instance to one of the ManagedScheduledExecutorService scheduler methods that are made available via the ScheduledExecutorService interface. The methods that can be used to schedule tasks are shown in Table 16-1.

Table 16-1. *ScheduledExecutorService Methods*

Method	Description
schedule(Callable<V> callable, long delay, TimeUnit unit)	Creates and executes a ScheduledFeature object. The object becomes available after the specified delay period
schedule(Runnable command, long delay, TimeUnit unit)	Creates and executes a one-time task that becomes available after the specified delay
scheduleAtFixedRate(Runnable command, long initialDelay, long period, TimeUnit unit)	Creates and executes a periodic task that becomes available after the initial specified delay period. Subsequent executions are then scheduled in increments of the specified period after the initial delay
scheduleWithFixedDelay(Runnable command, long initialDelay, long delay, TimeUnit unit)	Creates and executes a periodic task that becomes available after the initial delay period. Subsequent executions are then scheduled with the specified delay period in between each execution

In the example for this recipe, the scheduleAtFixedRate() method is called, passing the task class, along with the initial delay period of five minutes, and then the task is executed every five minutes thereafter.

16-6. Creating Thread Instances

Problem

Your application requires the ability to perform tasks in the background while other tasks are executing.

Solution

Create thread instances to run tasks in the background by making use of a ManagedThreadFactory resource. Before an application can use the service, it must be created within the application server container. To create a ManagedThreadFactory instance within GlassFish, issue the following command from the command line:

```
asadmin create-managed-thread-factory concurrent/myThreadFactory
```

In this command, `name-of-service` can be whatever you choose. The `create-managed-thread-factory` command has many options that can be specified. To see and learn more about each option, invoke the command help by issuing the `--help` flag after the command, rather than providing the name of the service to create.

To utilize a `ManagedThreadFactory`, the environment must be configured via XML or annotation. To utilize XML configuration, add a `<resource-env-ref>` element to the `web.xml` deployment descriptor. In this case, you need to configure a resource of type `jakarta.enterprise.concurrent.ManagedThreadFactory`, as shown in the excerpt from the following `web.xml`:

```
<resource-env-ref>
 <description>
</description>
<resource-env-ref-name>
    concurrent/AcmeThreadFactory
</resource-env-ref-name>
 <resource-env-ref-type>
jakarta.enterprise.concurrent.ManagedThreadFactory
 </resource-env-ref-type>
</resource-env-ref>
```

To utilize annotations rather than XML configuration, the `ManagedThreadFactory` can be injected using an annotation such as the following:

```
@Resource(name="concurrent/AcmeThreadFactory");
ManagedThreadFactory threadFactory;
```

In this example, a `ManagedThreadFactory` will be injected into a Jakarta Enterprise Beans so that a logging task can be used to print output to the server log when the Jakarta Enterprise Beans is created or destroyed. The following code demonstrates how to create a task that can be utilized by the `ManagedThreadFactory`:

```
public class MessagePrinter implements Runnable {
    @Override
    public void run() {
        printMessage();
    }
    public void printMessage(){
        System.out.println("Here we are performing some work...");
    }
}
```

To initiate the threading, call the `ManagedThreadFactory`, which can be injected into a using class via the `@Resource` annotation. The `ManagedThreadFactory newThread()` method can then be invoked to spawn a new thread, passing the `Runnable` class instance for which the thread should process. In the following servlet context listener example, when a thread context is initialized, then a `Runnable` class that was listed in the previous code listing, `MessagePrinter`, is instantiated and passed to the `ManagedThreadFactory` to spawn a new thread:

```
public class ServletCtxListener implements ServletContextListener {
    Thread printerThread = null;
    @Resource(name ="concurrent/AcmeThreadFactory")
    ManagedThreadFactory threadFactory;
```

```
    public void contextInitialized(ServletContextEvent scEvent) {
        MessagePrinter printer = new MessagePrinter();
        printerThread = threadFactory.newThread(printer);
        printerThread.start();
    }
    public void contextDestroyed(ServletContextEvent scEvent) {
        synchronized (printerThread) {
            printerThread.interrupt();
        }
    }
}
```

How It Works

To utilize threading within an enterprise application, you should create ManagedThreadFactory resource(s) within the application server container, and utilize those resources within application(s), as needed.

To create a ManagedThreadFactory resource within the GlassFish application server, invoke the asadmin create-managed-thread-factory command from the command prompt. At a minimum, the desired name for the resource should be included with the invocation of the command. However, there are a number of different options that can be specified to customize the resource. To learn more about those options, please see the online documentation at https://jakarta.ee/specifications/concurrency/.

As mentioned in the example, an application can make use of a ManagedThreadFactory resource by configuring XML within the web.xml deployment descriptor or by injecting via the @Resource annotation within the classes that need to make use of the resource. Once that resource has been injected, calls can be made against it to spawn new threads using the newThread() method. The newThread() method returns a Thread instance, which can then be utilized as needed, by calling the Thread instance methods, as needed. In the solution to this recipe, the thread is started by calling the thread's start() method, and when the context is destroyed, then the thread's interrupt() method is invoked.

By adhering to the use of the ManagedThreadFactory API, your enterprise applications can be made multithreaded using an accepted standard solution.

16-7. Creating an Item-Oriented Batch Process

Problem

You would like to create a job that runs in the background and executes a task.

Solution

Make use of the Batch Applications for the Java Platform API to create a job that handles item-oriented processing. Batch processing that is item oriented is also known as "chunk" processing. In this example, a batch process is created to read text from a file, process that text accordingly, and then write out the processed text. To begin, construct an XML file to define the job. The XML file for this example will be called acmeFileProcessor.xml. We will break down the lines of this file, as well as discuss the different options for writing job XML, in the "How It Works" section. For now, let's look at what a job process looks like. The following lines are from the acmeFileProcessor.xml file:

```
<?xml version="1.0" encoding="UTF-8"?>
<job id="myJob" xmlns="http://batch.jsr352/jsl">
```

```
        <step id="readingStep" >
            <chunk item-count="2">
                <reader ref="acmeReader"></reader>
                <processor ref="acmeProcessor"></processor>
            </chunk>
        </step>
        <step id="writingStep" >
            <chunk item-count="1">
                <writer ref="acmeWriter"></writer>
            </chunk>
        </step>
</job>
```

There are three tasks being performed in this job: acmeReader, acmeProcessor, and acmeWriter. These three tasks can be associated with Java class implementations within the batch.xml file, which is located within the src/main/resources/META-INF directory. The following code shows what the batch.xml looks like:

```
<?xml version="1.0" encoding="UTF-8"?>
<batch-artifacts xmlns="http://jcp.org.batch/jsl">
    <ref id="acmeReader" class="org.jakartaeerecipe.chapter16.recipe16_07.AcmeReader"/>
    <ref id="acmeProcessor" class="org.jakartaeerecipe.chapter16.recipe16_07.
AcmeProcessor"/>
    <ref id="acmeWriter" class="org.jakartaeerecipe.chapter16.recipe16_07.AcmeWriter"/>
</batch-artifacts>
```

Next, let's look at each of these class implementations. We will begin by looking at the following AcmeReader class implementation. This class is responsible for reading a file and creating a new WidgetReportItem object for each line of text:

```
package org.jakartaeerecipe.chapter16.recipe16_07;

import java.nio.charset.Charset;
import java.nio.file.Files;
import java.nio.file.Path;
import java.nio.file.Paths;
import java.util.List;

import jakarta.batch.api.AbstractItemReader;
public class AcmeReader extends AbstractItemReader<WidgetReportItem> {
    public AcmeReader() {
    }
    /**
     * Read lines of report and store each into a WidgetReportItem object.
     * Once all lines have been read then return null to trigger the end of file.
     * @return
     * @throws Exception
     */
    @Override
    public WidgetReportItem readItem() throws Exception {
        Path file = Paths.get("widgetFile.txt");
        List<String> fileLines;
```

```
        Charset charset = Charset.forName("US-ASCII");
        fileLines = Files.readAllLines(file, charset);
        for(String line:fileLines){
            return new WidgetReportItem(line);
        }
        return null;
    }
}
```

Next, let's look at the AcmeProcessor class. This class is responsible for processing each WidgetReportItem accordingly. In this case, if the line of text that is contained in the object has the text "Two" in it, then it will be added to a WidgetOutputItem object (see the following code for WidgetReportItem and WidgetOutputItem):

```
package org.jakartaeerecipe.chapter16.recipe16_07;

import jakarta.batch.api.ItemProcessor;
public class AcmeProcessor implements ItemProcessor<WidgetReportItem, WidgetOutputItem> {
    public AcmeProcessor(){}
    /**
     * Write out all lines that contain the text "Two"
     * @param item
     * @return
     * @throws Exception
     */
    @Override
    public WidgetOutputItem processItem(WidgetReportItem item) throws Exception {
        if(item.getLineText().contains("Two")){
            return new WidgetOutputItem(item.getLineText());
        } else {
            return null;
        }
    }
}
```

Lastly, let's see what the AcmeWriter class looks like. This class is responsible for writing the WidgetOutputItem objects that have been processed by AcmeProcessor:

```
package org.jakartaeerecipe.chapter16.recipe16_07;
import java.util.List;
import jakarta.batch.api.AbstractItemWriter;

public class AcmeWriter extends AbstractItemWriter<WidgetOutputItem> {
    @Override
    public void writeItems(List<WidgetOutputItem> list) throws Exception {
        for(WidgetOutputItem item:list){
            System.out.println("Write to file:" + item.getLineText());
        }
    }
}
```

The WidgetReportItem and WidgetOutputItem objects are merely containers that hold a String of text. The following is the implementation for WidgetReportItem; other than the name, the WidgetOutputItem object is identical:

```
package org.jakartaeerecipe.chapter16.recipe16_07;
public class WidgetReportItem {
    private String lineText;
    public WidgetReportItem(String line){
        this.lineText = line;
    }
    /**
     * @return the lineText
     */
    public String getLineText() {
        return lineText;
    }
    /**
     * @param lineText the lineText to set
     */
    public void setLineText(String lineText) {
        this.lineText = lineText;
    }
}
```

When this batch job is executed, the text file is read and processed, and then specific lines of text are written to the system log. The read and process tasks are performed as part of the first step, and then the write is processed as the second step.

How It Works

Prior to the inclusion of Batch Applications for Java EE, organizations and individuals had to write their own custom procedures for processing batch jobs. Utilizing the Batch API, developers can create batch jobs using a combination of XML for defining a job and Java for programming the implementation. In the solution for this recipe, a simple batch job reads text from a file, processes it using a comparison, and then writes out the processed text. The example batch program is simplistic, but the API makes it easy to write very complex jobs.

Let's begin the explanation by first taking a brief look at the API from a high level. A job consists of one or more steps, and each step has exactly one ItemReader, ItemWriter, and ItemProcessor. A JobOperator is responsible for launching a job, and a JobRepository is used to maintain metadata regarding the currently running job. Jobs are defined via XML, and the <Job> element is at the root of the job definition. Thus, a <Job> is the foundational element, which consists of one or more <step> elements, and also defines other specifics of the job, such as the job name and if it is restartable or not. Each <step> of a job consists of one or more chunks or batchlets. In this recipe, which covers item-oriented processes, each step has just one chunk, although in general steps could encompass one or more chunks. To learn more about batchlets, please see the specification or online documentation at

https://jakarta.ee/specifications/batch/2.1/apidocs/jakarta.batch/jakarta/batch/api/batchlet

As expected, each chunk of a step is defined within the XML using a <chunk> element. A <chunk> element defines the reader, writer, and processor pattern of a batch job. A chunk runs within the scope of a transaction, and it is restartable at a checkpoint if it does not complete. The <reader> element is a child element of <chunk>, and it is used to specify the reader for that chunk. The <reader> element can accept zero or more name/value pair properties using a <properties> element. The <processor> element is also a child element of <chunk>, which specifies the processor element for that chunk. Like a <reader> element, a <processor> element can accept zero or more name/value pair properties using a <properties> element. The <writer> element is a child element of <chunk> as well, which specifies the writer for the chunk step. Again, like the reader and processor, the <writer> element can accept zero or more name/value pair properties using a <properties> element.

The XML configuration for a job resides in an XML file that should be named the same as the batch job to which it belongs. This file should reside within a folder named *batch-jobs*, which in turn resides in the META-INF folder. An XML file named batch.xml should also reside within the META-INF folder. This file contains the mapping for the item reader, writer, and processor elements using <ref> elements and mapping the item names to a Java implementation class:

```
<batch-artifacts xmlns="http://jcp.org.batch/jsl">
    <ref id="acmeReader" class="org.jakartaeerecipe.chapter16.recipe16_07.AcmeReader"/>
    <ref id="acmeProcessor" class="org.jakartaeerecipe.chapter16.recipe16_07.
    AcmeProcessor"/>
    <ref id="acmeWriter" class="org.jakartaeerecipe.chapter16.recipe16_07.AcmeWriter"/>
</batch-artifacts>
```

The implementation classes should either extend abstract classes (reader and writer) or implement an interface (processor). The ItemReader implementation class, in this case AcmeReader, extends the AbstractItemReader and accepts an object into which the read items will be stored. In the example for this recipe, that object class is named WidgetReportItem. As such, the class should implement the readItem() method, which is responsible for performing the reading. The method should return the object to which the items are read or return a null when there are no more items to read:

```
public class AcmeReader extends AbstractItemReader<WidgetReportItem> {
...
@Override
    public WidgetReportItem readItem() throws Exception {
        Path file = Paths.get("widgetFile.txt");
        List<String> fileLines;
        Charset charset = Charset.forName("US-ASCII");
        fileLines = Files.readAllLines(file, charset);
        for(String line:fileLines){
            return new WidgetReportItem(line);
        }
        return null;
    }
}
...
```

The ItemProcessor class implementation, in this case AcmeProcessor, is responsible for performing processing for the chunk, and it should implement the ItemProcessor interface, accepting both the object containing the read items and an object to which the processed items will be stored. The ItemProcessor implementation class should implement a processItem method, which is responsible for performing the processing.

The ItemWriter class implementation, in this case AcmeWriter, is responsible for performing the writing for the chunk. The class implementation should extend the AbstractItemWriter class and accept the object to which the processed items will be written. This implementation must contain the writeItems method, which is responsible for performing the writing.

As mentioned in the introduction to this chapter, the Jakarta Batch API is very detailed, and this recipe barely scratches the surface of how to write batch jobs.

CHAPTER 17

Jakarta NoSQL

Microservices and applications built for the cloud sometimes benefit from a noncentralized database, and many of the most used are NoSQL databases. NoSQL means "Not Only SQL," and such databases do not follow the conventional Relational Database Management System (RDBMS) model. Jakarta NoSQL is a specification that aims to provide standardized Java APIs for connecting Java-based applications with some of the popular NoSQL databases. For further details, visit the project site at `https://jakarta.ee/specifications/nosql/`. This chapter provides a sneak preview of the Jakarta NoSQL specification, which includes two layers:

1. *Communication API*: A driver for most of the well-known NoSQL databases, the Jakarta NoSQL Database Driver. (To learn more about this, refer to `https://github.com/eclipse/jnosql-communication-driver.`)

2. *Mapping API*: A layer for integrating Java into NoSQL databases using annotations and CDI. It also integrates with other Jakarta EE technologies like Bean Validation, etc. (To learn more about this, refer to `https://github.com/eclipse/jnosql-mapping-extension.`)

The communication API consists of different modules for working with several NoSQL database types such as ArangoDB, Cassandra, Couchbase, DynamoDB, Elasticsearch, Hazelcast, HBase, Infinispan, Memcached, MongoDB, OrientDB, RavenDB, Redis, Riak, and Solr.

This chapter will not dive deep into the functionality of these APIs, but, rather, it will provide a brief overview for the utilization of Jakarta NoSQL with one of the most widely used NoSQL databases, MongoDB. It will also briefly touch upon the use of key value–oriented databases such as Hazelcast.

Note MongoDB is a document database, and it is helpful to know that while working with a document database, we refer to collections of data. A collection in a document database is analogous to a table in an RDBMS. To learn more about MongoDB, please refer to the online documentation: `https://docs.mongodb.com/manual/`.

This chapter will cover some high-level basics for using the Jakarta NoSQL specification. As the specification is not part of the Jakarta EE 10 release, portions of it are subject to change prior to its inclusion with the Jakarta EE platform.

17-1. Configuring for Jakarta NoSQL

Problem

You would like to configure your Jakarta EE application to work with a NoSQL database, rather than a traditional Relational Database Management System.

Solution

Add the appropriate dependencies to your project, depending upon the type of NoSQL database that you wish to utilize. Next, create a class to load the database and enable it for use within the application. In this example, a document database will be configured using MongoDB.

The first dependency that is required for working with Jakarta NoSQL is known as Mapping Extensions, which is the core API.

■ **Note**   Please refer to the Artemis documentation at `https://github.com/eclipse/jnosql-mapping-extension`.

```
<dependency
    <groupId>jakarta.nosql.mapping</groupId>
    <artifactId>mapping-core</artifactId>
    <version>1.0.0-b3</version>
</dependency>
```

The jakarta.nosql.mapping dependency that pertains to the type of database in use is also required. There are three such dependencies:

- Document

- Key-value

- Column

Next, the API for the database type will need to be added to the project. The following excerpts show the Maven dependencies for each of the APIs. Only one of the following dependencies is required to work with the API in a project, depending upon which type of NoSQL database is being used:

```
<--mapping-document -->
<dependency>
    <groupId>jakarta.nosql.mapping</groupId>
    <artifactId>mapping-document</artifactId>
    <version>1.0.0-b3</version>
</dependency>
<!-- mapping-key-value -->
<dependency>
    <groupId>jakarta.nosql.mapping</groupId>
    <artifactId>mapping-key-value</artifactId>
    <version>1.0.0-b3</version>
</dependency>
<!-- mapping-column -->
```

```
<dependency>
    <groupId>jakarta.nosql.mapping</groupId>
    <artifactId>mapping-column</artifactId>
    <version>1.0.0-b3</version>
</dependency>
```

There is a required driver dependency for supporting most NoSQL databases, and it is provided by Eclipse Jakarta NoSQL. Depending upon which type of database is being used, the correct driver needs to be pulled into the project. A list of each driver is located on GitHub: https://github.com/eclipse/jnosql-communication-driver.

In the following POM excerpt, the mongodb driver is being utilized:

```
<dependency>
    <groupId>jakarta.nosql.communication</groupId>
    <artifactId>communication-document</artifactId>
    <version>1.0.0-b3</version>
</dependency>
<dependency>
    <groupId>org.eclipse.jnosql.communication</groupId>
    <artifactId>mongodb-driver</artifactId>
    <version>1.0.0-b3</version>
</dependency>
```

Lastly, provide the appropriate configuration via a properties file on the CLASSPATH or as hard-coded values. The configuration should include the hostname, port number, and possibly credentials. In this case, hard-coded values are added to configure the database within a class. In the following source code, a class named DocumentCollectionManagerProducer is used to get the database configured and generate a DocumentCollectionManager, which can be used to work with the data:

```
package org.jakarateerecipe.chapter17;

import jakarta.enterprise.context.ApplicationScoped;
import jakarta.enterprise.inject.Produces;
import jakarta.nosql.Settings;
import jakarta.nosql.document.DocumentCollectionManagerFactory;
import jakarta.nosql.document.DocumentConfiguration;
import org.eclipse.jnosql.communication.mongodb.document.MongoDBDocumentConfiguration;

import java.util.Collections;
import java.util.Map;

@ApplicationScoped
public class DocumentCollectionManagerProducer {
    // setting the name of the database
    private static final String COLLECTION = "acmepools";
    private DocumentConfiguration configuration;
    private DocumentCollectionManagerFactory managerFactory;

    @PostConstruct
    public void init() {
        configuration = new MongoDBDocumentConfiguration();
```

```
    Map<String, Object> settings = Collections.singletonMap("mongodb-server-host-1",
    "localhost:27017");
    managerFactory = configuration.get(Settings.of(settings));
}

@Produces
public DocumentCollectionManagerProducer getManager() {
    return managerFactory.get(COLLECTION);
}
}
```

The DocumentCollectionManagerProducer can be injected into a class, and the
DocumentCollectionManager can then be called upon to work with the data.

How It Works

As with any database configuration for an application, a NoSQL database requires a bit of setup. The
configuration that is necessary for a NoSQL application can be equated to the DriverManager or
EntityManager configuration for JDBC or JPA.

To begin, there are several dependencies, but the nice thing is that the Jakarta NoSQL specification
contains all of them, so there is no need to rummage around the Web or Maven Central to find them. In
order to incorporate the appropriate dependencies for use with NoSQL, you must also know which type
of database is being used. There are different dependencies for each of the NoSQL database types, as
mentioned in the previous section.

The communication layer defines three modules: diana-key-value, diana-column, and diana-
document. Each of these modules corresponds to the respective NoSQL database type. The NoSQL mapping
databases are not covered by the communication module, as they are already handled by Apache TinkerPop
(https://tinkerpop.apache.org/).

■ **Note**　Apache TinkerPop is a graph computing framework for both graph databases and graph analytic
systems.

Each of the database types requires a necessary setting to be put into place, such as a database host
and port. In a document-, column-, or key value–oriented database, these settings can be placed into a
configuration file and then put onto the CLASSPATH. They can also be hard-coded within an application, as
follows:

```
Map<String, Object> map = new HashMap<>();
map.put("mongodb-server-host-1", "localhost:27017");
```

The next API, also known as Mapping Extensions, is used for mapping NoSQL database data to Java
classes, much like object-relational mapping with standard databases. The configuration dependency is
required to use the mapping API, as well as the corresponding Artemis driver for the database type that is in
use. In the case of using a document database, the artemis-document dependency is used. The important
piece of the configuration is to initialize the database by providing the host, port, username, and password
(if required). There are various methodologies which could be followed for initializing the database, from
using a main method in a Java SE application to using an @ApplicationScoped CDI bean in an enterprise
application.

In the example, an @ApplicationScoped bean contains the initialization of the database within a method annotated with @PostConstruct. Any methods designated as @PostConstruct are executed directly after the bean has been initialized. Since the bean in the example is application scoped, it is started up when the application starts. In this case, a DocumentConfiguration is instantiated from MongoDbDocumentConfiguration. A Map is then used to store some configuration settings, which could alternatively be placed into a properties file on the CLASSPATH. The Map of settings is then set into the DocumentConfiguration, and a DocumentCollectionManagerFactory is returned. This manager will be used by the application to perform database interactions.

17-2. Writing a Query for a Document Database

Problem

You have configured an application to utilize a document-based NoSQL database, and now you wish to obtain data by creating a query.

Solution

Utilize the DocumentCollectionManager of the configuration in Recipe 17-1 to initiate a query against a collection. In this example, the DocumentTemplate is injected into a managed bean, and it is used to query the collection of Pool within the acmepools database. The following example shows an excerpt of the code for a query within the managed bean:

```
package org.jakarateerecipe.chapter17.service;

import jakarta.nosql.mapping.document.DocumentTemplate;
import jakarta.nosql.document.Document;
import jakarta.nosql.document.DocumentEntity;
import jakarta.nosql.document.DocumentQuery;
...
@Inject
    DocumentTemplate documentTemplate;
...
DocumentQuery query = select().from("Pool")
                .where("_id").eq(id).build();
```

This particular query selects from the Pool collection where the _id is equal to the provided value. To obtain the value from the query, it can be passed to an injected DocumentTemplate instance, which will return an optional result:

```
...
Optional<Customer> customerOptional = documentTemplate.singleResult(query);
        System.out.println("Entity found: " + customerOptional.get());
```

How It Works

When querying with the Jakarta NoSQL API, it has a very similar feel to utilizing the `CriteriaQuery` API. Tables 17-1 and 17-2 show the various builder methods that can be utilized to help generate queries for a document database.

Table 17-1. *DocumentQuery.DocumentFrom Methods*

Builder Method	Description
`limit`	Defines the max number of results to retrieve
`orderBy(String name)`	Determines the order by which results will be displayed
`skip(long skip)`	Defines the position of the first retrieved result
`where(String name)`	Starts a new condition defining the column name

Table 17-2. *DocumentQuery.DocumentWhere Methods*

Builder Method	Description
`between`	Creates a between condition
`eq`	Creates an equal condition
`gt`	Creates a greater than condition
`gte`	Creates a greater than or equal condition
`in`	Creates an in condition
`like`	Creates a like condition
`lt`	Creates a less than condition
`lte`	Creates a less than or equal condition
`not`	Creates the not equal condition

The following example shows how to select all records of the collection:

```
DocumentQuery query = select().from("Pool").build();
List<DocumentEntity> entities = manager.getManager().select(query);
```

■ **Note** If using a different type of NoSQL database, there are similar builder techniques that can be used for retrieving the data. For more information on using Jakarta NoSQL to query each of the types of NoSQL databases, please refer to the documentation: `https://jakarta.ee/specifications/nosql/`.

One can either inject a DocumentTemplate into a CDI bean as shown in the example or obtain it from an SeContainer if using in a Java SE environment. Taking a look at the latter, one can obtain an SeContainer by calling upon an SeContainerInitializer and then obtain a DocumentTemplate from that container by passing DocumentTemplate.class to the container select() method:

```
try (SeContainer se = SeContainerInitializer.newInstance().initialize()){
    DocumentTemplate documentTemplate = se.select(DocumentTemplate.class).get();
    DocumentQuery query = select().from("Pool").build();
    List<Pool> results = documentTemplate.select(query);
    ...
}
```

The Jakarta NoSQL specification allows one to query document-oriented NoSQL databases, as well as other types of NoSQL databases, in a standardized manner.

17-3. Inserting, Updating, and Deleting from a Document-Oriented Database

Problem

You wish to utilize your application to perform standard CRUD operations against a document-oriented NoSQL database.

Solution

Utilize the DocumentCollectionManagerFactory that was generated as part of the configuration (Recipe 17-1) to obtain a manager which can be used for creating, reading, updating, or deleting data from the document-oriented database:

```
package org.jakarateerecipe.chapter17.service;

import com.mongodb.MongoWriteException;

import jakarta.inject.Inject;
import jakarta.nosql.document.Document;
import jakarta.nosql.document.DocumentDeleteQuery;
import jakarta.nosql.document.DocumentEntity;
import jakarta.nosql.document.DocumentQuery;

import jakarta.nosql.mapping.document.DocumentTemplate;

import jakarta.ws.rs.*;

import org.jakarateerecipe.chapter17.DocumentCollectionManagerProducer;
import org.jakarateerecipe.chapter17.entity.Customer;
import org.jakarateerecipe.chapter17.entity.Pool;

import java.util.Random;
import java.util.stream.Stream;
```

```
import static jakarta.nosql.document.DocumentDeleteQuery.delete;
import static jakarta.nosql.document.DocumentQuery.select;

@Path("acmepools")
public class AcmePoolsService {

    @Inject
    DocumentCollectionManagerProducer manager;

    @Inject
    DocumentTemplate documentTemplate;

    // ...
    // ...

}
```

Inserting

There are a couple of different techniques that can be used for generating new entities within a document-oriented database: utilization of the DocumentTemplate or utilization of a DocumentEntity.

When using a DocumentTemplate to create an entity, the workflow is very similar to that of the Jakarta Persistence API along with the Criteria API. Taking a look at the following code, which was excerpted from the AcmePoolsService class within the AcmePoolsNoSql project, one can see that objects are created using plain Java, and then they are inserted into the database using the document template. In this case, the DocumentTemplate has been injected into the CDI bean:

```
@GET
    @Path("testDocumentDb")
    public String testDocumentDb() {

        Random random = new Random();
        Long id = random.nextLong();
        StringBuilder builder = new StringBuilder("");
        Customer customer = new Customer("Josh", "Juneau", "123 AcmeWay", "JavaLand",
        "JJ", "12345");
// ...
```

Use the DocumentEntity construct along with a DocumentCollectionManagerFactory to generate a new entity for addition to an existing collection of data, and then use the manager to insert the entity. To verify this method, make a GET request to the following endpoint: http://localhost:8080/JakartaEERecipes_Chapter17-1.0-SNAPSHOT/rest/acmepools/testDocumentDb.

Updating

To update an entity, modify the DocumentEntity instance and then pass it to the insert() method. The following is the code excerpt from the AcmePoolsService class; here, a new entity is created and added to the existing pool collection of data:

```
@POST
    @Path("createNewDocument/{id}")
    public void createNewDocument(@PathParam("id") int id) {
        System.out.println("Insert new document with ID: " + id);
        if (id > 0) {
            // Utilize DocumentEntity to create a document
            try {
                DocumentEntity documentEntity = DocumentEntity.of("Pool");
                documentEntity.add(Document.of("_id", id));
                documentEntity.add(Document.of("length", 30.0));
                documentEntity.add(Document.of("width", 15.0));
                DocumentEntity saved = manager.getManager().insert(documentEntity);
                //Update Document
                saved.add(Document.of("Customer", "Juneau"));
                DocumentEntity updated = manager.getManager().update(documentEntity);
            } catch (MongoWriteException e) {
                System.out.println("Error: " + e);
            }
        } else {
            System.out.println("You cannot insert a NULL entity, please provide an id");
        }
    }
}
```

To verify this method, make a POST request to the following endpoint: http://localhost:8080/
JakartaEERecipes_Chapter17-1.0-SNAPSHOT/rest/acmepools/createNewDocument/{id}.

Replace the path parameter {id} with any number representing the document ID, for example, 1234.

Deleting

The DocumentDeleteQuery interface can be used to easily delete an entity from a collection of data:

```
public void deleteDocument(){
    DocumentDeleteQuery delete =         delete().from("Pools").where("length").
                                         gte(36.0).build();
    manager.getManager().delete(delete);
}
```

How It Works

In Jakarta NoSQL, DocumentTemplate can be utilized for performing CRUD operations against a NoSQL
database. The DocumentTemplate can be used to perform transactions against jakarta.nosql.mapping.
Entity classes, much like the Java Persistence API. When utilizing a DocumentCollectionManager,
persistence methods can be called upon to invoke behavior, passing DocumentEntity objects or
DocumentQuery objects.

A DocumentTemplate can either be injected via CDI or created from an SeContainer instance. Once
created, it can be used to perform operations with entity classes. In the example for inserting, the Pool
entity was created and then inserted using the DocumentTemplate.insert() method. Table 17-3 shows the
different methods available via a DocumentTemplate.

Table 17-3. *Methods of the DocumentTemplate Interface*

Method	Description
insert(T entity)	Inserts an entity into a collection
insert(T entity, Duration)	Inserts an entity with time to live
insert(Iterable<T> entities)	Saves a collection of entities
insert(Iterable<T> entities, Duration)	Saves a collection of entities with time to live
update(T entity)	Updates an entity
update(Iterable<T> entities)	Updates a collection of entities
delete(DocumentDeleteQuery)	Deletes an entity obtained via query
select(DocumentQuery)	Selects entities from a query
query(String query)	Executes a query
singleResult(String query)	Executes a query and returns a single unique result
prepare(String query)	Creates a PreparedStatement from a query
find(T entity, ID)	Find an entity class by ID
delete(T entity, ID)	Delete an entity class by ID
count(String documentCollection)	Returns the number of elements in a document collection
count(T entityType)	Returns the number of elements in a document collection
singleResult(DocumentQuery)	Executes a query and returns a single unique result

The remainder of the examples in this recipe demonstrated various persistence transactions utilizing a DocumentCollectionManager. This, too, can be injected via CDI or created from an SeContainer instance. In a Jakarta EE application, typically the configuration will take place within a single @ApplicationScoped bean, which @Produces a DocumentCollectionManager (see Recipe 17-1).

When using a DocumentCollectionManager, call upon the various persistence methods, passing either DocumentQuery or DocumentEntity objects.

In the examples, a DocumentEntity for a Pool is constructed and inserted using the DocumentCollectionManager. Taking a different approach in the next example, a DocumentDeleteQuery is constructed to delete an entity from the Pool collection. The DocumentCollectionManager delete() method is then invoked, passing the DocumentDeleteQuery object. Table 17-4 shows the methods available on a DocumentCollectionManager.

Table 17-4. *Methods of the DocumentCollectionManager Interface*

Method	Description
`close()`	Closes a resource
`delete(DocumentDeleteQuery)`	Deletes an entity obtained via a query
`insert(DocumentEntity)`	Inserts an entity
`insert(DocumentEntity, Duration)`	Inserts an entity with time to live
`insert(Iterable<DocumentEntity>)`	Inserts a collection of `DocumentEntity`
`insert(Iterable<DocumentEntity>, Duration)`	Inserts a collection of `DocumentEntity` with time to live
`select(DocumentQuery)`	Selects one or more entities from a collection using a `DocumentQuery`
`singleResult(DocumentQuery)`	Selects a single unique result from a collection using a `DocumentQuery`
`update(DocumentEntity)`	Updates an entity
`update(Iterable<DocumentEntity>)`	Updates a collection of `DocumentEntity`

Either way you choose to perform CRUD operations, the API is straightforward. The choice of which option to use is in the hands of the developer. It is time to choose the best tool for the job.

17-4. Working with a Key-Value Database

Problem

You wish to place values into a key-value database and also retrieve them at a later point. For example, you wish to utilize Hazelcast with the Jakarta NoSQL API.

Solution

Configure your application to work with a key-value NoSQL database. Once configured, utilize a `KeyValueConfiguration` to generate a `BucketManagerFactory`. The `BucketManagerFactory` can then be used to work with key/value pairs.

The following dependency will need to be added to your project in order to support Hazelcast with Jakarta NoSQL, along with the standard artemis-core dependency:

```
<dependency>
        <groupId>org.eclipse.jnosql.communication</groupId>
        <artifactId>hazelcast-driver</artifactId>
        <version>1.0.0-b3</version>
</dependency>
```

⬛ **Note** Hazelcast is an open source in-memory data grid based on Java.

Once the dependency has been added, configuration can take place. The following sample source code demonstrates key-value database configuration:

```
import org.eclipse.jnosql.communication.hazelcast.keyvalue.HazelcastKeyValueConfiguration;
import jakarta.nosql.keyvalue.BucketManager;
import jakarta.nosql.keyvalue.BucketManagerFactory;
import jakarta.nosql.keyvalue.KeyValueConfiguration;
import jakarta.nosql.keyvalue.KeyValueEntity;

// ...
KeyValueConfiguration configuration = new HazelcastKeyValueConfiguration();
BucketManagerFactory managerFactory = configuration.get();
BucketManager bucketManager = managerFactory.getBucketManager("Pools");
```

A Plain Old Java Object (POJO) can be used to contain the data, and the BucketManager is used to perform the transactions. In the following case, a Pool object has been populated, and a BucketManager is being used to insert the object into the database:

```
KeyValueEntity entity = KeyValueEntity.of(pool.getLength(), pool.Id);
bucketManager.put(entity);
```

How It Works

To refer back to Recipe 17-2, the key value–oriented database configuration is very similar to document oriented. Typically, in a Jakarta EE application, one would create an @ApplicationScoped bean in which to place the configuration of type KeyValueConfiguration. The bean also contains a manager, just like the document-oriented database. However, this manager is a BucketManager, and it will be the basis for performing transactions against the database. In a Java SE environment, the BucketManager can be obtained from the SeContainer instance. In an enterprise environment, the BucketManager can be injected via CDI.

In order to perform transactions against a key-value NoSQL database, utilize the various methods that are available when calling upon the BucketManager. Table 17-5 lists some methods of the BucketManager interface.

Table 17-5. *BucketManager Methods*

Method	Description
close()	Closes the resource
delete(Iterable keys)	Removes entities from keys
delete(K key)	Removes an entity from a key
get(Iterable keys)	Finds a list of values, given keys
get(K key)	Finds a value, given a key
prepare(String query)	Executes a query and returns the result
put(Iterable entities)	Saves the iterable of keys
put(KeyValueEntity entity)	Saves the KeyValueEntity
put(K key, V value)	Associates the specified value with a key

The utilization of a key-value NoSQL database can prove to make code easy to maintain and provides for a well-performing application. The Jakarta NoSQL API is a powerful means for working with key-value databases.

CHAPTER 18

■ ■ ■

Jakarta EE Application Server

The GlassFish application server is the industry standard for Jakarta EE. GlassFish 7 is the reference implementation for Jakarta EE, so it contained more up-to-date features than any other Jakarta EE–compliant application server available at the time of Jakarta EE 10 releases. It is a fully featured and easy-to-manage application server, making it a powerful choice for deploying modern and robust Jakarta EE applications. Although plenty of excellent application server choices are available, with many of them being Jakarta EE 10 compliant or working in that direction, GlassFish will remain the best choice for those who want to utilize the most current implementations in the Jakarta EE space since it is the reference implementation for the platform at the time of this writing. The downside to utilizing GlassFish is that there is currently no production support offered for the server, as it is open source and not a licensed vendor product.

Aside from GlassFish, there are a number of excellent Jakarta EE–compliant application servers that do contain vendor support. Many of these options provide commercially licensed implementations, as well as open source or "free to use" releases. Some servers of this ilk are Payara Server, Apache TomEE, WildFly, and Open Liberty. Some of these options provide paid support, and all of these options are fully Jakarta EE 10 compliant. Many others are also planning for compliance soon.

Another realm for delivering Jakarta EE applications and services is in the microservices and cloud space. Such applications and services in this space are not deployed to a traditional application server container, but instead deployed to micro-containers and cloud platforms. This chapter focuses on working with GlassFish 7, the reference implementation. It also covers the basics of developing microservices with Jakarta EE and working with container solutions such as Docker.

18-1. Installing GlassFish and Starting Up

Problem

You want to install the Eclipse GlassFish application server for Jakarta EE 10 development on your machine. Once installed, you want to start the server so that you can begin to use it.

Solution

Download a GlassFish 7 ZIP archive from the site `https://glassfish.org/download` and unzip the contents of the archive onto your operating system. If you are looking for the most current development releases of GlassFish, visit the download section of the project page. For the purposes of this recipe example, let's assume you are going to install the GlassFish 7 server into a directory named `/JAVA_DEV/GlassFish` on *nix systems or OS X or named `C:\JAVA_DEV\GlassFish` on Windows.

Once you have downloaded and unzipped the archive, you are ready to begin the installation process. The unzipped archive will be in a root directory named `glassfish`. Copy the `glassfish` directory and all of its contents into the `/JAVA_DEV/GlassFish` directory. The folder structure of the installation directory is as in Figure 18-1.

© Josh Juneau and Tarun Telang 2022
J. Juneau and T. Telang, *Java EE to Jakarta EE 10 Recipes*, https://doi.org/10.1007/978-1-4842-8079-9_18

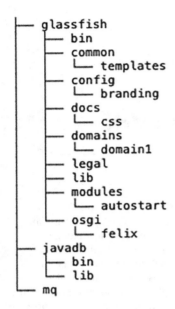

```
├── glassfish
│   ├── bin
│   ├── common
│   │   └── templates
│   ├── config
│   │   └── branding
│   ├── docs
│   │   └── css
│   ├── domains
│   │   └── domain1
│   ├── legal
│   ├── lib
│   ├── modules
│   │   └── autostart
│   └── osgi
│       └── felix
├── javadb
│   ├── bin
│   └── lib
└── mq
```

Figure 18-1. *GlassFish installation directory folder structure*

You are now ready to start the server and/or begin configuring your GlassFish application server.

How It Works

The GlassFish application servers can be installed by simply downloading the ZIP archive and unzipping it into the directory of your choice. Once this is completed, you are ready to begin configuring your server environment. The first step of configuring your environment should be to change the default administrator password, which is outlined in Recipe 18-2. However, if you are anxious to test your environment, you can traverse into the <<glassfish>>/bin directory and start the server using the following command:

*nix and OS X:

```
./asadmin start-domain domain1
```

Windows:

```
asadmin start-domain domain1
```

■ **Note**   The first time you start the application server using this command, it will not contain an administrative password. It is not recommended to start the application server without first setting the administrator password unless you are on an operating system with a firewall configuration, as doing so can leave your system vulnerable. For more information on setting or changing the administrator user password, see Recipe 18-2.

18-2. Changing the Administrator User Password

Problem

You want to add security to your newly installed GlassFish environment by changing the administrative user password.

Solution

Traverse into the server /bin directory within your terminal or command prompt and enter the following:

```
./asadmin change-admin-password
```

After issuing the command, follow the prompts accordingly to change the administrator password, as shown in Figure 18-2.

```
$ ./asadmin change-admin-password
Enter admin user name [default: admin]>
Enter the admin password>
Enter the new admin password>
Enter the new admin password again>
Command change-admin-password executed successfully.
$
```

Figure 18-2. *change-admin-password command*

18-3. Deploying a WAR File

Problem

You want to deploy a WAR archive to the application server so that your web application will be available for use.

Solution

Utilize the GlassFish application server's auto-deployment option by logging in to the application server host machine if you haven't done so already. Browse the file system to find the WAR file that you want to deploy. Copy the desired WAR file. Locate the auto-deployment directory (path) and paste the WAR file inside it. The application server will complete the deployment, assuming that there are no configuration issues with the application archive.

How It Works

To make a web application accessible to users on the Web, it must be deployed to the application server. GlassFish has a couple of very easy techniques for deploying applications for use. Java web applications can be packaged in a few different ways before deploying. To further understand the deployment process, it helps to look at the variety of possible deployment scenarios for a Java enterprise application.

In the early days of Jakarta EE, the most common package structure was an enterprise archive (EAR) file. An EAR file is an archive that consists of one or more modules, usually in Java archive (JAR) file format, along with XML deployment descriptors. The standard EAR structure contains two JAR files along with XML deployment descriptors. One of those JAR files contains the web sources, including the HTML, JSP, JSF, JavaScript, the WEB-INF directory, and other files used for displaying web content. This JAR file is known as the *web module*, and it corresponds to a web application as defined within the Jakarta Servlet specification. The second JAR file contains the Java sources that are packaged and used for the business logic of the application. Together, the two packages can be combined into an EAR file and deployed to a Jakarta EE application server, in which case the application server takes on the task of using the XML deployment descriptors to place the different modules into their proper locations within the application server. EAR files are still in use today, and most applications written using Java EE 5 and older are deployed using an EAR file format. Until recently, EAR files were the most common way to distribute and deploy Java EE applications.

Currently, the most common type of archive for Jakarta EE web application deployment is the web archive (WAR). WAR files are archives that contain all of the web markup and Java sources together under the same archive module. Typically, those Java web applications that contained no enterprise application structures, such as EJBs, web services, or the like, could be deployed using the WAR file format. Since Java EE 6, all enterprise applications can be deployed in the WAR file format as well, which makes it much easier to package and deploy an application. Although if you're using a Java IDE, the work is done for you, so deployment of WAR files is much faster than that of the EAR file, and it is much easier to work with all of an application's source files within the same module, rather than using more than one.

Both the EAR and WAR file formats are simply ZIP files that contain either the .ear or .war extension. As a matter of fact, you can easily view the contents of these archives by renaming them with a .zip extension and unzipping them to your file system. The GlassFish application server makes it easy to deploy each file type, whether using the administration console or the auto-deploy technique. When the application server is deploying the archives, it unpackages the contents of the archives into the deployment directory, which is located in the <GlassFish-Home>/glassfish/domains/domain1/applications directory.

▪ **Note**   It is possible to edit web files after an application has been deployed by updating the files that exist in the deployment directory. Any XHTML, HTML, JS, or other code files that do not need to be compiled, along with JSPs that are compiled on the fly, can be updated in place while the application is up and running. This can sometimes prove useful for making minor layout or JavaScript changes while in production. However, remember that if the application is undeployed or another application is deployed in place of an existing application, then all sources within the deployment directory are deleted.

18-4. Adding a Database Resource

Problem

Your application utilizes an underlying RDBMS, and you want to configure a database resource for this purpose.

Solution

Create a connection pool resource for the database to which you want to connect. After the connection pool has been created, define a new JDBC resource, which will be used to provide applications with a means to connect to the database. To perform these tasks, first log in to the GlassFish administration console (http://localhost:4848/) and then expand the JDBC menu under the Resources option within the tree menu on the left, as shown in Figure 18-3.

Figure 18-3. *GlassFish administration console: JDBC Resources*

Next, click the JDBC Connection Pools menu option, which will open the JDBC Connection Pools panel on the right side of the screen. Here, you will be provided with a list of the current connection pools, as well as buttons to add new pools or delete existing pools. Click the New button to initiate the creation of a new connection pool.

This will open the New JDBC Connection Pool (Step 1 of 2) panel, as shown in Figure 18-4. In this panel, specify the name of the pool you want to create, and then select a resource type and a database vendor from the selection lists.

New JDBC Connection Pool (Step 1 of 2)

[Next] [Cancel]

Identify the general settings for the connection pool.

* Indicates required field

General Settings

Pool Name: *

MyDataSource

Resource Type:

javax.sql.DataSource ∨

Must be specified if the datasource class implements more than 1 of the interface.

Database Driver Vendor: ∨

Oracle

Select or enter a database driver vendor

Introspect: ☐

If enabled, data source or driver implementation class names will enable introspection.

Figure 18-4. *New JDBC Connection Pool (Step 1 of 2) panel*

After clicking the Next button to continue, the second screen for creating a new JDBC connection pool will be displayed (see Figure 18-5), which contains a number of settings to help configure the connection pool. For instance, the datasource class name can be selected, pool settings can be adjusted, and transaction management options can be tweaked. I recommend retaining all of the default configurations unless it has been determined that something needs to be adjusted in order for application functionality. You can always revisit the connection pool settings and adjust them later if needed.

New JDBC Connection Pool (Step 2 of 2)

Previous | Finish | Cancel

Identify the general settings for the connection pool. Datasource Classname or Driver Classname must be specified for the connection pool.

* Indicates required field

General Settings

Pool Name:	MyDataSource
Resource Type:	javax.sql.DataSource
Database Driver Vendor:	Oracle
Datasource Classname:	oracle.jdbc.datasource.impl.OracleConnectionPoolDataSource ∨

Select or enter vendor-specific classname that implements the DataSource and/or XADataSource APIs

Driver Classname: ∨

Select or enter vendor-specific classname that implements the java.sql.Driver interface.

Ping: ☐
When enabled, the pool is pinged during creation or reconfiguration to identify and warn of any erroneous values for its attributes

Description:

Pool Settings

Initial and Minimum Pool Size: `8` Connections
Minimum and initial number of connections maintained in the pool

Maximum Pool Size: `32` Connections
Maximum number of connections that can be created to satisfy client requests

Pool Resize Quantity: `2` Connections
Number of connections to be removed when pool idle timeout expires

Idle Timeout: `300` Seconds
Maximum time that connection can remain idle in the pool

Max Wait Time: `60000` Milliseconds
Amount of time caller waits before connection timeout is sent

Transaction

Non Transactional Connections: ☐
Returns non-transactional connections

Transaction Isolation: ∨
If unspecified, use default level for JDBC Driver

Isolation Level: ☑ Guaranteed
All connections use same isolation level; requires Transaction Isolation

Figure 18-5. New JDBC Connection Pool (Step 2 of 2) panel

At the bottom of the form, you will find the Additional Properties table (see Figure 18-6), which is where you need to enter the specifics pertaining to the database connection you want to configure. While there are a number of properties listed in the table by default, you need to enter values only for a user, password, and URL in order to obtain a connection. Once you've entered this detail, you will be able to click the Finish button to create the pool.

Additional Properties (8)

Add Property | Delete Properties

Select	Name	Value	Description
☐	roleName		
☐	networkProtocol		
☐	User	app	
☐	DatabaseName	sample	
☐	serverName	localhost	
☐	PortNumber	1527	
☐	URL	jdbc:derby://localhost:1527/sample	
☐	Password	app	

Figure 18-6. Additional JDBC connection properties

■ **Note** You must have the database driver (JAR file) for the database you want to use installed within the application server. To do so, simply copy the JAR file into the `<GlassFish-Home>/glassfish7/domains/domain1/lib` directory. For instance, to enable the use of the Oracle database driver, download the JDBC driver file called `ojdbc7.jar` and use that.

Once the pool has been created, you can generate a JDBC resource for use from within your applications. The JDBC resource is basically a string identifier that references your database connection pool, and it is used from within a web application's `persistence.xml` unit to utilize an application server connection pool. To create the JDBC resource, click the JDBC Resources menu option from within the tree menu, which will open the JDBC Resources pane (see Figure 18-7), listing each of the existing resources. Click New in order to configure a new resource.

Select	JNDI Name	Logical JNDI Name	Enabled	Connection Pool	Description
☐	jdbc/DerbyConnection		✓	DerbyPool	
☐	jdbc/PostgresConnection		✓	PostgreSQL	
☐	jdbc/__TimerPool		✓	__TimerPool	
☐	jdbc/__default	java:comp/DefaultDataSource	✓	DerbyPool	
☐	jdbc/sample		✓	SamplePool	

Resources (5) — New... Delete Enable Disable

Figure 18-7. JDBC Resources pane

How It Works

Just about every enterprise application uses an underlying database to store and retrieve data. To connect to the database, you need to configure a database account for which to connect and code a connection utility that is responsible for opening and closing connections. Well, that is one way to do it; another way is to rely on the application server to manage the database connections. Utilizing an application server's database connection pool can be very useful because it takes away the burden of handling connections within the application's business logic, and it also helps the overall performance of an application by maintaining a number of open connections in a pool. When a process needs to work with the database, it grabs one of the open connection objects, uses it, and then places it back into the pool when finished. By maintaining this pool, the overhead of opening and closing connections for every single task is alleviated, helping your applications perform much faster. Another benefit to having the application server manage connections is that the username and password used to obtain the connection are stored in only one place, the application server. Usernames and passwords do not need to be hard-coded into applications that use application server JDBC resources. This can be helpful not only from a security standpoint but also from a maintenance stance. Isn't it much easier to change the password in one location when it expires, rather than fumbling around with each of the applications that use it?

Configuring a datasource within the GlassFish application servers is straightforward because you can manage everything from within the administration console. However, there are several configurations that can be altered in order to change the way in which your connection pool manages connections. On the first New JDBC Connection Pool panel of the connection pool configuration, you need to determine which type of resource you want to create. Table 18-1 describes the different resource types.

Table 18-1. *JDBC Connection Pool Resource Types*

Resource Type	Description
javax.sql.DataSource	Suitable for local transactions
javax.sql.XADataSource	Suitable for global transactions
javax.sql.ConnectionPool DataSource	Suitable for local transactions, possible performance improvements
java.sql.Driver	Standard driver

The Pool Settings section of the second New JDBC Connection Pool panel allows you to configure the number of connections that will be available for application use. By default, the number of open connections at application server startup will be eight. This means applications can grab and use eight connections from the pool without incurring any extra overhead, because the pool has already opened these connections.

The Maximum Pool Size option is set to 32 by default. When an application needs to use a connection, it goes to the pool and requests one. If there is a connection available in the pool, then it is given to the application. However, if no connection is available, then a new connection is made. The Maximum Pool Size value is the upper bound of connections that can possibly be made. So, by default, if there are 32 connections open and an application requests a new connection, then a database connection error will be thrown. Remember, when an application is finished using a connection, it is returned to the pool, so if an application is working properly and releases connections once it's finished using them, the maximum number of connections should be fairly difficult to reach in most environments.

A number of other configurations can be managed for your connection pool, such as determining when connections will time out and when to resize the pool. Adjust accordingly, if needed, after your application has been using the connection pool for a period of time. The transaction configuration for the pool makes it possible to set up an isolation level. It is recommended by Oracle to try to leave the isolation level alone if possible. If not, consider setting Isolation Level Guaranteed to false and make sure applications do not alter a connection's isolation level. The different isolation levels are listed in the following bullets, from best performing on top to worst performing on the bottom:

- READ_UNCOMMITTED

- READ_COMMITTED

- REPEATABLE_READ

- SERIALIZABLE

18-5. Adding Forms-Based Authentication

Problem

You want to configure authentication for your applications by utilizing a database table to hold usernames and passwords, along with user groups for different access privileges.

Solution

Set up forms-based authentication within your GlassFish application server by creating the necessary database tables to contain user accounts and groups and then configuring the application server to use those tables for authentication. The first step to setting up forms-based authentication is to create the necessary database artifacts to support the authentication. To do so, create two database tables. One of the tables will contain the usernames and passwords, and the second table will contain the groups, along with the users who have access to those groups.

The following lines of SQL can be used to generate these tables (Oracle syntax), along with the database sequences that will be used to populate the table primary key values:

```
create table users(
id number,
username varchar(150) not null,
password varchar(50) not null,
primary key (id));
create table groups(
id number,
username varchar2(150) not null,
groupname varchar2(100) not null,
primary key(id));
create sequence users_s
start with 1
increment by 1;
create sequence groups_s
start with 1
increment by 1;
```

For testing purposes, let's create a couple of user accounts along with a couple of different access groups. The following lines of SQL will insert these records:

```
insert into users values(
users_s.nextval,
'admin',
dbms_obfuscation_toolkit.md5(input=>utl_raw.cast_to_raw('jakartaeerecipes')));
insert into users values(
users_s.nextval,
'juneau',
dbms_obfuscation_toolkit.md5(input=>utl_raw.cast_to_raw('testpass')));
insert into groups values(
groups_s.nextval,
'admin', 'administrator');
insert into groups values(
groups_s.nextval,
'juneau','reader');
```

Now that the database has been set up for authentication, it is time to configure the database to use these tables for authentication purposes. To do so, log in to the GlassFish administrative console, navigate to the Configurations ➤ server-config ➤ Realms menu option, and click the New button. Doing so will open the New Realm panel, which is shown in Figure 18-8.

New Realm

Create a new security (authentication) realm. Valid realm types are PAM, OSGi, File, Certificate, LDAP, JDBC, Digest, Oracle Solaris, and Custom.

* Indicates required field

Configuration Name: server-config

Name: * JDBCAuth

Class Name: ⦿ com.sun.enterprise.security.auth.realm.jdbc.JDBCRealm

○

Choose a realm class name from the drop-down list or specify a custom class

Properties specific to this Class

JAAS Context: *

Identifier for the login module to use for this realm

JNDI: *

JNDI name of the JDBC resource used by this realm

User Table: *

Name of the database table that contains the list of authorized users for this realm

User Name Column: *

Name of the column in the user table that contains the list of user names

Password Column: *

Name of the column in the user table that contains the user passwords

Group Table: *

Name of the database table that contains the list of groups for this realm

Figure 18-8. *Creating a new security realm for GlassFish*

Within the New Realm form, enter a name for the realm, which you will call JDBCAuth for this example. Next, for the class name, choose com.sun.enterprise.security.auth.realm.jdbc.JDBCRealm from the drop-down menu. Once you've completed this first section of the form, it is time to fill out the properties specific to the class. For this example, use the values shown in Table 18-2 to complete this form.

Table 18-2. *Properties Specific to JDBC Security Realm Class*

Property	Value
JAAS	jdbcAuth
JNDI	jdbc/OracleConnection
User Table	users
User Name Column	username
Password Column	password
Group Table	groups
Group Name Column	groupname
Password Encryption Algorithm	MD5 (algorithm used in a SQL insert statement)

Once you're finished, click OK to save the values and create the realm. The newly created realm should now appear in the Realms listing, as shown in Figure 18-9.

Realms

Create, modify, or delete security (authentication) realms.

Configuration Name: server-config

Select	Name		Class Name	
☐	JDBCAuth		com.sun.enterprise.security.auth.realm.jdbc.JDBCRealm	
☐	admin-realm		com.sun.enterprise.security.auth.realm.file.FileRealm	
☐	certificate		com.sun.enterprise.security.auth.realm.certificate.CertificateRealm	
☐	file		com.sun.enterprise.security.auth.realm.file.FileRealm	

Realms (4) — New... Delete

Figure 18-9. *Realms listing in the GlassFish administration console*

That does it for the application server configuration. Now how do you use the new security realm? One way is to utilize the mature technique of creating a login view and making some configuration changes to your application's web.xml file to implement the authentication within your application. A more modern technique is to utilize the Jakarta Security API, which was introduced to the platform in Java EE 8. This recipe covers the older technique, highlighting some differences between it and the newer Jakarta Security API. To see a more modern example from start to finish, refer to Chapter 15. To begin, let's look at the changes that will need to be made to web.xml to configure the forms authentication. The following excerpt, taken from the web.xml configuration file in the JakartaEE10Recipes sources, demonstrates the updates that need to be made:

```
<security-constraint>
        <display-name>Admin</display-name>
        <web-resource-collection>
            <web-resource-name>Admin Tools</web-resource-name>
            <description/>
            <url-pattern>/faces/admin/*</url-pattern>
            <http-method>GET</http-method>
            <http-method>POST</http-method>
            <http-method>HEAD</http-method>
            <http-method>PUT</http-method>
            <http-method>OPTIONS</http-method>
            <http-method>TRACE</http-method>
            <http-method>DELETE</http-method>
        </web-resource-collection>
        <auth-constraint>
            <description/>
            <role-name>admin</role-name>
        </auth-constraint>
    </security-constraint>
    <security-constraint>
        <display-name>User</display-name>
        <web-resource-collection>
            <web-resource-name>Protected Users Area</web-resource-name>
            <description/>
            <url-pattern>/faces/users/*</url-pattern>
            <http-method>GET</http-method>
```

```
            <http-method>POST</http-method>
            <http-method>HEAD</http-method>
            <http-method>PUT</http-method>
            <http-method>OPTIONS</http-method>
            <http-method>TRACE</http-method>
            <http-method>DELETE</http-method>
        </web-resource-collection>
        <auth-constraint>
            <description/>
            <role-name>user</role-name>
        </auth-constraint>
    </security-constraint>
<login-config>
        <realm-name>JDBCRealm</realm-name>
        <form-login-config>
            <form-login-page>/faces/loginForm.xhtml</form-login-page>
            <form-error-page>/faces/loginError.xhtml</form-error-page>
        </form-login-config>
    </login-config>
```

Next, the GlassFish server security role mapping needs to be added to the sun-web.xml configuration file, which maps application roles to database groups. The following excerpt demonstrates the mapping configuration:

```
<security-role-mapping>
<role-name>admin</role-name>
<group-name>administrator</group-name>
</security-role-mapping>
<security-role-mapping>
<role-name>user</role-name>
<group-name>reader</group-name>
</security-role-mapping>
```

Lastly, the views that the user will see must contain specific names for the username and password input text fields, and the form action must be set to j_security_check, which will cause control to be passed to the application server for handling the authentication. The following login form demonstrates this process. You can see the sources within the login.xhtml form contained within the JakartaEE10Recipes project.

```
<?xml version="1.0" encoding="UTF-8"?>
<!DOCTYPE html PUBLIC "-//W3C//DTD XHTML 1.0 Strict//EN" "http://www.w3.org/TR/xhtml1/DTD/
xhtml1-strict.dtd">
<html xmlns="http://www.w3.org/1999/xhtml"
      xmlns:f="http://xmlns.jcp.org/jsf/core"
      xmlns:h="http://xmlns.jcp.org/jsf/html">
    <h:head>
        <meta http-equiv="Content-Type" content="text/html; charset=UTF-8"/>
        <title>TODO supply a title</title>
    </h:head>
```

```
<h:body>
    <p>
        <form method="POST" action="j_security_check">
            Username: <input type="text" name="j_username" />
            Password: <input type="password" name="j_password" />
            <br />
            <input type="submit" value="Login" />
            <input type="reset" value="Reset" />
        </form>
    </p>
</h:body>
</html>
```

When users point their browsers to the login.xhtml view, they will be prompted to log in to the application.

How It Works

Securing an application is a vital step for any enterprise application. Adding a username and password for login is one of the most basic forms of security that can be put into place. The combination of GlassFish application server, the underlying database, and some basic Jakarta EE application configurations make securing applications via username and password an easy task. The solution to this recipe demonstrates how to configure a security realm within the application server that will utilize a database table for storing username and password combinations. While some of the database code in this solution is specific to Oracle Database, the same technique can be applied to most RDBMSs with only minor modifications made to the code for securing the password within the database.

The first step toward configuring the security realm within GlassFish is to set up the underlying database table that will be used to contain the security credentials. It is of utmost importance to ensure that passwords stored within the table are encrypted; otherwise, they can be seen by anyone who has read-only access to the security table that is created for this solution. In the solution to this recipe, the Oracle database dbms_obfuscation_toolkit.md5 function is used in order to hash the passwords. However, if you're using another database system, there should be similar tools to use for encryption purposes. When configuring the database, a table should be created to hold the usernames and passwords, and another should be created to hold the groups or security roles. This will allow applications using the realm to contain a high level of security configuration in that various levels of access can be granted to different users based on the role.

Once the database objects have been created, the server must be configured to utilize the database for authentication purposes. This is done by logging in to the administrative console and setting up a new security realm. There are several pieces of information to fill out on the New Realm form that are used to map the realm to the appropriate database tables and columns. The name given to the realm can be any valid string, and the class name should be com.sun.enterprise.security.auth.realm.jdbc.JDBCRealm, since there are a number of different types of security realms that can be created, including LDAP realms, and so on. The remaining information on the form should be filled out according to the directions for each text field. It is important to be sure that the JDBC resource has been configured already and the name given for the JDBC resource matches the one that is provided for the JNDI field on the form.

To configure an application for use with a security realm, the security constraints and login configuration must be specified within the web.xml configuration file for the application. Security constraints are used to map designated web folders to different user roles for an application. This means that all of the administrative pages for an application can be placed into a folder, and a security constraint can be set up within the web.xml file to limit access to that folder, based on security credentials. If you look at the configuration example in the solution, you can see that there has been a security constraint configured with a display name of Admin. Any valid string identifier can be given to the display-name, web-resource-name, or description elements of the security constraint. The url-pattern element designates which folder should be protected by the constraint, and anything placed in that folder will be protected from unauthorized users. Each of the http-method elements lists the different HTTP methods that pertain to the resources within the given folder. The auth-constraint subelement contains the role mapping, which can be given a description along with the role-name that should be used for limiting access. The specified role-name should match one of the group values that was placed within the database table that was created to contain groups. Any usernames that correspond to the given group or role will have access to the resources contained within the protected folder, provided that they are able to log in to the application successfully. The sun-web.xml configuration file must be updated to contain the mapping of roles to groups if you are deploying to GlassFish. This is done by adding security-role-mapping elements to the sun-web.xml file, and each of the elements must contain a role-name element along with a corresponding group-name element.

The final piece of the puzzle is to create a login form. The form must contain an action by the name of j_security_check because this will pass control of the authentication to the application server. The username and password elements must contain the names of j_username and j_password, respectively. Doing so will allow these elements to be passed to the authentication mechanism properly. When the form is submitted, the username and password are sent to the authentication mechanism, which is handled by the application server via the security realm you created. If an appropriate username and password combination is used, the session is granted access to whichever resources have been designated for the authenticated user's role. If the given user's role does not permit access to certain areas of the application via the security-constraints that have been set up within the web.xml file, the user is denied access.

Configuring forms-based authentication is a good means of controlling access to an application. It allows each application to contain its own security infrastructure, providing the ability to limit certain areas of an application to designated roles. The only downside to the use of the JDBC realm is that the password must be stored in the database table. So as long as a good encryption algorithm is used to obfuscate the password, this should be a minimal risk.

■ **Note** To use LDAP authentication instead, set up a security realm using the com.sun.enterprise.security.auth.realm.ldap.LDAPRealm class. Specify a String value for the JAAS context, which will be used to reference the realm. The directory should be set to the URL for the LDAP server that you want to use for authentication. Base DN must be set to the base DN for the user who will be used for authenticating to the LDAP server (use a separate LDAP account for authentication that has read access to the LDAP directory). Additional properties that may be required for your LDAP configuration include search-bind-password, search-bind-dn, and/or search-filter. To learn more about LDAP configuration, reference the online documentation.

18-6. Deploying a Microservice to GlassFish

Problem

You want to deploy a Jakarta EE application to a lighter application server container that contains only a minimal set of specifications that are necessary to support the application. You also will develop the application that's targeted to provide a specific set of data via web services.

Solution

Develop a minimalistic application that is focused toward providing a set of web services for a targeted set of data. In the following example, a small Jakarta EE web application to host a set of web services for providing book author data will be developed. This small web application will be configured to use only those Jakarta EE 10 specifications that are required for the application functionality. The application will then be deployed to the GlassFish application server.

■ **Note** This example demonstrates the construction of the Java classes required for the solution. To see the entire solution, including configuration files, see the `AuthorService` project sources for this book.

To get started, create a new Maven web application named `AuthorService` and add the following dependencies:

- RESTful Web Services (JAX-RS) 3.1

- Jakarta Persistence (JPA) 3.1

- Apache Derby JDBC 10.15

- Bean Validation 3.0

- Jakarta Enterprise Beans (EJB) 4.0

- Eclipse Persistence 4.0

Once finished, the POM dependencies should look as follows:

```
<dependency>
        <groupId>jakarta.ws.rs</groupId>
        <artifactId>jakarta.ws.rs-api</artifactId>
        <version>3.0.0</version>
        <scope>provided</scope>
</dependency>
<dependency>
        <groupId>jakarta.persistence</groupId>
        <artifactId>jakarta.persistence-api</artifactId>
        <version>3.0.0</version>
        <scope>compile</scope>
</dependency>
<dependency>
        <groupId>jakarta.validation</groupId>
        <artifactId>jakarta.validation-api</artifactId>
        <version>3.0.1</version>
</dependency>
<dependency>
        <groupId>jakarta.ejb</groupId>
        <artifactId>jakarta.ejb-api</artifactId>
        <version>4.0.0</version>
        <type>jar</type>
</dependency>
```

```
        <dependency>
            <groupId>org.eclipse.persistence</groupId>
            <artifactId>eclipselink</artifactId>
            <version>3.0.2</version>
            <scope>provided</scope>
        </dependency>
        <dependency>
            <groupId>org.apache.derby</groupId>
            <artifactId>derbyclient</artifactId>
            <version>10.15.2.0</version>
        </dependency>
    </dependencies>
```

Next, add two Java packages: org.jakartaeerecipe.authorservice.entity and org.
jakartaeerecipe.authorservice.rest. Create entity classes for the AUTHOR_WORK, BOOK, BOOK_AUTHOR, and
CHAPTER database tables within the entity package. The sources for the Author entity class are as follows.
Follow the same technique for generating the other entity classes:

```
package org.jakartaeerecipe.authorservice.entity;
import java.io.Serializable;
import java.math.BigDecimal;
import java.math.BigInteger;
import jakarta.persistence.*;
import jakarta.validation.constraints.NotNull;
@Entity
@Table(name = "AUTHOR_WORK")
@NamedQueries({
    @NamedQuery(name = "AuthorWork.findAll", query = "SELECT a FROM AuthorWork a")})
@XmlRootElement
public class AuthorWork implements Serializable {
    private static final long serialVersionUID = 1L;
    @Id
    @Basic(optional = false)
    @NotNull
    @Column(name = "ID")
    private BigDecimal id;
    @Column(name = "BOOK_ID")
    private BigDecimal bookId;
    @JoinColumn(name = "AUTHOR_ID", referencedColumnName = "ID")
    @ManyToOne(optional = false)
    private BookAuthor authorId;

// Getters and Setters
    @Override
    public int hashCode() {
        int hash = 0;
        hash += (id != null ? id.hashCode() : 0);
        return hash;
    }
    @Override
    public boolean equals(Object object) {
```

```
        // TODO: Warning - this method won't work if the id fields are not set
        if (!(object instanceof AuthorWork)) {
            return false;
        }
        AuthorWork other = (AuthorWork) object;
        if ((this.id == null && other.id != null) || (this.id != null && !this.
        id.equals(other.id))) {
            return false;
        }
        return true;
    }
    @Override
    public String toString() {
        return "org.jakartaee10recipe.entity.AuthorWork[ id=" + id + " ]";
    }
}
```

■ **Note** Remember to annotate each entity class with @XmlRootElement, as this is the annotation that enables the entity to be converted into XML format. One of the common web service formats is XML, so you will almost always want to enable this feature.

Next, create a web service class that will query the database return data to web service clients in an appropriate format. To do so, create a class named BookAuthorFacadeREST that will contain a number of methods that will query the entity classes and return data to callers in a JSON or XML format. To begin, annotate the class with @jakarta.ejb.Stateless so that the class can perform transactional queries using JPA. Next, annotate with @jakarta.ws.rs.Path, providing a path for which the REST services will be made available via the URI. Inject a @PersistenceContext that references the persistence context unit name of your application. Note, you'll need to create a persistence unit for your application, so refer to Recipe 7-3 for more details, if needed. The persistence unit is used to query the data via the JPA API. Since this application will be deployed to Payara Micro instead of a traditional application server, it is a good practice to define the datasource within the web-xml and then refer to the defined datasource from within the /src/main/resources/META-INF/persistence.xml. Therefore, create a web.xml deployment descriptor containing the following configuration:

```
<?xml version="1.0" encoding="UTF-8"?>
<web-app xmlns="http://xmlns.jcp.org/xml/ns/javaee"
         xmlns:xsi="http://www.w3.org/2001/XMLSchema-instance"
         xsi:schemaLocation="http://xmlns.jcp.org/xml/ns/javaee http://xmlns.jcp.org/xml/ns/
         javaee/web-app_3_1.xsd"
         version="3.1">
    <session-config>
        <session-timeout>
            30
        </session-timeout>
    </session-config>
    <data-source>
        <name>java:global/DerbyDataSource</name>
        <class-name>org.apache.derby.jdbc.ClientDriver</class-name>
```

```
        <server-name>localhost</server-name>
        <port-number>1527</port-number>
        <url>jdbc:derby://localhost:1527/acme</url>
        <user>acmeuser</user>
        <password>yourpassword</password>
    </data-source>
</web-app>
```

Finally, write the methods that will be used to query the database and return the data in the appropriate format. In this case, the methods will return BookAuthor data. One of the methods will return all of the records in the BOOK_AUTHOR database table, while the other will return a BOOK_AUTHOR record that contains the matching ID.

```
package org.jakartaee10recipe.authorservice.rest;
import java.math.BigDecimal;
import java.util.List;
import jakarta.ejb.Stateless;
import jakarta.persistence.EntityManager;
import jakarta.persistence.NoResultException;
import jakarta.persistence.PersistenceContext;
import jakarta.ws.rs.GET;
import jakarta.ws.rs.Path;
import jakarta.ws.rs.PathParam;
import jakarta.ws.rs.Produces;
import jakarta.ws.rs.core.MediaType;
import org.jakartaee10recipe.authorservice.entity.BookAuthor;
@Stateless
@Path("bookAuthor")
public class BookAuthorFacadeREST {
    @PersistenceContext(unitName = "AuthorService_1.0PU")
    private EntityManager em;
    @GET
    @Path("{id}")
    @Produces({MediaType.APPLICATION_XML, MediaType.APPLICATION_JSON})
    public BookAuthor find(@PathParam("id") BigDecimal id) {
        BookAuthor bookAuthor = null;
        try {
            bookAuthor = (BookAuthor)
                    em.createQuery("select object(o) from BookAuthor o " +
                    "where o.id = :id")
                    .setParameter("id", id)
                    .getSingleResult();
        } catch (NoResultException ex){
            System.out.println("Error: " + ex);
        }
        return bookAuthor;
    }
    @GET
    @Produces({MediaType.APPLICATION_XML, MediaType.APPLICATION_JSON})
    public List<BookAuthor> findAll() {
        List<BookAuthor> bookAuthors = null;
```

```
        try {
            bookAuthors = em.createQuery("select object(o) from BookAuthor o")
                    .getResultList();
        } catch (NoResultException ex){
            System.out.println("Error: "  + ex);
        }
        return bookAuthors;
    }
    protected EntityManager getEntityManager() {
        return em;
    }
}
```

Lastly for the application, create the `ApplicationConfig` class, which will be used to configure JAX-RS for the application:

```
@jakarta.ws.rs.ApplicationPath("rest")
public class ApplicationConfig extends Application {
    @Override
    public Set<Class<?>> getClasses() {
        Set<Class<?>> resources = new java.util.HashSet<>();
        resources.add(org.jakartaee10recipe.authorservice.rest.BookAuthorFacadeREST.class);
        return resources;
    }
}
```

The application should now be ready to deploy to an application server. As such, it is deployable to GlassFish 7, and it should work without issue.

The bookAuthor service will be available at `http://localhost:8080/AuthorService/rest/bookAuthor/`.

How It Works

In this recipe, a simple Jakarta EE application "microservice" is created and deployed to GlassFish. To create the minimalistic application, create a Maven web application and include only the Jakarta EE APIs that are required for running the application as dependencies. In this case, those dependencies include Jakarta RESTful Web Services, Jakarta Persistence, Bean Validation, and Enterprise Beans. Two other dependencies are required for running the application, those being the Apache Derby JDBC driver and the Eclipse Persistence JPA implementation. As seen in the example, to create the SimpleService application, include the AuthorWork entity class. Create a web.xml deployment descriptor for the application and define a data-source within it, which will be used to connect to the Apache Derby database. A persistence unit can then be created for use by the application JPA calls. Configuring the datasource within the deployment descriptor makes it easy to deploy on Payara Micro, as no server-side configuration is necessary.

This simple application contains a handful of entity classes, which map to database tables that are required for querying the BOOK_AUTHOR database table. The entity classes are then used to create RESTful services in the BookAuthorFacadeREST class. This class contains two simple REST services, each of them @GET services. This means that these services will be used to retrieve data. The find() method creates a service that allows you to query for a BookAuthor entity that matches a given ID. That ID can be specified within the URI when calling upon the service. The findAll() method simply returns all BookAuthor results in XML or JSON format. For more details on developing RESTful web services, refer to Chapter 13.

The `ApplicationConfig` class registers the Jakarta RESTful Web Services classes with the API itself, so as to make the RESTful services available for use. The class extends the `Application` abstract class, which allows `getClasses()` to be overridden to return the list of JAX-RS resources for the application. In this case, the only Jakarta RESTful Web Service resource is `org.jakartaeerecipe.authorservice.rest.BookAuthorFacadeREST.class`. The `@ApplicationPath` annotation provides the path that should be used within the URI to access the RESTful services.

An exploded WAR is simply the contents of a WAR file extracted into a folder. A WAR file can be extracted by simply changing the `.war` extension to `.zip` and extracting the contents. If you are using a Maven-based application, the project directory will contain a target directory after compilation. Inside of the target directory will be the exploded WAR, along with several other folders, including the WAR file itself. It is sometimes beneficial to deploy an exploded WAR if you want to change those files that do not require recompiling (XHTML, JS, CSS, HTML, Jakarta Server Pages, etc.) without recompiling the WAR.

CHAPTER 19

■ ■ ■

Deploying to Containers

The world of containerization has erupted, and it is difficult to navigate technology without running into the word "containerization" or "Docker," to be specific. Docker is a technology which allows one to package a complete application environment into a small, portable container. This technology provides the ability to easily configure and customize containers to run various operating systems, virtual machines, databases, application servers, web servers, and so on, so that applications can be deployed once to the container and ported to almost any environment. With this ability, it is easy for developers to create applications that consist of multiple containers that communicate with each other, tightly integrating to produce robust and fault-tolerant applications.

One may ask questions such as "Why deploy to a container and then ship the container, rather than a web archive (WAR) file?" or "Why would one create multiple smaller applications deployed to multiple containers, in order to produce a single cohesive system?" These questions can be answered in a number of ways, depending upon the requirements of the solutions. In some cases, it does not make sense to deploy to a container, and a standard WAR file will do just fine. However, one of the main benefits of containerization is the creation of reproducible environments. This means that a container can be created and an application can be deployed to that container, providing a portable container that runs the same everywhere. When such a container is then shipped to a customer, it will run the same as it does on the developer's machine or on the testing environment. Reproducible. This is a major benefit. How many times have you developed an application, then deployed to an application server in a different environment, and ran into obscure issues? Lots of developers run into such plagues and spend countless hours trying to find a remedy... Containerization can help. This solution also makes it possible to share prebuilt images for other uses. Such is the idea behind Docker Hub, providing a library of prebuilt images for use. Images on Docker Hub can be used as they are, or they can be extended in order to customize them for use.

What about the reasoning behind developing a multicontainer solution? Fault tolerance can be easily provided when a system is constructed from multiple containers that run independently from one another. Each containerized application can perform just a single task (or a handful of related tasks) and communicate with the other containers. This type of solution is also known as "microservices," and many successful solutions have been developed with this methodology. If one of the containers goes down, the others will remain running, and only a single feature of the whole system will become unavailable. Better yet, a fault tolerance mechanism can be used to automatically spawn a new container to take the place of the one that is unavailable.

Docker and containerized solutions also provide a bevy of other benefits, including quick startup time, easily manageable CPU and container configuration, small portable solutions, and quick duplications and/or rebuilding of containers, just to mention a few. Noting all of the benefits of containerization, it is easy to see how one may get carried away and depend upon containers for everything. I cannot stress enough that containerization is not the best solution in all cases. You must be selective and choose the best strategy for the application at hand.

© Josh Juneau and Tarun Telang 2022

J. Juneau and T. Telang, *Java EE to Jakarta EE 10 Recipes*, https://doi.org/10.1007/978-1-4842-8079-9_19

This chapter will provide a brief overview of using Docker to create containerized applications. After reading through this chapter, you will have a basic understanding of how to create a Docker container and then deploy an application to the container. You will also have a basic understanding of how to make multiple containers communicate with one another, to create a cohesive solution.

19-1. Creating a Docker Image and Running Java

Problem

You would like to create a Docker image and run a small Java executable.

Solution

Create a Docker container using the following steps:

1. Create a new folder on your machine and name it **javaapp**. Change directories into the new folder:

   ```
   mkdir javaapp
   cd javaapp
   ```

2. Create a file within the new directory and name it **Dockerfile**, without any file extension. This will be the file containing the instructions for building your container:

   ```
   nano Dockerfile
   ```

   or

   ```
   vim Dockerfile
   ```

■ **Note**   Both the Nano and Vim editors are utilized from the terminal, and they are available for a number of operating systems.

---

3. Add the following contents to the Dockerfile:

   ```
   FROM openjdk:17
   COPY . /var/www/java
   WORKDIR /var/www/java
   RUN javac HelloDocker.java
   CMD ["java", "HelloDocker"]
   ```

4. Create a small Java program containing a `main()` method. Name the file HelloDocker.java, and place the following contents inside:

```
class HelloDocker {
  public static void main(String[] args){
    System.out.println("Hello Docker!");
  }
}
```

5. From inside of the jakartaeeapp directory, build the Docker image by executing the following command from the command line or terminal:

```
docker build -t javaapp .
```

6. Run the Docker image by issuing the following command:

```
docker run javaapp
>> Hello Docker!
```

This will yield the following output:

```
● ● ●                          jakartaeeapp — -zsh — 102×38
$ docker build -t javaapp .
[+] Building 36.9s (9/9) FINISHED
 => [internal] load build definition from Dockerfile                  0.0s
 => => transferring dockerfile: 156B                                  0.0s
 => [internal] load .dockerignore                                     0.0s
 => => transferring context: 2B                                       0.0s
 => [internal] load metadata for docker.io/library/openjdk:17         4.4s
 => [internal] load build context                                     0.0s
 => => transferring context: 310B                                     0.0s
 => [1/4] FROM docker.io/library/openjdk:17@sha256:74bad65c9e59d6410bdd6  31.2s
 => => resolve docker.io/library/openjdk:17@sha256:74bad65c9e59d6410bdd67  0.0s
 => => sha256:53f096d4aa0757c30613f325df1e03a90db9d9879 42.02MB / 42.02MB   9.1s
 => => sha256:921862a08fd8bc652539d62804daf06ab6464bd5b 14.30MB / 14.30MB   6.7s
 => => sha256:a8e5e67fcac32d1d4b20751372e66e4b457cc5 185.98MB / 185.98MB  28.1s
 => => sha256:74bad65c9e59d6410bdd67d71a14e14175ddd33d654 1.29kB / 1.29kB   0.0s
 => => sha256:8a99742c7c38a7b0826c8a47cacbca18af5c3a60e6eba18 954B / 954B   0.0s
 => => sha256:0b879b8a7f0a5eb2a13bd8c75e79c882d2b73959c62 4.47kB / 4.47kB   0.0s
 => => extracting sha256:53f096d4aa0757c30613f325df1e03a90db9d9879ea251b3   1.2s
 => => extracting sha256:921862a08fd8bc652539d62804daf06ab6464bd5b42061f5   0.4s
 => => extracting sha256:a8e5e67fcac32d1d4b20751372e66e4b457cc5644d145050   2.9s
 => [2/4] COPY . /var/www/java                                        0.1s
 => [3/4] WORKDIR /var/www/java                                       0.0s
 => [4/4] RUN javac HelloDocker.java                                  0.9s
 => exporting to image                                                0.0s
 => => exporting layers                                               0.0s
 => => writing image sha256:8aa7c49987cde38fa16580f5debc754276db053d38e50  0.0s
 => => naming to docker.io/library/javaapp                            0.0s

Use 'docker scan' to run Snyk tests against images to find vulnerabilities and learn how to fix them
$ docker run javaapp
Hello Docker!
$
```

How It Works

Creating a Java application and packaging it into a Docker image is quite simple. To begin, one must install the Docker environment onto the machine which will be used for creating the Docker container. On Windows or Mac platforms, this typically means installing Docker Desktop. On Linux, this is typically Community Edition or a Docker server environment, such as Docker Enterprise Edition.

■ **Note** For more information regarding installation of Docker on Linux, Mac, or Windows, please see the online documentation: `https://docs.docker.com/get-docker/`.

Once Docker has been installed, a container can be created and installed into the local image repository.

To begin creating a basic Docker image, create a folder into which any files that will become a part of the Docker image will be stored. Next, inside of the folder, create a file named **Dockerfile**, which will be used to configure the image. The **Dockerfile** is used to indicate the base image from which this image will be created, and it also allows one to specify configurations such as application entry point, ports for communication, database information, and so on.

In the example, the base Docker image is derived from OpenJDK 17 using the statement FROM openjdk:17. The next line of the example Dockerfile indicates that the contents of the current folder should be copied inside of the image's */var/www/java* folder. The Docker WORKDIR command is used to set the working directory for any subsequent RUN, CMD, ENTRYPOINT, COPY, and ADD instructions. In the example, the next line executes the Java program and creates an image:

```
RUN javac HelloDocker.java
```

A Docker container runs an image that is created via commands that are contained within a Dockerfile. The RUN command creates a container which incorporates an image on top of the OS image that is at the base of the container and runs it.

The RUN, CMD, and ENTRYPOINT instructions can be executed in either Shell or Exec form. In this example, the CMD instruction uses the Exec form. The Exec form uses the following format:

```
<instruction> ["executable","parameter1","parameter2"]
```

The Shell form takes the following format:

```
<instruction> command
```

In the example, the final line of the Dockerfile contains the CMD command. There can only be one CMD command per Dockerfile. If more than one CMD command exists, then the last one in the file is executed. The CMD command provides defaults for the executing container. In the example, the CMD command is written in the Exec format, which provides the executable, followed by any parameters:

```
CMD ["java", "HelloDocker"]
```

In this case, the executable is "java," and the parameter is "HelloDocker," which is the name of the executable Java application. The other possible formats for the command are "Entrypoint" and Shell forms. To learn more about the different formats, as well as the different Dockerfile commands, please refer to the online documentation:

```
https://docs.docker.com/engine/reference/builder/
```

Once the Dockerfile has been built, the docker executable can be used to build the image by invoking the docker build instruction from the command line or terminal. In the example, the -t option is passed, which specifies a name for the image. To see the many different options available for docker build, please refer to the online documentation:

```
https://docs.docker.com/engine/reference/commandline/build/
```

Lastly, to run the container, issue the docker run instruction from the command line or terminal. In the example, simply the image name is passed to the docker run command. However, there are more options that can be specified. Please refer to the online documentation to read about the various options:

```
https://docs.docker.com/engine/reference/run/
```

19-2. Deploying Images to Payara Server Utilizing an Official Payara Docker Image

Problem

You would create a container by utilizing a prebuilt Docker image of the Payara server and deploying an application to it.

Solution

Utilize a Docker Desktop installation to run a Payara Docker image that is stored on Docker Hub. The following command will pull down the official Payara image from Docker Hub, create a container consisting of the WAR files that are present within the "deployments" folder, and run the container:

```
docker run -d -p 4848:4848 -p 8095:8080 -v /Java_Dev/deployments:/opt/payara/deployments --
name payara-container payara/server-full:latest
```

How It Works

To easily spin up a container that is built on top of the Payara server, utilize the docker run command, optionally passing a number of operators or parameters to configure the container on the fly. The command in its most basic form adheres to the following format:

```
docker run <image name>
```

The image name is in the format of <community>/<repository>:tag.

Simply type docker run --help to see the available parameters. A handful of the most commonly used parameters are explained in Table 19-1.

Table 19-1. *Common docker run Operators*

Operator	Description
-d	Runs the container in detached mode
-rm	When used with -d, removes the container once it exits or when the daemon exits
--name	Provides an identifier for a container
-p	Publishes container port to host port in the format host-port:container-port
-v	Mounts a volume from host to container

In the example, the port 4848 within the container is mapped to the port 4848 on the host. Likewise, the port 8080 within the container is mapped to port 8095 on the host. The volume **/Java_Dev/Deployments** from the host is mapped to the container volume **/opt/payara/deployments**. Hence, if there are any WAR files residing within the host volume, they will be auto-deployed when the Payara server is started since they will be copied into the Payara deployments directory. The container in the example is named *payara-container*, which is more easily identifiable than a randomly generated number. Lastly, the container is based upon the latest Payara Server image.

19-3. Creating a Docker Container Running a Basic Jakarta EE Application

Problem

You would like to create a Docker container from an image and run a Jakarta EE application within the container.

Solution

Utilize a container image, such as Payara or WildFly, as the basis for a Jakarta EE Docker container. In this solution, Payara will be utilized to deploy a basic "Hello World" Jakarta EE application containing a Jakarta RESTful web service.

For the purposes of this example, a simple Jakarta EE application is packaged with the sources for this book. The application is named **HelloApp**, and the project can be opened and compiled into a WAR file using an IDE, such as Apache NetBeans or IntelliJ IDEA.

To deploy to a container, a **Dockerfile** needs to be constructed, which will pull a base image for the container, and then subsequent images can be layered on top to create a fully functional container. To begin, create a file without any extension in the root of the **HelloApp** project, and name it **Dockerfile**. Inside of the **Dockerfile**, place the following contents:

```
FROM payara/server-full:latest
COPY target/HelloApp-1.0.war $DEPLOY_DIR
```

Next, build the image by issuing the docker run command and passing a name for the image, along with a version. Be sure to include a trailing dot (.), as this indicates to include the contents of the current directory in the build:

```
docker build -t hello-app:1.0 .
```

Finally, run the container by issuing the docker run command, providing host port mapping, along with the image name and version:

```
docker run -it -p 8095:8080 hello-app:1.0
```

After issuing this command, the container will start, and you can visit the REST endpoint, which should be available at http://localhost:8095/HelloApp-1.0/rest/helloService/hello, and see the result:

```
Hello World
```

How It Works

Many application server container vendors package their containers in a Docker-ready format, usually on Docker Hub. As such, it is easy to build an image using one of these containers as a base and then deploy an application or service to that container.

In this example, the first line of the Dockerfile pulls the Payara Server, which is utilized to create a base image. Next, the HelloApp-1.0.war file is copied into an area within the Payara server referenced as $DEPLOY_DIR using the COPY command. There are a couple of things to note about this COPY command. First, it is assumed that the Dockerfile is contained at the base of the project directory. Therefore, there should be a target folder at the same level as the Dockerfile. Inside of the target folder should be the compiled HelloApp-1.0.war. Hence, the COPY command references target/HelloApp-1.0.war. Next, the $DEPLOY_DIR variable is a special variable to reference when using a Payara server image. This variable points to the container's /opt/payara/deployments directory. All in all, this command is telling Docker to copy the WAR file into the auto-deploy directory.

The image can be built by issuing the docker build command. In this case, the -t option is used to specify an image name and version. To see a complete list of options for this command, please refer to the online documentation: https://docs.docker.com/engine/reference/commandline/build/.

In order to run the container, issue the docker run command. In this example, the -it option instructs Docker to allocate a pseudo-TTY connected to the container's stdin. This essentially creates an interactive bash within the container. The -p option specifies the host-to-container port mapping. The last argument passed to docker run is the image name and version.

It is a piece of cake to create a container and deploy an application using your choice from a number of compliant Jakarta EE application server containers. Many vendors make Docker-ready containers available, allowing very minimal work.

19-4. Enabling Communication Between Containers

Problem

You would like to provide communication between multiple containers.

Solution

To provide communication between two or more containers, one must ensure that port numbers are being assigned correctly. Utilization of the Docker network feature can help achieve the desired result:

```
docker network connect hellonetwork
```

or

```
docker run —net=hellonetwork -it -p 8096:8080 hello-app:1.0
```

In this solution, a Jakarta RESTful Web Service named **HelloApp** is deployed to the hellonetwork on port 8096. A secondary Jakarta Web Service client service named **HelloAppClient** is deployed on the same hellonetwork on port 8097. In this case, **HelloAppClient** invokes the RESTful service that is exposed via **HelloApp** on port 8096.

To begin, let's take a look at the **HelloAppClient** code. One thing to note is that in this code, the URL for the RESTful service call is hard-coded for brevity. However, it is not suitable for production use in this manner. For a production environment, it would be best to set a property containing the RESTful URL which could be read from within the Jakarta RESTful Web Service client:

```
@Path("helloclient")
public class HelloService {
    @GET
    @Produces(MediaType.APPLICATION_JSON)
    public Response sayHello() {
      // Obtain an instance of the client
        Client client = ClientBuilder.newClient();
        Response res = (Response) client.target("localhost:8096/HelloApp-1.0/rest/
        helloService/hello")
                    .request("text/plain").get();
        return res;
    }
}
```

Next, build the **HelloApp** Docker image invoking the docker build command from within the **HelloApp** project directory. Once the project has been deployed, the container can be started by issuing the docker run command:

```
docker run -d --net=hellonetwork -it -p 8096:8080 hello-app:1.0
```

The **HelloAppClient** project image should be built in the same manner, and the container can then be deployed to the same network. To do so, change directories to traverse inside of the **HelloAppClient** project directory. Next, issue the docker build command, and then issue the following docker run command:

```
docker run -d --net=hellonetwork -it -p 8097:8080 hello-app-client:1.0
```

Open a browser and navigate to the **HelloAppClient** project, and the text which is made available from the **HelloApp** project service should be visible:

```
http://localhost:8097/HelloAppClient/rest/helloclient
```

How It Works

The docker network command allows one to create a network to which any number of containers can be assigned. Each of the containers within the network can communicate with each other by means of specifying a container name. There are a number of different ways to deploy multiple services to a Docker network such that they will be able to communicate.

In this solution, two of the techniques for joining containers to the same Docker network are presented. The first way to join a container to a Docker network would be to issue the docker network command in the following format:

```
docker network connect <<network>> <<container name>>
```

This technique works well if there are already containers running. The only downside is that one must know the container name in order to join it to the network using this option. The second option is easier to manage if containers have not yet been started, as the --net option can be specified with the docker run command, assigning the container to a network as it is started.

Joining two or more containers to the same network can be effective for providing container communication. This is a must if one of the containers is running a database and the other containers need to access that database. It is also essential for organizing microservices to provide a fully functional application. There are also tools, such as Kubernetes, that are available to help orchestrate and manage a number of services. If you plan to run many services, then it may make sense to look into one of these tools. For further documentation on networking Docker containers, please review the online documentation:

```
https://docs.docker.com/engine/userguide/networking/dockernetworks/
```

Jakarta EE Development with Apache NetBeans IDE

Developing applications on the JVM can be a fun job; however, it can also become cumbersome if you constantly need to be concerned with Java environment details. When developing an application using only a text editor and the command line or terminal, you need to constantly maintain the CLASSPATH in mind to ensure that all required libraries are available to your application. Moreover, organization can be difficult if you are working on multiple applications at one time, and you need to maintain some method of application separation. These are only a couple of reasons why development can become cumbersome if you are not working within a development environment. The Apache NetBeans integrated development environment (IDE) aims to ease the load on developers by abstracting the requirement to maintain CLASSPATH, organizing code effectively, and providing a plethora of features to make enterprise development much easier.

■ **Note**   This appendix covers the latest NetBeans release. It also works with Jakarta EE development.

A-1. Configuring Application Servers Within NetBeans

Before you can associate application projects with a server for deployment and testing, you need to register one or more application server containers for use within NetBeans. Even if you are developing microservices that will be deployed to a container, such as Payara Micro, you'll still need to register a server with the IDE for development purposes. Note that it is a good practice to only configure those application servers that are used for development purposes (not for production) within NetBeans.

© Josh Juneau and Tarun Telang 2022

J. Juneau and T. Telang, *Java EE to Jakarta EE 10 Recipes*, https://doi.org/10.1007/978-1-4842-8079-9

To add a local or remote server to NetBeans, perform the following tasks:

1. Navigate to the Services window and right-click the Servers menu selection. Click Add Server, as shown in Figure A-1.

Figure A-1. *Add Server to the NetBeans IDE*

2. When the Add Server Instance dialog appears, choose the server type that you want to add (see Figure A-2).

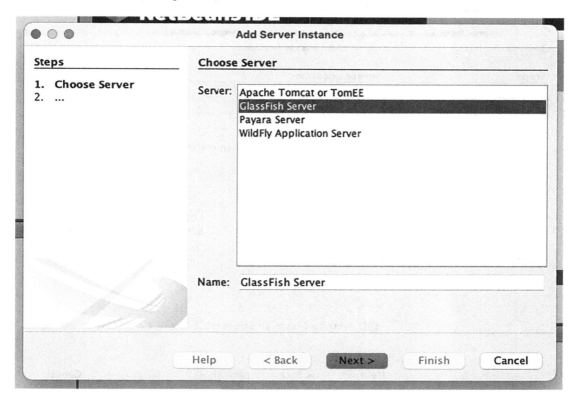

Figure A-2. Add Server Instance

3. On the next screen, enter the path to the application server installation that you would like to configure within NetBeans (see Figure A-3). Once you have chosen the location, click the Finish button.

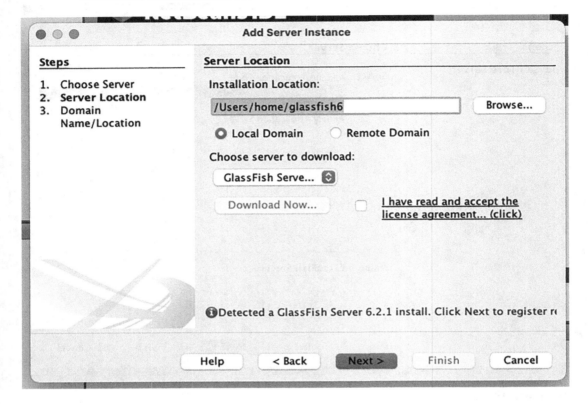

Figure A-3. *Set Server Location*

4. On the next screen, enter the domain location of the application server that you would like to configure within NetBeans (see Figure A-4). Once you have chosen the domain location, click the Finish button.

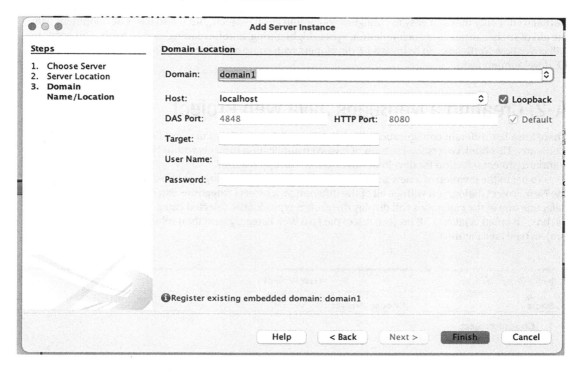

Figure A-4. *Set Domain Location*

5. You can now deploy applications to the server by registering it with a given project from within the project properties. Note: You can also perform some basic application server tasks by selecting the application server from within the Servers window in NetBeans, as demonstrated in Figure A-5.

Figure A-5. *Expand and administer the server in NetBeans*

Developing Java Web or Enterprise Applications

The NetBeans IDE makes it easy to develop Java Web or Enterprise applications. To begin, you first create a Jakarta EE project within the IDE and subsequently use the IDE to configure the project accordingly. NetBeans not only makes it easy to configure your application projects, but it also eases development with the aid of such features as autocompletion, syntax highlighting, autoformatting, and so forth. This section will cover how NetBeans can help Java EE developers with some of the most commonly performed Jakarta EE development tasks.

A-2. Creating a NetBeans Java Web Project

There are a few different configurations to choose from for the creation of a Java Enterprise project within NetBeans. This book covers the creation of Java Web application projects within NetBeans, which is the standard project selection for development of Jakarta EE applications.

To begin the creation of a new project, open the New Project dialog by choosing File ➤ New Project. In the New Project dialog, you will see all of the different Java project categories listed in the left-side list box. Selecting one of the categories will display the project types for the selected category within the right-side list box. To create a Jakarta EE project, select the Java Web category, and then select Web Application as the project type (see Figure A-6).

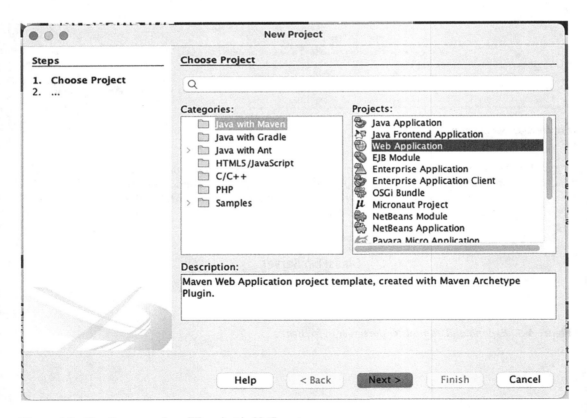

Figure A-6. *Creating a new Java EE project in NetBeans*

After selecting the project type, the New Web Application dialog will open. Enter a project name and location, as shown in Figure A-7. Once you're finished, choose Next.

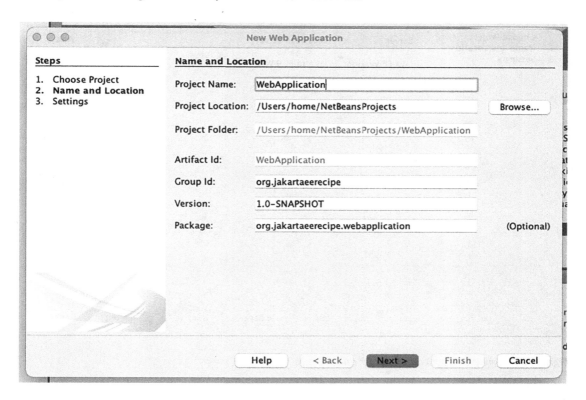

Figure A-7. *New Web Application: Name and Location*

In the Settings screen, choose the application server that you want to use for deployment (see Configuring Application Servers in NetBeans), along with the Jakarta EE version that you want to use (see Figure A-8).

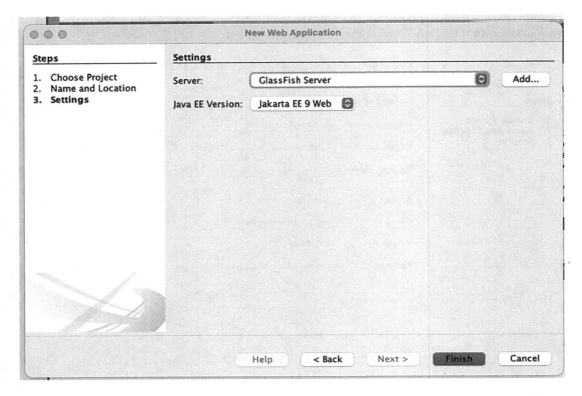

Figure A-8. *New Web Application: Server and Settings*

A-3. Creating Jakarta Server Faces Application Files

The NetBeans IDE makes it easy to generate files for Jakarta Server Faces application projects. To open the JSF menu, right-click an application Source Packages directory to open the context menu. From within the context menu, choose New and then Other... to open the New File dialog. Within the dialog, choose JavaServer Faces from the Categories list box to open the JSF file types within the left-side list box (see Figure A-9).

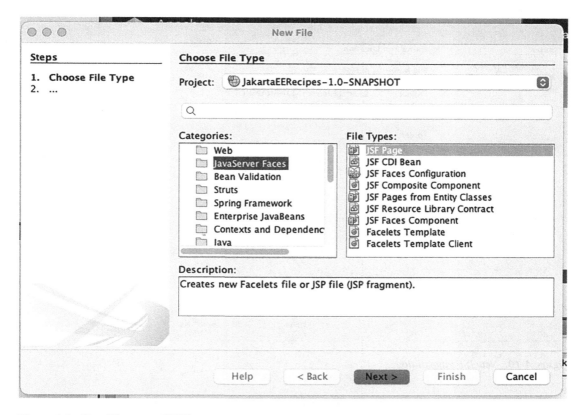

Figure A-9. *New File menu: JSF file types*

The JSF file types include the following options:

- JSF Page

- JSF CDI Bean (this is a CDI controller in Jakarta EE 10)

- JSF Faces Configuration

- JSF Composite Component

- JSF Pages from Entity Classes

- JSF Resource Library Contract

- JSF Faces Component

- Facelets Template

- Facelets Template Client

The JSF Page file selection opens a dialog that can be used to generate a new JSF page (see Figure A-10). The dialog allows you to choose a file location and name, and it also contains the ability to apply different options for the page type. The option choices for page type are Facelets (default), JSP File, or JSP Segment. The examples throughout this book feature the Facelets page type.

Figure A-10. *New JSF Page dialog*

The JSF CDI Bean file selection opens a dialog that allows you to generate a JSF CDI Bean controller class (see Figure A-11). The dialog provides the ability to choose to add the bean data to the faces-config file, as well as to choose the scope of the bean.

Figure A-11. New JSF Managed/CDI Bean dialog

The JSF Faces Configuration File selection is used to create a `faces-config.xml` file for a project. However, this option is not required if you choose to create a JSF project within the NetBeans Project Creation wizard.

The JSF Composite Component file selection opens a dialog that can be used to create a composite component file. The dialog does not provide many options other than the ability to choose a file location and name. The generated file contains the skeleton of a composite component, as listed in the following lines:

```
<?xml version='1.0' encoding='UTF-8' ?>
<!DOCTYPE html PUBLIC "-//W3C//DTD XHTML 1.0 Transitional//EN" "http://www.w3.org/TR/xhtml1/
DTD/xhtml1-transitional.dtd">
<html xmlns="http://www.w3.org/1999/xhtml"
xmlns:cc="http://xmlns.jcp.org/jsf/composite">
    <!-- INTERFACE -->
    <cc:interface>
    </cc:interface>
    <!-- IMPLEMENTATION -->
    <cc:implementation>
    </cc:implementation>
</html>
```

The JSF Pages from Entity Classes file selection can be quite powerful in that it allows you to choose an entity class from which to generate a JSF page, and then the resulting JSF page will be bound to the entity class upon generation. In order to use this option, the project must contain at least one entity class.

A-4. Developing Entity Classes

The NetBeans IDE provides facilities to help develop Entity Bean classes, either manually or based on a selected database table. To access the entity class wizards, right-click a project's Source Packages folder to open the context menu, and then choose New ➤ Other to open the New File dialog. Once it's open, choose the Persistence category from the left-side list box to display the file types in the right-side list box (see Figure A-12).

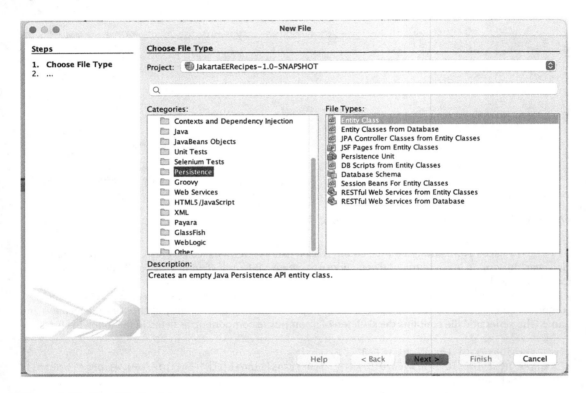

Figure A-12. *New File: Persistence*

The Entity Class option allows you to generate a blank entity class, and the Entity Classes from Database option allows you to generate an entity class from a selected database table. In doing so, all of the requisite code for mapping the entity class to the selected database table is automatically generated for you.

A-5. Using Jakarta Persistence Query Language

NetBeans includes a feature that allows you to query a database using Jakarta Persistence Query Language syntax. This can be quite helpful for those who are using the Jakarta Persistence Query Language in their session beans. To access the Jakarta Persistence Query Language query tool, expand a NetBeans web project that contains a `persistence.xml` configuration file in the project Configuration Files directory. Then perform the following steps:

1. Right-click the `persistence.xml` configuration file to open the context menu.

2. Click Run to open the Jakarta Persistence Query Language tool (see Figure A-13), type in your query, and click the Run button on the upper-right side of the query editor.

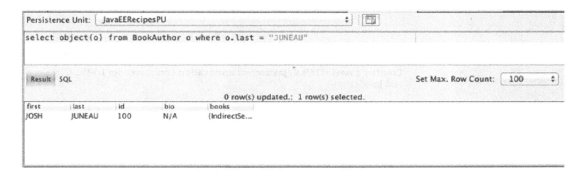

Figure A-13. *Jakarta Persistence Query Language tool*

A-6. Using HTML5

Many applications use HTML5. The Java community has taken note of that and has made it easy to begin working with HTML5 within NetBeans itself. NetBeans has an HTML5 project option, which enables developers to debug HTML5 pages using a Chrome web browser plug-in. To create an HTML5 project from within the IDE, select the New Project option and then choose HTML/JavaScript in the Categories selection list, followed by HTML5 Application from the Projects selection list (see Figure A-14).

Figure A-14. *Create a new HTML5 application*

Next, you are given the option to choose No Site Template, or you can select a template that you provide, or use one that you can download, as seen in Figure A-15.

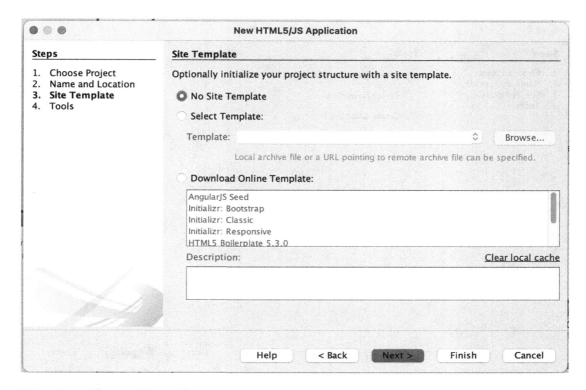

Figure A-15. *Choose a site template*

Lastly, choose the tools that you want to add to your HTML5 project (see Figure A-16), then click Finish.

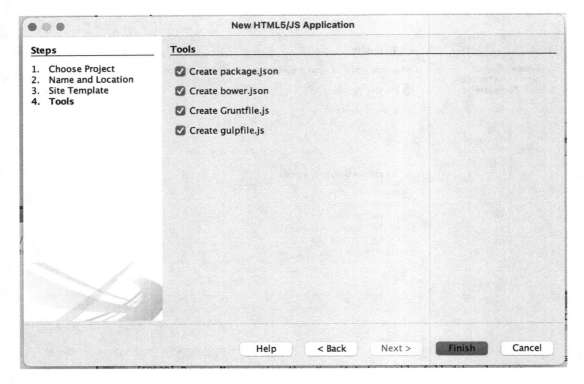

Figure A-16. *Add libraries to the project*

Once the project has been created, you can choose Run to have it opened within Chrome, assuming that you have installed the Chrome plug-in. If you have not yet installed the Chrome plug-in, you will be prompted to do so.

Index

© Josh Juneau and Tarun Telang 2022
J. Juneau and T. Telang, *Java EE to Jakarta EE 10 Recipes*, https://doi.org/10.1007/978-1-4842-8079-9

■ T

Printed in the United States
by Baker & Taylor Publisher Services